D0991097

# Hiding in Plain Sight

# Hiding in Plain Sight

*The Incredible True Story of a
German-Jewish Teenager's Struggle to Survive
in Nazi-occupied Poland*

———⇒●⇐———

BETTY LAUER

SMITH AND KRAUS GLOBAL

Smith and Kraus, Inc.
177 Lyme Road, Hanover, NH 03755
www.smithkraus.com

First edition: April 2004
Printed in the United States of America
9 8 7 6 5 4 3 2 1

Cover and text design by Freedom Hill Design, Reading, Vermont

Library of Congress Cataloging-in-Publication Data
Lauer, Betty, 1926–
Hiding in plain sight : a Jewish teenager's struggle to survive in Nazi-occupied Poland / Betty
Lauer. —1st ed.
p. cm. — (Smith and Kraus global)
Includes index.
ISBN 1-57525-349-6 (cloth)  ISBN 1-57525 348-8 (pbk)
1. Lauer, Betty, 1926– 2. Jews—Germany—Biography. 3. Jewish children in the
Holocaust—Poland—Biography. 4. Holocaust survivors—Poland—Biography. 5. Holocaust,
Jewish (1939–1945)—Germany—Personal narratives. 6. Holocaust, Jewish (1939–1945)—
Poland—Personal narratives. I. Title. II. Series.

DS135.G5L2985  2004
940.53'18'092—dc22
[B]
2003068623

FOR LARRY LAUER

*Ein Riss in der Schöpfung . . .*

A fissure in The Creation . . .

Nelly Sachs, in an address after receiving the Nobel Prize for literature in 1966

# AUTHOR'S NOTE

Though the first draft of this manuscript was completed in the 1950s, its contents were etched into my mind in the 1940s.

I should like to express my gratitude beyond measure to my friends and publishers, Marisa Smith and Eric Kraus. It was Marisa's steadfast support, her courage and understanding, that guided me through this final revision.

I would also like to thank Kate Mueller, whose professional editing and critique helped make the work more accessible to the reader, and Julia Gignoux for her design and production of this book.

The chronicle of the events I have witnessed and the many people who knowingly or unwittingly played a crucial part in helping me during those dark years I have truthfully portrayed. Some of the names I have changed because either I was unable to locate the persons and secure their permission, or in some cases to avoid embarrassing someone. Several persons gave permission to have their names used, and to some I have given their rightful names in the hope that they will read this book and contact me.

I could not have arrived at this point in time had I not been the beneficiary of the gift of love and loyalty of my husband Larry Lauer.

# GERMANY AND POLAND
## BEFORE AND DURING WORLD WAR II

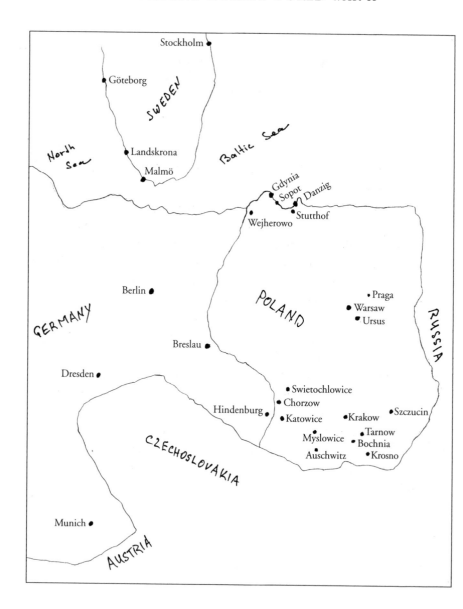

# CONTENTS

## *Part I  Descent into Hell*

# Part II  Hiding in Plain Sight

# Part III  Resurrection

PART I

*Descent into Hell*

1

# Expulsion

APRIL 1938 ✿ HINDENBURG, GERMANY

"Wake up." I felt Eva's hand on my shoulder and opened my eyes. "If you want to come along you must get up now." My sister's voice was firm.

"Where are you going?" I asked, but I quickly got out of bed because I knew.

"You have five minutes. If you are not ready to go, I will leave without you."

I hurried into my clothes. "Is there enough time? Do you think we will see him once more?"

"Don't talk now, just hurry. Here are your shoes."

Together we raced down Kronprinzenstrasse. We crossed at the Kochman-Ecke, took the shortcut through Peter-Paul Platz, and then turned left at Bahnhofstrasse. Eva ran into the railroad terminal; I followed close behind. On the platform stood our parents. They were crying. My father looked surprised. He let go of my mother's hand and put an arm around each of us.

"Why did you come?" he asked. "This is so difficult. We said our good-byes last night. I thought it would be better for you not to come to the station, easier for all of us." He looked at us while tears ran down his cheeks. My mother, her eyes red from crying, sobbed fitfully, her face distorted.

The previous evening, after we had eaten dinner, Father had said that Eva and I would say good-bye to him then and only Mother would accompany him to the terminal. Our parents remained in the dining room while Eva and I cleared away the dishes. When we returned from the kitchen, the dining room door was closed. Eva and I stood before the closed door, listening and trying to make sense out of the sentence fragments we could hear between sighs and whimpers. I started to cry. My hands clutched my aching stomach.

"Stop crying, they will hear us, you must stop crying," my sister said. She put her arm around my shoulder. "You must stop being silly. You heard what Papa said. It won't be too long, perhaps only two or three months, and then we will be together in America."

After what seemed a long time, my father came out. My mother stood behind him, both their faces red and puffy. My father put his hand on my head and recited a blessing. His hand felt heavy while he murmured the Hebrew words. Then he kissed me and hugged me hard.

"It will not be a long separation, I promise you. Believe me, it is for you that I am leaving. Don't cry. Think of your mother and your sister. You must sustain each other, and take care of each other. You must be courageous. If you get too upset, your stomach will ache, and that causes your mother to worry. You must be strong now, my brave, intelligent daughter. Don't get up in the morning to say good-bye. It's difficult now. In the morning it will be even more difficult." He led us into our room, and once again we hugged and kissed. I did not want to let go of his hand.

"Einsteigen," the conductor called. My father embraced us once more and then kissed my mother. He was crying hard. My mother watched him climb aboard the train. There was a strange look on her face, as if she had been beaten. The train began to move out of the station. Father was standing at the open window. Mother held onto his hand. She ran a few yards with the departing train, then let go. Father waved his handkerchief. For a long time Eva and I waved our handkerchiefs, our eyes glued to my father's head, then to the fluttering handkerchief, and finally to the back of the last disappearing car. Mother looked defeated, reduced in size.

Mother, Eva, and I: We mailed this photo to my father in New York in June 1938.
Hindenburg, 1938.

When there was nothing left to see, we started for home. We walked back
to our apartment, each of us holding one of Mother's arms as we climbed up
the two flights of stairs. Eva unlocked the door. My mother ran to her bedroom and slammed the door shut.

Wailing sounds came from the room. My mother could not make such
terrifying noises, I thought. They sounded like the howls of an animal in anguish. For hours we crouched at the door, fear paralyzing the urge to communicate. My big sister wept. I snuggled up to her and put my head on her
shoulder. She stroked my hair. "Mother will stop," she whispered. "You'll see.
Mother will stop."

I held Eva's hand and looked into her face questioningly. "Yesterday I overheard Mother say to Papa that he should not worry, that she will manage, that
she will take care of everything," I said.

"She will." Eva's voice was reassuring. "It has only been two weeks with
so much to do and so little time to think. Now Mother is reacting to the stress
and tension of the past two weeks." The Nazi government had sent my father
an *Ausweis*, an expulsion order. He had been allowed two weeks before he had
to leave the country.

In the late afternoon we finally went into the bedroom. Mother was lying
across the two twin beds, pushed next to each other, sobbing softly. Eva and

I lay down on the beds next to her. Together we remained there for two days, crying and sleeping. I could feel the fear; it was lodged in my stomach, dark and spreading. Eva was fifteen years old, and I was twelve.

## JUNE 1938 ✍ HINDENBURG, GERMANY

Our store was closed. Although my parents had closed the store before my father left for America, they had maintained the appearance that it was still open for business. They felt that it would be better for us if the date of Father's departure remained vague.

But now all pretense was dropped. Mother even stopped entering through the back door. She asked Herr Navrat to board up the store windows. Herr Navrat was the superintendent of the building, and it was through my father's intercession that he had gotten the position. He was a carpenter, and he had been an active member of the Communist trade union. When Hitler came to power, Herr Navrat was accused of treason and incarcerated. He was subsequently released, but could not find employment until my father stepped in and got him the job. He had three young children, all girls, and a wife who was very unhappy. Herr Navrat was always eager to help us, but his wife had told my parents that if he continued to associate with us, he would once again wind up in prison.

Each day when I passed the closed store I noted additional cracks in the store windows and broken glass from rocks thrown through the grillwork installed on the outside of the windows. We didn't bother to wash off the multiplying swastikas with their threatening messages.

Still, I felt relieved that the store was closed. There were daily torchlight parades through Kronprinzenstrasse, but our boarded-up store was no longer targeted. The marchers used the parades to harass the Jewish population of Hindenburg. During the parades, which occurred mainly in the afternoon, two SA, or Sturmabteilung, men, wearing black trousers, brown shirts, and black hobnailed boots, would position themselves in front of every Jewish store or office. Before the store closed, I would walk home from school while a parade was in progress and see two uniformed men standing in the recessed entrance leading to the front door of our store. The men stood erect, a red banner with a large swastika spread out between them. With burning torches held high in their outstretched hands, the menacing-looking Nazis were a blood-curdling sight. It took much courage for me to slip under the banner and into our store. This display of force kept even the most loyal customers at a distance.

In our apartment, across the street from our store, we were busy empty-ing drawers and bookshelves. Mother was paying surreptitious visits to neigh-bors and former friends. Jews were not permitted to sell their own possessions, but Mother decided to try and sell small items one could carry without call-ing attention to oneself. Since my sister left for work early in the morning, I would have to be the courier. I would have liked to work, but I was still too young. Within a relatively short time, Eva had learned shorthand, and she was a good typist. She worked full time for Dr. Schäfer, who had been my father's lawyer until Father left for America.

Mother gave me careful instructions. "Tomorrow, early in the morning, you will take these packages to Frau Pilne," she said. "Don't stop to speak to anyone and make sure no one sees you at Frau Pilne's door. Should you sense that someone is following you, or watching you from a window, don't stop to think and don't hesitate—just keep walking and return home."

"What should I say to Frau Pilne?" I wanted to know. I did not like the errand. Frau Pilne, the daughter of a meat-and-sausage merchant, was mar-ried to the owner of a bar, whose business had prospered. Both Frau Pilne's father and her husband had been customers in my father's clothing store, and for many years a friendly relationship had been maintained between our fam-ilies. I was aware that for the past year Frau Pilne had been avoiding us. She no longer responded to my greeting, and recently she had crossed the street rather than acknowledge Mother and me.

"There is nothing to say. Frau Pilne is expecting you," Mother replied. "She does not want you to ring the bell, and she urged me to warn you not to speak to her."

Earlier I had asked my sister if she thought Frau Pilne would buy the piano. Eva was sure that she would not. She knew that Frau Pilne had offered to store our paintings and the piano until our return to Hindenburg. "But we will never return. She knows that," said Eva. "Why should she buy the piano when she will get it for free?"

I carried parcels wrapped in brown paper and tied with string: a desk lamp, the metronome, and a tightly rolled small Persian rug. As I approached Frau Pilne's apartment, I saw the door was slightly ajar. The door opened, and

Frau Pilne received the first package without saying a word. I looked into her eyes. They were friendly, but she put a finger to her lips. I did not even say Guten Morgen. After the third trip, when I delivered the rug, Frau Pilne whispered, "No more today."

Our apartment no longer looked friendly. Shortly after Father's departure, Mother had taken all the paintings off the walls. My favorite picture depicting a tulip market in Holland—it was also Father's favorite—was gone. Only the photographs remained hanging. Over my parents' twin beds were portraits of my mother's mother and father on either side of a large portrait of my father's father. My paternal grandfather was dead now, and Father's mother had died shortly after the end of World War I. I longed to visit my remaining grandparents who lived in Poland. I did not speak about that because our parents had decided that there would be no more visits to Poland.

Saturday was the best day of the week. Eva and I, dressed in our nicest clothes, our hair carefully brushed, walked together to the synagogue to attend Sabbath services. At the steps leading to the main entrance of the synagogue, we met up with our respective friends, and Eva and I separated. Together, with our friends, we walked up to the women's section on the second floor. In the past, my friends and I used to gather in a spot that gave us

The synagogue community building with a large fenced-in garden and playground, before it was burned down during the Kristallnacht pogrom, Hindenburg, November 9, 1938.

a good view of the main floor, the male section of the sanctuary, and where we also could be seen. We must have giggled a lot, because often my father would look up and let me know that I was out of line.

Now, no one giggled. The seat where my father regularly sat was empty. The atmosphere was solemn, the faces of the worshippers serious. We read our prayers and sang our psalms responsively, but we all knew that everyone was waiting to hear the sermon. Our rabbi, Dr. Katz, was a fine orator and a very learned man. He selected readings from the Torah for his sermons, and through that biblical text, he instructed and guided us. If someone from the Gestapo had been listening, he would have had great difficulty in divining the portent of the sermon. However, we understood well what Dr. Katz was saying. He said it again and again, and most succinctly when he preached through the metaphor of Exodus. The message was: Don't tarry. Make your preparations carefully but expeditiously and leave "Egypt."

After our midday meal, we once again dressed carefully and took off for afternoon youth services, which were conducted in the main section of the synagogue. All the young people of our Jewish community wanted to be present at that service. It was the only place left where we could gather. After services, we would gather in groups according to age in one of the rooms of the Jewish Community Building, which was part of the synagogue complex. Without the constraining presence of adults or parents, we were able to speak about the matters that concerned us most. Many of the young adults, those in their late teens or early twenties, were leaving Hindenburg, and we wondered if we would ever meet again. Saying good-bye was difficult. Those departing friends were apparently heading to a brighter future, whereas for those remaining, the future looked bleak.

A number of Eva's friends had left, or were in the process of leaving, for Palestine, as were some of mine together with their parents. Both Eva and I would have liked our parents to go to Palestine. We were a Zionist family, and we dreamed about swinging a pickax and tilling the soil. My father had tried to emigrate to Palestine but had been unable to obtain a certificate, a permit issued by the British Palestine Mandatory government, which had the League of Nations mandate over Palestine. The permit was denied because England did not want merchants to emigrate to Palestine. However, young people with technical or agricultural qualifications had been able to obtain the coveted certificate.

During inclement weather, when it was not possible to gather in the fenced-in synagogue garden, all of us crowded into the narrow recreation room. We took turns playing ping-pong, we listened to group discussions led by the older members, and often we would sing together.

The person I was most eager to see during the Sabbath afternoons was Ernst Schäfer. We called him Zack—short for *zickzack* or zigzag—because he was constantly in motion and always eager to help. He had also become rather popular. In addition to leading the afternoon youth services, he had lately taken charge of deepening our appreciation of literature. Since Eva worked for his father, he knew our situation. Zack knew that I was sad and missed my father. I had confided in him and told him my dark thoughts. At night fear was gnawing away at my insides, and I did not want to burden my mother. Zack felt that reading could bring me some comfort. He brought me books, and we discussed them. In Jakob Wassermann's book, *Der Fall Maurizius* (The Maurizius Case), I perceived the powerlessness of the innocent individual when confronted by the limitless power of an accusing state.

It was not easy to find opportunities to discuss the books I was reading. My mother insisted that I walk to and from the synagogue with Eva. Mother always worried when we were out alone; it was dangerous to walk in our neighborhood park or to enter a playground. It was true that I had a penchant to linger or greet people, and the latter could have dire consequences. My non-Jewish friends, who had been my playmates, did not want to be associated with me, and they often joined their comrades in taunting or chasing me. Eva was unhappy about having me tag along. She told my mother that having an *Anhängsel* (appendage) nearby interfered with her social life. However, it was no use arguing the point since my mother backed all her decisions with the statement: "Your father left me an awesome responsibility, and until we are united again, I must do what I think best."

At the last literary meeting I attended, Zack read the whole short book of R. M. Rilke's *Die Weise von Liebe und Tod des Cornets Christoph Rilke* (The Bugler Christoph Rilke: How He Loved and How He Died). A very young officer is preparing himself for the ultimate sacrifice in the service of his country. I shuddered at his acquiescence to death, and I wondered about my own steadfastness. I did not have an opportunity to talk about the significance of Rilke's ballad poetry.

Oskar Weissberger. Photo my father sent to us in Hindenburg from New York.
August 1938.

## JULY 1938 ⤳ HINDENBURG, GERMANY

Mother was very nervous. No matter how good I tried to be, I was never good
enough. Though I knew that it upset her, I kept asking, "When will we hear
from Papa?" Mother's answer was usually, "You ask that question every day."
I wanted my mother to sit down with me, take me in her arms, talk with me,
and comfort me. Most of the time Mother appeared unreachable. She was busy
perusing and sorting documents. Often I found her deep in thought, her lips
compressed, her eyes distant.

We received two letters from Holland. In the first one, my father wrote
about his arrival in Amsterdam and of his attempts to communicate in English.
When he asked a policeman to direct him to a certain address, the policeman

smiled and told him to speak German so that he would be able to understand him better. The second letter was written on the stationery of the SS *Statendam*, the ship that would take my father to America. The letter was posted in Rotterdam.

I wrote letters to my father every day, letters I was unable to send. I told him how much we missed him, how lonely we were without him, and how I was keeping track of the days and weeks since his departure. I wrote to him about my friends: Margot Schneemann had left for Sweden; Gretel Neuman together with Elli, Gerda, and their parents had departed for Märisch-Ostrau, Czechoslovakia, enroute to New Zealand; and Erika Kochman, in preparation for emigration to Palestine, was attending an agricultural school outside Berlin. I told him that Hans Kaiser was now an orphan because his parents had committed suicide by inhaling gas. Heinz Prager, who was two years older than I, had been found hanging from a rope in the attic of his apartment building. I also told him that I was afraid. I kept the letters hidden in a cigar box in a secret place so that Eva and Mother would not be able to read them.


OCTOBER 1938 ⋙ HINDENBURG, GERMANY

Letters arrived from America. They were addressed to all of us, but there were also individual letters written to Eva and to me. Affidavits for the three of us had also arrived, and we received notification from the American consulate in Berlin that they were being processed. My father wrote that it was imperative for my mother to see the consul. But Mother had already made three trips to Berlin and had not yet been able to obtain an appointment. These trips were costly for us and difficult to finance. Most of our money was in a savings account, and we could only withdraw it for specific needs, such as food and rent.

Each time Mother left for Berlin, she dressed carefully and elegantly. She wanted to look her best for her appointment with the consul. Yet, each time when she appeared for the promised appointment, she was told that yet another document was missing, and until her file was complete, the consul would not see her. When Mother returned from Berlin, she would try to be optimistic. She would say that she had met the secretary of the consul, which itself was an accomplishment, since hundreds of people were waiting to get into the consulate building. However, after each trip, she looked very tired.

OCTOBER 28, 1938 ⚸ HINDENBURG, GERMANY

On Tuesday morning, at about ten o'clock, when Mother was once again in Berlin, perhaps with the last of the missing documents, the doorbell rang. Eva had left early for Dr. Schäfer's office. I was home alone, recovering from the grippe, and I must have dozed off. As I walked to the door, the doorbell rang once again and with greater urgency. There were men outside. Someone pounded at the door. A chilling voice commanded, "*Aufmachen, sofort auf-machen.*" Without removing the chain, I opened the door. It was the police. "*Aufmachen, aber schnell,*" said the policeman. I removed the chain. Five men walked into the hallway. Two of them wore the familiar navy-blue police uniform, two wore the black uniform of the SS or Schutzstaffel, and the fifth man was dressed in civilian clothes, with the Nazi armband on his sleeve. One policeman held a sheet of paper. He looked at me and snapped, "Oskar Weissberger?"

"That is my father."

"Where is he?"

"He is in America."

"That is a lie," he shouted. "His name is on the list."

"He is in America," I said again.

"Ilona Weissberger," he read from his list.

"That is my mother. She is in Berlin."

"What is she doing in Berlin?" the policeman demanded. He turned to the man dressed in civilian clothes and asked if that was permitted. The man shrugged his shoulders.

"When is your mother coming back?"

"Tomorrow afternoon."

He looked at the list again. "Eva Weissberger," he demanded.

"That is my sister. She is at work."

"Where is she working?"

"She works in Dr. Schäfer's office."

"You are Berta Weissberger?"

"Yes."

"So, they are all gone and left you alone—hmmm, a coincidence."

I could hear the other men stomping through the apartment, opening doors, moving furniture.

"I had the grippe," I explained, "and my mother wanted me to stay home from school for two more days."

I heard the snap of our front door lock. One of the black-uniformed SS men had left. The other returned to the dining room.

"No one in there," he said.

"Yes, we are doing very well, one out of four," one policeman said. Then he turned to me. "You come with us. There are some questions you will have to answer."

"May I get dressed?" I looked down at my pajamas. I did not want to cry.

"Take a coat, that's all."

He followed me into the room I shared with my sister. I reached for a drawer that someone had left open. "Only a coat!" It was an order.

Walking out of our room, I picked up the skirt and pullover I had left on the chair. There was no underwear. I slipped into shoes while walking toward the entrance hall. The policemen walked close behind me. My coat was hanging on a hook in the entrance foyer. I reached for it, and while putting it on, I managed to slip into the skirt. I stuffed the pullover into my coat pocket.

"The key!" The man with the armband held out his hand. "The key to the front door." The key was hanging on a hook. He looked in the direction my eyes indicated and put the key into an envelope and then into his pocket. As we walked out the door, Frau Raschke, our neighbor, was closing the door to her apartment.

"At what time do you expect your sister?" It was the policeman holding the list.

"She usually returns home around five o'clock."

We walked down the stairs and out of the house and turned right. People stopped to stare at us as we walked down Kronprinzenstrasse. I was walking between a policeman and a man from the Gestapo. The man in civilian clothes and armband walked behind us. I could feel the pajama bottoms I had rolled up slipping down my legs, but I did not dare bend down to fix them. It was a long walk. I could not see the names of the unfamiliar streets we passed because my eyes were full of tears.

We were heading for the new police station. From afar, I recognized the tall building of red brick and the adjoining prison with barred windows. Once inside, we walked down long corridors, past many offices with names on the doors. I could hear voices and the clatter of typewriters. All the doors were closed. We walked down a flight of stairs into another corridor, and then again down another flight of stairs. There were cell doors on both sides of the hallway. A guard opened a cell. The man in the black uniform pushed me inside, and the door was slammed shut and bolted from the outside. It was dark. There was a small barred window on the wall facing the door, but no light shone through, though I knew that it was still before noon. I was overtaken by fear. I called and banged on the door. No one came. I felt the urge to urinate. I pounded the door hard, screaming, "I must get out! Let me out!"

Through a barred opening in the door a voice shouted, "If you don't stop that racket, someone will come and help you stop."

"Please let me use the toilet," I pleaded.

"That's what the bucket is for. Use it." I wanted to see the guard who spoke. I stood on tiptoe, but I could not reach the barred opening in the door.

Hours later, two guards escorted me up several flights of stairs into an office. An official in civilian clothes wearing a red armband with a swastika sat behind a desk. He asked me the same questions I had been asked in our apartment. Then he turned to the guards, and said, "Next." The guards walked out. He motioned to me to come closer and leaned toward me across his desk.

"There is nothing I can do for you. The orders came from above," he said. "I know who you are and your father, well, I have known him for years. Let's see, must be eighteen years." He shrugged his shoulders.

The guards returned. With them were Herr and Frau Salomon. Frau Salomon was crying. As the guard led me out of the office, I heard Herr Salomon say, "Under which statute . . . ?" Back in the cell I felt somewhat comforted by having seen the Salomons. Apparently, they also had been arrested and brought to the prison.

After some hours the cell door was opened, and I was led to a large room filled with familiar faces. Most of them were members of the Ostjuden Verband, an association of Jews of East European background. My father had been the president of the organization for many years, and for the last several years, as a member of the board of directors of the Jewish community, he had actively represented the interests and concerns of this constituency. Frau Pasmanik saw me and walked toward me. Her husband and daughter Susie followed. Frau Pasmanik put an arm around me. She knew that my mother was in Berlin. Shortly before my father's departure for America, he had helped expedite the departure of her older daughter, Klärchen, to Palestine.

"So they did not manage to get Eva," she said with some relief. "You stay with us, and you will be part of our family until things get sorted out." There were chunks of bread and black coffee on a table. Frau Pasmanik urged me to eat. "You must eat something," she said. "You will need it." I couldn't swallow even a morsel. My stomach had been hurting, and when I looked at the food, it began to churn. Frau Pasmanik asked the guard if I could return with them to their cell. Then she appealed to him saying I was too young to be left alone. The guard was adamant in his refusal. He kept repeating *nicht erlaubt*—not permitted.

Back in the cell, after the door was locked, I could no longer cope with my mounting terror and screamed and cried. Hours later, the door was unlocked and my sister entered the cell. Eva was all over me. She hugged and kissed me and called me her little sister. She kept caressing me. "You look blue. Speak to me. Can you hear me?" she asked. She rubbed my arms and legs. I felt very cold. "Where are your stockings?"

"They did not allow me to take them," I told her.

She cradled my head in her arms. "What were they doing to you?" she whispered into my ear. "I could hear you screaming as I walked down the corridor."

"They didn't do anything," I said. I tried to tell her what had happened, but I could not put the words together. I became agitated, and I could not control my sobbing. Eva kept stroking my hair. She told me that when she returned home from work and opened the door with her key, she saw them. They were standing on the doorstep to the dining room—a policeman and a man dressed in civilian clothes with an armband. "Where is my sister?" she had asked. "I want to be with my sister." Eva did manage to stuff several pieces of clothing into a bag.

"Did you bring some clothes for me?"

"Yes, but why didn't you pack some yourself?"

Eva listened carefully while I recounted all that had happened—the interrogation at home and at the prison, seeing the Salomons, and the offer of help from the Pasmanik family. I was so glad Eva was at my side.

At about eight-thirty in the evening, there was a lot of noise all around us. Cell doors were opened and slammed shut. Children were crying, and guards shouted commands. Guards opened our cell and led us into a room filled with people. Everyone was standing, pressing against someone else, some holding the hands of children. The room was quite dark. There were people in wheelchairs I had not seen before. There were old people who could hardly walk and a man on a stretcher. I recognized most of the people. I had seen them in the synagogue, at community or sporting events, or on parents' day in school. Many families were no longer intact. Fathers had been taken away to concentration camps, and some of the older children had managed to find refuge abroad. No one really knew exactly what a concentration camp was; however, we understood that these facilities functioned outside the law and that legal recourse did not apply.

Frau Pasmanik was moving toward us. "Whatever happens," she told Eva, "let's try and stay together. Keep your eyes on us and stay near us." In past years, whenever Frau Pasmanik traveled to Hamburg to visit her parents, her husband and their two daughters would have Sabbath dinner in our house. In August 1937, Herr Pasmanik was picked up at his office and transported to a concentration camp. He was an accountant and respected member of our community. My father interceded on his behalf, and several months later, Herr Pasmanik was returned to his family. No charges had been made, but he had changed, and my parents said that the Gestapo had destroyed his spirit. Immediately upon his return, Herr Pasmanik and his wife began preparations for their daughter Klärchen's departure to Palestine.

Shortly after ten o'clock in the evening, the doors were opened and we were escorted out into the prison yard. The yard was brightly lit, floodlights illuminating all corners of the large enclosure. The evening was cold, and there were stars in the sky. After the darkness of the cell, and the near darkness of the holding room, the yard appeared eerie in its brightness. Orders were shouted for us to line up four in a row, and men in different uniforms, perhaps soldiers, surrounded us on all sides.

Moving slowly, covered trucks came into view. As the people ahead were loaded onto the trucks, and while Eva and I pressed against each other holding hands, we lost sight of the Pasmanik family. Through the rear flap of the covered truck pulling up in front of us, a suspended ladder was visible. The ladder was lowered to the ground, and families clinging to each other climbed into the truck. When the truck was filled with people, the stretcher was moved into the truck over the heads of the occupants. The man on the stretcher moaned and muttered a name. Just as the truck was about to pull away, two Gestapo officers with guns slung over their shoulders jumped aboard. They pulled up the ladder and lowered and secured the flap. The next truck moved up and stopped in the same place. The remaining people—there were now perhaps fewer than one hundred of us—were very quiet. Even the whispering had ceased. The only sounds one could hear were the clanking of the chains that held the truck flap open and the grinding noise of the bolts being shoved into iron slots.

As I climbed onto the truck, I noted that the yard was filled with uniformed men. I was afraid to let go of my sister's hand until I felt her presence on the rung beneath me. People in back of us were pushing us toward the front of the truck. It was very dark. There was a short whistle blast, the sharp command *abfahren*—proceed—and then sudden total darkness when the flap was closed from the inside. We heard our names being called: "Eva! Bertel!" Eva pushed toward the rear of the truck and called out, "Mother, we are here!" The people around us were calling, "Here! In here!" The truck never stopped rolling. A traveling bag was thrown into the opening, and then our mother was lifted onto the truck. The people around us made room as Eva and I moved to the rear of the truck. Mother was sobbing and panting. When she calmed down, she put her arms around the two of us and murmured, "We are together. Now everything will be all right. We are together."

We were standing propped by the other occupants who were pressing against us from all sides. In the dark I could sense the close proximity of the Gestapo officers with their guns. I planted my feet firmly so that I would not bump against them. We were told not to speak. I could feel my mother's arm around my shoulder. After several hours, the truck stopped. We were ordered to climb down, and as I did, I felt soft grass beneath my feet. There was noise as the people descended, stumbled, and fell in the dark. A hissing command told us to move silently. We were being pushed from behind across a large meadow until we reached the bank of a small river.

The sky was dark and it had started to rain. In the near distance, I saw the outline of a forest. We were ordered to cross in single file a plank that had been thrown across a narrow stretch of the river. I had to let go of my mother's hand. Eva crossed ahead of me, and mother came after me. The plank was too narrow for the people in wheelchairs, and the soldiers holding the stretcher were cursing as they struggled to get it across. Finally, all the occupants of the trucks had crossed over. We stood together on the other side of the river. The glare of the headlights from the trucks illuminated the shapes of the men facing us. A row of uniformed Gestapo officers and soldiers stood along the bank as far as my eyes could see, their rifles pointing at us. We were commanded to be silent and to listen carefully.

"We are standing on German soil," the speaker shouted through a loudspeaker. "You, however, having crossed this river, are now in Poland. You will march in the direction of the forest without looking back. Anyone attempting to turn back will be shot. This is a final warning. Whoever dares set foot on German soil again will immediately be liquidated."

The truck lights were turned off. We started to walk toward the forest. It had stopped raining, but the sky remained dark. We walked for hours. Intermittently, Mother sought out friends, and together they discussed our predicament. Though some of the people knew Polish, most did not. All conversation was conducted in German and whispered from one person to the next. Some men came over to speak to my mother. She had graduated from a Polish secondary school and knew the language well. She advised against continuing in a group and suggested that people separate and proceed in family units. Mother felt that we were bound to run into a Polish border patrol, and she wanted to avoid such an encounter. We moved toward some bushes and stopped while the other people passed us. I wanted to speak, but Mother put her hand over my mouth. In the stillness of the night, I could hear people stumbling, asking directions of each other, while children, afraid of the dark, were calling for their parents. "Too loud," Mother whispered. "Too much noise."

I was afraid to remain in the forest with Mother and Eva. When I finally asked Mother if she knew the way out of the forest, she answered, "Of course not." After everyone had passed us, she said, "This was an organized *Aktion**
to which the Polish government will surely respond. If we can avoid the border patrol and I can get to a telephone, I will call Uncle Zygmunt, but we will have to be very cautious while we move ahead." In the dark, Mother combed

* Nazi Germany created a unique dictionary, giving new definitions to common German words. The word *Aktion* became a euphemism initially for mass deportations, orchestrated persecutions, raids, and roundups and later, beginning in autumn 1941, for massacres.

our hair and straightened our clothing. She took off her hat and brushed off the moisture, combed her hair, and powdered her nose. After she had applied lipstick, we continued on the path alongside the forest. We took turns carrying Eva's briefcase and Mother's small traveling case. "Should we be stopped," Mother said, "I will speak Polish, and I will say that the carriage in which we were riding broke down. Don't slouch no matter how tired you feel. Don't answer questions addressed to you. Just look alert and pretend to understand what is being said." Neither Eva nor I could speak a word of Polish.

In the distance, through the early morning haze, we saw the outline of a village. We had walked throughout the night, and we were tired. Then we saw two men. They wore the khaki uniform of border guards and with them walked two policemen. They were carrying rifles. They stopped in front of us. In back of them was a police van. Mother spoke Polish to them, pleading with them not to put us in the van.

They took us in the van to the local police station. At the station, Mother again admonished us not to speak. She told the official seated behind the desk that, unless they allowed her to telephone her brother, she would wait for the captain and only speak with him. Since they did not let her use the telephone, Mother remained firm in her resolve not to give a statement. When the captain arrived, Mother went into his office, while Eva and I waited outside.

CHAPTER 2

# Sanctuary

I was later told that my uncle Zygmunt, Mother's brother, came to fetch us, but I only remember waking up in a bed in his apartment. Mother was bending over me and she was crying. Eva was hugging and kissing me, and Aunt Antosia came in stirring a cup of tea. Everyone was saying loving words. Two days had passed since our arrival in Uncle Zygmunt's home. They said that I had had convulsions and that during a nightmare I had screamed so loud and so long that the doctor who had been called had given me an injection. Though Mother had an official appointment to present herself at the police station in Sosnowitz, she had refused to go until I had regained consciousness. Neighbors drifted in and out of the room, and everyone wanted to know how I was feeling. I told them that I felt fine.

For many years Uncle Zygmunt had been a professor of classic languages at the Panstwove Gimnazjum, or gymnasium, the state secondary school in Lomza. He earned a comfortable salary, and he owned a vacation apartment in Bochnia, the town in which my grandparents lived. Every summer, for as long as I could remember, we had visited my grandparents for at least two weeks during our summer vacation. Uncle Zygmunt was the scholar in the

20

family, and everyone was proud of him. Sometimes when we visited, he was working, and we had to be very quiet while in the apartment. When Mother remained at home with Aunt Antosia, their son Salek, who was almost two years older than I was, took charge of us. He knew enough German to be able to communicate, and we enjoyed being together. My grandparents lived in the center of town, but from my uncle's apartment one could run into fields and a pine forest that were close by. We went blueberry picking or we gorged ourselves on wild strawberries. We laughed a lot, and we were happy.

In 1936, in the middle of the school semester, Uncle Zygmunt was advised that his teaching contract would terminate at the end of the school year. No reason was given, but it was not a great surprise. Poland was rife with anti-Semitism, and the Polish government wanted to fill all government posts with Christian nationals. Subsequently, Uncle Zygmunt obtained a position at the Jewish gymnasium in Sosnowitz at a considerably lower salary. At the Jewish gymnasium he taught Latin and history, and he also had administrative duties.

Since there were only two bedrooms, Aunt Antosia moved Salek into the living room and their five-year-old daughter Bronia into their bedroom, freeing up a bedroom for our use. The children were very happy to see us again, and they tried to teach us some Polish words. Late into the night, I could hear the adults discuss plans for our immediate future; however, most of the time they spoke Polish, so I could not understand what was being said. When Salek came home from school, he and Eva would go out and meet some of Salek's friends. I remained home because they said that I had had a "shock to the system." I did not even have to help with the dishes.

On the Sunday following our arrival, we were expecting guests. Mother washed and brushed our hair and did what she could to make our clothes look presentable. Libcia and Romek Landschaft arrived in the early afternoon. Libcia was my mother's cousin once removed, and the family lived close to the German border, in the town of Chorzow.

"Don't you remember me?" Aunt Libcia asked. "I came to visit you in Hindenburg, and I stayed almost a week."

"Yes, I think I do," I responded. "It was a long time ago."

"Let me see, it must have been in the autumn of 1932. Your hair was long and in pigtails."

I did not remember so well, but in those years we had frequent visitors from Poland. My mother's brothers, her sister, and her cousins often came with their families to visit us. Everyone liked to visit Germany. Once Hitler came into power, the visits ceased, and my mother preferred to travel to Poland and visit there with her family. Aunt Libcia spoke German fluently, her husband less so, and most of the conversation was conducted in Polish. After tea, Uncle Romek said to Mother, "We made the decision before we came here. We will take one of your daughters and keep her until you depart for America. We will treat her as if she were our own child. You don't have to worry, and it will be easier for you, but you must decide."

Mother looked at me, then at my sister, and again at me. "Bertel is the younger one," she said, "and she should be with me. Still, I don't know where or with whom I will be staying. If I can't go back to Germany, I will have to travel to Warsaw. It's best if Bertel goes with you." Mother smiled as she looked into my eyes then hugged me. "You must trust me," she whispered into my ear. "I know what I am doing. Believe me, it will be much harder for Eva."

I kissed Uncle Zygmunt and Aunt Antosia and said good-bye to my cousins. I hugged Eva long and hard. Aunt Libcia helped me with my coat. I walked up to my mother. "Will I see you again?" I whispered. "Now you are being silly." Mother's voice was firm and reassuring, but I did not feel reassured. She stroked my hair. She told Aunt Libcia that it was getting cold and that she would have to buy me a hat.

"I will write to you as soon as I am settled. Just keep in mind that shortly we will leave for America together."

"Will you come and visit me at the Landschafts?"

"I will come as soon as I can, but you must remember that we have no money, and it's expensive to travel. There is much that I must do, and it will be good for you if you get accustomed to your new surroundings. Do your best to learn as much of the language as you can. Perhaps Aunt Libcia will be able to find someone to help you continue with your English lessons. You always had a fine ear for languages." My stomach felt funny, and I forced myself not to cry. I embraced my mother. Aunt Libcia held onto my hand as we walked out the door. My other hand was in my coat pocket wrapped around a small piece of paper. On it was written my father's address in New York.

Two boys came to greet us as we walked into the Landschaft apartment. Sygmunt was one year older than I was and Maniek a year younger. Though

Aunt Libcia had told me that Sygmunt, they called him Syga, had had two years of German at the gymnasium, I found that neither of the boys understood what I was saying. Uncle Romek showed me around the apartment. In the kitchen I met Gertrud, the housekeeper. She lived in a room adjoining the kitchen. Everyone watched while I greeted the dachshund Bobek. They wanted to see if Bobek would like me.

The rooms were large and elegantly furnished. The Landschaft's bedroom looked like a bedroom I had seen in a film. The bed was large and covered with a rose satin bedspread embroidered with clusters of flowers. The window draperies were made of the same material. The boys' bedroom was furnished in white, and the furniture was similar to our bedroom furniture in Hindenburg. There was a dining room and a den. "Bertel will sleep on the sofa in the dining room," Uncle Romek said to Gertrud. "She should be comfortable there." Gertrud smiled at me encouragingly. "Everyone eats breakfast in the kitchen," she said.

"Let's empty a drawer in the boys' room for Bertel's things," Aunt Libcia said to Gertrud. Then she realized that I had nothing. "Not to worry," she added. "Tomorrow we'll go and buy some things girls should have."


NOVEMBER 1938 ⚭ CHORZOW, POLAND

During late morning hours, I wrote letters. Uncle Romek left for his office early in the morning, and at about eight o'clock, Syga and Maniek left for school. Aunt Libcia left the house around ten o'clock. The soup kitchen, sponsored by the Jewish community, where Aunt Libcia did volunteer work, was being expanded to accommodate Jews who had been expelled from Germany. There was much telephoning to gather clothing for people who had been forced to leave their homes without any possessions. Whenever the family gathered, they talked about the Jewish refugees. Just several miles west, across the Polish-German border, Hitler was taking unprecedented actions against German nationals who were Jews. The Polish press could not comprehend that the world had acquiesced in the German annexation of Czechoslovakia. During news broadcasts, there were frequent references to broken agreements and betrayals by the democratic countries of the West.

I wrote letters to my father, my mother, and Eva. I also wrote to Zack

Schäfer. I told him about my relatives, and that there were German books I could borrow from the local library. I also wrote that it was difficult to make do with clothes and things that were not my own, while my own treasured personal possessions were left behind. I spoke to him of my fears and of my loneliness. To my mother I wrote that though I was comfortable and treated well, I wanted to be near her. I asked her when I could go visit her in Krakow, or if she would come visit me.

From Uncle Romek's office one could make and receive foreign telephone calls. Zack wrote that he wanted to call me. Uncle Romek suggested I arrange to have Zack call me on November 10, at seven o'clock in the evening. I could come to his office then and wait for the call.

I never received Zack's phone call. In the early morning hours of November 10, news broadcasts informed Poland and the world of devastating attacks against Jews that had happened in Germany the preceding night. Days later a letter from Zack arrived. He wrote that terror had permeated Jewish communities throughout Germany since that night of pogroms. November 9, 1938, subsequently came to be known as Kristallnacht—the night of broken glass.

Zack wrote that our beautiful synagogue had been first vandalized and then torched, and that many Jewish homes had been destroyed. The streets of Hindenburg were littered with shattered glass. Many men had been arrested and transported to concentration camps.

Hooligans had assaulted our revered old rabbi, Dr. Katz, and cut off his beard. Jews who had made preparations to leave Germany were in a frenzy to depart. Those who were not able to accelerate their own departure made hasty preparations for their children. Jewish communities abroad were helping to arrange for sponsors and financial aid to help young children emigrate. This undertaking was called Kindertransport.

Toward the end of November the postponed telephone conversation finally took place. I was so nervous I could hardly speak, but I listened carefully to what Zack had to say. He told me that our apartment had been sealed, but that within the next few days he would try to enter it. He would already have done so, but his father cautioned that it was against the law. After Kristallnacht and the ensuing lawlessness, many empty Jewish apartments had been vandalized and plundered. I answered that we would be happy with anything he could salvage, but I admonished him to be careful. Zack told me that his uncle in Palestine was making arrangements to bring him and his brother Walter to a kibbutz and that he hoped to leave Hindenburg within a short time.

I also wanted to leave soon. I dreamt of my approaching boat trip to America. I imagined waving from train windows to my relatives who stood on the platform and watched the train depart. Before leaving, I would first say good-bye to all the people who had posed so many tormenting questions, such as why my father had left for America while his family remained behind.

On a cold and snowy Sunday my mother came to visit. She told me that she had decided to respond to my urgent requests for a reunion and had bought a railroad excursion ticket. She could only remain through the night and would leave before noon on the following day. We would sleep together on my sofa in the dining room.

Mother arrived in the same gray suit that she had worn when she left for Berlin and the appointment with the American consul. It no longer looked so nice. Next to my mother, Aunt Libcia looked elegant. The winter coat mother was wearing was warm but did not fit very well. Her face was drawn, and there were new lines under her eyes.

Everyone wanted to hear how our emigration was proceeding. Syga and Maniek listened attentively while Mother explained in Polish some of the problems involved with the transfer of documents from the American consulate in Berlin to the American consulate in Warsaw. Both she and my father in America were urging the authorities to accelerate our emigration.

When we were alone, Mother whispered, "Bear in mind that you are the lucky one. You live in a lovely apartment, and you eat fine meals at regular hours. Eva is not that fortunate, and I still have not been able to make appropriate arrangements for myself. You should be grateful."

"But I want to be with you."

"Where? You did not listen. I am moving from one place to another, and I know that while I am there everyone is inconvenienced. Fortunately, we have many relatives living in Krakow. You must learn to be more patient."

Before returning to Krakow, Mother told Aunt Libcia that she would like to see me more occupied. "Perhaps she could learn a trade," Mother suggested. "How about photography? That might be a good skill to have."

"She is too young," Aunt Libcia said. "Moreover, she doesn't speak Polish.

I don't know if anyone would be willing to teach her both the language and a skill. Eva was lucky that Salek was able to register her as his apprentice."

Salek was the son of my father's brother. He was a dentist and quite successful in his profession. At about the time of Eva's arrival in Krakow, Salek had been searching for a technical apprentice. He spoke German, and Eva was both eager to learn and eager to please. An apprentice did not get a salary, but I subsequently learned that Salek always made sure to keep Eva supplied with adequate pocket money.

## JANUARY 1939 ⤠ CHORZOW, POLAND

The Landschaft family observed Jewish dietary laws, but instead of changing the two sets of dishes, the family would spend the eight days of Passover in a small Jewish hotel in Zakopane, an internationally known ski resort in the Tatra Mountains. On a number of occasions, my parents had talked about the awesome sight of those majestic mountains.

My aunt and uncle were not sure whether to take me along or send me on a long-desired visit to my mother in Krakow. Though I was eager to visit my mother, the thought of skiing once again was a powerful temptation. Both

With my Aunt Libcia Landschaft on ski holiday, Zakopane ski resort. March 1939.

Eva and I loved to ski. From Hindenburg, a short train ride took us to Riesengebirge, where we could indulge in the joyous exercise. However, we hadn't used our ski equipment in several years. The increasing anti-Semitism, fueled by the daily newspaper *Der Stürmer*, had made it impossible for Jewish children to engage in this sport.

At about this time, the Landschafts received an important letter from my father. He urged them to travel with their sons and me to America on tourist visas to see the World's Fair. My father suggested that, after the annexation of Austria and the Munich Agreement, living so close to the German border was dangerous. He wrote that once in America on a tourist visa, Uncle Romek would have an opportunity to look around for a business association, and if successful, he could then return to Poland and liquidate his assets. With the proceeds, he would be able to obtain an immigration visa as a capitalist. Aunt Libcia was eager to discuss my father's proposal. The close proximity of Nazi Germany was giving her nightmares. Uncle Romek did not disagree, but he said, "If the World's Fair continues through 1940, it will give me time to make appropriate arrangements, but not this year. We just cannot leave this year."

The eight days in Zakopane were even more splendid than I had anticipated. The view of the tall mountains from the hotel bedroom that I shared with my cousins made me forget what was happening outside the charming mountain hamlet. Everything I brought along, including my long underwear, was borrowed. My boots did not fit well, and the skis were too long for me. However, after some minor discomfort, I was able to adjust the boots, and for the rest of the holiday, I was skiing hard to keep up with my two cousins, who were better skiers than I. During the day it got so warm I was able to ski in a pullover. The sky was often clear, and I could see the peaks of the three high mountains that surrounded us. We took the cable car only once because the tickets were expensive. Most of the time we either climbed or we took the cog railway.

One day while we were climbing, I heard my name being called. I turned and there was Ruth Wischnitzer, Eva's friend from Hindenburg. She told me that she had been forcibly detained and deported on the same fateful day, but we had not seen each other in the prison. Her family had real estate interests in Poland, and her life was quite pleasant. They lived in an apartment in a building the family partly owned. She had come to Zakopane as a guest of friends who were skiers. Her hosts invited me to come for afternoon tea, and both she and I tried hard to be sociable. We would have preferred to be alone. We were unable to speak about our lives in Hindenburg, about the indignity of our expulsion from our homes, and about the terror of the Kristallnacht. It was not that her friends would not want to know or hear about it, but we knew that they could not really comprehend the depth of our sorrow.

## JUNE 1939 ⋙ CHORZOW, POLAND

Aunt Libcia had made arrangements to keep me occupied in the beauty parlor she visited once a week. I was to look around and learn, and at the same time make myself useful to the staff. Though everyone tried to be friendly, it was immediately apparent to me that no one really wanted me to be there. Aunt Libcia was a regular customer at the beauty parlor, and they did not want to offend her. The daughter of the owners, Frania, ran a little business of her own in the front section of the store. She repaired celluloid dolls that were brought in with broken arms or legs. Frania had plenty of business, and it seemed to me she could use an extra pair of hands. She worked with glue, acetone, and round white elastic, and I was an eager apprentice. But Frania did not permit me to work with either scissors or pliers, and she never let me know if my work pleased her. I overheard her say that the whole idea of my being there was ridiculous.

When I heard my relatives discuss their upcoming summer vacation plans, I made the decision to go to Krakow and spend the summer near Eva and Mother. In her letters, Mother asked me to abandon my foolish idea. When she realized that I was adamant, she urged me to tell the Landschaft family that I would return after the summer. Aunt Libcia accompanied me to the train, and she repeated that, until I left for America, I was to continue to be part of their family. I held my little suitcase filled with my new possessions and I cried when I hugged and kissed my aunt. I was no longer sure that I had made the right decision.

At the Krakow terminal, a tall handsome man approached me as soon as I descended onto the platform. In his hand he held my photograph. He told me that he was Hennek Sternberg; his wife, Lusia, was my father's niece. I knew that Mother was presently staying in their home.

"Where is my mother?" I asked.

"She is waiting for you at home. She had a little asthma attack, and Lusia thought it would be better if I came to fetch you."

The Sternbergs lived in an elegant apartment house in a residential part of the city. We had to ring a bell and wait for a concierge to open the door before we could enter from the street. Lusia met us at the top of the stairs. She took me in her arms and kissed me lovingly. There were tears in her eyes. Lusia had long blond hair pulled back from her forehead. She was tall and heavy with child.

"I am very happy that you came," she said. "I read all your letters, and I was eager to meet my cousin who writes such beautiful letters. Your father and I were good friends when we were growing up, and whenever he came to visit the family in Krakow, he came to see us." My father was the second youngest of ten children and closer in age to Lusia than to some of his older siblings.

When I walked into the apartment, I saw my mother. She was sitting at the kitchen table, leaning over a plate with a burning coil. She was working hard to catch her breath by inhaling the smoke rising from the coil. She was coughing and wheezing, and her face was red from the sustained effort. Lusia held my hand, and with the other she stroked my mother's back. "It will be all right, Ilona. It will pass, if only you could calm down," she said soothingly. "Look, Betus has arrived."

I wanted to stand next to my mother, but Lusia urged me to follow her into the living room. She told me that Mother was under a doctor's care and that various remedies were being tried. "The attack will pass," she said. "They are scary, but not fatal. If you could make believe that you are not afraid, it will lessen your mother's apprehension." I said that I would do whatever was required of me if only my mother would stop making those frightening sounds.

That night and for the next several nights, I slept on a folding cot next to my mother, who slept on a couch in the Sternberg living room. I listened as my mother struggled to breathe, and I sensed her convulsive attempts to suppress the coughing. Dear God, I prayed, help us get to America and don't let my mother die. I will stay wherever Mother wants me to stay, and I will not complain.

On Saturday, Eva worked only during the morning hours, and in the afternoon she came to visit us. We went for a walk on the Plante Promenade and compared our respective living arrangements. Eva lived with Father's nephew Genek, his wife Sally, and their one-year-old son on Ulica Kremerowska

in the Karmelicka section. Eva was their au pair, in exchange for her room
and board. She did some housework and babysat during evenings when the
parents went out.

Eva was very happy to see me, and she was affectionate and forbearing;
however, when I asked her if I could live with her in Genek's apartment, she
got upset. She said, that it was time that I grew up and that I should have
stayed at the Landschafts.

"I wanted to be with Mother and you," I defended myself, "and now, how
can I leave when Mother is so ill?"

"It is an asthma attack, and the doctor said that once the attack subsides,
she should be able to live normally. There is no one in Krakow who lives as
comfortably as the Landschafts do, and Mother does not know where to place
you," Eva insisted.

"I will go back," I promised. "I'll stay for two weeks."

I loved being in Krakow because there were so many relatives there. Three
of my father's brothers and two of his sisters lived in the city. A fourth brother,
Salek's father, lived in Mielec, and he came to visit us. All father's siblings were
older than he was; some of their children were twice our age, and several had
little children. They lived modestly, in crowded apartments with few luxuries.
They talked to me about my father. I was happy to sit there for hours and listen to tales about their childhood on a farm and about my father—their re-
bellious and adventurous brother Oskar. After his discharge from the Austrian
army, my father had decided to remain in Germany rather than return to his
home in Poland. "He wrote to us," they told me, "and he came to visit as often
as he could. He came to every wedding, bar mitzvah, and funeral, and he always sent generous presents."

Sometimes I spent the night with the various relatives I visited, and invariably that caused problems. When I slept on a sofa or even on a folding cot,
I realized in the morning that someone had had to sleep on the floor. There
were never enough blankets or pillows, and when the time came to leave, I
gladly packed my little bag.

On Sabbath everything was different in Krakow. No one went to work,
and families gathered together. In Hindenburg our store had remained open
on the Sabbath. Most of the time my parents attended services at the synagogue. After services, we would go home for our midday meal. Following a
short rest, at about three o'clock in the afternoon, Father would return to the

store. In Krakow, it was mainly the men who went to the synagogue. Wives and daughters remained home and prepared for the Sabbath meal.

Our relatives welcomed us with much affection and urged us to stay for the big Sabbath meal. Following dinner, everyone sat around the table. There was singing, laughter, and talking. Everyone assured us that we would be leaving for America soon.

The two Sabbaths I spent at the Stiehls were the most memorable. Great Aunt Pepcia, and Great Uncle George—he was my grandmother's brother—lived on Ulica Brzozowa in the Kazimierz section. They were pious and observed the Sabbath with all its ritual traditions. Uncle George worked for the local Singer Sewing Machine Company. They lived very modestly, and my mother once suggested that perhaps in the territory he covered, everyone who could afford a sewing machine already owned one. Since Saturday was truly a day of rest and prayer, no one in their home was allowed to perform a task that would interfere with the sanctity of the day.

I arrived early on Friday morning, but for Ulica Brzozowa it was already late. The street was bustling with women carrying covered pots, covered baking pans, and bags filled with fruit. Most of the women of that neighborhood made their own challah. I helped Aunt Pepcia carry both the plumcake and covered challah to the communal bakery. The huge baking oven had separate sections for each customer's pots and pans. Everyone identified her creation by some personal mark. Women greeted each other and then proceeded on their way.

Back in the apartment, through the open window, one could hear the rhythmic sounds of knives cutting noodle dough and the click of cleavers against wooden chopping blocks. Aromas of chicken soup, fish, and chopped liver pervaded the air. Before Aunt Pepcia went into her room to prepare and dress for the Sabbath, she once again swept the two rooms and the kitchen. It was my task to spread white tablecloths on the dining table and the server. Then I set the table. Aunt Pepcia returned in a black alpaca dress set off with ecru lace around the neck and cuffs and with lace decorating her gray hair.

As soon as Uncle George returned from the synagogue, we sat down to eat. He said many prayers during the meal, and after dinner we prayed together and sang songs that glorified the Sabbath. Next morning when I awoke, Uncle George had already left for the synagogue. I went with my aunt to the nearby communal kitchen, where we fetched a hot covered pot. In it was our Sabbath meal, which had been kept at a low temperature on a stove at the kitchen. My mother came to eat with us, and after we had cleared the dishes, neighbors, friends, and relatives joined us. The men discussed the Torah portion of the day, while the women prepared the afternoon tea.

Men and women got together for the refreshments. Different cakes and cookies were tasted, and everyone toasted each other with the cherry wine that Uncle George distilled in large glass vessels. Toward the end of the Sabbath, the young people left. They walked in groups along the Plante Promenade. Sometimes they walked in pairs, but mostly they walked in foursomes. This was the time for introductions, for meetings with the opposite sex, and for making plans for the following Sabbath.


JULY 1939 ⤙ KRAKOW, POLAND

It seemed that everyone in Krakow was discussing the danger militant Germany posed for Poland. People lined up in front of cinemas to see the latest newsreel. Wherever folks gathered, I heard them discuss threats made by Hitler during his daily, angry tirades.

Zack sent us several packages from Hindenburg. There was clothing for the three of us—scarves, gloves, and some pullovers. Most important for Mother were the two Persian rugs from my parents' bedroom. Mother was delighted.

"They will bring us some money," she said. She was planning a trip to the American consulate in Warsaw, and she needed a means to finance it. Mother had received an official notification from the American consulate in Warsaw that acknowledged receipt of our affidavits and the accompanying documents from the American consulate in Berlin.

In his letter to me, Zack wrote that he was making final preparations to leave Germany. He was going to Palestine and had made arrangements to receive some missing documents in Italy. His brother Walter had already arrived in Palestine. Zack used metaphors that I readily understood. He said that the roof was burning, and the flames were spreading. He felt that if our departure for America was not imminent, Mother should look for alternate ways to get us out of Poland. He suggested that I inquire about Kindertransports that were leaving for Palestine. When I mentioned it to Mother, she said, "Don't divert my energy from the task I must accomplish."

Jewish refugees from Austria and Czechoslovakia were surging into Poland. The Polish government was a bit more hospitable than they had been with the Jews expelled from Germany. The Jewish community made a three-room apartment with a kitchen available to these refugees. This gathering place, located on Ulica Grodsky in the Radom section, was known as "the club." It was run communally, and everyone donated his or her talents. Talent was abundant. Since my sister was a good typist and also knew shorthand, she was immediately recruited to help write applications for various documents.

The common language was German, but within days, classes were given in Polish, English, and Ivrit, the spoken Hebrew language. In the same room, at the same time, three or four different groups gathered and pursued their respective tasks. In the evening hours, we would listen to lectures, and invariably the lectures about the growing menace from across the border drew the largest crowds.

At noontime there was always hot soup and some bread, and the members took turns preparing the meal. No one was to sleep at the club; however, whenever someone lost his or her sleeping arrangements, it was understood that he or she would spend the night at the club. The club was within a short distance of the Vistula River, and when it was very hot, those who had swimsuits went for a swim. We were told that the Vistula was polluted, but that did not deter us.

I met people at the club who had been prominent citizens in Germany, Austria, and Czechoslovakia. There were the brothers Robert and Otto Ball, from Vienna. Both had doctorates and were renowned in their respective disciplines. Robert was a psychoanalyst, and Otto a mathematician. Both had held university posts. One of the members had been a prominent nurse in the Prague Hospital. There were attorneys and teachers, and quite a number of students who had been preparing for advanced degrees. No one discussed his or her former lives; we were all in the same situation, trapped in a foreign country and trying hard to get out of Europe.

Eva was dating a young man from Prague. His name was Werner Lowy, and he was several years older than Eva. He was tall, very slender, with light brown wavy hair combed back from his high forehead. We had much in common. His married brother, several years his senior, lived in New York, and Werner was trying to leave Poland and join him in America. Werner's parents were elderly and had decided for the time being to remain in Prague. Werner told us that his escape from Prague had been dangerous and quite arduous and that his parents had not been well enough for such an undertaking. We decided that my father and Werner's brother Robert should get together, and both Werner and Eva sent letters to help facilitate a meeting between the two men.

I liked Werner and I enjoyed being with him and his friends from Prague. Eva thought I should look for friends who were nearer my age. I decided to stay out of Eva's way. I signed up for the English course that was given during the early afternoon. Whenever I could, I showed up for lectures, and no one thought that I was too young to be present.

Toward the end of July, Uncle Jacub came to Krakow. I knew him well because he had visited us many times in Hindenburg with his wife Regina, my mother's sister. When I was younger, we had visited them in Katowice whenever we took a trip to Poland. A few years back, they and their two-year-old son Dollek had left Katowice for Krosno, a town in the foothills of the Carpathian Mountains. Uncle Jacub told us that he had to go on a business trip to Tarnow, and since Eva was planning to visit them, Regina said that he should pick her up. "My problem is Betus," Mother responded. "For some reason I can't quite understand, she is unwilling to return to the Landschafts. I would be happy if you would take her instead." Uncle Jacub walked over to me, and said, "I guess you heard, and Aunt Regina is very anxious to see all three of you. We should leave now for our train ride to Tarnow in order to be on time for the afternoon bus from Tarnow to Krosno."

The bus was crowded, but Uncle Jacub managed to secure two seats together, and he arranged for my suitcase to be tied to the roof of the bus. The bus ride was bumpy; however, the landscape along the route was spectacular. Different crops were planted in adjacent fields. Seen from a distance, they looked like checkerboard squares. Next to a yellow wheat field would a green potato or vegetable field, and interspersed were orchards, the trees laden with fruit. Peasants with colored kerchiefs covering their hair were working in the fields, and often they straightened their backs and waved to the passing bus. Whenever the bus came close to a town or village, it would slow down to make room for passing cattle, and sometimes it would stop for a horse-drawn rack wagon. The stretches of pine forests were dark, fragrant, and mysteriously ominous. The majority of passengers on the bus were farmers returning from market. On their laps, in the aisle, or clamped between their legs were bundles and wicker baskets in all shapes and sizes. Despite the open windows, the air was rife with odors of cheese and wilting produce.

Aunt Regina listened attentively while I recounted the events of the past months. Her beautiful black eyes were sad, and they filled with tears when I described the anguish of the many inconclusive journeys my mother had made to the American consulate in Berlin. She kept murmuring "my poor sister."

That summer, during the month of August, it hardly ever rained. There were many days when Aunt Regina packed lunch and took my six-year-old cousin Dollek and me to nad Sztuki, the part of the river far enough removed from town not to be polluted. Since I was a swimmer and eager to take part in all sports activities, I met many young people. Most of them were gymnasium students on summer vacation, and they were supportive of my eager attempts to learn the intricacies of the Polish language. They included me in some of their day excursions, and several times I was asked to play tennis. On the Sabbath, or other dress occasions, the students donned their school uniforms: pleated navy skirts for the girls, navy trousers for the boys, and navy tunics with light blue trim. A chic beret, with silver insignia, mostly worn on the side of the head, completed the outfit. They looked very handsome as they promenaded in or around the town square.

On the two opposite sides of the square, stretching from one end to the other, were white stucco arcades. In back of arcades were shops. Uncle Jacub's store also was in the square though not under the arcade. On market days, Tuesdays and Fridays, the stores were full of peasants and small landowners from outlying districts, and Aunt Regina would help in the store. When it was very hot, or when it was raining, everyone rushed to find shelter under the arcade.

My best friend was Genia Springer. Together with her and her friend and classmate, Krysia Magierowska, we walked through the cool arcades while I listened to them giggle as they discussed their flirtatious encounters. Krysia, whose parents were devout Catholics, was rebelling against the strictures of her religion, and she questioned some of her teacher's prejudices. Both girls lived with their families in well-tended villas at opposite ends of the town. Aunt Regina lived in one of the few small apartment houses near the center of the town, and that was where the three of us would often meet.

The town of Krosno had a population of about fifteen thousand residents, of which perhaps less than one-fifth were Jews. The town was in a valley, and walking out of town in any direction one could see hills topped by oil rigs. The prosperity of the area was based on petroleum. Krosno residents proudly referred to the less-than-successful laboratory experiments of Wladislaw Dunikowski. A chemist and owner of a number of oil fields, Pan* Dunikowski had discovered gold dust in the petroleum. However, he had been unable to complete the process for refining gold due to inadequate monetary backing.

Genia's father was an engineer in the large refinery, and the family held shares in some of the oil rigs. On hot afternoons, Genia and I would sit in her bedroom and talk about being friends forever and of Genia visiting me in America. Genia had blue eyes, long blond hair, a fine athletic body, and a beautiful voice. I never tired of listening to her sing of romantic love and of sacrifice and patriotism. She also knew some Hebrew songs, but not as many as I did.

My return trip to Krakow was delayed due to my collision with a speeding bicycle. I was badly bruised, and the doctor, Romek Rosenberg, who attended to my wounds, was a friend of the family. He was also the most eligible bachelor in town, and during my recuperation period, when Dr. Rosenberg would make house calls, many single young women, who hardly knew me, would show up with flowers in the hope of meeting the doctor.

There were advantages in having to remain at home. I had a crush on Lutek Steigbugel, who came regularly to my aunt and uncle's apartment to tutor my cousin. An upper-class student at the gymnasium, Lutek earned money by tutoring the younger students. I longed to return to school, and in the Krosno milieu I was very conscious of not progressing with my education.

My six-year-old cousin, who had taken my invasion of his home in stride, was fascinated with my various relationships. Though I did not know it, he often mischievously listened in on my conversations. Later, he entertained my aunt and uncle with the bits of conversations he overheard while I was speaking with Genia or Lutek, conversations I had thought were private.

Throughout the months in Poland, letters from Zack arrived once a week, and I often wrote to him more than once a week. I would tell him of the

---

* *Pan* is the Polish form of address for a Polish man, equivalent to the English Mr. *Pani* is equivalent to Mrs., and *Panna* to Miss.

changes in lifestyle, as I moved from one relative to another, and of the people who had had an impact on my life. Through Zack I got news about my hometown. After Kristallnacht, all social life among the Jews in Hindenburg had come to a halt. In each letter I received, Zack wrote of yet another family who had gotten visas and left and of families who had broken up because the children had left Germany on a Kindertransport. A few lucky ones were claimed by relatives abroad. In a letter forwarded by my mother to Krosno, Zack again wrote of clandestine transports that were leaving Poland for Palestine. He urged us to make contact with the referring Jewish organization.

I had spent more than three weeks in Krosno, and the time had passed quickly. My friends were preparing to return to school at about the time I was to leave Krosno. When Uncle Jacub helped me onto the train in the neighboring town of Jaslo, my suitcase was bulging with new acquisitions. I had a new pair of shoes, a dress that was sewn according to my measurements by my aunt's dressmaker, a bathing suit, and some presents from my friends. When I arrived in Krakow, Hennek Sternberg was again waiting on the platform. He waved his magic pass, and we left the railroad station by some special exit ahead of the crowds. Hennek was attached to a governmental agency, and his work entailed a great deal of travel.

In Krakow everyone was now discussing the growing danger of a German military invasion. Along the German-Polish border, troop movement had been sighted on the German side. Crowds of Poles continued to line up in front of cinemas waiting to see the latest newsreel.

Mother was once again planning a trip to Warsaw to help speed up our emigration. Though it had been understood that I was to depart for Chorzow and once again be part of the Landschaft family, my mother kept delaying the day of my departure. She worried that there might be incidents of civil unrest because Hitler had called the Chorzow area "disputed territory."

I spent the last days of August at the club on Ulica Grodsky. The Krakow Jewish Community, through vigorous solicitations, had once again made available a collection of used clothing. An effort was made to distribute the items on an equitable basis, and I managed to obtain a winter dress and a woolen cardigan. The rooms were as crowded as they had been in early summer, and the number of lectures and classes were equally plentiful; however, now the atmosphere seemed more frenzied. People gathered in groups and whispered; one sensed an air of secrecy.

Finally I managed to corner Eva's friend Werner Lowy as he was leaving for the Vistula River for what I thought was an afternoon swim. "Can I come along?" I asked.

"We no longer go for afternoon swims," he replied. "I gather Eva did not tell you. We gather secretly and we train. We are in the process of forming a Czech legion that will fight alongside the Polish army should a war break out."

"How do you know that war will break out?"

"We do not know, and what we are doing is against the law. We could be arrested. No one must know about our preparations, and you should not speak about it to anyone."

"Yes, yes, I understand that, but the legion that is being formed, are all the members from Czechoslovakia?" I asked.

"No, Jews from Germany and Austria, and also several men who are not Jewish have joined us. This endeavor is beyond nationalism."

In the days following it was obvious to me that club members were saying good-bye to each other, but I was unable to ascertain where they were going, or where the legion would surface. The matter was complicated by the fact that all the club members were aliens, and therefore forbidden to engage in political or military activity.

CHAPTER 3

# Blitzkrieg

SEPTEMBER 1939 ⟶ KRAKOW, POLAND

Suddenly, on September first, the Landschaft family arrived in Krakow. The four of them came to see Mother at the Sternbergs. They were in traveling clothes, and they told us they had fled at a moment's notice. Someone had heard a radio news bulletin that German troops had crossed the border into Poland. "One radio announcement, and then all broadcasting ceased," Uncle Landschaft said. Mother had been listening to the radio, and Uncle Romek asked her what she had heard. "What have you heard? What are they saying?" he urged. Mother said that there had not been a news bulletin about an invasion.

Lusia had been speaking on the telephone, and now she was putting clothing into a suitcase. "Was that Hennek who called?" Mother asked. Lusia nodded and continued packing. She had recently had a miscarriage and was again pregnant. Mother and everyone in the family were concerned about her because she had had a number of miscarriages. She and Hennek were yearning to have a baby.

Mother rephrased her question. "Lusia, what did he say?" Lusia hesitated for a moment before responding.

"He said I should pack some clothes and walk over to my parents and stay there."

"What else did he say?"

"You know well, Ilona, he does not speak about his assignments, and certainly not over the telephone. He did say that he was asked to leave for Warsaw immediately, and he could not tell me when he would return."

Something was not right. We looked out the window and saw people rushing about carrying bundles and suitcases. Baby carriages were heaped with packages, and elderly folk were pushing the carriages. "One must guard against panic," Mother said as if to herself. She asked Uncle Landschaft about his plans.

"I will try to get to Wieroczyce," Uncle Romek said. "We want to be together with Libcia's family. Also, if there is a war, we will be safer in a small town. Here in Krakow people still don't know what has happened. We interrupted our journey to warn you, and I am surprised that by now you still have not heard a news bulletin about a German invasion at the border."

Mother thanked them for coming to warn us and said she was glad that they would be in Wieroczyce. Aunt Libcia's father owned the only flour mill in town, and he was a respected member in the community. While we were embracing and saying good-bye, Eva walked in. Her employer, our cousin Salek, for whom she was a dental assistant, had closed his office and had told her not to go back to the cousins where she was staying, but to go instead to Lusia and be with her mother.

Immediately after the Landschaft family left, Mother decided that we should pack a few of our belongings and head for the railroad station. The streets were filled with people. Streetcars were overcrowded, moving slowly, with passengers precariously perched on steps, hanging out the doors, or holding onto windows, their legs dangling. The Starowisla streetcar we had planned to board passed without stopping. The warning sound of the bell being pulled continuously filled the air. An occupied *droschke*—horse-drawn carriage—heading toward the railroad station heeded our pleas and stopped long enough to allow us to board. Traffic was congested, and the horse was intimidated by the throngs of people and barely managed to inch its way ahead. We were unable to get near the terminal. All the *droschke* occupants had to descend, and we were immediately engulfed in a sea of humanity moving in the same direction. We felt encircled, no longer able to proceed on our own. In the milling crowd, we kept an eye on each other, holding on as best we could.

It seemed that everyone had the same idea. In the event of war, there would be a better chance of surviving in the open spaces of the outlying districts rather than in the big city. Mother's parents lived in the town of Bochnia, which under normal conditions could be reached by train in one hour. The imminent threat of war was palpable, and though everyone was engaged in trying to reach a refuge, there was a sense of fellowship and an absence of panic. People were separated, and when they called out for their missing children, everyone stopped and looked around. Parents abandoned bundles and suitcases to lift their little ones off the ground. Strangers would help by picking up a bundle, or carrying a child.

When we reached the terminal, we saw a departing train. We heard contradictory rumors with regard to passenger trains, but there was agreement that the train that had just pulled out had not taken on passengers. The next train that pulled in stopped beyond the platform, and as the surging mass of people rushed after it, the stationmaster announced through a loudspeaker that the train was reserved for soldiers who were trying to join their regiments.

The three of us managed to secure a little space on the concrete platform and sat down. We had left the apartment after three in the afternoon, and we had not eaten since breakfast. Nearby, a woman who had been wise enough to bring along some food, gave each of us a chunk of bread. It was about ten in the evening and pitch-dark because of a blackout. I could not see the face of the woman who reached over and put the bread in my hand, but in my memory she will forever remain a beautiful person.

We sat, and at times I dozed off for a few minutes. Intermittently, we heard the same official announcement from the stationmaster, repeating, "There will be no passenger trains. All available equipment has been requisitioned for troop transports. People go home. There will be no trains because none are available." Everyone remained in place. I felt held in the grip of an imaginary vise. More and more people crowded onto the platform. By eleven o'clock it became impossible to remain seated on the ground. To avoid being crushed, one had to sit on top of a suitcase or better yet stand up.

Suddenly we heard the grinding sound of rails being switched. Someone nearby said that a train was being assembled beyond the platforms. What followed was a stampede, as people stumbled and fell over each other, rushing onto the railroad tracks. In the dark, the crowd propelled us in the direction of the passenger cars. The train consisted of three cars, and when we got close, we saw that they were filled with passengers. People were hanging out the doors and clinging to the windows. We realized that some of them had succeeded in climbing up and entering the train through the windows. Mother spoke to a man standing nearby, pleading for his help. Slowly the train began to move. A man picked me up and pushed me through the window. Arms received me at the other end. Next came Eva, and then the man helped my mother through the window. As the train picked up speed, two of our suitcases were thrown and landed in our arms. The third one missed the window, and we heard it drop to the ground. What should have been a one-hour ride took nine hours. Most of the time the train was stopped. When it started to move again, we would travel for a few miles and then stop again. All the time we knew we were heading east, and we never stopped close to a town.

On the following day when the train reached Bochnia, it did not stop but seemed to accelerate. The platform was jammed with people who tried to grab a door handle and gain a foothold that would help them board the train. On the outskirts of town, the train finally came to a stop; we managed to get to a door and get off. We walked back to Bochnia to my grandparents' house.

The little house was filled with our relatives, and everyone was happy to see us. Uncle Zygmunt, Aunt Antosia, and their children, Salek and Bronia, had arrived from Sosnowitz on the previous day. I had not seen them since the Landschafts had come to fetch me at their home. Uncle Willek who lived in Katowice, a town near the German border, was the youngest of mother's siblings. He had arrived several days earlier and had left his wife Frydia and four-year-old son Josef with his parents. He had been called up by his military unit and left shortly after his arrival in Bochnia to join his regiment at the specified assembly point. The atmosphere in the house was tense and charged with fear. Radio communication was sporadic, and telephone service was inoperative. There was certainty that the German army had crossed into Poland, and the possible arrival of enemy troops was imminent.

Though it could not be verified, there was a spreading feeling that the invader had attacked before Polish army units had had a chance to assemble and resist. My grandfather, Uncle Zygmunt, and Mother sat apart talking; we heard them discuss ways of getting some food into the house. Aunt Antosia gave us minor chores to do so that we would feel useful. Frydia held Josef on her lap. She was weeping inconsolably and frightening her four-year-old son by telling him that the advancing enemy may have overtaken his father's regiment. Aunt Antosia gently but firmly removed Josef from Frydia's arms and pushed him in our direction.

My grandmother sat quietly in her chair. She asked few questions, but her lovely wise eyes darted from one face to the other. It was obvious that she knew exactly what was going on around her. My grandmother had Parkinson's disease, and over the past six years, during our annual visits, I could see that her mobility was diminishing. Throughout the years of her illness, Grandfather ran his successful tailoring business from the large front room of the house. He employed three tailors, and since he was licensed in his craft, there were always several apprentices in the shop. This time when we arrived, all the sewing machines were covered, and the textiles were locked away in closets. The clothes that had been readied for fittings were hanging behind a curtain. The workshop looked as it always did on Friday at noon, when Grandfather closed the business in preparation for Sabbath.

Grandmother, with the aid of her helpmate, Kazia, ran the household. Grandmother directed Kazia in everything that needed to be done to maintain an efficient household. It was said in town that after having learned to cook from Grandmother, her helpmates would always find work as cooks. I knew that this was true because my father on many occasions had said how much he liked my grandmother's cooking, thereby implying that my mother did not quite reach that level of culinary achievement.

Aside from the large front room, the house consisted of two additional rooms—a large kitchen and a narrow dining room. Between the dining room and the kitchen was a small corridor, and on one side of the corridor was my grandmother's personal commode. One entered the house through a door that led into a square foyer. From the foyer one door opened into the workshop, and the other into the kitchen. It was understood that when the doors to the corridor were closed, the family did not walk from the dining room to the kitchen, but rather through the foyer to get to the kitchen. It was the unspoken rhythm of the household. All other members of the family, visitors, and customers used the toilet facilities located in the passageway outside the house.

Toward evening, on the day of our arrival, everyone had a bowl of soup and some bread. Following that, without undressing, I fell asleep on a rug on the floor. When I turned in my sleep, I realized that next to me, on all sides, were the sleeping bodies of my cousins. I knew that Eva and my mother were nearby.

I was awakened by the sound of explosions in the distance, and by the time I was fully awake, the explosions were so loud, it seemed the town was exploding. Chairs and small tables were crashing to the floor. Everyone jumped up, took the clattering dishes and glassware off the shelves, and wrapped them in towels and sheets. Grandfather, Uncle Zygmunt, and Mother took some bolts of cloth from the shelves. They wrapped the cloth in bedsheets, and the three of them left the house. Several hours later, they returned carrying small sacks of flour, sugar, and beans and several small bundles of other food items.

During their absence, the sound of nearby explosions never ceased. We could hear gunfire from field artillery. Mother rolled up her sleeves and together with Kazia, and with Grandmother supervising, they prepared to bake bread. It was very noisy inside the house, and all the adults were busy with preparations for baking and cooking when suddenly we realized that it had become very still outside. There were no longer explosions, and no artillery fire could be heard. The streets were empty. The sudden calm was unexpected and eerie. We did not have to wait long before we heard the sound of motorized vehicles on the cobblestones of the street. Everyone rushed to the open windows, and from behind shades and curtains we saw them.

Trucks and tanks were rolling through the street, and on top of them were smiling German soldiers. They were eating apples and chocolates, and they were waving to the people who looked out the windows. The motorized vehicles moved very slowly. The Nazi flags on both sides of the vehicles were fluttering in the wind, and swastikas were painted on the tank turrets. Trucks filled with singing soldiers passed, followed by antiaircraft equipment, field kitchens, and more trucks filled with soldiers. There were no foot soldiers, only endless columns of motorized vehicles and field artillery. Occasionally, important-looking officers of high rank rode by in open cars. The invaders were accompanied by the sound of heavy bombers flying overhead. No one dared to go outdoors to look.

The decrees that were to govern the frightened residents were issued in the late afternoon. The initial orders came over loudspeakers from passing trucks. A curfew, beginning at dusk, had to be strictly obeyed. The invaders told the vanquished population that they were fortunate to be occupied by such a benevolent army. They declared that the Polish army was a phantom that only existed in the minds of their rulers who had fled across borders to foreign lands. They announced that the German army had been unopposed and that the invasion had taken place without a fight and without casualties. The news was devastating. Everyone worried about Willek, but not much was said because Frydia was very upset and her little boy looked so sad. That night no one slept well, not even the children.

On the following day, the German army managed to hook up a public-address system. Loudspeakers located at strategic points blared continuous orders. Preceding each order was the bellowed command *aufpassen*—attention. Initially orders were issued in German to the Polish-speaking population. Subsequently, orders were also issued in Polish, and within days, one could read them on posters pasted onto kiosks all over town. We learned that a total blackout had to be maintained.

Each directive was accompanied by a threat of severe punishment for any infraction. The evening curfew was strictly enforced, and even before dusk, the streets were empty. No one wished to provoke the anger of the invader; everyone sensed that the present atmosphere of calm and order was but a reprieve.

Starting early in the morning, a never-ending procession of male refugees passed through our street. We saw them through the window, and some of them acknowledged us with a slight turn of the head or with a tired smile. We understood that they were trying to get back home and that they had to keep moving during daylight hours. Occasionally, a German army motorcycle with an occupied sidecar would pass along the column of refugees and pick out a man from the center. We soon realized that the person who had been removed wore one or two garments that had been part of the Polish army uniform. After four o'clock in the afternoon, Grandfather would unobtrusively position himself near the steps leading to his house. It was his way of signaling that refugees were welcome to spend the night. When there were enough people to fill the house, Grandfather came in and closed the door. Even after that, no person who knocked on the door was turned away.

The women of our household cooked soup throughout the day, and in the evening, Salek, Eva, and I would pass the bowls of soup to the men sitting cross-legged on the floor. The men slept on the floor, close to each other, and in the morning when I woke up, most of them had left to get an early start. All we could give them for breakfast was some tea or watery cereal. There was no bread. Many of the men were reservists who had been unable to reach their regiments, or who had reached their destination only to find that their regiment had been disbanded. Grandfather, Uncle Zygmunt, and Mother asked many questions, but they were unable to find out if a Polish front line had been established.

It was by now evident that the Russian army would not come to Poland's aid. Moreover, there were rumors that according to an agreement between the German and Russian governments, Russia would occupy a part of Eastern Poland. By now, Grandfather was certain that Willek had never reached his regiment, and all of us were concerned. While trying to assuage his daughter-in-law's growing panic, he opened his house to even more refugees, generously using the provisions we had been able to gather for ourselves. He kept saying, "I am praying that someone will do for my son what I am doing for their son."

The occupation army issued a decree forbidding the harboring of a Polish soldier. A fugitive Polish soldier would furtively enter the house, hiding parts of his khaki army uniform under a coat or blanket. He would slip into clothing we had hastily collected and give us his uniform to be buried in the ground. Army boots, however, were impossible to disguise. Many fleeing soldiers chose to walk barefoot rather than be picked up by the German army.

We were running out of provisions, but that was not an insurmountable problem. As part of his business, Grandfather had a considerable inventory of textiles. Peasants gladly exchanged flour, beans, peas, or even butter in return for cloth, but it was dangerous. Barter was strictly forbidden, and violators were subject to severe punishment. In addition, German soldiers, themselves eager for fresh country food, would intercept farmers on lonely country roads and relieve them of their parcels at gunpoint.

A proclamation announced that bread would soon become available. Rations would be distributed in some orderly fashion in conjunction with family registration. The head of every household would be responsible for registering the names of all its members, including children and infants. Peasants were advised that under the new law, the only legitimate outlet for their produce would be designated collection centers, and there they would be paid with newly issued occupation zlotys. The original Polish zloty had lost all value. Despite threats of punishment, both for supplier and recipient, farmers continued to come into town.

Though my grandmother was a fine housekeeper, my grandfather did most of the marketing. Some of his loyal suppliers continued to find their way to his door. They would walk through the kitchen into the middle room occupied by my grandmother, and there the women would lift their many skirts and untie sacks of provisions strapped to their bodies. Sometimes they would rest for a few minutes, just long enough to have a cup of tea. The association, even if no goods were exchanged, was fraught with grave danger.

Initially the family had decided not to register and to sacrifice bread rations, but subsequent orders made it impossible to abide by the decision. Apparently, other people felt as we did, and few came forward to register. A new decree informed the population that house-to-house searches would be instituted, and severe punishment meted out to all violators. We were now unable to avoid the registration. A special unit was set up for registering Jews. Certain age groups were classified for work assignments, and it was understood that the Jews would be the first group called. Once registered, Mother allowed us to stand in line for bread.

We were trying to get as many loaves of bread as possible. We had recently learned that the local army compound was filled to bursting with Polish prisoners of war, and they were not being fed. Bread was the only food that could be smuggled through the iron fence surrounding the barracks. The town elders decided that children should walk past the iron fence and try to slip the bread through the bars. I walked with Eva and her friend Hella Keller toward the barracks. We walked slowly, ostensibly just out for an afternoon stroll. Each of us carried under our open coats a loaf of bread tied with string to the sides of our bodies. When we got close, we saw the prisoners on the inside holding onto the iron fence with both hands.

German soldiers patrolled outside the fence. They walked in pairs with their guns at their shoulders, looking well groomed and well fed. The soldiers on the inside were a pitiful sight: faces haggard, uniforms disheveled. Deprived of their belts by the invader, they used pieces of rope to hold up their trousers. Prisoners unable to obtain a rope had to hold their trousers with their hands. All were in need of a shave and a haircut. Most devastating was the helpless look in their eyes. As we came closer, we were overcome by the stench of overflowing latrines. Clearly the remnants of the Polish army were dying of starvation. Nothing we had heard had quite prepared us for this spectacle. One needed a cool head and determination to keep walking. Fortunately for us, even the patrolling soldiers often turned their faces away from the gruesome sight, and that gave us the chance to quickly slip a loaf of bread into a prisoner's outstretched hand. A slight flicker in the recipient's eye acknowledged the gift.

On the way back into town the three of us felt elated. We had circumvented the decree that forbade bringing food to the prisoners and outwitted the hated invader. The next week, Eva and I once again strolled past the barracks and repeated the operation. It was the last time. The patrolling soldiers later intercepted some children carrying bread and other food items. The children and their parents were threatened. But we heard that the Jewish girl who was caught and her parents had been severely punished. They were being kept in a jail, and no one was allowed to go near them.

Our family unit—my mother, Eva, and I—were ordered to report for work assignments. Grandfather received a temporary exemption because his wife was an invalid. A day before we were to report for work, mother went to the Arbeitsamt—the labor exchange—and asked that Eva and I be exempted because we were needed to care for our disabled grandmother. My grandfather, Mother explained, could not take care of his wife. Mother received an immediate decision. She was told that for the time being she would be permitted to care for her mother; however, Eva and I would need to report on the designated day at eight o'clock in the morning. All her appeals to work instead of us—her argument that she was stronger, could work better, and was bilingual—were denied.

Mother admonished us to stay together, to watch out for each other, and, whenever possible, to make ourselves appear one year younger. As soon as we arrived at the army barracks, we were separated. Eva was marched to a kitchen, and I, together with other girls and some older women, was taken to a shed and shown how to stuff burlap bags with straw to make mattresses. The straw had to be evenly distributed so that the bag would fit into a cot. When the pile of mattresses was quite high, we were asked to carry them to the German soldiers' sleeping quarters.

On the third day at work, while I was alone in a barrack fitting a mattress into a cot frame, I felt hands grab me. Before I could scream, a hand covered my mouth and I was thrown onto the cot. A big soldier was on top of me; I could smell his repugnant breath and sweat. I fought myself loose and ran screaming through the door and into the narrow passageway leading to the stairs.

An officer stopped me and asked me what had happened. When I told him, he said, *"Das ist nicht erlaubt."* That is forbidden. He told me to calm down and said the soldiers would be instructed to keep their distance from the workers. He agreed that the attack had been frightening. When I asked to work near my sister in the kitchen, he wrote down my name and said he would arrange it. Throughout our short exchange, his voice was calm and soothing. However, when I tried to thank him, he became gruff, and I realized that he was not permitted to be kind.

Eva said that I should not have allowed them to separate me from the group, and I had to explain to her that each one of us could carry only one mattress at a time, fit it into a cot, and then proceed to the next one. Eva admonished me not to tell Mother. "It will upset her and nothing really happened," she said. I was angry with my sister for her unfeeling remark. I remembered too well the soldier groping at my underpants, trying to pull them down, but I agreed not to mention it to our mother.

We learned that the German army unit in Bochnia was a temporary occupation force. In the near future, a permanent occupation army would replace it. The Jewish community was ordered to provide a workforce for each day of the week, and all those able to work had to come forward to accept work assignments. The order stated that those who did not comply would be forcibly removed from their homes by the military authority. Although sexual assaults were forbidden, there were rumors of frequent incidents. It was prudent, if possible, to seek an outdoor assignment.

As the weather turned colder, the work became more arduous. For a number of days, we prepared beds for next year's vegetable planting. The soil was hard and crusty, but once broken, the task became easier. The stoop labor required to cultivate the larger tracts of land was very painful for some of my coworkers. Though I was very tired at day's end, on the following morning I felt strong enough to do my work and even help some of the older women. Whenever the guard walked away, the women chatted among themselves. They spoke Polish rapidly, and only occasionally did I manage to understand a phrase. At times I realized that they were speaking about me, but from their friendly smiles I knew that it was well meaning.

The first heavy snowfall brought an end to the work on the land. The army requisitioned all available snow shovels and ordered the Jewish labor force to clean the roads. I did not mind the work that much because I liked working outdoors, but I was cold all day long, and my fingers were numb. The three of us did not have appropriate winter clothing or warm gloves. Grandfather said that he would make up winter coats for us, but Mother felt that it would take too long and suggested that he instead alter some old garments that were in the house. The problem of gloves was harder to solve. Since none of us was good at knitting, Mother looked for someone who could do the task. One morning when we woke up, there were two pairs of mittens for Eva and me, fashioned from old cloth and lined with new gray flannel. Grandfather had worked throughout the night. We were grateful and lovingly hugged and kissed him.

Before Uncle Willek arrived, we already knew that he was making his way home. Someone had recognized him and told Grandfather that Willek was ill. Movement was slow because the men had to hide to avoid being taken away on work assignments. Returning reservists were not registered or classified for work. They could be arrested at the whim of the invader.

Tall, handsome Uncle Willek, who had to bend his head when he walked through our doors when he visited us in Hindenburg, was barely recognizable when he reached home. His four-year-old son ran from him, and his wife covered her face and cried. He looked gaunt and disheveled, and his feet were bleeding from blisters and wounds that would not heal. Though he needed a bath badly, my mother decided against it, because she saw immediately that he was running a fever. Grandfather and Mother undressed him, washed his face, hands, and feet as best they could, and put him to bed. On the following day, the doctor diagnosed pneumonia and exhaustion. He advised total bed rest and nourishing soup, and he left a document that would temporarily exempt Uncle Willek from being assigned to a work detail.

We learned from Uncle Willek that after dropping his wife and son safely with his parents, he had taken a bus to his army post near Katowice before the designated time. There he learned that his regiment had moved east. Together with several hundred men in the same predicament, he headed east in the hope of catching up with his regiment. When they arrived at the newly designated place, he learned that his regiment had again moved further east and that the German army had crossed into Poland and was advancing with overwhelming force and speed.

Hoping to locate their regiment and confront the enemy, the men kept heading east. All trains had stopped moving, and there were no buses. The peasants who usually could be seen with their horses and wagons throughout the countryside stayed off the roads. Finally, Uncle Willek caught up with his regiment, only to learn that the Polish government, which was about to cross the border and go into exile, had ordered the regiment to disband. As the inductees walked further east, they encountered hostility from the local inhabitants. Only a few peasants allowed them to seek shelter in their barns, and food was not available. While Uncle Willek was still too sick to coherently tell us what had happened, we learned from men staggering into town harrowing tales of hardship. After Russia had invaded from the east, roving bands of Ukrainian sadists attacked the reservists who were trying to get back to their families. When they were able to identify a Jewish soldier or civilian, their viciousness was unbounded.

## JANUARY 1940 ✍ BOCHNIA, OCCUPIED POLAND

The weather had become exceptionally cold. We were always busy getting food into the house. Obtaining coal, or enough wood, to keep Grandmother's room warm was a continuous struggle. Uncle Willek was moved into my grandfather's bed, and Grandfather slept with us in the big room. Mother, Eva, and I slept in one bed, and that was a blessing. We huddled close together, and we had a down comforter to keep us warm. Frydia and Josef slept in the third bed.

Uncle Zygmunt, his wife Antosia, their son Salek, and daughter Bronia occupied the other small room. They slept on two mattresses that took up all the floor space, and during the day they placed the mattresses against the wall. In spite of the cramped quarters, Uncle Zygmunt spent much of his free time in that room. Everyone tried to respect his need for a quiet space. Mother said that his scholarly pursuits had conditioned him to maintain separateness. With twelve people now living in a house previously occupied solely by my grandparents, moments of privacy were difficult to find.

Uncle Zygmunt had many friends in town, both in the Jewish and the Christian communities. He endeavored to keep informed, and sporadically he received clandestinely printed pamphlets. He also knew Poles who had access to a radio, though possession of a radio was considered an act of treason by the invader.

Frydia was very unhappy, and her eyes were always teary. Mother tried to explain to Frydia that Uncle Willek would heal more quickly if she would pull herself together and overcome her despair. Both Eva and I tried to engage Josef in games we invented, but it was difficult to communicate because we lacked a common language. It seemed to us that his beautiful dark eyes grew sadder with each passing day. Finally, Mother decided she could do no more, and she asked her brother Zygmunt to talk to Frydia. Whatever he said must have helped, because thereafter Frydia dressed more carefully and paid more attention to her son.

CHAPTER 4

# Occupation

On a very cold evening past curfew time for the Jewish population, some-one knocked at the door. A man in torn clothing limped into the room. He had walked for many days, and he was worried about his family whom he had not seen since he had left to join the Polish army. He brought us very sad news. The message was from Pan Majerowicz, a friend of Regina, my mother's younger sister, and her husband Jacub. The messenger told us that Regina's husband was dead. His headless, mutilated torso had been discov-ered in the Ukrainian town of Uszczycki in an open mass grave. A note taken from his vest pocket read, "Please take care of my wife and son." It was signed Jacub Vogelhut. The family's first reaction was disbelief.

Several months earlier, when I had been in Krosno visiting Aunt Regina and Uncle Jacub, I had met Pan Majerowicz, and I knew that he was a close friend of Uncle Jacub. He was a dignified and respected member of the Krosno community. He must have gone to a lot of trouble to get this message to us. Until that moment, we had had no word from Aunt Regina. With post of-fices closed, the vanquished population had devised a courier system: a mes-sage was transferred from contact to contact, moving in the general geographic direction, until it reached the intended recipient. The messenger also carried a note from Pan Majerowicz, "Urgent. Regina unbalanced. Community can

no longer care for her and son Dollek. Send member of family to take charge."
The note was written in telegram style and sounded like a command.

Grandfather, Uncle Zygmunt, and Mother decided that someone would
have to leave immediately. The logical choice was our family. In many of the
surrounding communities, Monday was market day. Mother decided to leave
on the following Monday. Even in the middle of the winter, some local peasants brought produce into town. Because of the Monday market activity, the
German soldiers as well as patrolling military police were less vigilant about
documents.

On the Sabbath evening preceding our departure, the twelve of us gathered in Grandmother's room, as had been the custom since our arrival; however, this Sabbath dinner was a very solemn occasion. Grandmother, wearing
her best dress, was seated at the head of the table. Though we had tried to
shield her as much as possible, there was a bewildered look in her dark brown
eyes, and the tremor from the Parkinson's disease was more pronounced.

Aunt Antosia had hardly left the kitchen since Wednesday evening; there
had been much baking, roasting, and cooking. Even Frydia was helping. In
spite of the carefully prepared meal, it was impossible to obey the com-
mandment of celebrating the beginning of Sabbath. The horrifying death of
Uncle Jacub at age thirty-four and Aunt Regina's resulting breakdown had
frightened and disheartened all members of the family. Invasive fear was like
a vise, and it was too difficult to speak about the murder. I was aware that
Uncle Zygmunt no longer disappeared into his room, but instead stayed close
to Mother or Grandfather. They spoke in low tones, and I could hardly hear
what they were saying. Mainly it was advice to Mother regarding our journey
to Krosno. There were also suggestions about Aunt Regina. They made plans
for communication between Mother in Krosno and the family in Bochnia.

Mother woke us up at about three o'clock on Monday morning. We
quickly washed and dressed in clothing we had carefully prepared days in advance. Jews were not allowed to travel, and different hours of curfew applied
to Christians and Jewish residents. Recent posters had warned that in the near
future all residents would be required to carry an identity document issued
by the German occupation government. We were fortunate that on the day
of our departure, this order was not yet in force. At about four o'clock in the
morning—dressed like peasants, kerchiefs covering our hair, our few possessions in various baskets—we surfaced at the outskirts of the town. We joined

a group of peasants, who, we surmised, were waiting for a vehicle to stop and give them a ride. It was very cold, and one had to keep moving all the time to avoid frostbite. The few items of clothing each of us carried were at the bottom of our baskets. Covering them were onions, beets, and dried beans.

After several hours a German army truck stopped. From within we heard women's voices speaking Polish and the voices of German soldiers. Several of the waiting peasants boarded the truck, but to Mother the vagueness of the destination was threatening, and we withstood the temptation. At about noon, we boarded a covered truck that seemed to be heading in our intended direction. In the dark we were able to distinguish the shapes of dozing German soldiers and three peasant women. Along with us, two more women and an old peasant climbed into the truck. Mother said, "Be with God," the customary Polish greeting, and they responded in kind. They wanted to know where we were from, what we were selling, and where we were headed. One woman gave Eva and me a carrot. I smiled and nodded my thanks. Mother had once again instructed us that whenever a Pole was nearby we were to act deaf. Mother explained that we were the deaf children of her dead sister, and that our father had been missing since the invasion. The woman who had given me the carrot stroked my head, but several of the other women eyed us with suspicion. A few laughed derisively and made me feel uncomfortable.

When one of the soldiers woke up, Mother asked him if we could be dropped off. He did not understand, and since Mother could only speak Polish, we had to wait until another soldier who did understand Polish woke up. He asked the driver to stop and let us get off. By then it was dusk, and we spent the hour until nightfall hiding behind bushes. Mother told us that two of the women had asked several hostile questions. Ever since we had come aboard the truck, these two women had hinted that we were not one of them. The meaner one of the two had wanted to know whether Mother was certain that she did not speak German.

Mother thought it was best to continue our journey on foot. She said it would keep our circulation going. We subsequently joined several peasants who were walking in the same direction, and together we hitched a ride on a German truck. At dawn we saw a sign indicating that we were twelve kilometers from Krosno. Shortly after the signpost, Mother asked the driver to stop and let us get off. We walked for about ten kilometers before we saw the outskirts of Krosno. It was past nine o'clock in the morning when we knocked at Aunt Regina's door. It took a while before my cousin Dollek finally let us in.

The three of us were overwhelmed by what we saw. My aunt Regina, so handsome, vibrant, and life affirming only five months ago, was almost unrecognizable. Her face was puffy, the hair matted and disheveled; her eyes stared vacantly into space. The torn and stained robe she wore must have been on her body for weeks. Dollek, who during my recent visit had been an irrepressible, mischievous six-year-old, had the confused look of a child who had suddenly lost his footing. He looked up at us with his dark eyes, then his sad gaze shifted to the face of his mother.

Aunt Regina started to tell us what had happened to her husband. She soon became hysterical, speaking incoherently and weeping and shouting. Neighbors walked in and tried to calm her. They told us she had had these attacks before. Aunt Regina kept shouting and no one could calm her down. The neighbors were afraid that an occupation patrol would hear her mad screams and storm the house. Mother said that she would take charge, and in a firm voice she asked everyone to leave. Mother closed the door, turned around, and in front of Dollek, Eva, and me, she slapped her sister's face. The screams subsided into whimpers. Minutes later, obviously exhausted, Aunt Regina was asleep.

Mother took a washcloth and washed Dollek's face and hands and combed his hair while he squirmed. Mother told us to clear the table, and the four of us sat down to a modest meal. Dollek did not want to talk. Mother's message to us, delivered via her expressive eyes, was that we should leave him be. The following morning, after a good night's sleep in a bed with a warm blanket, Mother assigned Eva and me the task of cleaning up the apartment. Neighbors drifted in and told us how happy they were that we had come.

For the next several days, Mother fed and bathed her sister and nursed her back to sensibility. Mother forcibly bathed Dollek, and then, holding him between her knees, she cut his hair. She sat him down, and in a firm tone told him that he was the only male in the household, and he therefore would have to take on some male responsibilities. To his mother's amazement, he fulfilled all his assigned tasks. Dr. Romek Rosenberg came to see us and told Mother that she had lifted a great burden off his shoulders. Uncle Jacub's friend, Pan Majerowicz, had heard of our arrival, and he walked over to see us. He told us that before Aunt Regina had received the report of her husband's murder, she had functioned admirably. Anticipating that their locked-up store would in time be vandalized, she had managed, with the help of Pan Majerowicz, to hide a considerable portion of the store's merchandise. Now with his help, Mother managed to barter some of the clothing for needed firewood and food. Pan Majerowicz helped us to find a tailor who was willing to make winter coats for the three of us in return for some additional cloth.

We learned the significance of the term *razzia* or raid. During these raids, Jewish men were rounded up and transported to an unknown destination. Ostensibly, this was due to a labor shortage, but everyone knew that was a lie: Christian laborers as well as Jewish could be found throughout Poland. And why didn't the men return home? Shortly after our arrival, Krosno restored its suspended postal service. The families of the men who had been taken away were told that news would soon be arriving from their missing relatives.

## FEBRUARY 1940 ⤙ KROSNO, OCCUPIED POLAND

We were able to resume contact with my grandparents in Bochnia. We had to be circumspect in our correspondence because we knew that all mail was censored. It was quite evident that letters had been opened and the contents examined. The letters were then stamped with an official seal. Mother and her brother Zygmunt would use Hebrew or Yiddish words to convey the prevailing situation.

Large posters issued by the German occupation authority directed the Jewish inhabitants of Krosno to divest themselves of their valuables. Initially, we were ordered to deliver to Gestapo headquarters all foreign currency in our possession. Thereafter, orders called for the surrender of jewelry, furs, and means of transportation, including bicycles. Inexorably, the decrees, with accompanying threats, brought about an ever-widening gulf between the Christian and Jewish residents of the town.

All residents had to obtain a registration card from the magistrate's office on which the holder's religion was prominently displayed. It was a very cold winter, and a subsequent decree, addressed to Jews only, ordered them to remove all fur collars and fur ornaments and deliver them to a collection center. We were advised that there would be home searches and should fur be found, the fines would be commensurate with the crime. For the rest of the

winter, Jews could immediately be identified by their coats, from which the
fur collars had been so obviously removed.

Decrees addressed to the Poles advised that cooperation with the occupation government was in their best interest. The ordinance against barter was
strictly enforced, and with Polish currency declared valueless, all commercial
activity was regulated by the German authorities. They established a quota
system that allowed the farmers barely enough food for their own subsistence,
while all excess produce had to be delivered to collection centers. This quota
system was strictly enforced, and food became increasingly more difficult to
obtain. German authorities permitted limited distribution of food items not
needed in the Reich. Nazi enforcement units patrolled farms and raided farm
cellars. If they found hidden produce that should have been delivered, the
farmer and his family risked incarceration and deportation. There were rumors that some stores, closed since the invasion, would be allowed to open.
The Krosno Agricultural Cooperative had voluntarily delivered to the
Sicherheitspolizei, or security police, a list of all businesses owned by Jews.
The Jewish community was stunned. Before the war when I visited Krosno,
relations between Christians and Jews had been friendly and cooperative.

I went to see Genia Springer. She knew that we had arrived in Krosno, and
she knew about Aunt Regina. When we had parted in late August, we promised each other that we would keep in touch and that after her graduation
from the gymnasium she would visit me in America. We embraced and wept.
The world had changed. We did not speak about the lovely days of the past
summer when we had swum, sung, and laughed, while planning our future.
Genia had many Christian friends, and one of her dearest friends was Krysia
Magierowska. When I asked about Krysia, Genia told me that she was being
pressured to distance herself from Genia. Krysia had sworn that she would
never succumb to the hate propaganda promulgated by the Nazis. Still, Genia
felt that she was no longer warmly received at the Magierowksi home.

"I try not to think about that," she said. "I am now concentrating on
improving my typing skills, and we really should speak in German, because
I need to work on my German language skills. You know, of course, about
the Arbeitskarte?

Everyone in the Jewish community knew about the Arbeitskarte, or record of employment, that had to be issued by the Arbeitsamt, or employment office. The problem was finding work that the Arbeitsamt would classify as useful employment. Several times I had been forced into a snow-removal detail. Our column of Jews, mostly females and some elderly men, was marched several kilometers out of town to perform the work. One time Eva was apprehended and placed in a snow-removal detail that had to clear the snow around Gestapo headquarters. One had a chance of being exempted from these street roundups if one possessed a valid Arbeitskarte.

Genia and I also discussed a recent disturbing development in our community that troubled all of us. The Jewish community had been ordered to form a Judenrat—a Jewish council. The German authority appointed Josef Engel as the chairman of the Judenrat. Before the war, Herr Engel had been a banker in Berlin, and his sister Hella lived in the apartment one flight above Aunt Regina. I told Genia that we knew him quite well. He had come to see us whenever he visited his sister. We shared a common experience: He had been expelled from Germany on October 28, 1938, as we had been. "That is good for you," Genia rejoiced. "Knowing him will give you connections."

Alas, our connection had limited value. I told Genia that Mother had said that the occupiers could not have chosen better. Herr Engel, she had told Aunt Regina, "was more Prussian than the Prussians and was a man who was certain that by dealing with the Nazis truthfully and honorably, he would be able to help the Jewish community." When Mother had asked him if he would help us, he said he would do all he could—once we had obtained useful employment.

I had heard about a nearby brothel and asked Genia about it. "Is it true that the Nazis opened a brothel near the airport?"

"Oh, it's true enough," Genia said, "but the Poles are so embarrassed about it, they make believe it does not exist." Apparently, no one knew where these girls came from. Dr. Rosenberg had told us that in the previous week a young girl had bled to death, but they did not call him to attend to her. "I did not know about that," said Genia, "but I have seen them in town. They come to get things from the stores, and from the apothecary. What I really find remarkable is that they go to Mass on Sunday, and as far as I know, there has not been a word of protest from the Catholic church or the Polish community leaders."

"Do they look like prostitutes?" I asked.

"Don't be so naïve," Genia chastised. "Germans don't want prostitutes for their young pilots. It's just another lie. These are young girls from nearby small towns and villages who were picked up for minor infractions of the laws."

"What laws? Do you know?"

"It seems these were curfew violations. Some of the girls were picked up while on a date with their boyfriends. You know, Betus, what really amazes me is that the Polish Christians seeing what is happening to the Jews are eager to distance themselves from us, but the Germans are taking Polish girls and confiscating their identity papers. Then they force them into prostitution. Now I ask you, can the Poles feel good about that?"

Late in February, several hours past curfew for Jews, we received exciting visitors—Uncle Jacub's brother Shimek and his new bride Margot Schwartzbad. Aunt Regina had lost all contact with Shimek. Margot came from Beuthen, a twenty-minute streetcar ride from Hindenburg. Mother had known her parents, and Margot knew my mother. Margot and Shimek had walked for days, most of the time clandestinely at night, and they were so tired they could barely stand up. They fell asleep in their clothing on some mattresses we hastily put together on the kitchen floor. The only luggage they had brought were two rucksacks filled to capacity. They were large and very heavy.

They told us that all their earthly goods were in these rucksacks, and that their arrival had been very carefully timed. They would leave in two weeks, about the middle of March, at which time they had arranged a meeting, in the town of Sanok, with the captain of a small riverboat. The San River was the official border between the German general government and the part of Poland Russia had occupied since September 1939. The captain, in return for a large payment, had agreed to smuggle them across the river into the Russian zone. Several of their friends had taken the same route and had safely arrived in Russian-occupied territory. "Of course, there are dangers," Shimek said, "but we have decided to take a chance. Nothing could be worse than remaining where we were." Mother asked many questions and took notes. "Besides," Shimek added, "we wanted to come and tell you about this escape route."

During the following weeks, late into the evening hours, we sat around the kitchen table making plans for our escape. We would have to wait for news from Shimek before taking to the road. I was very excited because Mother felt certain that once in Russia, we would be able to make our way to America and be united with our father. No one, except for Pan Majerowicz, could know of our plans because it was a crime for a Jew to even contemplate walking beyond the town boundary.

The distance between Krosno and Sanok was about eighty kilometers. We planned to wait until the spring before attempting our escape. The only problem that Pan Majerowicz could foresee was crossing the border between occupied Poland and Russia. There were rumors of border skirmishes and of shots being fired, but we decided not to let this deter us from our resolve to escape. The night Margot and Shimek left for Sanok, they both looked much better than when they had arrived. We embraced without tears, certain that we would soon be reunited and heading east toward a brighter future.

The only form of payment acceptable to the river smugglers was American currency, but possession of foreign currency was a serious criminal offense. The penalty for possession of dollars could be death. However, once over the border, the Russians could be bribed with German cameras, lenses, and watches. Most of these items would have to be obtained from German flight officers attached to the air base. We had heard that some of them were selling these items on the black market. Though these contacts were highly valued and very confidential, Mother did manage to buy a Leica. It was a first step. Following that she purchased two elegant leather wallets. The wallets were less desirable, but Mother hoped the smugglers would still want to possess them.

## MAY 1940 ⤳ KROSNO, OCCUPIED POLAND

News from Shimek should have reached us weeks ago, and we were worried. Had they been denounced to the Gestapo, caught by a military patrol, or had their smuggler betrayed them? We pondered these questions, while acquiring rucksacks and blankets for the five of us.

Then came devastating news. The Germans had invaded Holland and Belgium. A few days later we learned of their ultimate triumph: the invasion and occupation of France. The news came blasting forth from centrally placed loudspeakers. It was continuously repeated, interspersed with the Nazi national anthem. France's proud line of defense, the Maginot Line, had proved to be no obstacle to the victorious German army. The Jewish community was stunned by this overwhelming blitzkrieg success.

Christian Poles seemed equally devastated by the latest German triumph. For a short while, they seemed to understand that Jews and Christian Poles shared a common destiny, and some of them became more understanding of our plight. Repeatedly, I had to translate the song the German soldiers were singing as they marched through the streets. "*Wir marschieren, wir marschieren, gegen Engeland, gegen Engeland,*" they sang: "We are marching, we are marching, against England, against England." They were letting us know that England would be next.

Eva, Regina, and I: photos taken in Krosno, 1940. We were living with Aunt Regina and sent these photos to Father in New York, already with the knowledge that the anticipated reunion was no longer imminent.

Aunt Regina obtained a permit to open a tearoom, but neither tea nor coffee were available. Instead, we served a hot lunch. Aunt Regina and Mother, daughters of a Hungarian mother, knew how to cook an excellent Hungarian goulash. Mother obtained the beef, potatoes, and the onions, Aunt Regina cooked the stew in a huge pot on top of her kitchen stove, and Eva and I were the clean-up detail. Our activities began at five o'clock in the morning. At about ten-thirty, Eva and I carried the large, still-hot pot, each holding on to a handle, into our small restaurant on the main street. Bread was baked daily by a Jewish family and delivered by eleven o'clock. Word spread quickly, and within a short time, we developed steady customers who enjoyed our food. When we ran out of goulash, we closed the tearoom. Eva and I cleaned up, while Regina and Mother put aside the money they would need to purchase more food. Mother saved the remaining money toward the purchase of another Leica. As a result of our enterprise, the family was once again relatively well fed, which was a priority in view of our upcoming journey to the Russian border.

It was getting more difficult to get meat. Peasants trying to smuggle the forbidden commodity into Krosno were intercepted, deprived of their wares, and often punished. Aunt Regina was informed that her permit to run the shop would not be renewed, and that it had been issued by mistake. In the future, Jews would no longer be allowed to serve food to Christians.

The caretaker Maruszka, a hard-working Ukrainian woman, and her family occupied the basement dwelling of our small apartment house. Her son Michal was Dollek's best friend. It was a friendship Aunt Regina was unsuccessful in trying to end. Maruszka's common-law husband and the father of her two small infants was a drunkard. He turned vicious when in need of alcohol and was unpredictable when drunk. We were afraid that Michal might overhear fragments of conversation between us, or that he might see visitors in our apartment with whom we engaged in prohibited food barter. Though Dollek was forbidden to have Michal visit him in our apartment, my little cousin was welcome in Michal's home. Michal had no schooling, and Dollek was teaching him to read, while Michal taught Dollek to play cards. From Dollek, we heard that Maruszka, in addition to doing chores for various tenants and suckling her two baby infants, was also putting up cabbage for the winter.

In early autumn, we arranged with Maruszka to set aside a day and prepare a barrel of cabbage for us. Aunt Regina obtained a big wooden barrel, Maruszka scrubbed it thoroughly before putting it out in the cold air, and we bought the green cabbage. On the designated day, our whole family gathered in Maruszka's large kitchen to help shred the cabbage. The force and rhythm of the cleaver had to be maintained, and everyone took a turn and stayed with it until their arm got tired. Maruszka arranged the cabbage in layers and added salt, caraway seeds, and several apples. We took turns compacting the contents of the barrel with a heavy wooden rammer. The rammer was too heavy for me, and I was only able to lift it a few inches before bringing it down. When the barrel was two-thirds full, we all took a short rest. Maruszka nursed her infants, and then she put them to sleep. Following that, she went into a corner of the kitchen and washed her feet in a basin. Regina spread a clean heavy linen cloth over the cabbage. Maruszka climbed onto a high stool and from there she stepped into the barrel. We watched as she hoisted up her skirts and rhythmically stepped from one foot to the other, tamping down the cabbage. My mother and my aunt helped Maruszka get out of the barrel, and we resumed the cutting, filling, and ramming until the barrel was filled to the brim. After a final sprinkling of caraway seeds and salt, we placed a clean cloth on top, and Maruszka pounded a tight-fitting cover into place. Mother said if we could get a sack of potatoes, we could sustain ourselves through the coming winter.

We were receiving letters from my father, but they were so heavily censored we could hardly divine the meaning of his messages. We knew that Father would write nothing that would jeopardize us, so the heavy censorship could only be another form of Nazi harassment of Jewish people who received letters from abroad. During Hitler's angry tirades broadcast over loudspeakers, there were hostile anti-American remarks, in what seemed to be a determined effort to spread anti-American propaganda. In his letters, Father kept repeating that the war would soon end and that we would be reunited. In Hebrew he would add the words, "keep strong and steadfast," and he left it to us to interpret the meaning. I tried very hard not to think about my father. When I did, my stomach ached; I was afraid of never seeing him again.

Zack had stopped sending me letters, but I received several postcards from Italy. He advised me to stay strong, to keep up with my education, and to hold on to the belief that there would be a future. His words, as was his tendency, were vague. I hoped that he was implying a future together. I carefully hid his letters together with my dreams of joining him. I was wise enough to know that my dreams had no connection with reality. Zack's last picture postcard was mailed from Trieste, Italy, and though he did not say it, I was certain that he was about to embark for Palestine. I knew then that I would not hear from him again, but I was very happy for him.

FEBRUARY 1941 ✎ KROSNO, OCCUPIED POLAND

The tearoom was closed, and our family was once again assigned to do road-work. Eva and I were ordered to be part of a snow-removal detail. Once the snow disappeared, we were ordered to dig ditches on the outskirts of town. Occasionally we were driven by truck; however, most of the time we were marched through town in rows of six—a sad-looking column of about fifty Jews. Poles stopped to look, others looked away, while some of the children jeered, pointing fingers in mockery. The occasional news that reached us from Bochnia was devastating. Our relatives were unable to find food, and my grandmother hardly ever touched the food that was placed in front of her. The symptoms of her Parkinson's disease had grown worse, and the involuntary tremor was now in her leg as well as her arm. Uncle Willek was not well. His lungs were damaged by his bout with pneumonia. Poor nourishment and en-forced slave labor prevented him from regaining his strength. The family could do nothing but observe his declining health.

We heard rumors that new trenches were being dug east of Krosno. These special trenches appeared to be a more serious undertaking than the previous ones. A German engineering and construction firm, Kirchhof, Hoch & Tiefbau, established offices and workshops in Krosno. Subsequently, the Jewish forced labor was assigned to work for the firm. It was a cold winter. Sometimes I was assigned to kitchen duty in the Kirchhof canteen. When I returned home after hours of peeling potatoes, my fingers bloody from multiple cuts that I had been unable to avoid, Mother said I was lucky because I had spent the day inside.

In the early months of 1941, Jews were ordered to deliver all ski equip-ment and ski boots to a collecting center. The Judenrat was responsible for the speedy execution of this order. Mother had not yet been able to find a sturdy pair of walking shoes for me and was trying to get hold of a pair of forbidden ski boots. Pan Majerowicz suggested that we see Mennek Moszkowitz, the Jewish shoemaker. He thought that Mennek might be able to remake ski boots into walking shoes.

Since our arrival in Krosno in the winter of 1940, I had visited Mennek's workshop many times. One entered his dark, noisy workshop from the in-side of the house, and since the house belonged to the Moszkowitz family, the inside door was always open. In addition to Mennek and his four apprentices, who were grouped together in a semicircle facing the window, there were always customers. They waited for their shoes, sitting on makeshift crates or standing.

German civilians, who had heard of the Jewish shoemaker, frequently brought their shoes to be repaired. They never had to wait; all other work stopped to take care of their needs. The Germans brought sheets of leather for the repair of their shoes. They were able to obtain unlimited amounts of it, whereas leather was forbidden to Jews. When Mennek cut the leather for the soles of their boots, he managed to retain enough leather to accommodate some of his Jewish customers. The residents of Krosno, both Jews and Christians, were very fond of Mennek, because in time of war, a pair of sturdy shoes or boots was invaluable.

I always felt somewhat intimidated when I walked into that smoke-filled room. There was a pervasive acid smell of old shoes, new leather, and glue. The five men were each bent over an iron cobbler's form, hammering—it often seemed—in tandem. With mouths full of nails, Mennek and his apprentices pulled, shaped, and fitted leather vamps around lasts and molds. You had to wait until Mennek stopped hammering and lifted his head before you could speak over the noise. Not only was Mennek able to make new shoes, he was also capable of making a new pair of shoes from an old pair. Mother had spoken to him in advance of my visit, and this time he did not say to me, "So, our *yeke* needs to have her shoes fixed." This remark, though made in jest, was quite discomforting. *Yeke* was a mild pejorative for a German Jew. It denoted me as German, when what I wanted least was to be in any way identified with the hated oppressor. It also called attention to my heavily accented and awkward manner of speaking Polish.

Finally, Mennek got up and motioned me to follow him to the far corner of the room. He told me that he was still looking for a pair of ski boots that were about my foot size, but that nevertheless we should get started. In my stocking feet, I stood on a piece of cardboard, and Mennek made a tracing of both my feet. Next, I took off my socks, stepped into a basin of water, and then stepped onto a clean sheet of brown paper. "That's for your arch," he said.

When he looked up, I saw for the first time the expressive look in his radiant eyes. He had a strong, square jaw, abundant curly, blond hair, and a fair complexion. He remained with me while I dried my feet and put on my socks.

He seemed in no hurry to get back to his work. "Your father is writing to you from America. Can you tell from his letters if he knows what is happening?" he asked. I sat there for more than half an hour, answering questions about my family and myself. It seemed Mennek knew quite a lot about us, but he wanted to hear from me why my father was in America, while we were in Krosno. It seemed that in the small town of Krosno, far removed from large Jewish population centers, such as Krakow, Warsaw, or Lwow, little was known of the Aktion—the expulsion of Jews from Germany on October 28, 1938. When I left the workshop, I was happy that this young man was my friend.

What Mennek did not know was that I too knew a lot about him. Before the war, his parents had lived a rather comfortable life. His father ran a successful shoe-making business, and he managed to educate Mennek and his four sisters. The oldest daughter was married and lived with her husband and baby in one of the four apartment dwellings in the family house. An older unmarried sister took over the running of the household after both parents died. Another sister was a dentist, and the youngest sister was an accountant. Mennek, the youngest of the family, had attended the gymnasium in Lwow, and while there he also pursued his violin study. I knew that he was an accomplished violinist, and that sometimes, on the Sabbath, he played his violin for a select group of friends.

Mother secured work for me that would temporarily exempt me from roadwork assignments by the Judenrat. Moreover, she had already made certain that the work would entitle me to an Arbeitskarte. I was to work for the top dressmaker in town. Her name was Lutka Gomulka, and she lived in the Bialobrzegi district, about nine kilometers from the center of Krosno. The agreement was that I would become a junior apprentice in return for a small payment from Mother. Panna Gomulka insisted on receiving weekly payments until I proved to be useful in her workshop. Since I was quite good with my hands, Mother did not think that the payments would have to continue for long. I would, however, be required to translate from German into Polish and vice versa for her German customers. This assignment would qualify me for the Arbeitskarte and make it possible for Panna Gomulka to expedite her dealings with her German clientele. Ever since the invasion of France, the Germans had gained access to beautiful plundered silks and textiles. I would have to get up at five in the morning to start work at eight o'clock. Though the long walk, mostly on unpaved roads, would be arduous in inclement weather, I was quite happy with this new adventure.

Another benefit of the new job was the discontinuance of my mathematics instruction. Jewish children were not permitted to go to school or to receive private instruction, but that order was not easily enforceable. Mother was very aware that my education had been stopped at a young age, and she endeavored to further it by encouraging me to read. I loved to read. For a small fee, I had access to a well-stocked private library and reading was not a problem. However, my algebra and geometry skills were sadly deficient. Mother was determined that this situation should be remedied and that I should master the intricacies of algebra and geometry.

For months, I had been receiving tutoring from Professor Witepski at his home. Children of Christian Poles could only attend elementary school, and Professor Witepski had been clandestinely instructing a group of older Christian students. Because I was Jewish, I could not be part of that group. The professor would only see me early in the morning, before his breakfast and before his neighbors could see me arrive. Twice a week, at six in the morning, I knocked at Professor Witepski's door. Sometimes he or his wife would immediately open the door; however, most of the time it would take a while, and I would pray that a passing German patrol would not see me lingering at the door. The room in which the instruction took place was cold and dark. The professor usually wore striped pajamas over long gray underwear and a winter coat. Wound around his neck was a knitted muffler, and his sparse, disheveled hair hung down from beneath his cap. The stench of vodka emanating from his mouth was more powerful than the smoke from his ever-present cigarette. In spite of my pleas, Mother refused to stop the lessons. She believed what I said about his drinking and smoking, but kept reiterating how fortunate I was that the professor had agreed to tutor me. "It is well known that the professor is a drunkard and that he chain-smokes," she said, "but for many years he taught at the University of Lwow, and he knows how to teach mathematics."

Panna Gomulka's dressmaking business was thriving. In addition to the many German civilians employed by the occupation authority, employees of the German firm of Kirchhof, Hoch & Tiefbau had moved to Krosno. Jewish homes and apartments had to be vacated to make room for them and their families. The uprooted Jews had to leave their furniture and home furnishings behind and move in with other Jewish families in a designated area. The German women brought textiles for dresses, suits, and coats. The German men brought silks and satins to be fashioned into elegant lingerie trimmed with ecru or black lace for their Ukrainian and Polish mistresses. Panna Gomulka took much more work than she was able to complete. She usually put in a ten-hour day, and so did her seven apprentices. While she worked, she cursed the German pigs and their stinking sows, and she gave me the job of making up excuses for her tardiness. The German women, who considered themselves members of the master race, were outraged by their dressmaker's lack of punctuality. Their common refrain was to complain about how sloppy Poles were and to disparage the Poles and their slave mentality. I carefully edited my translations in both directions.

The Gomulka's household consisted of Lutka's elderly parents and Ryszard, an eight-year-old boy. Lutka was fair and blond, whereas the boy had an olive complexion, with black hair and dark eyes. Lutka was unmarried, and it was understood that Ryszard was her son. However, when the boy addressed her, he called her aunt. I was given to understand that questions were not welcome, and in the months that I worked there, Lutka's parents, though not antagonistic, never once addressed me directly.

The workshop was in the large warm kitchen. The seven of us, pinning, basting, and stitching, sat facing each other, grouped around two sewing machines. Much of the work was done by hand, but there were always two women operating the sewing machines. The cloth we were working on was placed on linen-covered plywood boards that were perched on our knees. Lutka made her own patterns on a large wooden table in the cutting room across from the kitchen-workshop, and when the pattern was totally satisfactory, Lutka would cut the cloth. Sometimes she called me in to help pin the pattern to the cloth, but when the actual cutting took place, Lutka wanted to be alone. The fittings for the German clientele took place in the cutting room, and I always had to be present. It did not take long before I realized that Lutka understood German and had devised this method to avoid the unpleasant task of communicating with the invader. Aunt Regina told me that all members of the Gomulka family were proud Polish patriots.

As I rushed through the streets in the dark, early morning hours, I often saw large troop movements. They were heading east in tarpaulin-covered trucks, with the rear flap open. Peasants coming to town whispered about seeing trains filled with soldiers. A regiment of the Wehrmacht would be in town for a day or so, and then the faces would change, as another regiment passed through Krosno. This troop movement, in addition to the miles of trenches the Kirchhof construction firm was digging, stimulated rumors and speculation. Even the Poles who had access to highly positioned German officers were unable to come up with an answer to the puzzling questions.

The Jewish population was ordered to wear a white armband with the blue Star of David on the upper right arm. The order came from Hauptmann Schmatzler, the commandant of the Krosno Gestapo. We were advised that the slightest infraction of this order would have dire consequences.

On a sunny Sunday afternoon, Genia Springer, her two Catholic friends, Krysia and Janka, and I met at the bank of the Vistula River. Genia and I were a bit apprehensive because it was our first meeting since we had been ordered to wear the armbands. Krysia told us that Polish patriots were sabotaging German troop trains, and that the Gestapo had accelerated arrests of the Polish intelligentsia. Krysia was indignant about the success the Nazis were having in driving a wedge between Jews and Christians. "Some of our people are so dense," she said. "They are aware of what is happening to the Jews, but can't see what the German pigs are doing to us. And then there are people who suddenly have become wealthy working for the Gestapo. They denounce Jews and still call themselves Poles." We knew that she was referring to Herr Becker, a man feared and despised by the Jewish community. He was seen walking in and out of Gestapo headquarters in his twill jodhpurs and elegant knee-high boots with the Nazi party insignia displayed on his lapel. It was no secret that his constant date was Maryla, a handsome young woman from a fine Polish family.

When it was time to return home, Genia and I urged that, for Krysia and Janka's sake, we should separate and not be seen together. "Because of the armbands?" Krysia scoffed. "Ridiculous." Together we strolled back toward the center of town, and I was conscious of Krysia hooking her arm around my upper right arm in such a way that she covered the armband.

Several days later when I returned home from work, my mother descended upon me with a tongue-lashing, heaping her pent-up anger and frustration on me. The Gestapo "gorilla," the scourge of Krosno, had accosted

Mother on the street. He was given that name because he was slightly stooped and his long arms reached down to his knees. He was known to be very mean. Whenever he was present at a roundup of Jews, he invariably found a victim whom he initially berated and then beat up until blood flowed. He had told Mother that he had seen me walking without an armband. "That's not true," I said, but I knew immediately the incident Mother was referring to. She did not give me a chance to explain or to defend myself. The gorilla had shouted at Mother, "You tell your daughter that if I catch her again without the armband, she is done for. You will never see her again." Mother was crying and telling me how much anguish I had caused her. I swore that I would always make sure that the armband was visible.

The last photograph taken of Eva, sent to Father in New York. Krosno, April 1941.

## JUNE 1941 ✎ KROSNO, OCCUPIED POLAND

Germany invaded the Soviet Union. They breached the Soviet-German Pact and marched in. The terrible news thwarted our plan to escape across the San River into the Russian zone. It shattered our dream of getting closer to America and a reunion with Father. Within days, Shimek appeared at our door with his wife Margot, broken in spirit. He told us that their passage across the San had been postponed several times by the smugglers, allegedly because of the agreement between Germany and Russia that all fleeing refugees would be returned to the Germans. The Russians never strictly enforced this agreement; however, lately the Germans had intensified their effort to prevent refugees from escaping into the Russian zone. By the time Shimek and Margot arrived in Sanok, the smugglers were busily fleecing the fleeing Jews with no intention of ferrying them across the river. Shimek and Margot had given their valuables to the smugglers without achieving their goal. "Now no one will be able to stop the Nazis. They have conquered all of Europe, all of Europe," Shimek kept muttering. They remained with us for about one week, before returning to Tarnow, Shimek's hometown. He was very sad when he left us. He had been so eager to help Regina, his brother's widow, and Dollek to escape the Nazi yoke.

The Germans wanted us to believe that another blitzkrieg had been successfully completed. Happy, laughing German regiments were marching through the streets accompanied by heavy artillery with exceptionally long gun barrels. Tanks, mounted on conveyor trucks, made the earth shake. The German soldiers were standing up in tank turrets, laughing and eating apples.

The young Jews who had fled Krosno in 1939, in a failed attempt to join their army units and who had succeeded in moving far enough east to come under Russian occupation, were now returning home. The Russian retreat had left them stranded. They told of other Jews attempting to reach their army units in 1939 who were intercepted by roaming bands of Ukrainians. These Jews were often tortured and killed and sometimes turned over to Nazi patrols. The men who reached the Russian zone were well treated, and despite severe food shortages, no one died of starvation. We learned that the German attack was so sudden and so unexpected that the Polish reservists as well as the local population were unable to flee east. The Russian army and its equipment had to be speedily evacuated to avoid capture by the invading Nazis.

The only positive news we had were the rumors that the German invasion forces were encountering Soviet military opposition.

Whenever I was able to find the time, I would visit Mennek in his workshop. I always felt welcome. The ski boots he had found for me had been taken apart, vamp separated from sole, and each component had been stretched, kneaded, and carefully fitted around a last. From the used, square-toed ski boots emerged new, round-toed walking shoes that could not be traced back to the forbidden original boots. Mennek would not hand over the shoes until he had succeeded in making them look old and worn. It was dangerous for a Jewish person to be seen in new shoes. Care had to be taken so that Mennek would not be caught.

Several times I was present in the workshop at a Friday evening musical gathering. Mennek's friends crowded into the workshop and helped move workbenches to the side of the room. Blankets were hung over the blackout shades and securely fastened so that neither light nor sound could penetrate to the street. Mennek, dressed in clean trousers and a white shirt and holding his violin, gestured toward stools and boxes where we could sit. The music he played expressed our common bond and yearning. It alluded to all that was inexorably escaping our grasp.

Occasionally Mennek played the violin just for me. He asked me to sing while he accompanied me on the violin. I sang German songs that my mother had sung when we were happy. He especially enjoyed the Hebrew songs that I had learned in the Zionist youth movement in Germany.

Mother was worried about Eva's health. The influenza epidemic that year had caused much hardship in Jewish families. All five of us had been struck with high fever and weakened so severely that we had been unable to help each other. Once Dr. Rosenberg got word of our situation, he came daily to look in on us. Twice he donned an apron and spoon-fed us cereal he had cooked in our kitchen. Dollek recovered quickly, and in time Mother, Aunt Regina, and I regained our strength. My sister, however, developed a bronchial infection, and subsequently Dr. Rosenberg told us that she had pneumonia. Mother was disconsolate. It was almost impossible to obtain the nourishment Eva needed to recover. Dr. Rosenberg supplied the medication required by Eva without charge. Several times, his nurse Stasia, a Christian woman whose family were farmers, appeared at our apartment with fresh butter, eggs, and even vegetables. She said that there was no charge because Dr. Rosenberg had taken care of it. When Eva was allowed to leave her bed and go outdoors, she looked pale and thin. Still, it was a time for rejoicing, because for a while, Eva had hovered between life and death. All of us were very grateful for Dr. Rosenberg's loving care. He knew that we could not pay him, but when Mother said something, he answered, "Of course, you will pay me. I expect that you will send me the fee from America." When he said it, he sounded as if he really believed it.

The Arbeitsamt notified my sister that the doctor's certificate exempting her from forced labor would no longer be valid. Herr Engel urged that she obtain a job on her own. He said his hands were tied, and he would not be able to help us.

Eva had brushed up on her shorthand, and she was able to take German dictation at relatively high speed. Her typing skills had always been excellent. She was able to secure a secretarial position in the office of a motor overhauling workshop. Pani Groszka, the wife of the owner, had previously done the office work, but she had recently given birth and wanted to remain at home with the new baby.

Pan Groszka, a Volksdeutsch, or ethnic German, was delighted to have found such a well-qualified secretary. "You will sit at a desk in a heated office, and that is better than scrubbing floors," he said. He requested that when she arrived at the office that she hang her coat or sweater in such a manner that the armband would not be visible.

Pan Groszka wanted Eva to know that in his heart he remained a Pole, but since his family was of German descent, it would be foolish not to take advantage of the privileges available to him. Not the least of those was the license to operate the workshop and own a motorized vehicle. Only Germans came to the shop. They brought trucks and cars, and Pan Groszka, in his own car, would drive them to their place of employment. It was understood that the German customers should not see Eva, but since she also manned the telephone, she knew that he had some highly positioned officials as clients.

One morning when I arrived at the Gomulka house, I was met at the door by Lutka and told to go home. She said that I should report for work on the following morning. She seemed very agitated and closed the door before I had a chance to utter even one word. When I came to work the next day, two new people, a man and a woman, were living in the house. In the days following, they would quietly walk in and out of the kitchen; no one addressed them by their name. All of a sudden, Ryszard was no longer the quiet, rather taciturn youngster he usually was. He addressed the visitors as aunt and uncle. He was skipping rather than walking about, and there was a sparkle in his eyes. In the workshop, knowing glances were exchanged, but I had to learn the truth in my own home. Reluctantly, Aunt Regina answered my questions, because the mere fact of knowing could jeopardize our family. The man, who had so suddenly appeared at the Gomulka's house, was Lutka's brother Wladislaw and the woman was his wife Zofia.

Wladislaw Gomulka was the man most wanted by the Gestapo and the Sicherheitspolizei. He was an important trade union leader and an activist in the prewar Polish Communist Party. He had been tried and convicted in a Krosno court for his Communist activities. He was also apprehended in Warsaw while in the process of organizing a general strike, and he had spent several years in Polish jails. Several days after the invasion of Poland, the Nazi security police had come looking for him at the Gomulka home. The Gomulka family had remained under surveillance for much of 1940. As months passed and more German women came to seek out the famous dressmaker, the Gestapo began to believe that the Gomulka family was in fact unable to supply information concerning his whereabouts. Aunt Regina told us that the Jewish community assumed that Wladislaw had been in Russian-occupied Poland when the recent invasion took place. The question no one could answer was why did the Soviet authorities leave him behind when they fled from the invading German army.

It was evident that Lutka and her parents were unhappy and tense. Lutka threw temper tantrums at anyone who crossed her path, and together with the other apprentices, I avoided asking for guidance in the work assigned to me. Lutka's private room, we called it her sanctuary, was now occupied by Wladislaw and Zofia. We also knew, though no one ever talked about it, that Ryszard was in fact Wladislaw and Zofia's son and not Lutka's out-of-wedlock child. Lutka slept in the fitting room, and in the morning, the cutting table was laden with her personal belongings, as well as food. It was my assignment to keep the cutting table clear.

Several times Wladislaw walked in while I was cleaning or sweeping. He would stop me from doing my work and question me about people in the Jewish community. He wanted to know if certain people still lived in Krosno and exactly where they were living. He asked me if I understood that no one must know that he had returned. When Wladislaw spoke to me, Lutka never interfered. Sometimes she just stood by, and at other times she walked out and left us talking. I never heard her speak to her brother in an angry tone, though the rest of the family, excluding Ryszard, was subject to her wrath.

Lutka reserved her most cutting remarks and nastiest manner for her Jewish sister-in-law. She never addressed Zofia by her given name. Zofia did not acknowledge the constant slights, but neither did she shrink from encounters with her mother-in-law and sister-in-law. Since Zofia prepared all the meals for her husband, the three women had to interact in an atmosphere of mounting tension. Zofia pretended to be unaware of the lack of help and cooperation she received when she came into the kitchen. No one responded when she asked for a saucepan or kitchen utensil.

Zofia was short, olive-complexioned, and energetic. Her dark wavy hair, cut in a bob, needed little attention. Her wardrobe consisted of one skirt and one blouse, and she often wore house slippers. By contrast, Lutka even during the early morning hours did not present herself unless her hair was carefully groomed and her feet placed in elegant high-heeled shoes.

Hardly ever was the work completed at the time promised. To the German women customers, I was asked to give the same excuses, and much as I tried to vary the language, the fact remained that most of the women had to leave without the promised fitting or the finished garment. Refusing to speak German, Lutka made no attempt at apology. It was up to me to invent elaborate explanations for the tardiness. After Wladislaw's arrival, Lutka tried to avoid these scenes by sending me to the customer's home with whatever excuse I could invent. The wife of a Gestapo official started to scream when she saw me with my armband at her door. "Tell her that if she sends you here again, I will personally throw you down the stairs!" she shouted after me, as I rushed down the steps. I did not report what the woman had said.

## AUGUST 1941  &#x223d; KROSNO, OCCUPIED POLAND

We received a very upsetting letter from my grandfather in Bochnia. He informed us that this would perhaps be the last letter he would be able to smuggle out of the Bochnia ghetto because the ghetto was to be closed off from the town. He wrote that my grandmother, not being able to receive the drugs necessary to control her Parkinson's disease, was dying. Uncle Willek had never fully recovered from pneumonia, and his wife and his five-year-old son helplessly watched his physical deterioration. Uncle Zygmunt, his son Salek, and daughter Bronia were exhausted because while the assigned *Zwangsarbeit*—slave labor—was getting more arduous, the food rations were becoming smaller. Mother wept while she read the letter over and over again.

In Krosno, the authorities were taking steps to force the Jewish population into a circumscribed area. Aunt Regina was ordered to vacate her apartment and find accommodation within this area. It was densely populated; two and three families were living in one small apartment, often sharing the kitchen with another family. Bathroom facilities were inadequate. Mother and Aunt Regina decided to split up and to make every effort to remain as long as possible outside the area obviously slated to become the Krosno ghetto.

A strange shift in population was taking place within the Jewish community. Street raids were becoming more frequent and more vicious. Men wearing armbands were stopped, herded together, pushed onto trucks, and whisked away. These street raids were executed with lightning speed. The sudden appearance of trucks and uniformed Gestapo units was so well synchronized that escape became impossible. Ostensibly, the men were taken to work. When they did not return, their wives or mothers would appeal to the commandant of the Gestapo, Hauptmann Schmatzler.

The commandant had dark shiny hair, was of short, compact build, and was severely bowlegged. Within the Jewish community, some people believed that if one had the appropriate connection to Hauptmann Schmatzler, he could be induced to help. In August 1941, he refused to see Jewish petitioners and instead referred them to the director of the Arbeitsamt, Herr Gehrhardt, who in turn was too busy to see them. At times the Jewish community, acting swiftly and with a supply of cash or jewelry, would succeed in releasing an individual. Often the victim had been tortured. He would not talk about his incarceration at Gestapo headquarters, concerned that he would thereby draw attention to himself and risk the arrest of himself and his family.

A transport of women, children, and some older men arrived from the city of Lodz. They reported that this densely populated Jewish textile-manufacturing center had been cleared of Jews. Their husbands, sons, and brothers, they were told, would be working for the infamous Todt Company building roads.

Infrequently we received a longed-for letter from father. He wrote that he had not received mail from us for several months, that he was very worried, and that we should immediately write to him. He also referred to a number of matters that he had written about, and he wanted us to know that he was writing to us several times a week. The realization that our letters, so carefully constructed, were not reaching my father filled us with dark foreboding.

Wladislaw Gomulka stopped me in the entrance hall of the Gomulka house. "Will you do an errand for me?" he asked. I nodded. "Don't tell your mother," he added. "It's better this way." Fleetingly, I felt his hand on my arm before he turned away. On the next day, Wladislaw gave me a message for Pan Osterweil. I thought it would be a note, but the message was verbal, and it made no sense to me. He noted my consternation and said, "Don't worry about that. Pan Osterweil will understand."

Pan Osterweil was one of the men who had recently returned from the formerly occupied Russian territory. On his way home, he had been captured by the Wehrmacht and subsequently released. Though I had never spoken to him, I remembered him well from my prewar visit to Krosno. An elegant, urbane man in his early thirties, he was a pharmacist and owned a pharmacy. I delivered the message to Pan Osterweil on a Thursday. When I reported for work on the following Monday, Katja, one of the apprentices, whispered in my ear, "Pan Gomulka is gone. May the Lord protect him." Wladislaw's wife Zofia remained behind. Pale and silent, she moved about in the hostile atmosphere. Several days later, Zofia also disappeared, and the tension in the workshop lessened. I noted that Lutka made a determined effort to control her temper whenever Ryszard was in the room. When she addressed the young boy, her voice was affectionate and soothing.

The wife of a highly placed civilian with the Todt Company was Lutka's most difficult customer. She was a woman in her fifties who suffered from a curvature of the spine. Frau Heinrich arrived for the fittings in a chauffeur-driven automobile and often her disposition was venomous. Each time she came, she brought a new supply of French silks, fine woolen textiles, and exquisite lace to trim her silk underwear. She kept a strict accounting of the material, and she brought along a tape measure to personally supervise the cutting of the lace. She told me to tell Fräulein Gomulka that she would not tolerate Polish sloth. As much as Lutka tried, it was impossible to camouflage the pronounced hump on Frau Heinrich's left side.

On Monday Lutka knew that the silk suit and matching cape she had promised to deliver to Frau Heinrich on Wednesday would not be ready. On Tuesday at two o'clock, Lutka told me to go home and on my way back to stop at Frau Heinrich's apartment. When I resisted, she said, "I don't want to see this witch in my home unless I absolutely have to."

"I am afraid of her," I pleaded. "She hates Jews, and she doesn't know I'm Jewish."

"Then take off the armband."

"But I am not allowed to do that."

"Well, so, don't take it off. But you must go." Lutka was adamant. "Besides," she added, "that was my agreement with your mother. I told her that I would take you on, that I would teach you, and that you would do the translating for me."

The maid opened the door to the Heinrich apartment, and just as I was delivering my message, I heard Frau Heinrich shriek. She stood before me, her face an angry red, her finger pointing at my armband.

"How dare you!" she screamed. "The effrontery to appear in my presence, you Jewish pig! A Jewess touching my garments. Fräulein Gomulka will soon learn that we won't tolerate this type of sabotage against the Reich."

I staggered backward, fell down one flight of stairs, got up, and ran down to the street. My heart was pounding, and my stomach heaved up the morning's breakfast. Both my knees were bloody, and I had scraped the palm of my right hand. I cleaned myself up in the Moszkowitz's kitchen before I went home.

When I arrived for work on the following day, Lutka was waiting for me. She directed me to the cutting room and closed the door behind her. "You were right," she said. "It was a big mistake. You should not have gone there."

On the previous day, at about four in the afternoon, Frau Heinrich, accompanied by a uniformed Gestapo officer and a translator, had driven up to the Gomulka home. She threatened and frightened the Gomulka family, and she made it clear that she had the power to back up her words. Lutka told me that she could no longer keep me. She had her own problems to cope with. She said that in the months I had worked at the studio, I had learned something about dressmaking. When I said good-bye, she looked straight at me for the first time, and we shook hands.


## NOVEMBER 1941 ⤝ KROSNO, OCCUPIED POLAND

The room Mother was able to rent was cold and damp. The owner of the little house adjacent to the riverbank, Pani Czszanowska, told us that the room had been empty because it could not be heated. She said that when it got really cold, she would keep the kitchen fire going through the night, and we could leave the door to our room open.

On a cold evening in late November, we heard a knock at our window. Mother extinguished our oil lamp and lifted a corner of the blackout shade. She recognized our friend, Dr. Romek Rosenberg. She let him into our room. He looked exhausted and appeared to be breathless. He was not wearing his armband. "It's a raid," he said, "and they are looking for me. May God protect Stasia. This is not the first time that she has kept me out of their clutches." Mother pointed to his right arm, and when he saw that, he smiled. "They are not rounding up Jews," he explained. "This time they are after Polish army officers, and it is not the first time. They have got me on their list. So far I have managed to evade them, but I know they will be at my house. I did not tell my wife where I planned to hide out. Better she should not know."

The house we lived in did not have an indoor toilet, and Mother went out to see if it was safe for Dr. Rosenberg to use the outhouse. Our landlady and her son must not know that we had a visitor. Eva and I slept in one bed, and Mother offered Dr. Rosenberg the other bed. He said he was too nervous to fall asleep, but that he would sit in the chair, and perhaps doze off a bit. Mother gave him a blanket, but neither of them slept. They talked through the night. Eva and I hardly slept, both of us preferred to listen to what they were saying. Mother mentioned that I complained of pains in my right shoulder and that I was running a low-grade fever. She told him that she was worried about me.

Early in the morning, before dawn, I was to go to the Rosenberg house, find out from his wife if the Sicherheitspolizei had been there to look for him, and report back. Dr. Rosenberg wanted to look at my shoulder before I got dressed. He moved my arm and my shoulder as I winced from the pain. Dr. Rosenberg diagnosed an inflammation of the shoulder joint and said that he would give me an ointment to ease the pain.

Together with Mother and Eva, he moved the heavy wooden bed away from the wall. "Look at that," he said, pointing at a wet fungus growing on the wall against which I slept. Like a giant mushroom, it had spread from the earth-packed floor along the wall. "It must have been breeding there for years. That's the source of Betus's rheumatic inflammation. There should be a stove in this room, but Pani Czszanowska is well known for her stinginess. One of her daughters died of tuberculosis, and her son has the same disease."

"Which son?" Mother wanted to know.

"The older one, Mjetek. Over the years, I think I have treated all the members of the family. But several years ago, when I told Pani Czszanowska that the family sickness was due to lack of proper nutrition, they stopped coming to see me. The woman owns quite a bit of land and the restaurant at the bridge that Mjetek manages also belongs to his mother."

"It was this or the ghetto," Mother said. She became upset while explaining the numerous frustrations she had encountered in her search for a room. What we were doing was against the law, because all Jews were ordered to live in the ghetto. In the ghetto we had been assigned a tiny room in an apartment occupied by two other families with small children and a set of grandparents. That was our legal residence and our address. Mother was afraid to settle in the confined area of the ghetto. She hoped to circumvent the latest Gestapo orders as long as possible. "What do you want me to say?" Dr. Rosenberg shook his head. "I know well what we are up against, still I must tell you to get out of this pestilent place as soon as possible."

"All I want is to survive through this winter" was Mother's sad rejoinder.

## DECEMBER 1941, KROSNO, OCCUPIED POLAND

Perhaps a day or two after December 7, we learned that America had entered the war. In angry tirades heard over the loudspeakers, Hitler and his henchmen declared that America had declared war on Germany and that "*Die Juden werden dafür büssen*"—Jews will pay for that.

During the winter months of 1941 to 1942, I developed a severe inflammation in my joints. The pain, especially in my right shoulder, was excruciating, and the fever remained dangerously high for several days. Dr. Rosenberg visited daily and brought drugs bought on the black market. Whenever Stasia, his nurse and assistant, returned from the country with fresh provisions, he brought some along. "For Betus," he would say, though it took weeks before I was able to properly digest the food. My recovery was slow and impeded by my intestinal problems. The stressful circumstances of our lives over the past several years had settled in my digestive system. I was too sick to go to the outhouse, and I could not move my bowels in the presence of Mother and Eva. Even when they left the room to give me privacy, I still could not manage because I knew they were waiting outside in the cold.

The Arbeitsamt assigned Mother to a work detail in the Kirchhof firm canteen. There she made the acquaintance of Herr Fährich, a middle-aged man from the Schwartzwald region. He had been discharged from the army after sustaining a leg injury, and he was in charge of provisions for the civil engineering firm with branch establishments throughout occupied Poland. He told Mother that he hated the Nazis and that God would never forgive them their inhuman treatment of the Jews. His family business was the linen trade, and in Krosno he devised what he called "his private linen business." He dropped off parcels of gray linen, and Mother and Aunt Regina dyed the linens different colors with dyes that Herr Fährich supplied. He subsequently sold the linens on the black market. For us it was a dangerous undertaking, but Mother and Aunt Regina were paid with food items, and once again the sisters were able to feed their families. Herr Fährich, well aware of our situation, never failed to include some canned vegetables or small sacks of flour or sugar whenever he dropped off his linen parcels.

According to Nazi propaganda progress on the Russian front was excellent. The Russians were laying down their arms and admitting defeat, and Feldzug Barbarossa—Operation Barbarossa—was yet another German victory.

The Polish underground supplied us with a different version. We heard that the Russian army was resisting, and that bloody battles were being waged.

From the beginning of Barbarossa, German trucks passed through Krosno, ferrying supplies to Russia, while truckloads of booty from Russia went in the other direction. The Kirchhof firm was also engaged in transporting goods to and from Russia. Twice Herr Fährich was sent to Russia, and each time he took along some of his own merchandise to sell on the black market. This private merchandise, we assumed, was stashed among the goods he was transporting for the firm.

Our families' association with Herr Fährich lasted two months and then came to an end. Herr Fährich suddenly stopped coming, and our food supply was cut off. Mother made careful inquiries, but all she found out was that Herr Fährich had not returned from his last trip to Russia. Neither he nor his Polish driver were ever seen again. We had to assume that he had been caught with the illegal merchandise. Though Mother had been very circumspect in her inquiries, we lived in fear that if Herr Fährich had been arrested, an investigation might lead in our direction.

MAY 1942 ⤙ KROSNO, OCCUPIED POLAND

Throughout the early months of 1942, while I was recovering from the rheumatic inflammation, Mother and Eva tried to shield me from some of the stresses of our daily existence. Though I lacked energy, I was at all times aware of our predicament. Shortly after we learned that America had entered the war, Mother came down with a severe asthma attack. It was the first time since that unforgettable sight of Mother gasping for breath in Lusia's kitchen in Krakow that Eva and I had seen her Mother in such a depleted state. Dr. Rosenberg told us that it was a nervous reaction, and that it would pass. I was very frightened. Eva tried to comfort me, and she assured me that Mother was not about to die.

Mother had a private meeting with Herr Engel, the president of the Judenrat. He urged Mother to move into the ghetto. He explained that only within the ghetto would we be protected from sudden attacks. Living illegally outside the ghetto would make us subject to incarceration and transportation

to a concentration camp. Moreover, he said that by being fraudulently registered at an address in the ghetto and not in fact living there, we were not only
jeopardizing the lives of the people in the apartment, but also the lives of the
officials of the Judenrat. Herr Engel told Mother that if questioned, he would
have to tell the truth, but he did agree that perhaps for the time being, if we
were discreet, the Germans would not discover our deception. Mother was
determined to maintain a domicile outside the ghetto. She felt that until the
ghetto was closed off and gated, we would be safer on the outside, and if arrested, we could make up excuses for being temporarily outside the ghetto.

Mother heard that rooms requisitioned by the German authorities at the
Dunikowski villa had been left unoccupied, and that the Dunikowski family
needed money and might be willing to rent one of the rooms. This highly esteemed family had successfully developed several local oil wells and, before
the German invasion, had lived comfortably on the resulting revenue. When
Poland was invaded, the mother, old Pani Dunikowska, was the only member of the family still living at the large house. One of the sons had emigrated
with his family to America, and the other son, a bachelor who managed the
oil wells, had been vacationing in Italy at the time of the invasion. A married
daughter resided with her family in Warsaw. The Krosno household consisted
of the old lady's housekeeper and Panna Wyszinska, the bachelor son's fiancée.
Though Panna Wyszinska was a civil servant who held an important position
at the post office, she did not earn enough money to support the three of them.

Mother found the three ladies gracious and receptive. Though they lived
in straitened circumstances, the rent they requested was modest. The available room was on the main floor and had a private entrance. However, the
bathroom could only be entered through the foyer of the Dunikowski apartment during normal waking hours. Mother was told that we could occupy
the room and assured that the Dunikowski household would go to great
lengths to keep the Germans living on the second floor away from our living
quarters. Panna Wyszinska and Mother agreed that we should make every effort to stay out of sight of the people occupying the second floor. Pani
Szczopack, the Polish administrative assistant to the German Bürgermeister
or mayor of Krosno, and her ten-year-old son lived in one of the three sec-
ond-floor apartments. The basement level housed several of the former servants of the Dunikowski household. They lived rent free, and since they were
loyal to the Dunikowski family, they could be trusted not to betray us. To

avoid the German tenants, it was also agreed that we would use the basement entrance to enter the house.

Within the ghetto, there was a continuous shift of population. Women with children and old people from other ghettos were brought in, while transports would leave the Krosno ghetto for other ghettos where, we were told, additional workers were needed. The employer with the inexhaustible appetite for Jewish labor was, purportedly, the infamous Todt Company. In past years, the families of Jews destined for concentration or labor camps would receive an occasional postcard; however in 1942, the Jews ostensibly transported to the eastern outposts to work for the Todt Company were never heard from again.

There were persistent rumors that the transports of Jews no longer reached a work destination. The duped workers were killed in forests by a unit called the Einsatzgruppen, or special commandos, and their bodies were disposed of in some grisly manner. There never was a witness who could confirm these rumors, but they persisted. People had heard, people had seen, and word was passed from community to community.

Pan Majerowicz, our dear friend who since our arrival in Krosno had been available to help and advise Mother and Aunt Regina, decided to share with us his most secret plans. He was in the process of preparing an escape for his wife and three daughters Ewa, Maryla, and Basia. He was planning to place them with Christian friends and then go into hiding.

The insurmountable problem that Mother had not been able to solve was obtaining false identity papers. It seemed that Pan Majerowicz had found a person who could create a fictitious birth certificate, as well as a marriage certificate. The person did not want to be contacted directly, and we could not know his name or address. He was engaged in what was considered a treasonable crime, and if caught, his punishment would be beyond imagination. We understood all that, and we were cognizant that Pan Majerowicz was sharing with us a most precious resource. The clandestine preparations would have to be carefully planned. Pan Majerowicz promised to facilitate contact with the person who could create the false identity documents. He told us to be ready with all the details concerning our new identity as Christians. Mother was once again full of energy and busy with plans for our escape.

I landed an excellent job. I could hardly believe my good fortune, but after my first day on the job, my boss, Pan Litewski, said that he was the fortunate one and that I was his *aniol*, the Polish word for angel. He was tall, a handsome man in his seventies with a handlebar mustache. Due to a slight limp, he walked with the support of a cane. He lived together with his wife in a small well-maintained cottage. Since his retirement from the Polish cavalry, several years before the invasion, he had supported himself on income from property that he owned, as well as a pension from the Polish military. With the collapse of the Polish government, all pensions ceased. Pan Litewski now earned his livelihood by running a petition office, licensed by the German authorities. He spoke German with some proficiency, but his German writing skills were limited. He was not able to compose in proper German the many petitions heaped on his desk.

I was replacing a Volksdeutsch girl who, without giving notice, had left with her German boyfriend. Most of the petitioners who came to the office were peasants appealing to the German authorities for a reduction of their assigned agricultural quota—produce they had been ordered to deliver. Pan Litewski had a number of form letters, and it was my job to draft petitions to the designated German governmental agency within the framework of the required form. Most of the clients could hardly read and write Polish, much less German.

On my second day on the job, Pan Litewski presented me with a genuine work permit that stated in clear language that my work was essential for facilitating the food supply for the German army from local resources. He had personally gone to the Arbeitsamt and obtained a temporary permit with the official swastika seal affixed. Aunt Regina was suspicious and wondered if my new boss was Volksdeutsch. He told me that he was a loyal Pole, a committed Christian who, however, never went to church. He said he was aware and very upset about what was being done to the Jews. I happily set to work typing almost until curfew time. I quickly reduced much of the backlog.

Since my knowledge of the German language was better and more thorough than that of my employer, I was often called upon to be present at many of the initial consultations. Petitioners pleaded for the release of a husband or son from prison or a daughter from forced labor in Germany. Some of the minor unpleasantness I encountered came from the petitioners. At times, especially when family members were involved, I would ask pertinent questions, and though a moment before the man or woman had wept, they would break out into laughter at my misuse of a Polish word or phrase.

Pan Litewski never addressed me by my proper name. Instead he called me aniol. Almost every evening I took home some desirable food items. Our customers brought chunks of butter wrapped in cabbage leaves, flour, eggs, and even strawberries. I received a small share of the produce, and as a result Mother, Eva, Aunt Regina, and Dollek were all eating well again. I also shared the food with the Moszkowitz family. I was happy to contribute to our continual efforts to obtain food.

Within days, I learned why Pan Litewski called me his angel. He knew Dr. Rosenberg well because he was his physician and both had been officers in the Polish cavalry. Pan Litewski was in dire need of prostate surgery, and Dr. Rosenberg had made arrangements for him to be operated at Holy Lazarus Hospital in Krakow. It would appear that my predecessor had not wanted to take on the responsibility of running the office during his absence, and Dr. Rosenberg said that I could do it.

During the second week of my employment, I was invited to the Litewski home for Sunday dinner. I met Pani Litewska, a dour and fanatically religious lady, their son Eugene, an unemployed schoolteacher, and his wife and their six-year-old son. Eugene was struggling to make ends meet, while keeping a low profile to avoid an undesirable work assignment. He lived with his family on the outskirts of Krosno. I was informed that while his father was in the hospital, Eugene would come to the office daily. Pan Litewski said that during his absence, Eugene and I would share equally all the produce received from the day's activity. Any money received by the office was to be delivered to Eugene. It was anticipated that Pan Litewski would be absent for one month.

The office was very busy, and though some of the customers balked at telling me rather than Pan Litewski about their problems, no one walked away, and the produce kept coming. Often before affixing their signature or an X to the petition, the appellant wanted to know what I had written. I got accustomed to the idea that my accent and my often clumsy translations were objectionable, but the laughter became more good-natured as it became evident that my petitions were achieving the desired goal.

When Mother mentioned my problem to Panna Wyszinska, she said she would help and arrange for an evening to tutor me in the intricacies of Polish grammar. Both Eva and I were working in offices where our knowledge of

German was the basis of our employment, and that caused Mother much anguish. In planning for our escape, one of the many dilemmas she faced was that her two teenage daughters did not speak Polish either fluently or correctly. Polish people often criticized Mother because as a graduate from a Polish gymnasium she had been remiss in not teaching her daughters Polish.

Pan Litewski returned to work wearing an old black evening coat that only partially camouflaged the drain emanating from the fly of his trousers. He had lost weight, but he vigorously clasped me to his chest and kissed me with much affection. "You have saved my business," he said, "and no one but you could have done it. In my absence you supported my family, and you assured my livelihood." Then, with tears in his eyes, and still holding my hand, and with his son standing by, he said, "I will never forget what you have done for me and what you continue to do for me and for my family. I know what has happened in Krakow. The Jews were taken from Krakow to a ghetto in Plaszow, and now the Nazis are getting ready to transport the poor Jews to concentration camps. Ha, concentration camps," Pan Litewski said derisively, "They invent these euphemisms to camouflage their ugly deeds. They bring them there by the thousands, and no one ever comes out." He put an arm around my shoulder, and he said solemnly, "This is my promise, and my son is a witness. I will not let them take you away. I will shelter you in my house, and I have friends who will help me find a hiding place for you."

"With my mother and my sister?"

He hesitated. "It is more difficult to hide three people, but for you I will try. I will talk it over with my wife."

When Pan Litewski made his offer, I immediately visualized myself giving Mother the good news. However, it would not be good news if he restricted his generosity to me and stopped short of including Mother and Eva.

The Friday evening gatherings at Mennek's workshop had been suspended during the winter months, and they were not resumed when the weather turned warm. It was difficult to meet with friends. All the news was bad, and everyone endeavored to cope with the pervasive fear. It took an effort to extricate the spirit from the ever-tightening grip. The realization within the Jewish community that the remaining elderly men, women, and children were trapped intensified everyone's despair. Daily and randomly, Jews were apprehended and transported to unknown destinations. In hushed tones, we referred to the ghetto liquidations that were taking place throughout Poland. How many weeks, or even days, separated us from the great void ahead of us? The fear gnawed at the organs and stopped them from functioning. Still, alone with Genia, my closest friend, we would speak of a future, of a yet unknown man who would come into our lives, and what it would be like.

The henchman for the Gestapo and their informer was Herr Becker. He was a Volksdeutsch who could be seen at different times in various locations dressed in civilian clothes and elegant brown leather boots that came up to his knees. He walked in and out of the ghetto, and he seemed well informed about the multiple families occupying each of the crowded apartments. A visit to a close or distant relative was suspect and could land the visitor, the host, or both in jail. Herr Engel told Mother that Herr Becker would show up in the middle of the night, pick up a person or a family, ostensibly for interrogation at Gestapo headquarters, and Herr Engel was powerless to obtain that person's release. He knew that he was ineffectual and no longer able to serve the Jewish community, yet the Gestapo chief, Hauptmann Schmatzler, denied Herr Engel's request to be released from his office as president of the Judenrat. Herr Engel told Mother that shortly the ghetto would be fenced in, but he was told total resettlement would not take place. "Can one believe them?" he asked Mother. "They tell me something, and next day's poster announces the opposite. All proclamations pasted on the kiosks are based on orders from Governor-General Hans Frank, but Schmatzler, or so he says, never knows of them in advance."

Some of the young Jews who had returned home from the Russian zone after the German invasion were attempting to hide, and it was understood that they should not be contacted. I had known several of them from my prewar visit to Krosno. The only one who had gotten a useful job and the requisite work permit upon his return was Dollek Zwiebel. At age nineteen, he appeared to be a fully grown man. Of olive complexion, six feet tall, and broad in the shoulders, he was by far the most handsome boy I had ever seen. His straight, thick, black hair was combed away from the forehead, and his eyes sparkled with vitality.

Though I knew that it was the one question he did not want to hear, I asked, "What made you come back to the German-occupied territory? We are trapped here, and we were trapped from the beginning, but you were free. Now you are one of us."

Dollek shook his head. "We too were trapped, because the German invasion was so sudden, so unanticipated, that only the Russian military and important dignitaries were allowed to be part of the Russian retreat. Who would have thought the Jewish refugees who previously had been transported to Siberia were the lucky ones?"

"I heard that the Kinder brothers and Genek Stiefel were sent to work somewhere in Siberia. Why didn't they take you?" I asked.

"In Russia one never knew who made a decision. It could have been the local commissar. I was afraid to tell them that my father owned a lumberyard, and I said that I had worked in a lumberyard, so they placed me in a cooperage, and I quickly learned how to make barrels."

"Why you and not some of the others?" I persisted.

"I don't know the answer, but they were shrewd. What the Russians did not want is a mass of refugees who would deplete their already meager food supply. I tell you, Betus, what is eerie is that we, living in the Soviet zone, and not far away from the German occupation zone, had no idea of the systematic dismemberment of Jewish communities throughout Poland and the deportation of Jews to an unknown fate."

"I find that difficult to believe," I said. "Just as I find it hard to believe that my father, living in New York, does not know what has happened here after the Germans invaded." We had been standing together for too long, and in parting Dollek said to me, "Be careful. Living in these conditions, you can't infer what your father knows or does not know. When I showed up at my parents' door, they greeted me without joy, without an embrace. Their shock was so great. All along the fact that I had escaped the Nazi yoke was a shining beacon in their lives. They felt that I had betrayed them."

I continued relieving Pan Litewski of much of the work at the petition office, while he slowly recovered from his surgery. He would show up in the afternoon, review my work, split up the food, and depart for his home, leaving me to lock up the office. Often he would look over my shoulder at the page in the typewriter, squeeze my shoulder, and bestow a kiss on my hair, murmuring, "I will not forget," or "You can count on me."

There were rumors that a small detachment of Einsatzgruppen, or liquidation squads, had remained in Krosno. It was also rumored that they were closely observing every movement within the Jewish community.

Large posters addressed to the Christian population appeared on kiosks all over town. They reminded the people that by a designated date everyone would have to be in possession of a new identity card. The application for a new identity card could only be obtained in person at the magistrate's office. The completed document accompanied by a birth certificate and two recent photographs had to be presented at the office of the German Bürgermeister of Krosno.

Mother obtained our forged birth certificates. Mother and Eva were now mother and daughter; their new names were, respectively, Jadwiga and Katia Dembicka. I became Krystyna Zolkos, Mother's niece and Katia's cousin. We constructed a relationship that made my deceased mother Jadwiga Dembicka's sister and wife of Stanislaw Zolkos, a Polish army officer missing since the invasion. My new place of birth was Iskrzynia, a village not far from Krosno, chosen in consultation with Pan Majerowicz. It was crucial that I pronounce the name of the village properly.

Next, we had to get photographs of ourselves for our forged identity cards. The arrangements with a photographer were made through Jerzy Hyp, a Christian and trusted friend of Aunt Regina. In the past he had helped dispose of merchandise from her prewar clothing business. On Saturday at dusk, when Polish families visited each other, we clandestinely went to see the photographer who worked in his home. We went separately. "Remember," Mother admonished, "when you see the photographer put his head behind the black cloth and his finger is about to push the release button, lower your eyelids."

When I reached the outskirts of Krosno, I slipped off my armband and located the country lane that would lead to my destination. I donned a large kerchief and, keeping my eyes down, greeted the occasional passerby with a muttered, "May God walk with you." No one stopped to speak to me, and I looked around carefully before slipping into the door of a cottage. To the young man in peasant garb, I said, "Jerzy Hyp sent me."

"I know who sent you," he responded gruffly, "but what I need to know is if anyone saw you walk into my house."

I watched him slide the glass plates in and out of the large box camera, mounted on a tripod. I noticed that his hands were pale, the fingers long and tapered—not the hands of a peasant. When he said, "Look into the camera," I did exactly that but with my eyelids lowered.

Jerzy Hyp, through his underground connections, had obtained a blank white identity card for Aunt Regina and Dollek. The card was then completed with their new identities, photographs, and a forged seal. Their photographs presented a vague, yet recognizable likeness of the bearers. The occupation authority had devised various security measures to foil attempts at forgery. Yet, we were looking at a document that to our eyes appeared genuine.

Jerzy was outraged by how some of his Christian brethren were treating Jews. He told Aunt Regina that the Nazis in their effort to separate and resettle the Jews were recruiting and bribing Poles to help them achieve their obscene goal. He promised Mother that he would use his connections to get forged identity cards for us. Doing this would require payment in advance. But within a few days, the required amount had tripled and was no longer within our reach.

Pan Majerowicz and Mother agreed that my mother, Eva, and I had no other option but to take our place in the long line of waiting Christian applicants. We did not think that the clerks working in the magistrate's office would recognize us since we were not native to the town. Applications had been issued for the past two weeks, and we hoped that townspeople who might recognize us had already obtained the required document. We thought we would be able to stand in line with people from outlying villages, strangers to each other.

We soon learned that this option was no longer viable. Disguised Jews waiting in line with their forged birth certificates had been recognized, reported, and imprisoned. They had been cruelly tortured because the Gestapo wanted to know how they had managed to obtain the false documents and who was behind this criminal deed. Two of the three Jews who had been caught were shot at Gestapo headquarters, and the third one was never seen again.

Pani Szczopack, administrative assistant to the German Bürgermeister, and her ten-year-old son Nikolaus occupied the largest apartment on the second floor of the Dunikowski villa. We were not sure of her nationality because she was residing in an apartment requisitioned by the German occupation authority.

We made every effort to avoid contact with this close associate of the German Bürgermeister of Krosno. We heard that Pani Szczopack was a fine cook and that the Bürgermeister was a frequent dinner guest at her apartment. Often his car could be seen near the house until late evening hours.

Pani Szczopack approached Eva and told her that she wanted both of us to work for her. Eva was to clean the apartment while she was at work, and I was to tutor her son, read to him, and put him to sleep on the occasions when she dined away from home. She also asked us to be available to carefully set her table and to prepare in advance some of the food she would cook when she entertained. She did not engage in conversations with Eva or me, but I gathered from what she said that she considered herself a loyal Pole who was trying to survive the war as best she could. She had settled in Krosno after having been expelled from the Posnan area, the western part of Poland annexed by the Third Reich immediately upon the invasion.

Nikolaus told me that he missed his daddy and that he had not seen him in many years. When I repeated this to Mother, she said, "Pani Szczopack, like most people living in a conquered land, has her secrets, and she knows well that with us her secrets are safe. She knows about us, and that by living outside the boundaries of the ghetto we are committing a disastrous offense. I don't believe she will ask questions, and you must be careful to reveal little." On vary rare occasions, Mother and Pani Szczopack would encounter each other on the path leading up to the house. Mother would incline her head, and our neighbor would just barely acknowledge the greeting. When we walked on the path leading up to the villa, we hid our armbands.

In nearby towns, ghettos were liquidated, and some of the inmates were temporarily brought into the Krosno ghetto. Time was of the essence in the task that needed to be accomplished. Mother located three persons who were all members of one family, close in age to the three of us, and who already possessed new identity cards. In return for payment, they would once more stand in line, but this time with our forged birth certificates and photographs. They would answer all questions in accordance with our assumed identity. Payment was made in advance, and shortly thereafter we were advised that the three applications had been successfully submitted.

Eva and I, in possession of validated work permits, departed for work early in the morning and returned home shortly before curfew. It was imperative to hurry when one walked through town to avoid giving the impression that one had time to linger, which was tantamount to loitering. Mother who was at that time without steady employment was subject to being called up for Zwangsarbeit, or slave labor. Whenever she worked at the airport, she seemed less exhausted when she returned home. She told us that some of the airfield officers were uncomfortable as they watched the Jewish women engaged in labor often beyond their strength and would themselves do some of the lifting or moving of heavy objects.

At night in our room, we talked about the submitted applications. Would a clerk recognize us from the photographs? Would a diligent official contact the respective village registrars to verify our birth certificates, which were, of course, unregistered documents? Did the counterfeit documents look genuine? Often while Eva and I pondered these questions, Mother was silent and distant. She had heard that the Bochnia ghetto had been liquidated, and there was a growing realization that liquidation meant elimination. What exactly was being done with the hundreds of thousands of Jews from the liquidated ghettos?

Mother had tried during the past several months to contact her father. In his last letter he had written that my grandmother was dying. Did she in fact pass away? we wondered. Mother hoped that she had, and that she would be spared falling into the Nazi killing mill. She did not know the fate of her two brothers and their families. Toward the end of 1941, some Jewish families from Krakow had been transported to Bochnia, among them Lusia and her eighteen-month-old son. Lusia, my father's young niece, had taken Mother into her home when we were expelled from Germany without money or clothing, and she had lovingly helped Mother through difficult times. She and her husband Hennek had longed for a child, and after several stillbirths and multiple miscarriages, Lusia had given birth to a healthy boy in March 1940. Mother wondered where they were and if they were alive. Mother in her powerlessness could do no more than grieve for her family.

Pan Majerowicz against his better judgment—he kept repeating—helped Mother obtain three cyanide capsules. It was a crime to be in possession of poison because only the Nazis could be in charge of the fate of an individual Jew. The capsules, oblong and of a greenish-blue color, were very costly. Mother justified the expense by telling us that she considered it to be our insurance; by means of the capsule we would be able, should the time come, to control our own fate. She hid the capsules in a secret place.

There was no question that "the time" was coming. Not only the Nazis and Jews knew, but also the Poles. The Christian residents had been encouraged, urged, even hounded to separate themselves from their Jewish friends and neighbors and sever, for their own well-being, all relationships with Jews. Word was out that the new white identity card, so recently acquired, would soon become obsolete. To make certain that no Jew could slip through the tightly controlled identity structure, the future identity card would require the bearer to be fingerprinted.

Eva's boss, Herr Groszka, told my sister that it would be difficult to find a replacement for her should the need arise. He said that while she was in Krosno, he would use his influence to keep her in his employ. "However," he said, "once the ghetto is closed off, my hands may be tied. If you can manage it, come and see me. I am sure I'll be able to help." Mother made Eva repeat this offer of help several times. Was Herr Groszka sincere? Would he remember? How did he say it?

Pan Litewski's assurances to me were continuous. Every day he repeated that he would help me, he would hide his aniol, even risk his life for me. And every other day there was a message from Pani Litewska letting me know that she had lit a candle for my family and me and that she was praying for us. She had asked the Holy Mother to keep us out of the clutches of the murderous Germans.

The first of the coveted identity cards had been approved and was to be handed to me by my proxy at an agreed meeting place. It was in my assumed name with the photograph of me in my changed hairdo—I could barely recognize myself. I was guardedly happy as we continued to wait for the other two identity cards. In a hiding place that we had prepared in the coal cellar of the Dunikowski house, Mother carefully placed my identity card amidst letters from Father and envelopes with his address, as well as several letters from Zack, written from Hindenburg, Berlin, and finally Trieste, Italy.

## AUGUST 1942 ✿ KROSNO, OCCUPIED POLAND

When I returned home after work I found Mother frightened and trembling. "We are discovered," she kept repeating. "Now they know." Once she calmed down, Eva and I learned what had happened. Walking up the hill to the Dunikowski house, Mother had come face to face with Pani Szczopack, who was on her way down. "Good day," Mother had greeted her. The response was, "Good day, Pani Weissbergerowa. Or should I say Pani Dembicka?" Evidently, Mother's identity card had come across Pani Szczopack's desk. Had someone brought the document to her attention? Had she informed her boss, the German Bürgermeister?

Together we examined various possibilities that could ensue. If someone other than Pani Szczopack recognized Mother's face in the photographs attached to the application, she would have to take action or be guilty of a crime. That, we were sure, she would not do for us. However, if she were the only one who had made the connection, she would not profit by denouncing us. She had attained the highest civil service position a Pole could aspire to, and she had nothing to gain from compromising her own conscience. How could we obtain assurance of her silence, and yet not ask for it? By asking for it, we would have to admit our criminal deed.

Mother remembered the two Persian carpets that Zack had clandestinely removed from our apartment in Hindenburg and sent to her while she was living in Krakow. They had been quite costly, and knowing their value, Mother had guarded them carefully. Over the past three years, wherever we were, Mother had periodically removed them from their paper wrappings, shaken and brushed them, and repacked them with fresh camphor balls.

Late in the evening, on the day the chance encounter had occurred, Eva and I walked up the stairs to Pani Szczopack's apartment, each carrying a rug. Mother had removed all vestiges of camphor, and she had carefully repacked them in the brown paper. Attached to the string was a note that read, "I should be honored if you could use these carpets." Two days later we got word that Mother's proxy had her new identity card, and I retrieved it on my way home from work.

Eva's document had not yet arrived, but we were packing. It was decided that each of us would leave carrying a small piece of luggage and a light coat. We wrapped and tied small bundles of clothing that Panna Wyszinska could send through the post office to our new address. Our winter coats, relatively new and fashioned from black melton cloth, were hanging in one of the wardrobes of the Dunikowski household. Panna Wyszinska told us she would pack and mail them separately once we had a forwarding address. We were careful to shield the Dunikowski family from knowing our planned escape, but we were aware that it must have been obvious to them what we were preparing to do. Everyone knew that it was better not to know. All three members of the Dunikowski family were always kind and agreeable to our requests. Yet, we also understood they wanted us to be gone before we were located and arrested in their house.

There were a limited number of ways to leave town. Three different types of foot patrols were guarding all roads. The Sicherheitspolizei, the Gestapo units monitoring the town and access to the town, were the ones we feared most. These security police, a unit working in cooperation with the Polish police force, employed a number of informers who had contacts in remote outlying localities. The peasants coming to the petition office could never understand how it was possible that the day after a calf was born, or shortly after a sow had dropped a litter, the German agricultural agent and his Polish translator would arrive in an open car with exact knowledge of when the animals had been born and how many. It was rumored that the German military police were less vigilant in checking civilian identity. We understood that though they examined documents and packages, they would not make arrests unless their suspicions were aroused by an obvious defect in the identity documents.

While mentally preparing for our lives as Christians and studying the catechism, asking each other the questions and answers a professing Catholic would have to know, we waited for Eva's identity card to arrive. We had to be prepared to answer searching questions about our background and to avoid appearing ignorant about the Catholic religion. Almost every day we heard that a Jew or a Jewish family had been caught while preparing to escape or intercepted en route. We prayed for the arrival of Eva's identity card before the Gestapo would come for us.

PART II

*Hiding in Plain Sight*

# CHAPTER 5

# Krysia Zolkos

On Saturday morning, during the last week of August, I stopped as usual at the kiosk near the ghetto on my way to work. Several people stood in front of me, and I had to crane my neck to read the print on the large white poster. It was a decree that ordered all Jews living inside and outside the ghetto to assemble on the following Monday at seven o'clock in the morning in the *rynek* or town market square. There were to be no exceptions. The decree applied to all Jews, including those who had tried to hide. If they reported at the market square, their attempt at evasion would be forgiven. Those Jews with documents indicating that their labor was necessary for the war effort, such as the group that worked at the airport, would after processing be allowed to return to work. All other Jews would be resettled to a different ghetto and put to work at tasks vital to the war effort. The last paragraph warned that any Jew who failed to report as directed would be shot on sight.

A final paragraph at the bottom of the poster was addressed to the Christian residents of Krosno and to the Christian population of the adjacent villages. It stated that it was a crime to help a Jew circumvent this decree. Any Christian caught aiding or hiding a Jew trying to evade this Aktion would be severely punished, possibly even with death.

As the people in front of me moved away, I had an unobstructed view of the ominous white poster. I read and reread it, trying hard to understand the portent of the threatening language. I thought I should rush home and inform my mother. Eva, who left for work shortly after I did, would already know, but Mother, who was energetically engaged in planning our escape, would have no way of knowing. Instead, I walked to the office and waited for Pan Litewski to arrive. When he walked in, I knew immediately that he had read the poster. "*Moja biedna Zaba,*" he muttered as he embraced me—my poor frog. I could see tears in his eyes. Because I always eagerly jumped to carry out his requests during his recovery period, he frequently called me his frog.

Before I was able to remind him of his promise, he said, "I have not forgotten, but you can see for yourself that we cannot hide you in our house. They might not even come after me. What could they do to such an old man? But I have to consider Eugene and my little grandson. We know the Germans; that's who they would go after." I was moving toward the door, but he stopped me. "You are coming with me. We will lock up the office, and together we'll go and see Pani Litewska." Perhaps he and his wife would do it. I must try and persuade them, I thought. It would only be for a few days.

Leaning heavily on the cane with his right hand and clasping my right arm with his left, obscuring, I thought, the armband, though I did not dare look, we slowly walked toward the Litewski cottage. The garden in full bloom had the verdant smell of late summer, with the peaceful calm of a world vastly different from my own.

Waiting in the parlor for what seemed an interminable time, I listened to the voices coming from the kitchen where Pan Litewski and his wife conferred about my fate. I could not make out the words, but from the tone of their raised voices, I inferred that there was a difference of opinion. Finally, Pan Litewski came back into the parlor. Their mutually agreed-upon decision was, he informed me, that I could take refuge for several days in the small toolshed in back of the garden. I asked to see it, and Pani Litewska went with me. She said that her husband wanted to hide me in the attic of their house, but she said, "You would not ask us to do that and risk our lives and those of our family, would you?" The only reply I managed was, "No one would know."

When I saw the shed, I knew immediately that it was a waste of precious time. There was not enough room for me to stand up, and both Mother and

Eva were taller than I. Still, I looked around and thought that if it didn't rain for the next few days, we might be able to stay outside and hide behind the lush branches of the chestnut tree. From our hiding place, we could see anyone who approached the garden gate, and in that eventuality, the three of us could squeeze into the shed.

When I told the Litewskis that I would tell Mother, and if there were no other possibility, we would arrive late in the evening and would make certain that we were not seen, both husband and wife looked astonished. Had they not made it clear that this fearful chance they were about to take was for me alone and not for my mother and sister? Did I fail to understand that it is easier to hide one person than three people? Hadn't I read the threatening paragraph addressed to the Christians? What did I expect of them? I did not answer. I no longer knew what I had expected. All I knew was that I was shaking, the tears were uncontrollable as they ran down my cheeks. I ran out of their house.

I looked at my watch and was horrified to see that it was almost two o'clock in the afternoon. It would take at least forty-five minutes before I reached home. As I was about to rush past Mennek Moszkowitz's workshop, he stepped out and, taking my arm, drew me inside. "I have been waiting for you," he said in a firm voice. "You are a pretty sad sight. It's better your mother does not see you in this condition. Now sit down, and tell me what has happened." After I told him, his response was brief: "You bet on the wrong horse."

"Now listen carefully," he said, "while we wait for Wladek to arrive." Wladek worked in Mennek's shop; he sat on the stool next to Mennek. I knew Wladek by sight only. Mennek wanted to know if all three of us had white identity cards with our assumed names and identifying us as Roman Catholics. When I told him that Eva had not yet received her document, but we were confident it would arrive, and Panna Wyszinska would forward it, I could tell that he was disappointed.

"You must proceed without it," he said. "The choice to wait for it has been taken out of your hands." Though Mennek was my dearest friend and I had confided many of my secret thoughts and fears to him over the past months, I did not tell him that Pani Szczopack had recognized Mother's face on the falsified application.

"I told Wladek that all three of you were in possession of the new validated identity cards, so I'll leave it at that," said Mennek. I felt his calloused fingers as he touched my hand. I looked into his eyes and saw the urgency in his glance.

"You must listen carefully. There is so much I need to say to you before Wladek gets back, and he will be here within minutes. You know that he and I have been friends for many years. For months now, he has been telling me that his family was prepared to shelter me in their home should the need arise. This morning after he read the order, Wladek came rushing to the workshop. He said that the time had come for me to walk out of my shop and make my way to his home. Subsequently, he would bring whatever I needed. They are truly good and decent people, and they have planned carefully. Wladek thought it would be best if he were to continue to run the workshop, repair German boots, and try to save, as we had done before, some of the shoe leather for our friends. If questioned, he would say that he didn't know what had happened to me—I had just disappeared and perhaps had been caught by the Gestapo."

I embraced Mennek. I was very happy for him. "It's great to have such a good Christian friend," I said. Mennek agreed.

"But, he said, "though I know the offer is generous and sincerely meant, you know, Betus, that I can't accept it. I have told you before that I will not hide and leave my three sisters without my protection. I have a number of German customers who still have their dress boots on my shelves. Perhaps one of them can get me a special permit so that I can continue my work. If I am successful, I will try my best to keep my family together in that camp they are taking us to. A shoemaker is still of some value, or so I tell myself. I will not abandon the girls."

I wanted to respond, but Mennek stopped me. "I told Wladek exactly what I am now telling you. I asked him to hide the three of you instead of me. Of course he did not want to do that, but I reasoned with him and I convinced him."

I was overwhelmed. "But the difference is one person. Why would he take us and not you and your sisters?"

"He was adamant about that. He said his parents are afraid to have three additional women in their attic as well as me, and they would not change their minds. I think they figured out that I could disguise myself because of my blond hair. I look like a peasant. My sisters can't with their Semitic features."

"How were you able to convince him to take us instead?"

"Well, it wasn't easy. I told him that the three of you have documents that state you are Christians. Also, the people in his village and the surrounding villages do not know your faces. But what convinced him was when I mentioned the obvious."

"The obvious?"

Mennek smiled. "I said it would be much less of a risk for him and his family to hide three women. After all, there is this matter of circumcision. They could not find proof of Jewish identity if they asked you to drop your pants."

This temporary solution to our immediate problem filled me with hope and cautious joy. I was completely aware of how awesome and generous his offer was. I wanted to tell Mennek how I felt. I wanted to tell him of my gratitude. His hand on my shoulder was firm as he stopped me.

"I know you and Eva and your mother. Yes, I do have other friends, and Betus you can believe me this was not a sudden decision. No one knew what I was contemplating, and no one, not even my sisters, will ever know about it. We must guard this secret so no harm will come to Wladek and his family. But I have this feeling that you are the ones who could, maybe, survive. You will be sustained by the certainty that at the end of the tunnel your father will be waiting and that he will bring you to America. That thought alone will give you strength, and it will bolster your determination to fight for your lives."

It must have been at least thirty minutes since I had walked into the shop and sat down on the stool. Mennek had given me a gift that would lift up my despairing mother. We would have a place to hide, whereas he and his family would face the treacherous Aktion and an unknown fate. The hot tears ran down my cheeks. The demands on me felt nearly overwhelming, beyond my years.

"You must pull yourself together," Mennek said in a firm voice. He was pacing in front of me. "You must. Here is Wladek, and there is much we have to talk about."

I wiped the tears from my eyes, stood up, and extended my hand in greeting. I knew immediately that he was unhappy with me and the mission he had agreed to undertake.

Mennek and Wladek had agreed that we should remain in the shop until sundown, and then I should carefully follow Wladek out of town to his house. There must be no indication that I knew Wladek, and while not letting him out of my sight, I must maintain distance between us. I was to pass him when he opened the gate to his garden and turn back after I had made sure that no one had noticed me. Under no circumstances was I to approach him or ask a question.

I listened attentively. Wladek did not speak to me directly. The only time he did address me, he said, "I am not happy about this. It is very dangerous, and I am doing it out of friendship for Mennek. My parents have no idea of what I'm about to spring on them."

Mennek put his arm around Wladek's shoulder and gave him a hug. "Come on," he said. "We've been through all that. We don't want her walking along looking like the weight of the world is on her shoulders, do we? She knows that you wanted only me and that I worked hard to persuade you. They will leave as soon as possible, perhaps Wednesday."

"The latest Wednesday," Wladek interjected.

"Don't do that, Wladek," Mennek soothed. "Proper arrangements will have to be made, and you know this. It would be the same in my case. The Aktion is so sudden, there was no time to negotiate for anything but a temporary shelter, and that is all they expect. Remember to tell your parents right away that they have documents issued by the magistrate, so your parents cannot be accused of aiding escaping Jews. I don't have Christian identity papers. Her mother will pay for everything, so please tell your parents that they should not worry about that. And don't forget to tell your mother that the three of them will eat less than I do—she knows my appetite." Wladek did not appreciate Mennek's attempt at humor.

There was little time. The men had agreed the three of us must be at Wladek's house that night. On Sunday night, the evening before Monday's Aktion, it would be much too dangerous to be seen walking on the street. Hauptmann Schmatzler, the Gestapo commandant, had advised the Judenrat that the ghetto would be closed, but it had not yet come to pass. However, outside the ghetto, patrolling units were more numerous, and members of the Einsatzgruppen, rumored to be killing squads, disguised in civilian clothes had been spotted near the ghetto. Herr Becker, the much-feared bilingual Gestapo agent, spent much of the day within the ghetto, listening, watching, and stopping visitors from entering. Great effort was made to avoid his attention. Once his suspicion was aroused, a raid on the suspected house followed within minutes. Residents were subjected to beatings at best, and at worst incarceration in Gestapo headquarters and subsequent disappearance.

I knew that I should be going home. Mother would not know where I was, or if something had happened to me. She would be worried, yet there was nothing I could do. Usually on Saturdays Pan Litewski closed the office early, and Mother expected me to be home by five o'clock at the latest. I decided not to think about it and also to ignore my stomachache. I had not eaten since early morning. Before me was the long walk to Wladek's village, and then back home. Mennek had mentioned that it took Wladek about an hour to walk to the workshop, and with me trailing behind, it would take even longer. The distance to Wladek's house was about eleven kilometers.

I needed to ask a number of questions, but I had to be prudent. From the conversation between the two men, I could tell that Wladek had not yet agreed to do it. His main concern was the reaction of his mother.

"You have been supporting your parents since you came to work for me," Mennek argued. "They will do it for you." "No," was the response, "they wanted to do it for you, and instead you are asking me to bring them three people they don't know."

Mennek reached for his hand; the two men looked at each other with much affection. "I know that my decision came as a surprise, but so did the decree. There had been rumors that a fence would enclose the ghetto. It's so sudden there is no time for other arrangements. Wladek, look at me. With or without Aryan papers I won't have a chance. You are not hearing what I am trying to tell you. Instead of one Jewish male, there will be three females with good documents who are relatively unknown in the area. They will stay out of sight for a few days, and then disappear."

Wladek said the decree states that the Aktion is for the purpose of resettlement, and that everyone should pack a small valise. "I don't want them to come with a suitcase. Just a small bundle tied up peasant style, or better yet a basket. They should pack some clothes and leave them in their room, and I will get them when I can. They should tie kerchiefs over their hair. A cardigan would be better than a coat.

I noted carefully the instructions for us, given to Mennek. We looked out the window, waiting for early dusk. It was time to leave. I wanted to put my arms around Mennek's neck, and I wanted to say some of the words that were crowding my mind. He waved a dismissive hand. No words.

"Will we see each other again?" I stammered. "Of course. You will send me an affidavit from America." Ever since my father left for America, I had heard these same words. They sounded hollow now. My faith in the future had been extinguished.

"It's time to leave," Mennek said. "Just walk behind Wladek as he told you and make believe you do not know him. Never let him out of your sight, yet give the appearance that you are aimlessly strolling along. When you get to Kroscienko Road, slip off the armband and roll up the sleeves of your blouse. He will stop long enough in front of his house for you to mentally mark the location. You know the rest. We have gone over it." I felt Mennek's lips on my forehead, then his hand pushed me out the door.

Maintaining an appropriate distance, I followed Wladek as he strolled out of town. Tired peasants passed us along the way. We walked alongside potato fields where women in colored kerchiefs, their backs bent, were hoeing the green plants. I heard voices of children at play and the barking of dogs. For about three kilometers, we walked along a railroad embankment, and then we passed over the tracks at a railroad crossing. It was unfamiliar territory, and I concentrated on memorizing various landmarks that would help me several hours later when I would have to retrace my steps. I hardly noticed when day-light settled into dusk. We must have walked on side lanes all along, because I began seeing cows grazing without having walked through a village. From a distance I could see barns and farm sheds. It was quite dark when we entered Wladek's village. All the houses looked alike. I noticed fruit trees and a pungent smell of manure.

Wladek stopped in front of a house that looked the same as all the others, and as I slowed my step, I saw him fondling an excited dog that seemed ready to jump over the fence. From the rattling of a chain, I gathered that the dog was restrained. A well-constructed doghouse stood next to the shed. As I walked past the house, I saw Wladek opening the wooden gate that led to his house. I tried to mark the abutting houses on either side, and I also looked for curtains, but it was too late. All windows had the blackout shades drawn, and there was not enough light or time to find distinguishing signs.

On my way back a few kilometers after leaving Wladek's village, sur-rounded by the anonymity of the fields, I felt in the pocket of my skirt for my armband, and holding on to it I ran until I reached the outskirts of Krosno. Mother and Eva must have seen me walking up the hill because when I reached the door it opened, and both of them were crying and hugging me, while simultaneously reproaching me. Where had I been? They were frantic with worry. Ominous news of Jews having been apprehended while attempting to escape had reached them. Genia Springer's best friend, Fayga Tepper, her mother, and a relative had made their way to the river, without realizing that Herr Becker had seen them leave the ghetto. In a shallow area, where during the dry days of August one could walk on rocks to the other side of the river, Herr Becker had shot and killed them as they were trying to cross.

Pani Tepper and her daughter Fayga had carried on their piece-goods and notion store as long as they were allowed to do business. Their store was in the town square, next to the arcade, on the opposite side of the square from Uncle Jacub and Aunt Regina's store. I remembered the store from my prewar visit. It was always stocked with merchandise that would delight a woman's or a girl's heart. I had purchased my barrette there and the belt buckle for a dress Aunt Regina had made for me. I also remembered market days when the store was so full that people had to wait outside for someone to leave before they could enter. Every female who came into town needed something they could only purchase at the Tepper store.

"We thought the worst. Do you realize what you have put us through?" Eva kept repeating, while holding me tight and kissing me. I looked at my big sister. Behind her eyeglasses I saw her red and swollen eyelids. Just wait until you hear what has kept me so long, I thought to myself, but instead I said, "I didn't know that you love me that much."

"Did you hear that?" Eva turned to Mother. "If she still does not know, then she is a silly girl."

Then I told them. Eva was dumbfounded. "I can't quite believe what you are saying. It is the miracle we no longer dared hope for. While you were gone, we began to pack. We were making plans to escape from the truck before it reached the work camp. Mother has all these ideas, and they are not realistic, because everyone would think of escape, and the Nazis have made plans that would make escape totally impossible."

I knew that Mother had heard everything I said. She had stroked my hair while I talked. Her eyes had a distant gaze, and her mouth was pursed. She looked this way when she was concentrating, making plans for the three of us. She still had not said anything, and I was so tired I thought I would faint. I watched as she moved toward the wardrobe. She took out a black cardigan and a dark kerchief.

"Mother, you didn't hear what I said," I remonstrated. "We must pack a few essential items, and we must be at our destination tonight by eleven o'clock. It is what I promised. You have no idea how difficult it was for Mennek to persuade Wladek to hide us."

"I do have an idea, and in my heart I feel overwhelming gratitude for Mennek and for Wladek," Mother said. "But I can't think about that. Now Eva is going to prepare dinner for you. You probably have been without food since this morning. This was not a day to think of food, but neither is it a time to get sick, and you must get something into your stomach. I am going to get Aunt Regina and Dollek."

Mother can't do that, I thought. She can't do it to Mennek or to Wladek and his unsuspecting parents. It will never work. We'll be stopped, the five of us together, and they will shoot us down just as they did Fayga and her mother. Even if we could manage to get to the house without being detected, Wladek would never let us in. These thoughts were racing through my mind, and as fast as they came to me, I spoke them. I pleaded and reasoned to my mother's deaf ears. Her response was, "I must do what I think is right. I will not hide and leave my sister and her child to face this sinister fate. I will not change my mind. You are wasting much needed energy, and I am wasting precious time." Mother left.

In one corner of our room we had fixed up a makeshift kitchen, and on the single gas jet Eva warmed soup for me. I was disconsolate. As I was running home, I had been thinking of how gratefully Mother would greet my news. I would walk in with the solution to a dilemma we had had no other means to resolve. Was it possible that my mother after all these years of maneuvering and staying alert was suddenly no longer capable of sound judgment? When I asked Eva, she said, "I have no idea how Wladek will react, or if he will let us in. You know Mother. If she thinks she is right, she can't be budged. No use asking me what I think."

We had approximately two hours before we would have to leave, and we had much to do. I did not think that I could eat, and I did not want to sit down; however, Eva insisted. She sat down to keep me company and make sure that I did not gulp down the soup. While I ate, she kept repeating, "So it was Mennek. I can't quite grasp it. So it's Mennek after all."

The first matter was the burying of our Jewish identity documents in the Dunikowski coal cellar. We found our hiding place and cleared it of coal and coal dust. Eva and I took turns breaking up the hard earth. No one had tampered with our treasured possessions. Carefully we removed the documents pertaining to our emigration to America and the letters Father had sent. At the bottom of the hole, we placed the documents marked "J," and we put the American papers on top. We replaced the earth, stamped it down carefully, and arranged the coal so that it would look like the rest of the pile.

Back upstairs we wrapped three tiny pieces of paper that contained Father's address in New York in separate, small squares of soft white muslin. With small safety pins, we each pinned one of the inch-square amulets to the inside of our brassieres. While waiting for Mother to return, we packed and repacked our three small bundles.

It was obvious that Aunt Regina was unhappy. Mother had given her and Dollek very little time to get ready, but she had agreed to come. During the day, her friend Jerzy Hyp had come to see her and had told her that he was unable to find a safe hiding place for her. He lived with his aging parents whom he would not ask, and everyone he had approached was afraid to take the risk. His advice to Aunt Regina and Dollek was to report at the town square as ordered, escape from the truck as soon as possible, and make use of the false documents he had helped them obtain. He was still holding a considerable stock of the merchandise Regina had given him for safekeeping, and he promised to carefully sell the merchandise and forward the proceeds.

Aunt Regina tried to persuade Mother to go along with her plans, but Mother had refused to listen. She told Regina that if she reported at the town square, she would forfeit all possibility of escape. Muttering to herself, but loud enough for all of us to hear, Aunt Regina said, "You really think that you can outwit them? I say all five of us will be shot." Mother responded angrily. "I did not force you . . ."

She stopped in the middle of her sentence. There stood Dollek, my little ten-year-old cousin with his dark, knowing eyes, a forlorn look on his face. This defiant, irrepressible child, whose hands were always in pockets bulging with little treasures, now looked frightened and overwhelmed. His hands, hanging uselessly at his sides, conveyed his turmoil. Mother embraced Dollek. In a low voice she told him that like the rest of us he should have courage and believe that what we were about to do must be done. She hugged him hard and said, "You are the only male among the five of us, and we treasure you."

The Dunikowski family was aware of our preparations. It was understood that the less they knew the safer they would be. They had also agreed that Mother should not leave our personal belongings with them because the Gestapo would search their apartment. Mother's last errand was to go see the Dunikowski family and tell them that we were leaving that night. Mother reported that they wished us well. They told her that they would be praying for God to help us.

With our bundles of possessions and carrying our shoes, the five of us left the house about twenty minutes after eleven, almost a half hour later than had been planned. Furtively, without talking, we slowly made our way down the hill, hiding behind trees and bushes as we descended. All the time we listened for the sound of hobnailed boots of the ever-patrolling Sicherheitspolizei.

When we reached Kroscienko Road, I had to stop. Clouds covered the moon, and I remembered Mother saying this was a good omen. But I was afraid the dark sky might make it difficult for me to see my previously noted landmarks. There were no road signs, and I found it difficult to identify the country lane at which we were to turn. Shortly after making the turn, I looked for the railroad embankment, but it was not there. Motioning to my family to stay put, I retraced my steps back to the road. I decided that I had made the right turn, and I returned to the family.

Mother came up to me and put an arm around my shoulders. "This is difficult," she said. "I don't know where we are, and you were upset when you followed Wladek this afternoon. You are my intelligent daughter, and I am confident that you will find your bearings. Just try to remain calm." While Mother said these words, her hand softly stroked my back. I felt a little better as I resumed walking, and there it was ahead of us, the railroad embankment. My relief was overwhelming, and I felt all choked up. I crossed the railroad tracks and walked into the narrow strip of pine forest that ran alongside the tracks. I stopped to let my family catch up, and when I looked at their faces, I could sense, even in the dark, their mounting distress.

The cloud cover was thick, and there was no starlight to help me identify Wladek's house. My outstretched hand touched a fence, and I stepped back. "What is it?" Mother whispered in my ear. "I don't think that I will be able to recognize Wladek's house, but I am certain that this is his village." Aunt Regina grumbled, "We will perish here, in a country lane. This is a mistake.

I tried to tell you. If they find us here, we will be killed. It was folly to risk our lives, to put our fate in the hands of a child." My aunt is right, I thought, as I concentrated my eyes and my mind on penetrating the darkness. My mother put her arms around me and hugged me. "I have confidence in you and in your ability to remember. My sister cannot think clearly when she gets upset. Don't listen to her. I know that you will find the way."

In the distance I heard the echo of boot steps. Mother had also heard it. She pulled me down and we crept back to the field. There we crouched until we knew that the foot patrol had passed. We walked back to the fence. From all directions, dogs started barking and pulling on their chains; it seemed as if the whole village had awakened. I still could not identify the house. Then I saw a light and an open gate. I entered, and there stood Wladek. I followed him into the house and through a narrow corridor. Mother and Eva walked in behind me. Suddenly Wladek turned, "How many of you are there?" he demanded. I did not answer. We followed Wladek as he led us through what seemed to be a stable attached to the house, and then we climbed up a narrow ladder into a hayloft. Wladek turned around and started counting. "Five of you," he said, "and I did not even want to hide three. And Mennek said there would be three females. You come and you bring a boy? We are lost. My poor old parents. Now all of us will perish. Because of me they will die in a German torture chamber. I never should have listened to Mennek. At dawn, all of you will have to leave."

We piled our bundles into a corner under one of the eaves, and as soon as I lay down on the fragrant hay, I fell asleep. On Sunday morning when I woke up, I saw Wladek standing on the ladder looking at us. He was angry, and though he spoke in a whisper, his accusatory words fell on me like the lash of a whip. He said that when he told his parents, his mother reacted so violently he feared she would have a heart attack. He said that his mother had a weak heart and would not survive if we remained. We had brought disaster into his house; he should never have opened the gate. He told us we would have to leave immediately before his parents returned from church.

Mother tried to stand up, but the roof was low and she banged her head against a crossbeam. Holding her head, she sat down and said to Wladek, "I am old enough to be your mother, and I find it difficult to impress upon you the reality of the situation, while you stand there on the ladder looking down on us and telling me what I must do." Wladek sat down. Mother explained that were we to leave now, we could not avoid being detected. His neighbors would see us; Nazi collaborators would denounce him. If we were caught by a foot patrol, how long would it take for them to link us to this village? she asked him.

"You have done such a brave deed, and we know that it was Mennek you wanted to shelter, but here we are, and we are very grateful," she said. "Now we must think clearly, and we must avoid panic. Your parents should know that no one saw us when we entered the gate to your house, and if we are careful, no one will suspect that we are here."

While Mother spoke, Wladek held his head in his hands. He looked up and said, "You brought a male child, a boy with dark hair and black eyes. No matter how good your documents are, you know well that if they examine him they will see his circumcised penis. You were wrong, and you betrayed my trust. Mennek said three females, Betus said three females, and you come with an additional female and a male child."

"This is my sister, and this is my sister's son." Mother introduced both by their Christian names. "Wladek, you do—you must—understand that we cannot leave here until this Aktion is over."

"How long will that be?"

"We will try and leave as soon as it is possible. We would not want to remain longer than we have to. You will be in town. You will tell us when the Aktion is over."

I remembered that on the previous day, when I was in Mennek's workshop, I had heard him say that he would meet Wladek at the workshop on Sunday morning while Wladek's parents were at mass. Mennek had given Wladek the workshop and all the tools in it, but he wanted Wladek to have a written and witnessed document, so that it would not be taken away from him. I reminded Wladek that Mennek was waiting for him at the workshop.

When Wladek rose to leave, Mother put some money into his hand. "Please give this to your mother. We have not eaten in a while, and perhaps we could have some soup this evening." Wladek shook his head. "You know five people . . ." he started to say, but Mother cut him off in midsentence. "It does not matter that much whether there are three or five of us; we have to eat. Would it be possible for you to bring up a pitcher of water and some bread? There is also the matter of using the outhouse. You told Betus that we would only be able to use it after ten o'clock in the evening, and after the dog is brought into the house. For daytime use could you please bring up a pail with a cover? We will take care of it when we go down at night to use the outhouse. Wladek, you have our assurance that our needs will be minimal and that we will do our utmost to be discreet."

Within minutes Wladek returned with a tray. There were slices of dark bread, some cheese, a large pitcher filled with water, and two glasses. He wore his Sunday clothes, and he had put on a jacket. Mother thanked him and reminded him not to forget the pail. "I'll bring it up in a moment," he said, "but there is another matter I must speak to you about before I leave. My parents will be returning home shortly, and it is our custom for my sister, her husband, and their two daughters to have Sunday dinner with us. Please be very quiet. We do not want my sister to know about this. Very quiet, no sounds. I shall remove the ladder, and I shall conceal it, but the girls like to play hide and seek, and they might stray into the stable below."

When we heard the dog bark, and subsequently the click of the shutting gate, we knew that Wladek had left and we were alone in the house. Mother cut up the bread and the cheese with the knife Wladek had put on the tray and prepared six equal portions. We ate slowly, savoring each morsel as if we were eating a delicacy. When Dollek finished eating his share, Mother handed him the sixth remaining portion. She put her arm around his shoulder and hugged him.

I had not paid much attention to my beloved cousin, but all along I had been conscious that, ever since we had climbed up onto the hayloft, he had been listless and had stayed in his space, hardly moving. However, his eyes were visibly engaged as he listened to the conversation between us and between Mother and Wladek. What could he be thinking, I wondered, when he heard the continuous references to his ten-year-old malehood and to his perilous penis that was jeopardizing our existence?

About seven o'clock in the evening after the visitors had departed, Wladek attached the ladder, climbed up the rungs, and sat down. He told us that all roads leaving Krosno were blocked and that warning posters addressed to the Polish population were pasted all over town. They threatened that any Pole who helps a Jew hide will share the Jew's fate. "They stopped me on Kroscienko Road," he said. "They wanted to see my identity card. Then a Gestapo officer searched my pockets."

"How is Mennek?" Mother asked.

"He appeared calm, but he is not. How can he be?" Wladek responded. "His sister Rutka asked me if I could muster the courage to hide her brother until the Aktion is over. I did not respond. What could I say? I had promised Mennek that I would not tell his sisters about my offer to hide him, and he did not want them to know about you. I was glad to hear that he decided to take along some of his tools. Even the stupid *Boche** will recognize a craftsman when they see one."

Wladek told us that he must get some sleep because on the following day, Monday, he would leave his house before six o'clock in the morning. We were unable to sleep. Though we hardly communicated with each other, the nervous tension between the five of us was palpable. We tried to engage Dollek in conversation, but he hardly responded. We were waiting for dawn, for the start of the fateful day, and then we were waiting for Wladek to return home.

In the early afternoon Wladek returned from Krosno. He reported that he had watched from a distance, behind a curtained window, the proceedings in the town square. Families stayed together while their names were checked off a list. In rows of four, they were then marched to the outskirts of town, where they were loaded onto trucks. Wladek was almost certain that he saw Mennek with his three sisters being marched out of town. The Aktion was completed by eleven o'clock. Wladek was visibly shaken. We could see that he resented our presence in his attic as he mourned Mennek's fate. The thought that it should have been us climbing into the truck, rather than his friend Mennek, was not put into words. Wladek also saw that a selected group of about eighteen Jews had been allowed to remain behind. We assumed they were the Jews who had been working at the Krosno airport.

On Tuesday, when Wladek returned from the workshop, he conceded that Mother was correct when she said that it would not be possible for us to leave. He told us that Germans were combing the countryside looking for escaped Jews and searching the houses of Poles accused of harboring Jews. There were rumors that Jews who had been caught hiding were shot on sight.

During the following days we developed a routine. We studied the

...................................................

* *Boche* is a French pejorative for Germans. It is derived from *Alboche*, a combination of *Allemande* (German) and *caboche* (cabbage or blockhead).

catechism and asked each other questions pertaining to the Roman Catholic liturgy and rituals. We would regularly stretch and go through a routine of exercises to keep fit. Each day Wladek brought us reports regarding the number of Jews apprehended. They were caught in fields, in the nearby forest, and also in cellars and attics throughout town. We learned that several Jews who were caught and executed had never been residents of Krosno, nor the subsequently created Krosno ghetto. We inferred that similar Aktion had taken place in neighboring towns and that Jewish escapees in their desperate flight had been trapped in the Krosno Aktion.

Since all communication with the ghettos was forbidden, we had no knowledge of what was happening even in the ghetto of the neighboring town of Jaslo. We had heard that the Bochnia ghetto, where my grandparents and Mother's two brothers and their families were incarcerated, had been liquidated and its Jews transported to what the Nazis euphemistically called a work camp. Several weeks ago, when Mother heard these rumors, she said she hoped her mother had died before the liquidation of the Bochnia ghetto.

At Mother's request, Wladek obtained a bottle of peroxide and a bottle of ammonia. She had decided to alter our appearance by changing our hair color. Since neither she nor Aunt Regina had any experience in preparing or using hair-bleaching formula, they could only guess at the proper proportion of the ingredients. Eva and I watched as the two sisters applied the bleaching tincture to each other's hair, and we were appalled at the result. Mother said that the application would have to be repeated several times before the hair would take the new color. Mother's former pitch-black, shining hair acquired a dull, rusty tint. When it was our turn, Eva categorically refused the procedure. For me, the fear of being recognized was greater than my reluctance to submit. The result was awful. Mother insisted that the proportions were correct and the harsh red hue resulted from our inability to properly wash our hair.

On September 6, Wladek told us that we must prepare to leave the house on the following day. "You are making a mistake," Mother said calmly. "If we leave now, we will be walking into the hands of the Gestapo. We have not been able to contact the people who could help us. Now we can, but we can only make arrangements through you. It would be safer for us and also for you if we wait another few days."

Wladek shook his head. "It was agreed that you would leave on Tuesday, and you are here almost a week. You have put us in an unbearable position.

Our neighbors are asking questions. They heard their dogs barking, and they wanted to know if we had any visitors. Do you have any idea of how this tension is affecting my mother? This is what I have done to my family."

"Perhaps I could talk to your mother and explain," Mother said.

"That is out of the question."

"No one has an inkling we are here. If dogs are barking it has nothing to do with us, and you know that. I beg you to allow us more time. We must plan carefully and all caution must be taken so neither you nor the people we will ask for help will run the risk of being detected."

On the following day Wladek reported that two more Jews were caught in a forest east of Krosno. Both were young boys, about fifteen or sixteen years old. He repeated that we must leave. Mother looked at him, but she did not respond. On September 8, Wladek contacted three friendly acquaintances who had access to transportation, and on whom Mother was counting to help us leave town. The return message was that they were no longer able to come to our rescue. Pan Litewski, who had called me his angel, when contacted by Wladek sent words of sympathy and God's blessings. He wanted us to know that Pani Litewska prayed for us and that in church she lit candles on our behalf. Eva's Christian friend, Edek Gonet, a student of the humanities and a Polish nationalist, was unable to give us temporary shelter because his parents refused to be involved.

At about that time, the Nazis were sidetracked from their Jew-hunting activities by a train derailment in the Krosno vicinity. Posters appeared on kiosks declaring that reprisals would be of such magnitude that the Polish swine who perpetrated this attack against the Third Reich would learn their lesson, and then no further attacks of sabotage would ever again take place. While we rejoiced that the Polish underground we had heard about for years had acted, Wladek felt that resistance was futile because innocent people would be punished.

While hunting for the perpetrators, initial reprisals were already in effect. Polish men between the ages of sixteen and forty were rounded up in random raids and shipped to slave labor camps. Wladek, though relatively safe due to his work permit in the shoe repair shop, was nevertheless adamant in his ultimatum to us.

"I want you out of here," he insisted. "I was tricked into this. My mother is sick in bed because she can no longer bear the threat that is hanging over us. I have done all I can." When he left, Mother said, "He is a very decent young man, and no matter what happens to us we must never forget that."

Throughout the night, Mother and Eva argued whether it was a good idea for Eva to contact her Volksdeutsch employer, Pan Groszka. "I have worked for him for almost a year," Eva pointed out. "Several times he told me he was outraged by the Nazis' brutal treatment of the Jews."

"He is not to be trusted; he is a collaborator. We don't know what he did before he came to Krosno," Mother warned.

"There is no one else. Everyone you thought would come to our aid has backed off. We are just wasting time. I will go to see him."

"I will not permit you to go." Mother was emphatic. "I will ask Wladek to contact him and find out if he is willing to help us."

"Wladek! What should Wladek ask him? Should he ask him if he would make transportation available to us so that we can leave the area? You don't even know him, and you want to make decisions about who should approach him? Pan Groszka would not even talk to Wladek, let alone trust him."

I listened to the argument. I felt helpless, defeated, and I touched my aching stomach. There was a hard bulge between my chest and my navel. Both Mother and Eva were crying, and Aunt Regina said, "We should have gone with the others. I tried to tell you, but you put your trust in a child."

Mother did not even look in her direction. Now her voice was calm as she tried to talk Eva out of her decision. "I will find a solution, I will think of a way. If you walk into town, you will be recognized. You are wrong. You refused to make changes in your appearance. Perhaps during the next few days you should work on that." Mother and Eva had been talking for hours, and finally, past midnight, I fell asleep.

On the following morning, Eva resolutely set about to change her appearance. She attempted to straighten her curly hair and change her hairdo. She carefully prepared the clothes she would wear and a kerchief for her hair. Mother watched, and several times, she repeated, "I am against this. You are doing this without my permission. I wish you would listen to reason. You know I can't forcibly restrain you."

"No, you can't," was Eva's response, "but I don't want you to be so upset. I have thought about this carefully, and I want to feel calm when I leave here at dusk. I plan to be among people as they rush home after work. Pan Groszka usually stays in his office until all the workers have left. He remains for another fifteen minutes or so, and he makes sure that the work for all the high Nazi officials is either completed or proceeding properly. No one will see me when I enter through the side door, and I am sure that he will not refuse his help."

Throughout the day we continued to weigh Eva's chances in view of the enormous risk she was determined to take. Mother was tearful, and Aunt Regina urged that since Eva felt confident about accomplishing the task, Mother should not undermine her courage. Aunt Regina mentioned that so far all other efforts were unsuccessful. Mother again reiterated that Wladek should initially contact Pan Groszka. Eva patiently explained that Pan Groszka, ostensibly a loyal Nazi, would never trust a Pole, and that such an attempt would ruin the only chance we had to leave Krosno alive.

Mother continued trying to dissuade Eva from going. "You cannot be sure that Pan Groszka would help us obtain transport, and I don't want you to leave because you think we are trapped, or because Wladek is pressing us. Our protection as well as his is that we do not get caught. Something will come up. I will think of something, I know I will find a way. Give me more time. The man is a collaborator. You don't really know him, and you cannot predict his reaction."

By the time Wladek came home, Eva was ready to leave. She had managed to change her appearance. She had removed the eyeglasses she always wore and put them in a pocket, and she had tied a kerchief peasant style under her chin. She had arranged to meet Wladek early the following morning in a sparsely wooded area immediately north of town and a considerable distance away from the liquidated ghetto.

I had not said much, but I could barely contain my mounting anxiety. My stomach ached and contracted convulsively, yet I kept myself from putting my hand on my stomach. Whenever Mother saw me do this, she got upset. I knew that the only immediate remedy was a heating pad or a hot water bottle. Since there was no electricity in the house, these were fleeting and idle thoughts. I also knew that I must not cry, but I wanted to tell Eva that I was afraid she would be caught and I would never see her again.

When Eva put her arms around me, the tears welled up in my eyes. My arms were around her neck. She hugged me and moved with me to a corner of the attic, while whispering in my ear: "I have spent most of the day convincing Mother that what I am about to do is right. It is our only chance, and this attempt must be made. At worst, Pan Groszka will say that he cannot help. If that happens, though I feel confident it will not, then I will arrange with Wladek to return tomorrow evening. I need you on my side. You know how difficult Mother can be. I can't make her understand. You must help." I couldn't control my tears and wept inconsolably. "Oh, my God, what are you doing to me?" she admonished. Her tone was gentle, her hand on my shoulder. "I spent hours arranging myself both on the inside and outside. Not only do I have to look like a peasant, but I also must project the casual appearance of a Polish Christian who is confidently rushing home after a day's work."

There was a quick hug, I felt her lips on my cheek. I watched my sister as she said good-bye to Mother, Aunt Regina, and Dollek. Then she was gone. We remained in the dark, looking ahead to a night we knew would seem endless. At about ten o'clock, Wladek signaled us that we could descend to the outhouse. I slept fitfully and several times during the night, I had to wake Mother because she was moaning in her sleep and I was afraid that in the still of the night the sounds could be heard.

## SEPTEMBER 10, 1942 ≈ KROSNO, OCCUPIED POLAND

That day we were unable to maintain the daily routine Mother had so carefully devised. None of us attempted to study the catechism. We did not even dare look at each other. Each minute was endless as we waited for Wladek to come home. We knew that he could not vary his daily schedule, yet we hoped that he would close the shop just a little earlier. In the silence about me I pleaded. I asked God to protect Eva from being recognized, and I asked for His intercession with Pan Groszka.

The message Wladek brought was disappointing. In the morning Eva had met him in the designated place. She looked well, he said, and she wanted him to tell us that we should not worry and that she needed one more day to accomplish her task. Pan Groszka was away on an overnight trip, personally delivering an overhauled motor to an important customer. This was an unforeseen obstacle, Eva had told Wladek, and she wanted us to know that Pani Groszka, his wife, had assured her that he would be back in the office by eight o'clock on the following morning. "Did Eva spend the night in Pani Groszka's house?" Mother asked. Wladek shook his head, no; he did not know where Eva had spent the night, but he was sure that it was not at Pani Groszka's house. Eva had mentioned that she had eaten there, but said Pani Groszka would not allow her to remain through the night.

Eva and Wladek had arranged that they would meet again on the following morning, though at a later hour, after Pan Groszka had opened his workshop and after Eva had seen him. This time their meeting place would be under a bridge that had become too dangerous for vehicular traffic and was only used by pedestrians.

Wladek also brought an envelope that had been dropped off at the shop by Ludmila, the housekeeper and companion to Pani Dunikowska. The envelope contained Eva's official identity card with the authentic Krosno municipal seal with a swastika. Now all five of us had the coveted document with an Aryan identity. The fact that Eva did not have the identity card had been a cause of much concern.

This second night without Eva was worse than the previous one. Mother's self-reproaches for having allowed Eva to leave were devastating to the rest of us. In addition, my mother, who prided herself on being a realist and on being able to assess facts clearly, kept talking about a bad omen. I countered by reminding her that the arrival of the identity card was a good sign because it meant that none of the officials behind the desks at the magistrate's office had recognized Eva from the photograph of her without her eyeglasses. Mother did not even look at me, and I felt that I could not reach her.

I tried to think of all the reasons why Eva's mission would succeed. She had been a satisfactory bookkeeper and typist for Pan Groszka, the best he had ever had—he had told her that again and again. He had been outraged by the Nazi treatment of Jewish residents, and he had told Eva that she could count on him for help. All thoughts of Pan Litewski, who had made similar promises to me, I pushed out of my mind. I spent most of the night praying.

That day Wladek returned home later than usual. We heard him as he entered the gate, we heard the dog bark noisily, and then we heard his footsteps as he entered the stable. He had not gone into the house to greet his parents. We knew when we saw his face that something had gone wrong. Eva had not kept their morning appointment under the bridge, and having waited as long as possible, Wladek proceeded to his workshop. He could not remember who told him, it just seemed that everyone knew, though no one could relate the exact circumstances. Three Jews had been caught that morning in the vicinity of the Groszka automobile repair shop. The three people were identified as Salek Weinfeld, Pan Hausner, and my sister Eva. Yes, he was definite that Eva was one of the three. It was dangerous to get too close to the place where the three people had been apprehended. The area was crawling with police and Gestapo agents, and the people who had stopped and lingered were ordered to disperse.

"What exactly did they see?" Mother wanted to know.

"I told you, they saw lots of policemen and Gestapo agents in uniform and in civilian dress."

"What else?"

"There was a truck with a metal roof, rather new and shiny. They saw it from a distance. No one was allowed to get close enough to really look at it, but everyone agreed that they had not seen this type of vehicle before. The Nazis threatened to arrest the bystanders who remained, and people left."

Wladek told us that he had closed the shop early and had gone there himself. He spoke to some of the neighboring merchants. He heard two versions of what had taken place. Everyone agreed that shots had been fired. Some said Eva and the two men had climbed into the truck, while others said three bodies were thrown into the truck. No one was able to say with certainty whether the three had only been injured or if they had been murdered. No one knew if they were alive when they were pushed into the truck. "I have told you all I know," Wladek said. Then he left.

During the night Mother was delirious in her sleep. She said words that made no sense. I thought that perhaps she had reverted to her native Hungarian, a language I did not understand. I was unable to wake her, and Aunt Regina pulled me away from Mother and said that she must be left alone.

At dawn when I awoke, Mother was sitting next to me. The night had changed her into an old woman. There were lines in her face I had not seen before. Her jaw was clenched tight, and her eyes were lifeless. "Do you know what day this is?" Mother asked. I did know; I had known all along, as did Aunt Regina and Dollek. It was the twelfth of September, and it was Eva's birthday. She was twenty years old, or was she? We did not know. Mother put her arm around my shoulder. It felt heavy. "Tonight, you and I will make our way to the Dunikowski villa," she said. "Wladek will go up first to make sure that we can enter the little corner kitchen. It will be quick, and then the three of us will be together. I now know that I made a big mistake. I should have brought the cyanide capsules. Betus, you must trust me, the gas is accessible, and it will be painless. We must make the decision while we still have the choice. I cannot see another way out, and I am certain that it is right that we do it ourselves, rather than let them torture us."

The three of us, Mother, Eva, and I, had discussed ending our own lives on numerous occasions. Rather than submit to what we had heard was happening to Jews when they were evacuated from the ghettos, we wanted to choose the manner of our death. The gas jet in our kitchen was an option we had considered. While preparing for our escape from Krosno, Mother had obtained cyanide capsules. She had promised the person who had supplied the capsules that under no circumstances would the cyanide be used in Krosno. It was imperative that every effort be made to protect the source of the cyanide so that it could not be traced. We understood that members of the Polish underground were supplied from the same source. We had hidden the capsules in the hem of our winter coats, between the lining and interlining. The coats were hanging in a wardrobe of the Dunikowski household.

Mother was waiting for my answer. "Aunt Regina and Dollek?" I wanted to know. "Are they coming with us?"

"No, she is not yet prepared to do it. My sister will make her own decision, for herself and for her son. You are intelligent and old enough to decide for yourself."

Mother appeared to be relieved when I told her that I was ready to go with her. That evening neither Mother nor I were able to swallow a morsel of the food Wladek's mother had prepared for us. Wladek agreed to visit the Dunikowski villa and informed us on his return that a German civilian now occupied the room we had used as a hideout.

After Wladek left, Mother straightened out the corner in which we had slept. I watched her as she sifted through our belongings, packing and unpacking some articles. "What are you doing?" I asked.

"Yesterday was Eva's birthday. She would have been twenty years old. She was talented and she was beautiful, and they murdered her. They murdered her for no reason, and all she wanted was to live. I no longer want to remain in this world. I can't go on fighting, not without Eva."

"Where are we going?" I asked.

"We are going to the villa. We will approach it from the back, you know, through the little pine forest in the rear of the house."

"Wladek just told us that it is no longer possible to go there."

"It does not matter; I even think it's better. The Dunikowski family will not see us, and this way they will not be implicated."

"What's better? What do you plan to do?"

"Wladek will give us some rope. There is that tree, the tall one in the back. Remember? Aunt Regina does not want to do it. She says she would rather risk capture and be sent to a concentration camp. They no longer transport Jews to concentration camps. I don't believe in their concentration camps. It is just the name they use to mislead us. Why should we allow them to torture us? We will end our lives ourselves. I will do it for you and for myself."

Yesterday when Mother broached the subject, I had been willing, and death by gas had not seemed such a frightening prospect. But I did not want to hang from a tree. In past months I had seen suicides by hanging, as well as murder by hanging at the hands of the Nazis or their helpers in an attempt to make it look like suicide. It was an awful, ugly sight, and I did not want to die this way. I also remembered Heinz Prager, my fourteen-year-old friend from Hindenburg. He was found hanging from an attic beam after he had learned that his parents had been taken to a concentration camp. I had learned about it from friends who had caught a glimpse of Heinz, dead and hanging from that beam. The image of him hanging from the rope had remained in the back of my mind.

"I don't want to die that way," I told Mother. "You talk about Eva as if she were dead. How do you know that? How can you be sure? We have no certainty that Eva was shot. And if she was shot, she could have been injured. For all we know, she could have been pushed into the truck without having been injured. And what if she is alive and finds a way to escape from her captors, and we are dead?"

"They have murdered her," Mother responded. "And if they have not done it, they will soon do it. It is their plan. They want to kill all of us, every Jew, so that no one will remain. If any of us remain, we would tell the world about their bloodthirsty killing spree. I wanted to live, because I felt that both you and Eva should have a chance to experience more of life. Now they have murdered my child, and I have no strength left to go on."

"You don't know that she has been murdered," I protested, "and yet you keep saying it."

"What do you want me to say? They are torturing her. You know they will want to know where she has been hiding for more than a week. We are here. Wladek goes to work every day, and no one came to question him. Do you understand what I am saying?"

I understood. Until Mother had put it into words, I had not wanted to think about it. I had known all along that Eva would not betray us. She would endure torture and die rather than betray us.

Later, when we went down to use the outhouse, Wladek mentioned that he had forgotten to tell us that the Springer family—my best friend Genia, her mother, father, and her father's sister, the beautiful Ester—were living outside the vacated ghetto in the Springer family home. I knew from Genia that the large Springer house had been occupied by Herr Ritter and his family for the past several years. Herr Ritter was a civil engineer employed by the Kirchhof firm. We also knew that it was Ritter who had intervened on behalf of the Springer family and who had secured work for them at the airport. With the work came the Arbeitskarte stating they were needed for the war effort and were therefore temporarily exempted from transportation to a labor camp. That evening Wladek did not urge us to leave his house.

Since Mother had not said anything more about the grisly deed she was contemplating, I thought perhaps she had changed her mind. When I crawled up to her and tried to put my arm around her, she said, "Don't," and turned her back to me.

"Mother, I am not going with you," I said. "I don't want to hang from a tree. I'd rather be shot in the back and die like Fayga."

"Do we have to go over it again?" Mother asked. "They will not allow us to decide how we will die. It will be their decision, and I want to decide for myself."

"And for me," I interjected, "but I'm not going with you. I've been thinking about this, Mother, and I've been wondering why you felt willing to make every effort to escape and not be caught while Eva was with us. I'm still alive. Have you no strength to go on for me?"

Throughout our exchange, Mother had not looked at me or turned to face me. During the past three days, she had completely withdrawn, and I had been unable to reach her. She had looked past me, and when I spoke to her, her responses were monosyllabic and arbitrary. Her unshaken resolve to commit suicide was reflected in her expressionless eyes and tight-lipped mouth.

But now I could tell she was weeping, her body shaking slightly. I felt a sense of relief. It was the first time since Eva's capture that Mother had yielded to her sorrow and allowed herself to come apart. I fell asleep next to her.

We decided to seek shelter at the Springer house. On the following evening, Wladek went to see the Springer family. He carried our plea for them to intercede for us with Herr Ritter. Wladek returned with an affirmative reply. It would be strictly a business arrangement. Herr Ritter did not want to know our Polish names or our destination. The money would be paid to the driver. Two days hence, after dark, we were to arrive at the Springer house, each one separately, about a minute apart. It was imperative that we must not be seen entering the house. There should be no luggage.

On the following evening when we walked down to the outhouse, Wladek told us that his father had a big kettle of hot water awaiting us in the kitchen. Behind windows carefully sealed with blackout cloth, trying to move as quietly as possible, the four of us washed properly, after fourteen days of sponging with a washcloth. Before washing our hair, we gave each other a final application of the peroxide-ammonia solution. We dried our hair, fashioning it as well as we could in front of the warm kitchen stove.

The last day in the attic was spent reviewing and rehearsing the details of our self-created background and memorizing landmarks in the towns in which we had allegedly lived. From that time on, Mother would be my Aunt Jadzia, short for Jadwiga; her full name was Jadwiga Dembicka. I would be Krysia, short for Krystyna; my full name was Krystyna Zolkos. Aunt Regina and Dollek would be strangers we had met and befriended.

I was born in Iskrzynia, but moved to Chorzow when my father was widowed at my birth. My father was an engineer and a Polish reserve army officer. Father had been away doing his yearly army service when the war broke out. His whole regiment had to flee when the German army advanced in their surprise attack. We decided on Chorzow, because it would be some justification for my strange accent. Chorzow was near the German border, had been part of Germany in the past, and it was known that residents of that area spoke with a different dialect. Krystyna had to be removed from Iskrzynia at birth and not have any memory of that village, and we did not know anyone who ever lived there.

The town of Chorzow I knew quite well since I had lived there with the Landschaft family for about eight months. While creating a background for the child, Krysia, we decided that during the summer weeks when her father did his army service, she visited with her beloved Aunt Jadzia, her dead mother's only sister. It was fortunate that Krysia was visiting her during the summer of the blitzkrieg invasion. Ever since that time, she had lived with her aunt. Jadwiga Dembicka, the aunt, was also the wife of a Polish army officer, a career officer who had achieved the rank of captain. He was on duty at the time of the German invasion and his whereabouts were not known.

According to Eva's new Polish identity card, Eva was Jadzia's daughter, but now it was painful to think of Eva's useless false document. Since Chorzow was in the part of Poland that Germany annexed to the Third Reich immediately upon the invasion, it was natural that all my contacts with Chorzow had been severed. The population of this industrial area, except for miners and mill workers, had been evacuated and dispersed throughout occupied Poland.

I kept the date of my birth, and the new document stated that I was a Roman Catholic. We practiced going down on our knees when we recited Our Father, or Hail Mary. We endeavored to make the sign of the cross with the same casualness as our Christian friends. We questioned each other regarding the tenets of belief contained in the catechism booklet.

That evening when Wladek came up, we shook hands with him for the first time. Mother wanted to give him more money, but he said that she had given him enough and that Mennek had been very generous in leaving him the workshop. Mother thanked him for all he had done, and she asked him to convey our gratitude to his parents. She said that we would never forget him, or what he had done for us, but when she said that should we survive she would want to do more, he stopped her in midsentence.

"All I want," he said, "is that you forget my name, my village, and that you never attempt to contact me. That is all I ask in return for the help we have given you."

Mother convinced him that under no circumstances would any of us reveal his name, his village, or even knowledge of his existence. Assured that the relationship he had not wanted and which his friend had forced upon him was coming to an end, his relief was evident. He said that he also would never forget us, and that he sincerely hoped that we would outwit the Nazi swine. When we had climbed down the ladder, he looked us over once more, and said, "It was what Mennek wanted, and it was more than I ever wanted to do. You were supposed to be here for one night, two at most, but never for two weeks. Now I am glad that you were not among the people who were caught, and I will pray for you. I wish you that with the Lord's blessing you will succeed."

While he was speaking and wishing us well, I was thinking of Eva, and I was sure Mother was also thinking about her. I was grateful that she did not say it.

We cautiously made our way to the Springer house avoiding the area that had been the ghetto. The door was unlocked. Mother walked in last, and we did not see members of the Springer family until all of us had come in. Then the four of them surrounded us. They looked at us, hugged and kissed us, and it was obvious that they were happy that we had managed to survive for two weeks. They did not ask where we had been, or if anyone had helped us. They knew about our Polish identity documents, and they knew about Eva. They repeated what Wladek had told us, that on the morning when the three Jews were caught, Eva was one of them. Yes, there were shots, they said. There was blood, and a strange-looking truck with a shiny metal roof was parked in the area. No, they did not know if the victims had been injured or killed. When Mother mentioned that Mennek had come to our rescue, all four of them were astonished because on the Monday when the ghetto was liquidated, Mennek and his sisters were seen in the town square.

From the Springer family we learned that perhaps thirty or forty Jews had managed to hide and had therefore disobeyed the order to assemble in the town square. The Gestapo informed the Krosno residents that almost all these criminals had been caught either while trying to leave town, or in hiding places that had been disclosed to the Gestapo by informers.

All of us were aware that in helping us the Springer family was not only jeopardizing their privileged status, but also their lives. Pan Springer said, "We did hesitate when we received your message because of the immense danger, but not for long. We had to ask Herr Ritter, our only resource, our protector. We decided the fact that you were alive after the Gestapo announced that no one had succeeded in escaping was perhaps an omen and that we would help you to leave town."

Both Genia's brothers, Eugene, the oldest, an excellent student and fine pianist, and Hennek, the handsome blond gymnasium student so popular with the girls during my prewar visit, had been taken to labor camps. The family had received several postcards from Hennek, but only one from Eugene. Eugene, due to a birth defect had a curvature of the spine, but he had a brilliant mind, much admiration from his circle of friends, and his impediment was hardly noticed. The Springer family had been unable to ascertain the name of the labor camp where Eugene was ostensibly put to work. The Nazi dogma regarding the handicapped, especially if they were Jews, was no secret.

It was about eleven o'clock in the evening. We huddled close to each other while Pan Springer's sister Ester revealed the plan and the extent to which Herr Ritter was willing to help. At four o'clock in the morning, we were to climb into a parked truck with an open back. We should move all the way to the front of the truck bed, near the cab, and cover ourselves with the canvas tarpaulins. There would be a number of tarps, and we should bunch them over us so that anyone looking into the truck would see only the tarpaulins. The rear of the truck would be loaded with building material the driver was delivering. The German driver would pretend he did know anybody was hiding in the back of his truck. We would not acknowledge the driver until he dropped us off, and only then could we pay him.

It was decided that the hours before our departure should be used to rest or to sleep. For the members of the Springer household, work at the airport started at eight o'clock in the morning. They did not know how much longer the Nazis would allow Jews to work for the military at the airport. However, there had been rumors that Jews would no longer be allowed to live in Krosno. Instead they would be housed at the airport.

Genia said that the two of us would rest in the attic, on the old army cot. It was a small windowless cubicle. Once we got up there, we held each other tightly and wept. We sat down on the cot and recalled all the wonderful moments we had shared in the faraway past. In the last months we hadn't seen each other as we were rushing to and from work, and there hadn't been an opportunity to talk. Perhaps we understood that avoiding each other was a true sign of our friendship. With fear eroding the last vestiges of hope, one had not much to offer except despair.

When I visited in the summer of 1939, Genia wanted to be my friend even though I barely knew enough Polish to put a sentence together. Through her intercession, I met other girls and boys, and within days I was included among a group of intelligent and sophisticated gymnasium students. For me the most joyous times were the days when we swam in the river and sunbathed on the grass. But then there were the hours that just the two of us shared. They were usually spent in Genia's bedroom, or on the grass in the back of their villa. Genia would sing to me, and I would try and learn the sad songs of love and loss inherent in Polish nostalgia, with its dreams of the irretrievable.

That was the past, and though we had remained friends, there hadn't been very many happy moments during the last two years. We looked into each other's eyes, and we knew that we would not see each other again. Then we put it into words. We would try to live, but we knew that they would find us and that they would kill us. One could not possibly prevail against the might of the Nazi war machine with its omnipotent military branches, the vicious Gestapo officials—the Schutzpolizei, the Sicherheitspolizei, and, of late, the infamous Einsatzgruppen—all of them committed to the annihilation of the Jews. We wondered if perhaps it would have been better in the town square. At least tortured, we would have been together and not alone, as Eva and Genia's brothers had likely been. We wondered if Fayga when shot by Herr Becker had died immediately or later by drowning.

"We will never know what it is like to be with a man," Genia whispered. "I know at this time I should not have these thoughts, but I do. I would have liked to experience the sexual pleasure we were not even allowed to know about. Now I am sure that I will never know, and I do regret that I did not permit myself to try."

"Yes," I agreed. I had asked myself similar questions, but not lately. Ever since that Saturday morning when I read the poster, my life had changed. The fear that convulsed my stomach had pushed aside all other thoughts. "Genia, all I can say is that there have been times when I had thought about it. Now that they took Eva, it no longer matters. I am not even sure that I really want to continue the struggle. But I did not want to hang from a tree. Now that my mother has regained some of her courage, and since your Aunt Ester was able to secure transport for us to leave town, I dare think that perhaps there is a chance."

We did not sleep, nor did we want to close our eyes. We wanted to share our remaining time. At three o'clock when Pani Springer walked in to wake us, we assured her that we had slept for several hours. We had some bread and tea. There was no exchange of words between Genia and me. We did not hug or kiss. It was as if we understood that our raw emotions would not serve us well. We looked at each other long and hard before leaving the Springer house.

# CHAPTER 6

# Escape to Szczucin

Though we made sure that we had left some air space, we were unable to see the road the driver had taken. Twice we were stopped by military patrols. We heard the questions, and the answers from the driver. The first interceptors wanted to know what the driver was carrying and the location of the delivery. The driver got off the truck, produced the required documents, and pointed to the materials on the truck. We kept going until stopped by the second military patrol. There was a similar exchange, except for a warning to the driver to beware of escaping Jews. They told him that the Tarnow ghetto was in the process of being liquidated and that some Jews had escaped. They reminded the driver that the Jews are a wily lot and that some even have the effrontery to acquire false papers in the hope of being able to pass as Christian Poles. There was some raucous laughter as they agreed that one does not have to worry about Jewish males, but one has to watch out for the females—they are liable to trick you.

The truck stopped. Through the little glass pane, the driver signaled to us that we were to get off. We adjusted our clothing and moved to the back of the truck. It had been agreed that we would act like a group of hitchhikers who had gotten a ride from a friendly driver. The four of us attempted to smile and to look carefree as we helped each other descend. We were, Aunt Regina said, in a suburb of Tarnow, on the main road leading into the center of town. The driver accepted the money and nodded when Mother expressed our appreciation. "This was tougher than I thought," he said. "I think I need a drink." We moved to the side of the road, and he followed us. It was still quite dark. He said, "You probably heard what they told me. The Tarnow ghetto is being liquidated. Most of the women and children have already been removed. Some have managed to escape, and even the army is cooperating in hunting them down. My advice is that you get off this road as fast as possible."

The truck drove off, and we started to walk in the direction of the town. Several trucks passed, and we knew that it was dangerous to ask someone to give us a ride out of the perilous area. Apparently, German drivers of the passing vehicles had been alerted to watch for Jews escaping from the Tarnow ghetto. Pedestrians turned to look at us as they hurried past. We sensed they were avoiding us. Compared to the peasants passing us, we looked like town folk.

On both sides of the road were meadows and harvested fields. There was a garbage dump on the left, and within sight some broken-down shacks. A village had to be nearby. We walked in pairs, Dollek and I in front, the two women a few paces behind us. Ahead of us we saw an area of modest dwellings. Suddenly Aunt Regina screamed. I turned around and saw my mother lying on the road. She had fainted. I ran back and called, "Mother." I felt Aunt Regina's elbow in my ribs. "It's Aunt Jadzia, and you better remember that."

Aunt Regina ran to a nearby house to ask for some water. I was on my knees, bending over my mother, saying, "Mother, Mother," when I heard her whisper, "You must remember that I am not your mother." Mother responded to the water Aunt Regina gave her. Two women had come out of the house, and from a distance they watched us. Regina rolled up her coat, and put it beneath Mother's neck. She turned to the women and asked whether they would let us come in so that Pani Capitanowa—wife of a captain—could recover from the fainting spell. The younger woman shook her head. Aunt Regina pleaded, telling about heart problems, the breakdown of the vehicle we had been traveling in, and the need for food and drink for which the women would be compensated. The women reluctantly agreed, but stated firmly that we would have to be out of their house by early afternoon and before the younger woman's husband returned from work. We learned that the husband worked for the railroad, under German command, at a nearby milk stop, where he pumped water for the passing locomotives. Aunt Regina said we would probably leave earlier, just as soon as she returned from town after contacting friends who would help us.

The women wanted some assurance that we were not Jews who had escaped from a ghetto. Regina was astonished. "Jews! Do I look like a Jew? Does Pani Capitanowa, or her niece? Her father is with the Polish regiment that got into England, an officer, you know. Oh I forgot myself! We are not to talk about that. Can you imagine what the Germans would do to her if they knew that her father was with the enemy?" Shortly thereafter, Aunt Regina left. Mother was resting on a sofa in an adjoining room, and Dollek and I remained in the kitchen.

The two women were baking bread, and we watched. It was the first time I had heard my "father" was in England. I noticed that the women appeared to be impressed when the secret was revealed to them. They asked me how old I was when my father left for the war. I said I was thirteen years old. They said I was lucky, because if my father was alive then I was not an orphan. My eyes filled with tears. It was a rather new phenomenon I did not seem able to control. After that there were few questions, and I was glad. I felt insecure speaking Polish and awkward with the details of my newly acquired background.

After several hours, Aunt Regina returned. She seemed confident and informed the women that we would leave before four o'clock to meet her friends who would have transportation waiting for us near the local milk stop, where the husband worked. The women were unhappy. The husband should not see us. He would be very angry. Aunt Regina asked if we could have one more meal. She put a considerable amount of money on the table. Pani Capitanowa, my "aunt," came to join us in the kitchen. My mother felt much better, and she apologized profusely for the inconvenience she had caused. She wished them God's blessing for their kindness, which, due to circumstances, she could not repay. The older woman said, "I know," and later, "I understand." Something about the way she said it, or the way she looked when she said it, made me wonder if she sensed the truth. There was no reaction on our part.

At dusk we were going to board a train, and we would disembark at a country stop, near the town of Szczucin. There we were to be met by a man. Since we had to leave the house and it was dangerous to linger on the road, we proceeded in the direction of a small forest. Suddenly, Mother was not in charge, instead it was Aunt Regina. Uncle Jacub had been born and raised in Tarnow, and she knew the town and the surrounding area quite well.

We learned that Aunt Regina had been able to contact her brother-in-law Shimek, with the help of a Pole from the outside and a Jewish guard on the inside. She had spoken to him while she stood outside the tall iron fence that surrounded the ghetto, and Shimek stood inside. Their conversation was conducted under the watchful eye of a German guard, who patrolled outside the fence. The guard had instructed her to keep her hands away from the fence. Still, Shimek had managed to surreptitiously pass Regina a considerable amount of money that he said she could put to better use.

For Shimek it was too late. On the previous day, his young and beautiful wife Margot had been forcibly torn from his side and sent off with a women's transport. He asked Regina if she knew what that meant; Regina knew. He was hoping on that evening he would be transported to the alleged collection center, perhaps in time to see his wife once more. He told Regina that the trucks transported the Jewish human cargo at dusk or at dawn.

Shimek was happy to once more see Regina. He was almost certain that he would not be there on the following day. He told Regina that initially thousands of Jews from Tarnow and the neighboring towns and villages had been forced into the Tarnow ghetto. At the time of their meeting, there were perhaps less than two hundred people left. "From the beginning when the ghetto was closed, transports of Jews were being brought in, while almost simultaneously transports of Jews were taken to other locations," Shimek said. "They think that no one knows what they are doing, and that we will not be here to tell. But the Poles know, and if you survive you must tell the world of the carnage that took place in Poland. Shimek told Regina that people are forbidden to bring food to the ghetto inmates, but, he said, "Some Poles are willing to take the chance. They remember that we grew up together, and they know that Nazi tales of alleged labor camps for Jews are lies.

Shimek gave his sister-in-law his most precious possession—the name of the man who had promised to help him and his wife. "Bolek, the man who will meet you when you get off the train near Szczucin, is my friend, he has always been my friend, and he knew Jacub," Shimek said. He urged Regina to listen carefully. "Bolek and I attended business school together. Bolek is not his name, and for his protection it is better that you don't know his real name. He hates the Nazis, and he fights them whenever there is an opportunity. He is very smart. He left Tarnow because he did not want to work for the Germans. He lives in Szczucin. His father-in-law owns a house there, and in the house is a neighborhood bar frequented by the local bureaucracy. German officials drop in, also military patrols. The latter make sure that the beer allotment is delivered. I can't tell you more, because I don't know if he can help you, or how he can help you. But I know he will try, and you have no other option. If things go sour, whatever you do, don't betray Bolek. There are not many around like him. His wife just had a baby, and when I sent some money for the baby, Bolek brought it back. They felt that I may need it, and they still believe that I'll manage to escape and they could then help me. This tall iron fence is escape-proof. Besides, without Margot, I would not even make the attempt."

Regina and Shimek could not hug or kiss, but when they were sure that the guard's back was turned, their hands met in a final parting. Though the encounter had been devastating, it had somehow strengthened Regina's resolve to survive. She told us that when she saw Shimek walking toward the fence, she thought she would faint, and she had clenched her hands around the iron bar. That was when the guard told her that she was not allowed to touch the fence. Shimek's once dark and lustrous hair was gray, his red-rimmed eyes were dull, and his look of helplessness and defeat made him appear smaller than he was. In the ghostly looking creature walking toward her, she barely recognized what had once been her young, handsome brother-in-law. He immediately cautioned her to pretend she was just passing by, perhaps had recognized a face, and had stopped to visit. No intimation of a relationship. She was the Gentile on the outside, he the Jew on the inside.

At the country railroad stop, we boarded the train for Szczucin, but our destination was a town twenty miles beyond Szczucin. The man whom Aunt Regina had contacted by telephone was there to meet us when we arrived. "To you I will be Bolek," he said. Then he asked for the slip of paper Shimek had given Aunt Regina. When he had read the few words, he motioned toward a horse cart and told us to put our luggage inside. He appeared to be astonished that there were four of us. When Aunt Regina had called from the public telephone, she said only what Shimek had told her to say: "The package is arriving on the evening train."

Bolek told us that he had seen Shimek and Margot on the previous Sunday and had expected to hear from them, "but not this, and not by train." He told us that he lived with his wife and in-laws above the bar. His wife was presently recovering from giving birth to their second child and above all she must be protected. He said he did not know what to do with us or where to place us: At this time of day there was much activity in the bar, and he should be there to help.

"You cannot spend the night in the house. It is not my house," he said in a firm voice, but the tone was not angry. "I will think of something." Laughter and loud voices could be heard before we reached the bar. Bolek told us that once we entered the apartment above the bar, we were to say as little as possible. We were not to mention our names, nor divulge where we had come from. He cautioned us to be careful and to stay in the side lane until we were sure that we were not seen entering the house. The three of us should walk up separately. He took Dollek's hand and went in through the outside door.

Two women were in the apartment. The younger woman indicated that we were to sit down. The older woman ladled soup into four bowls and motioned to us to eat. The women smiled at us, but their faces were tense. The only words addressed to us came from the younger woman. "These are very difficult times," she said. We sat and dozed in the warm kitchen, then were suddenly wide awake when we heard Bolek's resounding steps coming up the stairs. He said something to his wife that we were not able to hear. He hugged his mother-in-law and said good night, then he made a sign to us that we thought signaled that everything was going well and descended back to the bar. Shortly thereafter, the two women said good night and disappeared into adjoining rooms.

From down below, we heard the cocky voices of men who had drunk too much. We heard the door to the pub close and the opening of the door that led out to the street as people left the bar. It was after ten o'clock when a detail of soldiers with hobnail boots entered the bar. Aunt Regina turned down the wick in the kerosene lamp, while we sat up and reached for our coats. We breathed easier when the sounds of tipsy male conversation accompanied by bits of German marching songs wafted up to our ears. Sometime later, we heard the soldiers leave the pub. I dozed off. I was awakened by voices and saw Bolek preparing to start a fire in the kitchen stove.

He looked tired, and it was obvious that he had not slept. He told us that we would be leaving shortly. He had arranged to take us to his friend's small farm. Eight months ago, the friend was accused of having committed sabotage against the Third Reich. Although the man was innocent, and after a hearing, the county court in Tarnow had pronounced him innocent, the Gestapo refused to release him and hauled him off to Germany. Now he was tending a German farm while his own farm deteriorated.

"His wife and their seventeen-year-old daughter do all the farm work," Bolek told us, "and they need help in the house. Besides," he added, "Pani Jowanczyk said she needs money to pay her taxes. They have been trying to evict her because she could not come up with the tax money." He told us she had sold her horse and was able to make a part payment, but now she has to borrow a horse to plow her fields. Furthermore, each month she has to deliver the required farm allotment they had assigned when her husband was working the farm."

"Ever since her husband was accused, the other farmers have kept their distance," said Bolek. "Pani Jowanczyk thinks it's just as well because she never found out who the accuser was, and she is suspicious of everyone. Two more women in the house will allow them more time to tend to the three cows and the fields. The place is falling apart. The boy should stay out of the way, and during the day he must remain inside the house. Now the young girl . . ."

He turned to me and asked me about my skills. I told him that I knew how to sew by hand and by machine. He waved his hand as if to say that in this village everyone does their own sewing. I added that I had worked in a petition office that wrote letters and applications on behalf of the peasants.

"So you know German?"

"Yes," I answered.

"You mean to say that you picked up enough of the German language since the invasion to enable you to write a letter, to compose a petition?"

Everybody was looking at me, and Mother, it seemed, was staring straight into my eyes. I said that I had lived in Chorzow since I was three years old and until the invasion. "Yes, and . . . ?" Bolek prodded.

"In Chorzow many people spoke German," I continued. "I knew some German even before I started school. In school, each grade had a German class that everyone had to attend, and at the time of the Nazi invasion when I left Chorzow to live with my aunt, people would ask me how to write sentences in German. Also, my boss in the petition office tried to speak German with me because there were occasions when he had to represent a petitioner at a hearing in the agricultural administration office. He said both he and I needed the practice."

It was the first time I used the alibi we had so carefully constructed. I knew that Mother and Aunt Regina had urged that I avoid talking about my language problem, and that only if absolutely necessary was I to reveal the Chorzow connection to justify my unusual accent. Bolek said, "Ah! That's the reason. You don't say very much, and I was wondering why some words sounded a bit strange. Now I understand."

I did not dare look at Mother. Was she satisfied? Did I do well? Was I the liability my aunt insisted I was? While in the hayloft, Aunt Regina had said that everyone was concerned about Dollek, but she thought my strange pronunciation was the greater problem.

Before we left for the farm, Bolek told us it was imperative that we forget he had met us at the country railroad stop and that we had been to his house. We must erase from memory the name Bolek (though that was not his real name) and forget his existence. My mother assured him that we were fully aware of the risk he had taken and that we would obey all his instructions.

"Should you be asked why you are at the Jowanczyks," Bolek instructed, "or how you managed to find your way to Pani Jowanczyk's farm, be prepared to say that someone told you she had a room to let and that she was in need of help. I told her that the older woman is recovering from a lung ailment and needed the country air. Do not attempt to contact me. In an emergency, Pani Jowanczyk or her daughter Halina will know where to find me. The girl must work. She was sixteen in March, and this is September. She must have work papers or she will be picked up and transported to work somewhere in Germany. That must be avoided. I do have contacts in the municipal office. I will see what I can do."

We walked for almost an hour in narrow lanes among fields. Some had been harvested, and some looked in need of attention. Bolek pointed to a small farmhouse. "Just walk in. You are expected. I don't think the dog will bark, but in any case there is no one living close enough to hear the dog, or to see you."

Mother wanted to thank him, but he waved his hand. "I know," he said, as he turned to leave us. Then he stopped and added, "One last thought. Pani Jowanczyk does not want to know who you are or where you came from. She does not say much, but she is a smart woman, and she hates the Boche."

## OCTOBER 1942 ⤳ SZCZUCIN, OCCUPIED POLAND

The farmhouse we entered consisted of two rooms. Adjacent to the house was a barn. The room we were to occupy had two beds, a table, and several chairs. Behind a flowered curtain were several wooden pegs for clothes. The woman motioned to Mother to follow her to the other room.

Subsequently, Mother told us that the Jowanczyks, mother and daughter, slept in their kitchen-living room. They were barely able to support themselves from the proceeds of the farm and from their livestock. They had been unsuccessful in getting their assigned allotment reduced. Pani Jowanczyk said that her husband had been imprisoned before he was transported to Germany. She was very angry because they still demanded the quota that was assigned when her husband worked the farm. Mother told us that Pani Jowanczyk urged that we remain in the house throughout daylight hours because someone could see us from the road. For the time being she felt that it was best that only she and her daughter remain the registered occupants of the farm.

Between us we agreed to establish a routine that would keep us mentally and physically alert. The four of us resumed our study of the catechism, and Mother insisted that I spend the early morning hours reading aloud whatever Polish material we could obtain. We prepared vegetable and potato soup for the household of six, and Mother and Aunt Regina took turns grinding wheat for our bread on the makeshift flour mill. During the day, we watched Pani Jowanczyk through the window as she plowed her fields. The plow was hitched to a neighbor's horse, and the woman walked behind, watching the furrows and adjusting the plow. At dusk the daughter, Halina, mounted the horse and rode it bareback back to the owner's stable.

On Sunday morning, after the Jowanczyks left to attend early Mass, Bolek came to see us. He brought us good news. Through an address Aunt Regina had given him, he had been able to make contact with our loyal friend Pan Majerowicz, who was living as a Polish Christian under the name of Jerzy Krawczyk. His message was that he would contact us.

Bolek informed us that there were rumors in town that the Jowanczyks had new tenants, or perhaps visitors. He wanted to know if someone could have seen us. He added that both mother and daughter were clever, and if someone asked them directly in church, they could deal with it.

Then came the surprise. "There is a job opening at the magistrate's office," Bolek said. "They are looking for a German-speaking person with some secretarial skills, and I think Krystyna can do it." My mother and her sister looked at each other, then both looked at me. "Yes, yes," Bolek said. "I know she has an accent, a foreign accent, but country folk know that city people don't speak the way they do. Besides, she does not have any trace of what we call a Jewish inflection, and that is important."

Bolek told us that an older man, a former schoolteacher, who had been in charge of the correspondence addressed to the German administration offices, had suffered a severe hip injury. He had been absent for several weeks and was not expected to return for the next few months.

Bolek turned to me and queried me about my background. In response to his questions, I gave short answers. My mother died when I was born. When I was three years old my father took me with him when he got a job in Chorzow. Until the invasion, I had lived in Polish Silesia. My father, a reserve army officer, had not returned to occupied Poland after the invasion. No, I had not heard from him. I heard rumors that some regiments managed to escape across the border to a foreign country. Why did I think that? Because we would have been notified if he was taken prisoner or had been killed. Other people had received such notification. Bolek supplied me with a number for my father's regiment, and I wrote it down. Since the invasion I have lived with my aunt, who now, according to her physician, needed to live in the country. She was recuperating from a tubercular infection.

"It will do," Bolek said. "No matter what they say, just stick to your story, and keep your answers short." He put a hand on my shoulder, and I knew he expected me to look at him. I did. "You will manage," he said. "You won't let me down. You are the cornerstone of this structure. It will depend on you whether you can remain and be registered in the village."

It was agreed that I would present myself at the magistrate's office at eight-thirty on Tuesday morning. Bolek gave me the name of the woman I should contact, and he told me that he would make the arrangements on the following day. The strain of the interrogation had depleted me. By the time Bolek left, the cramps in my stomach had become unbearable. Only after Aunt Regina heated some pot lids on the stove and Mother had applied them to my bulging stomach did I feel an easing of the spasm. I heard Aunt Regina say it was ridiculous for me to present myself at the magistrate's office. "I don't believe that she could convince anyone in that office of her new identity." Mother's rejoinder was curt: "She always did what was expected of her, and she will do what she has to do." The sisters exchanged some angry words. Mother accused Aunt Regina of being negative at a time when I needed encouragement, and Aunt Regina said that Mother made decisions without consulting her and was domineering.

On Tuesday morning I presented myself to Panna Russek, the magistrate's secretary. The woman was tall and gaunt, perhaps in her late thirties. She asked me a few questions, and when I said that I came to Szczucin with my aunt, she said, "What a coincidence. Ever since Christmas, my niece has been staying with me. The two of you should meet. She is younger than you are, but I think you would like each other." After a few minutes, she took me to the person in charge of all matters relating to the German administration of the district.

Her name was Pani Wozek. She was of medium height and trim, and she had beautiful blond hair. She was dressed sedately in black, and I wondered if she had recently been widowed. She exuded an air of confidence, and I was a bit surprised to find such an elegant woman working in the mayor's office. She asked me few questions, and I felt that she hardly heard my answers. All she wanted to know was whether I could do the job. Her eyes never smiled, and I was apprehensive. The Szczucin district was under the supervision of the German occupation administration authority in Tarnow. I learned that the county seat, the county commissioner, and offices of the mayor and magistrate were all housed in the same building. Except for minor local administrative matters, all correspondence from the combined offices had to be channeled to the German supervisory offices in Tarnow. Pani Wozek told me that her ability to read and speak German was limited and writing a German letter was beyond her capability.

Pani Wozek led me to a typewriter. Next to it on a small desk were two high stacks of letters. The letters were written in Polish, and most of them were handwritten. The smaller stacks contained letters addressed to the magistrate. The other stack contained correspondence addressed to the county clerk, and it dealt for the most part with matters familiar to me. The petitioners asked for relief from the heavy burden of the agricultural allotment. There were also letters begging the German authority to divulge the place to which family members had been transported.

Pani Wozek instructed me in the office procedures. If my translation of a document met with her approval, she would present it to the appropriate authority, either the county clerk or the mayor's office, for signature. I noticed that a number of rubber stamps and official looking seals were in the locked drawer of Pani Wozek's desk. Shortly after I sat down to work, I asked if I could look at copies of letters that had been filed. I said that I wanted to have some models of previous German correspondence from the Szczucin office.

Glancing through the letters written by Pan Wroblewski (the person I was temporarily replacing), I saw immediately that his knowledge of German was limited. Following his example, I worked slowly and carefully at misspelling words and distorting the grammatical structure of the paragraphs I was writing. I was aware that in my assumed identity as a native-born Pole, I could not display fluency in German. My workday started at eight-thirty in the morning and ended at five in the afternoon. At the end of the day, the departing workers often expressed discontent. Their complaints focused on the amount of work that was expected, the inadequate salaries, and, most important, the insufficient food rations. Having just been hired, I thought that by lingering a while after work and socializing and by being attentive, I might avoid being rejected by my coworkers. The walk back to the farm took about fifty minutes, but if I ran part of the way, I was able to arrive before the seven o'clock curfew.

It did not take me long to realize that Pani Wozek was perhaps the most important person in the whole office. She was addressed as Pani Directorowa—Mrs. Director—and both the magistrate and the county commissioner signed without reading all the letters she presented for their signature. Frequently, Pani Wozek would come and interrupt my work because official documents required an immediate response. For the main part these documents dealt with German occupation rules and ordinances that were not adequately enforced by the Polish local administration. There were also new laws with specific instructions for execution.

One document warned about escaped Jews who may settle in an agricultural area with forged Aryan papers. These Jews must, the document stated under a specifically numbered paragraph, be apprehended, arrested, and, within a period of not less than twenty-four hours, delivered to the appropriate Gestapo headquarters in Tarnow. Just as Pani Wozek was phrasing the response she wanted me to type, the mayor passed by. After they discussed the content of the document, he said, "Now they want us to do their Jew hunting for them. I wonder what they'll ask next."

Pani Wozek was requested to appear in Tarnow at the office of the province administrator. The administrator was the direct link to Governor-General Frank. It was an overnight trip. Upon her return, a clerk with a horse-drawn carriage met Pani Wozek at the train station. When they arrived at the office, the clerk deposited two heavy briefcases in the conference room. After a few minutes in her office, Pani Wozek, dressed in a black suit with matching hose and shoes, followed the clerk to the conference room. When I left at about five o'clock, Pani Wozek, the mayor-magistrate, and the county commissioner were still in the conference room. They were not accepting telephone calls.

Pani Wozek had brought a document from the governor-general instructing the mayor's office that, as of January 1943, all people residing within his district must have a new identity card. The white identity card issued during the past eighteen months would then become invalid.

The briefcases Pani Wozek had brought from Tarnow contained applications for a new identity card called a Kennkarte for all staff members presently employed in the two offices. Pani Wozek had to pledge that she would personally examine each application and scrutinize the applicant before issuing the Kennkarte. The new document's safety measure would be a fingerprint of both the right and left index fingers in the spaces provided on the Kennkarte next to the person's photograph.

Pani Wozek told the mayor's secretary that she would take a few days off and charged Panna Russek with the task of distributing the applications to every person employed in the offices, including the cleaning personnel as well as the driver. The applications were written in both German and Polish, and though they were self-explanatory, everyone was to feel free to ask for help. A photographer would be on the premises for two days, and each applicant was required to have his picture taken. Once completed, Pani Wozek was to personally bring the Kennkarte forms to the Kreishauptmann, or district military commissioner, in Tarnow for final scrutiny and signature. The whole process was to be completed within a short period of time, and only after the employees of the Polish local offices were successfully processed could all people residing in the district register.

On an evening when we were ready to go to sleep, there was a gentle tap at the outer door, and when Aunt Regina went to see who it was, she returned with our dear friend Pan Majerowicz. We all wept with joy. We had tried to contact him through the person who had agreed to facilitate communication between us, and since there had not been a response, we feared the worst. He brought money for Aunt Regina that Jerzy Hyp had been able to channel to him. The message that Aunt Regina's friend sent was that he had experienced some difficulty in disposing of the merchandise he held for Aunt Regina because people preferred barter; since the occupation, the Polish currency was nearly worthless.

Pan Majerowicz, whose assumed name was Jerzy Krawczyk, looked very tired when he walked in, but he refused to lie down and rest. We had so much to tell each other. We had felt very isolated since coming to Szczucin. Jerzy, we had to address him by his Christian name, told us that various individuals had tried to find out where the Jews from the Krosno ghetto had been transported. All efforts had been unsuccessful. "There were hundreds of people," Jerzy said, "and they have disappeared without leaving a trace."

Jerzy told us that he had been able to find a hiding place for his wife and that someone had arranged for his ten-year-old daughter Basia to be enrolled at a convent boarding school. He had managed to find a furnished room in Tarnow, and for the time being he lived there with Ewa and Maryla, his two older daughters. He said that it was their third lodging since they had left Krosno. Tarnow was an extremely dangerous location. Since the liquidation of the Tarnow ghetto, Jew hunting was relentless. For some Poles it had become a lucrative business to denounce Jews, because the Gestapo had instituted payment for each Jew that was captured. Jerzy solemnly gave us a precious gift: his address in Tarnow. He told us to guard it carefully and to only use it under extreme circumstances. Other than that we would make contact through the previously designated person, but only if there was a change of address on either side.

Our guest was to depart on the following evening, and he said that he would sleep during the day. He was surprised that I had been able to get a job at the magistrate's office. When I told him about the newly arrived applications for the Kennkarte, and that the documents would be processed within days, he asked me several times to repeat what I was saying. He said that there had been rumors about a new identity card and about the invalidation of the recently issued white identity card. The realization that our identity cards would become obsolete within weeks was an unexpected threat to our existence. The Gestapo had let it be known, Jerzy informed us, that because of sloppy *Polnische Wirtschaft*—Polish management—too many Jews had been able to fraudulently obtain the white identity card. Henceforth the German occupation authority would issue the new Kennkartes, and all stages of the process would be supervised by the governor-general's office.

Jerzy was eager to know if there had been a comment when my birth certificate was inspected and if there had been specific questions. He was much relieved to learn that my falsified birth certificate had been collected together with the documents from other office staff members and that it had been returned to me. Jerzy had access to the source that created these documents, and since Jerzy's family had obtained their white identity cards based on birth and marriage certificates from the same source, he felt that he and his family members could now feel a bit more secure when asked to present their documents.

It was agreed that I needed several hours of sleep before leaving for work. I was so excited that sleep would not come. As I dozed off and woke up again, I could hear Jerzy, Mother, and Aunt Regina whispering throughout the night.

They talked about the war in Russia. In Tarnow there were continuous dispatches issued by Hitler and his general staff proclaiming victory in the east. "Though occasionally one hears," Jerzy reported, "that there are some minor clashes or skirmishes between the Wehrmacht and the Russian army, the Wehrmacht always wins. That is what they report, but no one really knows. A blitzkrieg it's not." All three seemed to agree that we could not remain in Szczucin for any length of time and that Jerzy and his daughters could not remain in Tarnow. The whole province is riddled with informers, Jerzy said, and one can't know who they are. Mother felt that Krakow might be a town where we could disappear, and she knew the city. Jerzy disagreed. He said that the news from Krakow was devastating. In the Krakow-Plaszow ghetto, the Nazis were reducing the number of Jews that would have to be transported by killing them in the ghetto.

When I left for work on the following morning, Jerzy embraced me in a bear hug. I wanted to express my gratitude for his friendship and for his fortitude in daring to visit us in our hideout. My eyes filled with tears, and once again the overwhelming feeling of fear and foreboding left me in want of words. Jerzy said that it would be a stroke of good fortune for all of us if I were to obtain a legitimate Kennkarte. He also said that I was a courageous girl.

In the evening when I returned from work, Jerzy was gone. Mother said that the Jowanczyks must know that we had had a visitor, but when she gave them the rent money for the next two weeks, neither mother nor daughter made any reference to his visit. We would have liked to know that Jerzy arrived safely in Tarnow, but we had no means of communication. With Gestapo patrols checking documents in trains and on platforms, all travel was fraught with danger. Mail was not an option for contact because it was censored by Gestapo agents at the post office. They were charged with the task of finding submerged Jews.

The Kennkarte, filled in by Pani Wozek, stated that Krystyna Zolkos, born in Iskrzynia, on May 1, 1926, was a Roman Catholic. She was employed as an office worker in Szczucin, District of Tarnow, in the Province of Krakow. The photograph was a poor likeness. I had forgotten to lower my eyelids, and there was a serious, perhaps sad look in my eyes. In addition, the lighting had been poor, and the photograph was underexposed. My dark blond hair looked almost black. Pani Wozek aided me in properly fingerprinting the document. When all the Kennkarte forms were completed, Pani Wozek packed the processed applications and documents into her briefcases. She told us that she would be gone for several days because the Kreishauptmann's office would want to scrutinize each document before affixing the official seal and signature.

Mother, Aunt Regina, and I worried that, as part of the scrutiny, the authorities might contact the registrar's office in Iskrzynia. I prayed that it would not. Dollek listened to our conversations and refrained from asking questions. With each passing day, I noticed Dollek becoming more withdrawn. I hugged and kissed him, though that was not what he wanted. In the morning, as I was getting ready to leave for work, I caught the wistful look on his face. Our little prisoner was not permitted to leave the room until it was dark. Even then, he could only move within a limited area. We played checkers, dominoes, and games that required only paper and a pencil, but we knew all he wanted was to run through the fields and nearby forest.

On the morning following Pani Wozek's departure for Tarnow, while I was trying to compose a letter according to a form I had found in the files, a man I had not seen before walked up to me and looked over my shoulder. "So, you are making use of my labor," he said.

I knew immediately that it was Pan Wroblewski, the man I had replaced. In my eagerness to find the right words, I almost stuttered. I said that I was glad he had recovered from his illness and that I knew I had been hired on a temporary basis and only until he was able to return to work. "So you know that," he said, and walked away. I sensed that this older man in his late sixties, quite gray, almost bald, and rather unkempt, did not like me. I knew that my days in the magistrate's office were numbered, and I hoped that Pani Wozek would return in time for me to receive the invaluable document.

That evening as I was preparing to leave, Panna Russek stopped at my desk. "Pan Wroblewski is coming back to work," she said. "Yes," I responded. "I met him, and I told him that I was hired on a temporary basis and only to help out while he was ill."

On my way back to the farm, I tried to discover the source of my turmoil. Why did I fear Pan Wroblewski's return to work? Had there been a hidden message in Panna Russek's statement of fact? Was my response adequate? Should I have asked if I could stay and continue working in one of the offices? It was of utmost importance for a young Polish girl to be employed, and being employed by a municipality granted the employee an additional layer of protection. Did I appear appropriately eager to remain employed there? I thought that I should discuss the situation with Mother and Aunt Regina.

However, when I arrived at the farm, I found the sisters engaged in making plans for our near future. I learned that Jerzy, during his visit, had urged us to leave Szczucin. He felt that the village was too small for people not to wonder and ask questions. Mother and Regina were attempting to find a suitable new town and a route to get us there without being apprehended.

Compounding our anxiety was that no one knew where the Jews from the Krosno ghetto had been transported. The Tarnow ghetto, which had sheltered thousands of Jews, had also been liquidated. In Tarnow, Jerzy reported that obliteration of the ghetto had evolved in stages. The original inmates had been shipped to another ghetto, or transit center, and from that camp to a mysterious destination that could not be traced. While this was going on, Jews from smaller ghettos were brought into Tarnow to remain there until relocation. Jerzy said there was no longer doubt what the words *transport* or *liquidation* meant. They were euphemisms for murder. Rumors of the mass murder of Jews were confirmed daily by Poles escaping from work details, or by eyewitnesses who happened by chance to see what the Nazis tried to keep secret. Through contacts with the Polish underground, Jerzy had learned that one evening, in the freight yard of the Krakow-Plaszow ghetto, Jewish inmates had been loaded into a van. When the van was opened on the following morning, it contained corpses. There was talk of a time-release gas that could efficiently kill people.

Jerzy's message from Aunt Regina's friend Jerzy Hyp was that he wished to help. He wanted her to know that he was trying to convert her remaining hidden merchandise into transportable currency. He was also in the process of trying to activate a contact that might provide a temporary hiding place for Aunt Regina and Dollek. Jerzy urged us to separate into two units: Aunt Regina and Dollek in one, Mother and I in another. Before leaving he admonished both Aunt Regina and Mother to pay more attention to our little caged sparrow—his reference to Dollek.

On the following day, I overheard one of my coworkers say that Pan Wroblewski had wondered aloud about my sudden appearance in their small community. Later in the day I became aware that he was sitting across from my typewriter, watching me. "I'm learning from you. I heard you are a good worker," he said. I continued with my work, but whenever I looked up, I felt his eyes piercing mine. Remember, keep your eyes down, I kept admonishing myself.

Though Pan Wroblewski was not to resume work until the following week, he appeared daily, always shortly before noontime. On Thursday, he stopped before my desk, and asked, "Why did you come to Szczucin?"

"I came with my aunt," I answered.

"Yes, but why Szczucin?"

"I don't know."

"It is rather surprising that your aunt should want to stay at the Jowanczyk's farm. Why not settle in the village? Pan Jowanczyk was in prison. They are troublemakers."

"I know nothing about that."

"Everyone here knows that the family is suspected of having contact with partisan groups."

"That is not possible. They are nice people. They work very hard," I said.

"In times like these one can't be too careful about the company one chooses."

His last sentence, with its barely veiled threat, caused turmoil in my intestines. I was drenched in perspiration, and the pain in my stomach was severe. Yet, during our conversation, I had not felt pain or discomfort. My total concentration had been on remaining calm, on keeping my eyelids down and my answers short.

On Friday, Pan Wroblewski informed me that, as of the following Monday, he would once again be in charge of the German correspondence. I smiled and nodded my head. "Poor Panna Russek is inundated with work," he said, "and she is looking forward to your capable help."

"I will do my best," I responded.

"Yes, of course. It certainly is much easier to write in one's native language, even if one is a poor typist."

In my mind I reviewed the sarcastic tone in Pan Wroblewski's voice. How much did he know? Aunt Regina had been right after all. The problem was my diction and strange syntax and my frequent hesitancy when I tried to put my thoughts into Polish. If Pani Wozek returned by Monday, would Pan Wroblewski prevent me from obtaining the Kennkarte? How would I be able to excuse my faulty spelling when faced with Polish correspondence? A native Pole would welcome with relief the change from German back to Polish. For me, the shift from the phonetic German language that I knew to vowels and consonants accented with a variety of dots, dashes, and squiggles was fraught with danger. I had never learned the basic rules of the Polish language that a child learns in elementary school. My lack of fluency did not match my invented identity as a native-born Pole.

Mother listened attentively as I recounted the events of the day. She agreed that I would have to proceed with extreme caution and that Pan Wroblewski was the enemy. She stated firmly that I must use whatever ruse I could devise to hold out until Pani Wozek's return from Tarnow.

On Monday, before leaving for work I intentionally cut the index finger of my right hand. By the time I arrived at the office, blood had seeped through the gauze bandage. "Please excuse my predicament," I said to Panna Russek. "May I make myself useful indexing and filing the accumulated documents?"

"Yes, of course," she replied. In back of me stood Pan Wroblewski. "Hmmm, an accident," he murmured sarcastically, loud enough for me to hear.

In the late afternoon, I heard someone say that Pani Wozek had returned from Tarnow and that she would be in the office on the following day. On Tuesday when I arrived at the office, with my right index finger covered by a clean gauze bandage, I came face to face with Pan Wroblewski. He was coming out of the mayor's office and was in the process of closing the door. "Let's get to work," he said. "There is no room here for slackers." The look in his eyes was hostile, the tone of his voice cutting. I sat down at the typewriter, and he took the chair across from me. He murmured to himself while I typed the address. Then he began to dictate a letter. The pace was deliberate, the words pronounced clearly. I tried to keep up with his dictation, knowing all along that almost every other word I typed was misspelled. Altogether he dictated three letters, while I attempted to shield the pages from his view. While I was typing the conclusion of the third letter, Pan Wroblewski suddenly leaned over my shoulder and hissed, "Do it over." Then he walked away. I spent the remainder of the morning checking the dictionary, correcting my mistakes, and retyping the three letters.

I still had not seen Pani Wozek, but I had heard that she was in the mayor's office and had been there for most of the morning. During lunch break, I saw several staff members waiting in front of Pani Wozek's office. I stood in line behind the others waiting to receive their Kennkartes. Pani Wozek looked tired and harassed, but I was sure that Pan Wroblewski had not spoken to her. I took an oath that all the statements I had made were true. After signing a receipt, Pani Wozek handed me the document. I was in possession of the Kennkarte.

During the rest of the day, I answered several simple letters that required no more than a sentence or two. When I presented the finished correspondence to Panna Russek, she seemed to indicate that there were no problems. She smiled as she bade me a good evening.

When I returned to the farm, both Mother and Aunt Regina were delighted that I was now the owner of the much-desired document. They scrutinized all three parts of the gray identity card, and Dollek perked up when he saw the imprint of my index finger and thumb next to my photograph. He surprised us with his awareness of the tactic. It had been devised, he said, to identify criminals.

I did not want to go back to the office. I sensed danger, and I tried to remind Mother that dealing with Polish correspondence was beyond my ability. I cannot pretend to know what I don't understand, I said. Pan Wroblewski had set a trap when he sat down across from me to observe my dismay. "Mother, he knows," I pleaded.

"He cannot be certain unless he contacts the village registrar in Iskrzynia," Mother urged. "Your application for the Kennkarte was scrutinized by several officials, and you received the document. You have been courageous, and you can't run away now. You have to go back tomorrow, face Pan Wroblewski, and pretend that nothing of consequence has happened. Your position should be that you are a poor typist and that you have never before taken dictation."

Since I told Mother that applications for the Kennkarte for the general public were to commence on the following week, Mother felt that all she and Aunt Regina needed were an additional two weeks. It was of utmost importance that they should have the document in hand before we left Szczucin.

On Saturday, camouflaging my anxiety as best I could, I left for the office. Despite Pani Wozek's instruction that I carry the Kennkarte with me at all times, I decided to hide it at the farm. I was afraid that I might be asked to return the indispensable document. When I arrived, I learned to my great relief that since the office closed at noontime on Saturday and Pan Wroblewski had a bit of a walk to get there, he had made arrangements not to work on Saturdays. I felt that God had given me a respite. Pani Wozek gave me several letters that needed to be answered, and the hours passed quickly. All seemed well when I said good-bye and left for the farm.

On Monday morning, almost immediately upon my arrival, I was called to the mayor's office. Pan Wroblewski stood in front of the mayor's desk, watching me.

"Panna Krystyna," the mayor said, "a complaint has been made that we are harboring a Jewish fugitive." With my eyelids lowered, I looked at the mayor. I did not respond with words but conveyed my surprise.

"Panna Krystyna," he said, "I must be blunt. It is you who has been accused. I want you to answer truthfully. Are you a Jew?"

"No, I am not a Jew," I stated firmly. I wanted to add something, but the mayor raised his hand in a gesture that implied no further discussion was necessary.

"That's all for now," he said. "Let's go back to work, all of us. We will explore the matter at another time. I am very busy now. But one thing I am certain of, we don't need this type of rumor in this office."

I walked out and down the stairs to the bathroom. I felt dizzy and a bit nauseated. I knew that I was not going to faint. It was just a matter of calming down. I returned to my desk, but I cannot recall what I did during the next several hours. Before lunch break, the mayor himself stopped at my workplace and said, "Stop by my office."

"Now?" I asked. He nodded. He was alone in the room when I walked in. He was quite tall, and I was glad that he was standing, because I did not have to look into his eyes.

"When you walk out of this office, go home," he said. "Don't ever come back here. You told me that you are not Jewish. You are an orphan. I want to believe you, but these are difficult times, and we are an official agency. I want neither examinations nor investigations. The county commissioner agrees with me. For your own good, it would be best if you leave this area altogether."

I felt the tears, but they did not start coming until I had closed the door

of his office. I walked down the stairs and out of the building. I strolled through
the main street until I had left the village behind me, then I started to run.

Mother and Aunt Regina behaved as though they were not surprised at
what had happened at the office. I could not control my weeping, and Mother
kept urging that I pull myself together. The Jowanczyk women must not divine what had transpired, she said. It was imperative that I immediately leave
the area.

CHAPTER 7

# Escape to Krakow

It was agreed that I would take a late afternoon train to Tarnow from a neigh-boring town. It would be too dangerous for me and the rest of the family if I took the train from Szczucin. We spent the remaining time packing the little suitcase and bundle I was to take with me. Days were getting cooler, and lately there had been evidence of early frost. We agreed that I must travel light. Our winter coats were still in Krosno, and Mother insisted that I would have to wear whatever warm clothes I owned. Mother baked a chicken and wrapped it in brown paper, then she put some bread cut into chunks and an additional loaf into a cloth pouch.

Both Mother and Aunt Regina kept assuring me that Jerzy Krawczyk—our Pan Majerowicz—would help and advise me. There was no one else, and I would have to use the address he had left with us. Mother and Aunt Regina took turns telling me how fortunate I was to have a Kennkarte. They kept re-peating that if asked I must confidently take it out of my pocketbook and pres-ent it to the examining authority. I was to memorize Jerzy's address but just in case I forgot, I wrote it on a small scrap of paper, which I stuffed deep into my pocket. Aunt Regina had an idea where the street was located. She told me to ask directions to a major thoroughfare that she thought would be near Jerzy's street, and then find my way to his apartment. Mother once again reminded me that in case of capture, both Jerzy's and my father's addresses must be destroyed.

The train in which I was riding made many stops. At each stop, milk cans were loaded into a freight car. Sleepy and grumbling peasant women pushed at each other to secure space for their respective baskets of produce. It was past nine o'clock in the evening and past curfew when the train entered Tarnow. Since the train arrived after curfew, all disembarking Polish passengers were required to spend the night in the station. Along with everyone else, I headed toward a bench. Leaning against my neighbors on each side, I dozed off. Several German patrols passed by and scrutinized the resting passengers. I pretended to be asleep while the soldiers randomly inspected documents. Several men were taken away to an office for further scrutiny of their documents. Only once was I asked to present my Kennkarte. The examining officer, speaking German to his colleague, said, "This is the new one," and returned the document. Early the next morning, I checked my one piece of luggage and the greasy food bundle at the railroad station, and unencumbered I proceeded toward my goal.

Walking purposefully, as if I knew where I was going, I managed to locate the apartment house. I was certain that I had not been followed when I entered the house. When I approached the apartment door, I could hear noises within. However, when I knocked, all sounds stopped. I knocked again, louder this time.

"It's Krysia. It's me Betus," I whispered through the keyhole. There was total silence. I did not move. After several moments, Maryla opened the door, her eyes wide with fear. She pulled me inside. She closed the door and locked it. In back of the room stood her older sister, Ewa. She beckoned to me to move away from the door and toward the back.

"How did you know where to find us?" Ewa asked.

"Your father told us."

"When did you see our father?"

"About eight days ago."

"Do you realize the jeopardy you are putting us in by coming here? The house is being watched. It has been raided several times. Early this morning we watched as they raided the house across the street. They brought out a man. It was frightening. You must leave now, so that whoever saw you enter, sees you leave."

"But there is no other place I can go," I said, taken aback. I hadn't expected Jerzy to be gone. "Where is your father?"

"He's not here," Maryla said.

"When will he be back?"

The sisters looked at each other "Not today," Ewa said. "Maybe tomorrow. No one was supposed to know this address. I can't understand why Father gave it to you."

"I would like to wait here until your father returns. May I sit down?"

"Why sit down? You can't stay here. It's out of the question. It's best for all of us if you leave immediately." Ewa's voice was brusque, her tone unyielding. "Every day Jews are being discovered, apparently denounced to the Gestapo by neighbors when they see a stranger who they suspect of being Jewish. Yesterday we thought that the police patrol walking toward this house was coming to pick us up, but they went into the next house. When they came out, they were pushing a young woman and a little boy into a car that was parked in front of our house. Whenever Jews are spotted, the police comb the neighborhood, and they search through all the apartments."

"No one saw me enter, therefore no one knows that I am here," I said. I was standing and so were both sisters. I turned toward Maryla. She had not said much, but I could tell that she was not happy with Ewa's rancor. I repeated with emphasis that I was certain that no one had seen me when I entered the house.

"How can you know that no one saw you enter?" Ewa demanded before Maryla had a chance to respond. "The landlady is very suspicious. She watches from her window all the time. If she sees you leave, we will be all right."

"Yes, Krysia, you must understand." Maryla's voice was soothing and conciliatory. "All Ewa wants is to hold on to our hiding place. It wasn't easy to find this place, and if we were forced to leave, we would have no other place to go. I hardly recognized you. You look so different with your blond hair. Honestly, you look like a Christian girl."

"You didn't tell us why you are here. Why did you leave Szczucin?" Ewa asked. I recounted the events of the past days while deemphasizing the language aspect. I showed them the Kennkarte. Both girls were impressed.

"You are the lucky one," Ewa said. "At this very moment our father is looking for contacts to help us obtain forged Kennkartes. Yours is legitimate; you can manage with that. For your own safety, you should leave now. Tarnow becomes even more treacherous toward evening when everyone is looking for shelter, with secret police and informers where one least expects them."

"But I don't know Tarnow. How can I go about looking for shelter? Please just let me stay until your father gets home," I pleaded. "He will be able to guide me." I looked appealingly at Maryla. My mind was working fast, wondering what I could say about our past that might get her to relent. Though Maryla was a year or two younger than me, all her Krosno friends had also been my friends, and we shared the memories of a happy summer.

Aside from Genia Springer, she had been the best-looking girl in my group of Krosno friends. She was tall and slender. Her naturally blond hair and delicate features gave her the desired Aryan appearance. Ewa, a year or two older than me, was darker complexioned and taller than Maryla and somewhat heavy, though she too could pass.

Maryla turned to her older sister. "Let her sit down for a moment," she said. Maryla suggested that perhaps I should have a bite to eat before I was turned away.

"I'll prepare something for you to eat, but then you must leave," Ewa said.

"No, thank you. I could not swallow a morsel of food. I just want to stay here until your father returns."

"You are putting us and our father in grave danger. Because of you, all of us will be picked up. That is selfish. You have the Kennkarte, you will manage." There was a note of finality and command in Ewa's voice. She was moving toward the door.

I was desperate. "Please Ewa, let me stay until your father arrives. I beg you, there is no one else I can turn to." I went down on my knees. I wept as I implored Ewa to reconsider. I poured out my fear, my anguish, and I kept begging.

"You must leave now." Ewa was adamant.

I got up from my knees. I dried my eyes and straightened my skirt. "Where will you go?" Maryla whispered to me as I walked to the door.

"I no longer care," I answered. "If I make it through the day, perhaps to Krakow."

When I left the house it was late morning. I proceeded at a brisk pace, focusing on a destination I selected. When I reached that goal, I randomly decided on another, keeping in mind that I couldn't retrace my steps. Suddenly I felt very tired. I was passing a church. I would have liked to enter, but decided against it because in a neighborhood church, a strange worshipper could be noticed. I would look for a larger church, a cathedral if I could find one. The next church I sighted was larger, and as I approached, I saw several women with kerchiefs covering their heads, enter through the main portal.

I made the sign of the cross, genuflected before the altar, and slid into a pew. I went down on my knees, and for the first time, after days of reacting to encounters that threatened my existence, I fastened on this moment of respite and proceeded to order my thoughts.

For days I had not thought about my sister Eva. What had been done to her before she was murdered? Had she been murdered? Was it possible that, in spite of the threat that any Jew who dared to escape the ghetto liquidation would be shot, they had let Eva live? The order on the poster stated that all inmates would be transported to labor camps where they would be put to work. Despite all the rumors we had heard, no one had seen Eva's dead body. Was she killed on sight, or was she taken into that closed truck, questioned about her missing family, and tortured? Not that, I prayed fervently, rather let her be shot.

What chance did I have in a town where the capture of escaped Jews was an almost hourly event according to Ewa and Maryla? The green pills, the cyanide tablets that Mother had obtained in the hope of giving each of us the power to end our lives on our own terms, were sewn into the lining of our winter coats, which were hanging in the Dunikowski wardrobe. Mother's total reliance on Jerzy was a misjudgment. She had not anticipated he might be away and that his daughters would refuse me shelter. Did I mean it when I told Maryla that I might take a train to Krakow? It had just come into my mind at that instant, perhaps because I knew Krakow better than I knew Tarnow. When Jerzy had visited us in Szczucin, he had told us that the Krakow-Plaszow ghetto had been partially evacuated and that Gestapo officials daily committed vile atrocities.

When I turned to look around in the dimly lit church, I noted that the priest had left, as had most of the worshippers. I genuflected before the altar and made the sign of the cross. I repeated the process, as I had observed others do, once more at the exit and left the sanctuary. I untied the kerchief and retraced my steps to the railroad station.

In the afternoon I purchased a ticket for an evening train to Krakow. Since there were several hours before the departure of my train, I thought that I should retrieve my luggage so I would not be suspected of loitering. Suddenly I felt quite weak, and I thought I might faint. I had not eaten since my arrival in Tarnow that morning, and it was after four o'clock in the afternoon. I walked into the restaurant, and standing at the counter, among other travelers, I tried to slowly eat the soup I had ordered. I took the partially eaten roll that had come with the soup, and while chewing on it, I walked toward the baggage checkroom.

I felt an arm gently placed on my shoulder, and simultaneously a kiss on my head. I looked up, and there was Jerzy, tears in his eyes, and I felt mine pouring out beyond control. "God, am I happy I found you," he murmured. "I have been combing the whole station, looking for you."

"I suddenly felt very hungry, and I went to the restaurant to get something to eat."

"I looked in, but I did not see you."

"We must have just missed each other. You cannot imagine how happy I am to see you," I said. I felt overwhelmed with gratitude.

"Hardly more happy than I am to find you. I was horrified when Ewa and Maryla told me what had happened in our room. Maryla remembered that you said that you might take a train to Krakow, but that was about eleven o'clock this morning, and there was a train departing in the early afternoon. I was beside myself with worry and very angry with my daughters. As soon as I heard what had happened I left, and I have been looking for you ever since. Do you have luggage?"

"Yes, it's in the baggage checkroom."

"That's good. We will leave it there, because it is safer to walk around without it. We'll walk together, a father and daughter walking home before curfew."

I looked at Jerzy. Like Maryla, he was tall and slim, and though he had a large bald spot on top of his head, the golden blond hair framing his oblong face gave him the much-desired Aryan appearance. He was well dressed wearing a tailored suit, white shirt, and a conservative tie. He had been a good friend of my uncle Jacub, and I remembered the two men, my uncle even taller than Jerzy, walking together on Sabbath, when all business was put on hold, their hands clasped behind their backs, engaged in serious discourse. After my

uncle was murdered, we did not see him often, and though all of us were occupied with our own survival, we somehow knew that Jerzy's protective hand
was always within our reach. I was groping for a way to tell him.

"I bought my ticket for the train to Krakow."

"That's good. It's valid for tomorrow, or next week, or even next month.
Now you are coming home with me. We are going to have a bite to eat together, and you will spend the night. You are expected. I told my daughters
that if I can find you, I am bringing you back."

"You know I am not wanted. Ewa and Maryla are afraid that my presence will put you in grave danger."

"Indeed, we are in grave danger, all of us. Their reaction was stupid, totally unreasonable. You don't think that they can decide for me? I am in charge
of my house, and I decide who may stay. Besides, I have not even had a chance
to think. Where should you go? Krakow, I hear, is even worse than Tarnow
because Jews have also escaped there, and the hunt for them is unremitting."

"I don't think I can go back. It was very difficult for me. I spent several
hours in a church, and even if I come back with you, I still have to strike out
on my own—perhaps tomorrow, or the next day. I have made the decision to
do it tonight."

"Now you are speaking like my girls, with total disregard of the circumstances. Both Maryla and Ewa have led protected lives, under the watchful
eye of a mother who was dedicated to the care of her family. It has been different for you. You know well that without a plan, without a place to go to,
you are imprudently putting yourself in danger. Are you listening to me?"

Throughout this exchange we had kept walking and were now walking
out of the terminal. I hooked my arm around Jerzy's arm and explained to
him why I could not go home with him. I told him that when I had walked
out of his house without a destination, there were a few moments when I en-
vied my sister and when I thought that it would be best to let things take their
course. It was the torture I was afraid of and the questions: Where had I been?
Who had helped me? How did I obtain the Kennkarte? I wondered whether
I would be strong enough to withstand it. So many people were involved. The
pill was out of my reach. Then in the church, while I was thinking about my
options, I knew that I would have to be on my own, and suddenly I felt my
resolve strengthen. I told Jerzy that I felt strong now. If I went home with
him, I wasn't certain I would feel the same strength tomorrow or the day after.

Jerzy squeezed my arm. "I will tell your mother," he said. "Don't contact her for several days. I will write to Pan K. You can contact him as soon as you have an address, and in time he will reach her." Pan K. was Jerzy's contact; we did not know his name.

Jerzy looked at his watch. Though my train was not to depart for another several hours, he had to be back in his apartment before curfew.

"Krakow is probably as dangerous as any other town," Jerzy said, "and I don't know a place, or an address, that I could send you to. Buy the early morning paper and look under *nocleg*—night lodging. These are inexpensive places where people who are stranded can spend one night, two at most. I don't know how often they are raided, but having the Kennkarte will help you. The owners of the lodgings are careful to abide by the law. The law is that anyone who spends more than one night has to be registered with the police. You want to avoid that. The best chance for you would be to find a bed in someone's room and a job to go to. And Krysia, no secretarial work for you."

"I know. I would rather do housework."

"Not the best idea either, you don't have that look. I must leave you now. There is nothing more I can say, except that I would feel better if you were coming back with me. On the other hand, it could be us who are picked up today or tomorrow. Now go back inside. Buy a newspaper and find yourself a seat." Jerzy kissed my forehead, turned, and walked away. I watched him go, and he never looked back.

While I sat on a bench, awaiting the departure of my train, the woman next to me asked me if I would watch her luggage for a few minutes because she wanted to use the toilet. Shortly after she returned, I thought that perhaps I should do the same. She said it was a good idea because the toilets on the train were not very clean. On my way back to my seat, I felt a glance in my direction, and then a detail of uniformed German occupation police approached me.

"What are you doing here at this hour?" a policeman asked in Polish.

"Waiting for the train to arrive," I answered. I realized my voice sounded quite hoarse, as if I were coming down with a cold.

"From where? Who are you expecting?"

"Oh no, I am departing. I am leaving for Krakow."

"For what purpose?"

"Perhaps to have surgery," I said on a sudden impulse. "I seem to have a growth in my throat."

"Identification paper," he snarled.

I rummaged in my purse and handed it to him. He looked at the photograph, then at me. He handed the Kennkarte, to another policeman and said something in German. The German policeman tried unsuccessfully to pronounce the word *Szczucin*. He shrugged his shoulders and said, "Your Polish names are enough to drive one mad."

OCTOBER 1942 ↞ KRAKOW, OCCUPIED POLAND

Squeezed between my neighbors in a third-class car, I tried to doze. The train made repeated stops: to take on water, to uncouple a freight car, or to just wait for a signal to proceed. Before the war, the train ride from Tarnow to Krakow took about three hours. My fellow passengers grumbled about the constant delays, but for me it was more advantageous to arrive in Krakow during early morning hours, rather than sit in the terminal waiting for daybreak.

Since Poles were not permitted to ride second-class, my fellow passengers were both well-dressed people traveling on business and poorly dressed workers and peasants, the men often in need of a shave and haircut. Several men were drunk and derelict-looking, and their foul smell allowed them to take up additional space as people moved away. I never looked in their direction because it was known that people of that type could be informers in disguise, working for the Gestapo.

When the train arrived in Krakow, I checked my baggage and proceeded to the bathroom. I washed and groomed as best I could, bought a morning newspaper, and made my way to a church. Having said my prayers, I found a pew with enough light coming through the window to enable me to read the nocleg vacancy advertisements. Jerzy had said that I must get there early and reserve my space, because by late morning all available beds would be spoken for.

I proceeded in accordance with my checkmarks and found that the three places I had thought most advantageous had no vacancies left. That was discouraging because it was only about eight o'clock in the morning. When I rang the doorbell at the fifth place I had checked off, the woman who opened the door grinned at me with a toothless smile and beckoned for me to come in. She said that it was late and that all available space had been taken but there was one room that was permanently rented to an elderly invalid, and he would be willing to share his room with a nice person. "There is even a sofa you can sleep on," she said, "and that is better than sleeping on a rug on the floor." Before I had a chance to decline, she opened up a door, and there propped on pillows was an old man. He was smiling at me, beckoning with his hand, and saying, "Come in my child, come closer." I turned and ran and did not stop until I had left the building.

The woman who answered the doorbell on my next attempt looked me over, placed her hands on her hips, and said with fury, "How dare you come knocking at my door? Get back to your own people and take your punishment." There was something more about calling the police, but I was gone.

I had to breathe, I had to think, and I had to get to a church. Finding my way from one place to another by streetcar had taken several hours. It was past noon. I had to find shelter for the night. After having been stopped by the police patrol in Tarnow, I dreaded spending another night at a railroad station. I decided to once again peruse the advertisements for nocleg. Perhaps I had missed something, or because I had been frightened, I had given up too quickly.

There were several advertisements I had yet to follow up. I stopped at a soup stand and ate a bowl of soup that came with a slice of bread. Then I felt better. After several further rejections, at about three o'clock in the afternoon, a well-groomed lady answered the door and asked me to come in. She said that it was rather late and that all her spaces were taken, but that she liked my appearance and might be able to help me. Her friend, a widow, lived with her son in a nearby suburb and had a vacant bed in her bedroom. The friend had told her that if the right female person came along, she should send her over. She asked me if I had a valid identification card, and I said yes. She told me that her friend's name was Pani Szklarzewicz and that she had a telephone, though my interviewer did not. However, she had access to a telephone and would advise Pani Szklarzewicz of my interest in her vacant bed.

Pani Szklarzewicz lived in a residential neighborhood in an area I did not know. I had to transfer from one streetcar to another and ask several times for directions before I arrived at the address. The outer door was locked, and the bell was answered by a concierge, who wanted to know who I was visiting and if I was expected.

An elderly lady, tall and gaunt and clothed in a well-fitting, knitted, sea-green dress, opened the door and asked me to come inside. She looked me over from head to foot, starting at my hair and continuing down to my clean shoes. She seemed to be pleased with my appearance and repeated several times that she had to be very selective and that she had never before shared her bedroom with a sixteen-year-old. "You know, I am sixty," she said. I smiled. The lady looked as if she were past seventy years old, and the black henna dye, inexpertly applied, poorly disguised her white hair.

"How long do you plan to stay?" she asked, while leading me into her bedroom.

"Perhaps one week, I am not sure. I came to see the doctor." The idea had worked with the police at the railroad terminal, and I thought that it would satisfy the skepticism of the woman and provide the reason why a girl of my appearance was looking for nocleg.

"Are you ill?" she asked.

"I keep getting these headaches. There seems to be a problem with my throat, or perhaps my ear. My aunt felt that my problem requires the attention of a specialist."

Pani Szklarzewicz shook her head disapprovingly. "Why didn't your aunt accompany you?" she wanted to know.

"My aunt is not well. She has a weak heart, and it is better for her not to travel. However, she told me that she would come if I needed to stay longer or be admitted for surgery."

"Since you plan to stay the week, I would like to be paid in advance. I could use the money." I carefully counted out my money. I wanted to convey the impression that I too had very little money, which was true, but was willing to pay in advance because I did not wish to incur a debt.

"Aren't you going to unpack?" Pani Szklarzewicz asked. "What are you carrying around in that greasy brown paper?"

I opened the suitcase and pulled out the bag of bread and the greasy package. "This is a roasted chicken my aunt baked yesterday."

"Ah, country bread. It is so expensive. I can no longer afford to buy it."

"Perhaps, should I need to stay longer, my aunt will send us another one," I ventured.

Later, while we were sitting at the kitchen table drinking tea, I returned to the delicate subject of my illness. "My aunt thinks that I may require treatment. If that is needed, and my aunt says it is always preferable to surgery, I will have to look for a job. My aunt has very little money."

"Money. Who has money?" Pani Szklarzewica's replied. "They have all the money, and we have to survive without it as best we can."

When Pani Szklarzewicz and I had each eaten one slice of the bread, she proceeded to pack away the rest. "I am going to leave some for my son," she said.

"Does your son live close by?" I asked.

"He lives with me. If not for him, I could not afford to pay the rent for this apartment. I have lived here for more than thirty years. They stopped my pension. They are our rulers, and they are turning us into beggars. These are bad times."

The bedroom was long and narrow. The two beds were pushed against the wall with their headboards against one another. It felt wonderful to put my head on a pillow, and I slept soundly and late into the morning.

Pani Szklarzewica, dressed in a bathrobe and shuffling around in worn slippers, her hair in pin curls, seemed less friendly than on the previous evening. "Don't expect us to feed you," she said. "You may have some tea with the bread you brought. About the chicken—how long have you been dragging it about?"

"It was cooked the day before yesterday."

"It's tasty, but not very fresh. My son said it must be eaten by today."

"Of course, please share it with me so that it will be gone by this evening."

The lady wanted to know the name of the doctor I was planning to consult. I explained that, due to our depleted resources, it would have to be a hospital clinic.

"Yes, I thought so. Your best bet is the clinic at the Holy Lazarus Hospital. They will have a throat specialist on the hospital staff. Did your aunt tell you to go there?" I had heard the name before, and I was grateful that Pani Szklarzewicz had given me a name and a location I could fasten on.

"Yes," I answered. "Aunt Jadwiga thought I should try that clinic, but she warned me that I shall have to be patient, because it might be difficult to gain access to a specialist if I register as a clinic patient."

I spent most of the next day trying to find the Holy Lazarus Hospital. Having located the outpatient clinic, I observed that there were a large number of patients sitting or standing inside the waiting room, with an overflow waiting outside. The people I saw were in various stages of distress. All were holding numbers. A woman told me that I was wasting my time: the clinic was closed for the day but would open again on the following morning. While contemplating my next step, I saw a nun in a white habit ushering some people out of the office. She turned to the waiting crowd and informed them that, except for emergency cases, all waiting patients would have to return on the following day. She said that the clinic was inadequately staffed, and the few available doctors were working to capacity. Everyone should hold on to their numbers because they would be honored in sequence.

When I returned to the apartment in the late afternoon, I met Pani Szklarzewica's son. He was in his late forties, tall and dark haired like his mother, but he was fat and soft looking. He worked in the municipal department of weights and measures, in what he referred to as a demoted position. He said that German civil servants were now in charge of the department and that his immediate superior was a Volksdeutsch. He asked me many questions—too many, I thought—and I was careful not to say anything that would be at variance with what I had said on the previous day to his mother. Though I faced him while he was addressing me, I was mindful to keep my eyelids lowered.

"Strange. I think it is strange," he said to his mother, "to send a young girl from a good family without supervision to our large city."

"It's the war. Nothing is normal," his mother responded. Changing the subject suddenly, he turned to me, and asked, "What makes you think your father is alive?"

"After the invasion my aunt had word that his regiment had crossed a border."

"Where was that?"

"My aunt thinks it was perhaps Rumania, but she was told that to know less would be better for everyone."

"Why look for work in Krakow?" he continued. "There are enough unskilled people looking for work."

"We were advised that I would need surgery, but my aunt thinks that perhaps with appropriate medical treatment surgery could be avoided."

"What kind of work will you be looking for?" he probed.

"I shall have to see the doctor first. If surgery is necessary, my aunt will come, and she will decide what I must do. If lengthy treatment is involved, I might be able to find work as a nursemaid."

The son did not like me. He informed me that he was law abiding and that the law required him to register with the police any visitor who spent more than one night on his premises. He asked to see my Kennkarte, and he told me that he would return it to me on the following day. Throughout the night, I slept fitfully. I awoke several times, my heart pounding, to the soothing, snoring sounds of Pani Szklarzewicz. In the morning when I walked into the kitchen and saw my Kennkarte on the table, I felt reassured that I had succeeded in camouflaging my anxiety.

## NOVEMBER 1942 ✍ KRAKOW, OCCUPIED POLAND

In an attempt to make myself inconspicuous, I stayed out most of the day. I studied the employment columns, and I investigated leads that I deemed safe. Several of the Polish mothers or grandmothers who were looking for help did not think that I would be the right person for the job. There was something about me that immediately put them on guard. They did not want to interview me, or even ask me to come in. I decided that I would say only the bare essentials. That, too, backfired. One woman, who appeared to be less antagonistic than some of the previous prospective employers, told me that I seemed to be a rather pleasant person, but that her little boy and her five-year-old girl, who was a chatterbox, would not be happy with some one who was less than articulate.

When at a loss of where to go, or when I felt tired because I always needed to walk at a brisk pace, I entered a church. I carefully monitored my money, but since most of the time I was in a state of anxiety, I hardly ever felt hungry. However, I did suffer from the lack of warm clothes. I had, in accordance with my arrangement with Jerzy, written to our contact person, Pan K. I enclosed my address in the hope that my aunt Jadwiga—Mother—would write to me. I knew that Mother would find a way to acquire some warm clothing. Perhaps she had by now arranged to have our winter coats forwarded.

I dreaded the evenings. Invariably Pan Szklarzewicz wanted to know if I had managed to see the laryngologist at the clinic. I had in fact spent another day at the Holy Lazarus Hospital clinic—without registering as a patient.

There were always large crowds of people waiting to see the physicians. I learned that at times it took weeks to get an appointment to see a certain specialist. I realized that my unresolved situation could not continue in view of Pan Szklarzewicz's mounting suspicion.

On Monday morning, after spending an uncomfortable Sunday sitting and kneeling in cold churches, I registered at the clinic of Holy Lazarus Hospital clinic. For years I had suffered from adenoidal distress, but my physical discomfort, compared to the turmoil of our lives during the past five years, was of such low priority that I hardly mentioned it. I decided to use this discomfort to justify an appointment with an ear, nose, and throat specialist. I was given a number. I would have to show up every morning and register, and I would then receive instruction concerning the rest of the day. It meant that either I could not be seen that day and could leave, or I would have to stay and wait to see if a doctor was available. The hospital routine would give me a respite for the next several days. I was able to return to the Szklarzewicz home without having to make up excuses. One afternoon I managed to sit in a chair for more than two hours and read a book from a bookshelf in the hospital waiting room. But on the following day, reality shattered my illusion of safety.

I was sitting in the hospital waiting room, crowded between a heavy-set peasant woman and a well-dressed young man in a dark velour hat that covered most of his face, when a Polish police detail marched into the room. My hand over my ear, I pretended to doze. I sat up when a light was flashed on my face. A policeman barked, "Identification papers." He wanted to know the nature of my illness and the duration of my visit to Krakow. I was holding the registration number in my hand, and I made sure that it was visible. Since I was in "pain," I confined myself to monosyllabic responses. There were perhaps forty people in the waiting room. I noted that the persons who were questioned and whose documents were examined were randomly selected: the woman on my right was passed by; the well-dressed young man on my left was thoroughly interrogated. He was suffering from a heart ailment. When the police left. I heard the nun grumble, "Is there no sacred space and no protection from them?"

The young man was visibly shaken and whispered in my ear, "This time lucky." He was handsome, an educated Pole. He reminded me of the young men I had known in Krosno—before the armband made it difficult for me to consort with Gentiles—who were smarting under the German yoke. It was not his remark that had jolted my nervous system to an extra alert; it was the look in his eyes that frightened me. He was telling me that he knew. During our short exchange, following his remark, he indicated that he, too, had something to hide. I was suspicious because since the occupation one did not speak to a stranger about such matters. The older woman sitting across from me said to her neighbor, "They were looking for Jews." I heard a male voice say, "They are finished with the Jews. Now they will come after us." I felt relieved when I was told to come back the following morning. I rose, nodded to the young man on my left, and hoped that I would not see him again.

Pan Szklarzewicz asked me if I had written to my aunt, since I might shortly be admitted to the hospital. He wanted to know who would be giving consent for my surgery. I had not thought of this, but on the following day I mailed a letter to Mother. I wrote that I thought it would be beneficial for me if she would make a brief appearance.

The doctor who examined me, Dr. Leszczynsky, was chief of the laryngology department, and I learned that after examining the patients, he referred them to his assistants for treatment or surgery. He examined my throat, nose, and ears, and then he checked my heart. He looked at my chart, and once more he examined my heart. My fear of being found out was great. He placed a hand on my arm and said, "There is good reason for your headaches. Relatively minor surgery will give you considerable relief." Then he added something about being safe. Had he said that surgery would be safe, or I would be safe? I was almost certain that it was the latter, but I did not acknowledge this, not even with a glance. He sat down behind his desk, and he made some notes, while I dressed. He pressed a buzzer, and a Sister responded. He gave her the chart and told her that he would perform the surgery. He called me Krystyna and told me that from now on all further arrangements should be made with Sister Ursula.

Sister Ursula gave me a note stating that I was scheduled for surgery. She advised that for the next three days I could not be admitted because all beds were occupied. I would have to come in daily to affirm my availability. She thought that on the third day a bed might be vacant, and I would be informed in advance when I was to arrive for surgery and what personal articles I should bring.

I felt immensely grateful. I had somehow cleared a hurdle that had seemed insurmountable. Though I had not eaten, I felt no hunger, only a guarded sense of elation. I needed to be in a church to send up a prayer of gratitude and review what the doctor had said, and I wanted to delay for several hours being questioned by Pan Szklarzewicz. Even though I had previously seen Germans visiting Kosciol Mariacki, the big Roman Catholic cathedral and a Krakow landmark, I recklessly entered the heated church.

Next day, when I opened the apartment door with my key, I heard voices coming from the dining room. There was laughter and the voice responding was my mother's. I knocked on the dining-room door and entered. There was my mother having tea with Pani and Pan Szklarzewicz. During the interminable hours of the past week that I had spent in Pan Szklarzewicz's company, I had not seen him smile or heard him utter a kind word to me. All of a sudden he had become a charming man. I thought he was even flirting with my mother.

I kissed my aunt's hand, as was the custom, and she embraced me and stroked my hair. She was carefully dressed, in accordance with Polish wartime elegance, which meant that every piece of clothing had been turned inside out and then refashioned. Mother was wearing the same navy velour hat that she had worn on her last day in Germany when she had returned from her visit to the American consulate in Berlin. It had been remade and reshaped. Knowing Mother and her determination once she decided to do something, she had probably accomplished the task herself. I had not seen Mother since my departure from Szczucin. She looked different. Perhaps it was the hat.

Pani Szklarzewicz said that since Pani Dembicka was spending but one night in Krakow and I had much to tell her, she would spend the night in the apartment. Both my aunt and I could sleep in my bed. I was delighted. Mother had brought along the desired country bread and also a small amount of butter. Mother wanted to keep me company in the kitchen while I ate some of the bread with my tea, and since Pan Szklarzewicz left early in the morning, Mother walked up to him to bid him good-bye. I was astonished. The man was suddenly standing upright. He almost looked handsome as he bent over my mother's hand and kissed it. He urged her to return soon, to stay at the apartment, and to sleep in my bed while I was at the hospital. He even called her Pani Capitanowa—wife of a captain in the armed forces. Mother waved a finger and said not to call her that. This was not the time for titles, but with God's help, the time would surely come.

I sat down at the kitchen table. Mother sat down next to me. She still had not removed the hat. I reached up and took it off, and my mother reflexively slapped my face. I felt unnerved. It was not the sharp slap on my face that shook me up—in the past Mother had used this tool to enforce obedience—it was the condition of her scalp. Except for a red stubble, all her formerly black beautiful hair was gone.

"What happened?" I whispered. Before Mother answered, she lectured me about the dangers of being thoughtless. What did I think would have happened if I had done that in the dining room in front of the others? Well, I hadn't, I said to myself, but I had been tempted, and I should have known better.

Mother told me that she had tried to use the same proportion of peroxide, water, and ammonia that she had used on my hair, but while my hair turned blond, her hair became even redder. It was rumored that many black-haired Jews who tried to dye their hair blond in an attempt to pass as Christians had become redheaded instead. Mother seemed to be one of these casualties. In an attempt to overcome the problem, Mother changed the proportions. On the morning following the new application, her abundant hair was on her pillow. She had become totally bald.

She had not dared to leave the house, but upon receipt of my letter, she had decided to take a chance and come to Krakow to affirm my legitimacy. She had not intended to spend the night, but since I returned so late in the afternoon, she agreed to accept the Szklarzewicz hospitality. Mother wondered whether I appreciated the good fortune that had directed me to the Szklarzewicz household. They considered themselves to be part of the Polish minor aristocracy. Pani Szklarzewica's husband had been an army officer in World War I, so the ladies had much in common. Also, both she and my mother had graduated from a Polish gymnasium. In contrast to my limited Polish vocabulary, Mother's was vast, and while my accent was strange, Mother's diction was perfect. I hoped Mother's visit would assuage Pan Szklarzewicz's suspicions regarding my speech, and that his questions about my past would cease.

During the short time we had alone, before we went to the bedroom I shared with Pani Szklarzewicz, Mother and I exchanged important news. The doctor had not asked for my aunt's consent to do the surgery, so Mother would not have to appear. Mother told me that Bolek had come out to the farm when he knew that I was gone. He told Mother and Aunt Regina that the county commissioner had questioned him. He was told that someone in the office had accused me of being Jewish and of hiding out. He had answered that this was nonsense, pure invention, and the same thing could happen to anyone who finds himself in need of work or a place to live. Before leaving, he advised my mother and aunt to leave Szczucin as soon as possible because too many people knew about Pani Jowanczyk's tenants.

Mother told me that soon Aunt Regina and Dollek would be leaving for a village near Myslenice. They had an address that Jerzy and Pan Hyp had helped them get. Both Mother and Aunt Regina felt that the change would be good for Dollek. He had matured rapidly, and he said that he wanted to hide his identity just as his cousin Betus had done. Mother said that Jerzy had been to visit them a second and, perhaps, last time. He told them that he no longer could stay in Tarnow and that boys and men suspected of being Jewish were stopped and forced to drop their trousers. He was afraid that his walk or demeanor would betray him. Looking frightened was an immediate giveaway. He told Mother what had transpired in the Tarnow apartment when I came looking for his help. He explained that Ewa and Maryla thought that for the sake of their safety, Betus would have to leave.

"What did you say?" I asked. Mother shook her head. "It's all part of the Nazis' plan," Mother said. "Everyone is terrified. First they forced us to give up all our possessions; now they are coming for our lives."

I wanted to tell my mother about the fear and the anguish I experienced as I walked the unfamiliar streets in Tarnow, but her only response was that I should not dwell on it. She said that Ewa and Maryla acted as they did because they are struggling to stay alive. Next morning when I left for the hospital, Mother remained behind. We decided that it would be dangerous for us to be seen together, and Mother should depart an hour or so after I had gone.

On Wednesday, Sister Ursula informed me that I would be admitted during the afternoon and that surgery would be performed on Thursday morning.

When I returned to the Szklarzewicz home to pick up my pajamas and some toilet articles, I heard Pani Szklarzewicz mutter to herself, "That will teach my son not to jump to hasty conclusions." When I said good-bye, I kissed her hand, and she kissed my forehead.

The hospital was administered by nuns, and the nurses were Catholic Sisters. After I was admitted, a Sister led me a large ward that contained twenty-four beds. To my surprise, I registered a fever. During the night, I had suffered from uncontrollable vomiting, with simultaneous diarrhea. The doctor said he would postpone surgery until Friday. The medication I received soothed my stomach. Throughout the morning, there were visits from various nuns. Mainly they were concerned about my soul. When did I last confess? I was asked, and how long was it since I had received communion? Why did I not appear at prayers at all times? Why was my spirit troubled? Did I endeavor to live in a state of grace?

After the surgery, for a full twenty-four hours, I did indeed experience a state of grace. The dull pain in my head, in addition to the sharp pain in my nose and throat, obliterated the anxiety that was my steady companion. Fearing that my clumsiness would be readily apparent, I had been avoiding going to confession. But now that I felt drowsy and weak and it was difficult for me to speak, the time was propitious: My condition would disguise my ignorance. I let Sister bring me to the confessional. The elderly priest guided me through the ritual. I could not see his face, but I knew that he could see me, and I prayed that he would not realize something was amiss and that this was my first attempt at confession.

"Father, I have sinned," I mumbled, but even as I said it, I knew that I had not sinned; I was sinned against. Sister met me when I staggered out from behind the drapery. She kissed my forehead and said, "I will wake you early, and you will take Holy Communion on an empty stomach. After that, with the grace of God, you will recover." Compared to going to confession, where I had to worry about saying the appropriate words, as well as confess suitable sins, taking Holy Communion was easy. All a recipient had to do was kneel and in that passive state receive the wafer.

On Sunday afternoon, both Pani and Pan Szklarzewicz came to visit me. It was a very kind gesture. They had to transfer from one streetcar to another to get to the hospital, and on Sunday the streetcars ran on a reduced schedule. I was very grateful because most patients had visitors during visiting hours, and now I was no longer an exception.

Mother came on Monday. She had arrived on Sunday in the late afternoon and slept in my bed. She had brought some of my clothes. She had told Pani Szklarzewicz that it would be good for me to find a position in Krakow. She said that she found it difficult to support me on such a sustained basis. Pani Szklarzewicz agreed. She said that Mother was exceptional; rarely does one find an aunt who takes such good care of a niece, and during wartime even young ladies from families such as ours must find work to eat.

Mother told me that Aunt Regina and Dollek had left Szczucin. The sisters had agreed not to communicate directly. Jerzy would contact Mother whenever Jerzy Hyp thought it was safe to pass on information.

"Regina needs me," Mother said. "Her nerves are shattered, and the weeks of hiding have taken its toll on Dollek. He still pretends to be cocky, but inside he is just a scared little rabbit." Though the Jowanczyk farm was no longer safe, and Pani Jowanczyk was urging Mother to vacate the room, Mother kept delaying her departure because she needed additional time for her hair to grow. When I caught a glimpse of the reddish fuzz of hair, I thought it was an improvement over the red stubble I had seen previously. Still, I had to agree that she could not be seen without her hat.

I was glad when Mother told me that our winter coats, mailed in two separate parcels, had arrived from Krosno, but disappointed that she had not brought my coat. The temperature was dropping, and I felt chilly all the time. Mother explained that we could not wear our coats until the two rabbit fur collars she was presently having dyed gray were ready. Mother feared that the lack of a fur collar could be an identifiable sign.

That night I awoke to being shaken, and when I looked up, I saw Sister bending over me. "You were screaming," she whispered. "What is the matter? Were you dreaming?" I shook my head, and I said I did not remember, but I remembered only too well. I dreamed that my bald Mother was walking between two Gestapo agents. They were leading her away, out of my sight, while I desperately ran after them, trying to reach her.

On the following day I was to be discharged. I went to early Mass, and after chapel I caught the eye of my favorite Sister. "What is it my child?" she asked. "You seem to be troubled."

"Doctor said that I would be discharged today, and I don't have a home to go to. Would it be possible for me to remain here for a while and work in the hospital for my room and board?"

"We cannot employ our patients," Sister said patting my shoulder. "We hardly have enough provisions for our staff, and the number of workers employed by the hospital is regulated by the German occupation authority. They register and supervise all personnel. I wish I could help you, my child."

By noontime, I still had not been discharged. Dr. Leszczynsky, while making his rounds, stopped at my bed. "Sister notes that you have been running a slight temperature," he said. His eyes met mine. "We will make it Thursday. You will have to leave on Thursday."

"Thank you, Doctor," I whispered.

The fact that I had lived for almost a week among Polish women and girls without being subjected to questions regarding my strange pronunciation or faulty grammar had given me some measure of assurance. I thought I was ready to face the task of looking for employment. A young girl in the next bed who had been admitted to the hospital for removal of a kidney stone took the Szklarzewicz telephone number and said she would call me.

When I returned to my temporary home, Pani Szklarzewicz told me that someone named Bogosia had telephoned me. "When you came to us, you said that you did not know anyone," she added. I had thought that having a friend would assuage suspicion regarding my unprotected and friendless predicament, but perhaps I had been reckless, and I decided not to return the call.

The hospital discharge legitimized my unemployed state for several days, and I knew that I had to use the interim to find employment. At a newspaper stand I purchased a newspaper with help-wanted advertisements. My attempts to find work as a housekeeper were not successful. Either the position was already taken, or I did not appear sturdy enough to do the work. My inability to produce letters of recommendation was an additional obstacle. All I could show was my hospital discharge, and that was not sufficient. Moreover, I was reluctant to be contacted at the Szklarzewicz home.

It was out of the question that the aristocratic Pani Szklarzewicz would share her bedroom with a housekeeper. Both she and her son assumed that I was looking for work in an office. They could not understand why someone of my intelligence was rejected for employment. I responded that I was unsuccessful because prospective employers were looking for someone with previous office experience and who knew how to type. Mother and son agreed that perhaps, since I had no office skills, I should look for a position as a nursemaid.

For several days I responded to advertisements in the Polish newspaper for nursemaids. I was not successful. Several of the mothers in need of help rejected me on sight. When I was asked to come in and sit down, I was rejected after answering two or three questions. I tried to revise my answers, but there was something about me that did not meet with approval. In two instances, I was immediately recognized. One prospective employer asked me if I realized that I would put the whole family in jeopardy. Another one called her maid to the door and asked her what she thought. Both the mother and the maid looked me over, and the maid said, "I think what you think." They closed the door before I could respond.

I was desperate. I kneeled on the stone floor in several small, unheated churches, and I fervently prayed to my God not to forsake me. The Szklarzewiczs were unable to understand why after so many days of looking I had not yet landed a job, not even as a nursemaid. I made up a variety of excuses: I did not have experience; I could not produce a recommendation; the position was filled before I got there. I dreaded their questions upon my return to the apartment.

After I had been searching for employment for a week, an advertisement in the Polish newspaper caught my eye. The prospective employer was looking, on a temporary basis, for a companion for a four-year-old boy. There was a proviso: The candidate would have to be able to speak enough German to communicate with, and also to entertain, a young boy who did not speak Polish. I read the advertisement several times before I decided to pursue it.

The address given in the advertisement was in a fashionable neighborhood, and when I rang the doorbell, a Polish housekeeper led me to an elegantly furnished living room and asked me to wait. As she was leaving, she turned back and said, "They are Germans." Within minutes a tall, statuesque woman with heavy, blond hair gathered into a bun at the nape of her neck entered the room. She smiled, stretched out her hand, and said, "*Sprechen sie Deutsch?*" I quickly decided to answer in hesitant, slightly accented German.

She sat down across from me and asked me if I understood that it would be temporary employment.

I said that I did. Frau Ludwig asked me several questions regarding my family and my experiences since the German occupation. She wanted to know if I was bitter and whether I hated all Germans. I phrased my answers carefully, saying that indeed I was bitter and that I had lost my home when all Poles were forced to evacuate the annexed part of Poland. However, I could not say that I hated all Germans, because I had no contact with German people, except for officials of the German occupation authority.

Frau Ludwig was pleased with my proficiency in German. She said that it would be good for Hans, her four-year-old son, to converse with someone who spoke German grammatically. Reflexively my brain sent a warning signal. Since I did not know how to speak German incorrectly, I would have to speak slower and search for less than appropriate words. My interviewer agreed that it was good if children learned a foreign language during their early school years, especially if one lived near the border. She told me that her family had lived in Bremen for several generations and that everyone had studied French in elementary school.

I learned that Herr Ludwig was a highly placed official in the occupation authority. Frau Ludwig was occupied with social engagements and official receptions frequently hosted by Governor-General Frank, which of late she was remiss in attending. For nearly two months she had been recovering from her confinement, after giving birth to little Helmut.

I followed Frau Ludwig through the apartment, past rooms with walls covered with works of art and floors layered with thick Persian rugs. She introduced me to the housekeeper, whom I had met when I rang the doorbell, and to a young woman named Wanda, who was cradling a tiny infant in her arms. I learned that the baby, little Helmut, had arrived early and had been delivered by cesarean section. Fräulein Wanda had been hired three months ago to care for young Hans, because the baby nurse who was expected to come from Bremen had not arrived. Frau Ludwig said that the baby had stopped crying and been content ever since Wanda took him into her arms. Frau Ludwig told me that now everything was falling into place, she would be able to resume her responsibilities, and though Wanda spoke some German, she felt sure that Hans would be better able to communicate with me.

## DECEMBER 1942 ⤳ KRAKOW, OCCUPIED POLAND

I was working. I had a letter, signed by Herr Ludwig, stating that I was a *Kinderfräulein*—a nanny—employed by him. I told the Szklarzewiczs that my employers were Poles. The truth, in their eyes, would have been tantamount to betrayal of Poland. I constructed an elaborate story of a Polish family with two children and both parents working. I made up an address, and I checked the exact location and house number to be sure that it in fact existed. I kept repeating the story to myself to familiarize myself with its details. Each night, I found a different hiding place for Herr Ludwig's letter. During the day, I carried the letter with me. I was sure that if the Szklarzewiczs found the letter, I would immediately be thrown out of their home.

It had been agreed that I would receive only one meal—*Mittagessen*, the main meal at lunchtime—to be eaten with Hans in his room. The housekeeper supplied us with a snack about midmorning before we left for the fresh-air outing in the nearby park. During midafternoon, there was an additional snack. When I left the Ludwig apartment, around six o'clock in the evening, before Herr Ludwig returned home, I was never hungry. I now would be able to earn enough money to pay my rent.

After having searched several weeks for employment in a Polish home and having failed to secure a refuge, it was ironic that I had found respite in a German household. Hans was a delightful little boy, and he reminded me of Dollek when he was that age and of my cousin Josef, who must have been close to seven years old when the ghetto in Bochnia was liquidated. Suppressing these thoughts as best I could, I tried to be responsive to the little boy in my charge. Little Hans was fascinated by the city's transportation system. Horse-drawn vehicles transported all freight for the local population. Residents with means, especially German occupation personnel, did their errands in hackney carriages. "In Bremen," Hans said, "we travel in automobiles. Here in Krakow, my father travels by automobile. He has a chauffeur, but it is not our car."

After working for almost a week in the Ludwig household, I still had not met Herr Ludwig. By the time I arrived in the morning, he had left the apartment. One morning as I approached the house, I saw a tall man dressed in civilian clothes enter a large, dark limousine. The chauffeur stood by, closed the door, and walked around to the driver's seat. I was sure that this was Herr Ludwig.

Sometimes I had the impression that Wanda was avoiding me, though there was little time for conversation. Most of the time when the baby was sleeping, Hans and I were out walking. Both the housekeeper and Wanda lived in the Ludwig apartment. The housekeeper slept in a little room connected to the kitchen, and Wanda slept in the nursery.

During the second week of my employment, Frau Ludwig asked me if I would be able to sleep over on the following Friday. I said that I could, and Frau Ludwig was delighted. She said that with both Wanda and me in the house, she would be able to leisurely get ready for an important late dinner engagement. On Fridays, the housekeeper left after noontime and did not return until Saturday morning. Frau Ludwig had prepared a basket of clothes that needed mending, and she assured us that she did not expect us to complete the task. At about nine o'clock, after having given Hans his bath and made certain he was asleep, I sat down across from Wanda. Between us, on the floor, was the laundry with the clothes that needed mending.

Within minutes I learned the reason for Wanda's reticence toward me. Though Frau Ludwig had been definite when she informed me that I was hired on a temporary basis, she had told Wanda that she had not yet decided which one of us would be let go and which one would remain as the Kinderfräulein for both children. Wanda said that I seemed to have a place to go to after work, whereas she had no other home. She had been given to understand that her position was permanent. I was horror-struck when I learned that Wanda had come from Lwow, after the German army invaded the territory, formerly occupied by the Soviet Union. Her mother had died in childbirth, and she had learned German in school. There was only one difference. While my fictitious father had escaped with his regiment to England, or so it was hoped, her father had been killed during the invasion. Wanda also had an aunt who had been her protector. I steadied my voice as I assured Wanda that I would not jeopardize her position and that if there was even a hint that Frau Ludwig might consider me for the permanent position, I would give notice and would subsequently leave the job, perhaps even the town of Krakow.

Wanda told me that she was twenty years old. During the time of the Russian occupation she had been able to continue with her studies and had graduated from the Lwow gymnasium. I kept sewing and silently nodded occasionally to let Wanda know that I was paying attention to what she was telling me. I decided that I would not reveal more than was already known by the Ludwigs. I told Wanda that I was tired and had not slept well during the previous night. I stood up and was about to walk toward Hans's room where I was to sleep when Wanda stopped me.

"I knew the moment I heard you speak," she said. I shrugged my shoulders, hoping to indicate I did not know what she meant. "You can stop pretending," Wanda insisted. "I am certain."

"I don't know what you mean, and I don't know what you know. Could we leave it at that?" I asked.

I was eager to be alone. I had to assimilate this new and totally unexpected information: Two Jewish girls were living in this German household. I decided to carefully prepare for giving notice. I felt that I had acted properly when I decided not to reveal myself to Wanda, even though she had been willing to put her trust in me. Initially, I had not felt that Wanda was Jewish. What was it about me that awoke suspicion? If only I could identify the foreign aspect, I might be able to camouflage it. I needed to speak to my mother. I needed her counsel, but she had told me that she would hide in Szczucin until her hair grew back.

On Saturday, both of us were engaged in our respective tasks. Sunday was my day off. On the following Wednesday morning when I came to work, I noticed an automobile parked in front of the house. It differed from the limousine I had seen earlier. Perhaps Herr Ludwig had not yet left. I rang the doorbell. The door opened and facing me was a Gestapo agent. I thought he was leaving, and I stepped aside. He had indeed been in the process of leaving, but Frau Ludwig called him back. Pointing to me, she said, "This is Fräulein Krystyna, and this one I am sure of." I felt a piercing stare measuring me from my head to my toes.

"Again you are sure. You said that last night when we came to pick up your nursemaid," the Gestapo agent berated Frau Ludwig. "There is not a shadow of a doubt her documents were forged, and that filthy swine of a Jewess was hiding here, polluting a German family. If it weren't for the letter that was sent to your address, which we were able to trace, she would still be here—perhaps in the process of poisoning your children."

Frau Ludwig was leading the way to the dining room. I heard the baby cry. I looked at Frau Ludwig and asked if she wanted me to go and pick up little Helmut. The Gestapo shouted, "*Stehen bleiben!*"—don't move. He asked to see my documents. I reached for my handbag and was about to extract my Kennkarte, when he pulled the bag out of my hands and emptied the contents onto the table. My Kennkarte, keys, a hospital receipt, a pencil, Herr Ludwig's letter regarding my employment, a rosary, and a small prayer book with colored pictures of the holy family spilled out. He examined my Kennkarte, turned it around, examined it some more, and put it into his jacket pocket. While he was doing that, I kept telling myself to remain steadfast and not to betray myself by showing fear. Frau Ludwig had walked out and was returning. She asked the Gestapo agent if I could take off my coat and go to work. "She is not a Jew," Frau Ludwig declared. "Of that I am certain." He looked at me, took my Kennkarte from his pocket, and looked again at my photograph, at me, and at the information. He turned to Frau Ludwig, and said, "I would not even bet a groschen on her."

Frau Ludwig asked what had happened to Wanda. He answered that she had already been dispatched to Saint Peter. He watched me to see if I had heard and understood his comment. My Kennkarte was still in his hand, and he put it on the dining-room table. Frau Ludwig told him that he would not have to come back because the housekeeper had gathered all of Wanda's possessions and that he could now take them. I was standing there in my coat and hat, trying to look like a young Polish girl with a clear conscience.

"I realize now that I was not careful enough when we hired Wanda," Frau Ludwig said. "She did not have a Kennkarte, but Herr Ludwig said that in the large cities it would take longer before the task of issuing the Kennkarte to every legitimate resident was completed. I should have paid more attention to the documents Wanda showed us."

"Well, all one can say is that it is hoped you have learned your lesson."

"Indeed we have. My whole household is in a turmoil," Frau Ludwig responded. "But you can see for yourself that Fräulein Krystyna's Kennkarte is genuine."

"How can you be so sure? Jews will go to any length to avoid their just punishment."

"You can't assume that every Polish girl is Jewish just because Wanda managed to deceive us," Frau Ludwig reasoned. "We have to hire some Poles to do the work. We can't live here and do all the work ourselves. Besides, you have the means to verify the allegations made in the document. If there is a falsehood, you can find Fräulein Krystyna here during the day, and we have the address of her home."

"I can't agree." The Gestapo agent was adamant. "The only way to be certain is to take her along to Gestapo headquarters. There we will be able to get to the truth. If everything checks out, she will be back, but like I said, I would not bet on it."

He looked at me and barked, "Come with me." I prepared to follow and turned to Frau Ludwig to say good-bye. I heard Hans calling for his mother, and simultaneously the baby crying. Frau Ludwig was clearly upset, and she looked harassed. "My husband is not going to think that this was necessary, since it is really a matter of verification," she insisted.

"When do you go to confession?" he asked. He spoke Polish, and I answered in Polish that I tried to go during the week, mostly Friday after work.

"Communion?"

"Sunday early, before breakfast."

"Recite the Hail Mary," he commanded.

I went down on my knees, crossed myself, looked toward the ceiling, then down at the floor, and recited the Hail Mary. I did it twice and was about to start again, when he stopped me. "Stand up," he directed. "Our Father." Down on my knees again and making the sign of the cross, I prayed fervently. Each word came from my heart as I prayed to "Our Father" to deliver me from the awaiting evil.

I stood up, and I saw that he was sitting, copying information from my Kennkarte. The apostles, he ordered. I recounted the names. There were twelve. Would I remember all the names? He stopped me before I got to all of them and said, "That's strange. It's been years since I last went to church, and I still remember that you start with Peter and Paul when you recite the names of the apostles." He asked several more questions regarding the Epistles in the New Testament. I hoped that I supplied the answers he was looking for.

The Gestapo agent turned to Frau Ludwig, "I want you to know that I am doing this against my better judgment and in deference to Herr Ludwig. I have taken enough information to make the necessary telephone calls, and we will clear up this matter soon enough." He asked for my address. I started to give him the name of my street, but he interrupted me, "Not from you. I'll take that from Frau Ludwig." He wrote the name of the apartment owner and the street and house number into his notebook, verified the information on my Kennkarte once again, and then closed his notebook. He put the Kennkarte back on the table and told Frau Ludwig to expect him back within the next two or three hours. Frau Ludwig responded that she certainly wanted to hear from him, especially since she knew that his suspicion was unwarranted.

He clicked his heels, shouted Heil Hitler, and stood at attention until Frau Ludwig raised her arm, then he left. I took off my coat and asked if I should pick up Helmut. Frau Ludwig said that it would be better if I read to Hans and kept him entertained until noon, and thereafter we could go out for an afternoon in the park.

I reasoned to myself that I had less than an hour to spare. I did not know where the Gestapo had its headquarters, but I thought that by car the distance could be covered within minutes. It would not take long to contact the municipal registrar that covered the village of Iskrzynia, the alleged place of my birth, and ascertain that Krystyna Zolkos did not exist.

Shortly before lunchtime, I approached Frau Ludwig, my hand on my forehead. She knew that I had recently undergone surgery. I told her that I often got headaches that could bring on a nosebleed. I asked her if I could leave for about fifteen minutes to go to the apothecary. The doctor had prescribed drops for my sinuses, but I had stopped taking them.

"It was not an easy morning," Frau Ludwig responded. "I, too, have a headache. Perhaps I can find something in our medicine cabinet."

"I am afraid to take something other than what the doctor prescribed. It's because of the nosebleed. It comes on suddenly, and I would not want Hans to be frightened," I ventured.

"I think you will feel better once you get some food into your stomach. Still, a nosebleed can be messy. There is an apothecary not far from here, on the other side of the street," Frau Ludwig suggested.

"Yes, I know, I have passed it several times."

"All right then, run along, but hurry because I need to rest while Helmut is taking his nap. Hans will be waiting to eat Mittagessen with you." I was heading for the foyer to retrieve my coat and hat. As I walked out, I said, "I won't be long. It will just take a few minutes."

I knew exactly what I had to do. I realized that, subconsciously, I had long ago carefully prepared for it. First of all, I had to get away from the Ludwig neighborhood. I could not go back to the Szklarzewicz home, because they probably had already been, or shortly would be, contacted. I could not be seen rushing through the streets, and I had to walk deliberately, as if on an errand. I would not be able to carry out my plan until early dusk, about four-thirty in the afternoon. I heard church bells and checked my watch. It was noontime. The Ludwig household would be expecting my return.

I took a streetcar, exited after several stops, and tried to orient myself. I vaguely remembered the area. It was not far from Ulica Kremerowska, where Eva had stayed when she lived as an au pair with our cousin Genek. I felt quite weak, and I needed strength to carry out my plan. I stopped at a stand and bought a bowl of soup. I entered the refuge of a dimly lit church, and after genuflecting and crossing myself, I sat down in a pew. I reviewed my options. I could not return to Mother in Szczucin. Jerzy, Ewa, and Maryla no longer lived in Tarnow, and I would not have gone there in any case. All I had to do was to survive until dusk. Then I would take charge of my destiny: I would lie across the railroad tracks and wait for the train that would unite me with Eva. I vaguely remembered the streetcar and subsequent transfer I would have to take to leave town. We had done that several times during my short sojourn in prewar Krakow when, together with friends, we had picnicked in the fields or nearby forest.

I reasoned that Mother would understand my decision because she had on several occasions assured me that, were it not for me and my desire to continue, she would have ended her life after Eva was taken from us. Death, I reasoned, would put an end to my fear and the constant danger. It would be a relief. My one regret was that I could not inform Mother.

It looked as if it was about to rain when I left the church. I thought that was a good omen, because everybody would be intent on getting home. By the time I reached the last stop of the streetcar, it was raining. I kept walking until I saw an embankment in the distance. The railroad tracks were elevated. I took the footpath below to avoid being seen. When I saw the outline of an overpass in the distance, I climbed up and continued walking between the tracks. In the far distance I saw the light of an approaching train. I put down my handbag and stretched out across the track. Though the light was moving closer, there was very little noise. I closed my eyes.

The light was on my face. I was being pushed. I opened my eyes and looked into the face of an old man dressed in overalls. The man had pushed me off the track. He helped me get to my feet. My joints felt stiff, and it was difficult for me to stand. I realized that I was wet to the skin and shivering. The man kept muttering, "Not on my track, no, not on my track." He cursed occasionally, but I did not feel that the curses were directed at me.

By the time I entered his small shack, I had learned that the man was a railroad worker responsible for a line of tracks and that he preferred the night-shift because his supervisor did not like to come out at night. The cabin was very small, and the square space was filled with a narrow cot, a rickety table, a chair, and, next to the chair, a little iron stove. When he threw some coal onto the fire, the flame shot up high and illuminated the shack. I saw that the old man walked with a limp, and I realized why I found it so difficult to understand what he was saying. His mouth was toothless, and he had lit his pipe. Between puffs, I heard him say, "The Germans are doing a good enough job of ridding Poland of young people, and they don't need help from us." He gave me a blanket, and I took off my coat. When I hesitated, he urged me to remove all my wet clothes so that they could dry. He told me that he was old and that there was no need to be afraid. He spread my garments over a clothesline, said something that I did not understand, and walked out.

I remember sitting down on the cot, but must have dozed off because when I woke up, I was curled up on my side. The man was sitting on the chair, and the aroma of ersatz coffee, made from roasted barley grain, filled the cabin. He had not asked me, but he assumed that I had wanted to end my life because of what he called man-trouble. He hinted that even if I was with child, and the man responsible would not marry me, that still was not reason enough to take my life.

"Not only would it be a sin, but isn't there enough killing on Polish soil?" he asked. He had hung my coat and dress upside down. I could tell that they were almost dry. He gave me a tin cup of steaming coffee. I gratefully drank all of it. When I had emptied it, he poured a cup for himself. It was the only cup in the cabin. I looked at my watch. It was four o'clock in the morning. The man said that his shift ended at six o'clock, but that the relief sometimes showed up early. He wanted me to be gone by five o'clock, because if anyone saw me, he would be in trouble on two counts: that he did not detain me and that he did not report the incident.

When I was ready to leave, I thanked the man. He told me to go with

God, and I told him to remain with God, as was the Polish country custom. I quickly bent down and kissed his gnarled hand. He waved a crooked finger at me and said, "No more of this nonsense. Not on my track, or any other track."

I did not feel grateful. As soon as I stepped out into the cold dark morning, the futility of continuing overwhelmed me. I had no place to go to. I was certain that the Gestapo had invaded the Szklarzewicz apartment and confiscated my few belongings. There was nothing in my luggage that could be traced, but the Gestapo agents would find out all they needed to know from the registrar in Iskrzynia. They would be hunting for me. I reasoned that only the Gestapo agent who had so thoroughly looked me over at the Ludwig residence would know what I looked like. The problem was my coat. It could easily be described, and I had no other clothes to change into. It was too early for the streetcars to be running, and it would be dangerous to walk into an empty chapel at this hour in the morning. Was the fact that it had stopped raining a providential message? Could I have contacted my mother without endangering her life? Should I prepare more carefully for the next suicide attempt? I was certain that with no action on my part, I would be picked up on the street as my sister had been. That was the fate I wanted to avoid.

The sky had turned gray, and when I got closer, I saw a streetcar standing at the end terminal and boarded it. Aside from me, only the driver and two passengers were in the streetcar. When the streetcar reached its terminus, instead of transferring to the trolley that would take me back into town, I entered a nearby chapel for morning prayer. It was not yet seven o'clock, and there were too few pedestrians in the streets. Later in the morning when there were more people rushing about, I would feel safer.

At about nine-thirty, I found myself near the Szklarzewicz apartment house. I knew that Pan Szklarzewicz left for work shortly after eight o'clock, and until about ten o'clock in the morning, Pani Szklarzewicz would be busy with her morning routine. I did not go past the house. I walked toward it, turned, walked around the block, and came back from the other end. I did not see a Gestapo officer in uniform, and I carefully looked to see if there was someone loitering about who could be a Gestapo agent in civilian clothes.

The key to the Szklarzewicz apartment was in my purse. I did not dare use it. On my third attempt to search out anything that might be threatening,

I saw a woman walking toward me. She was carrying a heavy bag. It was my mother. She was wearing the elegant, hardly worn winter coat fashioned of black melton cloth, tailored for us from Aunt Regina's hidden textiles. The collar was trimmed with gray fur. She wore a hat I had not seen before. The coincidence was overwhelming, and I needed to exercise all my restraint to hold back my tears and refrain from showing surprise. I pulled Mother from the street into a church that had sheltered me on several occasions.

Mother said that she had to leave Szczucin suddenly because Bolek came to tell her that there were rumors a woman was living at the Jowanczyk farm who must be a Jew. He had told Mother that he was glad he had been able to help, but unless she disappeared now and was not seen there again, his family's lives, as well as that of Pani Jowanczyk, would be in jeopardy. Mother told me that she had left a suitcase in the Krakow railroad terminal and that the bag she was carrying contained my winter coat. She could not return to Szczucin, and she thought she would stay with me at the Szklarzewicz apartment for several days, just long enough to devise a plan of escape.

I told Mother what had happened to me on the previous day, and Mother agreed that since the Gestapo agent had the Szklarzewicz address and telephone number, it was no longer a refuge. I changed into the warm winter coat made of the same black cloth as that of my mother's and trimmed with the same gray fur; the style, however, differed. We agreed that we should not be seen together. Mother said that she must first find a place for us to spend the night, and I told her about the difficulties I had encountered while looking for a nocleg. We parted, and when we met again, Mother told me that she had found a place. She had paid in advance for two spaces on the floor, and the payment included the use of two blankets for each, one to serve as a mattress and the other as a cover. The proprietor had said that her night guests were not permitted to arrive before dusk.

In the early afternoon, Mother telephoned Pani Szklarzewicz. The lady was very upset that I had not returned the previous evening and that I had not even telephoned. She told Mother that her niece did not uphold the standards that her family was accustomed to. Mother answered that something had happened to me, that I was back in the hospital, and she would come and explain. In a public pay lavatory, Mother carefully applied her makeup and brushed her still short, but now passably colored hair. She looked well put together when she donned her black hat. She took the country bread she had brought along as a present and left me with the now considerably lighter bag that contained only my spring coat.

It took several hours, longer than I had anticipated, before Mother arrived at the church we had designated. It had been a difficult afternoon. All my confidence had evaporated, and on several occasions I had caught myself looking over my shoulder to see if I were being followed. I knew that the ever-present informers looked for this reflexive, nervous movement, signaling fear. In addition, Mother had left me with the bag to carry, another sign identifying someone on the run.

Mother had told Pani Szklarzewicz that I had been caught in a street raid that targeted unemployed young Poles who were then shipped to work in Germany. My weakened state, resulting from the recent surgery, had caused me to faint, fall, and have a nosebleed. She said I had been taken to the hospital, which had contacted her, and she had immediately taken the train to Krakow. The two ladies agreed that these raids had accelerated in the last few months. Almost daily one heard of Poles picked up off the street and enlisted in forced labor details under the guise of some minor infraction of the law. Pani Szklarzewicz told Mother there had been a telephone call for me. The caller had been female, but had not identified herself.

Mother told Pani Szklarzewicz that she would have to go to work because her means of support were vanishing, and she had heard from friends that it would be easier to find employment both for herself and for Krysia in Warsaw. Pani Szklarzewicz agreed and added that she herself was fortunate because of the important position held by her son and his dependable salary, they had been able to retain her apartment and a measure of security. The ladies parted on friendly terms. Mother told me that she had packed up my few belongings and had checked them under my name in the railroad station.

When it started to get dark, we walked on opposite sides of the street toward the nocleg address. The woman ushered us into a dimly lit room, pointed to two spaces on the floor, and walked out. The room was filled with men and women of various ages. After we sat down, Mother and I looked at each other, and I could tell that Mother had noticed the same thing I had: Most of the people around us were Jews. There were several Gentiles, and an informer could easily be among them. Mother was afraid that it was a trap,

and she whispered to me that the woman had said she had twice been subjected to Gestapo raids, but then so was every other nocleg. Each nocleg was
registered with the police and was allowed to operate according to strict rules.
The registered owner was forbidden to harbor anyone for more than one night
unless that person was registered with the police by name and a permanent
address. The rule against giving shelter during the day needed to be maintained by the person operating a nocleg. The law against harboring a Jew was
strictly enforced. It was the proprietor's responsibility to recognize a Jew and
to immediately inform the police.

Exhausted from the previous day and night, I stretched out on the blanket and fell asleep. Mother kept vigil throughout the night, and she could
hardly wait until we escaped from what she called a lethal trap.

When I woke up, at about four o'clock in the morning, Mother whispered that she was determined to leave Krakow as soon as possible and that
we would take the train to Warsaw. "Where in Warsaw?" I asked. "We don't
have an address to go to." Mother told me that Jerzy and his daughters, Ewa
and Maryla, had departed for Warsaw. Living in Tarnow had become too dangerous, Jerzy had told Mother, and he believed Krakow was equally dangerous. For hundreds of years in both cities, Jew and Gentile had lived peaceably
together, but during the past three years, with prodding by the Nazis, many
Poles had made it their business to search out Jews, denounce them, and often
make a profit.

"Jerzy feels that it would be easier to disappear in Warsaw," Mother said,
"and though I do not know the capital well, I did note during my few short
visits that it has a much more cosmopolitan atmosphere than Krakow and perhaps the residents would be less inquisitive into other people's lives."

"Do you know where Jerzy and his daughters live?" I asked.

"No, but even if I did, we could not go there. Jerzy left me a telephone
number of a person who would know where I could reach him, but I have
another resource that I am going to pursue."

Mother told me that during my sojourn in the hospital, while she was
staying at the Szklarzewicz apartment, Pani Szklarzewicz had asked her to come
along and be a fourth at a bridge game. One of the ladies she met there was
Pani Wojchiechowska, whose husband, a colonel in the Polish army, had also
been declared missing. He was presumed to have crossed several borders and

perhaps arrived in England. The women had much in common. Their husbands were officers in the Polish reserve army, and both women were childless. Mother told her that she had assumed the care of her niece, and she was doing all she could to help the young girl. Pani Wojchiechowska said that she also was concerned about her two nieces. Her brother and his wife and two daughters had been expelled from the Baltic region when that sector was annexed to the German Reich. The lady owned an apartment on the outskirts of Warsaw presently occupied by the brother and his family. However, Pani Wojchiechowska said she retained one of the bedrooms for herself. Presently, while she was engaged in a small business venture in Krakow, the room remained locked and at her disposal. Only she and a close friend who lived in the center of Warsaw had the key to the locked room.

Mother told me she remembered Pani Wojchiechowska say that, were she to remain in Krakow through the winter, she might consider renting out her room because she could use the rent money. I was amazed. Mother had managed to plan our escape, and I was more than eager to leave Krakow. When I started to express my elation, Mother immediately stifled my enthusiasm. "I have to tread very carefully," she said. "Ladies meet, they play cards together, and they idly chat. I doubt that Pani Wojchiechowska will remember who I am. I may have to ask Pani Szklarzewicz to intercede for me."

Throughout the day, Mother was busy cajoling and negotiating, but she did manage to obtain from Pani Wojchiechowska a letter of introduction to and the address of Pani Mozejkowa, the woman in Warsaw who had the key to Pani Wojchiechowska's locked room. Mother gave Pani Wojchiechowska the rent for the month of January, plus an extra month's rent as security in case of damage to her property. Pani Wojchiechowska warned Mother that her brother was not going to like this, but that there was nothing he could do about it.

"He lives in my apartment," she said, "and he knows that the room I am renting to you belongs to me. Still, there is the problem of the kitchen and the bathroom. You will have to use the bathroom facilities, but please stay out of my sister-in-law's kitchen. She is not an easy woman to get along with, and you should be prepared for some difficulties."

We spent the night in a different nocleg, and again we were certain some of the people around us were Jews. From muted conversation nearby, we

inferred that the nocleg had been raided the previous night. The speaker reasoned that, since both the owner and her crippled daughter, as well as all the
guests, had been hauled to the police station and the woman had promised
that she would be more careful in the future when she examined the documents of prospective lodgers, one could be relatively safe for the night.

The following day, our last in Krakow, I kept busy rushing from one street
to another, attempting to give the appearance of being purposefully occupied.
Mother was actively engaged preparing for our journey to Warsaw. We planned
to depart in the evening because we wanted to reach our destination on the
following morning, Christmas Eve day.

CHAPTER 8

# Escape to Warsaw

The train ride was long and uneventful. I secured a seat near the window, and Mother sat next to me. We anticipated that our documents would be checked, and it would be better if I refrained from speaking. I would be a mute, a congenital defect, and Mother would speak for both herself and me. I was very tired and quite relieved to have Mother take charge. I wanted to use the time to improve my proficiency in Polish, and I read an adolescent novel I had purchased at a secondhand bookstall. The train made many stops, once for more than two hours. Mother agreed with the other passengers that, though they took our good money for the tickets, no one bothered to come and tell us why we were being delayed. Everyone was cautious, and the grumbling did not go beyond remarks that we were an occupied country.

Twice Mother woke me when a railroad police patrol entered the compartment and asked to see our documents. In both instances, the patrol consisted of two men in uniform and two men in civilian clothes. The latter wore leather trench coats, which marked them as secret police. During the first document check, the policemen asked Mother about the nature of my problem. He wanted to know why I did not sign, and Mother answered that I was not her child and she did not know. She added that I was an orphan and that I had come to live with her after the occupation.

During the second interrogation, the men from the secret police compared our identity documents for what seemed to be an unreasonably long period of time. They asked why my documents were up to date and issued in Szczucin, whereas those of the woman I was living with were issued in Krosno and would soon become invalid. Mother explained that she had been ill with pneumonia and had been recovering on a farm in Szczucin. Mother added that she had been too ill to walk to the municipal office, and there had been no means of transportation. The two plainclothes policemen discussed Mother's white identity card. One of them said Mother should not delay obtaining the Kennkarte once we arrived in Warsaw. While our documents were being scrutinized, the uniformed policemen checked the documents of the other passengers. It seemed to me that after the second document check, the atmosphere in the compartment changed. The other passengers spoke to each other, but no one addressed Mother directly. There had been too much explaining, and perhaps suspicion had been aroused. Mother, her eyes closed, pretended to rest.

Though we had been scheduled to arrive in Warsaw in the morning, due to the many delays, we did not reach our destination until afternoon. The Warsaw railroad terminal was vast and intimidating. Harassed passengers, carrying luggage, boxes, and crates, were arriving and departing. German civilians and members of the German armed forces traveled in separate railroad cars. They were elegantly dressed and did not carry heavy baggage, but all travelers merged while rushing to the numerous platforms. I had not seen a railroad terminal of such vastness since my childhood visits to Berlin. There were numerous tracks for long distance as well as local trains.

While we were waiting in line to surrender our train tickets, we noticed several groups of people talking to each other. Suddenly, a member of a group would dart toward an individual and ask to see identification papers. In one instance, the group member apparently signaled the others, because within seconds the individual accused was surrounded and taken away. The atmosphere was treacherous. An elderly woman who had stopped to see what was happening was approached while we rushed past her. As we walked toward the baggage check, we saw people picked out of the milling crowd and led away.

Because I was ostensibly mute, I did not dare speak until after we checked our luggage and walked out onto the street. I felt as if I had been holding my breath, though I knew I had been breathing all along. I was no longer sure that Mother's decision to move to Warsaw was well thought out. I told Mother that I did not think the people we had seen being led away looked Jewish. Mother told me this was not the time to think about what we had witnessed, and I would have to compose myself because my anxiety was showing. "How?" I asked.

"It's in your eyes and your movements," Mother said. "You keep looking sideways as if wondering whether we are being watched, and even in the way you move you project fear and insecurity. Look at the Poles surrounding us and try to emulate their carefree attitude. For most of them life is difficult, yet they chat and laugh easily. We must adapt no matter how difficult in order to avoid detection."

Mother added that since the moment she found me walking near the Szklarzewicz house in Krakow, she had noted a change in me and she was unhappy about it. I tried to explain what I had been through during that devastating encounter with the Gestapo agent and that I had wanted to end my life. Mother put up her hand to indicate that she did not want to hear about it.

"That's in the past," Mother said. "I hope that you have not forgotten what you said to me when Eva was taken from us. I thought we had agreed that we would make every effort to avoid being caught. Think of Mennek and the trust he placed in us. Does a sixteen-year-old Polish girl look as if she were carrying the weight of the world on her shoulders? That is what you have been projecting, and that has to stop. Besides, if the worst should come to pass, you now have the capsule, and your fate is in your hands. There will be no more railroad tracks."

Mother had spoken in a low voice, but her tone was curt and the reproach stinging. Still, I knew she was right. I straightened my shoulders, and I attempted to stride out, rather than drag my feet. Within, my heart felt shrunken, and the dull pain in my stomach was ever-present.

Mother was stunned when she saw the damage this once proud and elegant Polish capital had sustained. The upper stories of some of the tallest buildings were missing. A blanket of dirty snow covered mounds of debris. It was dusk on Christmas Eve, when we arrived at Pani Mozejkowa's building. This fashionable area had been spared during the invasion. Mother rang the bell. After a short interval, the street door was opened by the concierge who informed us that Pani Mozejkowa was not at home and would undoubtedly return before curfew. He said we should come back later. He wanted to know if we were expected, and when Mother hesitated, he grumbled, "It's Christmas Eve." Mother said she was sorry; Pani Mozejkowa had been apprised of our arrival, but several train delays had prevented us from arriving in the morning. Mother said that we were tired and would like to sit down, and as she said this, she put some money into the man's hand.

We followed the man into a courtyard and down a staircase to his living quarters below ground level. He opened the door to a kitchen, and when we entered I saw his wife standing at a table chopping cabbage. I got a whiff of clean, soapy steam coming from a huge laundry kettle standing in the middle of the kitchen stove. Diapers were drying on lines strung throughout the kitchen. The man placed a narrow bench against the wall in the passageway leading to the kitchen. Mother and I sat close to each other in the cold, dimly lit, narrow cellar hall. We pressed against each other for warmth, and we encouraged each other to keep our hands and feet moving.

While we waited, the doorbell rang several times. Each time, the man went up to open the outer street door and returned several minutes later. In prewar Poland, I had observed that it was important to tip the concierge each time he opened the door. Omitting the expected tip could seriously jeopardize the comfort of the dependent tenant. One tipped only when entering a building. A departing tenant or visitor could open the door himself from inside.

Shortly before seven o'clock in the evening, the concierge walked toward us with the elegantly attired Pani Mozejkowa. She was angry, and she immediately berated Mother for her impudence. Even after she read Pani Wojchiechowska's letter, she was unable to control her temper. She asked, in front of the concierge, if we realized it was Christmas Eve.

Mother was at her best. She calmly explained that we did know that it was Christmas Eve, but our arrival was delayed due to circumstances beyond our control. After all, we were living in an occupied country, and since the invasion, for many of us the celebration of Christmas was severely circumscribed. In a more subdued voice, Pani Mozejkowa explained that she could not possibly accomplish anything after curfew, and knowing Pani Wojchiechowska's sister-in-law, she was loath to contact her by telephone on Christmas Eve. She said as sure as "ice in winter" there would be severe resistance and angry tantrums. Mother said that due to the late hour, we were rather helpless and we would only need a corner to get us through the night. The lady responded by telling us that she could not take us up to her small apartment because there was no vacant corner. After conferring with the concierge, and after the concierge had consulted his wife, Pani Mozejkowa informed us that both the man and his wife had agreed, in the spirit of Christmas, to let us spend the night sitting in their warm kitchen.

The wife supplemented their income by taking in laundry and was ironing shirts with an iron filled with charcoal. There was no Christmas tree, and the little three-year-old girl, I was certain, would have liked for me to speak to her. In return for some additional money, the woman gave each of us a slice of bread and some black coffee. The husband told us that Pani Mozejkowa was an important person. She was the official block warden for the apartment house and for several other buildings on the street. She was required by the occupation authority to register all transients with the police, even those who stayed only for one night within the area of her jurisdiction. It was her task to report all people whose documents seemed suspicious.

Early on Christmas Day, Pani Mozejkowa came to fetch us. She was dressed in a well-tailored fur-trimmed gray suit and green felt hat with a red feather. The heavy scent of her perfume seemed out of place amidst the poverty of the kitchen. She took us up to her apartment to examine our documents. The door to her bedroom was closed; however, the room we entered was furnished luxuriously. White French provincial chairs covered in rose-colored damask were grouped around tables with fine wooden inlays. The uncomfortable looking sofa was also covered with a damask textile. The paintings on the walls and the many crucifixes looked like museum pieces. We stood and admired our surroundings while Pani Mozejkowa scrutinized our documents.

"We might as well get it over with," she said. "It's almost a one-hour ride, and we must take two streetcars to get there. I expect you to pay for me, also for the return trip."

"Of course," Mother answered.

Pani Wojchiechowska's apartment house complex was located in the Mokotow section, a suburb of Warsaw. There were about twelve three-story attached or semiattached gray stucco buildings. They were arranged in an oblong design, facing each other across a grass-covered interior courtyard framed by bushes and evergreens. All apartments were individually owned. The Mlodzianowski family who occupied Pani Wojchiechowska's apartment consisted of mother, father, and two daughters. Pani Mlodzianowska, the sister-in-law, greeted our escort with a scowl before even learning the nature of her mission. She was a severe-looking lady in her late forties. Everything about her—face, hair, and the peasant-type clothing on her broad frame—was gray and forbidding. An argument ensued between the two women, with the husband and the two daughters standing within the apartment and the three of us in front of the door.

Pani Mlodzianowska, her hands on broad hips, shouted, "We abided by our agreement, and we have allowed the room to remain empty, while we are crowded with two grown daughters in two and a half rooms and a kitchen. We don't want strangers living with us."

"You only pay rent for two and a half rooms and the kitchen," Pani Mozejkowa answered, "and you never pay the rent money on time. How do you expect your sister-in-law to cover the expenses? Besides, you seem to have forgotten that she took you in when you were homeless."

"Another two people to use the bathroom when we experience difficulties in getting enough bathwater for ourselves."

"The niece will only remain until after the New Year," Pani Mozejkowa explained, "and you should trust your sister-in-law to have been careful when she selected someone to use her room and her personal possessions. She needs the money. Would it have been better had she selected a man to come and live in her room? Please remember that Pani Dembicka must be a good and trustworthy friend."


## JANUARY 1943 ⋘ WARSAW, OCCUPIED POLAND

The narrow well-furnished room was unheated. Mother and I slept in the single bed, our bodies pressed against each other for warmth. The radiator under the large picture window was ice cold. The rest of the apartment was heated, but since we were forbidden to use the kitchen and our use of the bathroom was frowned upon, the only relatively warm refuge remained churches.

To reach the center of Warsaw, one took the Rakowiecka streetcar at the

Mokotow terminus, the last station of that streetcar line, and transferred at Ulica Pulawska to the streetcar that terminated at Ulica Marshalkowska, one of the main boulevards of the city. From there we could walk, and as we did, we got to know the city. Mother remembered important landmarks from her prewar visits to Warsaw, and she also remembered that throughout the city there were well-maintained pay bathrooms for men and women.

Mother told me that our money was running out. I would have to go to work as soon as something suitable could be found. Pani Mozejkowa had mentioned that one of her many friends might be in need of a servant. Mother and I agreed that it would be better if I could get a position as a nanny. Children would notice less my awkward grammar and diction. Mother must, Pani Mozejkowa had warned, secure the Kennkarte. The original deadline to obtain the document had already passed, but due to some early snowfall and resulting transportation problems, that deadline had been extended. Mother was also eager to make contact with our friend Jerzy. She hoped that the telephone number he had left with her would help her trace him. We were alone, without money, and living in a hostile environment.

We retrieved our luggage and registered with the block warden. Once registered, we were also able to obtain a limited number of food stamps. A more adequate number of food stamps could only be gotten through a qualified employer who contributed to the war effort. The headlines boasted that the war on the eastern front was going well for the Wehrmacht and poorly for the Russian army. During the next several days, our refuge on Ulica Falata, though very cold, was a treasured respite. Through our large casement window, we looked at the exact duplicate of our building. Between the two buildings was a wide strip of grass with benches and shade trees. Though covered with snow, it was a lovely setting.

We tried to be as unobtrusive as possible, but Pani Mlodzianowska retained her hostile stance. When we met face to face, she would not acknowledge our greeting, and her dislike of us was obvious. Her husband remained aloof. He did incline his head when we crossed his path, thus acknowledging our existence. He even murmured some words that could be construed as a greeting. The older daughter, Krystyna, my namesake, referred to by the family as Krysia, was perhaps two years my senior. She slept in a small room, the prewar maid's room, adjacent to the kitchen. She was about five foot three, well proportioned, and quite attractive. The curly blond hair framing her ob-long face was swept up in the back and pinned at the top. This type of hairdo was in vogue because it made costly professional hairstyling unnecessary. When we did exchange some pleasantries, I kept my guard up, because I noticed that, though her green eyes would light up at times, the corners of her mouth re-mained turned down.

Danuta, the other daughter, was one year younger than I. She was called Danka, and we knew immediately that we liked each other. Danka was tall and broad framed like her father, but unlike her stolid-looking father who walked with a heavy gait, Danka was light-footed, graceful, and chic. It was obvious that she spent much time on her appearance. Her light blond hair was attractively short—she cut it herself, she told me—and obviously bleached. She used eye makeup to darken her eyelashes and emphasize her large green eyes. She wore a short winter coat that displayed her long, straight legs to advantage. Mother said that she was handsome as well as charming, just like her aunt, Pani Wojchiechowska. Danka and I knew that attempts to know each other better should be kept hidden from her family, as well as from my Aunt Jadwiga.

Mother and I were now very careful when referring to each other. At all times, even in the privacy of our room, I addressed Mother as Aunt Jadzia. Mother in turn tried to treat me as one would a niece. When I mentioned to her with some enthusiasm my pleasant encounters with Danka, Mother cau-tioned against any type of intimacy, even in casual conversation. I disagreed, but Mother was adamant. She felt that I would not be able to camouflage my inadequate Polish vocabulary, and my strange accent could lead to questions that might entangle me in a web of unwanted fabrications.

My mother's worry regarding my language problems, as well as my own constant fear, was renewing my violent stomach cramps. Mother wanted me to refrain from speaking, and she tried to explain my silence by saying that I was shy. On the other hand, it was crucial that I find work. Mother had as-sured Pani Mozejkowa, and she in turn had assured the Mlodzianowski family, that the only tenant occupying Pani Wojchiechowska's room would be Pani Jadwiga Dembicka, and that her niece would depart shortly for a sleep-in position.

Mother did not seem to realize that each time she referred to my language problems, she diminished my already shaky self-confidence. I felt immediately drawn to Danka, and I perceived that Danka liked me. She had not mentioned my accent, and when I told her that I had been brought up in Polish Silesia and expelled when the territory was annexed to the German Reich, she reacted with sympathy and without a trace of suspicion. Still, Mother was unyielding in her insistence that I distance myself from Danka while at the same time urging me to begin going out for job interviews.


Mother and I were very careful when we walked in the streets. We did not walk together. Wearing winter coats fashioned of the same cloth emphasized our connectedness. Though I had some of my father's features and Mother was taller than I, there was a physical resemblance. In addition, both of us had bleached, not quite natural-looking hair. When we boarded the overcrowded streetcars, we used different entrances. After noticing that some people turned around to get a better look at us, we made a decision to maintain an even greater distance between us when outside our room.

That January the temperature in Warsaw dropped to a record low. Except for Poles connected to, or working for, the German occupation authority, the residents of Warsaw endured great hardship. It was beyond our comprehension that, in spite of lack of coal, inadequate clothing, and the continuous effort needed to get enough food, so many Poles were helping the Nazis round up Jews who had escaped from the Warsaw ghetto. A small number of ghetto inmates, perhaps those with resources or those who were fortunate enough to contact sympathetic Polish friends, had managed to escape. The danger that they, as well as we, needed to avoid was the large number of Polish informers. To the average German soldier or bureaucrat, a Polish Jew looked the same as any other Pole and spoke the same incomprehensible language; the Nazis depended on Polish informants. There were, of course, specially trained German units, such as the Gestapo, who were charged with the task of carrying out the avowed Nazi mission to not allow a single Jew to survive.

We knew at that time that almost all the ghettos in Poland had been liquidated without leaving a trail that would disclose the fate of the evacuated inmates. The only news that we had been able to obtain about the large Krakow-Plaszow ghetto, into which most members of my father's immediate and extended family had been herded, was that people had been separated into useful and useless groups and subsequently shipped to unknown destinations. The Warsaw ghetto, located in the Nalewki section, an area that had been home to the Jewish poor, was in the process of being liquidated. Ghetto inmates were being transported to what were euphemistically called work camps. By that time, the inmates knew that Treblinka and Auschwitz were not work camps but death camps for Jews. It was rumored that Jews within the Warsaw ghetto were refusing to leave on daily work details, because transports, ostensibly going to work, had not returned.

Mother could not locate Jerzy. She did not know if Aunt Regina and Dollek had succeeded in reaching their destination. I was supposed to banish all these dark thoughts from my mind while outside the walls of our room. Mother continued to urge me to look for a job. She was unable to provide food for us. At about that time, I missed my period twice. Mother asked silly questions, and when I assured her I could not have been impregnated, she decided that the cause was lack of nourishment.

On a brisk Wednesday morning toward the end of January, I boarded the two trams that would take me to the Warsaw business district. We had seen an advertisement from a florist in the help-wanted section of a Warsaw daily newspaper. The flower shop was located on Aleje Jerozolimski, the most fashionable sector of Warsaw. The two shop windows displayed a profusion of exotic flowers in the depth of winter. Within the store, the warmth, moisture, and floral scents were intoxicating. I just barely had a whiff before a woman, perhaps the manager, said that the position was no longer available. In back of the store, in an adjacent office, sat an elegantly dressed man. I had glanced in that direction when I entered, and I had seen the man incline his head in a negative motion. Once outside, the cold air quickly dried the tears that had sprung up in my eyes. I attempted to comfort myself by telling myself that the job could have been filled, but I knew better.

Walking briskly, I observed the busy activity of people rushing in all directions. On both sides of the broad tree-lined boulevard the buildings were tall and well maintained, and the shop windows displayed fashionable clothes and hats. There seemed to be quite a lot of fraternization between Polish civilians and the German military. Though there were a considerable number of

German women, it seemed to me that the majority of the elegantly clad women escorted by German officers and leather-coated German civilians were Poles. It was alarming to note that the hated invader, the German occupier of Polish soil, was so comfortably entrenched amidst the Polish population of Poland's capital.

At about eleven o'clock on that same morning, I rang the doorbell at an apartment on Ulica Wspolna. A working mother was looking for a nanny with some experience and references to care for an eighteen-month-old. I thought that I would be able to satisfy the experience requirement, and I would somehow overcome the lack of references. The young woman did not even want to hear about my work experience. When she found out that I had not brought references, as had been requested in the advertisement, she walked me back to the door.

I answered a number of help-wanted advertisements during the next week and encountered rejection in various guises. There were some prospective employers who looked me over and said that they did not think I could fill the position. One prospective employer berated me for entering his establishment. Another interviewer, a poorly dressed man in his early seventies, cursed at me while reaching for the telephone. Several times I thought I was being followed. I turned around to look. I knew that by turning I was betraying myself. Mother said that I should, for the time being, stop going on job interviews. She would try to contact Pani Mozejkowa by telephone, our only available resource. Reluctantly, she agreed to help. She had heard from an acquaintance of someone who was looking for a sleep-in maid. When she gave Mother the name and address, she added she wanted nothing further to do with the matter.

Pani Mozejkowa told Mother that Pani Gregormirskowa, an aristocratic Russian woman, would be a demanding employer but would treat me fairly if I worked hard. The lady lived on the fourth floor of an old, well-maintained apartment house in the vicinity of Kosciol Swietego Krzyza—Church of the Holy Cross. She immediately told me that she had not placed an advertisement in the newspaper because, "I do not want some Jewish escapee from the ghetto to use my home as a refuge." She said that she usually required references from someone who was to live in her home, but because her friend said that Pani Mozejkowa had interceded on my behalf, she would make an exception.

I was to sleep in the kitchen on a folding cot that must be returned to an adjacent closet by six o'clock, when I was to start the fire in the kitchen stove. Breakfast was to be brought to the bedroom on a tray, no later than seven o'clock. My other responsibilities were to keep the kitchen, large living room, and three bedrooms spotlessly clean, to daily empty the ashes from the four tiled heating stoves, to care for Pani Gregormirskowa's personal laundry, and to cook. The lady looked me over and remarked that she was not sure that I was strong enough to do all the work. Smiling bravely, I assured her that I was strong and that she would be satisfied with my work.

Standing tall and proud, the tightly corseted woman led the way to the living room and stopped at the threshold. Two book-sized pieces of carpet were stationed just past the threshold. Placing each foot on a carpet square, Pani Gregormirskowa sailed across the highly polished parquet floor, turned, and then glided back toward me and stopped, without either foot slipping off the squares. "Now you try it," she said. Though one or the other foot kept sliding off, Pani Gregormirskowa felt that I would get the hang of it. "It is my rule," she said sternly, "that whenever you enter this room, and you will enter it often, your feet must be positioned on the rugs because that's how I keep the floor well polished." The old wood parquet floor did indeed shine like a mirror.

A considerable number of valuable icons were displayed throughout the living room. Fragrant odors of drying herbs pervaded the room. The herbs were on shelves in a sideboard, in divided compartments, and quite a number of herbs were hanging from the ceiling. Pani Gregormirskowa was an herbalist, and I was required to usher in and out the many patients who came to consult her during the afternoon.

Pani Gregormirskowa said that her professional name was Kama, and I was to address her as Pani Kama. I liked that a lot because her last name was not easy to pronounce. The lady frequently referred to her White Russian heritage and spoke with disdain about Bolsheviks and Poles.

Two bedrooms were rented to a team of trapeze artists—a couple and a man. These subtenants slept till afternoon and performed late into the night at cabarets frequented by the Germans. The tiny woman and her husband occupied one bedroom, and their working partner, whose prewar residence had been Berlin, the other. All three were White Russians. I was to clean their rooms in the evening after their departure. Both rooms were filled with photographs and memorabilia from many of Europe's cities. Newspaper clippings and posters recounted recent successes in Paris. Their lifestyle was unconventional. Sometimes they did not leave their room for twenty-four hours whereas at other times they would not return for two or three days.

Every day my employer wore the same ankle-length black dress, her feet clad in the same black tie boots reaching up to midcalf. Only her white collar and sleeve cuffs were changed in accordance with the importance of the visitor. These neck and cuff pieces were made of linen, satin, or voile, and it was my job to wash and iron them.

Pani Kama informed me that I was to eat the same food she did, but that she ate sparingly, and she expected me to do the same. The main meal was to be served at about twelve-thirty, and thereafter the kitchen stove door was to be tightly shut and no further coal to be added. She said that it was very difficult to acquire coal; we were an occupied country, and the Germans requisitioned all the coal extracted from the mines.

A large tile stove heated the consultation–living room. Early in the morning, coal briquettes were added and the stove door tightly shut. After that, the tile stove kept the room warm for the rest of the day. Coal briquettes were also delivered to the subtenants for their tile stoves.

At about eight o'clock in the evening, often without even a crust of bread to assuage my hunger pains, I crept fully clothed under a thin blanket. The kitchen, by then, was ice cold. Pani Kama retired with a cup of tea that she brewed on an electric plate in her bedroom. Most of the time she appeared to be oblivious that I had had nothing to eat after the midday meal. I knew that frequently her subtenants supplied her with delectable food items, but they never reached the kitchen.

During my second week on the job, I came down with a severe grippe. Pani Kama brewed a special concoction of herbs for me that contained a healing substance. She allowed me to ease up on some of my responsibilities, but I still had to keep the kitchen fire going.

Every other Sunday, on my day off from work, I could leave immediately after having served breakfast and return at curfew time. When I arrived on Ulica Falata, Mother would help me to get undressed because all I wanted to do was to sleep under the warm covers. I looked at the food Mother had prepared and fell asleep. When I woke, I saw Mother sitting next to me applying an oily substance to my burned and bruised hands. The skin was raw from the constant washing of collars, cuffs, and handkerchiefs. Invariably, Danka would knock on the door and ask to see me. Mother would say either that I had the grippe, was exhausted, or had a stomachache. But the more Mother tried to keep Danka away, the more eager she became to visit.

Mother had told the Mlodzianowskis that I was employed as a nanny and in charge of two little girls. The family would have been horrified to hear that their subtenant was working as a common maid and sleeping in a kitchen. Mother kept insisting that my hands should not be seen. "Your hands will give us away," she said. In the afternoon, after washing my hair thoroughly in a basin filled with warm water, Mother prepared the peroxide-ammonia mixture to touch up my hair. I was coughing and wiping my running nose. I seemed unable to shake off the recent respiratory infection. I looked worn and thin, and I knew that Mother was worried about my weakened condition. "If only that woman would feed you properly," she said. Mother was so relieved I had found a hideout that I could not tell her the conditions of Pani Kama's employ were very difficult to bear.

## MARCH 1943 ⤳ WARSAW, OCCUPIED POLAND

After about six weeks on the job with no comments on my manner of speaking and my stuttering diminishing in frequency, I was beginning to regain my self-confidence. Having lived for a number of weeks without being interrogated about my background was a good omen. Mother agreed that my Polish speech had become less awkward, but she still urged caution. "Most of Pani Kama's associates are Russian exiles," Mother said, "and they are also deficient in their Polish language skills."

Escape from the Warsaw ghetto was no longer possible because high walls and barbed wire enclosed the area. Police and Gestapo units patrolled the perimeter of the ghetto. Sentries at the gates were continuously changed to avoid arousing sympathy for individual Jews within. Pasted onto walls and newspaper kiosks throughout Warsaw were posters warning Christians against harboring Jews with false identity papers. Poles, under threat of severe punishment, were warned not to withhold knowledge, or even suspicion, of Jews hiding in their midst. They were urged to denounce all persons suspected of being Jewish to either the block warden or to the nearest police or Gestapo official. Listed in large print were addresses and telephone numbers one could contact without revealing the caller's identity. People stopped to read the posters, and I also stopped to read them. The large posters were headed by the exclamation, "*Uwaga!*"—attention.

Often, while standing in the tram, I became conscious of being watched. Perhaps I wasn't camouflaging the anxiety that was my constant companion. I immediately composed my facial expression into a more carefree look, lowered my eyelids, and moved toward the exit. When I thought I was being followed, I sped up my steps, without breaking into a run, and weaving in and out of densely populated streets, I kept going until I was certain that I had shaken my follower. In two instances, I knew who my pursuer was. Once it was a man; the other time two middle-aged women. My pursuers were Poles.

Mother's encounter was worse. A man looked into her face and said, "How dare you board a streetcar, you dirty Jew." Though we always tried to remain near the exit door, Mother had been pushed toward the center and was surrounded by other passengers. She drew herself up, she told me, and said, "How dare you accuse me falsely. You should be more careful with this type of slander."

"Slander, ha?" the accuser said, while looking around for approval. He said he needed to find a policeman. Mother made a remark about the man being too eager to provoke a police encounter, and some of the passengers nodded in agreement. Mother moved toward the exit and plunged through the large crowd of people waiting to board the tram. She was badly shaken and did not tell me about the incident until some days later, when she had calmed down. She subsequently avoided that particular tramline because she feared that the man, a Pole, would be watching for her.

Toward the middle of March, when I came to visit on my day off, my Mother greeted me with a big hug and a smile. "You can give Pani Kama one week notice when you return tonight," she told me. She recounted how she had searched and finally managed to find our friend from Krosno, our patron Jerzy Krawczyk. His temporary address was an apartment off Plac Narutowicza, a square known for its proximity to the Warsaw Polytechnic Institute, an architectural landmark bombed during the invasion.

Professor Glowacki, a widower and the owner of the apartment, had sublet one of the rooms to Staszek Winiarski, known to us in Krosno as Janek Haftel. Janek's father, a pious Jew, had been a printer, and his shop in Krosno had been adjacent to my uncle Jacub's store in the town square. While visiting Aunt Regina in July 1939, I had seen Janek Haftel almost every day. He had learned the printing and stamp-making business from his father and worked with him in the shop. Janek was perhaps ten years older than I, and though I had met a number of young men that age during my summer holiday, I had only a nodding acquaintance with the young neighbor next door. I would smile at Janek when our paths crossed, but though my uncle had proudly introduced me to all his neighbors and friends, he had barely acknowledged my existence.

Jerzy had been able to find a hiding place for his wife and daughters, Ewa and Maryla, in a distant village. He had succeeded in arranging shelter for Basia, his youngest child, in a Catholic convent. Jerzy shared Staszek's room while looking for a place of his own. It was too dangerous to keep three people hidden, and he wanted to bring his daughters Ewa and Maryla to Warsaw. Jerzy was delighted that Mother had found him, because he had been unable to trace us.

The professor, who had sublet the room to Staszek, had taught music at the University of Warsaw. Mother said he was a kindly and cultivated man, exuding old-world charm. Each morning, he played on his grand piano for several hours. He was noninterferring, and perhaps even forthcoming, whenever Staszek had company. He also had a resource that provided him with enough coal to keep the apartment heated. Staszek in turn was more enterprising than he was in obtaining food provisions. Staszek cooked nourishing vegetable, cabbage, or potato soups that he would share with the professor and Jerzy.

Jerzy told Mother that she would be welcome to visit and that it was detrimental to live in such isolation. It also would be good for me to come and for several hours be relieved of the strain of living the fiction of my assumed identity. Staszek disagreed. He told Mother that he already had too many visitors, and he must protect his hiding place. Too many visitors would make it dangerous to live in the building, or worse, would arouse the professor's suspicion. Jerzy was adamant, Mother told me, and he said that he would not disavow a good friend. Jerzy told Staszek that he had the good fortune of having a contact in Warsaw, and since Mother and I were totally isolated, without a friend or contact in a city full of Nazis and Nazi informers, they must try and help us whenever they could. Staszek reluctantly agreed to Mother's visits, and he urged that she space her visits carefully and refrain from visiting if she had the slightest suspicion that she was being watched or followed. When Mother was preparing to leave, Jerzy told Staszek that he thought it would even be beneficial if Mother came to visit. Two bachelors living in the apartment of another bachelor might arouse suspicion if no woman came to call. He told Mother, in Staszek's presence, that both men agreed her visits would be good for all three of them, and the only condition was that she be vigilant in making sure she was not followed. "But that goes for all of us," he told Staszek. "Jadzia has been alone for too long. She needs a place to come to, a destination, someone who is a friend."

Mother explained to me that Jerzy did not give Staszek a chance to object, because he would have. In addition, Jerzy told Mother that I should quit my job, and he would urge Staszek to use some of his contacts to find a more suitable job for me. Meanwhile, I was to recover and get my hands back to normal, and when I had regained my stamina to come and show my face at the apartment.

My mother had even discussed with Jerzy her worry about the disappearance of my monthly period. I could not understand why this should be a matter of such great concern. Mother felt that were I to survive, I would not be able to bear children. I had great doubts that either one of us would survive. The Nazi policy that no Jew must survive was successful. Every day Jews who had been hiding within the city were caught, and that action was visible to all. When I saw the victims, who looked like everyone else around me, being marched through the street to the nearest police station, I felt certain that my days were numbered. Aside from the many traps set by the Nazi pursuers, there were too many contemptible Poles waiting to ensnare me. I made certain to always keep the cyanide pill within reach. I also kept my father's address, though without his name, rolled in a bit of muslin, pinned inside my brassiere.

With help from several of his sources, Jerzy had found out that Aunt Regina and Dollek had managed to reach their destination. They had found refuge in a village near Myslenice, and Mother was beside herself with joy. She had always felt protective toward her younger sister, and after the brutal murder of Uncle Jacub, when Aunt Regina had suffered a nervous breakdown, Mother had become the mainstay of Aunt Regina's existence. Little Dollek was very dear to her heart. When the sisters parted in Szczucin, both of them knew that to survive they would have to separate. Still, I was aware that Mother felt guilty because she was no longer able to give Aunt Regina the emotional support her sister so badly needed. When Mother learned that Aunt Regina and Dollek were alive, she began to hope that perhaps Eva had managed to escape. Mother conjured up scenarios in which her older daughter was alive and had found a kind-hearted soul to give her shelter.

While recovering from physical exhaustion in the room on Ulica Falata, I received a valuable gift—the friendship of Danka. Tall and handsome, her bleached blond hair set in tiny curls that framed her high cheekbones, Danka departed each weekday early in the morning, usually with a rolled-up newspaper sticking out of the pocket of her short black coat and a quart-size milk can dangling from her hand. In the afternoon, when Mother was absent, Danka would visit me in our room. When Mother was home, she urged us to go out for walks. Mother felt that I needed to be out in the fresh air, and walking with Danka would provide protective cover.

Danka told me that her mother had been trying to discourage her feelings of friendship toward me. But she had reproached her mother for her lack of understanding and empathy. Danka told her mother that, like them, I had been chased from my home when it was annexed to the Third Reich. Like her family, my family had fallen on hard times. I was her contemporary, but in contrast to her, I did not have the good fortune to have my father's protection. Moreover, I had become motherless at birth. She argued that my father was an officer who had fought the Germans, and for all we knew he could have died or become a prisoner of war. If he were fortunate, he may have landed in England. Eventually, her mother had surrendered and given her consent to the friendship.

Since her sister and I were both called Krysia, Danka named me Mala Krysia—Little Krysia—though I was not even an inch shorter than her sister. When Danka came into our room, she never stayed for long. She said it was too cold to sit down. One day I overheard her say, "Mother, this has to stop. It has gone on long enough." On the following day, an old man from the superintendent's workshop walked into our room while I was there. He turned a screw in the radiator and within minutes the room warmed up.

Swearing me to secrecy Danka revealed to me her morning activities. Though it was strictly forbidden, she was going to "school" and continuing her secondary school education. Though she would not specify the exact location of this clandestine undertaking, she did mention that she and several other students were receiving instruction in the basement of an inconspicuous building near Pomnik Mikolaj Kopernika, the monument to the Polish astronomer Nicolaus Copernicus. The building was within walking distance of the Gestapo headquarters on Aleje Ujazdowski. The German occupation authority had closed all facilities of higher education. Only primary education, with subjects taught under scrutiny of the occupation education department, was permitted. The pursuit of study beyond the primary grades was forbidden to Poles and was considered treason. If discovered, professors, students, or administrators faced imprisonment and possible transportation to concentration camps.

For me, the knowledge that a Polish underground organization, dedicated to defying Nazi laws, truly existed was a life-affirming revelation. Danka concealed her notes beneath her garter belt, stuffed inside the elastic band of her panties. The rolled-up newspaper sticking out of her pocket was a diversionary tactic. If she was stopped, the first thing the police would look at was the material she was reading. The small milk can swinging from her hand was legitimate. Since Pan Mlodzianowski was employed in the office of agriculture, he was entitled to a certain amount of milk for his family. Unless a seventeen-year-old girl could provide a paper showing that she was usefully employed, she could be subject to forced labor. Danka was in possession of a permit that stated that she was needed to do the household work because her mother was ill. Krystyna, her nineteen-year-old sister, was employed in an office.

I was now able to visit with the sisters in their living room. Though Pan Mlodzianowski remained aloof and did not address me directly, the fact that he did not object to my presence in his living room somewhat eased my anxiety. In his official-looking briefcase he often brought home small amounts of flour, sugar, and sometimes several eggs.

On Saturday, the girls asked me if I wanted to attend eleven o'clock Sunday Mass at Kosciol Swietego Anne—Church of Saint Anne. On prior occasions when asked where I worshipped, I answered Kosciol Trzech Krzyzy—Church of Three Crosses. It came to mind at that moment because I had gone there several times to keep warm. I gathered that both girls had boyfriends, and they met when attending Sunday Mass. I felt that I had become sufficiently acquainted with the Mass ritual and the responses in the liturgy to go along.

The sisters dressed up before setting out for the church. They agreed that the hat I was wearing was dowdy, suitable for a girl of fourteen or fifteen but not chic enough for me. Both girls pulled out boxes stashed behind the furniture and, while laughing, tried Danka's white-and-green pillbox hats and a black derby on me. The hats did not suit me at all. Danka was wearing a kerchief, beneath which her bleached blond hair was rolled up in paper curlers. She removed the curlers efficiently, combed her hair, now frizzled at the ends, and proceeded to don the various hats. On her, all hats looked great. "Do you use something to bleach your hair?" she asked me. "No, I don't," I lied.

Krystyna favored a more conservative look. She invariably wore dresses and hats in dark, muted colors. One of her hats, the color somewhere between moss green and gray, was a perfect fit, and the sisters insisted that I wear the hat on a permanent basis. They told me Krystyna had not worn it for several years. I was not comfortable with their decision, and I urged that they ask Pani Mlodzianowska's permission. The girls brought their mother into the room, all three of them laughing and approving of the way I looked in Krystyna's old hat. When I said that I could not pay for it, Pani Mlodzianowska told me, "The hat is not for sale. Krystyna is lending it to you, and you can wear it as long as she wants you to."

At the church we met Danka's and Krystyna's boyfriends. Daniel, Danka's friend, was as tall as Danka, slender, with delicate features and chestnut-colored hair. His expressive eyes were stunning. They were almond shaped, dark and deep, and they radiated kindness and intelligence. Krystyna's friend, Mjetek, was tall, broad shouldered, and athletic looking. He had strong features and wavy blond hair. He was the prototype of a young and handsome Pole. Both young men sang in the church choir, and we did not see them until after Mass. The men greeted me in a friendly manner. They said that they had heard about me. Then there was a whispered exchange between the respective couples. The young men kissed the girls' hands, mine also, and waving a friendly good-bye disappeared into the departing crowd. Months later I learned that Daniel and Mjetek, as well as three other members of the Church of Saint Anne choir, belonged to an underground cell that held clandestine meetings on prearranged Sundays in the church cellar.

Mother was worried and despondent. She had applied for her Kennkarte in January through the appropriate office. She had stood in a long line, first to get an application, and then to submit the completed application to the clerk. He scrutinized her white identity card, issued by the Krosno municipality. He wanted to know why she had moved from Krosno to Warsaw. Mother answered that her husband had been reported missing after the invasion. She had not been able to find work in Krosno and had imposed on the charity of friends. She had exhausted all her means, but she had been assured of employment in Warsaw. The clerk took all the information, including Mother's present address, and said that she would be called if more information was needed. If everything checked out, she would receive the document. Two months had passed since she had submitted the application, and without the Kennkarte, Mother was unable to find employment. Our room was on the ground floor and faced the inner courtyard. At night when we heard the sound of boots on the sidewalk, Mother sat up to listen. I prayed.

The nightmares I had first experienced in Szczucin, and then in Krakow, returned with increased frequency. When I woke up, often drenched in sweat, running ahead of my pursuers who finally caught up and reached for me, I felt Mother's hand either placed gently over my mouth or on my arm. I could not recall having such traumatic nocturnal assaults while sleeping in Pani Kama's cold kitchen. But in the afternoon, when with Danka or with both sisters, I tried to appear as carefree as they did, and I must have been convincing enough.

I reported to Mother the strong anti-Nazi and patriotic sentiments of the Mlodzianowski family. The family condemned the fraternization of Polish females with the German invader, and they cursed the Philistines who profited from the occupation. The killing of the Jews that was taking place in the Warsaw ghetto was seldom spoken about but referred to as the "abomination." Pawiak, the name of the Warsaw prison where unimaginable acts of torture were taking place, was mentioned in a whisper. There were constant reports of Jews being caught and brought to the infamous prison, where they were tortured, often to death, in order to extract the names of people who might have helped them. It was known, too, that Poles suspected of acts of sabotage, or those who for no apparent reason were found to be undesirable in the eyes of the Nazis, were brought there on trumped-up charges. They were tortured and maimed, and if they survived, they continued to languish in the underground cells of the feared prison.

All members of the Mlodzianowski family read *Nowy Kurier Warszawsky*, the Polish daily newspaper, before it was cut up for use as toilet paper. Almost every issue of the newspaper gave brief accounts of failed attempts by Jews to evade incarceration and deportation. In these newspaper reports, the Nazi authorities alleged that Jews were managing to hide because of the negligent attitude of the Warsaw population. The newspaper articles urged the residents to be vigilant and to report escaped Jews from the Warsaw ghetto. Diligent informers pointed out people they suspected of being Jewish as the fugitives passed them on the street. Frequently they were denounced by former neighbors or business associates, who had recognized them despite a changed appearance. The informers received compensation. Danka spoke with disdain of the scum that would stoop so low as to denounce anyone to the Germans.

Within the Ulica Falata apartment complex, the Szczupanek family regularly baked bread for the other tenants. The father had worked for the Warsaw municipality. When he lost his job, the family managed to pay their rent from the meager income generated by their baking. The entire family—father, mother, a daughter perhaps twenty years old, and a son of about twenty-three—did the baking during the night.

Twice a week at dusk, Danka and I, and sometimes Krysia, walked up the three flights to their apartment. Invariably, the record player would be in action, and the records, popular prewar hit tunes from Polish, German, American, or Argentinean films, filled the apartment with music. On the cleared parquet floor, couples danced the tango, foxtrot, and even the Lambert walk. It was important that we stay a while to create the impression that we had come for an hour of socializing and dancing and not for the loaves of bread we hid under our coats upon leaving the apartment. The possession of flour, beyond the amount needed for personal consumption, was labeled hoarding, a crime considered an act of sabotage against the war effort. If caught, the whole Szczupanek family could be punished. By the time we arrived for these social gatherings, all traces of the bread baking had been removed.

Being able to obtain fresh bread was an important event, and a nutritious addition to our meager diet. Mother did worry that we might get caught and be interrogated, but we were sworn not to divulge our source. Mother and I did not want to overindulge in such luxurious eating, and we used only one loaf a week. Mother took the other loaf of bread to Staszek's apartment, where it was gratefully received and shared with the professor.

Some months later when we no longer lived on Ulica Falata, three members of the Szczupanek family were caught baking bread and arrested by Gestapo agents. Only the son, who had been absent at the time, avoided capture. He sublet the apartment and left Warsaw. It was said the family had been denounced.

I had visited Staszek's apartment several times, and Jerzy was delighted when he saw me. He hugged and kissed me and told me about his wife and three daughters. He visited them infrequently to avoid endangering their lives. He hoped that Maryla, the middle daughter and my friend, might be able to find shelter in the same convent that was harboring little Basia. Staszek was more reserved. Yes, he said, he remembered me from Krosno. It was true that he had kept his distance when I lived in Krosno because he thought that I had too many friends. I did not know what he meant, but I smiled. I was eager to gain his friendship. He had valuable connections in Warsaw, and he was the person Mother hoped might be able to find suitable employment for me.

At Staszek's apartment I learned that Dr. Romek Rosenberg, with his wife, his sister, her husband and son, and their friend Shulek Axelrad, were hiding in an apartment in Warsaw. When I asked if it was possible that I go and visit our beloved doctor from Krosno, I was told that I should put the thought out of my mind because it was not possible. Romek Rosenberg, an athletic, tall, and handsome man with his gray eyes, abundant straight hair graying at the temples, and a strong square jaw, looked the prototype of a Slav. In spite of that, he had been harassed, followed, and denounced.

The good news from Aunt Regina was almost beyond belief. Dollek had found favor in the eyes of the local priest, who had appointed him as an altar boy. It seemed that Dollek, together with several other little fellows, was performing small duties in the village church, and he was often in attendance, waving the censer, when the priest was officiating at sacramental events.

## APRIL 1943 ⚘ WARSAW, OCCUPIED POLAND

Walking on Ulica Marshalkowska, one of the main thoroughfares in the Warsaw business sector, I suddenly found myself face to face with Dr. Rosenberg. He did not see me, but I recognized him immediately. He kissed my hand in greeting and said my blond hair had changed my appearance. He did not know that I had managed to evade transportation when the Krosno ghetto was liquidated, and he was very happy to see me. Almost immediately, I observed Dr. Rosenberg disobeying the cardinal rule of the fugitive: He kept jeopardizing us both by constantly glancing nervously around and appearing frightened. Though I told him gently what he was doing, his head kept jerking in both directions. This handsome, once powerfully built man appeared shrunken, and it was obvious that his nerves were badly damaged. Asserting myself, I took his arm and forced him to walk alongside me at a fast pace. My heart reached out to him, but simultaneously I knew that walking with him, being seen with him, put me in grave danger.

He told me that he was on his third set of falsified documents. Obtaining the papers—one set gathered with Staszek's help—and finding shelter for his family had exhausted a large part of his considerable fortune. He had been pushed into a doorway and forced to drop his pants. Each time he was caught, he had to pay bribes. Even if a bribe was accepted, he had to move to a different hideout because his captors wrote down his address after examining his papers. Faithful Stasia, his former nurse who had worked at his side for many years, had access to his money and his possessions. She lived in the Krosno area and was selling off the doctor's property. Dr. Rosenberg endeavored as best he could to provide for his wife, his sister, her husband and child, and his brother-in-law's brother. I knew all of them. They lived together in a small apartment someone had rented for him. This man—who, with his calm and reassuring voice, had treated and counseled us through numerous illnesses and bouts of malnutrition and had supplied us, without charge, with medication and food—had come undone. The rudder was gone, and I perceived that he could barely keep himself afloat. He spoke too fast and too loud, and his continuous need to make sure that he was not noticed called attention to both of us. I knew that I could not help, and I felt relieved when we parted.

The Warsaw ghetto was burning. There were rumors that a large group of Jews, the remnant that was about to be taken away to one of the death camps, had managed to obtain arms and attack their persecutors. The Jews had dared to rebel against the mighty tyrant. It was an outrageous act, and the Gestapo wanted to keep it a secret. Still, there were rumors that a Polish underground organization had supplied some of the weapons. Besides, there were visible signs that could not be erased. There had been shooting, and German guards and soldiers had been killed. The Nazis decided to burn down the ghetto, together with the activists within, including women and children. One did not even have to go to the center of the city in order to see the distant black columns of smoke in the blue sky and smell its pervasive odor.

Jewish females hiding out in Warsaw were coloring and lightening their hair to change their appearance. Some people within the Christian community seemed rather adept at identifying Jewish fugitives by the color of their hair. Since our arrival in Warsaw, Mother and I had been conscious of that fact. Whenever we needed to replenish our supply of peroxide or ammonia, we went to an apothecary we had not previously frequented. It was fortunate for us that there were many apothecaries in Warsaw.

Toward the end of April, on a clear spring day, I entered an apothecary on Plac Swietego Zbawiciela—Square of the Holy Savior. The clerk was talking with a male customer. I waited until he turned to me, and I told him that I wanted to buy some peroxide. He shot a glance at the other man, and then he asked me if I knew what was going on outside. I shook my head and indicated that I did not.

"Do you mean to say that you don't know that the ghetto is burning with all the Jews within?" he asked provocatively. I nodded that I knew. "So you did see," he continued. I shrugged my shoulders, indicating that I did not know what he was talking about. He came around from behind the counter, and said, "You mean to say that you have not seen the Jewish mothers throwing their children from the windows into the flames and jumping down after them? You can see it from here. Come." He walked toward the door, pulling at my arm, while the other man walked out behind me. There was nothing to see. It was a ploy. They had hoped that by showing emotion, I would reveal myself. The burning ghetto could not be seen from Plac Swietego Zbawiciela; only the distant smoke was visible. I calmly walked away, and once at a safe distance from the apothecary, I broke out into a sweat.

Pani Mlodzianowska gave us notice that we would have to vacate our room. She informed us that Pani Wojchiechowska, the owner of the apartment, was planning to return to Warsaw and would need her room. Until her arrival, Danka could sleep in the room, Pani Mlodzianowska said. She produced a letter from her sister-in-law, and Mother gathered that the topic of our leaving had been discussed in their correspondence for quite a while. Danka was delighted that, even if only for a few weeks, she would have a room of her own with a door that would remain closed if she so desired. She hugged and kissed me and said that our friendship would not be diminished, but rather enhanced, because now we would be able to get together without being subjected to her mother's and my aunt's surveillance.

The prospect of finding, at this treacherous time, an apartment owner who would rent a room to an aunt and her niece was at best perilous. Still, Mother said we had managed to live in relative safety through the bitter cold winter months, and she was almost certain that the Mlodzianowskis would give us a letter stating that we were unobtrusive tenants who paid their rent on time.

Mother received her Kennkarte. It was a momentous event. Staszek scrutinized the document carefully and compared it with his own forged Kennkarte. The small circle of Jews who came to see him and Jerzy in the professor's apartment had forged Aryan papers. Staszek, and even Jerzy, had expressed grave doubt that Mother would succeed in her daring attempt to legitimately obtain the coveted document. They also knew that Mother was totally without means or resources and could not buy a forged Kennkarte. They agreed that Mother's courage in presenting herself in person to the issuing authority had paid off.

Because some Jews, and other persons who were hiding their identity by means of forged documents, had managed to evade the Gestapo units charged with the task of apprehending each and every one of them, a new decree was issued. The law stated that every person in possession of a Kennkarte must now have the document validated. The document was to be submitted to the block warden, who was responsible for registering every person within his or her assigned jurisdiction. Residents who attempted to evade the process would be immediately taken into custody. Any block warden who was less than diligent in carrying out the task would be suspect of abetting sabotage. The large posters, outlining the procedures to be followed, were pasted onto kiosks.

Mother determined that the ceasing of my menstrual period for the past six months was connected to my malnutrition. I was convinced that the night I lay down on the railroad tracks, I let go of life and froze my natural cycle. Mother dismissed my conclusion as nonsense. Staszek reported that he had not yet succeeded in finding work for me because of the problems I presented. Jerzy kept assuring Mother that he was working at it and that she must be patient. We could not pay for the minimal amount of food we needed to sustain ourselves. Mother urged that I find live-in work in order to eat. Once again I answered help-wanted advertisements. Prospective employers who were ceaselessly warned to report escaping Jews, scrutinized my appearance, my downcast eyes, and my validated Kennkarte and informed me that the job had been filled.

When answering ads, I tried to stay as far away from the ghetto as possible. In desperation, I did apply for a position as a live-in maid at the cluttered office of a trucking firm on Ulica Grzybowska. The address was within walking distance of the ghetto. With me I carried a letter of recommendation from Pani Kama, in which she praised my diligence and honesty. From behind a desk, a young woman informed me that she was presently engaged in screening prospective job applicants for her employer.

"The position to be filled is in Ursus, a suburb located about thirty miles south of Warsaw," she said.

"That would be fine," I answered.

"Your aunt will not mind your being so far away?"

"No, she agrees that I must support myself."

"You will be able to go home for a two-day weekend, but only once a month. Won't you be lonely?"

"No. I will look forward to my two-day visit with my aunt."

"There will be a lot of work. My employer and his wife expect a set of twins sometime in May. They have a little boy of five. Pani Kucharska enjoys looking after him, but she no longer can manage her household. They are looking for an intelligent girl who would teach their son letters and numbers and who would keep him occupied."

"I will do my best to relieve Pani Kucharska of the household chores, and I will be happy to instruct the child."

"How old did you say you are?" My Kennkarte was on her desk.

"I just turned seventeen, on March first."

"You realize that there will be a confinement, perhaps complications. You will have to fetch the midwife and doctor and take little Stefan to the neighbor."

"I feel confident that I can handle whatever may come up."

The long interview had robbed me of whatever self-confidence I had when I walked into the office. These feelings were within and not visible to the interviewer. I was eager to obtain the position. The location was ideal, I thought. It would make it possible for me to leave informer-inundated Warsaw. Perhaps I might find a shelter where I could remain for a while. The woman said that she was waiting for her boss. She thought he should see me. I sat in the chair waiting and alert. Pan Kucharski arrived shortly. He was too well groomed for someone in the trucking trade. He was of medium height and build, his dark hair was combed back and kept in place with greasy hair pomade, and there was polish on his fingernails. His Hitler-type mustache attempted to hide a harelip. He was a vain man, and I was cautious.

"You are old enough, I guess," he said. "Also you look intelligent, but quite frail. There will be a lot of work."

"I grew up without a mother. I learned early to do housework and to be responsible."

"Well, you seem like a friendly sort that makes for good company. I guess we'll take a chance."


MAY 1943 ⤳ WARSAW, OCCUPIED POLAND

The Kucharski family lived in a comfortable apartment on the upper floor of a two-family house. Pani Kucharska, large with twins and in her final weeks of pregnancy, regarded my intrusion into her home with suspicion. Pani

Kucharska did not want anyone near her who had been selected and dispatched by her husband's secretary. She wanted her husband to come home for the night, rather than spend his evenings in their Warsaw studio apartment, perhaps with the secretary. Her frustration was compounded by her weight and ungainly gait and by the puffiness that had distorted her features. Usually at about six o'clock in the evening, the husband called from the office to speak with his son. Reluctantly, Pani Kucharska walked to the phone located on the kitchen wall. There was no telephone in their Warsaw apartment, and the presence of the secretary prevented a private conversation.

The twins arrived in advance of the anticipated due date. They were born at night in the apartment in Pan Kucharski's absence. The midwife delivered the twins with a neighbor and me standing by to help. Toward evening of the following day, the father of the new twins arrived with his secretary. During the night, the argument between the new parents was so loud and angry that I was asked to run and get the doctor. He had been at the apartment in the early morning hours to check on both mother and the babies. He wanted me to tell him what had caused Pani Kucharska's setback, since in his opinion the delivery had progressed along a relatively normal course. I was careful not to divulge what I had heard. Several hours after the doctor had given instructions that the new mother needed to rest, the secretary took the morning train back to Warsaw.

Two days later, Pan Kucharski informed me that the midwife was sending a nurse and I was free to leave when she arrived. The little boy cried when I hugged him and bade him good-bye. He turned to his father and said that he did not want me to leave. Pan Kucharski shrugged his shoulders, paid me the agreed salary, and said, "My wife is too weak to see you. She insists that you were not the right person and that she wanted one of her own kind." The little boy walked me to the door, and I pretended that I had not heard that last sentence.

I had not been able to visit Mother since I left for Ursus, and I returned to Warsaw with almost four-week's salary in my pocket. I immediately saw that Mother was changed. I saw it mainly in her eyes. She was unable to control what they reflected. They did not focus, not even on me. They betrayed her fear and gave her smile an artificial cast. She looked weary, the resilience in her gait was missing, and it seemed that the effort of maintaining an erect posture was more than she could muster.

"The Warsaw ghetto was liquidated," Mother said.

"What does that mean?" But I knew.

"That was the term they used. It came over the radio, and they also announced it through loudspeakers. They wanted everyone to know that this ridiculous attempt by ghetto Jews to stage an uprising against their mighty captors could only end in a bloodbath."

Mother said that the Nazis proudly proclaimed that in the Warsaw ghetto all Jews had been killed. They had also succeeded in apprehending and killing a number of Jews who had attempted to escape through underground sewers.

I had not yet taken off my coat. Mother's face was turned to the window. She had not even looked at me. Tears were running from her eyes, and I noted that her hand, hanging limp from her arm, had a slight tremor I had not seen before. I moved to embrace her, but she turned away. She did not want me to touch her.

"They killed Regina," she said.

"Aunt Regina?" I asked.

Mother nodded. "And Dollek?"

Mother barely nodded again. I sat down on the unmade bed. I suddenly felt very cold. It seemed as if my heart had turned to ice. I held the money in my hand. Though we had tried as much as possible to push it from our thoughts, both Mother and I felt that her brothers Zygmunt and Willek and their wives and children had been murdered. We tried hard to hold on to the hope that a miracle might have occurred and Eva had survived. Perhaps a Nazi with heart, or perhaps a Pole with underground connections. The knowledge that Aunt Regina and Dollek were alive, living incognito in a small village, and that Dollek was an altar boy to the village priest had brought us much comfort. Now both of them were dead, Mother was in mourning, and I knew what she was thinking. Was it worth it? Could we possibly survive in the face of this relentless onslaught? There was, of course, the solution. We could swallow the cyanide pills and circumvent all further suffering.

I wanted to know what had happened to Aunt Regina and Dollek, but I realized that Mother was not able to give me coherent answers. It was too painful. Several days later, when I visited the professor's apartment—our euphemism for Staszek and Jerzy's hideout—I learned the grisly details. There had to have been rumors regarding Aunt Regina's and Dollek's identity, because what else could have compelled a group of his fellow altar boys, between the ages of ten and twelve years, to peek through the cracks between the wooden boards of the outhouse? Several days after the boys had glimpsed what their parents had suspected—Dollek's circumcised penis—the Gestapo arrived during the early morning hours at my aunt's door. Aunt Regina and Dollek were shot and left to die on a country road, not far from their hideout. There was a lot of blood.

I remembered an early evening in Szczucin, when I came home from my work in the municipal office. Dollek appeared to be angry, and both Aunt Regina and my mother were holding on to him while he tried wriggle out of their grasp. They wanted to be sure that he heard what they were telling him. He could not understand why I was able to go outside, while he had to be cooped up in the room until the late evening hours. His mother and his aunt were telling him that it was because of his penis. No one could see his penis, because if someone caught a glimpse of it, all four of us would be captured and taken away. I had the distinct impression, and I could read it in his eyes, that my ten-year-old cousin had grasped the severity of the danger. Mother and Aunt Regina had the same feeling. They hugged Dollek and kissed him to the extent that he would allow it, then let him go. But they had not prepared him for cracks between the boards of an outhouse, where he believed himself unobserved behind a closed door.

I was lonely, and I felt comforted when I visited the professor's apartment. I needed to talk about Aunt Regina and Dollek. Jerzy took me in his arms and said that he had been contacted and told about the murder, and how difficult it was for him to tell Mother what had happened to her sister. I told Jerzy that I was afraid. Mother hardly spoke; she was like a stone. Jerzy told me to give her time; the loss of her sister was a severe assault on her stability. "Your mother is a strong woman. She is a fighter," he said. "She needs time to recover."

On one of my visits to the professor's apartment, I was briefly introduced to a handsome young girl who was just leaving the apartment. Her name was Stefa Sobolewska. She was perhaps two or three years older than I, and she looked like many of the Christian Poles I came across in Warsaw's more prosperous neighborhoods. She wore an elegant tailored suit and a chic hat. I noticed that she walked and spoke with an assurance I did not possess.

Shortly thereafter we met again, this time in the street. She asked me if I was Jewish. I was astonished. Just asking the question was dangerous. I said that I was not, and I told her I could not imagine why she would ask. I said I was in a hurry and rushed off. I was upset that, in spite of my changed appearance and my self-monitoring, she had asked such a question. Mother said that since I had seen her in the professor's apartment she was safe, and I need not worry. Mother remembered Staszek mentioning Stefa's name, and Mother thought there had been a hint of the young woman's underground connections. We subsequently learned that Stefa was Jewish and knew Pani Kazimira Zulawska who had direct contact with the Polish underground. Just like Mother and me, Stefa liked to come to the professor's apartment. Later, in the spring of 1944, I attempted to initiate a relationship. I was eager to have a Jewish friend, especially one who was as safe looking as Stefa. But I quickly realized she was not interested in associating with me.

## JUNE 1943 ⤳ WARSAW, OCCUPIED POLAND

Pan Mlodzianowski told Mother that he understood it was difficult to find a room to rent, but his sister, Pani Wojchiechowska, would be arriving in Warsaw within the next few weeks. We must vacate the room before the end of June.

My mother hand-delivered the monthly rent for our room to Pani Mozejkowa. She was well aware of our predicament but had as yet been unable to help us find a room. When Mother brought the rent money for June, Pani Mozejkowa said she was expecting a visit from Duchess Woroniecka. Pani Mozejkowa, Mother told me, referred to her friend often and with much pride. Though the two women were well acquainted, Pani Mozejkowa never omitted her friend's title whenever she spoke about her. The Duchess, whose title had descended from her family and whose brother was a Duke, had a large country estate in Poznan, the western part of Poland that had been annexed to the Third Reich. The Duchess and her brother were evicted from their estate. They were living in straitened circumstances in Warsaw and had managed to survive by selling off some of their disposable property through the black market. They also received financial help from old friends.

When they met, the Duchess and Mother found they had much in common. Both women had been forced to leave their homes. The Duchess was a widow, and Pani Dembicka's husband was missing, his whereabouts were unknown. Both had had the benefit of a higher education, and both were conversant with Polish history and literature. Mother told me that the Duchess and she recited poetry to each other, and Mother was amazed that she had been able to remember lines of verse she had read when she was sixteen years old. The Duchess said she would help us. She told Pani Mozejkowa, "We must try and find a place for Pani Dembicka and her niece."

# CHAPTER 9

# An Address, A Job, An Ally

Our new address was a large six-story apartment house complex on Ulica Marshalkowska, near the Square of the Holy Savior and within walking distance of the professor's apartment. Our landlords were Pani Cybulska, a cantankerous old lady, and her daughter. The latter was in her early forties, Mother's contemporary. She was tall, slim, rather elegant, and distant. It took quite a bit of persuasion, we learned, to convince the two women that renting a room to us was not only a patriotic gesture, but also a good deed in the eyes of God. One entered the apartment house through a wrought-iron gate that was locked at dusk and could only be accessed by ringing a bell to summon the concierge. The front door of the apartment house was in an archway where the staircases to both sides of the building were located. A walk through a spacious courtyard led to a more modest archway and staircases to the back entrances, from which we entered our room.

Mother told me that it was not so much patriotism or a good deed in the eyes of God that made the arrangement possible, but the monthly rent Mother agreed to pay for the small room. The Cybulski family was struggling to make ends meet. The married son, who lived with his wife and children in a Warsaw suburb, contributed to the maintenance of the household. Still, Pani

Cybulska and her daughter wanted to meet Pani Dembicka's niece before they gave permission for us to move into their apartment. Mother urged me to refrain from speaking, but to convey intelligence. Mother said the Cybulski ladies would not want anyone who was dull within their orbit. Since returning from Ursus, while Mother was trying to find shelter for us, I kept busy reading books and newspapers aloud, practicing the difficult pronunciation of the multiple Polish double consonants. I thought that my diction had improved considerably, but Mother said that I would have to work harder because I still did not sound like a native Pole.

Pani Cybulska hardly ever went outside the apartment, which was located on the third floor. She hobbled about, leaning heavily on a rubber-tipped cane. The two women lived surrounded by heirlooms. They shared a bedroom and ate their meals at a small round table located in the alcove of a large living and dining room. The table was invariably set with exquisite china and crystal goblets, but we quickly realized that their meals consisted of watery pea or lentil soup. The ladies subsisted on a starvation diet similar to our own. This graciously decorated room faced the grass-covered part of the courtyard. A tall chestnut tree stood in its center. We were forbidden to enter the living-dining room and the kitchen.

Our small room was in the rear of the building. Across the hallway from our room was the library and music room. We were asked not to enter that room as well. However, through the open door I could see a shiny black grand piano and along the walls glass cases filled with elegantly bound books. Near the window stood an exquisite nineteenth-century, green-leather-topped desk. There were two brown-leather-upholstered club chairs, and rolled up against one wall was what looked to be a large Persian carpet. A telephone was mounted on the wall near the back entrance door.

Our room contained a narrow bed, a sofa, two dainty chairs, and a mirrored vanity that was hidden from immediate view by a three-paneled damask screen. Behind the screen was also a tiny table, and on it, and most important for us, a single gas burner. The gas outlet immediately above the vanity was installed for a lady's hair-curling iron. The fact that we would be able to cook in our room would make our daily life easier, and we were grateful for our good fortune. There was no heater for the room, but we had survived the previous winter in an unheated room. We had found a shelter.

When Panna Cybulska went to see the concierge, who was also the block warden for the apartment complex, to register her tenants, she encountered some difficulties. Though my Kennkarte was validated and Mother's Kennkarte was relatively new and not yet subject to validation, he had viewed our documents with suspicion. He passed out ration cards for minimal amounts of food. To get a more generous ration card allowance, one had to work. The employer had jurisdiction over supplemental ration cards. The warden wanted to know why I was not working, and when Panna Cybulska was unable to provide an answer, he said that I should find work or else. We did not know what the *else* meant, but Mother assured Panna Cybulska that I had been working all along, and that I was recovering from pneumonia—which, of course, was a lie.

We subsequently learned that the son, Pan Cybulski, was an attorney, but that information was secret. It was dangerous for a noncollaborating Pole to belong to the educated classes, because at unexpected moments, on some pretext, the Nazis would round up members of the Polish intelligentsia. Some of these Poles were sent to forced labor assignments, while others were incarcerated and subsequently released. Lately, a number of them were kept as hostages because of acts of sabotage committed by the growing Polish underground movement.

About that time there were rumors that now that the Jews had been eliminated, the Poles would be next on the agenda. The Nazi regime wanted to destroy Polish academicians and members of the professional classes who might in the future aspire to leadership positions. The rest of the Polish people would be needed to perform manual labor for the master race. Mother and I spoke about it, and Mother discussed the matter with Jerzy and Staszek. How would this rumor affect the Polish residents of Warsaw? There were many mean-spirited Poles who still collaborated with the Nazis in finding the hiding place of Jews and reporting them to the Gestapo. Would these Poles now become more tolerant toward the few Jews still hiding out?

There were Poles who helped or gave shelter to Jews. Jerzy had managed to gain refuge for his youngest child in a convent. He was presently attempting to place his daughter Maryla in the same convent. He also had found a temporary hideout in the country for his wife and oldest daughter Ewa. We had heard of Poles who volunteered to help their Jewish friends.

Since we did not have access to Poles who might be able to help us hide, Mother and I were subject to constant harassment. My month in Ursus had provided a respite from the never-ending self-surveillance I had to maintain whenever I was on the street. Someone's eye would fasten on me, and I would feel myself being observed. My mind raced ahead as I searched for the nearest place to hide. Mostly the pursuers were men; only seldom was it a woman. The people I feared most were male, ranging in age from eighteen to sixty. When trying to get away, I moved fast, just short of running, because I knew what they wanted: They wanted to know where I lived. I kept running until I was certain I had left my pursuer behind.

Shortly after we moved to the Cybulski apartment on Ulica Marshalkowska, I had a searing encounter. The man was about thirty years old. I sensed his glance passing over me, while I stood in the middle of a crowded streetcar. Suddenly he was at my side. "*Zydowka*" —Jewess—he said loud enough for everyone who was nearby to hear. I did not respond and pretended he could not possibly have referred to me. Moving with the passengers to the exit door, I was about to step down, when once again he repeated the accusation. I jumped off the running board and attempted to lose myself in the crowd. Though I did not turn my head, I knew that I was being followed. I kept running until I lost my pursuer. I must have run and walked for a good number of kilometers. By the time I got back to our apartment house, I was certain I had lost my self-appointed henchman. I was drenched in sweat. I lay down and finally fell asleep, but throughout the night I kept running. Twice Mother woke me. She said I was moaning so loud, she feared the Cybulskis might hear me. I did not tell her what had plagued me throughout the night.

Mother was subject to these encounters more frequently than I was. Our Jewish friends agreed that with my long blond hair and half-closed eyelids, I looked like a Christian Pole, as long as I did not speak. Mother's hair color did not take as well as mine and looked more artificial. Mother had dark eyes, an aquiline nose, and an aristocratic bearing if she kept an erect posture. When I carefully scrutinized her appearance, I could not see that she looked different than her friends—Pani Wojchiechowska, Pani Mozejkowa, or Duchess Woroniecka. Yet, she was accosted, pursued, and several times held by the arm, in an attempt to point her out to a policeman or a Gestapo agent.

On Ulica Hoza, on my way home one day, I saw from a distance three men entering a doorway. I was not sure at first, but it seemed that the two on either side were holding on to the man in the center. I crossed to the other side of the street, but as I passed the doorway, I discreetly looked across. One man held the victim's arms, while the other one bent down over and pulled down the victim's trousers. From a distance, when I first spotted them, all three men had looked alike and all were similarly dressed. What caused them to fasten on that man?

Romek Rosenberg, our physician and dear friend, was dead. The Gestapo had managed to find his hideout. They had come in the early morning hours, and Dr. Rosenberg, together with his sister, brother-in-law, their little child, and another relative, were picked up and taken away in a covered green truck. His wife Wanda had not been in the apartment when the Gestapo arrived. She was returning from an errand and saw the truck from a distance. She did not go near the building until the truck had moved on. Only then did she learn that the people who had been picked up were her husband and all remaining members of Romek's family.

## AUGUST 1943 ⤳ WARSAW, OCCUPIED POLAND

I was always hungry, and it no longer mattered whether my stomachaches were caused by ever-present fear or the need for food. I desperately needed to find work. Jerzy told Mother that Staszek had an important contact in Warsaw. Through this contact I might be able to obtain work. Though the men were good friends, Jerzy had no access to that person. Staszek was quite secretive about this connection, and Mother kept urging Jerzy to use his influence to help place me in a factory. Staszek kept postponing his promise to secure an appointment for me with his Polish contact. Jerzy tried to convince him that my language skills were much improved and that the risk he would take by introducing me was mainly in his own mind.

Intercepting foreign news broadcasts, as well as disseminating news other than that promulgated by the occupation propaganda machine, was punishable by death. In spite of these threats, underground cells received radio messages sent by the Polish government-in-exile. News of a German army defeat in North Africa sparked new acts of sabotage in Warsaw.

In the summer of 1943, ostensibly to aid in the German war effort, Poles were transported to German work camps. Men and women who could not produce a document showing they were usefully employed were randomly taken off the streets and sent to German mines and industrial plants. Women who did not have young children to care for and especially young girls were sent to Germany to replace German farmworkers who had been inducted into the Wehrmacht. However, Polish women and girls could circumvent the street raids and resulting forced labor if they voluntarily relocated to Germany. All they had to do was register at the German *Jedz znami do Niemiec* office (Travel with Us to Germany). The office was located on Nowy Swiat, and the invitation—"Travel with Us to Germany"—was printed in large letters on a white canvas banner above the storefront office. On either side of the door were posters depicting a happy blond girl with pigtails picking fruit in an orchard, and another one sitting on top of a pile of hay in a horse-drawn cart. Ostensibly, a person sent from this office lived with a farm family and was well treated, especially at the present harvest season.

Since my unemployment posed a continuous threat, and the office was asking for farm help, I decided to take a chance. I had heard that the "volunteer" bureau was funded by the Arbeitsamt and administered by a Polish-speaking staff. It sought to encourage prospective applicants to relocate to Germany. A bell rang as I opened the door. From behind a desk facing the door, a man rose and looked at me. It was only an instant, but it felt as if he had stripped me naked. I had let go of the door handle but had not yet advanced into the room. I noticed that there were other desks, and there must have been ten or twelve people in the room—interviewers and applicants. "*You* want to go to Germany?" the man shouted. "What—" he snarled, as his hand reached for the telephone. I backed out of the room, my eyes on the finger that was dialing a number. When I reached the street, I disappeared into the swirling crowd around me. Fortunately, Nowy Swiat was always bustling with people going and coming from Warsaw's Old Town, a restored historic neighborhood.

The longed-for appointment with Pan Walter, Staszek's important contact, finally took place. Pan Walter was a Pole who had the power to open doors closed to us. I thought I looked quite well when I walked at Staszek's side to Pan Walter's apartment.

With Staszek who produced the birth certificates that were crucial in our struggle to survive in Warsaw. He is taking me to the job interview with the director of the garment factory where I subsequently worked. Warsaw, autumn 1943.

Pan Walter, a man in his fifties, was a musician and composer. He had written the musical scores for some of the finest films the Polish film industry had produced. After the invasion of Poland, Pan Walter had moved to a modest neighborhood where he lived with his two sons, one married, the other single. During the Great War, from 1914 to 1918, Staszek's father, a soldier in the Austrian army, had been the orderly to Pan Walter, a cavalry officer. The men became friends, and the friendship continued throughout the postwar years. When Staszek came to Warsaw, he contacted his father's friend, and Pan Walter had arranged for the room in Professor Glowacki's apartment. The relationship became increasingly more important. Staszek, a printer and stampmaker, supplied some of the forged documents the Polish underground needed. Staszek had no direct contact with the Polish underground; Pan Walter and his sons arranged for the needed documents.

The well-groomed and immaculately dressed man who opened the door for us radiated old-world charm. He took my hand and I could see in his eyes that he liked me. He introduced me to the older son. It was the son who took me to an interview with the female owner of a small cosmetic factory. The woman was friendly. She asked a number of questions while leading me to the adjacent workroom. There were three large oblong tables with about eight women sitting close to each other at each table. They were engaged in filling small jars from an assortment of larger jars. They used little shovels. The factory consisted of an office-shipping room, a kitchen-laboratory, and the workroom. Back in the office, the woman said she felt I could easily manage the required tasks and that she would keep me in mind when the next opening became available.

Shortly after we returned to Pan Walter's apartment, Staszek and I got ready to leave. The elder Pan Walter kissed my hand and said, "Perhaps it's better this way. I will find a job for you. Now that I have met you, I know that we will find a job for you." I was surprised. I had been so careful, and I couldn't figure out what had gone wrong.

I subsequently learned that the owner of the cosmetic factory was young Pan Walter's wife. She said that she was certain I could do the work, but less certain that I could handle working closely with women who were bound to ask too many uncomfortable questions.

Though my apprenticeship with Panna Gomulka had been mainly confined to basting and finishing, I had managed to learn the rudiments of operating a sewing machine. When Staszek asked if I could successfully work in a garment factory, I answered that I could.

Pan Walter sent me a letter of introduction to a woman who was the director of a garment factory. Staszek accompanied me to a well-maintained building on Aleje Ujazdowski and remained in an outside office while I was ushered in to meet the director, Pani Garzynska. When the lady—she was addressed as Pani Directorowa, or Mrs. Director—asked me if I could operate a sewing machine at a rapid pace and turn out a perfect garment, I answered in the affirmative. She said that if a garment was less than perfect, and if the damage could not be properly repaired, the cost of both materials and labor would be deducted from the operator's wages. I nodded. A new branch was to open within several weeks. I was to report on October first, at eight o'clock in the morning, at the second floor of a building on Ulica Chmielna. It was definite. I had a piece of paper that said so. Nothing else mattered. I had a job, and I knew that I would do all I could to hold on to it.

I decided that since speaking had, on so many occasions, brought me close to the abyss, I would be reticent without appearing unfriendly. My ration coupons would be increased, and more important, my earnings would ease our constant fear of losing our room for not paying the rent on time. Perhaps if I made enough money, Mother could stop being a volunteer for a laboratory experiment in the Mokotow section, to which she traveled every other day, except Sunday.

Mother told me the laboratory operated in conjunction with a blood bank located in the same building. When I first asked Mother what she was doing there, her answer was evasive. When I insisted, she said I should stop pestering her. Apparently through the Duchess, Mother heard of a group of women who had volunteered to be part of an experiment. One of the women had been unable to fulfill her commitment, and a replacement was needed. The incentive was food. Mother made the necessary connections, her blood was tested, and she had been deemed a satisfactory substitute. The experiment was to last three months. Mother guarded her secret carefully. She did not want the Duchess, our landlady, or even Staszek to know about it. She did tell Jerzy. The laboratory assignment commenced in August. In the afternoon, when Mother returned from "work," she was quite pale and tired. Waiting for me on our little table was either an egg, an orange, or, on a few occasions, a piece of cheese. The food Mother brought home never exceeded one portion, and though I knew that it was meant for her, upon seeing it I couldn't restrain myself from eating it. Mother sat on the sofa and watched me eat. Every day she wanted to look at my sore gums, and she kept asking me if they had stopped bleeding. A recent respiratory infection had left me with a cough I was unable to shake off. Maintaining our health was a constant worry.

The monetary compensation Mother received was minimal, but she received coupons that entitled her to one meal in the laboratory eating facility. Each morning, laboratory technicians fastened little boxes, the size of small matchboxes with rubber bands, to Mother's exposed thigh and upper arm. After the midday meal, which Mother ate sparingly, another batch of little boxes was attached to her other thigh and arm. Only when I saw Mother apply cold compresses soaked in a liquid she brought home from the laboratory, did she tell me what she was doing to obtain food. When she lifted the compress,

I saw that sections of the skin on her arms and thighs were dark red. Within the sections of red were tiny pinpricks. Mother told me that she did not know the purpose of the experiment, and as far as she was able to ascertain, neither did the technicians who administered the protocol.

The small boxes contained lice that fed, through a mesh netting, on the blood of the volunteer. Despite safety precautions taken by the Polish technicians who carried out the experiment, there were instances when lice escaped. Neither the technicians nor the donors knew the source of the lice. The supervising German authority supplied the lice. Mother reported that the atmosphere in the laboratory was always tense because in recent months a number of volunteers had contracted an unidentified illness. They had to be treated in the hospital. Once a volunteer was infected, she was not allowed to return to the laboratory. The technicians were male, Mother said, but all the volunteers were female.

On a Saturday evening the doorbell rang at our end of the apartment. Since we hardly ever received visitors, we were immediately alert, our adrenaline pumping. Mother went to open the door, and I heard her speak in a low voice. There was a man's voice. I could not hear what was being said. After a while Mother returned. In her hand she held one hundred zlotys. She told me that the man, a tall, handsome, well-dressed Pole, had been an emissary from a clandestine organization.

I was stunned. "Did he say that?" I asked.

"He did not," Mother replied, "but that's what I inferred. Someone must have contacted the underground and interceded on our behalf."

The visitor let it be known that he was aware that we were without means and starving. "This is a one-time payment," he said. "It's all we can do, so please don't ask for more. Should you ever see me on the street, do not acknowledge me. Do not betray me with even a glance in my direction. You do understand." Mother had nodded that she did. He opened the door leading to the staircase and was gone before Mother was able to express her gratitude. We had heard that the Polish underground was making counterfeit banknotes and circulating them into the market. We examined the money the man had brought. It was real. We had no idea who had initiated the good deed.

A number of times Danka had asked me to come along when she went swimming in the Vistula River. She knew that I did not own a bathing suit, but she assured me that between her and her sister's old swimsuits, one would be found to fit me. Mother wanted me to see Danka, and she said it was good for me to be in her carefree company. One warm Saturday morning in late summer, I telephoned Danka and told her that I would be coming to visit. My friend was delighted, and she was waiting for me when I descended from the streetcar. "I am so happy that you came," she called out. "Let me take a look at you. Poor Krysia, I can see you were ill. How pale you are, and slimmer than ever."

Her genuine friendship enveloped me like a warm cloak. Happily, her eyes sparkling, she put her arm through mine. She had shed the mannish black coat she wore when I last saw her and wore instead her father's cast-off long-sleeve cardigan. As always, she looked stunning. The short, pleated skirt showed her shapely legs to full advantage. She chattered gaily about a new man she liked, who so far did not know of her existence, gramophone records of dance music circulating among her friends, a party she wanted to bring me to, and how all summer I had declined her invitations to go swimming in the Vistula. We were approaching her building in the Falata Apartments complex when Danka said, "You must ask your aunt's permission to come swimming with me tomorrow after Mass, and I will pray that you receive the sardines."

"Sardines?" I asked.

"You haven't heard? The sardines are sent from Portugal but commissioned from England. They are safer than letters, and whoever receives sardines from Portugal has confirmation that someone in England had made the arrangements."

Dear Danka. She did not have the slightest idea how valuable the information she had so casually given me was. The sardines would help us establish our alibi with our landladies and would assuage lingering suspicions among Mother's friends. If Polish army personnel were using this surreptitious method to inform their families in Poland that they were alive and well, we would use the information to hint that we also had received such a communication. Since Poles seemed to know about this arrangement, all we had to say was that we had received a tin of sardines.

Early on Sunday afternoon, Danka, her sister, and I boarded two streetcars and walked for about three kilometers to a place on the bank of the Vistula

River the girls referred to as their "club." I had entered a different world. The riverbank was an expanse of green grass, and borders of trees and bushes provided shade for families out for a Sunday picnic. The river was broad. In Krakow I had been able to swim across to the opposite shore, but in Warsaw that was impossible. I followed my friends to a broken-down shack. We undressed in a corner, folded our clothes into a pile and stored them on a shelf alongside the wall.

The delight I felt when I submerged myself in the gentle waves of the river was boundless. Magically, I had gained access to this heretofore inaccessible world and was now experiencing its delights. Both Danka and Krystyna were happy to note that I was a good swimmer. Danka bubbled over with joy as we swam out into the river. Krystyna wanted to know where I had learned to swim so well. Perhaps I should have been less of a good swimmer, but it was too late to alter that fact. I decided to be more careful. It was not wise to be too proficient at any task.

Danka introduced me to several people and referred to me as little Krysia. When we were ready to leave, both girls stopped to speak with Stefan, a young man who was in the process of disassembling his kayak. Danka helped by holding on to the plywood boards, while he peeled off the canvas that held the kayak together. He kissed her hand and thanked her. Then he turned to me and said, "You are a good swimmer, but you should work on your endurance. You should practice breathing exercises." As we were leaving, he called after us and said that he hoped the days would remain warm because he wanted to see us again. Danka told me that Stefan kept the disassembled kayak at the shack, and that several times during the summer he had taken Krystyna for a ride in his small boat.

Before the cold weather made swimming impossible, I managed to experience several more of these glorious days. I began to look accordingly: My hair recovered its normal luster and I acquired a becoming tan. Suddenly, after a ten month's absence, my menstrual period returned. Mother was overjoyed. I did not think Mother would approve, but I decided to give Stefan our telephone number. He said that he enjoyed meeting me and that he would call me. I knew I wanted to see him again.

On the designated Monday, I reported for work in a three-story apartment building, on Ulica Chmielna. An older woman, dressed in a kimono, opened the door. "You must be the new one. I figured as much," she said. "You are fifteen minutes ahead of time." She closed the door in my face. Moments before eight o'clock, women of all ages came rushing up the stairs, and together with them I entered apartment 2G.

The woman who had slammed the door in my face had changed into a gray, belted smock that covered her knees. Her gray hair, pulled back tightly into a neat knot, framed a tired and wrinkled face. Her name was Pani Ulaszewicz, and she was the owner of the apartment and manager of the factory. I learned from coworkers her husband was a dentist whose whereabouts were unknown. What served as a factory during the day were living quarters during the night for Pani Ulaszewicz, her married daughter and son-in-law, and a single daughter. From the time of the invasion, German personnel had occupied her home. The apartment that now housed the factory had, in prewar times, been her husband's dental office. I never learned what kind of managerial task Pani Ulaszewicz was charged with, but her tall stooped figure was visible throughout the day. She looked worn out and defeated, while Pani Garzynska, the director, was regal-looking and self-confident.

A forelady, Pani Jaworska, an aristocratic-looking woman in gold-rimmed spectacles, was responsible for the work output. She told me that until a machine became available, I would have to sew buttons on dresses. I would be paid by the garment. The shirtwaist dresses required four buttons down the front and one at each cuff. When everyone had settled down to work, the noise of the sewing machines—most of the machines were ancient—was ear shattering. There were two double rows of sewing machines, arranged so that the machines and their operators faced each other, almost touching. I was eager to work at a sewing machine because sewing the actual garment was paid at a higher rate than sewing buttons. At twelve-thirty, during the one-hour lunch break, we were encouraged to pray in a nearby chapel and to take advantage of the adjacent soup kitchen, run by nuns from a Catholic mission. The factory had made the arrangements, and the payment was minimal. The cabbage soup, more nourishing than anything Mother or I could prepare on our burner, was most welcome. I was overjoyed and grateful that after searching for ten months I had finally landed a steady job, but I had to be on guard lest I appeared too eager. My coworkers felt underpaid and overworked.

The finished dresses were shipped to Germany. Before leaving the factory, each garment had to meet with the approval of Pani Wyszynska, who supervised production. She was directly responsible to the director, Pani Garzynska. After approving the garment, Pani Wyszynska dispatched the dresses to the presser who worked on the floor below in an apartment that also housed the shipping division. Pani Wyszynska's eagle eye was able to detect the most minor defects, and she concluded all reprimands with the threat that competition was keen and should garments not live up to German expectations, the factory would have to close down and everyone would be out of work.

Pani Wyszynska was very pious. Suspended from a silver chain around her neck was a large crucifix. She encouraged us to murmur our prayers while we were working, and she frequently initiated the singing of hymns. It was she who had arranged for the bowls of soup we received in the chapel. Often while I worked at the factory, I would see Pani Wyszynska on her knees at the chapel, praying fervently at the feet of her patron, Saint Teresa. She knew who did or did not attend Mass at the chapel before coming to work. She let me know that she approved of my frequent attendance. She also encouraged weekly confession and the subsequent communion.

I had no problem attending chapel. The church had been my refuge since I had assumed my false identity. I felt comforted when I was on my knees speaking to and pleading with the only God that I knew. Whenever possible, I tried to avoid going to confession. Receiving the wafer was less hazardous than being in the confessional, subject to questions by the priest. Still, the act of receiving communion caused me considerable distress, because accepting communion signified that I had been to confession. To myself I reasoned that I was not hurting anyone by kneeling and pretending to be what I was not. I had no sins to confess.

Behind her back, my coworkers mocked Pani Wyszynska for her piety. They said that she moved from one novena to the next. Yet, these same women brought their prayer books to work and discussed their personal connection to the holy pictures they had placed inside. At times I felt that my coworkers were waiting for me to participate in their ridicule of Pani Wyszynska, but I tried to convey that my religious beliefs would not permit that. I had always known people who had a deep need for prayer. I did not dare think about them, or their whereabouts. If Pani Wyszynska lived her religion passionately, then I respected her method of worshipping. Each day when I left for work, I carried my prayer book and rosary with me.

## NOVEMBER 1943 ✋ WARSAW, OCCUPIED POLAND

In the late autumn of 1943, German broadcasts kept insisting that total victory at the eastern front was imminent. Polish broadcasts received clandestinely over the BBC reported that it was the other way around. In the factory, these events were commented on, but always in code. There was a rumor or someone had mentioned to a shopkeeper that railroad personnel had glimpsed hospital trains loaded with Wehrmacht casualties, and Polish patients had been forced to vacate Polish hospitals to make room for wounded soldiers returning from the eastern front. I was glad to hear the rumors, but I kept my eyes on the buttons I was sewing. I did not dare believe the good news of German military reverses. Despite my fervent prayers during the past five years, all available data had confirmed the Nazi propaganda. Enriched by the conquered countries they plundered, the Nazis had devastated Europe and brought it to its knees. German expansion appeared limitless.

Then, in late November 1943, while rushing home from work along snow-covered Aleje Jerozolimski, there they were—column after column of wounded German soldiers shuffling along the broad boulevard. They were no longer the strutting, invincible army heading east in hobnailed boots that I had first seen in Krosno in the spring of 1941. Though they were heading east, the lyrics of their marching songs referred to the west. I remembered the ominous words, bloodcurdling in their portent, the ever-repeated refrain: " *Wir marschieren, wir marschieren, gegen Engeland, gegen Engeland.*" We are marching against England. Or "*Heute England, morgen die ganze Welt.*" Today England, tomorrow the whole world.

Orders to look sharp and march in step, shouted by officers accompanying the column on motorcycles, were disregarded. Slack-jawed, dejected-looking soldiers trudged along the broad boulevard, from which all vehicular traffic had been banned. Many walked on crutches, some soldiers with the supporting arm or shoulder of a comrade. Blood-encrusted bandages covered heads, arms, and legs. Relatively few soldiers were in possession of an army overcoat. What had happened to the well-constructed, and always polished boots of the German soldier? The straggling feet were shod in torn boots with dirty cloth strips wrapped around legs.

I walked briskly, with downcast eyes, and the columns kept coming. In spite of orders from patrolling police detachments warning pedestrians not to stop or stare, for some Poles the temptation to look was greater than the fear of punishment. In passing I noted that some who had dared to disobey were accosted by the police and taken away.

For the first time since my arrival in Warsaw at Christmastime in 1942, I felt part of the larger community. Though anonymous in the crowd, I sensed that my secret jubilation was shared by many of the people around me. I was aware of fleeting attempts by others to make eye contact with me, an invitation to acknowledge with some gesture that what we were witnessing was what we had prayed for. I resisted the urge to exchange an affirmative glance. Agents provocateurs were watching us all the time. No one knew what these people looked like because nothing distinguished them, or their secret mission, from the average citizen. They could be walking alongside you, or trying to catch your eye. I would not succumb.

The latest addition to our clandestine group of those who had evaded the liquidation of the Krosno ghetto was from Warsaw. Ninka, the young girl whom Professor Glowacki had brought to his apartment, had escaped from the Warsaw ghetto. The professor apparently had no idea of the true identity of his tenant Staszek Winiarski and Staszek's friend, Jerzy Krawczyk, yet he had trusted them enough to enlist their help in rescuing this Jewish girl. How Ninka, one of the ghetto fighters who had escaped via an underground sewage canal, had survived, when most of her comrades had been caught and murdered, was a miracle. She told us there had been a lot of shooting, and the corpses of her dead comrades were all around her as she ascended from the sewer canal. Despite being wounded, she managed to evade her pursuers. On a cold October evening, a friend of the professor, who was also a fellow tenant in the apartment house, had found Ninka at the foot of a monument near Ulica Filtrowa. The girl was nearly frozen, scarcely breathing, and she had lost consciousness. Her savior had taken her to his home and told the professor that, had he not come upon her, "the young girl would surely have died that night." Having saved her life, her rescuer was determined to protect her from falling into the hands of the Gestapo. However, the man who had rescued Ninka, and his family who had fed and sheltered her while her wounds were healing, were afraid to keep her in their home. Their two children were too young to be let in on so dangerous a secret. He asked his friend, Professor Glowacki, to share the burden and allow Ninka to further recover in the professor's apartment.

Ninka was perhaps a year or two older than I was. She was less than five feet tall, and a bit stocky. Her exquisitely formed eyebrows framed her almond-shaped eyes. Her short black hair enhanced the handsome oval of her face. When I met Ninka, perhaps several months after she was rescued, the men who had sheltered her were preparing to place her with a family that needed help and lived in the same building.

Everyone who met Ninka was astonished to hear how she had managed for these many months, all alone, to outwit her pursuers. Her desire to report what had taken place during the liquidation of the Warsaw ghetto had given her a fierce determination to survive. While Ninka talked, I listened and wept. Her diction was flawless, and it was immediately apparent that she had received a fine education. She told us of the uprising in the Warsaw ghetto, of the spirit of community that had pervaded the starving, besieged prisoners, and about the death of the immediate members of her family. She spoke about the heroic determination of a relatively small and exhausted group of activists to obtain or fashion weapons and to fight and resist until the end.

Neither Mother nor I knew that the factory where I worked was located in the infamous red-light district of Warsaw. Not being native to Warsaw, we were unaware of the notoriety of Ulica Chmielna. Only when the name of the street was mentioned to Panna Cybulska, did Mother gather that something was amiss. When I told Danka where I had found work, she broke into giggles before telling me what she found so comical.

Not until I was assigned to a sewing machine near the window was I able to look down and see the activities Danka had intimated. Now I understood the expressive glances I had previously been unable to decipher. Whenever Pani Wyszynska was nearby, no one dared look out the curtainless window. There were no red lights, but from early afternoon, the ongoing commerce became visible. The prostitutes, mainly young women of various shapes and attire, all wearing high-heeled shoes, were standing in doorways or walking the street. Frequently in pairs, they strolled on the sidewalk along Ulica Chmielna across from the factory and propositioned the passing males. If the man accosted stopped, we knew that within minutes the couple would disappear into one of the doorways. Prostitutes were registered with the municipality and subject to police raids when least expected. In accordance with Warsaw municipal health regulations, police agents would examine the booklet every prostitute was required to carry and verify that the woman had undergone the obligatory medical examination. If a woman had failed to present herself for the mandatory health check, she was led away in full view of her fellow practitioners, and people watched the sad spectacle from the windows. I learned that the red-light district in Ulica Chmielna had existed before the war. The majority of the patrons were native Poles. On rare occasions one could see a German civilian, or even a soldier, trying to make contact, despite the visible reluctance of the women to accommodate the occupier.

Shortly after I graduated from sewing on buttons to operating a sewing machine, I heard rumors that the factory might close down. It was devastating news. Just when I had mastered operation of the machine and the swelling of my ankles, caused by the fierce pressing of the foot pedals, was beginning to subside, I might lose my hard-won anchor.

Pani Wyszynska solemnly informed us that Pani Garzynska, the director, was presently bidding for a contract that might keep the factory operating. The contract she was bidding for involved sewing uniforms worn by a German workforce. Pani Garzynska was encountering fierce competition, we were told, and if she obtained the contract, wages would have to be cut to remain in business. Also, the factory would have to be enlarged and would therefore be moved to a different location. Pani Wyszynska told us that not all the operators presently employed would remain with the firm. She admonished us to pray fervently.


## DECEMBER 1943 ~ WARSAW, OCCUPIED POLAND

Since being introduced to Stefan on the bank of the Vistula, I had met him several times. We arranged to meet at street corners or in front of a store. I knew that during the previous summer he had several times taken Krystyna for a ride in his kayak. When I asked Danka why he had taken Krystyna and not her, she shrugged and answered he must have liked Krystyna more. "And Krystyna," I wondered, "did she like him?" Danka laughed. "Both of us like him," she responded. "But now Krystyna likes Mjetek better."

Since my ardent friendship with Zack Schäfer, which we expressed almost exclusively in the letters we exchanged until December 1941, when America entered the war, no other male had shown a special interest in me. I found Stefan's friendship comforting. He was mature, in his mid-thirties, and he did not ask invasive questions. Stefan was handsome and tall, and when I looked up, I looked right into his gray eyes, focused on me. I liked the way he looked at me. I detected warmth and kindness. Just walking by his side gave me an illusion of normalcy. Having been accosted a number of times while rushing through the streets and subjected to interrogation when I presented my Kennkarte, I was always worried that next time my luck would run out. Stefan's presence provided some welcome protection.

Whenever I met Stefan, usually on my way home from the factory, he would walk with me toward, but not quite to, the gate of my apartment house. I had told Stefan that I was living with my aunt who was very strict and would not permit me to date. I also told him that we had to assume that my father was in England because twice I had received sardines from Portugal. He knew about the sardines and said he was happy that my father was alive.

At night, when I reviewed the previous day's conversation between us, I was absolutely certain about one fact: Stefan Broda did not have even an inkling that I might be someone other than Krystyna Zolkos. Aside from Danka, he was the only person who did not question my odd speech. When we were together, Stefan asked questions about my prewar life. Cautious though I was, I could not avoid spinning a web concerning my past. He said I was very mature for my age. I needed to be careful; Polish girls my age did not carry my burden.

Christmas was approaching, and when questioned by Stefan, I recounted the Christmas celebrations I had enjoyed during my childhood. In Hindenburg, I had spent many happy hours around the decorated Christmas tree at Fräulein Hedel's home. Each year among presents for their family there were gifts for Eva and me. Using these good memories as my model, I created for Stefan a myth about our Christmas tree in Chorzow, where I lived in a comfortable household, within the secure orbit of my father's love. When Stefan asked if my aunt, Pani Dembicka, would have a tree for Christmas, I answered no. I had previously alluded to our precarious finances, and I had mentioned that between my aunt's and my earnings we barely managed to scrape along. Our impoverished state was nothing to be ashamed of. After four years of tyrannical occupation, the Poles who were rich were suspect. Patriotic Poles of Warsaw were in a constant struggle to survive and outwit the invader.

Native Warsawians had advantages over recent arrivals because of family relationships and friends who could be called upon to help.

I learned that Stefan rented a furnished room in the same building where his widowed mother lived. His father had died when he was in his early teens, and the man his mother subsequently married had been a professor at the Warsaw Polytechnic Institute. Before the war Stefan, a civil engineer by profession, had been employed by the Warsaw municipality. Not wanting to work for the Nazis, Stefan did not claim his prewar position once Warsaw was invaded. He thought it was safer to remain unaffiliated and thereby avoid invasive scrutiny by the occupation authority. To earn his livelihood, he relied on his hobby, photography. He told me that he had fixed up a windowless chamber adjacent to his room for a darkroom, where he developed film and produced enlargements whenever he was able to obtain commissions from his Polish resources. He took all photographs with a Leica. Though the camera was always with him, he took great care to avoid being noticed, and he was quick and efficient when he took a picture. Most of his work was done in people's homes. His steady income came from an arrangement with the resident theater company and the Parnell dance ensemble. Until I met Stefan, I had not heard that there were resident companies that were permitted to give performances for the citizens of Warsaw.

The semiannual validation of our Kennkartes was again due. We heard that the documents were scrutinized more severely. Gestapo agents intensely interrogated applicants they deemed suspicious. Several people hiding Jews, as well as Poles suspected of political activity, had disappeared after presenting their documents for validation. After discussing the peril with Jerzy, Mother decided that it was more dangerous to have the Kennkarte validated than to have a lapsed validation. We heard of young Poles who let the deadline for validation pass, because young people, especially males, were often suspected of being involved in forbidden organizations. There was speculation that after the defeat at Stalingrad, the war at the eastern front would soon end in German defeat, and if that should come to pass, the Nazis would turn on the civilian population. Danka told me that more Poles were joining the underground and were being trained for combat.

The Gestapo once again let it be known that despite a concerted effort

Sunday after attending mass. Warsaw, winter 1943–1944.

to round up every single Jew, they had caught several passing themselves off as Christians. They reaffirmed their determination to rid the city of all Jews, and they enlisted Warsaw residents to help in that effort. Both monetary and food compensation were promised for informers and complete confidentiality.

The superintendent of our apartment house was charged with making sure that the Kennkarte validations were up to date, and he had orders to report residents who failed to comply with the law. Mother knew that our landlady, Panna Cybulska, had not yet validated her or her mother's document. She said that due to the inclement weather she intended to postpone getting the validation. The superintendent had approached Mother on several occasions, and he told her to obtain the validation. When Mother failed to comply, he registered his impatience with Panna Cybulska, even though she was in the same predicament.

Jerzy, our loyal friend and advisor, had become less accessible because he had moved out of Warsaw. He had rented a small house north of Warsaw, in Miedzeszyn. The town could be reached by commuter railroad. It took about forty-five minutes to get there, and another fifteen minutes to reach the house. The professor's apartment had become too crowded, and Jerzy felt it had also become too dangerous. Jerzy, his older daughter Ewa, and Pani Jutta, a Jewish woman who needed shelter and who would be the housekeeper, took possession of the house in October. His younger daughter Maryla continued to work as a nursemaid with a Polish family who did not question her identity. Moreover, Staszek now had a female friend who had moved into the apartment. Her assumed name was Kazimiera, and she was the widow of a renowned surgeon who had been killed in the Warsaw ghetto. Mother met Jerzy when he came to Staszek's apartment, but with Kazimiera present it was somehow understood that visits should be curtailed.

In the late afternoon, on Christmas Eve, our doorbell rang. When Mother opened the door, our superintendent stood, smiling at her, and handed her a small decorated Christmas tree. Mother asked him to wait, rushed back into the room for a generous tip, and wished him a Merry Christmas. He wished Mother a Merry Christmas, and for the first time since we had moved into the building, he smiled and chatted a bit before he left. The tree, perhaps three feet tall, was in a wooden stand. It was decorated with tinsel and white cotton puffs, and it came from a florist. The card read, "For Pani Dembicka and Panna Krystyna, with best wishes for a bright Christmas." It was signed Stefan Broda.

In the ensuing question-and-answer session between Mother and me, I tried to be as evasive as possible. I said that Stefan was a friend of the Mlodzianowski girls. I had first met him when I went swimming with the sisters, and since that time I had run across him several times. "But the tree. A considerable expense—" Mother wondered. I could not respond to her puzzlement, but I said that I might have mentioned to Pan Broda that we could not afford a Christmas tree. Mother had to admit that the superintendent had been friendly and forthcoming, whereas before Christmas his antagonism toward us had been clearly evident. "Well, we should be grateful," Mother concluded, "Perhaps the generous gesture from your friend will buy us some goodwill from the superintendent."

That evening, while I was reading before falling asleep, Mother asked, "How old is your friend, Pan Broda?" I hesitated and said, "I think he must be in his late twenties." Stefan was thirty-six years old, but I thought it wise to be vague. Ever since they took my sister away, Mother's outbursts of anger had become more subdued. Still, every so often when walking the tightrope became unbearable, Mother's fear and frustration would erupt, and on some pretext I became the focus of her anger. Even while in Krosno, when Eva or I deviated just a little from what Mother considered the norm, she would trot out her trump card—my father. She would say he left her the mandate to care for us and she was charged to uphold standards as she saw fit. In Warsaw, we hardly ever mentioned my father. That indulgence was no longer available. The miracle we had hoped for, an assassination of Hitler and his henchman, had not occurred, and a victory by the Allies had not taken place.

Jerzy invited Mother and me to spend New Year's Eve in his house in Miedzeszyn. He thought it would be wise to project an air of normalcy, and since he learned that a number of his neighbors were having friends in for New Year's Eve, he should do the same. We happily accepted the invitation. Due to curfew we were to arrive at dusk, and leave on the following morning after breakfast. It was to be a lovely evening with friends. Aside from Jerzy, Ewa, Pani Jutta, Mother, and me, there were three other guests. Staszek and Kazimiera had been asked but they could not come.

Our host, Jerzy, conceived the idea of an evening with friends, because an initially vague perception that he was being watched had gained momentum. We were aware that in Warsaw the peacetime custom of spending New Year's Eve with friends had been observed throughout the years of occupation. Jerzy hoped that a small timely gathering would help create an image of social ties. The idea of being part of so daring an enterprise was anxiety provoking, but exciting at the same time. Mother and I took the precaution of arriving separately.

Pani Jutta, a woman in her fifties, was an early escapee from the Warsaw ghetto and was no longer able to finance a hiding place. Among ourselves, we referred to this phenomenon as "coming out." When a person had exhausted all means of financing a hiding place, his or her hidden state ended. The struggle to survive yet one more day on the streets became the sole focus of existence. The other guests, Janka and Hela, women in their early twenties, were not from Warsaw. They had managed to evade liquidation of the Lublin ghetto and had fled before transportation from that ghetto was put into action. They had invited Mjetek, a young Pole, to help add legitimacy to Jerzy's daring enterprise.

Mjetek brought a portable turntable and several records we could dance to. Throughout the evening, anyone passing by could hear soft dance music coming from Jerzy's house. We took turns watching the street from the unlit upstairs room. Although Jerzy and his family were the sole occupants of the detached suburban dwelling, we did not dare relax our vigilance. We spoke in whispers, addressing each other by our assumed names, and we used abbreviations when it was necessary to mention a name or an address. In spite of the pleasant sound of the dance music and the comfort of spending the evening with friends, it was an anxiety-fraught night. We were worried that the sounds on the inside might camouflage sounds on the outside. From the upstairs window, we watched a foot patrol pass the house. Though for that one night we had hoped for it, feeling safe was not an option.

## JANUARY 1944 ⚜ WARSAW, OCCUPIED POLAND

The factory on Ulica Chmielna was closed, and I was among the lucky ones asked to report for work at the new location. Our new quarters were above Café Aktorow, or Actor's Café, in an elegant gray stucco building located at a corner immediately off Napoleon Square. Since the one-story structure was set back from the sidewalk, closed off by a wrought-iron fence, and fronted by a well-kept lawn, a passing pedestrian would never imagine that the building housed a garment factory. In time we learned that the administration of the Actor's Café could no longer afford to maintain the empty upper story, and there was fear that the German occupation authority would convert this facility for its use.

All sewing machines were checked by mechanics, and six of the old machines had been motorized, making it a total of ten. We were informed that the firm was trying to obtain additional motors, and that the ones presently in place would be assigned to the workers who were most productive. I was one of the six who had the good fortune to be assigned to a newly motorized sewing machine. Pani Jaworska handed each operator stacks of cut-out parts, which, when assembled, would become a type of overcoat called, in German, a *Joppe*. The garment consisted of an outer dark-gray shell made of reprocessed

wool, a wool interlining, and a rayon lining. All garments were made of the
same textile and fashioned on the same pattern. An operator was required to
complete five garments during the day. The cloth was heavy and difficult to
maneuver. Especially difficult was the sewing in of the epaulettes and pocket
flaps and the tedious task of sewing the buttonholes.

On the first day in the new location, not knowing how to regulate the
thread tension of the bobbin in relation to the speed of the machine, I wasted
a considerable amount of time until I mastered it. I subsequently encountered
other obstacles. When I turned to Pani Jaworska for help, I learned to my surprise that the forelady of production knew even less about operating a sewing
machine than I did. She told me that I would have to learn what I needed to
know from the other operators. However, it would be better by far, she added,
if I were to address my questions to the mechanic. Once a week, on Saturday
afternoons, a mechanic visited the factory. He repaired broken belts, oiled motors, and took care of minor adjustments.

I wondered what Pani Jaworska had heard; perhaps there had been hints
or complaints that I, who had so little experience, had been given a motorized machine. Pani Jaworska, always kind and soft spoken, suggested that I
remain after work on Saturday and ask the mechanic. Winking at me conspiratorially, she added, "I'll be at your side. In time I may need to know how
to operate a sewing machine."

In January we were overwhelmed by a catastrophic event. Jerzy's house in
Miedzeszyn was raided, and our beloved friend, his oldest daughter Ewa, and
Pani Jutta were murdered, their frozen bodies left in a ditch at the side of the
house. No one dared to go and claim the dead bodies. Only after Staszek had
word that the corpses had been removed, did he inform Maryla. I could not
even go near Maryla because her employer had no idea of her real identity,
and a wrong move by a well-meaning friend would have jeopardized her safety.
We subsequently learned that Jerzy, uneasy in his new residence, had been trying to relocate. He told Staszek that Pani Jutta had been questioned in a neighborhood store and that there had been overt harassment. Two days before the
assassination, while Jerzy was absent, an "electrician" had rung the doorbell,
ostensibly to check on some wiring. The man had meandered through the
house, and by the time he left, Pani Jutta was certain that the man was an
impostor.

Not since the murder of Aunt Regina and Dollek did I see Mother in such a state of utter despair. Unable to find words of comfort, I spoke to Mother about Jerzy's multiple acts of friendship. He had been the only one who still staunchly believed that she would live to see her husband, and I, my father. He encouraged Mother to keep fighting when she felt she could no longer endure. He helped us to obtain forged documents, and he interceded for us with Staszek, when the latter thought that our visits to the professor's apartment would jeopardize their safe haven. He never wavered in his opinion that I could pass as a Polish girl and would be capable of handling the language. We mourned Jerzy in our hearts, our sorrow hidden away, as we mourned for my grandparents, uncles, aunts, and my many young cousins. It was gnawing at us, grinding us down.

We did not acknowledge to each other, not even to ourselves, that my sister might be dead. We knew that she did not die naturally because she was young and healthy and wanted to live. Was she murdered? Since we never found out what had happened to her when she was caught in those early morning hours in Krosno, we had decided to hope. My mind invented scenarios of Eva escaping, of Eva being rescued, and of Eva being hidden by a compassionate Polish woman. During my incessant nightmares, I would see Eva's face. She was holding my hand, and we were running. In the morning I was grateful to escape from our cold room and embark on the fifty-minute walk to the factory along the icy and snow-covered streets of Warsaw.

I worked at a feverish pace, turning out well-sewn garments with straight seams. Since the factory operated on a piecework system, all operators endeavored to complete as many coats as possible. The two most experienced seamstresses were Zosia and Stacia. Both in their late twenties, they had met in the factory on Ulica Chmielna and were good friends. They were seated across from each other, and as in the previous location, they were next to the window. Seated on my left, between Zosia and me, was Pani Byk, a protective buffer—or so I thought. She was faster than I, and her output even exceeded that of Zosia and Stacia. The operator across from me, Pani Grub, was a middle-aged woman who was the sole support of an invalid husband and six children. She did not engage in conversation, and she never smiled. Whenever I looked up, I saw her tight-lipped almost toothless mouth. A look of anger never left her face. The woman seated between her and Stacia, Pani

Zawacka, must have been in her late sixties. Her gaze was shifty, her disposition mean, and her manner ingratiating. Stacia, Zosia, and Pani Zawacka formed an alliance whose main focus was belittling and ridiculing their coworkers, supervisors, and even the young assistant presser who had recently joined our workforce. Whenever the young man came near them to pick up the completed work, they would utter words that made him blush, and I saw the three women snicker at his discomfit.

My head bent over my work amidst the loud noise of the rotating motors, I pretended not to hear the derisive remarks, the backstabbing, and the giggling that accompanied the nasty assaults. I feared the threesome and modeled myself on Pani Grub, who appeared oblivious to all attempts at communication. On several occasions, while rushing out of the factory, Stacia and Zosia came at me from both sides and attached themselves to me. It took all my presence of mind and my ingenuity to fend them off.

Warsaw residents knew that the Gestapo kept a list of Poles who would be arrested in case of sabotage or civil disorder. The fact that some had already been arrested came as a surprise. Large pink posters listing the names of two hundred potential Polish hostages appeared suddenly, pasted to kiosks throughout the city. They were academicians, lawyers, writers, doctors, and artists—educated Poles, who, by living unobtrusively, had hoped to avoid contact with the Nazi invader. Twenty-five people from the top of the list, all men, had already been arrested, the Gestapo announced, because of an act of sabotage committed by a "deranged" underground organization. The other targeted hundred and seventy-five Poles still enjoyed their liberty, but were advised that they would pay with their lives if further acts of sabotage were to occur. Within days after their arrest, the twenty-five hostages were put against a wall on Nowy Swiat and shot dead. The bodies were left in the snow. After they had been taken away, the blood-spattered wall became a place of pilgrimage for patriotic residents of Warsaw. One could pass by, but was forbidden to stop or offer a prayer. Yet, during the weeks following the murder, and despite strict orders to refrain from such acts of "treachery," candles were lit each night at the murder site, and they illuminated the bloodstains of the Polish martyrs. I saw the candles flickering in the early dawn when I passed at a safe distance on my way to the factory.

Danka told me her father had said that since the posting of the hostage list and the subsequent killings, Poles had come to realize that the Nazi doctrine did indeed adhere to a master plan. People feared, he said, that now the Jews were exterminated, Christian Poles would be next. Her father remembered reading that Hitler listed Poles and Slavs immediately beneath Jews and Gypsies as races that were inferior and expendable.

I overheard our landlady warn her brother during a telephone conversation. She told him not to visit and to consider a change of address. The killing of the twenty-five hostages, the blood-spattered wall, and the explicit threat to Warsaw residents presaged calamity. Several of the women at work were teary-eyed, and Pani Jaworska and Pani Wyszynska were openly weeping and wiping their eyes. Having a legitimate reason to mourn, my tears came easily. During the following days, the menacing threesome refrained from ridiculing their coworkers.

Zosia and Stacia were able to carry on a continuous conversation, while at the same time turn out a record number of garments. With my motor running, and all the other machines working at the same time, I could not hear what they said, or rather, I pretended not to hear. When asked "Krysia, did you hear that?" or "Krysia, what do you have to say about that?" I shrugged my shoulders. No, I did not hear. I did not know what the conversation was about. Frequently the conversation was about Jews who were discovered hiding in the most unlikely places. About Jews who were caught running from a cellar, and about the rewards offered by the Gestapo to Poles coming forward and turning in a Jew, or someone sheltering a Jew.

Though Pani Wyszynska had pointed out the nearest chapel, a ten-minute walk from the factory, few of the workers made the effort to rush over during the lunch break. The fact that there was no adjacent mission serving soup was an added deterrent. Most workers brought food from home, ate it quickly, and returned to their work. For me, the lunch break was a time of torture. More often than in the previous months, the two bullies badgered me about my strange accent. They asked questions about my parents and the towns where I had lived before moving to Warsaw. But what almost stopped my heartbeat were the questions addressed to Pani Byk. "Did anyone ever tell you that you look Jewish?" they asked her. "That could be," responded Pani Byk. "Did anyone ever tell you that you did?" Were they joking among themselves? I wondered. Shortly thereafter, during lunch break, when Pani Byk had walked away from her machine, Zosia turned to me and asked, "Does Pani Byk's voice sound Jewish?" I shrugged my shoulders.

"What do you mean you don't know?" she prodded.

"I did not know there was such a thing as a Jewish voice."

"Stacia, you must hear this." Zosia motioned to her friend to come closer. "Krysia never heard that you can recognize a Jew by the way he speaks."

"Then Krysia must have led a sheltered life," Stacia said.

"Maybe there were no Jews in Chorzow," Zosia interposed. "Krysia, were there Jews in Chorzow?"

"Yes, I think there were," I responded.

The giggling on the part of my two tormentors seemed to increase with the offensiveness of their remarks. The only avenue of escape was to remain at my machine, hiding behind the noise of the motor. My nervous energy propelled me to turn out a record amount of uniforms. Since the two bullies were also the two operators who turned out the highest number of garments, I made certain to turn out fewer garments than they did.


## MARCH 1944 ⤳ WARSAW, OCCUPIED POLAND

There was a new man in Danka's life, and she wanted to talk about him. She told me that I was the only person who understood her, and indeed I did. Danka enjoyed the excitement of meeting an attractive man and testing her charm and the possibility of a conquest. It never went beyond a short flirtation because her boyfriend Daniel was her only true love. There was an understanding between them, though more vague on Daniel's than on Danka's part, that they would in time marry. Daniel did not want to make a commitment, and he encouraged Danka to socialize with other young people. Aside from meeting her at Mass on Sundays, communication between them was confined to the telephone.

Daniel, who had been a year short of graduating from the gymnasium when the Germans conquered Poland, was a committed enemy of the invader. During the day he worked as a mechanic in an auto repair shop, and evenings, together with his father, he repaired various household items in a workshop his father had set up in the cellar of their apartment house. Daniel was aware

Danka, my loving friend who never knew my true identity, gave me this photo. Warsaw, February 26, 1944.

of the poverty around him and of his inability to help. He talked about the fatherless children throughout Poland, the atrocities going on in the camps, and the disappearance of the Jews. A serious young man from a working-class background, he found it difficult to cope with Danka's middle-class femininity. Though delighted with her attractive appearance, he objected to her flirtatious disposition, her provocative way of dressing, and her teasing sensuality.

Danka knew that her attraction to Daniel was not casual. She wanted to hold on to this caring, self-possessed young man, but she also wanted to hear him say that she was his girl. During the winter months, my friend telephoned several times during the week to discuss with me what Daniel had said and what I thought it meant.

Occasionally, I would meet the sisters, Danka and Krystyna, for morning Mass on Sunday at the Church of Saint Anne. Whenever I came along, Daniel, Danka's friend, and Mjetek, Krystyna's friend, made sure to bring along Bobek, a third young man, when we met after Mass. I knew by then that all three men belonged to the Polish underground and that they were involved in such clandestine activities as planning and carrying out acts of sabotage. We were aware that police agents pretending to be ordinary worshippers were monitoring church activities, and one had to be very careful. The three young men, all members of the male church choral society, came to greet us after Mass. Then they disappeared. Danka complained that Daniel was too busy to see her. He hardly telephoned.

Bobek, a tall, lanky man who was about twenty-two years old, would come over to me, kiss my hand, and engage in some casual conversation with me, just long enough to give the two couples time to exchange some private thoughts. At first glance, one would say that Bobek was not an attractive man. His elongated face, gray skin tone, protruding buck teeth, and thick eyeglasses, in addition to his stooping gait, contrasted sharply with the handsome appearance of both Daniel and Mjetek. Yet, I knew that Bobek was highly esteemed, and the reason for this became quickly apparent. The glance of his deep brown eyes was intelligent and penetrating. He was a man of few words with a well-trained, disciplined mind. I felt privileged to know him, though I would have been unable to articulate the reason why.

Due to the accelerating acts of sabotage in different sections of Warsaw, which targeted unlikely locations, just knowing that an underground cell existed was becoming almost as dangerous as knowing the hiding place of a Jew. Moreover, the Gestapo was disseminating propaganda that tied the Polish underground activities to both Communists and Jews. Many times, while waiting for the streetcar on my way to work, I was stopped by German police and requested to produce my work documents. The police appeared suddenly, in groups of six or eight men, and within seconds that many people would be simultaneously stopped, scrutinized, and questioned. My Arbeitskarte stated that I was sewing uniforms for a civilian task force. The assignment came directly from the Reich, and it suggested that the bearer not be unduly delayed because the factory was required to produce, on time, a designated quota of uniforms.

During the impromptu roundups, the police were always successful. Invariably two or three victims would be led away, while I was among the fortunate ones who were released. It was mainly a matter of luck. Most people had proper documents or work passes, either forged or legitimate. Without them, one could not venture into the street. What was unpredictable was the interrogator. His power was limitless, and the decision to honor the work pass or detain the bearer was his alone. Only on very rare occasions did I take the streetcar after work. I felt safer rushing home on foot, though it was hard on the soles of my one decent pair of shoes.

Since the days were getting longer, I decided to accept Danka's offer to meet me after work. I gently suggested that she meet me inside the gate. Danka would have preferred another meeting place, but when it came to our friendship, she easily acquiesced. She had no idea of the gift she bestowed upon me. She gave me a yearned-for respite from my two tormentors, Zosia and Stacia. Whatever suspicion they harbored against me was somewhat assuaged when they saw my best friend embracing and kissing me. Without a glance at my coworkers, Danka, the prototype of a young, handsome, and self-assured Polish female, linked her arm with mine, and smiling happily, she whisked me away.

At times when I walked with Danka, I experienced fleeting moments of fellowship. Fleeting indeed they were, because I knew that I could not relax my vigilance for even a moment. We were at all times surrounded by enemies, and my sole protection was my intuitive sense of danger. I had trained myself to keep my eyelids lowered whenever I was among people. In Danka's company, I had to make certain that the role I was playing coincided with the convoluted past I had created. Once while walking with Danka, her arm linked with mine, I recognized from quite a distance a young man walking toward us: He was Tadek Wolsky from Krosno.

During the early years of the war, perhaps it was the summer of 1940, the Wolsky family moved into an apartment in Aunt Regina's building. We soon learned that they were Volksdeutsch—ethnic Germans. Frau Wolsky, the German part of the couple, acknowledged our existence, returned our greetings, and occasionally even smiled when I passed her in the hallway. Her children, the boy Tadek and the girl Halina, were friendly enough when we met on home ground. Eva and I had a number of conversations with them, and they were charmed by Dollek's irrepressible personality. It was understood that we would not recognize each other on the streets of Krosno.

The father, Herr Wolsky, was a dangerous man. A Ukrainian and a drunkard, he had gained advantages through his wife's German ethnicity. Within weeks of his arrival in Krosno, we learned that he had unceremoniously displaced the Jewish owner of a lumber mill and that he had replaced the workers with Jewish slave labor recruited through the Arbeitsamt. Aunt Regina and Mother, as well as Eva and I, had the impression that Frau Wolsky and both children were not proud of Herr Wolsky and his treatment of the Jewish workers, or his publicly displayed, drunken anti-Semitic tirades. By the time we were forced to vacate the apartment, the Wolsky family had moved out of the building and taken possession of an elegant villa, from which the Jewish owners had been expelled.

I made certain that my face was turned toward Danka when Tadek passed us. Still, I sensed his eyes scrutinizing my face. There was a momentary hesitation on his part; perhaps he slowed his step. I never hesitated or stiffened. I kept my pace, and I was sure, as we continued on our way, that I had in no way betrayed myself.

"Do you know the guy that just passed us?" Danka asked.

"No, I didn't really look, but I'm sure I don't," I answered calmly.

"You did not see the way he looked at you? Sort of quizzically?"

"Now Danka, don't be modest, his glance wasn't meant for me, but for you. You should be used to that by now," was my rejoinder.

Within I felt anything but calm. My stomach knotted into a spasm, the piercing pain inhibiting my breathing, and my heart, it seemed to me, was beating so loud and wild I was afraid Danka might hear the pounding. Without giving it adequate thought, I agreed to the long postponed visit to Stare Miasto, the famous Old Town of Warsaw. The sudden unanticipated encounter had left me shaken, and I reasoned to myself that seeing Old Town with Danka would somewhat help restore my equilibrium.

Danka was proud of that quaint part of Warsaw, which I had never seen. It was not difficult to succumb to the charm of Old Town. The tree-lined streets we passed through were teeming with people on this late afternoon of an early spring day. In recessed front yards, the grass was once again green, and buds were sprouting from recently dormant trees. The center of Old Town consisted of two large squares divided by a walking street. There were side streets that were part of Old Town; however, the heart of Old Town was the treasured ancient buildings surrounding the two central squares. Most of the structures were renovated within and kept up to date with modern conveniences. The facades of the buildings were maintained in accordance with a strict code of architectural conservation. Though parts of Warsaw had been ruined during the blitzkrieg, Old Town had not been damaged.

Danka pointed out houses whose existence could be traced to the Middle Ages standing in harmony with adjacent houses that were no more than one hundred years old. It was apparent that careful planning by the Warsaw municipality had successfully achieved a balanced architectural unity for Warsaw's famous landmark.

I had been reluctant to visit Old Town because it was known that, since the invasion, the Polish owners and tenants had been forced to move out and most of the gracious dwellings were occupied by German families. A number of Polish artists and craftsmen maintained studios or shops in the side streets. We stopped to look at a display of handmade cork-soled sandals. Danka said that the shops in that area were for Germans only because Poles could not afford such luxury items. The Germans we saw looked like SS men in civilian clothes. Still, I had to agree with my friend: It was, ironically, an area where one could feel relatively safe, because the Germans wanted to provide a pleasant, normal atmosphere for their families. German housewives with mesh shopping bags were busy doing their marketing in the side streets, and German children, supervised by mothers and nursemaids, were playing in the square or sitting on benches surrounding the fountain.

Despite the apparent tranquil atmosphere within Old Town, I could not wait to leave it. There were too many Germans about, and I sensed danger, though Danka did not. She contended heatedly that it was her town and she would not let the Boche intimidate her. Danka used that word often, and she did not lower her voice when she said it. When I remonstrated that she was courting danger, she agreed to substitute another word. She thought *pasozyt*—parasite—expressed her sentiments just as well. I marveled at Danka's self-assurance. To my knowledge, she had never been to Warsaw until her family was expelled from Wejherowo when that area was annexed to the Reich, and they were forced to move to Warsaw. For Danka, all of Poland was her country, and Danka was certain that she would be present to rejoice when the invader was chased out. My reality differed sharply from hers. At the end of each day, I did not know if I was going to make it through the night, or if I would survive the following day.

## APRIL 1944 ⤝ WARSAW, OCCUPIED POLAND

It took a lot of persuasion to convince Mother that it was safe and advantageous for me to see Stefan Broda. Mother found it difficult to trust a Christian
Pole, especially one whom she had never met. I kept repeating that it had nothing to do with trust, since I would never reveal my true identity to him or
anyone else. What was important, I urged, was that Stefan believed me. He
had little money, yet he had sent us the small Christmas tree to help make
our holiday brighter. For the past several months, the apparent hostility of our
building superintendent had been somewhat mitigated. Wasn't that an advantage? I asked. Mother continued to express her apprehension, but she did
not stop me from seeing him. Several times Stefan met me after work. He was
inside the courtyard when I left the factory. He was a handsome, self-assured
man, and he projected a cultivated image. Subsequently, one of my tormentors asked if it was my uncle who had come to pick me up. I ignored the snide
remark. It was of utmost importance that I project an image of being connected. I was not alone. I had friends.

## MAY 1944 ⤝ WARSAW, OCCUPIED POLAND

The Polish underground, in a daring attempt to destroy Gestapo headquarters, invaded its fortress on Aleje Ujazdowski. Warsaw's Polish population was
eager to learn the minutest details of what the news broadcasts labeled a treacherous and cowardly attack. There was one issue about which everyone was in
total agreement: Repercussions would be swift and severe and directed mainly
at Polish men. It took days before we learned what in fact had taken place.
Apparently at dusk, two Gestapo trucks pulled inside the gate of the fenced-
in Gestapo headquarters. Out of the trucks jumped Poles disguised in Gestapo
uniforms. The attack was so unexpected that before the baffled guards could
sound the alarm, and amidst flying bullets, the courageous attackers managed
to rid Warsaw of several of the Gestapo's infamous torturers. A number of Gestapo
officers were killed, and some severely wounded. Contrary to news broadcasts,
the raid had been well planned, and although there were many casualties
among members of the underground, one truck had managed to escape.

On the day following the attack, the Gestapo, in reprisal, killed one hundred Poles from the list. Warsaw residents were informed that it was only the

beginning. Hundreds more could expect the same fate. It would be up to the families of the assassinated hostages and families of prospective hostages to make clear to members of the Polish underground that their cowardly actions would result in the death of their innocent compatriots. Throughout the city, new pink posters pasted to kiosks listed the names of hundreds of additional prospective hostages. The Gestapo decreed that each week one hundred people would be assassinated until the perpetrators of the attack on Gestapo headquarters were found and brought to justice.

The attack resulted in an acceleration of street raids. Poles, both men and women, even those with a validated Arbeitskarte, were taken in for questioning at police stations. Men, especially, were detained for no apparent reason. Both Danka and Stefan informed me that it was not an auspicious time for meeting me after work.

One evening during the latter part of May, our friend Staszek came to see us. He was pale and agitated. Mother immediately urged him to sit down. A family living under assumed names, based on documents forged by Staszek, had been picked up and taken to Gestapo headquarters for questioning. They had not been released. The term *questioning*, though used by everyone, was in fact a misnomer. Interrogation by the Gestapo meant questioning under torture. In response to Mother's inquiries, Staszek affirmed that he was certain it was not the police, a lesser evil, but indeed the Gestapo. Staszek had stashed all the forging implements in the deep pockets of his winter overcoat, on this mild May evening. He wanted us to hide them. Before Mother hid them, I saw the tools of his secret enterprise. There was a small stack of printed forms—blanks for birth and marriage certificates. From little boxes Staszek removed rubber rings and discs covered with tissue paper. To create the official seal of a Polish municipality, Staszek would spread a special glue onto a wooden hand piece, place the disk that contained the distinctive Polish eagle onto its center, and affix the rubber ring listing the name of the Polish municipality, or parish, around the disk.

We spoke in a whisper while Mother, under Staszek's watchful eye, hid the tools separately in shoes, jars, and among our clothing. For the benefit of our ever-watchful landlady, we staged an exit of our visitor. However, that night, as well as the two nights following, Staszek slept on the little sofa that was my bed, while I slept with Mother in her bed. While I went to work and

Mother was busy with errands for her friend, Duchess Woroniecka, Staszek remained in our room. It was not easy to have a male visitor in our tiny room, but I sensed that Mother was very glad to help. She was eager to reciprocate in some manner for the many favors Staszek had done for us, even if chiefly due to Jerzy's constant prodding. After three nights and two days, Staszek left. His precious materials remained with us for more than one week.

The errands Mother was running for her friend, the Duchess, were part of an effort to float items stolen from a German warehouse into the Warsaw black market. The Duchess had an unknown German or Polish source who was connected to the shoemaker supply department. She enlisted Mother to help sell rubber heels, leather soles, nails, and small tools. It was a dangerous undertaking, but Mother was careful. She said it helped pay the rent for our room. The meetings with the Duchess, Mother remarked, were more treacherous than those with the entrepreneurs who helped Mother dispose of the stolen goods. It was not so much that the Duchess was suspicious of Mother's identity, but her curiosity about Mother's background was insatiable. She was obsessed with pedigree. She could spend hours talking about her own genealogy, and she was frustrated by Mother's vagueness regarding her line of descent on either her side or her husband's side. She wanted to identify the Dembicki branch of Mother's family.

Neither the heroic act of sabotage by the Polish underground against Gestapo headquarters, nor the Gestapo street raids directed at the Polish residents of Warsaw, deterred the two bullies, Zosia and Stacia, from their vicious attacks on Pani Byk. I wanted to tell Pani Byk that her strategy was wrong, that it was not working, but alerting her would betray myself. Pani Byk, who was several years older than I was, and certainly mature enough to know better, made the mistake of engaging in the taunting, giving back better than she got. She had a fine command of the Polish language, and she often used it in a self-deprecating manner. The translation of *byk* is bull, and Pani Byk would at times refer to her husband as Byk. I was terrified for her when I heard her say, that by late autumn there would be a baby *byczek*, a little bull. I thought it unwise to reveal this type of intimate information to her tormentors, even in the hope of buying surcease. I felt that she should distance herself, that she should use her ingenuity to direct their attention elsewhere. I was certain that she was employing the wrong tactic. In addition, to my ears, her attempt to put herself on an equal footing with these two low-class women had a false ring. She was skirting danger. She responded to their anti-Jewish heckling by turning their confrontational remarks against them. There were three of them, in fact, because Pani Zawacka, seated directly across from Pani Byk, never failed to contribute her sneaky remarks whenever the topic turned to Jews who were still hiding in Warsaw.

Moreover, I did not believe for an instant that Pani Byk was in fact pregnant. It had to be a subterfuge. My initial perception that Pani Byk was perhaps Jewish had become almost a certainty. If she was Jewish, then she was not pregnant. Her name was a fiction, as was mine, and I even doubted that she was married to a Pan Byk. I wanted to help her, to say something to her that would make her see that she was not accomplishing the goal she needed to achieve. I did not act. I did not know how to tell her that she must divert their attention away from herself.


## JUNE 1944 &sect; WARSAW, OCCUPIED POLAND

Because of the tormentors—Stacia, Zosia, Pani Zawacka, and lately several other recruits they had managed to enlist into their campaign—my workdays became a time of agony. Daily, there were remarks about Jews in their midst, about the need to clear the atmosphere, about danger to everyone if indeed the factory harbored Jews. When I returned home I was exhausted, unable to eat. When I did give in to Mother's urging and managed to swallow some food, within a short while I would throw it up.

Mother knew the reason for my anguish, and she did what she could to help me cope with the situation. Mainly she would speak of news snippets that had come her way. Ever since the Russian army had liberated Stalingrad, Leningrad, and several other major areas within the Soviet Union, it had kept marching forward rapidly. Presently it was engaged in liberating the Ukraine. We knew nothing of these events from official news broadcasts. From clandestine radio stations, Polish underground operatives were able to intercept news from England. The Allied armies were finally succeeding. They were winning battles and gaining territory. They were mounting attacks on several fronts. They were now the aggressors. Mother kept reiterating these good omens and said that all I had to do was hold out. This news portended the eventual fall of the Nazis, which should soothe and strengthen me. She also spoke to me about my father, whose name, it seemed to me, we had not mentioned in months. The constant fear, the anguish of witnessing the disappearance and killing of our fellow Jews from Krosno, did not leave room for this type of indulgence. Mother wanted me to believe that once again it looked as if we might live to be reunited with my father. She was afraid that I might give up hope, that I might weaken in my resolve to survive.

Each day, on my way to work, I planned a strategy that might anticipate and perhaps circumvent the snares set for Pani Byk—or was it me they were after? I kept reviewing the multiple comments that contained messages, innuendoes. Why didn't I complain about the low pay? they wanted to know. Why did I seem to be so accepting of a work regime that approximated slave labor? The mean-spirited threesome noted that I avoided a closer relationship with my coworkers. Why did I shy away from social intercourse with my fellow workers? Perhaps there was something I needed to hide? And why did I fail to report the protruding bone in my wrist that was so obviously inflamed? Perhaps I was less sturdy than the other workers. I smiled, shrugged my shoulders, and hoped that the answers I gave satisfied the questioner.

The inflammation, I knew, was the result of straining my wrist. It had begun shortly after we were given the materials for the winter uniforms. The heavy fabric plus lining, interlining, and stiffeners were bulky and therefore unwieldy when the completed garment had to be maneuvered through the machine during the stitching of the closing seam. Getting a straight seam severely strained my right wrist.

In observance of a saint's day, Pani Wyszynska requested all operators, finishers, and pressers to gather in the neighboring church for early Mass before starting the workday. It was her wish that we join together in prayer. I found myself on my knees near Zosia and Stacia. I sensed I was being watched while we moved up to take Holy Communion. The priest's arm moved so fast that I barely had time to bow my head. As I lifted my head, I wondered if they had noted my ineptitude. On our way to the factory, they asked invasive questions regarding the sacraments and whether I had been to confession before taking Holy Communion.

JULY 1944 ⤳ WARSAW, OCCUPIED POLAND

On a bright, clear day in early July, at the end of the workday, I hurried down the stairs in my usual manner. As I opened up the iron gate that led into the street, I saw that Zosia and Stacia were behind me. Neither Danka nor Stefan were there to extricate me. Acting companionably, they each took an arm and, laughing conspiratorially, announced, "Come, we are taking the streetcar to Zoliborz."

"Zoliborz? Why would one want to take a ride to Zoliborz?" I asked. "It takes over an hour to get there, and my aunt is expecting me. What in heaven's name is there to see in Zoliborz?" The two conspirators smiled and signaled to each other. I knew. Zoliborz was home to Pani Byk. She had mentioned that distant section of Warsaw on numerous occasions and always in conjunction with the long distance she had to travel to and from the factory. Then I saw her. She was ahead of us, hurrying toward her streetcar, unaware that she was being followed. The women knew that I had seen Pani Byk.

"We are going after her," Zosia said.

"After whom? What are you talking about"?

I was no longer on my accustomed route home but instead forced to walk to a different streetcar stop. "We are following Pani Byk. We must know where she lives," Stacia said. "There is not much we can do unless we know where she lives." Unable to extricate myself from the tight lock on my arms and hemmed in by the entering crowd, I felt myself propelled into the interior of the second car and seated between my two enemies. Sitting in the front car, Pani Byk was apparently oblivious of our presence.

Forcing myself to calm down and appear carefree, I said, "Come now, tell me what this is all about. You know I really should not be here, but on my way home."

"It's about finding out where Pani Byk lives."

"Why would we want to know where Pani Byk lives?" I asked.

"We have decided to act," said Stacia. "Krysia, don't tell us that you are that naïve. She must be Jewish. It's so obvious."

"What is obvious? I don't know what you mean. Did she tell you that she was Jewish?"

"You're not just naïve, Krysia, you're stupid. You mean to say, you can't hear it in her voice, or see it in her manner? She thinks she is so smart, but we are going to show her that we are smarter than she is."

The streetcar made frequent stops, people were exiting and entering, and I was still seated between the two girls who were plotting this evil deed. I knew I had to act fast. "If she is Jewish," I said, "and you really don't know if that is so, then why would you want to know where she lives? It's not for us to investigate. Poles don't help the Nazis. You wouldn't be doing this for the promised compensation?"

There was no direct answer to my question, just body language—a shrug of the shoulder, a turn of the head. The conductor announced the last stop for transfer to the Zoliborz trolley. Standing at the trolley stop, among a crowd of waiting people, I hoped, I prayed, that Pani Byk would turn, that she would see us and find a way to shake off her pursuers. Within minutes the trolley arrived, and once again Pani Byk entered the first car, and the three of us mounted the second car. There were far fewer people, almost everyone was seated, and there was more room to breathe. Speaking slowly, seriously, I said: "You do know that God is watching us and that he knows what we are about to do. It is contrary to Christ's teaching, that I am certain of. There will be punishment. I will have nothing to do with this. How would I be able to go to confession? What do I tell the priest? No, I am getting out at the next stop. You can do what you want. I have to answer to my own conscience."

"You mean to say that you don't care if she is a Jew and pretends to be a Christian? She should not be here. She should be with her own people and not trying to make us believe she is a devout Catholic. All we want is to find out where she lives and if she really has a husband."

"Then you do it," was my response. "I am getting off. My priest said that the Jews are not our affair, but that of the Nazis. I will not help the Nazis. Poles are being murdered every day. Why should I be concerned with the Jews?"

I forced myself to break through the terror that had plunged me into a state of paralysis. Projecting determination, I stood up and made my way toward the exit. I did not turn around. When I got off the trolley, both Zosia and Stacia were behind me. The trolley moved on. Pani Byk was safe. While waiting for the streetcar that would return us to the stop where we had started our journey, I was the only one who had something to say. Zosia and Stacia were silent, sullen looks on their faces. About to leave them, I smiled, and said, "Till tomorrow."

"Well then, till tomorrow," Zosia replied, "but don't think that this is the end of it. Maybe we will ask Pani Wyszynska if she knows that she is harboring a Jewess. Or maybe we will let the police take care of the matter."

Leaving the plotters behind, I ran through the streets to the safety of our room and into my mother's arms. She had been waiting for me, and she was worried. I told her that I could not go back to the factory. I fell asleep in my street clothes, without washing, or brushing my teeth. I woke up in the middle of the night, and I saw that Mother was awake. While I undressed, Mother told me that my exhaustion was due to the extraordinary ordeal I had been through. She said I had handled myself well. I had managed to dissuade the plotters from their gruesome undertaking, and now I should go back to sleep so that I would be able to get to work on time.

Mother refused to accept my explanations that I could not return to work because my reaction to their plot had left Zosia and Stacia frustrated and angry. I was terrified of yet another encounter. I doubted that invoking Christ to justify the dictates of my conscience had been persuasive enough. I knew that they were waiting to entrap me, and I knew that I must evade them at all cost. My terror, my arguments, my pleas did not persuade my mother that she was wrong. Her reason, she told me firmly, was that we had no place to go to. The factory office had our address. I had not been directly accused. I would just have to continue to be courageous. She said I must carry on as if nothing of great consequence had taken place, and she expressed confidence in my ability to sense danger and to innovate the ruses that had so far kept me alive.

Huddled together in Mother's bed, I could understand her reasoning, but I felt that she was wrong. Mother said that against all odds we had survived for one and a half years in Warsaw under a Nazi administration that prided itself in having caught every Jew that had attempted to evade them. We were still alive. It was not a time to stop fighting or to lose courage. She wanted me to keep in mind that the Nazis were sustaining severe losses and that they could not continue the war on three fronts for an indefinite time. The end was in sight. Not appearing at the factory would be tantamount to self-incrimination was Mother's concluding argument.

The next day was Thursday. By the time I sat down at my sewing machine, everyone—or so it seemed to me—was already working. The welcome noise of the many droning motors enveloped me, and no one could really tell whether or not I had said a word of greeting with my smile and the nod of my head. I knew that I had not uttered a word. My throat felt dry and constricted. Pani Byk was at her machine. Everyone was engaged in turning out the requisite number of garments. There was, I was certain, tension in the air. The atmosphere was hostile.

On Friday, as arranged between us, Danka was in the courtyard waiting for me, with her carefully curled, bleached hair, and slightly outrageous makeup. Her happy disposition and obvious affection for me would, I prayed, give my enemies pause to reflect. On Saturday, at one-thirty in the afternoon at the conclusion of my workday, I saw Stefan come through the gate and walk toward me. He kissed my hand, took a good look at me, and asked, "Are you ill?"

I did not tell him that I suddenly felt much less ill because he had come. Just being with Stefan, as well as being seen with a Christian Pole, gave me comfort. We walked for hours, through neighborhoods I did not know, and talked. When we saw an unoccupied park bench, we would sit down for a few minutes to rest our feet. We could not remain for more than a few minutes. It was dangerous, even late in the day on a Saturday, for a Polish couple to seem idle. Stefan's analysis of the losses sustained by the German army on three fronts paralleled that of my mother. He also was certain that the end of the Nazi occupation of Poland was in sight. He touched the red swelling on my wrist and said, "Soon your father will be able to return to Poland. You won't have to sew German uniforms in a factory. Instead, you'll go to school and work toward your matriculation."

Stefan expressed regret that there was no place we could go to. It was dangerous, also expensive, to go to a restaurant for a meal. When he took me to a café, we only stayed long enough to finish our coffee. To linger would tempt fate because Gestapo agents were all around us, watching. Stefan lived in a furnished room and was subject to numerous restrictions imposed by his landlady. I lived in a tiny furnished room with an aunt who did not approve of going out on dates in an occupied city ruled by the Nazis. We could not visit each other.

When I came to work on Monday, I saw immediately that Pani Byk was not in her usual place. On Tuesday, a woman who had worked as a finisher replaced Pani Byk at the machine. Pani Wyszynska let it be known that Pani Byk's husband called to inform her that Pani Byk had suffered a miscarriage with a severe hemorrhage. Pani Wyszynska implied that it would be a while before Pani Byk could resume work. Zosia and Stacia did not, in my presence, mention Pani Byk's name again. Their attitude toward me remained distant, perhaps hostile, and, I was certain, suspicious.

In the middle of July, during our midday break, as I was passing through the office on my way to the bathroom, Pani Wyszynska walked up to me and said, quite casually, "Krysia, on your way home, please stop by my office." I had never been in Pani Wyszynska's office, though many times I had seen her disappear through a door into a small room that could only be accessed from the main office. Did she know? By the time I reached the bathroom, I hardly managed to get to the sink before my recently eaten meal came gushing out of my mouth. I returned to my machine and resumed sewing, while trying to calm my agitated stomach.

When I entered Pani Wyszynska's office, she rose from her chair and walked toward me. "Krysia, I'll come straight to the point. There are rumors floating about. Rumors that I can no longer ignore. I don't really believe them, but now I have no choice but to ask you outright. Are you Jewish?"

"No, I am not Jewish," I answered, my voice firm. Pani Wyszynska's eyes, dark and penetrating even through her eyeglasses, dug into mine. "Is this the truth? Would you swear, in the name of Christ, that you are not Jewish?"

"Yes, I would."

"Then Krysia, can you tell me why, if you are not Jewish, these rumors that you are Jewish are circulating throughout the factory, jeopardizing our very existence?"

"I can't answer that. I don't know who is spreading these rumors or why. No one has ever accused me of being Jewish, though I remember hearing some operators accusing each other of being Jewish."

"Well, at this time I am not concerned about others. Do I have your firm assurance that you are not Jewish, but are indeed a girl baptized into the Catholic religion?"

"Yes."

"Yes, what?"

"Yes, I give you my firm assurance that I was baptized into the Roman Catholic religion."

Pani Wyszynska regarded me silently, her eyes never leaving my face. It was less than a minute, but it seemed interminable. I was waiting for the verdict. Then it came. "Krysia, you give the impression of a sincere and truthful girl. I have watched you in church. I know that you are pious, and you are a good worker. Still, we have a situation here that must be stopped. My decision is that you take sick leave. I have noticed your swollen wrist. It could use a rest. Please do not come back to the factory, better yet, don't even come near it. I will instruct the office to pay you for the completed garments. You can wait for the envelope outside." I am certain that I was not crying; however, there must have been tears in my eyes when I stretched out my hand to say good-bye and uttered some words of appreciation.

On my way home, each time I turned a corner, I made certain that I was not being followed. Would the office reveal my address? Would they be forced to reveal my address? There was no doubt in my mind that I had been denounced. The question was, had the accusation gone any further than the administration of the factory? Were the police or the Gestapo informed? As I was leaving Pani Wyszynska had said, "I am certain that I made the right decision." Had I been skillful enough to convince her, or did her statement convey uncertainty? What would Mother say when I told her that we were no longer safe in our room? Where would we find a place to hide?

Mother only wanted to know if I had revealed my address to the evil threesome. She asked whether one of them had ever accompanied me on my way home, or if there was a possibility that they had followed me, without my knowing it, as they had followed Pani Byk. I had been very careful, I assured her. I never trusted them. I have never trusted anyone, I told Mother. "And Pan Stefan? You trust him. You let him take you right up to the door of the building, and you even gave him the Cybulski telephone number. Was that being circumspect?" Mother demanded.

I don't know what else Mother said next, or if I gave an answer. When I opened my eyes, I was lying on the floor, and Mother was applying cold compresses to my eyes and my forehead. She told me that I had passed out and that she was barely able to catch me before I landed on the floor. She was contrite. She told me that she had been very upset, but she knew what had happened in the factory was not my fault. She expressed confidence in me, and she said that she trusted me.

My mother had never been near the factory, and no one there knew what she looked like. She proceeded with her careful outings, often on behalf of the Duchess. When she returned, she frequently had small packages of food hidden in her purse. I had no appetite, and if in response to Mother's urging, I swallowed some food, I gave it right back. My stomach refused to accept nourishment.

We decided that for the week following my dismissal, I should remain at home. Under no circumstances should I leave the building, and it would be best if I were not called to the telephone. So that I would not trap myself in further lies, Mother, when at home, would say that I was ill with a severe respiratory infection. Several times during the day, while I was alone, the telephone would ring, but I did not answer it. It was agreed between Panna Cybulska and us that we would answer the telephone because if they were in the bedroom or the kitchen, they could not hear the phone. The ringing was audible in their living room, but it was a room they hardly ever used. The Cybulski ladies received few telephone calls, and Panna Cybulska usually called her brother late in the evening. The only people we knew who had the Cybulski telephone number were Danka and Stefan.

In time I came to the phone, but only if Mother first answered it. I told both Danka and Stefan that I was recovering, but was not yet well enough to meet them. Danka, as always, accepted my subterfuges without doubt or suspicion. She let me know that she would be there for me when I recovered. When I asked if she had seen Daniel at Mass, or if she had managed to get him to meet her for an outing, she became vague and evasive. She said that this was no longer a matter she could discuss with me over the phone. She added that if I really wanted to know, I had better get well soon and meet with her because it was "bubbling." Danka would not elucidate what was bubbling.

Stefan was not that easy to put off. He wanted to know the exact nature of my illness. He did not quite believe me. He asked me if my aunt had forbidden me to see him. He even asked me if I were certain the factory would take me back after such a prolonged absence. "They might replace you," he said, "and it is very important that your Arbeitskarte is validated."

The truth was I really was ill. I had developed a bladder infection, and my discomfort was severe. Mother was certain I had run a temperature during the previous week. I was suffering from dehydration, and it had caused the bladder infection. She said that I had contributed to my condition because I had not listened to her when she urged me to drink more water. Mother was determined to act. Not having recourse to a physician, she checked around and found a remedy and an apothecary that would dispense the medicine without a prescription. It was called Brontosil, and it came in a liquid suspension and in tablets. Mother obtained both. Within a day my urine turned red, but with it came relief. The pain became less severe, and so did the urge to urinate. I dutifully, gratefully, consumed all the glasses of water Mother wanted me to drink.

After about a week of confinement in our room, I had lost weight, and Mother decided I should resume going out among people. She said that she did not think the house was being watched. Since the window of our room opened into the courtyard, we were able to see and recognize tenants and their visitors.

PART III

*Resurrection*

# CHAPTER 10

# The Warsaw Uprising

I had been out several times, but never for long, because I was afraid to be too far away from a toilet. On the first of August, a warm pleasant summer day, I was at home. Mother had taken the streetcar to Mokotow where she could get bread in a small, clandestine bakery on Ulica Rakowiecka. For her own safety and that of the bakery, she had to hide the bread on her person. We shared the bread with the Cybulski ladies. It was one of Mother's many attempts to retain their goodwill; however, obtaining the bread and getting it home was a dangerous undertaking. I was always worried when Mother went on that errand. While I waited for her to return, I tried to keep my mind on the book I was reading. I was quite concerned. I was to meet Danka later, but I was unable to reach her. There was a strange buzz on her telephone line. I also called Stefan, but his landlady said that he was not home. I did not leave my name.

Throughout the afternoon, I heard rumbling sounds. The window was open, and I could see the blue sky above. It could not have been thunder. Unable to concentrate on the book I was reading, I once again looked out the window. The rumbling sounds I was now hearing were more powerful, different. Suddenly, the floor beneath my feet moved, and the windowpanes rattled. Then came a thundering detonation. It was a bomb. I looked across the courtyard to the front of the building. It was standing; still, the bomb's target had to be close by. I was scared. I had been unable to reach either of my two friends. And where was my mother? My mounting anxiety caused my stomach to spasm.

In the late afternoon I decided to leave the house and go out onto the street. The library on Ulica Marshalkowska, between Wilcza and Hoza streets, would be a good destination. I needed to hear a human voice, and the librarian knew me by sight. Ulica Marshalkowska appeared to be deserted: no street-cars or buses in sight. I walked perhaps for a block and a half toward my destination and saw only a few people rushing by. For a moment, the earth beneath my feet trembled. Was it an earthquake? I wondered. I had seen the American film *San Francisco* in Hindenburg. Perhaps Warsaw also had a history of earthquakes? There were three women in the library when I arrived. They were on their knees, packing books into cartons.

I told them I was alone and worried: I was living with my aunt and she had gone on an errand and should have been back several hours ago. "Could the rumbling and thunder we are hearing be an earthquake?" I asked. One of the women looked at her companions, then at me, and said, "We think we are hearing Russian artillery. The Russian army has chased the Wehrmacht from most of the territory east of Warsaw. No one really knew that they were that close to the capital. One thing is certain: The Germans are not about to hand over Warsaw without a fight. So my advice to you is to leave immediately for your home and wait there until your aunt returns."

When I opened the back entrance door leading to our room, I saw that the door to the Cybulski living quarters was wide open. I no longer needed anyone to tell me that the earth-shaking explosions were the sounds of bombs hitting targets. Or was it antiaircraft fire? It certainly was reminiscent of the Nazi blitzkrieg invasion on September 1, 1939. If only Mother would return, I could allow myself to feel jubilant. I felt like getting down on my knees and thanking God for allowing me to survive—if only Mother would come home. The euphoria was short lived: Would there be a life for the two of us unless we found Eva and my little cousins, aunts, uncles, and grandfather? I pushed the thoughts out of my mind. Please give me my mother back, I prayed, don't abandon me now.

I heard movement on the staircase, and I knew from the snatches of conversation I overheard through the closed door that tenants living on the upper floors were descending to the cellar. Panna Cybulska looked through the open door of our room. "You went out," she said. "What did you learn?" She walked to the window. "Can you smell it?" she asked. The strange smell that pervaded the room was part smoke, part gunpowder. "Listen," she said. "Do you hear it?" The sounds were different, no longer detonations and bombs dropping. I could hear machine guns and grenades. It sounded as if the shooting was taking place in front of our house. Were the Russian army and the Wehrmacht fighting in the streets of Warsaw in front of our building?

I recounted what I had seen. I had not seen soldiers, just several people rushing by, and I had not seen a streetcar. "Of course not," Panna Cybulska said. "My neighbor Pani Barecka told us that the last time she heard a streetcar pass was early this morning."

"My aunt went to Mokotow to buy bread."

"I know, I asked her to buy a loaf for us."

"Two loaves! How will she hide them? May God protect her. I am very worried. Do you think she will be able to get back?" I asked.

"Who can answer that? I would not have gone, but then, I can't go anywhere. I am chained to my mother. Your aunt is always going some place." There was resentment in Panna Cybulska's voice. She looked at me with her usual air of detachment and added, "Everyone has to look out themselves. I am taking my mother down to the cellar."

Throughout the night I listened to the sounds of heavy artillery, exploding bombs, and salvos from antiaircraft weapons. The ear-shattering sounds came in waves. Among those noises, I was able to distinguish the deafening noise of low-flying airplanes and seconds later the sounds of explosions. As the bombs hit their targets, antiaircraft responded with salvos of gunfire. I was alone in the apartment, perhaps even in the building, but I was not afraid. I could now use the bathroom whenever I wanted to. Several hours past midnight, the low-wattage lightbulb we used at night went out. I flicked the light switch and discovered there was no electricity. My litany now consisted of two prayers: for Mother's safe return and total victory for the Russian army. I decided to telephone Staszek early in the morning. He did not like to receive telephone calls because the telephone was in the professor's bedroom. Since Jerzy's horrific murder, our access to Staszek had been more circumscribed;

still, I was certain that he would advise and help me. I picked up the phone to dial; the line was dead.

In the morning, after I had removed the blackout shades, I heard through the wide open window the exhilarating news: Warsaw had been liberated. The lyrical melody of the Polish national anthem, a tune strictly forbidden during the past five years, was blasting from a neighborhood loudspeaker. I ran out into the street, just in time to hear the incredible announcement. The speaker said: "The Armia Krajowa [the Home Army] to be henceforth referred to as A.K., in cooperation with the Polish army-in-exile, under command of General Wladislaw Anders, has liberated Warsaw. Not all of Warsaw, but most of it, and the Hitlerowcy* are on the run." The speaker concluded by saying that the A.K. would issue hourly news broadcasts, and that everyone was expected to follow all forthcoming directives and abide by the rules issued from A.K.'s military headquarters.

The announcement was repeated again and again, preceded and followed by the Polish national anthem. I looked at the people surrounding me on all sides. There must have been over a hundred people, my immediate neighbors. I looked at their beaming faces with tears of joy running down their cheeks, and I, too, was awash in tears. It was an overwhelming moment. United in joy, we imbibed the heady wine of liberation. We locked eyes and embraced whomever we happened to be standing near. Overnight, all the vicious Poles, the collaborators who had wanted to hunt me down and denounce me, had disappeared. There was no one around who threatened my existence. I felt safe and protected among people beaming with goodwill for each other. No one scrutinized my features and my hair, and nobody cared about my diction. I asked questions, received answers, and for the first time since my escape from Krosno, almost two years earlier, I now spoke freely, the Polish language at my command.

The next announcement over the loudspeaker instructed us to keep off the streets and to descend to cellars and air-raid shelters whenever the warning siren sounded. Since fighting would happen close by, there might not be time for more than one warning signal. A young A.K. soldier appeared and

---

* A Polish pejorative for the Nazis. It literally means "Hitler people."

urged us to return to our homes without delay. He wore regular clothing. Only his black beret and a white armband with the letters A.K. distinguished him as a soldier. The young soldier's joyous optimism was contagious. Everyone wanted to shake his hand or hug him. People wanted to know which part of Warsaw was in the hands of the A.K. and which still remained under the control of the German occupation forces. We learned with dismay and sadness that the liberated sections of Warsaw were not contiguous. We were assured that it was just a matter of days before all of Warsaw would be in the hands of the A.K., provided, of course, that the Red Army would shortly, perhaps within days or even hours, cross the Vistula River.

It was understood that minor problems remained. The word *minor* was somewhat vague, somewhat stressed. The Red Army had captured and occupied the east bank of the Vistula River, but that colossal army was not moving. The Home Army, which had chased the German occupation forces out of a large part of Warsaw, was now eagerly waiting for the Russian army to cross the river. The A.K. plan was to offer aid and hospitality to the victorious Red Army and to fight alongside the Red Army to liberate the rest of occupied Poland. However, Warsaw, the beloved capital of the nation, had to be liberated by its native sons. It was a matter of pride. The residents of Warsaw were assured that ongoing negotiations between London and Moscow would shortly bring about the anticipated crossing of the Vistula River.

On August third, 1944, in the late afternoon, Mother came home. She had been gone for two nights and almost three days. She was accompanied by a woman in her mid-twenties, and I watched in horror as the two women, supporting each other, dragged themselves up the stairs. For miles, they had crawled through cellars and underground sewage passages. Their disheveled appearance and bloody knees attested to the hardship they had endured. All Mother managed to say that night was that she had lost the bread. Mother pointed to my sofa for the woman to rest on, while she sat down on the bed. Within seconds, both women had stretched out and fallen asleep.

Panna Cybulska came rushing in, and even her mother came hobbling behind her. Both women seemed genuinely glad that Mother had returned home. They wanted to know how Mother had managed to circumvent Plac Swietego Zbawiciela, since we knew that the region south of the square was still in German hands. That was the area Mother had to get through to come home.

I stood between the bed and the sofa. There wasn't enough room for me to stretch out on the floor. Panna Cybulska, without asking her mother's permission, opened the door leading to the library and music room and invited me to sleep there.

The young woman Mother brought home had been with her since the first day of August. After obtaining the bread—only one loaf due to a flour shortage—Mother had boarded the streetcar and sat down next to Pani Halina, our temporary guest. The young woman had also taken the trip to buy food. She was on her way back and eager to return to her little daughter, whom she had left in the care of a neighbor. The women had traveled only a few minutes when the streetcar was stopped. A Gestapo unit boarded, and an officer ordered all passengers to leave the car. Both Pani Halina and Mother managed to kick the bread and food away from their seats. They were body searched and marched to the area lockup. When they arrived at the lockup, they saw hundreds of prisoners surrounded by a small number of guards in uniform. Mother's group of about twenty detainees, mostly women, was directed to a different location.

While walking ahead of the strutting guard, who prodded those lagging behind with his gun, the two women tried to remain near each other. Both wanted to get back to the city, and both were willing to take risks if an opportunity to escape presented itself. They had no idea what had happened. From the irate curses of the Gestapo officers and the guards, and from their remarks about Polish treachery and deceit, the two women assumed that an act of sabotage by the Polish underground had brought about this Nazi attempt at mass incarceration. While walking from one place to another, more people and additional guards were added to the group. In time, Mother said, there must have been more than sixty people, some women with children and a few old men. The young men were immediately separated and marched away. Mother's group was led through residential neighborhoods. Although adjacent houses were obviously occupied, there were no people to be seen. Entrance doors to the buildings appeared to be locked. Whenever the group was directed onto the sidewalk to avoid impeding passing German cars and trucks, they came so close to the doors of buildings, they could touch or turn a doorknob.

As they were passing one of the dwellings and were about to be directed back onto the street, Mother noticed one of the doors was open a crack and heard the almost imperceptible click of the doorknob turning. She pulled Pani Halina near her. Mother saw an elderly woman in the doorway. She motioned the woman to step back, while putting a warning finger to her lips. Mother and Pani Halina slipped through the door. Pani Halina thought one of the guards had turned his head in her direction just as she entered. When Mother and Pani Halina were sure that the group and the soldiers guarding it had moved on, they thanked the good Samaritan who had left the door ajar.

The sector in which the two women found themselves was in German hands. The population had been warned to keep off the streets and to keep their doors locked to everyone but German units. Since all persons living in the buildings were registered with the German police and several police raids had already taken place, with more expected, the two women were urged to leave at nightfall. The residents gave them many helpful suggestions, urging them to take an underground route. The two women proceeded through underground passages and sewer tunnels. They spent a number of daylight hours in churchyard cemeteries, hiding behind large gravestones.

Once Pani Halina was awake she wanted to leave immediately. No one could tell her if her home was on our side or on the German side. Everyone assured her that she would find her little girl; Pani Halina's friends would be watching over her. Mother persuaded her to take some of the lentil soup I

Building a barricade during the Polish uprising; people just stopped and helped. (Betty on left.) Warsaw, August 1–October 2, 1944.

had cooked. When the women parted, they were so overcome with emotion that for minutes they stood together, holding each other in a tight embrace. They vowed to find each other when the war was over, and they called on God to protect and bless the other. Then they parted. After Pani Halina had left, Mother told me that she too had caught for an instant the eye of the German guard who had accompanied the group during the latter part of the journey.

"Were you afraid that he would stop you? Come after you?" I asked.

"It all went so fast, it was just an instant, and Pani Halina was afraid that he would send the Gestapo after us. But I felt, I somehow knew, that he would not pursue us. Not this guard. The first one, the one who was cursing us, would have shot us dead. Still, I was frightened; I could not be sure."

Mother listened intently while I recounted everything I had seen and heard during the past four days. She was puzzled and concerned to learn that the sounds of heavy artillery from the other side of the river—the reassuring pounding of the Russian katyushas—had ceased.

On the fifth day of August printed leaflets issued by the A.K. called for an all-out mobilization. Residents were urged to register at neighborhood draft boards for induction into the volunteer Home Army. All able-bodied people were urged to help, to do their part. Tunnels were being dug, and more barricades were essential. All hands were needed. A special appeal was directed to Jews. It read:

> We urge all Jews who are in hiding to come out into the open; to take their places alongside their Polish fellow citizens; to give freely of their effort and their talent in this last, final struggle to rid the Polish homeland of the Nazi invader. We call upon you to be part of the effort to build a free and democratic Poland.

The manifesto was signed by Bor Komorowski, the commanding officer of the Home Army. I read and reread the large black print. People were reaching for the leaflet; there were not enough of them for everyone. I did not relinquish the paper until I had committed to memory every word of that paragraph.

Mother knew. She had read the paragraph. There also had been an order directing the civilian population, the people not actively engaged in the fighting, such as mothers with children, the old, and the sick and disabled, to fashion temporary living quarters in cellars and air-raid shelters. Mother thought it would be best to comply with the order. She was not feeling well and was suffering from diarrhea. The A.K. had liberated a generator and was able to generate electricity for several hours a day for our building. We could once again boil our water. I was certain that Mother needed rest, and I thought that she would be able to rest in the cellar. She appeared to be totally spent, exhausted from her escape.

I was about to offer my services at the recently opened emergency health station on Ulica Koszykowa. I had filled out an application, and I was ready to do whatever needed to be done. I had answered yes to questions about giving first aid. Mother would have liked for me to remain near her. She was afraid that I would be misled by the appeal directed to Jews and might succumb to the temptation of brotherhood and disclose my identity.

Intermittently, the street, even our courtyard, was deluged with leaflets dropped by the Luftwaffe. Mostly they contained demands for immediate surrender. The enemy threatened that the many innocent residents of the city would pay the price for the treacherous deceit of a few. The German leaflets informed us that the A.K. was fighting a lost cause, that it was running out of both ammunition and food. They urged Warsaw residents to ally themselves with the occupation authority, especially since that authority had endeavored to be fair and considerate in its treatment of the population. Then came the threat: If, however, residents persisted in their mistaken loyalty to a bunch of rebels and Communists, they should not be surprised when the full wrath of Nazi power descends upon their heads. In addition, the ominous, previously made declaration, expressed by Nazi leader Fritz Sauckel, that "the German army would only leave Warsaw when no stone was left standing on top of another stone," was once again in circulation.

Despite these threats, and contrary to Mother's firmly stated injunction that I remain at her side, I decided to take an active part in the liberation of Warsaw instead of descending with her into the cellar. Mother had managed to secure a small space on the floor of the cellar, with about forty inches of wall space, just enough room for a pillow. I assured Mother that unless I was on night duty, I would be home each evening before nightfall. I would see her installed in her space in the basement, but I would sleep upstairs in our room as long as possible. I realized my stance was unreasonable and that I was causing Mother anguish, but I persisted. Mother needed the respite. She would not be alone. She would not be threatened. Preparing to live in the underground shelter, making the necessary adjustments, was a cooperative undertaking. She would be part of it and, knowing my mother, an integral part of it. There was a communal spirit in the endeavor, and, I hoped for Mother's sake, some healing power. She was so very tired.

For the first time in my life, I felt I had the power to make a decision for myself. I was determined to exercise that freedom. During daylight hours, and sometimes late into the evening, I ministered to the wounded that were brought into the first-aid station in ever-increasing numbers. I took a crash course and quickly learned to prepare splints, apply tourniquets, and give injections. I assisted in cleaning wounds and lacerations. A large part of my time was taken up scrubbing and sterilizing instruments. The older doctor who supervised my training and who decided which of the wounded would have to be transferred to the hospital told me what I myself feared: The bladder infection I had tried to ignore needed to be taken care of. The doctor told me I needed to keep taking Brontosil, the medication Mother had gotten for me. However, when I told him I had used all the tablets and asked him where I could get more, he shrugged his shoulders. He did not have the medicine. He suggested I canvass apothecaries within our area of liberated Warsaw.

People directed me to a number of drugstores, but when I got there, I found the store either demolished or shuttered. In some instances, there was only rubble where the apothecary had been. When I entered through the open door of one damaged drugstore, I was greeted by a middle-aged man who stood amidst the broken glass of a showcase. The druggist thought that he might be able to help me, but that he would need some time to find the medication. When he returned, he held several vials of the medicine and put them into my hands.

"What do I owe you?" I asked. "Owe me?" he responded. "Everything I have is for the *powstaniks*.* Tell them, tell everyone, that I am staying at my post and that I am ready to serve." Apparently, since I was wearing my Red Cross armband, the druggist assumed that I was a soldier in the A.K.. I did not attempt to explain my situation.

--------------------------------------------------

*Powstanik* is derived from the Polish word *powstaniec*, which means "insurgent."

Confrontations between the A.K. and the German military were increasing, with heavy losses sustained by our side. We talked about the victories. We rejoiced when the A.K. liberated an area and discovered a large food storage depot. They also captured stores of petroleum and sometimes a car, or even a truck, but no ammunition—and that was what the A.K. needed most. The Home Army was in constant contact with the Polish government-in-exile, based in England, but clear communication over the BBC from London was difficult to achieve. The Home Army was unable to ascertain why the urgent requests for an airplane drop of ammunition had not been acted upon. Radio broadcasts sent to us over the BBC were full of static, compounding the frustration of both the leaders and population. Several times we were advised that parachute drops were being dispatched to our beleaguered city: They were to reach us at nightfall or before dawn. When, once again, scheduled parachute drops failed to arrive, we rationalized that the distance between London and Warsaw was considerable, visibility had been poor, and German aircraft was preventing the British planes from coming down low enough to execute the drop.

At intersections in our neighborhood, soldiers were constructing barricades to the accompaniment of national tunes that wafted from loudspeakers. Though the pervading mood was festive and we kept assuring each other of imminent victory, we were all hiding our foreboding. The A.K. insurgents

A Polish soldier behind an emplacement during the Polish uprising. Warsaw, August 1–October 2, 1944.

had counted on the Red Army to arrive within days, but there had been no agreement between the two parties that they would come. We knew they were there; all they needed to do was to cross the river. We also knew that the signal to launch the uprising had come from the Polish government-in-exile. General Berling, a Pole and the commander of the First Polish Army, the unit fighting alongside the Russian army, had failed to acknowledge the insurrection, which added to our consternation. It appeared that from the day the uprising was launched, communication with the Russians, who were to liberate us, had ceased. The question on everyone's mind was: Why had the Red Army stopped its offensive before entering Warsaw, especially since the army was well aware that most of the city was liberated and awaiting its arrival? On all sides, except to the east, we were surrounded by the German enemy, and we were running out of food.

We no longer dared express our main concern. Will the leaders who had decided on and timed the insurrection find the crucially needed support? Will either London or Moscow come to our aid? We knew that without help from the outside, we were doomed. A German offensive would overrun us within days, and they had threatened us with a bloodbath. Everyone was aware of how destructive this type of speculation could be to morale. We diverted our anxiety by taking an active part in the defense of Warsaw.

Due to the ever-present static, BBC communications were frustrating, and it was difficult to ascertain whether our inquiries for drugs and weapons had been received and if the requests would be acted on. When communication was successful, we were advised that parachute drops were being dispatched, yet on the morning following the good news, we heard that again the nightly vigil had been in vain. We learned that the Russian army had refused permission for British aircraft to land for refueling, which compounded transportation difficulties.

Confusion intensified when we learned that although large parts of Warsaw had been liberated by the A.K., as was the case in the sector in which I lived, there were other parts of the city that had been conquered by the Armia Ludowa, or the People's Army. The A.L., a revolutionary underground unit I had not heard of before, was socialist- and Communist-inspired and received support and directives from Russia. They declared that, until the onset of the insurrection, they had been in direct communication with General Berling.

The A.L. headquarters pointed out that waiting for help from London

or the Allies was totally unrealistic. They were too far away, and it was folly
to rely on them. London would not make the all-out effort that was needed.
Even if they wanted to, which they probably didn't, military logistics would
make the attempt very difficult. The A.L. contended that the residents of
Warsaw had been misled. Help could only come from the Russians, and
Moscow had received no warning that the insurrection was about to take place.
A.L. leaders advised that it was not true that the Russian army and the Berling
regiment had refused to come to our rescue, but that the Germans had
launched a counterattack at the Vistula River and had driven the Russian army
back and further east from the river. Ostensibly, the Russian army was unable
to cross the river until army reinforcements had strengthened their strategic
position.

It appeared that although both the nationalist A.K. and the socialist A.L.
insurgents were united in their struggle to drive the enemy from their land,
they were unable to bridge the ideological gap. To understand at least some
of the implications resulting from the political predicament, one had to listen to both the A.K and A.L. news broadcasts and extrapolate from them some
truth regarding our fate.

The threatened German blockade was totally successful. Food and ammunition supplies could only be augmented by parachute drops. In the early
days of the insurrection, both A.K. and A.L. units had managed to liberate a
number of food and ammunition warehouses that had been hidden by the
German occupation authority. In the ensuing weeks, additional food caches
that were discovered were small and insignificant.

Mother and I were adept at surviving on a minimal amount of food. Our
main hardship was lack of potable water. Whenever we were fortunate enough
to fill a pail or a pot at a nearby water pump, it was almost impossible to get
the rusty looking liquid to a boiling point.

The nights continued to be clear, a prerequisite for parachute drops, yet
supplies failed to arrive. Although radio broadcasts from London assured us
of eventual victory, we wondered how this victory could be accomplished.
There was no indication that the Russian army was moving closer. The
Germans increased their leafleting. They threatened to level Warsaw to the
ground and kill all insurgents unless there was total surrender. All that would
remain, the leaflets informed us, would be rubble and corpses.

Filling vessels at a below ground water source during the uprising. Warsaw.

In our section of town, A.K. units continued to implement a defense strategy. Cellar walls were dynamited to connect underground passages, and street barricades were elevated and reinforced. Throughout the night, working in shifts, A.K. units dug deep trenches amid the barricades. The enemy kept abreast of all our activities. Reconnaissance planes would appear suddenly. They swooped down low enough to take close-up photographs, then quickly zoomed back into the sky. The insurgents did not have antiaircraft equipment.

Strafing from airplane machine guns increased the number of wounded. Injuries were more severe than in the first days of the insurrection because the Germans were now using tanks and other motorized artillery. Occasionally due to some lucky circumstance or superior strategy, our side would capture a tank and turn it against the enemy. My Red Cross station was inundated with civilians caught in crossfire. Often, after receiving first aid, they returned to their units to again volunteer their services. Our drug and first-aid supplies were rapidly dwindling, and we were advised to use painkillers sparingly. Frequently the only comfort I could offer was kindness and words of encouragement. Just a few blocks north of our first-aid unit, the powstaniks, in successful combat against the Wehrmacht, liberated a section of the city where a recently vacated hospital was located. We were informed that our unit would be housed in or near the hospital.

Our side forcing Germans to vacate a building. The "Travel with Us to Germany" office was an attempt to entice Polish workers to voluntarily work in Germany.

Upon Mother's insistence, I slept in the air-raid shelter of our building. It was difficult to get a few hours of sleep, even if one managed to secure a spot near the wall. The bombings were incessant. The bombs were not hitting our immediate area, though by the boom of the detonations it felt as if they were falling onto the neighboring building.

Mother was very popular in our basement air-raid shelter. She was called on continuously. I would be awakened by someone touching her shoulder and asking Pani Dembicka—my mother—for help. The main problem was lack of water, and the dehydration suffered by victims of the ubiquitous diarrhea. Once again there were remarks such as "one does not often see an aunt who is so solicitous of her niece." Now these remarks were uttered in a tone of respect, and Mother no longer felt called upon to justify the relationship. She ministered to the sick people. She helped them wash and comb their hair, and when necessary, she emptied chamber pots.

At the first sign of dawn, Mother and I would return to our room. Toward the latter part of August, there were instances when we heard the air-raid siren as we walked up the stairs. Before we had time to turn back, we would hear the droning of heavy bombers flying overhead, dropping their load as they passed over us. We would stand paralyzed, our hands over our ears, stunned by what had just happened. We knew the target was our neighborhood. Usually the attack lasted only minutes. Often, before we reached the cellar, another squadron dropped their loads—and yet another. We would stretch out flat on the staircase landing, our hands over our heads, shielding ourselves from the shattering glass and flying debris.

After the first all-clear signal, Mother always admonished me to remain in the cellar. But I would embrace her and rush to my assignment. I knew wounded civilians injured by bomb shrapnel would be crowding into the emergency room. I spent most of my time directing prospective blood donors to newly established makeshift blood banks. There was no shortage of volunteers.

I could see, smell, and taste the black smoke that engulfed the city. Whenever the smoke lifted, the glow of burning fires was clearly visible. We learned that several buildings had collapsed onto their crowded air-raid shelters and that A.K. units were bringing out the wounded. At my aid station, my coworkers whispered about careful preparations in anticipation of a large parachute drop. I gathered that in recent days there had been a number of drops, but we could not discuss this openly. For some reason, even though great care had been taken to keep the drop sites secret, supplies meant for us had been captured by German units, and our weapons were now in the hands of the enemy.

A successful parachute shipment from England. Warsaw.

Once I watched as A.K. soldiers disentangled a parachute's white cords and disconnected the strings attached to an aluminum cylinder that looked like a giant cigar. I noted with amazement that the canister held enough drugs and medical supplies to save the lives of more than a hundred people. Occasionally, after a canister was disconnected, the A.K. left the parachute on display to bolster our courage and let us know that we were not alone in our fight. Passersby greeted the isolated floating parachute, its cords stuck in a wall, with guarded optimism. It signaled that in faraway England attempts were being made to help us.

On the night of a large and eagerly awaited drop, more than twenty containers were dropped at the agreed-upon lit area. But an unexpected wind carried off almost half the supplies into German territory. A.K. soldiers managed to salvage the rest by jumping for them in midair. It was discouraging. People asked why German bombers were able to unerringly drop their load on us, while English airplanes carrying supplies so often missed their mark. We asked, but we knew the answers. Supplies for beleaguered Warsaw could only arrive in the dead of night, whereas our enemy targeted us mainly during early morning hours.

When several buildings that housed Red Cross units were once again bombed, the military unit decided that the Red Cross emblem, though prominently displayed, did not provide enough protection. Perhaps it could not be seen clearly enough from above, whereas a bona fide hospital with a huge Red Cross painted on its roof would better ensure the protection guaranteed by the Geneva Convention. My aid station was closed, and the injured were moved to a nearby hospital. There were not, however, enough hospitals in the liberated parts of Warsaw to minister to the casualties.

Since the beginning of the insurrection, and Mother's return from Mokotow, our movement had been confined to our immediate neighborhood. To be able to cross underground, past enemy-held territory, one had to possess a military pass. The underground passages that connected buildings and the above-ground crossings between barricades were supervised from checkpoints and manned by security guards. At times, even people in possession of a pass were turned back because combat units were expected to pass through. After the closure of my aid station, Mother urged me to stay at her side, but I wanted to be useful and continue the work I had been doing. I went out and tried to secure a military pass so that I could continue working in a different neighborhood. After I returned to our room, I happened to look out the window and saw the familiar figure of Stefan Broda. He was crossing our courtyard. I ran down the stairs and into his arms. He was wearing a gray suit, an open-neck shirt, and a black French beret. The white armband with the black A.K. letters was on his sleeve. Hanging from his left shoulder was his treasured Leica, and a gray haversack was slung over his right shoulder.

For the first time, Stefan met my mother, whom he believed to be my aunt. He kissed Mother's hand and made some complimentary remark regarding her niece. Mother was thrilled to finally be able to discuss the political situation with someone who was officially connected to the A.K. and who had come to us from the other end of town. It had taken Stefan three days and two nights to reach us. Due to direct bomb hits, several underground passages were filled with debris, which had to be cleared away before people could pass through. Noncombatants were recruited to help rescue the wounded trapped below, or put to work clearing the tunnels. The section of town Stefan had come from was east of Nowy Swiat, a part of Warsaw that for days had been the target of incessant bombardment. All that was left of his building were the outside walls. Some of the neighboring buildings were smoking ruins. His mother, his landlady, and her children were among the fortunate ones who had not been wounded.

Stefan was exhausted by his journey, and he gratefully accepted Panna Cybulska's offer to sleep in the library. In the week before Stefan's arrival, the off-limits room had become a transient rest stop for acquaintances of our landlady who were fleeing their burning homes. There were many questions that I would have liked to ask Stefan, but Mother and Panna Cybulska and her mother did not give us a chance to be alone.

Later in the day, I learned that Stefan had a special pass as a roving reporter. The pass, issued by A.K. headquarters, asked military personnel to facilitate his assignment, which was recording on film the battle of Warsaw. The haversack Stefan brought contained his Rolleiflex, film for both cameras, and several rolls of exposed film, as well as a shirt, a change of underwear, a toothbrush, and a razor.

"Is that all you were able to salvage?" I asked.

"No, there is a suitcase with some clothing. I left it with my mother."

"Nothing else?"

"I am glad I was able to get out two of my cameras and the film before the building collapsed."

That night in the cellar, Stefan remarked upon the resemblance between my aunt and me. "It's not that you look alike; still there is a resemblance. One can tell that you are related. She is your mother's sister, right?"

"Yes."

"A good-looking woman. There is such sadness in her eyes."

"It's been difficult for her these past years."

"I can believe that. It's been difficult for most of us."

## SEPTEMBER 1944 ⚔ WARSAW, OCCUPIED POLAND

Stefan needed an assistant to take close-up photographs, while he took shots with a telephoto lens from rooftops. "It would be good to have you work alongside me," he told me. "I brought an application form, but you must get a photograph. It need not be standard size, as long as your face is identifiable. We'll fill in the application before I leave, and I'll try to have the pass ready by tomorrow. What do you say, Krysia? Would you like to be a reporter?" It was a rhetorical question. I loved the idea of being out in the open and active and contributing to the communal effort.

"Do you think your aunt will give her permission?" Stefan asked. "I would hate to get on her wrong side. How are you going to broach the subject?"

"I will speak to her after you leave. It will take some convincing, but she knows how much I fear being underground. Whenever I am in the cellar, I feel trapped and in a state of panic. I only agreed to go down at night after nearby buildings were bombed. She knows the anguish it causes me and that I will not go down into the cellar during the day."

My stomach cramps and frequent diarrhea, which sapped much of my energy, caused Mother incessant worry. Mother did realize that when I went out to work, I felt much better. And since Stefan's arrival, I felt relief from some of my symptoms. I was certain that this fact alone would help me support my argument.

On the morning following Stefan's departure, Mother surprised me by being moderate in her opposition. I had prepared a number of arguments to convince her to let me go, but apparently I forestalled the main thrust of her objections when I mentioned the improved state of my digestive system. There was only one condition.

"You must promise me that you will come back at night, and that you will sleep here, in the cellar."

"Mother, I promise," I said solemnly. "I will come home to sleep every night if it is within my power. You probably heard Stefan say that it is now almost impossible for him to return to his former neighborhood, and he might come back with me at dusk unless he is able to make other arrangements."

"There is room in the basement for one more person. I will arrange it," she said. Then came the warning. Did I understand what we were up against? Did I realize that the Nazis were using a strategy to force surrender? After destroying an area, leaving people homeless and dispirited, they moved on to the next sector.

"I no longer believe that victory is possible," she said. Her voice sad and her eyes full of tears, Mother continued, "Stefan did not say it, no one wants

Crucifix monument in front of the Church of the Holy Cross. Warsaw.

to say it, but he also worries about it. He said that the Nazis bomb an area until it is leveled to the ground, then they move on. I want us to be together when it's our turn."

"We will be together at night," I repeated. "Did I tell you that Stefan met a woman who cooks cereal for the sick and the elderly? He said we could eat there whenever we are nearby. He said that type of food would soothe my stomach. I'll be so glad once I start to work with him. I only hope that he will return with the press pass."

Mother reached for my arm and pulled me close enough to look straight into my eyes. I knew what was coming. "Did you tell him?" she asked.

"No, I did not," I answered truthfully.

"Be careful," Mother warned. "Resist the temptation to share our secret. For a while I too felt that we were near the end. The euphoria was seductive, but the poor boys are fighting a losing battle. Without help from the Soviet Union, victory is no longer possible."

I was immediately immersed in my new assignment. Stefan knew precisely what he wanted to achieve and the exact place from where the photograph had to be taken to accomplish his goal. Most of the time we did not work side by side. Napoleon Square was a favored Nazi target. On one of its corners stood a once proud landmark, the only skyscraper in Poland. Shortly after our arrival, in the winter of 1943, when I looked up to the top of the building, I saw its decapitated top. The top three stories had been destroyed during the blitz invasion in September 1939. Since the start of the insurrection, several bombs had hit the building, but it was still standing tall. Stefan felt that the Nazis would not be content to let this building stand.

I knew the area well. The skyscraper was still used as an office building, and Lucynka, one of Danka's friends, had a secretarial job in one of the offices. I was never in the building, but when the Garzynska factory, where I worked for almost a year, moved its quarters from Ulica Chmielna to the former Actor's Café building, the skyscraper was always within my sight.

One day when it seemed likely the skyscraper would once again be targeted, Stefan spent three hours, his lens cocked at five hundredths of a second, on the roof of a nearby building, his camera focused on the skyscraper. A barrage of bombs hit the heart of the building, and Stefan captured the event. I

Bomb hitting the skyscraper on Napoleon Square—a favorite German target and the
only skyscraper in Poland. Warsaw.

was standing in the middle of Napoleon Square, taking close-up photographs
with the Rolleiflex camera. After this earth-shaking event, when several more
stories of the skyscraper collapsed, there was little left to remind one of its former graceful architecture. Only rubble remained. To take photographs, I had
to disobey the air-raid warning siren. I lay prone on the ground, my hands
over my head, my body shielding the camera. The droning sound of the heavily laden bombers was ominous. The earth shook each time a bomb exploded.
I could see nothing through the heavy black smoke. It entered the nostrils and
blackened the clothes. When I was able to look around, it seemed that I was
all alone in the square. I knew that Stefan was on a nearby roof, though I could
not see him. I prayed to God to help him stay alive.

Once when Stefan took me to A.K. headquarters, he showed me newspaper articles in which his photographs were featured and lauded. Before his
apartment had been bombed into oblivion, he had worked in his darkroom
and supplied headquarters with photographs ready for publication. Now we
could not tell if our efforts were successful. All we had were the exposed rolls
of film. Locating an abandoned photographic studio was still on Stefan's
agenda, but he no longer spent time searching for one. There was too much
to do. The heaps of rubble around us were mounting. The Cathedral of the

Three Crucifixes, a proud Warsaw landmark, was destroyed, each tower broken off.

Though I was unable to see the results of my efforts, Stefan kept assuring me that I was good at my work. I learned that, as a rule, air attacks came in waves of three. Between raids, first-aid units worked at fever pitch to get the wounded out of the area. That was also the time for me to position my camera in anticipation of the next bombing raid. In September we knew that the enemy had strategically positioned the heaviest artillery tanks in the German arsenal. The cannon, according to their size, were called Czolg, Tiger, Karl, which packed a 600-millimeter mortar, and Goliat, the largest of them, which could fire electrically controlled incendiary material.

To the left of the door to the gutted central post office of Warsaw, a parachute was hanging from the third floor. Only the outer wall was still standing. Within, everything was rubble and ashes. Someone must have detached the tube, while taking care not to damage the parachute. It was an eerie sight, perhaps a signal, a conscious decision made in the early days when there was still hope for a paratroop landing. Although Stefan had cautioned me to use film sparingly, I decided to cover that telling site from several angles.

A parachute drop from the Polish government in London. The parachute got stuck on the ruin of the midtown post office on Napoleon Square. Warsaw.

A Polish soldier leading a group of German prisoners of war. Warsaw.

A platoon of German soldiers and officers was lined up in front of a soup kitchen. It was a new experience to see the conquerors as prisoners. They were unshaven and shabby looking, and since their belts had been taken away, some held their trousers up with their hands. It was difficult to believe that these were the same men who only weeks ago with a wave of their hand could determine whether one lived or died. Though several civilians stopped to either talk or jeer, all I did was take a photograph. I subsequently photographed a column of German soldiers, with officers marching in front. There were only a few A.K. guards. Another prisoner group I encountered and photographed was clearing away rubble. I never saw a German soldier or officer who had been beaten or otherwise abused. Some of them had clean bandages on a hand or an arm in a professionally set splint. Yet, I had seen the inhuman beatings Gestapo officers and, yes, German soldiers had administered to Jewish prisoners in Krosno and to Poles in Warsaw. And it was the Germans who had called the Poles pigs.

Stefan occasionally spent the night in our cellar. He had many friends who were glad to give him shelter. He also spent several nights with a two-man camera crew. Before the war, they had been part of the Polish film industry. Now in their black berets, movie cameras on their shoulders, they were filming documentaries. Mother wanted me to report on the minutest details, and I tried to convey to her whatever I had seen or heard. Though I tried to convince her that my position was enviable, the only affirmation I could get out of her was "if you say so," or "if this is what you think."

One morning, on my way to my assignment, I passed a group of pow-staniks digging a trench. There were eight of them, seven men and one woman. They worked with picks and shovels, excavating one small area at a time. A dim kerosene light alerted passersby to the ditch. On their sleeves were white armbands with black A.K. letters. Stuck into the ground next to the lantern was a small Polish flag alongside a small white flag with the blue Star of David in its center. On two or three occasions, since the insurrection, I had seen individuals wearing the familiar white armband with the blue Star of David. Obviously, the armband was now worn with pride, and I wondered what made the wearer feel so secure, while I still felt certain that I must hide my identity. Now here was a group of eight Jews, and I could not resist the strong impulse to stop and talk with them.

I identified myself as a reporter for the A.K., and I asked if I could take a photograph. To my surprise they answered that I could. I pretended to press the shutter. An inner voice told me not to record the encounter. They thanked me and continued with their task. They had no time to talk, and I would have felt dishonest to stay and not reveal myself. For the remainder of the day, I was unable to get the image of the credulous Jews out of my mind. At night, when I told Mother, she said, "They are making a mistake. They did not need to reveal their identity to take part in the uprising. No, the war is not over." She was glad that I had resisted the temptation to tell.

Although the accelerating death rate was not publicized, it seemed that more and more families were grieving the death of loved ones. Throughout the liberated areas of both the A.K. and A.L units, small plots of earth were studded with shallow graves and makeshift crosses. There were so many, I stopped taking photos of the sites. The turning point for me, the realization that the insurrection was doomed, came after the bombing of Warsaw's Philharmonic Hall.

The attack took place in the early morning hours before dawn. The relatively modern and well-constructed building, which provided shelter in its basement for children, the elderly, and the disabled, was reduced to rubble, even though a Red Cross flag had been prominently displayed. Several hundred victims were caught below when the attack took place and were buried alive beneath the debris that broke through the ceiling. Rescue squads, aided by family members and residents, rushed to the site and worked until late in the afternoon before the first bodies could be brought out. The black smoke rising from the ruins prevented me from getting close to Philharmonic Square. The workers, their heads covered and bandannas over their faces, looked like ghosts as they struggled within the enveloping black smoke. At dusk, when some of the smoke had cleared, figures in gas masks carrying dead bodies groped their way out of the debris. Throughout the day, I saw Stefan rushing about. He told me I could either go home or stay, but I shouldn't take photographs. He felt that under the prevailing conditions, I would not be able to get close enough to record the horror, but he wanted to document the tragedy from other perspectives.

On the following morning, I returned to the grisly site. On two sides of the square, laid out in rows, were the dead bodies of the victims. Doctors, nurses, and an ambulance stood by ready to tend to the wounded, but there were no wounded. The bodies were covered with sheets, and when sheets were no longer available, with brown paper, and after the brown paper ran out, with newspaper. A light wind had sprung up and kept blowing the newspapers off the corpses. Young children took on the job of keeping the bodies covered, a futile task in view of the increasing wind. Relatives, friends, and neighbors were walking among the dead, lifting the coverings from mutilated faces in an effort to identify the victims. A powstanik, holding pad and pencil, was crying while he wrote down names. All self-control shattered at the sight of the dead children, some no more than three or four years old. A few dolls lay near the bodies. It was a heartbreaking sight. There was a consensus that the bodies should not be buried until all possible identification marks of the victims could be registered.

A few steps away, a special unit of soldiers were huddled over a bomb that had not exploded. Though the people crowding the square were alerted to the danger, no one hurried to leave the area. The men attempting to defuse the bomb were volunteers, none older than twenty-two. I took several photos of this group of heroes engaged in the task of separating the mechanical fuse from the deadly explosive material.

Though no one talked openly about our lost cause, tragedy was in the air and could be read on people's faces as they rushed about, trying to find water or food.

A volunteer diffuses a bomb. Warsaw.

At dusk, while Stefan and I were walking back to my house, my foot slipped and I fell. When I got up, I looked at Stefan and saw the black soot on his face streaked white from the rivulets of tears that had run from his eyes throughout the day. When I told him about it, he said that was exactly what my face looked like. He put an arm around my shoulder and said, "Victory for us is no longer possible. General Komorowski is attempting to make arrangements for contact with General von Bach to negotiate an armistice."

"Why are you calling him *General* Komorowski? We were supposed to refer to him as Bor Komorowski—his nom de guerre."

"That has changed. The Nazis keep referring to us as rebels, criminals, and savages. He would want to negotiate as a general with a general of the Wehrmacht. He wants the A.K. participants to be considered soldiers and for them to be treated in accordance with the Geneva Convention." As an aside, Stefan added, "Once again the Gestapo is spreading rumors that the insurrection was a combined Communist and Jewish conspiracy in order to slow the German war effort. They must be desperate to come up with such ridiculous propaganda. They killed all the Jews. As far as the Communists are concerned, not only did they not come to our aid, they want no part of us."

"I am Jewish," I said.

"What did you say?"

"I said I'm Jewish."

"You can't be. You're joking. That's not possible."

"Would I be joking at a time like this? It's the truth. I have wanted to tell you ever since you came to find us, but I just could not muster the courage to do it."

"How about your aunt? Your father—is he an officer with the Polish army in London? What's your name? You have to give me a minute to take this all in. It's astounding. I never suspected it."

We were passing a burned-out building, and we sat down on the stoop. It was quite dark. We could no longer see the face of the other, and that was good. Stefan was silent, and there was nothing I could add. Mother would be anxious, I knew. She liked Stefan. She told me that she thought he was a decent guy, a fine and proud Pole. Yet, she was certain that she did not want him to know.

"You have to forgive me, Krysia," Stefan said. "It's been a very difficult day. So many innocent people dead. Now this. I find it hard to comprehend. It must be a year ago that we met—and you keeping this secret. I always knew that there were a number of Jews hiding in Warsaw. They probably escaped before the ghetto was demolished. I thought it was best for everyone, especially for them, if no one took notice."

"I am one of them. You never mentioned the Jews of Poland and what had happened to them. I did not know how you felt. How do you feel?"

"About the Jews? Before the war I did not even know who was and who was not a Jew. I studied with some of them at the engineering school, and later there were colleagues when I worked for the Warsaw municipality. There were not many of them. We never discussed religion, though we did discuss politics. I don't go to church, but I know that you do. Judaism is just another religion. No one could imagine what the Germans would do when it all started. There is nothing Jewish about you."

"What does that mean?"

"That was a stupid remark. Please forget it. Let's start from the beginning. What is your real name?"

"Bertel Weissberger."

"Bertel?"

"It's Berta. You know, during World War I they referred to the largest cannon as Dicke Berta—fat Berta. My birth certificate said Berta, but I was always called Bertel."

"Berta. That's not a Polish name."

"No, I am not Polish. I was born in Germany, and I lived there until I was twelve years old. In October 1938, the Nazis forcibly transported us to Poland."

Stefan was silent. I wondered what he was thinking, and I was no longer certain that I had made the right decision. "It's all very strange," Stefan said. "I don't think I quite understand, though it does explain your accent. You never wanted to talk about your childhood. I thought that there were painful memories. And your aunt?"

"She is not my aunt. She is my mother."

"Wait a minute—your mother? She does not speak with an accent."

"I know. My mother was raised in Poland. She attended the gymnasium, and after that she studied dentistry in Krakow. She moved to Germany when she married my father."

"Your father? He is not a Polish officer with the Anders army in London, is he?"

"He's in America. I think he is living in New York."

"You think? You don't know?"

"The last time we heard from him, it was before America entered the war. He was living in New York. We have an address. I only hope that he still lives there, that he has not moved. He did not yet have his own apartment, and he was living with a family in a rented room. I also have an older sister. Her name is Eva. We do not know if she is alive. She was captured by the Gestapo on the street. We were told that shots were fired. There were witnesses, but we were unable to find out if she had been hit. There was a truck nearby, and there were two Jewish men who were seized at the same time. We keep hoping that Eva is alive."

For the first time, since my father had left for America, I had made a decision that could crucially affect our immediate destiny. After I returned to the cellar, I huddled next to my mother for the remainder of the night, mentally preparing my argument for justifying my disclosure. What did I know about Stefan? He was thirty-six years old; he was born and educated in

Warsaw; his father had died when he was at the university; he owned Gershwin records, though he did not dare play them during the war; at great cost, he had obtained a ticket for a performance by Josephine Baker when she performed in Warsaw; he never referred to his engineering degree because he refused to work for the Nazis. His kept a low profile to avoid being noticed by the German authorities, and he earned just enough money to maintain himself in his rented room.

When I told my mother, she was surprisingly accepting; our immediate survival was a more important concern. We knew that the surrender of the Home Army was imminent, and soon we would be under the Nazi yoke again. In the morning, on the way up to our room, we saw the German leaflets in the courtyard. They had been dropped from airplanes during the night, and as always they contained a message and a threat. This time the language was different. It admonished the "hoodwinked" residents of Warsaw to acknowledge defeat. "It is hopeless," the message read. "Your ill-fated rebellion is over. Put your fate into the hands of the Wehrmacht, and tell the leaders of this criminal rebellion that as soon as they lay down their arms, the siege will be lifted and food distributed. However, if you persist in your support of this treachery, civilians will also be treated as traitors and punished accordingly."

Stefan had gotten hold of a developing tank and the chemicals necessary to develop the rolls of film we had taken during the last several weeks. We worked rapidly to get the task done. We worked in the ruins of the adjoining bombed-out building. Fortunately for us, the charred ruins gave off some warmth, and we were able to dry the film. We rolled the films as soon as they were dry and stored them carefully in glass jars intended for preserving fruit. We secured the glass lid with drippings from paraffin candles. In the cellar of the ruins in which we were working, we dug a deep hole, and using ashes for insulation, we buried the two glass jars.

# CHAPTER 11

# Spellen Internment Camp, Germany

OCTOBER 1944 ⚔ REOCCUPIED WARSAW, POLAND

On October 2, a spokesman for General Komorowski announced the surrender of the Home Army. The broadcast was short and crisp. It stated that the German authorities had agreed to give the insurgents prisoner-of-war status and treat them accordingly, as provided by the Geneva Convention. The documents of surrender were in the process of being signed. All residents must relinquish their arms. Henceforth, residents must submit to the laws of the victor. The reassuring sound of the Polish national anthem that had accompanied all previous news broadcasts was not heard again. Only moments after this frightening announcement, the loudspeaker was under German control.

Orders were issued in a bone-chilling voice accompanied by multiple threats. We were advised that this treacherous act, a rebellion against a benevolent ruler who was in the process of winning a war, had to be paid for by its perpetrators. Because the German army had been forced to divert manpower and weapons from the eastern front, the rebellion had interfered with the German timetable for winning the war. Punishment for this outrageous crime would be commensurate with the damage inflicted. On orders from the high command, Warsaw, the capital of Poland, would be reduced to ashes. The rubble would serve as a reminder to all people who contemplate rebellion against German occupation forces.

German occupation forces were well aware of the nearly total cooperation that had taken place among Warsaw residents. Within the next few days, they announced, orders would be issued that would address this evil belligerence. Ulica Marshalkowska was teeming with people. There was an understanding that the city would be evacuated. What they would do to us was on everyone's mind.

Stefan left to find his mother. We did not know when, or if, he would return. Movement from one sector to another was prohibited. Everyone was to remain in place. Before Stefan left, we noticed in the courtyard of an abandoned ruin some people standing around what appeared to be a pail with a fire burning inside. They were burning the A.K. armbands. We took ours from our pockets and threw them on the heap.

Despite the explicit order to stay put, people lugging bundles were rushing through the streets in an attempt to unite with family members. The sense of panic that had been mounting was now released in a frenzy of activity. The freedom we had so thoroughly enjoyed had come to an end. Refugees from Krakowskie Przedmiescie, the section Stefan had lived in, were in need of food and temporary shelter. The damage our building had sustained was moderate, and its residents opened their doors to the tired people. There was no food to share. We learned from the refugees that during the last days of September, large areas of the city had been recaptured by the Germans and systematically incinerated. Only ruins were left standing. The densely populated areas, housing masses of people, had been organized into transports, in preparation for shipment to some unknown destination. There were conflicting rumors regarding the fate of family units. Since all males between the ages of seventeen and fifty were suspect of having been active in the rebellion, they were separated from their families and dispatched to special camps. Married men and fathers of small children were either taken away or left with their families. Apparently, the German unit in charge decided their fate.

Stefan returned with his mother and her friend. There had been a directive in their neighborhood, not yet in ours, that residents who voluntarily reported at a designated gathering place for transportation out of Warsaw would be accorded better treatment. Stefan was unable to persuade his mother to remain with us. She, on the other hand, urged him to accompany her, even though he had not been listed for this transport. She was crying all the time, except when she stopped to light another cigarette. The lady could not have been more than sixty years old, but she looked older. Her shaking hands and brimming eyes indicated a nervous system at the breaking point. "Stefan, we have lost our home. There is nothing left," she kept repeating. Stefan walked with them as far as possible, then returned.

One or two days after Stefan's mother had left, we received our orders over the loudspeaker. Two days hence, we were advised, all residents of the buildings in our sector would have to vacate the premises. Everyone was to stand on the sidewalk in front of their building by nine o'clock in the morning and remain in place awaiting further orders. Everyone must present his or her validated Kennkarte to the examining officer. There was, however, an alternative. The people who voluntarily submitted to transportation out of Warsaw would be treated more leniently. Everyone was allowed to bring along a small suitcase or bundle, light enough to carry for long stretches at a time. That instruction applied to both groups. Mother and I decided to pack only some warm clothes and carry our winter coats because their bulk would take up a whole suitcase.

On the evening of the day the directive had been issued, Stefan met Pan Klucz, a well-known men's tailor who lived in the front part of our building. Shortly before the invasion, Pan Klucz had made a sports jacket for Stefan. The men exchanged thoughts with regard to the evacuation. Pan Klucz had decided to go with the transport that left voluntarily. Stefan felt that it was not wise to volunteer for anything the Nazis proposed. Pan Klucz asked Stefan if he needed anything. Stefan said that he was concerned because he did not have an overcoat. Pan Klucz told him to go to the apartment on the next day after they had left and pick up a winter coat. He told him exactly where to find it.

On the following day, we watched as some of our neighbors departed. Mother and Stefan agreed that she and I would be better off in a large crowd, rather than among a relatively small group of people. In 1944, when the Nazis once again required all Poles to have their identification papers revalidated, neither Mother nor I had submitted our Kennkartes. Now we tried to prepare explanations for our lapse that would sound reasonable to the officer in charge. Stefan suggested that Mother and I should be at a distance from each other when documents would have to be presented. It would be best if we were among neighbors who did not know us or our relationship.

It was with great relief that we learned that Panna Cybulska and her mother wanted to take advantage of the preferred treatment of residents who voluntarily submitted to transportation out of Warsaw. Aside from the superintendent of our building, a morose man whom Stefan had befriended, our landladies were the only people who had questioned our identity.

A young couple passed us on the street. Stefan knew the woman, and we stopped to speak with them. They told us that although there was no explicit ruling, there were rumors about that if neither husbands nor wives had taken part in the insurrection, being married would give the couple a better chance of remaining together. They were on their way to be married in Kosciol Swietgo Zbawiciela—Church of the Holy Savior—and they asked us if we would be their witnesses at the ceremony. The woman told Stefan that the priest of the church on nearby Plac Swietego Zbawiciela was coming to the rescue of distraught unmarried Polish couples. On numerous occasions, when suddenly in need of a hiding place, this church had provided me with a refuge. The priest was issuing marriage certificates to couples whose plans to be married had been thwarted by the outbreak of the insurrection. There were estimates that close to a hundred thousand men had lost their lives during the past two months, and it appeared that the Catholic Church, in an attempt to help the men who had survived, was willing to make some compromises.

We readily agreed, and as we accompanied them, Stefan and I exchanged some thoughts. "As a married couple," Stefan said, "they might send us to a labor camp rather than a concentration camp. We might be able to remain together. Without this type of document, neither of us stands a good chance. If we stay together, I may be able to help your mother. So what do you say, Krysia, should we try?"

Should we try? Stefan had asked. I was overwhelmed by gratitude. I could not speak. I smiled and nodded my head in happy acquiescence. Ever since the A.K. capitulated to the Nazis, I had not been able to shake the feeling that our efforts to survive, to outwit the Nazis, were doomed. Every other order to the defeated Poles included some reference to the Jews in their midst, who had been the instigators of this Polish calamity. Much of my energy was spent in combating my fears. It was churning up my insides and pulling me down. All of a sudden there was a glimpse of light.

I knew the priest, Father Stanislaw. On several occasions I had heard him celebrate Mass. I was astounded by his humanity. In black garb without the elaborate vestments, addressing him as Father somehow seemed natural. He addressed us as "my children," and he questioned Stefan with regard to some of the events he knew about but had not witnessed. At first, upon hearing that neither of us had been a member of his parish and that at no time had there been a posting of the banns at any church, I feared that our request would be denied. Stefan was doing most of the talking, but while he did so, the priest's eyes, so it seemed to me, never left my face. He was a man in his sixties, tall and gaunt and slightly stooped. His eyes were gray, tired looking, and wise. He asked each of us a number of questions. I told him that I was Jewish and that my mother was alive.

"So your mother knows that you are here. I am so glad that you have a mother, my child. There has been too much suffering. So much killing. I must not deny you. The Lord is full of compassion."

"I am so grateful, Father," I whispered.

"I cannot enter your marriage in the registry, but I will issue a document of marriage. I pray that it will help you. But you must promise me," he put his hand on my head, "you must promise me, both of you, that when the war is over, and if you are sure that this is what you want to do, you will come back to this church with the certificate I will give you, and that you will enter into a marriage as prescribed by the Roman Catholic Church."

"Yes, I will, Father," I said.

"Thank you, Father," Stefan said. "The Lord willing, we will be back."

On a piece of paper we wrote down our respective names, places and dates of birth, and the names of our parents. The priest understood that all the information I gave him was false, but when I wanted to explain, he just waved his hand and said "No, not now. Once the war is over, and you come back. It is better for me not to know."

We watched as he carefully filled in the blank spaces on an official-looking form. He signed the document and affixed the seal of the parish. "As far as the Nazis are concerned, and whatever German authority you will have to face, this document is legal. I know, you know, and the Lord knows that it is not. I will pray that it may save your lives."

When I looked around, I saw other people waiting to see the priest. He had given us a great deal of his time. I felt very grateful. I reached for his hand.

I wanted to kiss it as was the custom, but he did not want that. "I am not a bishop," he said. The document stated that on October 3, 1944, Stefan Broda and Krystyna Zolkos had entered into the holy state of matrimony, in accordance with the laws prescribed by the Roman Catholic Church. It was not the third of October, but we were sure that the priest knew what he was doing. Both of us felt that we had been most fortunate to have met this wise and kind man.

When we returned, and before I had a chance to tell Mother, she told us about the latest order issued by the authorities. Residents were instructed that on the following morning they would be marched out of the city on ten minute's notice. No one would be able to return to their vacated buildings, a bellowing voice had informed the residents. At all times identity documents must be ready for inspection.

During the night I managed to tell Mother about my marriage. She was very distracted. "We know about the strategy employed in the final liquidation of the Warsaw ghetto," Mother told Stefan. "The best one can do is not call attention to oneself. They follow a preconceived master plan. Their promises of better work assignments or conditions are just a ruse to deceive victims into submission."

Neither Mother nor I were able to sleep during that last night in our room. Mother was concerned about Stefan's idea that the three of us should stay together as a family unit. Ever since our arrival in Warsaw, we had taken various measures to avoid being seen together. Though Mother's diction was precise and elegant, her bleached hair or perhaps her features had caused problems on many occasions. My bleached hair looked natural enough, but my inability to speak Polish fluently was often a cause for suspicion.

Mother could not understand how Stefan was able to sleep through the night in view of what was awaiting us. At five-thirty in the morning when I went to the library to wake him, he said that he was very tired and needed all the sleep he could get.

At seven o'clock in the morning, the loudspeaker repeated all the previous instructions, with an additional caveat: Residents were now ordered to open all windows and upon exiting their apartments to leave the door wide open. A warning followed: "Noncompliance will be severely punished."

Mother questioned the wisdom of trying to stay together. Stefan disagreed with Mother. He said that during the past months, I had continuously interacted with Poles, and no one had remarked upon my diction. The most important rule to observe was not to act self-conscious. "All of us are now in the same boat," he said. "It would seem that for our people survival and not ferreting out hidden Jews will be the sole objective." Mother and I looked at each other, and we knew that we would continue to be cautious. Stefan had heard that a Einsatzkommando detachment had been called in from the eastern front to help with the evacuation of Warsaw. He wondered aloud what that meant. We did not react.

In front of each building, and also in our courtyard, German soldiers with guns at ready watched the scurrying residents as they rushed back and forth. Families struggled to stay together while lugging their bundles and suitcases. Crying children refused to relinquish their mothers' hands for even a second. Once out in the street, we saw soldiers in battle dress patrolling the growing columns of people. They stopped anyone who had forgotten something and wanted to return to an apartment, or even to step back to retrieve a fallen item. Requests to use sanitary facilities were denied. However, after standing for a considerable time, we were allowed to sit down on the ground or on our suitcases or bundles. At two o'clock in the afternoon, there was a renewed flurry of activity. A number of soldiers dressed in black uniforms, running on the double, moved toward each building. About eight of them entered our building, and four of them moved through the courtyard to our part of the building. There was a burst of shattering windowpanes. Within minutes they returned. From the front part of the building two angry soldiers dragged an old man who appeared to be senile. From the building across the street, a pregnant woman was brought down on a stretcher. She was moaning and cursing the soldiers.

Commands to stand up and to be ready to march were issued, but we had only moved a few steps from the sidewalk onto the street when we were stopped. We were ordered to face the building that had been our home. A long and strange-looking truck moved up to the front of our house. Soldiers in rubber suits and helmets jumped off the vehicle, dragging thick white hoses, six inches in diameter. An open car came into view, and everyone craned their necks to catch a glimpse of the four officers, all of high rank, that were standing up in it. One of the officers held a microphone and a sheet of paper. It was very quiet. He read in German; a translator repeated each sentence in Polish.

"Your punishment: For starting the mutiny; for supporting the criminals who led this ridiculous rebellion; for refusing to put down your arms and surrender to the occupation authority; for wasting precious German manpower and equipment; but most of all for daring to believe that the victorious Third Reich would be defeated by a misguided horde of Polish peasants, you will leave this cursed city. Before your departure, you will see with your own eyes that you will never be able to return. Anyone found within the city of Warsaw after orders to march out have been issued and anyone who dares to return will be shot on sight. There will be no exceptions. The punishment for your treachery will serve as a lesson to anyone who engages in treason or sabotage against the Third Reich."

The open car with the four officers still standing rolled past our column. Seconds later, I watched in disbelieving horror as the white hoses held by the helmeted soldiers stiffened into upright columns and red flames erupted from them. Within minutes our house, as well as all the adjacent apartment buildings on both sides of Ulica Marshalkowska, and as far as the eye could see, became part of one huge inferno, crackling and hissing. Not a sound was heard from the people surrounding me on all sides. The muttering, crying, and complaining had ceased. It seemed as if breathing had stopped.

When we were ordered to move, everyone picked up their bundles and pointed their feet in the indicated direction; however, eyes remained glued to the burning buildings. As if mesmerized by the awesomeness of this wanton destruction, I kept looking up at the dark smoky sky long after the burning buildings had passed from my view.

We walked for hours. Although the armed soldiers surrounding us on all sides tried to prod the stumbling mass of people into a marching pace, their orders were not heeded. I had to watch my step to keep from stumbling over abandoned parcels of food, pieces of clothing, and even suitcases. My little carrying case that had seemed quite light at the beginning of the march was getting progressively heavier. I tried to hold on to it as long as I possibly could, before shifting it to my other hand. At intervals, Stefan would carry my winter coat. I concentrated all my attention on not surrendering to exhaustion and on keeping my feet moving forward. I avoided thinking about what lay in store for us. Stefan, Mother, and I communicated with our eyes only because to speak would have expended precious energy. We knew that people were falling down, and we heard shots being fired. We were now part of thousands of people; all of us in the same predicament. We had not eaten since we left our room.

I told myself that unless we were recognized by someone who knew our true identity, we would share the fate of the Polish population. I was married to a Roman Catholic Pole, and we had pledged to help each other. Besides, there had to be some truth to the rumor that Germany was losing the war. As we walked through various sectors of the city, I tried to discover some familiar landmark to help me orient myself, but the city had changed too much. I could not tell which direction we were heading. There were ruins, remnants of red brick buildings with their interiors gutted, and along the streets, piled-up rubble, perhaps two stories high.

"I know that there were areas our people never managed to access," Stefan said. "They were not touched by the insurrection, and they were inhabited throughout by German troops. They decided to take us along this route to further intimidate us and destroy whatever morale is left."

"Where do you think they are taking us?" I asked. "We have been walking for hours, by now we should be out of the city. In which direction are we headed?"

"We are walking in circles. We started out going in a southerly direction, then we turned west, and now it seems we are going back north."

Evening had turned into night. It was dark and damp, and the moon, visible during the early evening hours, was now covered by clouds. I kept my eyes riveted on Mother's and Stefan's silhouettes; I feared that if I lost sight of them, I would not find them again. Whenever someone raised his or her voice above a whisper, the order "*Kein Reden!*"—no talking—was thundered in an angry tone by a patrolling guard. Children pleading for food or water were hushed and threatened by distraught parents.

It was after ten o'clock at night when we were directed to trudge up a rather steep hill toward an embankment. From the top, as far as the eye could see, were open freight cars. We were ordered to climb aboard. The three of us managed to get onto the same flatbed car. Squeezing us from all sides were bodies, bundles, and valises. "*Rein, rein*"—get in, get in—the guard kept shouting, long after every available inch of space had been filled. The slight drizzle that had begun when we mounted the train turned into rain by the time it started. I was grateful to be out in the open and to get wet. I thought that in a closed car, among the mass of pressing bodies, I would suffocate.

Over the ensuing hours, whenever I dozed off, the person I leaned against nudged me back to consciousness. On several occasions I heard the puffing of a steam engine and the rhythmic clicking of a passing train. At three o'-clock in the morning, our transport halted. There was much shouting in German, and I was able to make out that our guards were ordered to report to Pruszkow, but that the authorities in Pruszkow would not allow us to leave the train because their facilities could not accept such a mass of people. They were overcrowded and overextended, and they wanted our train to keep moving. Once again our train started, and we traveled perhaps for one more hour.

In total darkness we were led into a huge, dimly lit barrack. The relatively new structure resembled an indoor arena, or a hangar for housing airplanes. The structure was rectangular, there were no beams, and a row of small windows touched the roof.

The barrack was bare except for blackout shades, which covered the windows. Every foot of space appeared to be occupied by the time we managed to orient ourselves. We did what everybody was doing, dropped our belongings to the ground, thereby securing a place for our bodies. We had been standing for over twenty hours. The dirt floor beneath my body felt like a feather bed. Several hours later I awoke to a bright dawn that illuminated a ghastly sight. The people surrounding me looked like cave dwellers rather than the inhabitants of the gracious residential buildings they had lived in a short while ago. The stench of stale urine assaulted the senses, and I could barely keep myself from retching by pressing a kerchief against my nose and my mouth.

Wherever I looked, I saw gray faces framed by disheveled hair and bodies covered with grimy rags. To determine the source of the foul stench, one had only to look at one's feet. We had been without toilet facilities for more than twenty-four hours.

A self-appointed committee of four women drew up a list of requests they would present to our wardens when the door was unlocked. It was decided that all men, including the teenage boys, should maintain a low profile, and that the women should deal with the soldiers. Among the several hundred people locked into our barrack, less than an eighth were males. In spite of the hardship caused by lack of food and water, it was agreed that the matter of sanitary facilities would be on top of the agenda.

The door was unlocked, and a platoon of soldiers, guns held in the crooks of their arms, stormed into the barrack. While still in the flatbed railroad car,

I heard voices urging escape. Later in the dark, as we were hurried into the barrack, we were guarded by soldiers on all sides. It was inconceivable that this mass of exhausted prisoners could offer even a semblance of resistance. After the soldiers had reviewed the scene, it was obvious that several of them were embarrassed. The others kept busy shouting commands in German that few could understand. Every sentence contained the favored pejoratives *Polnische Wirtschaft* (inept Polish housekeeping or management) or *Polnische Schweinerei* (Polish pigsty) reserved for conquered Poland. The soldiers demanded that a translator come forth and on the double. There were no volunteers. Mother and I had prepared for all sorts of possibilities, and that was one of them. We neither understood, nor spoke, a word of German. We did learn that the barrack we occupied was located on the outskirts of Ursus, a suburban community about an eighty-minute train ride from Warsaw.

The soldiers told us that our kind, though totally undeserving, were the beneficiaries of the most benign treatment. Several transports out of Warsaw had been shipped to Treblinka and Auschwitz. We inferred that all prospective camps in the vicinity were severely overcrowded with prisoners from Warsaw, and that a number of infectious diseases had crossed over and infected the Nazi prison guards.

We agreed that we would refer to ourselves as evacuees, in the hope that it would persuade our guards to treat us as victims rather than as criminals. We organized ourselves into a number of units that took turns cleaning the makeshift latrine and the dirt floor in our barrack and regulating access to a water pump. After we had cleaned the floor, we petitioned the officer in charge for straw to spread over the dirt floor. We had gained access to drinking water, but we were denied food. Before we were driven out of Warsaw, we had been told to bring along a bowl for food and a spoon to eat with. Our guards told us that not only had we sabotaged the war effort, but the insurrection had also caused a monumental breakdown of the rail network. We were told that our transgression had caused incalculable damage, and as punishment we should starve to death. However, when the matter of the bowl and spoon was brought to the officer's attention, he reluctantly admitted that we were supposed to be fed, but that the field kitchen and the food supplies had not yet arrived.

From local people employed at the Ursus camp site, we heard that hundreds of transports, the German name for freight trains filled with human cargo, had passed through Ursus and its vicinity. All prisons, concentration camps, and work camps within a radius of a hundred miles, including the dreaded Treblinka, were overcrowded and unable to take more prisoners until some of the inmates could be relocated. Relocated! How many among the hundreds of people around me understood the true meaning of that euphemism? In addition, residents of the neighboring communities had been warned against giving shelter to escapees from transports and threatened with severest punishment if that decree should be disobeyed. Polish railroad employees passed on reports that trains filled with Warsaw's defeated insurgent army, ostensibly headed for prisoner-of-war camps, had in fact arrived at the unloading platform in Auschwitz for what they were told was a temporary work assignment.

Since our unit of three had been unable to secure a squatting place adjacent to a wall, we felt hemmed in and kept communication between ourselves to a minimum. It was difficult to move in any direction without stepping on a person or a blanket, at times spread out in excess of the needed space. The women expected Stefan to be more knowledgeable than they, and he was frequently called upon to give advice or to venture an opinion. To the right of us, a woman, clearly in charge of a family of six, made several attempts to draw us into a conversation. Mother, whom I addressed as aunt and whom Stefan addressed as Jadwiga, responded only when directly addressed. I pretended to be ill because I feared that in such close proximity my language problem might touch off questions and further expose my deficiency. When asked about my silence, Stefan said that he thought a nearby detonation had affected my hearing and that we had been unable to consult a doctor.

The woman's family consisted of her elderly mother, a sister who appeared to be retarded, a boy of perhaps fifteen and a girl several years younger, and a female friend. The woman was blond and robust, and she resolutely assumed charge of her family unit upon entering the barrack. She spread out three blankets, and then stood guard over every inch of space until each member of her group had managed to lie down. On the second day after our arrival, while we were still waiting to receive some food, she extracted from a small sack a number of cooked unpeeled potatoes, an onion, and a jar of oil and prepared what to my nostrils appeared to be a sumptuous feast. I refrained from looking in the direction of the tempting odors lest my eyes betray the yearning of my empty stomach.

The woman looked up suddenly, and addressing Stefan, she said, "You got yourself a young wife, eh?" Stefan did not answer, however he nodded his head as if to say, that might well be so. "What's the matter with her?" the woman persisted. "She doesn't say much, does she?"

"She is ill," Stefan answered. "She needs to rest."

"Then she will not be of much use to you should there be a chance to escape," the woman insisted. Stefan lifted his hand, the motion implying she need not concern herself. "We are going to escape," the woman continued. "We have relatives who live nearby. They will take us in. I am not going to let them herd us around as if we were cattle. They may take us to Oswiecim. That's where they took the Jews. If you don't try to get away, you'll wind up in Oswiecim with the Jews."

"I don't think anyone really knows where we will wind up," Stefan said calmly. "I heard that there was no space left in the concentration camps, and that the transports who came through yesterday were directed to a labor camp. We were told that this is a temporary camp, and that they can't keep us here for long. I do hope that you will succeed in getting away," he concluded.

The woman's reference to the Jews in Oswiecim had sent cold shivers down my spine. The Polish town of Oswiecim had been renamed Auschwitz by the Germans, the notorious death camp for Jews. I had not moved my head, nor could she have had a glimpse into my downcast eyes. In my mind I analyzed each word of her many statements and the context in which each remark was made. Had there been a threat, or had it just been our misfortune to be next to such a vicious woman? From Stefan's body language, I could sense that he was annoyed, yet I felt certain that he could not divine the turmoil I was experiencing.

Late in the afternoon, we were ordered to line up and to bring along our bowls and spoons. Some of the inmates were so weak that they were unable to stand in line. Stefan took the bowl an old man with tremulous hands held out to him, and he promised to bring back his allotment of food. From a large kettle on top of a field kitchen, a soldier ladled out soup, and the soldier next to him gave each person a chunk of bread. Once he understood why Stefan was holding up the additional bowl, the soldier turned to his companion and said, "If he is so weak, then let's just give him half a portion." Since it was obvious that Stefan did not understand it was meant to be a joke, the soldier laughed and filled the bowl with a generous portion.

On the following morning, as I was preparing to line up for the pump in order to wash, the blond woman turned toward us and said to no one in particular, but loud enough to be heard by all who were nearby, "I am willing to bet that there are Jews right here among us. It was the Jews and the Communists who started this cursed insurrection. If I had some of the dollars the Jews are hoarding, I could bribe our way out of this mess."

The woman looked at my mother and said, "What did you say your name was?" Mother did not reply. She was occupied searching for her toothbrush and other items, preparing for her turn at the pump. The woman repeated the question. Mother lifted her head and said, "I did not say. Neither did I ask for your name. As for the Jews, I should think that in view of our own predicament, we will need all our energy to worry about ourselves."

Mother's tone had been low, but firm, and I noticed that some of the people nearby were nodding their heads. I felt once again able to breathe. The thought that my mother was a wise woman flashed through my mind.

That night, sleepless and frightened, I felt Stefan reaching for my hand, and I saw that the index finger of his other hand made the sign of silence across his lips. I knew that Mother was awake. Her open eyes never left my face. When we were certain that the people around us were asleep, Stefan and I drew the blanket over our heads to muffle our conversation.

"The first thing that we will do once we get out of this barrack will be to put distance between ourselves and that vicious woman," Stefan said. "Until then, we'll just sit tight. You did fine," Stefan said to me, "but I now realize that your aunt—that is, your mother—was right. She had said that you must separate, that you should not be seen together. I did not think that there would be a problem. Frankly, I am stunned. I thought all of us knew the enemy. Who would have thought that this inoffensive-looking housewife, with children to care for, would be willing to become an instrument for the Nazis?"

"Speak to Mother. She must be in a dreadful state," I whispered. "I'll do whatever you say. We always knew that it was dangerous for us to be seen together. I wanted to believe that, after the Warsaw insurrection, Poles would stop hunting Jews to gain favors from the Nazis. But nothing has changed."

"Now Krysia, be fair. Are you going to judge all Poles, the beautiful and heroic young Poles you have met and worked with, by the implied threats made by this mean-spirited woman?"

Stefan turned to discuss our situation with Mother, and I was left alone with my trepidations. The feeling of living in mortal danger, which had left me during the insurrection, even with bullets, bombs, and shrapnel coming at me from all sides, had once more taken hold of me. There now was an additional problem. Would Stefan be willing to stay with me? Were the worst to happen, should someone denounce us to the Gestapo, I knew that Stefan, though not Jewish, would be forced to share our fate. I decided that should he want to separate, I would not say a word to dissuade him. On the other hand, I wouldn't bring up the matter; I would allow him to evaluate the prevailing conditions.

Two incidents freed us from our persecutor. Her retarded sister stole something, and the woman was blamed for her inadequate supervision. Moreover, her young daughter developed a fever, and she came to ask us if we had a thermometer. Mother said she had not brought one along, but she would look at the girl. The woman was very grateful, almost obsequious. Mother assured her that it was a slightly elevated temperature, and since the girl also had a stomachache, the mild fever would pass.

After several days we knew our situation was about to change. While queuing up for the latrine, for washing at the pump, or for the soup line, we learned from remarks dropped by Polish workers employed at the camp that our next hurdle would be the selection process. Having been subjected to the selection process in the Krosno ghetto, and familiar with the evil of that operation from events in the Warsaw ghetto, I knew that selection was a euphemism for separating families and dispatching each member in different directions toward an unknown destiny. The only question was, Would the Germans dare to do to the Poles what they had done to the Jews? On numerous occasions, the Nazis had proclaimed that the Poles would become their slaves. To do that, I reasoned, they would need to keep them alive.

In the late afternoon, eight uniformed Nazis, with Gestapo insignia on their shoulders, arms, and hats, strutted into the barrack. In an angry tone, the officer in charge once again reiterated the crimes we had committed. They apparently wanted to prepare us for the punishment we were about to receive. "You are to be ready to march out of this barrack by seven o'clock tomorrow morning," he bellowed. "For your own good, obey all orders promptly, as all of you will be held accountable for even the slightest deviation from my orders. Just look at this Polish pigsty. I expect it to be scrupulously clean when you leave. Don't you dare leave any of your Polish filth behind. Upon leaving, each person is to carry his own belongings. The barrack will be inspected, and each person will be scrutinized."

In the dim light, amid the frenzied activity around us, Stefan, who had talked with Mother, was now ready to tell me her plans. "Your mother said," Stefan told me, "that we must separate immediately upon leaving the barrack. She said that once we leave here, she will not speak to you again, and she vowed that she would not look at you. She wants you to do the same. I must say," Stefan confided, "that while we were queuing up, I did notice glances directed at you and me and Jadwiga. Some of them I did not like."

"What else did Mother say?"

"She said that she will try and stay near us, within eyesight, but I promised her that you would not look in her direction. She said that I should take care of you. We divided our money, though I doubt that the occupation currency will do us much good. Did you know that your mother has a twenty-dollar bill? She said that she would be glad to give it to us, but should we be searched, she would prefer that it is found on her person than on one of us."

"Yes, I know about it. It is for one purpose only. Even when we thought that we would die of hunger, we agreed that we would not touch it. Mother has the twenty-dollar bill, and I have my father's address in America."

"I am glad you reminded me," Stefan said. "About the address—your mother thinks that the slip of paper could be more fatal than the dollar bill. She urged that both of us memorize the address, and then destroy the paper." I touched my brassiere and felt the tiny safety pin fastened to the piece of muslin that held my most precious possession. I did not trust my memory, and I knew that I would not take Mother's advice. I noted that Mother had not told Stefan about the little green cyanide capsule that my father's address was wrapped around. I resolved not to mention it to Stefan. I reasoned it might scare him away. The pill would remain my secret.

"When next you speak to Mother," I said, "please tell her that I will be careful. For now I shall leave the address in place, because this is not the time to take it out and commit it to memory. Tell her that I will make believe that I don't know her. Tell her that I am praying for all of us."

Since the day they took Eva, my Mother had refused to speak with me about God. When I told her that my prayers were comforting to me, and that

I had prayed on my knees each time I entered a church, all she managed to say was that she was glad that prayers brought me comfort, but that she would not talk with me about God.

The lineup, in rows of six with family groups together, was completed shortly after seven o'clock in the morning. Officers seated at a number of tables examined the documents of each person. Other officers standing nearby moved from one person to the next asking questions. Commands were shouted directing the people to move forward, and the mass of people was soon organized in accordance with a swift and orderly procedure. As we moved closer to the tables, I was able to see the dispersal method. Families with children were directed to one side, elderly people to another. There were screams of anguish as families were forcibly separated. Mother was no longer near us. I could not see her, but she must not have been far behind us, because I could feel her eyes glued to my back. I did not dare turn around.

The order "*rechts, links, vorwarts*"—right, left, forward—was upon us. In front of us was a truck with the motor running. I could see men boarding the truck. Stefan and I were in front of the Gestapo officer who did the directing. He held a riding crop in his outstretched arm pointing in one direction or the other, and whipping it occasionally against his shiny boot. Holding hands, Stefan and I moved forward. We gave our name, and the name was checked against a list held by an officer standing to the left of the commander. A soldier, in field uniform, did the translating. Another soldier reached for our respective Kennkartes. He questioned me about the missing 1944 validation stamp. I pretended to be confused, and Stefan said I had had a mild shock, but that since the day we left Warsaw, I had shown continuous improvement. He wanted to know what I did during the uprising. I pretended not to understand. I said I was a sewing machine operator and that I had been sewing German uniforms. Which kind? he asked. Black ones, I answered. He asked to see our marriage certificate. He compared the names, glanced at the parish seal, and returned the document.

He wanted to know what was Stefan's occupation. Stefan said that he had worked in a photography studio. He asked Stefan if he owned a camera. Stefan answered in the affirmative. When asked where the camera was, Stefan said that it had been in his mother's apartment when her building was bombed and destroyed. It must have been the right answer, because the officer was pleased. Stefan, who had a tendency to lean forward, sometimes gave the appearance of a stoop-shouldered man. The officer said to his assistant, "I don't think this specimen is the warrior type. What do you think?" The other man agreed, and both of us were directed to the left side.

Several minutes later, Mother was directed to our side. Families with children were directed to the right side. I looked around and to my great relief the blond woman, our enemy, was nowhere in sight. Our group was the larger one by far, and more and more people were directed to our swelling ranks. At noontime we were given some soup and an extra ration of bread. We were told that it would be wise not to eat the bread, because from now on we would be under a different administration, and it was not certain when we would receive our next meal.

We were ordered to march forward, four abreast, and to keep the rows neat. It felt good to be moving again and to be in the fresh air, on a country road, surrounded on all sides by open fields. Ahead of us, though still in the distance, was a long freight train. Walking toward it I counted twenty-three boxcars. I had not finished counting, when I felt myself pushed from behind to climb onto the boxcar facing me. Stefan climbed up behind me. He immediately moved to the left, lunged against the side of the car, dropped his suitcase, and sat down to ensure possession of the space. When I pushed through to his side, he moved over to make room for me. I leaned my back against the side of the car.

It was late in the afternoon. There was no illumination inside the car, and the light coming from the outside was quite dim. Rain had started to fall as we climbed aboard. Stefan said that we were in a cattle car, meant to transport at most six horses. There was straw on the floor of the car. We watched in horror as ever more people climbed aboard. They were angry and wet. There was quite a lot of pushing and cursing from our tormentors. I counted about forty-four people. My mother was the forty-fifth. I was so relieved, I stopped counting. I was not sure if Mother had seen us, but she immediately moved over to the right side, and with more people climbing aboard, I lost sight of her. I knew that she was there.

Outside, the guards were talking, but the noise within the car was so loud, I could not clearly understand what they were saying to each other. I did hear one of them say that it was going to be a long night. Not being near the opening, but from the sound, and the sudden total darkness, we knew that the sliding panel door of the car had been slid shut in its track. On one side of the car, placed high, but within a tall person's reach, was a vertically grated opening, with a sliding panel on an inside track. Some of the men succeeded in opening the sliding panel. We knew fresh air must be coming in, but because of our distance from the opening, it would take a while for the air to reach us. A guard pounded on the door, and said, that if they continued to hear noises on the outside, the window would be shut and padlocked.

I woke up in the middle of the night feeling chilled. Cold air was coming into the car through four small slatted vents located near the corners, slightly below the roof of the car. It was early October, and the weather had been relatively mild. Perhaps lack of food caused me to feel so cold. In the stillness of the night, I could hear people breathing. Some of them were snoring. I would have liked to see the faces of the men and women who were near us. The fresh air seeping through the vents did little to disperse the stench of human waste. I observed some women putting kerchiefs overs their mouths and noses, and I did the same. I slipped my arms into the sleeves of my winter coat and dozed off.

Early in the morning, a guard opened the sliding door a crack and fastened it in place with a chain. For the next two days, our boxcar remained at the siding where we had climbed aboard. It was difficult to move or turn around. The stale odor of unwashed bodies was pervasive. Cramped legs and arms needed to stretch out. People were beginning to lean against each other, and irritation was mounting. Some people were saying that we had been abandoned and that except for the Nazis no one knew of our existence. Stefan and I agreed to refrain from speaking to each other and thereby conserve our energy. Near the opening, someone had been able to communicate with the patrolling guard, and we learned that we were waiting for a locomotive.

The arrival of a puffing steam locomotive was received as a good omen. Coupling the locomotive to our transport took several hours. It seemed that the same locomotive had passed our train convoy several times. We speculated that the engineer was receiving conflicting orders with regard to direction. We heard the hissing of the steam and the clanging of the coupling and felt a tug as our car moved a few feet, then once again the boxcar stood in place. The people near the opening saw the same locomotive pass us on an adjacent rail. Subsequently, the sounds of the coupling procedure could be heard from the other end of the train.

Once we were moving, the people close to the opening, were able to observe from station names that we were headed west. We had been traveling for about forty minutes when our train transport approached a station platform and suddenly reduced its speed to a crawl. The platform was filled with Polish women who were throwing loaves of bread into the cars. A guard stepped up on the crossbar of our slowly moving car and pushed the door wide open. As the train rolled out of the station, another group of women and children ran up the embankment, and then ran alongside the accelerating train. Their hands reached into baskets and out came loaves, aimed at the opening, into receiving arms. Stefan caught one loaf, then another, and passed it along. Others did the same, freely sharing the bread. With this unexpected gift came the clear realization that we could only survive by helping one another. It was a supreme moment.

All of us knew that hoarding flour and baking bread was a punishable crime, strictly enforced by the German occupation authority. The baking and delivery of all those loaves had been a heroic effort made on our behalf. This act of defiance had to have been organized and carried out by at least thirty or forty people. Preparations had been made, and communication had been transmitted regarding the time when our train was expected to pass through the town. The mouth-watering aroma of fresh-baked bread filled the car. There were tears and prayers. Our plight was known.

When the train stopped to take on water for the locomotive, we were permitted to dismount and remove the fetid straw. In the process of replacing it with fresh straw, we discovered that the floor of the car slanted down to a central, grated drain, six inches in diameter.

We had not been allowed access to a latrine since leaving the camp in Ursus. The men had managed to make their way to the crack in the door and relieve themselves while the train was moving. For the women, it was an agonizing and degrading situation. Once we discovered the drain, our situation improved. We evolved a system whereby several women formed a circle around a person squatting over the drain. The women turned their backs to the woman using the drain, providing as much privacy as possible.

Except for very short periods when we were allowed to dismount, we remained in our boxcar for eleven days. Most of the time our car was left at remote sidings without a locomotive. We were told that we were cargo of the lowest priority, and our locomotive was needed for transporting troops and supplies. On several occasions a large vat of water and a long handed ladle was wheeled to the car opening. Using the ladle, a person on the inside was able to reach the water in the vat and fill the cups that were passed from one person to another.

Once or twice when the steam engine had to be uncoupled to take on coal or water, the boxcar inmates were allowed to climb down and use a latrine. Only one car at a time was processed. The women used their turn in the latrine to wash themselves. They urged the men to shave out in the open, thereby allowing the women additional time.

On two occasions we were aware that we had crossed into the German Reich, but hours later we were once again at the border and back in occupied Poland. Once, during the day, when our transport was passing through a German town, I heard German women insisting that our transport be stopped. The officer in charge argued that he had orders not to stop, but to pass through. He said that we were the prisoners from Warsaw. We were being punished, the officer said, for having assisted a group of rebels and criminals who had attempted to sabotage the German war effort. The German women prevailed. One woman said they were Red Cross volunteers and knew their mandate. Our sliding door was opened all the way. We were not permitted to step down, and the German women were not permitted to board the train. However, some of them managed to look into the car. The women were clad in gray uniforms and hats, with Red Cross armbands on their sleeves. I understood from what they were saying to each other that they were not happy with what they had seen. They gave us hot coffee and chunks of bread. They said that they were sorry, but there was no soup left.

Sometimes, in the middle of the night, moving very quietly, I would stand up against the wall. All around me people were lying on the floor. Across the car I could feel Mother's eyes looking at me. I could not see her, but I knew that she too was standing up. It was the only signal that passed between us.

Though we comforted each other that the ordeal would in time pass, at night when the large door was slid shut and locked into place, despair descended on us. During the day, the optimists among us insisted that before destroying us the Nazis would want to work us to death, and that with God's help, by then the war would be over. All of us were aware that Germany was fighting the war on two fronts. According to their propaganda, they were winning ground all the time, but we knew that was not true. Though we had not seen them, we knew Soviet troops were outside Warsaw, positioned along the eastern bank of the Vistula.

At times there was talk about the Jews. In whispers our fellow prisoners talked about rumors they had heard of mass killings in concentration camps and of other camps where death was an industry. I heard a man say, "They took the Jews away in transports. What did they do with them? There were hundreds of thousands of them, maybe millions. Now they are transporting us in closed cattle cars. What are they planning to do with us?"

During the early hours of the night, when I was unable to sleep, I could hear our guards talking. They were complaining about a shortage of locomotives, about receiving conflicting orders, and about a breakdown in organization. One of them said, "Didn't they know that by setting this mass migration into motion they would deprive our own people of transportation equipment?" One guard grumbled that he'd rather be a soldier than a prison guard, but another one said that this was far better than fighting the Russians on the eastern front.

In the middle of the night, one person was removed from our car. People said that it was an old man who had been ill for several days. No one knew whether the man had been alive or dead when the guards came in to carry out the body.

We were certain that we were passing through the Third Reich when we heard heavy bombers flying overhead and antiaircraft guns firing from the ground. We were stopped at a passenger terminal, and our engineer was accused of disobeying the order to pass through freight terminals. I could hear him defend himself. He said that he had obeyed the switchman's signal. When ordered to reverse course, the engineer answered that if he was ordered to reverse course, he would collide with the train that was coming up behind us. The exchange was conducted in heated tones, accompanied by angry threats. The favorite German slang *verdammte Schweinerei*—damned foul-ups—was heard again and again.

When the train was moving, and the rhythmic click of wheels against rail masked sound, I whispered into Stefan's ear what I had heard. He asked many questions that I could not answer. Most of all he wanted to know if anyone on the outside had mentioned the heavy bombers that were continuously flying high above us. Who did they belong to? The Germans, the English, or the Americans? I did not know, but I told Stefan that from the sound of the voices I could tell the atmosphere was very tense.

It must have been on the twelfth or the thirteenth day since our incarceration in the boxcar when we had a distinct perception that we must be close to the western front. Men who climbed on each others shoulders to get a better view through the grated window reported that the blackout was so severe that our train passed through tunnels and depots without ever encountering a signal, or position light. There was the thunder of exploding bombs, and simultaneously we heard firing from antiaircraft batteries. One detonating crash followed another. For seconds at a time, though it was nighttime, our car was so brightly illuminated that we were able to see each other. Everyone was fully awake. The rejoicing was subdued but fraternal.

No one spoke; we were all eager to determine which direction the sounds were coming from. In our excitement, we touched each others' hands and shoulders. The bombs were hitting German targets on German territory. Throughout, our train kept moving ahead. Bombs were exploding close by. Our train rocked on the rails, on the verge of toppling over. We were no longer able to stand and crashed on top of crouching bodies. Stefan and I tried to hold on to each other. There was an explosion. Our train was hit; it stopped.

We heard inhuman howls. Bright flames illuminated the inside of our locked car. As fists pounded the locked door, we heard the sound of a chain being removed. Our door was slid open all the way. We surged toward the opening, jumped, fell on each other, and crawled under the boxcar. There must have been more than thirty people beneath the car. Once I knew that Mother and Stefan were near me, my eyes focused on the two boxcars that had been turned into flaming torches. People were locked inside. The guards had not been able to get there in time. Nearby on his knees was one of our guards. He was murmuring Hail Mary, repeating over and over again, "*Heilige Maria, Mutter Gottes.*"

While the bombing continued, I was free. I went down on my knees and I prayed. I pleaded, I begged Him to please have mercy on us and to continue the bombing. I told Him that I did not care if I got hit by a bomb, if my Mother got hit by a bomb, to just please keep the bombs exploding, and bring an end to the Nazi carnage. I told Him that the murder and the killings would not end until the Nazis were defeated.

I looked at the praying guard. He turned in my direction and said, "I opened up my car." He looked toward the burning cars. "That's not my fault," he said. "I opened up the doors of my cars." I translated for Stefan, and he said I should tell the guard that the crime all the guards had committed was to lock human beings inside boxcars. Stefan had forgotten that we had agreed that I could neither understand nor speak German.

The sirens sounded the all-clear signal, and we climbed out from under the boxcar. The cars that had been burning were wide open shells. There were a number of boxcars between the one we occupied and the two that had been hit. From a distance, the burned-out cars looked like flatbed cars filled with glimmering ashes. The roofs had fallen in, and I was able to see the smoldering red embers. The crackling and spitting fire was burning itself out. There were still a number of locked cars, and the people on the inside were screaming to be let out. In time all the doors were slid open, and the inmates, clearly in a state of panic, tumbled out into the open air.

We were in a large cargo depot on the outskirts of the town of Essen, Ruhr district, the industrial center of western Germany. Nearby were chimneys whose tops reached into the sky. Through the black smoke that engulfed us, there were signs of a gray dawn. A few of our fellow inmates who had found shelter near us beneath the boxcar had made the decision to escape. We watched them as they stealthily made their way out of sight Quite a number of guards were patrolling the area, and they were motioning to us to get back into the cars. We did not move. When our guard crawled out from under the car, knowing that some of the prisoners in our car understood German, he said in a low tone while motioning in the direction of the escapees, "They will be caught soon enough. There is no place to hide here. I did not want to be the one to catch them."

When it was again quiet, I could hear the soldiers say two words: *Arnhem* and *Nijmegen.* I had not heard these words before, and I did not know what they meant. German officers riding in open vehicles were slowly passing by, assessing the damage. They wanted our transport to move out, to leave the area. Near us, a bombing expert, speaking through a bullhorn, was directing the separation of the now barely smoldering cars from the train and of another car that had been damaged during the bombing. There were a number of wounded. One of the burning cars had been opened in time to save the inmates. Some of the casualties had to be taken to hospital. There were people who were in shock and appeared to be either blind or deaf. They were separated from the rest of us, but it was not possible to understand the instructions regarding their disposition.

The engineer was unable to start the locomotive. The count of prisoners revealed that aside from the victims who had burned to death, thirty-two prisoners were missing. Speaking in an ominous voice, the officer said, "They won't get far. You can be sure that they will live long enough to regret this attempt to escape."

It was very cold, yet we were loath to get back into the smelly confines of the boxcar. I saw Mother and Stefan near each other, casually exchanging some words.

In the early dawn, moving slowly, several feet at a time, our transport made its way out of the severely damaged freight yard. We took turns at the crack of our car door to look at a site that closely resembled the burned-out district we had been forced to abandon three weeks ago. In the gray haze of the early dawn, the white-clad figures digging in the rubble were a ghostly sight. Helmeted firemen dragging invisible hoses moved cautiously among the ruins. It took several hours before our transport lurched through the partially bombed passenger terminal of Essen.

The train picked up speed. Fellow passengers positioned near the door called out the names of the towns we were passing. It seemed that the train was traveling north, perhaps along the Rhine River. The train slowed to pass through the town of Wesel, and once outside the town, it came to a stop.

We were advised that arrangements were being made and that shortly we would be permitted to leave our boxcars. Permission was granted for two persons from each boxcar, to bring back containers of water filled at the nearby pump. At dusk, holding our belongings, we were ordered to form a column of six abreast. There were several hundred of us, and it took a while before the exhausted and disheveled captives managed to line up in the orderly rows our captors demanded. Someone I was unable to see advised us to keep in mind that we were prisoners and that our immediate future would depend on our deportment. We also were told to stop shuffling like useless cripples because we were brought here to work.

The camp compound we were approaching was even larger than the one that had housed us in Ursus. There were a number of huge brown barracks enclosed by a tall wire fence. In time we learned that the compound was a former prisoner-of-war camp, but that since early autumn 1944, it had become known as the internment camp in the village of Spellen an der Wesel.

At the time of our arrival, the camp was being vacated by people who spoke a language I could not understand. Stefan wanted to know if the people were speaking in a German dialect, but I was certain that they were not. Our attempts to speak to them, our questions regarding the compound we were entering, were rebuffed. It was evident they wanted nothing to do with us. Most of them averted their eyes as they rushed past us. They walked erect and purposefully, in fur-trimmed coats and hats. Mainly they were women, also some children. The few men among them were either old or disabled. Compared to our emaciated and grimy appearance, they looked vigorous and well groomed.

A fellow prisoner who spoke Russian as well as German managed to engage a woman and her daughter who had responded to her German greeting. We learned that the people leaving the camp were Estonians. They said that rather than be subject to the imminent invasion of the Soviet army, which was about to overrun Estonia, a large number of Estonians had preferred to claim a Germanic heritage, work in Germany, and help to defeat the Russians. Most of their men were already engaged in the German war effort.

Nina, our Russian-speaking fellow prisoner, recounted the conversation to her husband and to Stefan. She and Karol, her husband, had spoken before with Stefan. I had also seen them speaking to my mother. I was careful in my resolve not to speak with anyone. Stefan was my cover. To the insistent questioner, Stefan would explain that his wife had apparently suffered from shock. He did not want to seek medical advice from the Germans, and as soon as this accursed war came to an end, he would get appropriate medical care for me. Stefan always added that my condition was much improved. Nina said that the Estonian women had read accounts of the Warsaw uprising in German newspapers. They knew that the whole city of Warsaw had been leveled to the ground. "You should never have done that," the Estonian women told Nina.

We were not permitted to enter the barracks because several Estonians were still in the process of packing. Apparently not until early morning of the day of our arrival were they informed that they would have to leave the camp. While waiting, Stefan obtained as much information as he could regarding our present location and camp conditions. I stood with downcast eyes, projecting detachment, and all the while listened carefully for snippets of conversation that might prove useful. Between us, we learned that the departing Estonians did not want to have anything to do with us because they were voluntary refugees, whereas we, they had been told, were prisoners because we had supported a criminal element that had dared to attack the German army and slow the German war effort.

Even at a distance I could see Mother's exhaustion. Her face was gray, her eyes deep in their sockets, and she was limping. I did not know how I looked. I did not have a mirror. For the past two weeks we had been deprived of even the most elementary sanitary facilities. Next to Mother were three young women, all in their mid-twenties. One of them was carrying Mother's suitcase. They passed by me without looking in my direction. They were engaged in a barely audible conversation. Until we tumbled out of the boxcar in the Essen freight yard, I had not seen the three women before. However, since that time, they had spoken with Stefan on several occasions. Like everyone else, they were seeking information, a clue, regarding our immediate future. Other than that, their unit of three kept to themselves. I was happy to see that they had now opened up their ranks to include my mother.

By the time we entered our assigned barrack, we saw that all the wall space was already occupied. We moved toward a pole. It was important to have some sort of anchor in that vast open space. Next to us were Nina and Karol. Was it serendipity, or somehow propelled by either Stefan or Mother, that while we were in the process of claiming our space and spreading out our blankets, Mother and her new friends—Anna, Janka, and Irena—approached. They placed their possessions adjacent to the pole and proceeded to spread their blankets next to ours.

From outside, the barrack appeared similar to the one we had occupied in Ursus, with one crucial difference. In Ursus we were lodged on a damp dirt floor, whereas the floor in the Spellen internment camp was wood. Adjacent to our barrack were two latrines, and the one assigned to the women had several washbasins. When I returned from the washroom, I saw that Stefan, Karol, and the five women were engaged in conversation. When I approached, Stefan explained that a decision had been made that our group of eight would form a unit for mutual assistance.

Both Mother and I acted our respective parts during the ensuing introductions. Within, I began to feel more positive. I allowed myself to smile, to project that I was recovering from my shock. By the time we made ready to go to sleep, the eight of us had spread our blankets in a manner indicating that we were a family. It appeared that a number of other groups had the same idea. We agreed to pool all the information we could glean. The thought that we would help each other and rely on each other as would members of a family was both reassuring and strengthening. We agreed that the war could not last much longer and that we should carefully explore our options and means of escape.

I fell asleep to the droning sound of heavy bombers overhead flying east. I knew that Spellen was located at the very edge of the western front, and from snippets of conversations I had overheard in the freight yard at Essen, I was certain that German bombers were no longer flying west. Now a defensive strategy was being waged within the German Reich. Hours later I woke again. This time the Allied airplanes were flying west. They were flying closer to the ground, accompanied by heavy barrages of antiaircraft fire—the much heralded *Deutsche Abwehr*, or German defense. I rejoiced because it was obvious to me that the success the Abwehr experienced in Warsaw, while defending against a powerless army of freedom fighters, would not be duplicated when deployed against the combined forces of the British and American military.

## NOVEMBER 1944 ⤝ SPELLEN AN DER WESEL, GERMANY

The blackout shades that covered the high windows of the barrack must have been controlled by a central switch, because I awoke to bright daylight. A soldier speaking for the commandant ordered us to make both ourselves and the barrack presentable and ready for inspection. We rolled up our blankets and proceeded to line up for the washroom. Upon returning from the washroom, I was permitted to pick up one chunk of bread from a pile heaped on a table. My eyes devoured the bread, while my fingers broke the crust into tiny morsels. There had been no solid food for several days, and my stomach felt like an open sore. I prayed that I would not get sick and disabled while in this propitious location. Across the river, in Holland, were the Allied armies: only a few kilometers separated our camp from freedom. That was one of the options for escape we had discussed the previous night.

Feldwebel, or Master-Sergeant, Storch, attended by the same soldier who had previously transmitted his orders, arrived at about ten o'clock in the morning. He walked leaning sideways, as if compensating for an immobilized hip joint. He held a riding crop in his right hand, and while addressing us, he intermittently slapped it against his boot to emphasize his words. When standing straight, he appeared to be six feet tall. He looked like an intelligent peasant. He had a sturdy frame, a square face, and a ruddy complexion. Gray-blond hair sparsely covered a balding pate. Below the epaulettes of his uniform were rows of battle ribbons. He did not call for attention, neither did he shout; still, the message he delivered was terrifying. He began, in a tired voice, by listing the crimes we had committed.

"You are here because you dared to attack us. It was your misfortune to side with a gang of rebels. You caused a great deal of harm, and you have been trouble ever since. Had you done otherwise, you would have been treated like the friendly civilians who just vacated the camp. Instead, you committed high treason against the Third Reich. Ah, yes, and there is a message for you. All the prisoners who escaped from this transport thought they could outwit us, but they have been apprehended, both dead and alive. They will be punished in accordance with their crime.

"Look at yourselves: You come into our clean country bringing your filth and your Polish lice and your diseases. Tomorrow morning, at eight o'clock sharp, your barrack is scheduled for the delousing center. All your possessions, including your blankets, are to be brought along. No suitcases and no eating utensils."

Months before the insurrection, Mother and I had heard rumors about the murder of our people in bathhouses and shower facilities. My eyes searched for Mother's eyes, and we exchanged glances. For the first time since our separation in Ursus, our mutual recognition of imminent danger induced us to disregard our agreement to not look at each other. In the ensuing hours, and throughout the night, my stomach ached from convulsive contractions I was unable to control. I knew they were caused by fear. When I tried to tell Stefan about my forebodings, he shook his head in disbelief and said, "That's preposterous."

The women were to go first. Before I left to line up for the shower, I hugged and kissed Stefan. Reaching up to his ear, I whispered, "Thank you." He looked at me without comprehension. He would not believe that in the language of the Nazis the words *bath* and *shower* could be euphemisms for murder.

The large, gray concrete structure that housed both the delousing center and the communal shower looked like a fortress. Hundreds of women silently entered the cavernous hall; the only audible voice was that of a man who directed our movements. We were ordered to face a bench and put our opened bundle of clothing on it, to hang our coats and the clothing we were wearing on a numbered hook above the bench, and to place our boots beneath it. Behind our backs, soldiers marched back and forth while we disrobed, making certain that the commands were scrupulously obeyed. Surreptitiously, I detached the tiny muslin talisman containing my father's address in New York from the center of my brassiere and slipped it into the tip of my boot.

Upon walking through the door of the communal shower, we were ordered to pick up a pail of kerosene. Each shower column had six extended metal rods with showerheads at the end of each rod; each showerhead served two people. Riding crop in hand and wearing tall rubber boots, Feldwebel Storch walked among the naked females. Using the crop, he prodded the women to spill the kerosene onto their hair and to splash it under their armpits and onto their pubic hair. Only after Feldwebel Storch was certain that everyone had doused herself properly with the kerosene did he give the order to turn the water on. Hard soap that could not be induced to lather was passed from hand to hand.

When I returned to the dressing room, I was engulfed in a gray cloud. The odor of strong disinfectant invaded my nose, throat, and eyes. A white dust had settled on each piece of clothing. My talisman was safe, and the shower had been used for its appropriate purpose. How could I have thought that Poles, though prisoners, would share the fate of the Jews? I resolved to better control my fears.

A high-ranking official from the slave labor resource division was expected to arrive within several days. He was to bring orders for our work assignments. There was a rumor that some of the prisoners had obtained permission to walk into the town of Wesel to make minor purchases. The secret of how to acquire this type of permit was jealously guarded. However, Janka and Irena persevered and obtained a slip of paper with written permission to walk into town. On the following morning, immediately after receiving their daily ration of bread, the two young women, looking rather chic, set out to walk into Wesel.

In the afternoon they returned elated, but not until evening, after we had received our soup ration and when the lights were dimmed, did our unit of eight huddle together to listen to their adventures. Janka, who grew up in the Polish part of Silesia, had learned German in school and was therefore able to communicate with the residents of Wesel. The people they met were friendly, and Irena and Janka found them to be quite different from the Nazis who had persecuted us during the past five years. When pressed to elaborate, Janka described some of the encounters. When approached in the street, residents were willing to answer questions. They knew who we were. News had spread quickly; however, there were no accusations, and apparently the residents were horrified by the wanton destruction of Warsaw. They considered us to be victims rather than prisoners.

"The day of reckoning is getting closer," Stefan said, "and they are as aware of the nightly bombings as we are." The women reported that the stores were empty. The only item they brought back were sanitary napkins they had bought at the pharmacy. I wondered if I would be able to find the peroxide and ammonia I needed to touch up the dark hair that was beginning to show.

They left the most fabulous news till the end. While making their purchase at the apothecary, Janka and Irena had made the acquaintance of three Dutch sailors. The three young men, all in their mid-twenties, were part of the crew of one of three small interned naval training vessels. Their ships were anchored in Wesel, quarantined in a channel that was part of the Wesel River and apparently subject to some international agreement. The river separated Germany from occupied Holland. The sailors reported that parts of Holland were no longer occupied, and that German news broadcasts had not yet acknowledged the partial liberation of Holland by the Allied armies. The nightly flights of loaded bombers flying east, the sailors reported, were taking off from airports located immediately across the channel in the cities of Arnhem and Nijmegen.

The sailors had walked into town to obtain their allotment of medicine and drugs. It was remarkable how well the Nazis treated the western European nations, compared to the punishing cruelty they inflicted on the defeated peoples in the east. Shortly after the invasion of Holland, the German navy had apprehended the three ships and towed them into the channel in Wesel. They had been there ever since, awaiting further determination. The sailors were confident that the total defeat of the Third Reich was imminent. They did not know that the Russian army had driven the Nazis out of a large part of

Poland and were positioned at the Vistula River ready to invade Germany from the east.

Both the sailors and our friends, Janka and Irena, found the exchange of news from the eastern and the western fronts exciting. The sailors had permission to walk unguarded to and from town, on a prescribed route, and the two women accompanied them almost to the quay at which their small ship was anchored. While walking back, the sailors were hailed by some of the residents. Several times they stopped for a brief exchange of words. They greeted each other in a friendly manner and, to our friends' consternation, apparently without animosity. The three sailors spoke German fluently, and they urged the two women to walk with confidence. Their appearance, they said, in no way differed from that of young female residents of the town.

Janka and Irena told us that they had seen the three ships. "They were small, more like boats," they reported. They confided to the sailors that they were planning to escape. With the war so close to an end, they were determined to take risks to avoid being shipped to some steel mill work camp. The sailors listened attentively. Together, they weighed possible routes of escape. Janka and Irena made a point of emphasizing that there were three of them. The sailors briefly conferred in their native language and suggested that it might be possible for the three women to surreptitiously board the boats and stow away until the collapse of the Third Reich. The sailors apparently received secret dispatches from across the border. They were certain that it was but a matter of weeks, perhaps even days, before the arrival of the Allied armies. The young men were eager to help and willing to risk this act of defiance. However, they would need to consult with their superior officer. Without his permission, they felt they would not be able to successfully accomplish the task of hiding the three women.

Irena unfolded a small piece of paper on which one of the sailors had drawn a map. It showed the route to the anchored boats. On another piece of paper, the sailor had written out the name and address of Frau Petersen, an old woman who had befriended them. She lived alone and could be counted on to help should the need arise.

Irena and Janka and the sailors made an appointment for three days hence. The three women would meet the sailors in town, immediately across from the apothecary, and together they would casually proceed toward the quay. They should come prepared to board the ship, as if to visit. In the past year, on several occasions, local women had done just that, and they had not been stopped. All their belongings would have to be left behind.

"The questions are," Stefan cautioned, "did they mean it and can they get away with it?"

"We think so, but we can't be certain," was the response. "But we thought we should talk it over with you. There is of course the matter of getting permission. The sailors said that it was not explicit permission they were hoping for, but rather some sort of sign that the commander would look the other way while they carried out this rescue mission."

"The act of outwitting the enemy," Nina speculated, "of initiating an action after years of enforced inactivity could be a boost to their morale. I am happy for you." She added, "If Karol and I had had the good fortune to meet up with the sailors, I can assure you that we would not hesitate for a minute. We would leave everything we own and go aboard."

On their way back to Spellen, Irena and Janka had ventured to ring the doorbell at Frau Petersen's small house. As soon as Frau Petersen knew who had given them her address, she asked them to come in. The women declined the cup of tea Frau Petersen offered and said they had to be back at the camp. They only stayed for a few minutes and remained just inside the entrance door. Frau Petersen spoke of the sailors in a motherly tone. She called them "*die lieben Jungen*"—the lovely boys.

"What sort of woman?" Stefan wanted to know. "A German woman?"

"Oh yes," was the reply. Frau Petersen had told Irena and Janka that she was "a true German, not a Nazi."

There was so much we wanted to know. Each member of our group was seeking an answer to a different question. Irena and Janka had walked into town and had experienced a truly remarkable chance encounter. We learned that Frau Petersen lived alone and was in her mid-seventies. She was alert, a no-nonsense type, and she was well informed. She was up to date on frontline news and knew about us and our forced evacuation from Warsaw. The sailors had told Janka and Irena that Frau Petersen's son was a soldier, but that she didn't want to talk about him.

Unable to fall asleep until late into the night, we listened to the reassuring sound of heavily loaded bombers flying overhead. We also heard the explosion of bombs and the firing of antiaircraft guns—sounds familiar to us. But now we were not the target. Would the three young women succeed? we wondered. Would the commanding officer of the small Dutch navy ships be willing to look away, and thereby permit the women to board ship? Would he agree to jeopardize the lives of perhaps thirty cadets? What about the druggist who had seen the women leave with the sailors? Could the German woman be trusted? Stefan decided to bring up these matters on the following day, but he said he would not attempt to dissuade the women if they decided to proceed. As for myself, I was certain that if this offer had come our way, I would not hesitate.

On the day following Janka's and Irena's propitious meeting with the sailors, a number of important-looking officials were sighted at the camp. Some were in uniform, and some in civilian clothes. They remained for several hours and left. On the next day, when we lined up to receive our bread ration and coffee, it was readily apparent to all of us that the atmosphere had changed. There were rumors that a decision regarding our work assignments had been made. A directive from a central command post had been received, ordering the liquidation of the camp in Spellen. We understood, as did our guards, that they did not want us so close to the front line.

Several of our fellow prisoners had made contacts with the German soldiers guarding us. We learned that orders for our transportation had been previously given and rescinded because trains able to ship such a mass of prisoners were no longer available. Instead, we would be separated into smaller groups and shipped to work camps in need of additional laborers. Everyone agreed that within the next days crucial decisions would determine our fate. Hanging over us was the threat of a concentration camp. I was certain that my false identity papers and language liability would not withstand the scrutiny of concentration camp guards. Neither would my mother's appearance. The telltale evidence of our darker hair growing out at the roots was a concern.

At dusk our barrack door was locked, and no one was allowed to leave. One had to ask permission to go to the toilet. Permission was granted grudgingly by the guard, and only after urgent pleading. That evening, to our dismay, there were only six of us. Nina and Karol had not yet come in. On several occasions Nina had reported on her encounters with Feldwebel Storch. He had confided that he was tired of the war and suffering from injuries. He worried about his two sons who were engaged in front-line battle. He was unhappy with his present assignment and the barrage of conflicting orders, and he was responsive to Nina's flirtatious attentiveness.

When the two of them finally arrived, they made discreet signs to us, signaling that we refrain from questioning them until after lights were dimmed. Both Nina and Karol had received a work assignment from Feldwebel Storch. The assignment directed them to travel on their own to the town of Bielitz—a formerly Polish region, now annexed to the Third Reich. Feldwebel Storch had not been able to tell them the type of work they would be doing, but he was certain that it was above ground, and he told Nina that she would be wise to take the assignment. When Mother and Stefan excitedly asked whether we could obtain this type of work order, Nina responded that she did not know, but that she noticed Storch consulting a list. Storch had emphasized that he was doing something that was against the law, and he could be punished if Nina and Karol talked about it or showed the permit to the wrong person.

Karol nudged his wife to reveal the rest of the information. We learned that Feldwebel Storch, in an effort to liquidate the camp, had made inquiries about work at factories and steel mills and had received many affirmative responses. "After all," Feldwebel Storch told Nina and Karol, "within days this area will become a battleground, and I don't want to be stuck here with hundreds of prisoners on my hands. I want you out of here. We have lost the war. Who knows what's to become of us. I have a family. I have to look out for myself. I can tell you when this war is over, it will be every man for himself."

Nina and Karol had gotten the permit in return for a piece of diamond jewelry. "But don't even attempt to try that," they warned. "Storch made an exception for us. He wanted dollars, American dollars. He hinted that two women from the camp had come to see him with dollars." How many dollars, we asked. Nina and Karol were not sure, but thought it might be ten dollars per person. "If you have the money," Karol said, "you better be there tomorrow and early in the morning."

Irena, Anna, and Janka announced that they had made the decision to keep their appointment with the sailors; they would walk into town on the agreed day and not return to the camp. That left only the three of us without a method of escape. Mother told our group that she had a twenty-dollar bill, and she had no intention of giving an extra ten dollars to Feldwebel Storch for her work permit. Karol said Storch apparently had dollar bills in various denominations, and Karol thought he was a decent enough man. "I think he would give you ten dollars change," Karol ventured.

Speaking slowly, thoughtfully, Mother said, "I don't feel right leaving Krysia and Stefan. We made the decision to help one another, and there is no doubt in my mind that in the type of camp they have in mind the newlyweds would be separated. Who knows what could happen to them?" Mother addressed Nina: "I was thinking . . . What do you think Storch's reaction would be if I went to see him with Stefan and Krysia and asked him to accept the twenty-dollar bill in return for helping the three of us obtain better work assignments?"

The consensus was that it was worth trying. They were all impressed by Pani Dembicka's generosity. Not everyone, they said, would part in times like these with much-coveted dollars and bestow them on strangers befriended in a camp.

"Oh no," Mother answered. "Krysia and Stefan appear to be an honorable young couple, and there is no doubt in my mind that once this war is over, they will return the money. It is," Mother said, as she turned toward Stefan and me, "meant as a loan. You do understand that?"

Stefan and I nodded in agreement. There were tears in my eyes. My tears were not a reaction to Mother's apparent magnanimity, but to tension—the dangerous audaciousness with which Mother had involved the rest of the group. That night I could not sleep, not even for an hour. I knew that Mother was also awake. I could hear Stefan's regular breathing. At times, I knew, he forgot who we were and the additional burden of fear that we carried.

On the following morning, after careful attention to our appearance, the three of us made our way to Feldwebel Storch's office. We had carefully rehearsed what we would say, and we decided that Mother would be the one to initiate the request since she had the twenty-dollar bill.

One of the first laws enacted immediately upon German occupation of Poland was the currency decree. It called on all residents of Poland to exchange their foreign currency, especially dollars, into occupation zlotys. The population was advised that possessing dollars after the deadline for exchanging them for worthless zlotys would be considered an act of treason. The threatened punishment was incarceration, or even death. However, throughout the years of occupation, the extremely dangerous but profitable trade in dollars had been a flourishing business.

Storch was sitting behind his desk when the three of us filed in. His assistant closed the door behind us and remained outside. Mother said that we would like to apply for a pass that would grant us permission to leave the camp and allow us to report for a work assignment. She said Nina had alerted us to the possibility and we hoped Storch would help us.

"And why do you think I should grant permission?" Storch asked.

Mother responded by saying that she had not implied that he should, but that she appealed to him on humanitarian grounds. Our work assignment would be less rigorous, she suggested, if we were not part of such a large mass of people. And of course, we would not expect him to help us without receiving a token of our appreciation.

"Yes, and what did you have in mind?"

"I have twenty dollars," Mother said, "and I would like to help this young couple I have befriended since our evacuation from Warsaw. There were times when they helped me, and now I would like to help them. They were married shortly before we were ordered to leave the city."

"In gold?" Storch asked.

"No, in paper, but it has the same value."

"Don't tell me about value," Storch thundered. "After a war, there is but one value, and that is gold. Besides, you will have to do better than that. I am jeopardizing my career, perhaps my life, and you will have to come up with another ten dollars—and in gold."

While Mother tried to formulate a response, we watched as Storch retrieved a key from his pocket and unlocked a desk drawer. He removed a cigar box and opened it. There were indeed several gold coins, but mostly there were dollar bills. Stefan, speaking Polish, told Mother to say that American gold coins had been taken out of circulation and that paper was of equal worth. Mother translated, but Storch shook his head.

"You believe that?" he asked. "I don't. It's an American trick to enable the government to get their hands on the gold."

Mother had taken out the twenty-dollar bill. There we stood, three petitioners, while Feldwebel Storch limped back and forth in front of us, ostensibly reviewing our situation. He reached for the twenty-dollar bill, moved to the window, and held it up to the light.

"It's genuine," Mother said. "You can be certain."

"I know it's genuine. I can recognize a counterfeit. I am an expert." Storch slipped the twenty-dollar bill into the cigar box and sat down behind his desk. He put the cigar box back in the drawer and locked it. Then he called for his assistant and motioned him to sit down at the typewriter. His face expressionless, the soldier sat down.

"You first," he said pointing at me.

"*Zusammen*," I said—together. I put my hand on Stefan's arm.

"Katowitz," Storch bellowed, naming a Polish town formerly called Katowice, now annexed to Germany. He ordered us to hand over our respective Kennkartes to the soldier at the typewriter. The soldier looked at my Kennkarte, looked at me, then turned to Storch and said that the last validation was missing. I responded immediately, explaining that I had been sewing German uniforms and the lines of people waiting to have their Kennkartes validated were long and would have kept me away from work that needed to get done. The soldier continued to type.

"What type of work?" Stefan whispered to me. "Ask him what type of work in Katowitz."

When I asked, Storch got angry. "How would I know that?" he asked. "All I know is that I have been notified that the Arbeitsamt in Katowitz needs workers of some intelligence to help in the war effort. There are a number of armament factories in that area. I am certain that they will make use of two able-bodied Poles."

The piece of paper that we held in our hands stated that Stefan and Krystyna Broda, deported Polish civilians from Warsaw, were ordered to report to the director of the employment office in Katowitz. Two-days travel time had been granted to allow the bearers of this official document to reach their destination. Storch signed the document and affixed the official seal with a swastika to the bottom half of the paper. He said it would be best if we left at dusk. He had been advised that a special unit had already been dispatched and would take charge of liquidating the Spellen work camp. Then he dismissed us with a wave of his hand. We thanked him and left his office. Once outside, we reviewed the information we had just received. Stefan folded the document. and put it into his pocket. We waited for Mother.

When she came out, we saw immediately that she was upset. Mother had asked Storch to please issue for her a work assignment near Katowitz. He got angry, she told us, and shouted, "For God's sake, woman, where is your gratitude? Do you want to bury me? Don't you understand the danger, the risk I run, when I sign these permits? Two people to the same destination are more than enough. You, I'll send to Austria. You'll report to the Arbeitsamt in Schönbach."

Both Mother and I were worried. We knew that once separated we would no longer be able to look out for each other, to support each other.

When we returned to the barrack, we learned that Nina and Karol had left. Something had alarmed them. They had said they planned to walk to a neighboring village and board the local train there. They were afraid to board a train at the Wesel railroad station, but our three young friends were unable to tell us what had caused the sudden decision and what it was they feared.

When Janka read our document, she got very excited. She told us that her aunt, her mother's sister, lived in Katowitz. Janka said she would much prefer to be near her aunt than a stowaway on a boat. I asked if her aunt was German because only German people were permitted to live in the annexed territory. Janka told us that her aunt was a Pole at heart, but that she was married to a Volksdeutsch, a Pole who had claimed the privileges of his German ancestry.

"You can't blame them," Janka explained defensively. "He has relatives who live all over Germany. He is a decent enough guy. When my family was asked to leave the territory, he helped us as much as he could. He remained in his apartment, and he is keeping some of our valuable possessions that we couldn't take along."

The two young women, Janka and Anna, decided to go and see Storch and ask for a work permit that would land them in the Katowitz region. Irena was adamant in her resolve to stowaway on the boat. Within minutes of their departure, Janka and Anna were back in the barrack. From their crestfallen appearance, we knew their visit had not turned out well. They told us that work-release passes were no longer available. It appeared that Storch had no authority to issue passes to prisoners. There was a strong possibility all work-release passes would be remanded.

We hurried to gather our few possessions. Our three friends helped. Janka wrote out the address and telephone number of her aunt in Katowitz. She gave one piece of paper with the address to us and one to Mother. "Please don't let this fall into the wrong hands," she urged, "and remember, you must first telephone. When you call, say that you send regards from me and that we are friends. Nina and Karol also have my aunt's address. Let's keep in touch. None of us know what's in store for us. Perhaps we will meet again once the war is over."

"Are you going through with the plan to stow away?" I asked.

"Oh, yes, if it's possible. We'll leave everything here. It's better this way. We may have to come back. No one but you knows where we are going, and that is a protection for us, as well as the cadets."

# CHAPTER 12

# A Visit to the Third Reich

At about four o'clock in the afternoon, Stefan and I walked out of the camp. All we carried were the small suitcases we had brought from Warsaw. We left our blankets rolled up and propped against the pole. It was decided that it would be safer for the three of us if Mother left thirty minutes after our departure. We did not know the name of the village Nina and Karol had walked to board a train, and we did not want to find ourselves in a situation where we would have to ask for directions. Projecting self-assurance, we walked into the Wesel railroad station.

The one-story red-brick building was a typical small-town German train station. Opposite the entrance door was the gate leading out onto the platform. On the right side of the door was the ticket window. Affixed to the wall near the ticket window were a number of timetables. Stefan and I pretended to study the timetables. We had no German currency and did not know how to proceed. A woman and a young boy walked in and sat down on a bench.

I asked Stefan to give me the work-release pass, and I walked up to the ticket window. "You are from the camp?" the ticket agent asked.

"Yes."

"If you are planning to spend the night here, you have picked the wrong place."

"No," I said, handing him the pass.

"Another one of those," he said. "I've had five of them already, but it's all over. A train is being assembled. Tomorrow the camp will be emptied, and they'll ship you back east where you belong."

Attempting to keep my voice calm, I asked which train we would have to take to get to our destination. The ticket agent looked at the paper, then he looked at us. He mumbled something, and I thought he said, "I don't want to be the one . . ." He wrote on the pass that we should be permitted to travel on the railroad until we reached our destination.

We had a ninety-minute wait and sat down on a bench. Stefan was very proud of me, and he told me so. He could see how tense I was. I had addressed the ticket agent in German, trying to speak haltingly, like someone speaking a foreign language.

"Try not to be so timid," Stefan said. "Nina spoke German, and Janka spoke German, and they were not at all afraid. The Germans know that educated Poles studied foreign languages, and German was one of them. You just happen to be one of the lucky ones whose parents had the foresight to have you study German."

It was difficult explaining to Stefan the complexity of my situation. My German pronunciation and grammar, which had been drilled into my head, were almost flawless. In addition, my vocabulary was extensive. A Pole who had learned German in school and who had not lived in Germany could not possibly speak German as fluently as I did. I mentioned to Stefan my failure to speak Polish fluently despite my earnest efforts. But Stefan was confident that I could make the necessary speech adjustments. To accomplish this, he suggested I remember at all times that I was a Polish Christian married to a Polish Christian and that, henceforth, my fate would be that of a Polish Christian.

Shortly thereafter I passed another test. Out of the corner of my eye I saw Mother walk into the train depot. Stefan also saw her enter. The three of us never acknowledged each other, not even with a glance. I was afraid to look in Mother's direction lest I reveal my agitation. I had not said good-bye to her. I would have no way of knowing how to reach her, how to find her, and neither would she know how to find me. Our only link was Janka's aunt in Katowitz. There was Mother, sitting alone, about to embark for some unknown destination.

It was quite dark when we heard sounds of an approaching train. The ticket attendant motioned to us, and we boarded the train. I did not look back. Not until we were seated in a compartment, did I permit myself to take a deep breath. There were blackout shades on the windows, and the compartment was lit by a single partially shaded blue lightbulb. The luxury of sitting on a polished bench molded to accommodate my back in a warm compartment, my coat hanging securely from a hook, was overwhelming. There were stops, and people entered and departed without light and with barely a sound. When at last we were able to sit next to each other, Stefan said, "I am relieved that we are alone, and that is the truth. It will be easier for me to shield one Jewish woman than to protect the two of you. Don't worry about your mother. She was more worried for you than she was for herself. She is a wise lady, and she will do what has to be done to survive. Now try to lean back and sleep, and don't forget what I told you."

I was unable to sleep. It seemed to me that the train was proceeding at a very slow pace, and I wanted to be aware of the passengers who entered the compartment. I needed to see what they looked like so that I could anticipate danger. Stefan asked me if I was awake because there was something he had to tell me. "I just realized that I am totally dependent on you," he said. "Are you aware of the fact that here I am in the land of the Boche, and I don't speak a word of German? You will have to speak for both of us and make decisions for both of us. Just remember who you are now, don't think back. I depend on you to get us through."

I nodded and said of course I understood. I thought about my changed role. I had been a native German masquerading as a Pole in Poland, trying to convince native Poles that I was fluent in Polish. Now I would be pretending to be a Pole in Germany—a Pole who could speak German, but poorly. I would have to disguise my fluency in my native tongue.

We were supposed to change trains in Essen, but we never reached the city. The closer we came to our destination, the more we realized that through the closed compartment of the moving train we were hearing the sounds of heavy bombers flying low, with powerful detonations of exploding bombs. We could hear antiaircraft in action and the wailing of sirens. With all that bombing, surrender can't be faraway, I thought. With that happy thought, I fell asleep.

Minutes later Stefan woke me. Directions were being shouted, and he could not understand. The instructions were to vacate the train immediately, and passengers were advised that the emptied train would depart within minutes to an undetermined destination. People were instructed to seek the safety of nearby bomb shelters.

By the time we descended from the train, we heard the all-clear siren. We were not at a central terminal, but at the site of a freight depot in a suburb of Essen. Nearby, we could see the smoking ruins of a bombed area. I asked for directions to the main railroad station. The woman I asked shook her head. She said she was unable to give us directions because she did not know the area. She pointed to a nearby streetcar stop. She thought the conductor would be able to help us get to our destination.

We boarded the streetcar. It was very crowded. No one came to ask for tickets. When I asked the elderly man who stood squeezed against me where we should get off to get to the railroad terminal, he looked at me quizzically.

"You can get out at the third stop and walk from there," he said, "but I doubt that you could even get close to the terminal."

I translated for Stefan, and we decided to get off as instructed and to see for ourselves. The streets were crowded. People were scurrying around, moving in different directions, and most of them carried bags and suitcases. There were baby carriages filled with household goods. I suddenly realized that the people around us were refugees—German refugees. Except that Stefan was wearing a beret, there appeared to be little difference between them and us. They looked harassed and worried and did not resemble the triumphant, boisterous members of the civilian occupation force that had descended upon Poland.

The railroad terminal could not be approached. It was cordoned off, and no one was permitted to go near it. From a distance, one could see the smoking remnant of what had been the main railroad terminal of Essen. "Does it remind you of Warsaw?" Stefan asked. It did indeed, but it also complicated our situation. I asked for directions to a suburban railroad depot and was told to go to a travel booth. To get to the booth, we needed to take a streetcar.

The streetcar was crowded, and people standing in the center aisle were pressed against each other. Almost immediately we were approached by the streetcar conductor selling tickets. He asked our destination. I said that we had been directed to the travel information booth and that we had no money.

"No money," he said in a stern voice, loud enough for all nearby passengers to hear. "People who do not have the money to ride on the street-car use their feet. You'll have to get off at the next stop."

I reached for Stefan's arm. I knew he didn't understand what the conductor had said, but I felt sure he realized it concerned our fare. While speaking to me, the conductor had jangled the metal change frame perched on his stomach. Speaking softly, I attempted to explain to the conductor that because of the air raid we had had to disembark from our train.

"Yes, yes, I know all that, but rules must be obeyed." Before he had a chance to continue, an outstretched hand held out the appropriate change to the conductor, and a young girl who had been standing nearby said, "Two tickets, please." She gave the name of a streetcar stop, and then turned to me and said, "I will tell you where to get off."

The unsolicited offer, this act of kindness, brought tears to my eyes. I thanked the young girl. She was tall, blond, and handsome, and she could not have been more than seventeen years old. She said that she sympathized with us, because she too had been on a train during the bombing raid. She was eager to get home. "These are difficult times," she remarked. She added that she was sure she had made her mother unhappy.

I looked at her, my eyes questioning. She told me that she had taken the train to visit her favorite uncle, who lived alone and who had not been well. Her mother had not wanted her to go. It was a time for staying close to one's family, her mother had said, and not a time for traveling on a train. "Where are you from?" she asked.

"We are from Warsaw."

"Refugees?"

"In a way. We were deported."

"Oh yes. The papers were full of news about Warsaw. Some members of my family were very angry with you, but there were others who felt that your surprise attack was more than the treacherous attempt to stab us in the back, as our newsreel kept reporting. You wanted to liberate your city."

The girl appeared to be well informed, but she refrained from mentioning the Soviet army deployed at the Vistula River.

The streetcar proceeded at a slow pace through partially bombed streets. Frequently we passed large mounds of rubble. Workers in uniform were loading the debris onto trucks. "We are beginning to learn what it's like," she remarked. "This streetcar is full of refugees."

"Are you a refugee?" I asked.

"No, I am a native of Essen."

She moved close to me, her lips almost touched my ear. "I shall get off at the last stop, and you will disembark before that. Yesterday I went to visit my uncle and I had to stay the night because of the air raid. Today is my birthday. I just turned eighteen."

"Heartiest congratulations," I ventured.

"How old are you?" she asked.

"I turned eighteen in March."

"So we are contemporaries. I thought you were older. I only mentioned my birthday because this morning when I got ready to leave my uncle's home, he gave me fifty marks. It was his birthday present, and I want you to have it." Once again tears filled my eyes, and before I could control it, my eyes were brimming over. This malady of mine—my eyes betraying my emotions, tears rushing into my eyes before I had a chance to control them—had plagued me ever since the liquidation of the Krosno ghetto. It was a reflex reaction to a generous gesture, or even a kind word. I was holding on to the leather strap above my head, the girl's hand was next to mine. In an instant, she slipped the fifty-mark bill into my other hand.

"What is your name?" I whispered.

"Brigitte Schultz."

"Please jot down your address," I said. "I am much more grateful than you can ever imagine. Shortly my husband and I will be working, and I promise you that I will return the money."

"You don't need to do that. It is my gift to you. I know you need the money. I'll just make believe that I never got the money, so I won't miss it. Still, I'll give you my address. I will be happy knowing that I helped you reach your destination. Thinking about that will make me feel better during the difficult times ahead. This is where you get off."

We shook hands. I looked into Brigitte's eyes. I too felt that during the difficult times ahead it would be important for me to remember her face. After we had stepped off the streetcar onto the sidewalk, I opened my hand. Folded into the palm was the fifty-mark bill. It was a great deal of money. Poor Stefan was dumbfounded. He wanted to know what had I said to the girl. What had impelled this German girl to act so generously? I told him that I had in no way encouraged her action. Stefan was troubled. He said that he felt like a mute. He was disenfranchised, unable to understand the words of the people around him.

It was close to ten o'clock in the morning. We had evacuated the train at dawn, and it had taken hours to reach the queue at the travel information booth. The line was almost as long as some of the bread lines I had encountered in years past. I thought that it might take more than an hour before we would get our turn at the counter, but Stefan agreed that there was no alternative. Apparently, several railroad depots and locomotives had sustained enough damage to bring train movement to a standstill. We needed information that would help us orient ourselves in this partially gutted city.

We were tired and hungry, but encouraged by the amazing sights all around us. There could be no doubt that we were seeing a mass migration. People were fleeing from the western front, but a considerably larger number of refugees were flooding in from the east, the occupied territories. Most were women. Whenever we saw a male, he was either old, wounded, or a young boy.

The woman at the travel information booth consulted a chart and said that there would be a train going to Berlin. It would depart in the late afternoon, but not before five o'clock. She wrote down the name of the terminal and said it would take twenty-five minutes to get there. She also wrote out the number of the streetcar we would have to take. She was curt and efficient. Before I could ask an additional question, she said next, and I was dismissed.

While translating for Stefan I felt dizzy. The fitful stomach cramps that I had learned to live with were excruciatingly painful. Stefan was sure that I needed some nourishment, and we did have fifty marks. We headed for a nearby restaurant. The owner, a corpulent man with his right arm amputated at the elbow, the empty sleeve tucked into the right-hand pocket, looked us over and said, "*Lebensmittelkarten, bitte*"—ration cards, please.

"We don't have any," I replied.

"That's what I thought, and I am going to tell you right now—and I will not discuss it—I cannot feed you unless you present ration cards." He consulted the watch on his left wrist. "You look like you could use a meal. There is only one place, the soup kitchen. But you better hurry."

"How do we find this soup kitchen?" I asked. He gave us directions and said that we should take the streetcar.

When the streetcar conductor called "Tickets, please," I motioned to Stefan to pay the fare. The conductor looked at the fifty-mark bill and requested small change. I told him that we didn't have change or marks in smaller denominations. Pointing to the bill, he muttered, "I can't change that," and moved on.

When we disembarked at the designated stop, the fifty-mark bill was still intact. We were standing in a small square. I looked around and saw the sign mounted on corner of a building. In large black letters on white canvas were the letters my parents had feared most, NSDAP—National Sozialistische Deutsche Arbeiterpartei, the umbrella organization of the Nazi Party. Beneath the abbreviation was the letter V placed in the center of a W. The symbol stood for Volks Wirtschaft, or social welfare. A cardboard sign tacked onto the inside of the glass-paneled door read, *Volksküche*—soup kitchen. I stopped. I was certain we should not enter.

"What's the matter?" Stefan wanted to know.

"Can't you see? Don't you know what those letters stand for?"

"No," was the answer. Stefan had no idea what the letters meant.

"This kitchen is run by the Nazi Party. We cannot go in there. Even standing here is dangerous."

"We must. Pull yourself together. We can't go on unless we get some food. This is not the time to lose courage. You saw yourself that the Third Reich is disintegrating. Right now they are busy coping with their own refugees."

I felt that Stefan was wrong. A Polish maxim came to mind: "Beware, before the fat one gets thin, the thin one dies." From what he had observed, Stefan deduced that the Boche was on his knees and ready to capitulate. I knew better. I felt certain that wherever the German Wehrmacht would decide to locate their imaginary Maginot Line, they would dig in and fight to win. Stefan had no idea that even in the midst of battle, the Nazis could muster the means to empty whole towns of their residents in a matter of hours. They could move people to some unknown destination from which no one would return. Stefan did not know what had happened to the Jews of Germany, of Poland, and of Russia. But I didn't want to tell Stefan what I knew; his close association with me was enough of a burden for him.

Stefan picked up my bag. Holding both suitcases, he pushed me ahead. When we got to the door, he handed me my small suitcase and declared, "You must do it for both of us." There were people ahead of us, and within seconds people lined up in back of us. A man in his late thirties, dressed in civilian clothes, greeted each person in line with a "Heil Hitler," raising his right arm to shoulder level. A round enameled pin with a swastika encircled by the letters NSDAP was pinned to his lapel. We had entered a vestibule and followed the moving line of people to a room below ground level.

A woman seated behind a desk said, "Heil Hitler. Your ration cards, please."

"We don't have any," I said.

"Would you repeat that?"

I reached for the work-release pass and handed it to her instead. I told her that we were very hungry and unable to get food. She motioned to us to stand aside. She addressed a young woman seated at a nearby desk. "Herr Strauss will have to come down."

Within seconds, Herr Strauss, the party member we had encountered at the entrance level, the one who had snapped up his arm with every Heil Hitler greeting, was standing next to us. He carefully read the writing on our work-release pass and turned it to read the note added by the railroad ticket agent in Wesel.

"Ah yes," he said, "the enemy from Warsaw. You are the people who stabbed us in the back. Is that not so?"

"We are residents of Warsaw. We were deported," I said.

I looked at his face and forced myself not to let my eyes stray to the party insignia pinned to his lapel. I watched his movements while he continued to greet the people who were coming down. One family after another handed the woman ration cards. She cut out the coupons and ushered the people into the nearby dining hall. Whenever the curtain was pushed aside, the pungent odor of steaming meat soup filled my nostrils. Herr Strauss turned to us, our work-release pass still in his hand. He moved the curtain to the side. Pointing to two vacant seats at the end of a bench, he said, "Over there."

"Could we please have the pass back?" I asked.

"See me when you have finished your meal. I'll hold on to it until then."

We had barely sat down, when a woman carrying a tray smiled at us and put two soup bowls in front of us. They were filled to the brim with divinely smelling soup. Two generous pieces of army bread were placed next to the bowls. It was a vegetable barley soup, and in it were small chunks of meat. I knew that I had to eat very slowly so that my sore stomach could digest this feast.

I looked around. We looked like everyone else. Refugees in need of food and shelter. Considering that over a hundred people were in the dining hall, the noise level was low and the atmosphere subdued. My stomach rebelled against the nourishing *Eintopfgericht*—a whole meal cooked in one pot. The Eintopfgericht method of cooking was one of the early measures of thrift instituted by the Nazi Party. I refrained from eating the meat. Stefan assured me that he too felt nauseated, but he managed to finish what was in his bowl, and then he proceeded to eat what remained in my bowl. Unobtrusively, we packed the two pieces of bread.

We walked up to the entrance level. The door through which we had entered was closed, the vestibule empty. Herr Strauss, telephone in hand, was seated at a desk. Was he telephoning about us? I wondered, as we approached him. Our document was on his desk. He put down the telephone and smiled at us.

"Thank you for allowing us to eat here," I said.

"Ja, Ja," he said, waving his hand dismissively. "Your husband is very fortunate to have a wife who speaks German," he added. He turned to Stefan and asked, "You have no knowledge of our language?"

Stefan understood that much. "*Tylko troche*," he answered in Polish—just a little. I translated, "*Nur ein wenig.*"

"This is what I did for you," Herr Strauss said. Holding the document he leaned toward me and pointed to the multiple notes he had added. "I extended your travel pass for another three days. You'll never get to Katowitz by Friday, and it would not be to your advantage to present yourselves at the Katowitz Arbeitsamt on a Saturday. You might find yourselves in a lockup. I also made a note that you should continue to receive free railroad transportation. I think you might have a circuitous route ahead of you."

"We are very grateful," I stammered.

He shrugged and said, "I just happen to be the person with authority to do it. I have here a map that will help you with rail connections. Can you read it?" I nodded. "What did your husband do before the war?"

"He was a civil engineer. He was employed by the Warsaw Municipality."

"Do you have money?"

"Yes, we have a fifty mark bill. A young girl gave us the money when we were unable to buy our streetcar tickets."

"A German girl?"

"Yes, a German girl from Essen."

"There is another thing I am going to do for you, but it means going a bit beyond my jurisdiction. Still, I shall make a note of it on your document, because otherwise you could be in trouble." He held out two German ration cards. "Each one has enough coupons to provide you with food for a week," he said. "Use the coupons with care. Either purchase your provisions yourself, or keep your eye out for a Volksküche."

I was concentrating on his words and gestures. Only minutes before he had been a strutting, intimidating Nazi, exclaiming one "Heil Hitler" after another, and here he was acting like a decent person, bestowing gifts on us.

"Could you change the fifty mark note?" I asked. "We encountered difficulties." He reached into his pocket and gave us the change.

"One last warning," Herr Strauss said. "Take care to adhere to the curfew for foreign laborers. We are very strict about that. And stay off the streets during evening hours."

"We thank you for your help," I said and stretched out my hand, "and for your kindness to us. We will never forget that we had the good fortune to walk into this Volksküche and that you were in charge."

He took my hand, then he shook Stefan's hand and said, "Tell your husband that perhaps despite everything he is the lucky one. I have just been notified of an order recalling me to military service, and who knows."

"I wish you a safe homecoming," I said.

"Thank you, and you, too."


We walked out into the November cold, and I realized that I was wet with perspiration. Everything had gone so well. Meeting Herr Strauss had been a stroke of good fortune for us, and yet for me it had been an encounter of excruciating tension. I realized that my nervous system was stretched to its limits. Even though we still had time before our train was to depart, I wanted to be within the anonymous confines of a railroad terminal. My accelerated heartbeat needed to calm down.

Storch had made it clear that he had no authority to issue the work-release passes. He had decided on his own to issue the passes to reduce the number of prisoners housed in the Spellen camp. Just before we left the camp, word had reached us that Storch's superiors wanted the passes remanded. Stefan and I agreed that our nominally legal document had gained additional legitimacy. The added notes, to which Herr Strauss had affixed his title and signature, as well as the official stamp with the prominent swastika of the NSDAP, had been a stroke of good luck.

"You are too timid," Stefan said. "You must stop acting like a Jew who is hiding and who is being chased by Nazi bloodhounds. This attitude could harm us, and what both of us want is to survive the Nazi carnage. You must learn to feel and act like a Pole. As far as we know, no decision has been made to annihilate us."

Of course Stefan was right. Still, he did not quite realize that since the Warsaw uprising, the Nazis, with their penchant for cruelty, had put Poles, at least Poles from Warsaw, into a new category. Though the Germans were fighting a war on two fronts, they had nonetheless managed to destroy Warsaw and forcibly transport a large portion of its residents out of Poland. Stefan could not understand that I, as a Jewish girl in hiding, had been living a different reality than he. During the early weeks of the uprising, German propaganda had to some extent exonerated Polish insurgents, while falsely putting the blame for the rebellion on Jews and Communists. The Nazis had vowed to find these alleged criminals and punish them accordingly.

Stefan was astonished that Germans had been willing to help us. Our fortunate encounters with Feldwebel Storch, Brigitte, and Herr Strauss had persuaded Stefan to change his view about the German people. He had thought that all Germans were Nazis, and therefore all Germans were evil. That was the crucial difference in our view of the Germans. I had always known that there were decent Germans. However, I had to admit that I, too, was surprised by Herr Strauss's willingness to help us.

At the Essen railroad station, the ticket agent informed us that the train going to Berlin would depart as scheduled, and that in Berlin we would have to make the appropriate connection to our destination. He issued one voucher for both of us in lieu of tickets. Once again we were scheduled to arrive early in the morning. We had not slept in days, and both of us were very tired. I looked at Stefan, and I was surprised to see him in such a happy mood. "What is it?" I asked.

"Have you ever been in Berlin?" he wanted to know.

"Yes, I visited Berlin when I was quite young. Both my sister and I were there with our mother."

"I have never been in Berlin, and I am not going to miss this opportunity."

"Berlin is the most dangerous of all the German cities. I am afraid to even set foot there. That's where decisions are being made, and all the high-powered Nazis live in Berlin."

"Krysia, you must stop that. We have a voucher that lists Berlin as our temporary destination, and this is my chance to see Berlin."

Except for several delays, due to repair work on bombed railroad trestles, the train ride to Berlin was uneventful. Passengers disembarked as we traveled east, and in time I managed to secure a window seat. The majority of the people waiting to board the train were men in uniform. The sight of so many green uniforms, trimmed in black, with skull-and-crossbone insignia on shoulders, lapels, and hatbands, sent shivers down my spine. Stefan on the other hand kept looking out the window, and he barely managed to conceal his excitement.

"I know that you are afraid," he said in a low voice. "But it was something that you yourself said that affirmed my decision to stop in Berlin."

"What could I have said?"

"You said that while you were hiding, you found it easier to hide in a city than in some provincial town."

"Yes, but we were talking about Poland and not about the capital of the Third Reich."

"But we are no longer in Poland; we are in Germany now. Essen is not a provincial town, and as Poles, were we not treated well, even by the Nazi Party?"

"No, Stefan, it was not the party. It was one member of the party. A party official beset by German refugees coming at him from all sides. He had the power to make dispositions, and we just slipped by."

"Krysia, I know you've been out there making decisions for both of us, and I don't know where I would be now if not for you. Still, Berlin is my decision, and I know that I am right. We are arriving on a Friday morning, and Strauss extended our appointment date until Monday morning. We'll deposit our luggage at the terminal. I'll take off my beret, and you'll see how well we'll blend into the crowd."

We disembarked at a central railroad terminal of Berlin. The terminal was huge, and masses of people flowed in all directions. We followed passengers leaving our train, hoping they would lead us to an exit. I was jostled from all sides, and I took care not to bump into anyone. The atmosphere was different than the one we had encountered in Essen. People appeared to be annoyed, ready to pounce at the slightest provocation. The faces I glimpsed were closed off. Most of the people were well dressed. There was a great deal of luggage on the platform and not enough porters to handle it. Huge crates that one would expect to be forwarded through a freight yard were crowding the walkway. From loud remarks exchanged between family members, it was clear to me that many of the people were Germans fleeing from the occupied territories and the advancing Russian army.

At the baggage depot, we were advised to carry our luggage because the facility was filled beyond capacity. Out in the street, the crowd was less dense. A woman in her fifties put her suitcase onto the sidewalk, pausing to shift the burden from one arm to the other. I made the snap decision that she could be a native of Berlin, and I stopped to say good morning. She responded in a friendly manner. I asked her if she would know where we could find a night's lodging.

"If it's a hotel you want, you can just forget about it," she said. "All hotels are full."

"We are looking for a rooming house."

"You could try Friedrichstrasse. It's the only possibility I can think of. I hope that you find something."

The woman gave us directions and pointed out the Untergrundbahn, or subway, station. She told us where we should get off. I was very grateful, and I said so. The Untergrundbahn, or U Bahn, was close by, identified by a large letter U edged into the concrete wall.

Walking along Friedrichstrasse, I saw a number of signs that read "*Mobilierte Zimmer zu vermieten*"—furnished rooms to let. I also noted that most of the apartment buildings displaying the sign were run down, the windows dirty and the curtains torn. There was an unsavory aspect to the area. Without hesitating, I kept walking because I sensed eyes watching from behind curtains. My first two attempts were unsuccessful, and Stefan's sense of adventure diminished considerably. The third attempt was alarming. The sign directed us to the second floor, but when we arrived at the landing of the first floor, I looked up and into the gross and pasty face of a huge woman. She wore a torn housedress and the perspiration under her armpits reached down to her middle.

"Deutsch?" the woman barked.

"No."

"We don't want you here. We'll take care of our own, and you go back to where you belong." Additional diatribe accompanied our retreating steps. Before we reached the door leading out to the street, we heard her shriek, "*Keine Juden und keine Ausländer!*"—no Jews and no foreigners.

Once out in the street, I took a deep breath and sent up a thank you. The woman must have been watching us, and she had concluded that we were not German nationals. We walked at a brisk pace, neither stopping nor looking until we were certain we were out of her sight.

We passed up several "room to let" signs because I needed time to gather my flagging courage. We were still on Friedrichstrasse, but the neighborhood had improved. I inferred that we had come into a working-class area. An effort had been made to keep the street as well as the buildings neat looking.

The next attempt went smoothly. We mounted three flights, and I rang a doorbell. The woman who came to the door said that she had already rented two rooms of her apartment. I thanked her, and we started down the stairs.

"Did anyone send you?" she called out softly.

"No, we saw the sign below."

She beckoned to us to return and enter the apartment. "How many nights?" she asked.

"Two nights."

"Are you fugitives?"

"No," I responded, my voice firm.

"Documents in order?"

"Of course," I said.

"I would keep you," the woman continued, "but my rooms are taken. My sister-in-law does not believe in putting out a sign, but she could use the money. As a matter of fact, she needs money badly. I will give you her address; it's not far from here. I know she is home, still I will telephone, just to prepare her a bit."

We thanked the woman, and I said that we appreciated her help. I added that after spending the previous night on the train, it would be a great relief to stretch out and get a good night's rest in a bed.

The sister-in-law, Frau Globke, led us into a sparsely furnished room. Not much daylight entered the room through the single window, but it was clean.

There were twin beds joined together by a single headboard. I said it would be fine. Everyone sleeping here, even if only for one night had to be registered, Frau Globke informed us.

"We are monitored, and they always have their eye on me," she complained. "That will come to four marks per night. Three for the room, and one for the linens. It will cost fifty pfennig for morning coffee and rolls for the two of you—that is, if you have the coupons."

"We would like to have the breakfast, please." I took out the ration cards.

"Your identification cards, please."

She looked at the work-release document and shook her head. "That's not good enough," she remarked.

I pulled out my Kennkarte and I asked Stefan to do the same. I hoped that those official documents with our fingerprints and swastika stamps would allay Frau Globke's concern regarding the work-release pass. She looked at them and shook her head again.

"Hmmm, Pollacks," she muttered, the German pejorative for Poles. "I'll have to keep these for a while. They have questionnaires one meter long, and if I don't answer all the questions, I will be accused of disloyalty. I have done nothing wrong, still they have threatened to revoke my license."

Stefan was eager to see Berlin, but we could not walk the streets without our documents. He didn't want to wait for Frau Globke to process our application. He asked me to ask her if we could leave our luggage and keep our documents while we toured Berlin. We would return during the early evening hours and leave the documents with her at that time for processing.

"Oh no, you can't do that," she bristled. "Do you know what would happen to me if I let you do that? They spot-check at all hours and each room has to be accounted for. There are neighborhood supervisors and then there are the informers. And don't think for a moment that your arrival in this house, the duration of your stay in my apartment, and the fact that you came carrying luggage was not noted."

I felt reassured by her repeated references to "them." She felt no part of the Nazis. I quickly told her that we would wait while she processed our application. I suggested we go ahead and unpack our suitcases while we waited.

"It's just too much for a woman alone," Frau Globke complained. "They gave me a telephone number. They told me to call immediately if I had reason to be suspicious—you know what I mean."

I kept the expression on my face blank to convey that I, as a foreigner, could not understand the local customs. I did, however, assure her that our documents were in order. I explained that train delays had forced us to stop over in Berlin.

Documents back in our possession, we walked down the stairs and retraced our steps to the entrance of the U Bahn. We were off to view the famous landmarks. I tried to impress upon Stefan that a surveillance patrol could arrive at any time at our lodgings on Friedrichstrasse, or we could be stopped and interrogated while walking. I was certain that we needed to prepare an explanation to justify our audacious stopover in Berlin. My voice was firm when I said there were two precautions we must adhere to: We could not stroll, but must at all times walk purposefully toward a destination, and we could not ask for directions. No sight in Berlin was worth seeing if it required that I ask for directions.

My sense of direction was poor, and several times we had to retrace our steps. Some of the U Bahn platforms were as much as four stories below ground level, and all of them, I noticed, were registered bomb shelters. The tunnels and passageways were brightly lit, and trains arrived within minutes of each other. We obtained a U Bahn map, and though we were often caught up in throngs of people rushing in all directions, we managed without much delay to transfer trains at several stations.

We surfaced not far from the Brandenburger Tor and walked for a while along Kurfürstendamm. Stefan insisted on seeing the linden trees of Unter den Linden. He also wanted to catch a glimpse of the "notorious" activities on Alexanderplatz, but I was adamant in my refusal to even go near the square. Alexanderplatz invoked visions, recounted by my father, of bloody engagements between Social Democrats and early Nazis, with government secret police disguised as beggars spying on the combatants.

"No, not Alexanderplatz," I said.

"All right," Stefan agreed, "but cheer up. How I wish you could share my excitement. It's fantastic to be here. The variety of architectural styles and periods is overwhelming. And those skyscrapers! Did you see all that glass? I should not have buried my Leica. I would like to take photographs, to make notes."

I was unable to appreciate the architectural splendor of Germany's wretched capital. I also marveled at Stefan's naïveté. He really believed that as a foreigner, an enemy, he would be permitted to take photographs. Since his camera was buried in the ground in Warsaw, there was no need to dwell on the matter. While Stefan stopped to admire glass, iron monuments, and grill-work, I unobtrusively scanned the faces of the people walking by us. I felt I should be prepared. By being alert, I would gain additional time if we were approached. The faces I glanced were either mean-spirited and threatening or anxious and closed off. And I felt there was something odd about some of the buildings Stefan was admiring. I expressed my misgivings to Stefan. He said my anxiety was affecting my perceptions.

But when we passed yet another strange-looking building, Stefan studied the buildings more carefully and decided my perceptions were accurate. The buildings had windows and an entrance door, and at times statues, columns, and even friezes. However, on closer scrutiny, one realized that it was only a carefully restored façade. Beyond the door and the windows facing the street, there was nothing but mountains of debris. Only if one stopped long enough to look through a crack did one realize that it was a façade. A pedestrian rushing by, unless he knew the site, wouldn't realize that something was amiss. The restoration was so expert, one had to conclude that the bombing had taken place a while ago.

We had never heard of an air raid over Berlin, and since we knew that the attack could not have come from the east, the realization that the Allied armies had at one time penetrated that far into the Third Reich was uplifting. I had the feeling that every Berliner knew the extent of the camouflage, and that there was an understanding between them that the pretense had to be maintained. Although we had stopped but once and for what could not have been more than a minute, hostile glances in our direction made it abundantly clear that the façades were not to be stared at.

This time Stefan understood the angry looks. He reached for my arm, and we quickly moved on. "It's ridiculous," he said, "to make believe it does not exist when it's all over Berlin. I felt they might attack me if I lingered one moment longer. There must have been some sustained bombing. I wonder when it took place."

We entered a modest restaurant and sat down. We ordered the pea soup that was featured and the portion of bread permitted in accordance with the ration coupon for that day and that meal. At five o'clock, ostensibly to see the film *Rigoletto*, starring Benjamino Gigli, we entered a movie theater. All we really wanted to see was the current newsreel that was shown before the featured film.

Had we not just arrived from the western front, where nightly bombings had become a way of life for the population living in that area, we would have been devastated by the news report. According to the commentary accompanying the snippets of film, Germany, aside from occasional minor setbacks, was winning the war on all fronts. In southern Italy, the German army was gaining territory. A short news flash showed a battalion of Polish powstaniks surrendering. They were referred to as the criminals of the Warsaw uprising. They were the young men who just weeks ago were lauded as heroes by their countrymen, but were now a sad sight. The brief film segment showed mountainous heaps of rubble surrounded by burned-out ruins, the remnants of what had once been the proud capital of Poland. I reached for Stefan's hand. I knew he was weeping—and that was dangerous.

On our way to the underground, Stefan said he was more than ready to return to the safety of our room. I asked him if some of the areas shown could have been the site of the obliterated Warsaw ghetto. Stefan didn't know, but he was certain, however, that we had seen the ruins of central Warsaw. Stefan had recognized the debris of monuments that had graced Krakowskie Przedmiescie, his vanished neighborhood. Of Warsaw University, the bohemian quarter, and the elegant residential areas Warsaw residents liked to show visitors, nothing remained. Stefan was disconsolate.

"Hitler has won," he said. "He will lose this war, but as far as Poland is concerned, he has won. Warsaw cannot be rebuilt; he made sure of that. He destroyed the heart of the country. And no one really knows to what extent he destroyed other cities. They called it a blitzkrieg, but there was no krieg, only an invasion for the purpose of rape and plunder."

Along with many of his compatriots, Stefan had never analyzed the fate of his Jewish fellow countrymen. The Polish intelligentsia had retained some vague attachment to the prewar myth of a German culture. There had been an unwillingness to acknowledge the horrific crimes that were being committed. During my two years in Warsaw, I felt that some of the people I got to know believed all one had to do to survive the war and the German occupation was to avoid the Boche and thereby the accompanying contamination.

When Hitler had proclaimed that Warsaw would be obliterated, that no stone would remain standing, Mother and I understood that it had not been an idle threat. Poles on the other hand, especially in Warsaw, had never fully experienced the Nazi horror, and they were stunned by the total destruction. The devastation of Warsaw had put an end to the wishful delusion of a common humanity with the invader.

On the way back to our lodging, we once again had to walk through the loathsome section of Friedrichstrasse we had traversed that morning. A number of rowdy soldiers were entering and exiting the unkempt dwellings. It was obvious that most of them were drunk. Females of all ages could be seen in doorways. Walking at a fast pace, we quickly left that unsavory part of the neighborhood. Stefan smiled and said, "We were lucky. This morning we tried to find lodgings in an area that caters to prostitutes."

When we got back to our room, I asked Frau Globke if we could take a bath. She said she would have to charge an additional fifty pfennig for the hot water. If we had wanted a bath, Frau Globke informed us, we should have been back before seven o'clock in the evening. She said we should have known that. We had no idea what she was talking about, and I didn't ask. However, at eight o'clock on Saturday morning, we would be permitted to have our bath, she added, one after the other. At nine o'clock, as previously agreed, there would be coffee and rolls for our breakfast.

Our first night in Berlin was also the first night that Stefan and I shared a room and a bed. For more than three weeks we had slept on the floor, and most of that time in cramped positions. I woke up in Stefan's arms, my head buried in his neck. I was glad the long awaited event had finally happened. There had been a fleeting moment of joy, but it was gone before I could fully savor it. Stefan said I was too tense and that next time it would be better.

The bathtub was clean and inviting. After the makeshift hygiene I had had to make do with over the past years, my luxurious minutes in the bathtub were dreamlike. The hot ersatz coffee was served in a china cup with a matching saucer. The rolls were fresh and crisp, and there was margarine as well.

In the early afternoon we once again retraced our steps to the busy central section of Berlin. Stefan's sense of adventure had evaporated. I did not think that the ubiquitous red flags and buntings with swastikas had increased in number since the previous day, but now the sight of them affected Stefan. His professional interest had apparently been satisfied. The treachery I had felt on the previous day, he now sensed. He was ready to leave Berlin. It would have been exciting to go to the Berlin Zoo. It was world famous, and I had vague memories of strange and large animals in beautifully maintained jungle habitats. I did not know if Stefan even liked going to zoos, and I did not mention it.

We decided to once more view the city, this time at a somewhat slower pace since it was Saturday afternoon. We noted that some people were strolling, holding hands, and stopping to view window displays. We walked to Bahnhof Ost—the east railroad terminal—for the last leg of our journey to obtain official permission to board the train. The unusual aspect of our work-release pass was once again remarked on, but the notation, permitting rail passage to our final destination, was officially entered, signed, and stamped.

On Sunday morning, as we walked toward the information window to inquire about the appropriate departure platform, I saw four people walking toward us. A young couple, perhaps in their late twenties, was being prodded forward by two men in belted overcoats. Their self-righteous demeanor and strutting gait and their fine, well-polished boots left no doubt as to their identity: It was the Gestapo. The two men made hand motions, signaling to people nearby to move out of the way. The foursome walked fast and within seconds they were out the door. I had not looked at them, and like everyone around us, I made believe I had not noticed that something was amiss. I squeezed Stefan's arm, and he let me know that he knew, that he also had seen. A couple had been caught and taken away. There had been nothing about them that looked different than the other travelers milling about. The attractive-looking woman had been well dressed, wearing high-heeled shoes and a simple, rather chic hat.

Both Stefan and I felt unnerved. We could not imagine why these two people had been selected. Could they have been Jews? What would have denoted them as such? Both of us had a definite impression that they had not been criminals caught performing some illegal act. I realized we had been lucky so far; we had slipped by. Would our fabricated document pass inspection were we to be stopped?

The train ride from Berlin to Breslau took about six hours. We must have been on an express rail because we passed a number of towns without stopping. In Breslau, we needed to change to a local train. Janka, who had given us the address of her aunt's apartment in Katowitz, had warned us about the treacherous atmosphere of what once had been the provincial capital of Polish Silesia. At the time of the invasion, that part of Poland was annexed to the Third Reich, and all Poles, including Janka's immediate family, had been forced to leave. The only Poles who had been permitted to remain were miners. Coal was needed to support the German war effort. The miners had been exempted from the mass evacuation, and there were special laws that applied only to them.

Aside from the miners, Poles were not permitted to live in the annexed territory, and that law was strictly enforced. Though ostensibly part of Germany, the area had a different set of curfew rules. People were stopped in the street, Janka told us, and their documents checked. Janka had emphasized that her aunt was a good person, albeit timid. Her husband discouraged visits from his wife's relatives from occupied Poland. He felt that even though he had pledged his loyalty to the German nation, he was still considered a Volksdeutsch, an ethnic German, and was looked upon with suspicion.

As we neared our destination, I realized we had not correctly calculated the time of our arrival. We would be arriving in Katowitz after seven o'clock in the evening. Curfew for foreigners was seven o'clock. How would we find the neighborhood we needed to go to or the building without asking questions, I wondered aloud. We wanted to avoid drawing attention to ourselves by asking directions. Stefan agreed with me but pointed out that we would need to ask directions to find a place to spend the night.

We would be passing Hindenburg, the town where I was born and grew up. I would be able to orient myself without having to ask for directions. But would I be recognized? Six years had passed since the raid on our apartment and my expulsion. I was a different person. I had not grown much taller, but my hair was blond, my features more mature. It would be a daring undertaking; still, it could be the answer to our immediate problem.

"The only hotel I can think of is the Admiralspalast on Kronprinzenstrasse," I said.

"What can I say?" said Stefan. "Only you know and can weigh the risk we are taking. I should think Hindenburg would be the better choice, but only if you think you can carry it off."

On several occasions, when my parents had had important visitors, such as the Polish consul who came from Oppeln to have dinner at our house, my father had reserved a room in the Admiralspalast. I knew the owner of the hotel by sight, though I was certain that he did not know me. His name was Würfel, and his daughter Ursel, several years Eva's senior, knew my sister, and she also knew me by sight. When Herr Würfel joined the Nazi Party, Ursel renounced all her Jewish friends.

Stefan had two questions. He wanted to know if, were I approached, would I have the presence of mind to deny any relationship to the young girl who had grown up in Hindenburg. The answer was yes. Then he asked me if I would look at the building where I had lived or at the building that had housed my father's clothing store. For his second question, I answered no. I would not go near my home, not even near that neighborhood. Neither would I walk past the site of the burned-out synagogue. The large tree-shaded garden that had been part of the synagogue complex, the place where I had spent so many memorable hours during my childhood, was off limits. Stefan questioned me about a nostalgia that I did not feel. No, Hindenburg was not my Warsaw.

It was after seven o'clock when we arrived in Hindenburg. My heart was pounding when I stepped off the train. Once out on the familiar Bahnhofstrasse, I was glad to see that all street illumination had been dimmed. There were few stars. Other than the blackout, nothing much had changed. We walked past the taxi stand down to the end of Bahnhofstrasse. I pointed to the big corner building ahead of us. For the city of Hindenburg, it was a massive structure with windows looking out in three directions. At the top of the eight-story hotel was the infamous roof garden from which in 1937 a woman had hurled herself to the street.

There used to be a uniformed doorman guarding the swinging gate at the front of the building that led into the restaurant. We entered through a side door because it was lit. A room clerk sitting behind the counter greeted us, and he asked if we had reservations. I explained that we were passing through, and that we only needed a room for one night.

He shook his head, looked over the counter at our luggage, and said, "I am not really the room clerk. Just doing nightshift, double duty. You didn't reserve a room? I cannot accommodate you without a reservation. Where are you headed?"

"Katowitz."

"That's not far. Why did you come here?"

"A lady we met in Berlin told us that due to curfew hours we may need to spend a night in a hotel," I lied. "She said that the Admiralspalast in Hindenburg was a large and gracious hotel."

"So, we have a good reputation. Well, I am not surprised. Let me see. I might be able to arrange something."

He took a sheet out of a folder, examined it, and then he looked at the pages of the reservation book at the counter. I had taken special care to accentuate the German words as a Pole would and to modify the grammar in a manner that would be natural for someone speaking a Slavic language.

"Are you German?" he asked.

"We are Poles," I said, as I handed him the work-release pass.

"Polski—well, what do you know. And from Warsaw? I had relatives in Otwock, my father's side. His uncle. We don't even know if he is still alive. Must have been tough, eh? Speak to me in Polish, I'll understand. My father speaks both German and Polish, but ever since the Poles went to war against us, he only speaks German."

I translated for Stefan. He was about to react to the outrageous twisting of history. I placed a subduing hand on Stefan's arm. No need to argue. We were in no position to antagonize the young man.

He had noticed Stefan's discomfort. He smiled and raised his hand in a mitigating gesture. "I know, I know," he said, "but we must believe what we are told. We had reports that you had attacked the radio station in Gleiwitz, and now we are fighting a war on three fronts."

Once again he perused our work-release document. "I need more than this piece of paper. You must have other identification documents. Every night we get special visitors who come to examine the guest list." We produced our respective Kennkartes.

He took the three documents and put a paperweight on top of them. When I started to say that we would like to keep the documents, he interrupted me and said that there were laws he had to obey. If we wanted to remain for the night, the documents would have to stay in possession of the room clerk, subject to examination by the surveillance inspector. "There will be an inspection," he said. "There always is. You read German, yes? Be careful to obey the blackout instructions, all of them. We don't need a visit from the neighborhood warden."

He gave us a key and told us our room number. I thanked him, and as we were leaving he wanted to know if we had ration cards. I said that we did, and I asked if he wished to see them. He said that was not necessary, but that he had to know if we had them. The room was spacious and well furnished. The window was covered with blackout shades, in addition to damask drapes that were lined with a dark cloth. The air was stale. We turned off all the lights and opened one of the windows.

Standing next to each other we looked down into the dark street below. Stefan wanted me to talk about Hindenburg. He said that he knew very little about my past. I pointed in the direction of our apartment house. Both the house and the location of my father's store were beyond our range of vision. I knew every building, the shops they contained, and most of the owners of the shops. My mind was full of images from my former life, but only one loomed so large that it crowded out all the others. I saw myself as a young child, surrounded by police and Gestapo officers, being marched along Kronprinzenstrasse toward the prison, the bottoms of my pajamas hanging below my coat.

Unlike the two nights in Berlin when I fell asleep as soon as my head touched the pillow, I was unable to fall asleep in the comfortable surroundings of our hotel room. Each time I heard footsteps or the sound of voices in the hallway, my senses sprang to alert and my body stiffened. It felt as if someone were thrusting knives into my stomach. From the soles of my feet came a wave of panic that threatened to obliterate me. While in the street, I had not lifted my face. Who could have recognized me?

I awoke to Stefan shaking me. I must have dozed off. He lifted my shoulders off the pillow, and I heard him say, "You must stop this! For God's sake stop this!"

He let go of me, and I slumped back onto the pillow. I was very tired. "What did I do?" I asked. "What must I stop doing?"

"You were moaning so loud, it sounded as if you were being tortured. I was afraid that anyone passing through the hallway would hear you. You were dreaming. I had to wake you."

My pillow was wet, as was my hair and my back. I had been running, faster and faster, and they were catching up with me. It was a familiar dream, but it was the first time that Stefan had been subjected to it. He was frightened. He said he now realized stopping in Hindenburg had been a mistake. He looked at his watch. It was two-thirty in the morning. We should remember Jadzia's—my mother's—last advice, he suggested. She and I had not said good-bye to each other; only Stefan had spoken with her.

"Jadzia said I have to remember, because you tend to forget. She said that we must eat whenever food is available and must rest if there is a possibility. Krysia, don't let go now. You must hold out until the end. You can see for yourself that it can't go on much longer. You know that, don't you? Now try to get some sleep."

I stretched out on the comfortable bed and pretended to sleep. Stefan's words of comfort, his soothing tone, were reassuring. Still, from the look on his face and in his eyes, I could tell that he was disturbed. I had tried to shield him from the grim reality of my illegal existence. I did not want him to know about the nocturnal ghosts that haunted my sleep. There was nothing preventing him from leaving me. Our marriage certificate was a sham, and we both knew it. Would he continue to stay with me as I stumbled from one reprieve to the next? Without me, the worst scenario that could befall him was a stint in a labor camp. Shielding me was a death sentence. Did he know that? I wondered. He admired me for being able to speak with the Boche, for having been able to communicate in a manner that had provided us with this remarkable interlude. He wanted me to forget that I was Jewish. He wanted me to feel like a Pole. I knew that I had lived up to his expectations during the day, but I did not know how to prevent the dreams that assailed me during the night. My name is Krystyna Zolkos and I am a Christian, I kept repeating to myself. It must have worked because the next thing I knew was Stefan waking me and telling me that it was time to get ready for our appointment at the Arbeitsamt in Katowitz.

# CHAPTER 13

# The Health Clinic at Myslowitz

Upon arrival in Katowitz, we left our luggage in the baggage depot and walked out into a bright and cold late November morning. Everywhere I looked I recognized familiar buildings. Though the street signs had changed, they were the same streets, and yet it was immediately apparent to me that the population exchange had had a crucial effect on the atmosphere of the city. I remembered that during my many visits to prewar Katowitz the streets were teeming with pedestrians of all ages. Especially on Sundays, sidewalks and squares were filled with residents, jostling each other and apologizing amidst laughter, while church bells tolled. The display windows of the many cafés had been crowded with trays of delectable pastries. Shop windows featured duplicates of the latest Paris couture, fashioned by skilled Polish dressmakers.

On the Monday morning of our arrival in Katowitz, there were no strolling pedestrians to be seen. People in drab-looking clothes, looking tired and harassed, rushed past us. Teenagers were not to be seen, and when I did see a small child, it was dragged along by its hurrying mother. The former Polish city that was now part of Germany had been plundered; its splendor, sparked by the melding of Polish and German cultures, obliterated. Its residents were scattered all over occupied Poland while transplanted German residents filled the vacuum. The streets, sidewalks, and empty storefronts looked remarkably clean. The former tantalizing odors of Polish cuisine, coming from bakeries and restaurants, were gone. Compared to the disarray I remembered—traffic jams caused by horse-drawn carriages, automobiles, pedestrians, and clanging streetcars—the city was now repellently hygienic.

The main office of the Katowitz Arbeitsamt was housed on the street level of a three-story building. A secretary took our work-release document while motioning to us to remain standing at the side of her desk. Crowded together on the wooden bench near the entrance door were five elderly people and a woman cradling an infant. The woman was sobbing and simultaneously hushing the baby to stop it from crying. The office workers who manned a number of desks and typewriters in an adjacent open area never lifted their heads to look in our direction. The secretary, who had taken our document, returned and resumed her seat behind the desk. A guard stuck his head through a door and called a name. The woman with the infant shuffled through the room and past the guard. He closed the door behind her. Subsequently, two of the seated men were called and motioned to walk past the guard. Three people had walked out of the room, and not one of them had returned. By that time, we must have been standing for more than an hour. Stefan took my hand as he moved to the vacated seats. All I could think of was that the document, our life-line during the past days, was no longer in our possession.

When our name was called, I sprang to my feet. It had the sound of a command. Stefan stood up more slowly. He looked as if he were walking to his doom. I threw him a look of encouragement. The guard closed the door behind us, and we followed him through a long office, past desks and typewriters, and into a hallway. In the center of the hallway was a large double door made of light oak. The black letters etched into a brass plate affixed to one of the doors read Hübner. The door and the brass plate looked new and shiny. On either side of the imposing double door were doors of regular size. The massive door was ajar, and the guard snapped "*Reingehen*"—enter.

We took several tentative steps toward a man seated behind an impressive-looking desk. He was seated on a swivel chair, his back to us, talking on the telephone. He turned suddenly, shouted Heil Hitler, and banged the telephone onto the cradle. The man, who appeared to be in his early sixties, had an egg-shaped head and a pale and puffy face. His sparse gray hair was oiled and combed to the side. He wore the regulation black tie and Hitler brown shirt and over it an English tweed jacket. From behind his rimless eyeglasses,

I felt for an instant the icy stare of his bloodshot eyes. Then his eyes fastened on the document.

"That's a new one for me," he sputtered. "I have not seen one of these before. Do you know the penalty for forging documents? We are making inquiries."

I did not reply; I knew that he was bluffing when he mentioned forgery. Three of the five official seals, thanks to Herr Strauss's kindness, carried the telling NSDAP insignia.

"Do you understand nothing of what I am saying?" he screamed.

"Yes, I understand." My voice was tentative with a Polish accent.

"And you?" He was strutting toward Stefan in his black breeches and high, custom-made brown boots.

"He . . . ," I started to say, but the man's raised hand stopped me.

"Are you dull-witted?" he shouted, his face red with rage.

"I don't understand," Stefan said in Polish.

"I don't understand, I don't understand," the man mimicked, his voice dripping malice.

The man was quite small; Stefan towered over him. Stefan did not step back. The man turned, marched back to his desk, and as if exhausted by his fit of temper, he slumped back into his chair. He grumbled about decisions. He said, once made, they should not be altered, not by anyone. Again the watery eyes focused on me, and with a beckoning index finger, he motioned for me to step forward. I took Stefan's hand as we moved closer to his desk.

"It's either Buna or Farben for you. There you can serve your sentence in the company of your fellow countrymen."

At that time I did not know what either Buna or Farben meant, but since he had used the word *sentence*, I thought it referred to a prison.

"We were advised that we would be allowed to work and that you would give us the work assignments," I ventured timidly.

"You were told," he mocked. "And who told you? Herr Strauss? Poles from Warsaw? What is your connection to Herr Strauss?"

I decided not to answer, to pretend not to have understood. An acquaintanceship with Herr Strauss would have been in our favor, but Herr Strauss, if questioned, would not remember the incident. Our work-release pass was one of many documents expediting travel that he had probably signed that day. To my knowledge, no copies were made.

"For a Pole you speak German rather well," Herr Hübner said. "Did you work for the occupation government?"

"No."

"What did you do?"

"I worked in a clothing factory. I sewed German uniforms."

"Not for the Wehrmacht?"

"No, but since they were all fashioned according to the same pattern, it was assumed that they were uniforms."

"What else?"

I quickly reasoned that my work in the petition office in Krosno and my emergency Red Cross work, if combined, could explain my facility with the German language.

"I worked in a health clinic," I lied.

"A German health clinic?"

"No, but the clinic was supervised by the health department of the occupation government. Since there was a shortage of staff, I helped expedite forms and inquiries."

"You know how to read, write, type?"

"Yes."

Herr Hübner shuffled through some papers that were piled high in a wire basket on the right side of his desk. He extracted a sheet of paper, read it, and then dialed a telephone number. He identified himself, saying, "Heil Hitler, Hübner hier," and said to the person on the other end that it's disgraceful, that he did not like it at all, but that there was a shortage of qualified personnel. If Herr Doctor could make do with a Pollack, a Pole from Warsaw—not too stupid—for perhaps a week, Herr Hübner felt sure that the right person—a German national, of course—could be located. Signing off with a Heil Hitler, Hübner hung up.

Speaking to no one in particular, he said, "He expects me to perform miracles. Two days without a second nurse, and he runs amuck." To me, he said, "Dr. Kostka said to make sure that you know how to spell, because he never met a Polack who was able to write and spell correctly."

Herr Hübner handed me a pad and pencil, and while strutting back and forth through the room and stopping occasionally to look over my shoulder, he dictated several sentences. I wrote with care, but inserted several minor spelling and grammatical errors. He took the pad out of my hand and sputtered, "It's not exactly free of errors." From my experience, both in the petition office in Krosno and later in the county office in Szczucin, I knew that correspondence from German offices was far from flawless. I did not apologize, but I suggested that given more time I would have corrected some of my mistakes.

"Dr. Kostka will just have to make do until we can find the right person. Present the appropriate identification documents to my secretary. You did bring your Kennkarten?" I said that we did. "She will give you further instructions and a letter for Dr. Kostka. We can't have Polish criminals running loose in our country. The rest is up to Dr. Kostka." He turned toward Stefan. "Now to you. What can you do?"

"He is a civil engineer," I said. "But in the past years he has worked in photography."

"Worthless!" Hübner bellowed. "What good is it? But you do know something about chemicals. I.G. Farben would not mind getting a worker who knows something about chemicals, right, ha, ha, ha."

The tone was menacing, and Hübner, his face flushed, once again moved toward Stefan.

"Herr Director, please do not separate us. So many families have been broken up. We were permitted to remain together, and both of us were designated able-bodied workers," I lied. "I beg you to allow us to remain together."

"Are you asking me to act against the national interest? I am duty bound to see that everyone gets the work he is most qualified for. All that husband of yours is qualified for is to work in a mill."

"My husband is very capable. Please give us a chance. I feel certain that if the doctor decides to employ me, my husband will also find work."

"In Myslowitz? There is nothing there for someone who does not speak German." Herr Hübner's tone sounded adamant. Then suddenly, he relented.

"Three days," he said. "If Dr. Kostka agrees to employ you, he will notify me. Your husband has three days to find employment, doing work that will benefit the Reich." He gestured toward Stefan, but continued to look at me. "In three days I want to hear where you are and what you are doing. Now get out of here before I change my mind. I thought I was through dealing with Polacks, and still you come here—ingrates that you are—after attacking us."

"You are most kind," I said. We rushed out of the office.

I hardly had a chance to calm myself before a young handsome woman ushered us to her desk. She asked to see our respective Kennkarten, inserted a printed form into her typewriter, and typed in the information she needed. She noted the lapsed validation date on my Kennkarte, looked up at me, and continued typing. It took a while before she completed the two-sided questionnaire. She put my Kennkarte down and proceeded to transcribe the needed information from Stefan's Kennkarte. From a drawer she retrieved our work-release pass. I assumed that the Arbeitsamt had made a copy, because Herr Hübner had held one in his hand, but with much relief I saw that the young woman was transcribing from the original.

"Are you really from Warsaw?" the young woman asked. I answered in the affirmative. "It was a beautiful city, yes?" I said that it had been very beautiful. The woman handed me a sealed envelope, addressed to Dr. Kostka in Myslowitz. She returned both our identification documents and the work-release pass. She got up and said, "I call that luck, that is if Dr. Kostka approves. It's a busy office, and he has had his problems. I called him, and he said he wants you there tomorrow morning, the earlier the better. You can take the train; it takes about half an hour. There is also a streetcar going to Myslowitz. It's cheaper, but you would have to transfer and it would take much longer."

"Thank you," I said. "You are very kind. Good-bye—till we meet again."

"Better that we not," was her response—a gentle acknowledgment on her part that, as Poles, we would want to stay far away from that malignant place.

Back in the street, both of us breathed a deep sigh of relief. Stefan said that he felt as if he had escaped from the edge of a precipice. He thought that Hübner could not stand the sight of him, and twice he felt that Hübner was about to strike his face.

"I never want to be in that office again," Stefan vowed. "The man is not normal, one of those German sadists." I was certain that the director of the Arbeitsamt was a vile man. It was quite astonishing, but he did resemble the director of the Arbeitsamt in Krosno, the one who had assigned me to work on the street-cleaning detail.

Though it was early in the afternoon, I did not think it wise to embark on the trip to Myslowitz. We needed a place to spend the night, and we thought that this was the right time to contact Janka's aunt, Frau Mandola. We had both her address and her telephone number. I would first telephone, and I mentally prepared what I was going to say. I made the call from a telephone booth, and Frau Mandola, Janka's aunt, answered. Her voice sounded friendly when she picked up the receiver but changed immediately when I identified myself. In a clipped tone, she urged that I tell her Janka's message over the phone, adding that Janka should have known better than to send messengers. She then asked if I knew where Janka was and if her parents were with her. I said that I could not answer these questions over the phone, but that I would be able to if I could see her. Only when I said that Janka had given me the address, did Frau Mandola relent. She gave us explicit directions to her house, and she urged us not to stop and ask for help. She insisted that we appear without luggage. She made me repeat the number of the trolley we were to take and the names of the streets we had to traverse.

The door opened before I touched the bell. Behind Frau Mandola stood her daughter, a young woman about Janka's age. Both women appeared frightened. They looked at us as if we were intruders from another world. They motioned us to not speak and to follow them through the hallway and into the dining room. Once in the center of the room, the daughter asked if we wanted to remove our coats, while the mother, her eyes darting around the room, drew the curtains and moved several chairs so that we could sit facing each other. We introduced ourselves, and Stefan, in accordance with Polish custom, kissed the hands of the women. When we were seated, Frau Mandola lifted her arms, her palms turned outward, and murmured in German, "That's the way things are." I translated for Stefan.

"It's all right to speak Polish now," Frau Mandola said, "but please keep your voices low. We are being watched all the time, and they are keeping track of our visitors. They are just waiting to trap us, to denounce us for something we either said or did. That's how they get hold of a nice apartment or well-paying employment—foreigners, you know. They don't even speak German properly, but they have Nazi friends. Their power is without limits."

"Your neighbors?" Stefan asked.

"Yes, next door, and they have powerful Nazi connections. That's why I did not want you to come here. If my husband had been home, he never would have let you come."

Both women were eager to tell us that the Warsaw uprising had been a terrible blunder, and they wanted to know if we, or Janka, had taken part in the rebellion. We assured them that neither Janka nor we had taken up arms against the Germans, but that we had fully supported the valiant effort of the insurgents. When Stefan mentioned the relentless bombing and artillery attacks coming at us from all sides, Frau Mandola interrupted and said, "But not from across the Vistula. The Russians watched you bleed from across the river."

Stefan and I looked at each other in amazement. While in Germany, we had heard references to the Warsaw uprising, the carnage residents had been subjected to, but the Soviet army watching from across the Vistula River had not been mentioned.

"Whatever stupidity caused you to trust the wily Russians?" said Frau Mandola. We did not respond. We were seated across from people who had trusted the wily Germans and had been living in fear ever since. All along Stefan had tried to elicit some feelings of sympathy for the Warsaw residents, with whom the two women shared a common heritage, but he had not succeeded. I felt relieved that I did not have to speak, and I retreated to the safety of my lowered eyelids—the timid Polish wife who lets her husband speak for her.

"What was the message you felt you could not relay over the telephone?" Frau Mandola asked. When Stefan told them what Janka and her two friends were planning at the time of our departure, the two women perked up. They were unable to hide their astonishment. Would they be caught? they wondered. Could they succeed? How was it possible, they wanted to know, for Dutch nationals to move freely in the German town of Wesel? Why had these Dutch training ships not been confiscated? They criticized us for recounting the tale as if it was a daring feat. Didn't we know the penalty Janka would be subjected to if apprehended? Besides, was it not equally dangerous for both sides? Did we realize, they wanted to know, what would happen to the Dutch naval cadets if the girls were discovered aboard ship? Did we really believe that the three girls could circumvent German surveillance? The penalty for escaping, for avoiding work assignments no doubt would land the girls in concentration camp, Frau Mandola concluded.

Stefan led the conversation back to our own problem. He showed the Mandola women our work-release pass, and he told them that on the following day we would be leaving for Myslowitz and my work assignment with a doctor. The women hardly looked at the document, and they quickly returned it as if divesting themselves of contraband. Once again their impatience with us was evident.

"What is it you want from us?" Frau Mandola said. "Here, you are despised, and regardless of your pass, you would be considered traitors, as well as fugitives from the camp. Here, they don't ask questions when they arrest you."

"*If* we get caught," Stefan responded. "So far we have been lucky. We traveled straight across the whole of Germany, and we found to our relief that we blended in rather well, with the thousands of German refugees presently on the move."

"That may have been so in the Reich, but here there is little movement. Unlike the German refugees, we have no place to go to. You don't seem to realize the damage your visit may cause us. How could we explain your visit to our home? Or why we did not contact the police registry, as we are pledged to do? A visit from a foreigner has to be justified. I entreat you to leave before my husband returns. He is a law-abiding German citizen who lives in accordance with the rules. He would not be happy to know that we were conversing in Polish."

Stefan continued to hesitate. "If it is money or food coupons that you need," said Frau Mandola. "We might be able to scrape up something. All I ask is that you leave our home and that you not come here again."

"Thank you very much, but we don't need money or food coupons," Stefan assured the woman. "All we ask is that you allow us to remain here through the night. We can sleep on the floor, any place you can put us. We must be off the street at curfew time. You said yourself how treacherous the town is."

"That is out of question. I knew it when you called. I should never have permitted you to come."

We were at an impasse. Both women were standing, and we had not yet gotten up off our chairs. The women moved to the side and whispered among themselves. Finally, Frau Mandola said that she would call her cleaning woman. Perhaps she would be able to put us up, and she could use the money. It wouldn't be much. Could we pay? Stefan said we could.

While the mother went out to make a telephone call, the daughter, who so far had said very little, told us about Pani Lischka, the cleaning woman. Frau Lischka and her husband were Poles. At the time of the German invasion a special law had been passed exempting Polish coal miners and their families from the deportation of Polish residents of Katowitz. Pan Lischka worked in a nearby coal pit, the daughter informed us, though at the moment, due to an injury, he was temporarily unable to work. The daughter also mentioned money: The Lischka family was struggling to stay afloat.

Frau Mandola returned with an affirmative answer. Frau Lischka had agreed to let us spend the night. We got up to leave. We explained to the Mandola women that we were not the only ones who had her address. There was a woman, Jadwiga Dembicka, who had received a work assignment in Austria and who would contact us by sending her address to the Mandola family. Of course, her niece Janka, our friend, would also contact us through the same channel. Stefan assured them the mail would come from Germany and Austria, not from Poland. Stefan and I had to promise that we would not contact the Mandola family until we were properly employed and registered in accordance with the law.

We retrieved our luggage and boarded a trolley. It was getting dark, and we were grateful that there was still enough light to enable us to read the street signs. The address we were seeking was in a neighborhood I did not know. The streets were narrow, and the odor of mildew and sewage was pervasive. Identical three-story red-brick row houses lined both sides of the street. The poverty was palpable.

Pani Lischka, a petite, dark woman with large, sad eyes, opened the door, and immediately from the landing we entered a dimly lit, steamy kitchen. Two laundry lines fastened to hooks in the four corners of the kitchen intersected beneath the shaded lightbulb that hung low in the center of the room. Beneath it a table was set with four plates. We ducked to avoid the hanging garments and walked toward a large iron stove. A man in a wheelchair sat near the stove.

Although it was quite warm in the kitchen, the man was wrapped in a blanket. He lifted a hand to his cap and greeted us in Polish. "God be with you," he said. I wanted to embrace him and kiss the woman. We were strangers to them, yet they had opened their home to us, and we knew we were welcome. Pan Lischka pointed to a pot bubbling on the stove. "We would have liked to offer something better," he said. Stefan told him how happy we were that they allowed us to spend the night. We shed our coats and sat down, this time feeling at ease.

"After the accident, they once again reduced our food ration," Pani Lischka told us. "All they want is your muscle, and if you get hurt while working for them, they say it's your own fault. For all they care, we might just as well rot. And we were lucky. Last year when two of the miners got hurt, they were accused of having caused the accident themselves—an attempt at sabotage."

"Yes, yes, we have our problems," the husband agreed, "but for them"—he pointed at us—"it is worse. My God, Warsaw! All our Polish people—it was a slaughter, that's what it was." He addressed his wife, "Mariechen, now you can ask."

Pani Lischka told us she had cabbage soup cooking on the stove and that she would fix some potatoes to go with it. She wanted to know if that would be all right. She also said that she was sure that the Mandolas had not even offered us a cup of tea. I said that we would be happy to eat whatever she prepared and that we were very grateful to them for wanting to share their food with us.

Pani Lischka put fried potatoes on the plates and placed a bowl filled with cabbage soup in the center of the table. She spooned the cabbage soup over the potatoes, and we did the same. Suddenly I felt very hungry. We had not eaten a morsel of food since breakfast. I tried to eat the food in a mannerly fashion when all I wanted to do was to gulp everything on my plate.

"We are grateful beyond words," Stefan said. "I don't know what we would have done had you not come to our rescue."

"You don't have to be grateful. The Mandolas have lost all their humanity, if they ever had any. We shall retain ours till the end. And the end is near." Pan Lischka turned to Stefan. "Don't you agree?"

Pan Lischka wanted to know about everything that had transpired during the two months of the Warsaw uprising. How did it start? Where had we been at that time? How did the Polish underground manage to hide arms while subject to incessant Nazi surveillance? Had we ourselves taken up arms? Stefan answered the questions as best he could. He said that since neither of us had belonged to the clandestine underground organization we had not known when the uprising would occur.

He told the Lischka couple that it had been his task to document the historic event as best he could and that I had initially ministered to the wounded at a Red Cross station and subsequently assisted him in taking photographs. Pan and Pani Lischka expressed their sadness regarding the bloody defeat of the insurrection and the heartbreaking imprisonment of the young fighters. It was difficult for them to comprehend the forced evacuation of residents from Warsaw and subsequent destruction of the Polish capital. Still,

Pan Lischka ruminated, even the temporary setback of the ostensibly invincible Nazi war machine had uplifted them.

Stefan had spoken freely, and now Pan Lischka allowed himself to vent some of his accumulated frustration. He told us that our perception of a pervasive treacherous atmosphere in Katowitz was correct. "All the Poles were chased out," he said. "And who do you think moved into the empty apartments? Germans from the so-called Third Reich? Not really. Well, some came—but believe me, not too many. The people who came were German-Poles, German-Slovakians, German-Rumanians, German-Ukrainians. That's what they call themselves, but the Nazis call them Volksdeutsch—ethnic Germans. The Nazis don't really trust them or their avowed loyalty to Germany. And you know what's strange? They don't trust each other. Neighbors denounce each other, and they spy on each other for some imaginary gain. They have given up their honor for extra ration cards."

Exhausted by the intensity of his emotion, Pan Lischka slumped back into his chair. Pani Lischka removed the plates, placed cups and saucers on the table, and poured mint tea for the four of us. Then she sat down.

"Wouldn't you say," she said, "that it's strange that the Mandola ladies can only trust us? After the invasion, we were ready to leave, you know, but we were ordered to remain. They needed the coal. They could not bring miners here from Germany. They needed them to work their own mines, or to serve in the Wehrmacht. Here, the ethnic Germans treat us like pariahs—but look what just happened! Frau Mandola trusted us with their secret. The terrible secret! Homeless Polish nationals were sent to them, and all they wanted was to sleep over for one night. One single night!"

Stefan said that we would have to get up very early on the following morning, and he asked how we could do it without disturbing them too much. Frau Lischka insisted that she would get up to make us a cup of ersatz coffee. There was no bread in the house. They had used up their bread coupons and could not purchase bread until the day after next. Pan Lischka would not be up in time, she told us; he now stays in bed until midmorning because the days were so long.

When we bade Pan Lischka good night, he kissed my hand. He had tears in his eyes, and he told us to remember that we were welcome to visit or even to spend the night. "I hope you will be allowed to travel," he added. "You will feel very lonely among the ethnic Germans. That's all you will find in

Myslowitz: ethnic Germans and Polish coal miners. The latter, just like here, live in fear and in poverty. I am not afraid. I know my coal, and they know it. So you come and visit, but call first. We never know how the law might change from one day to the next."

The apartment consisted of a bedroom, living room, kitchen, and bathroom. Though Pani Lischka said that we could sleep in the living room on the sofa, we declined. The unheated living room was ice cold. We slept quite well in the warm kitchen on the floor near the stove. The following morning, we took leave of Pani Lischka. Both she and I had tears in our eyes when we embraced and kissed. Each time I came across genuine kindness, my fractured faith in some remaining goodness in the world was vaguely bolstered.

There were few passengers on the early morning train to Myslowitz. During the journey, we saw numerous steel elevators leading to mine shafts. Clusters of tall brick chimneys, bellowing black smoke, dotted the sky. Steel mills proliferated, and steel in various dimensions was piled high. Dr. Kostka's office was located in a two-story red-brick semiattached dwelling, a five-minute walk from the railroad station. It was about nine-thirty in the morning when we arrived at the doctor's office.

The waiting room was crowded with people of all ages. Chairs and benches were occupied. Patients with despondent-looking faces, dressed in threadbare clothing, were waiting their turn to see the doctor. I spotted an empty chair near a file cabinet in a corner, and I motioned for Stefan to sit down. We shoved the two suitcases into the corner. I moved toward the desk while at the same time a young woman, dressed in a white nurse's uniform, approached the desk from the other side of the room. She looked at me and said, "You are the one they called about?" I nodded. "You have to wait." She gave me a guarded smile. "You can remain right here," she motioned. "The doctor will see you next."

My first encounter with Dr. Kostka was brief. All he wanted to know was whether I was ready to start right away. I said I was. He pointed to a door and said, "In the bathroom on your right, you will find clean uniforms. They belong to my wife, but she should no longer assist me in the office. Leave your coat in there and walk out through the hallway back into the office. Hedwig will show you what to do."

I must have looked at him questioningly, because he added, "I can't tell; we'll just have to see."

Hedwig, his assistant, pointed to the file cabinet and explained the filing system with few words. For each patient, both long forms and short index cards had to be filled out. She said that all questions had to be clearly answered and that often I would have to insist to obtain the appropriate answer—there were questions on the questionnaire that patients would rather not answer.

"Most of our patients have been to the office before," she said, "and all you will have to do is locate their record. The majority of patients belong to the German National Health Service, and the document designating them as members must accompany the index card when they walk into the doctor's office."

"There were also patients who qualified under welfare," she continued. "Everybody likes Dr. Kostka. But unless they are registered with us, they must go and see the other doctor. There is one other physician in town, and Dr. Kostka can't be expected to carry the load all by himself. Then there are the prisoners of war—French prisoners of war and others—we will talk about that another time."

For the next several hours I located files, interviewed patients regarding their complaints, and filled in forms. Occasionally, Stefan and I made eye contact. His glance was questioning, and I had no answer. At two o'clock in the afternoon, there were still four people seated in the waiting room. Frau Kostka stuck her head out and said, "The doctor has been called away." Patients still waiting to see him would have to return the following day. If they presented themselves no later than nine o'clock in the morning, they would be seen first. Hedwig would give them the appropriate voucher.

I continued working until I had listed on the dated form going to the German National Health Service the names and addresses of all the patients the doctor had seen. From a coded chart, I filled in the nature of their complaints. My task completed, I went into the doctor's office and watched while Hedwig and Frau Kostka cleaned and stored the instruments. All instruments were washed with soap and water and rinsed in a large glass cylinder filled with disinfectant. The syringes and needles were then stored in separate stainless steel sterilizers located on a side table, while the larger instruments, such as scissors, scalpels, and curettes, were put in a large, free-standing, oblong-shaped sterilizer. Frau Kostka told me to observe carefully what was being done because the sterilization of instruments would henceforth become my task.

"We take great care to sterilize everything that might possibly lead to an infection," Frau Kostka said. "In this office we take every precaution to prevent the spread of disease. Besides," she smiled, "I want my husband to remain alive. We all want to stay alive."

Frau Kostka, a handsome woman of medium height, was in her late twenties. Curly, dark blond hair framed her oval-shaped face. Her complexion was fair, and the alert look in her smiling eyes gave the impression of a self-possessed and charming woman. She was walking around in an unbuttoned white coat, and when she saw that I had noticed her swollen abdomen, she patted her belly and said, "The doctor says I should take it easy, but it's hard when I see that they are working him to death."

At about three-thirty in the afternoon, the clean-up job completed, Hedwig declared, "I've had it," and went into the hallway to get her coat. On her way out, she turned to me and said, "Until tomorrow."

"When was the last time you had a meal?" Frau Kostka asked.

"This morning," I responded.

"That's what I thought. I heard that in Warsaw you learned to get along without food. Go through the hallway to the kitchen and tell Marta—she's our housekeeper—to make you a couple of sandwiches."

"Thank you very much. May I introduce my husband, Stefan Broda?"

Stefan bent over Frau Kostka's hand and kissed it. She said something about old customs that have long been set aside, but it was evident that she liked the greeting.

"Now both of you to the kitchen," she said. She told us that Marta was waiting for us, and that she had to clean both the office and the waiting room before dinnertime. She added that the doctor should be back within the hour and that our situation would then be assessed.

Marta was expecting us. She could have been in her late thirties, perhaps early forties. She was dark haired, short, and squat—her oily complexion marred by numerous protruding moles.

She said the doctor told her that we were Poles from Warsaw, prisoners out on parole. Though Marta spoke German, there was no question in my mind that she was Polish. She spoke a strange dialect; some sentences included more Polish than German words. I needed to be careful. I told Stefan what Marta had said and encouraged him to speak with her in Polish.

"I don't know what is being said about us because I don't understand

German," said Stefan. "We were residents of Warsaw, and when they forced us to leave, they declared us to be prisoners."

"Everyone? The whole city?" exclaimed Marta. "Were they ever angry! You should have seen the newsreels! How stupid to start something you can't finish." Ignoring me, she addressed Stefan. "You sure married a young woman. I, for one, could never see why a man would marry a younger woman. Asking for trouble, I dare say."

Marta's Polish was as fractured as her German—an amalgam of German and Polish words. It was immediately apparent that Stefan had made a friend. Whenever Marta addressed him, she became quite animated. Toward me, however, she did not convey the same warmth. Marta wanted to know if we had been married for a long time. She asked too many personal questions, and I was afraid of her. She wanted to know how come a young woman from Warsaw spoke German much better than she did. So far I had not said much, and I determined once again to speak guardedly and to pause more often, as if I was searching for the right words.

Dr. Kostka returned in the late afternoon. He was a good-looking man in his middle thirties—jovial and brimming with energy. There was a twinkle in his eye. Though a bit fleshy, he carried his weight well, and the vest of his well-tailored suit managed to camouflage his belly. He embraced his wife, and she asked about something as they moved to the side. Moments later he smiled at me and said, "My wife tells me that this time we won the big one in the lottery."

The doctor told me that there was a flu epidemic abroad, and he wanted his wife to stay out of the office. He once again mentioned the need to sterilize. He said that he expected me to be scrupulous in taking all the necessary precautions.

"We are just not up to it," the doctor said. "There are diseases we never had before. They are coming at us from all sides, especially the camps. I use a lot of rubber gloves. We request them whenever we order supplies. My wife will show you how I like my rubber gloves. Always go easy with the powder. Twice a week in the afternoon, I do house calls. Hedwig is overworked. We need assistance with routine laboratory work. We do our own urine and blood analysis. In our office, first aid consists mainly of disinfecting and bandaging cuts and bruises. I expect you to attend to this unless stitches are required."

## DECEMBER 1944 ✎ MYSLOWITZ, FORMERLY POLAND, NOW ANNEXED TO THE THIRD REICH

On the day of our arrival, Marta had been dispatched to go and see the widow Ptak. She was on welfare and one of the doctor's patients. She was desperately in need of money and wanted to rent her bedroom, while she would sleep on a makeshift bed in her kitchen. We desperately needed a bed and made arrangements through Marta to rent her room.

Frau Ptak was in her eighties and stone deaf. She was lonely, and she talked incessantly, hardly ever in German. One did not need to know what she was saying, all one had to do was nod. Once she was asleep, we rejoiced in the silence and opened the bedroom door to garner warmth from the coal-burning kitchen stove—the only source of heat in the two-room apartment. There was no telephone. On Sundays, my one day off from work, the widow went to church early in the morning. That was our only opportunity to heat water and wash.

There was one photographer in Myslowitz. He was Volksdeutsch, and one of the doctor's patients. He suffered from diabetes. Frau Kostka said that she would call him about work for Stefan. She subsequently informed me that he had agreed to see Stefan. She smiled and said, "Herr Pawelek was reluctant, but he knew that he could not refuse my request. He complained that business was slow, that he did not need additional help, and that by employing a Pole from Warsaw he was courting trouble."

Frau Kostka told me that she had been prepared to remind him of the numerous times when, during the night, the doctor had been called to come to his home, but she was glad that it did not come to that. She said that Herr Pawelek was overweight and self-indulgent; he forgets to take his insulin, and then the doctor is called in the middle of the night.

Dr. Kostka called Herr Hübner, the director of the Arbeitsamt, and said he was prepared to keep me and that my husband had found employment. Herr Hübner answered that he had not stopped looking and would find an appropriate German assistant. Dr. Kostka was a perceptive man and noted my involuntary fearful reaction when he told me Hübner's response. "You don't have to be afraid," he said, "not for the next few months, while I am still here. After that . . ." His voice trailed off.

Within days I knew what "after that" meant. Several months before our arrival, Dr. Kostka had been designated as fit to serve in the Volkssturm, or home guard. The Volkssturm was made up of men and women who had previously been exempted from serving in the Wehrmacht army. Since every able-bodied German man had already been called up for army service, the people exempted were either too old or too young, disabled, or doing necessary work on the home front. According to the snippets of conversation I heard, I inferred that the time had come when everyone, even the old, the young, and the disabled, could no longer be exempted from defending the Fatherland.

Initially, Dr. Kostka had obtained deferment because of his patient load and because he was ministering to local miners who needed to return to work as quickly as medically possible. His deferment had now been canceled; the current deferment was the last one. The doctor had been notified that he would be allowed to continue his medical practice until Frau Kostka's confinement. After the birth of the baby, Dr. Kostka would be needed at the front. I understood that to get this latest deferment, Dr. Kostka had used all the influence he could muster.

Once registered in the Myslowitz municipality, we were allotted the ration coupons allowed for foreign workers. Very little food was available. Store shelves were almost empty. We bought whatever was available on that day. Sometimes it was bread, other times potatoes or a beet preserve to be used as a spread. Even cabbage, the Polish mainstay, was rationed. With our shrunken stomachs, our need for food was considerably decreased. When I worked late into the evening, Marta was asked to prepare a meal for me. Frau Kostka said that whenever I worked late, which was at least twice a week, Stefan could come and eat with me in the kitchen. Those meals were nourishing and well prepared. Marta was an excellent cook, and at times we even had meat. I was very grateful. After dinner, at about eight o'clock in the evening, I left Stefan with Marta—because I knew she liked that—and went back to the office to set up for the following day.

Even though Stefan despised the German milieu of the Kostkas, he did like the comfort of their kitchen and bathroom whenever it became available. We did not have a corner of our own in the Ptak apartment. The widow rummaged in our belongings and did not even bother to cover up her trespass. The bathroom was located in the hallway of the building and it was difficult to gain access. There was not one comfortable chair to sit on. In the Kostka apartment, even the chairs in the kitchen were comfortable, and Marta was happy to speak Polish and with a man. Occasionally Marta slipped a small package into Stefan's coat pocket. Often there was a piece of sausage or some bacon. Apparently, Dr. Kostka had patients in the countryside, and they supplied him with food items no longer available in the grocery stores.

Once a week, on Thursday afternoons—and those were days that seemed endless—we ministered to patients infected with syphilis. The word *syphilis* was never mentioned. We referred to Thursdays as the "S days." Before the patients entered the doctor's office, Hedwig and I arranged them in groups, according to the severity of the infection. Within the office, careful preparations were made in advance. The groups were comprised of men, women, and sometimes children. Salvarsan the drug we injected, came in glass ampoules marked in different colors. Immediately before injecting the Salvarsan, the neck of the glass ampoule was broken and its contents emptied into the syringe. The doctor administered the Salvarsan, while Hedwig or I, working in tandem with him, injected an antigen solution into the buttock; the latter, I assumed, enhanced the effect of the Salvarsan.

Most of the afflicted patients were miners or mill workers and their families, and almost all the men were employed. In spite of the frenzied activity generated by the coming and going of such a large number of people, the process was remarkably efficient. Everyone knew what to do, and I just followed along. The patients lined up in two rows, about six in a row. The people in the front row bared one arm and one buttock, and the doctor methodically swabbed the arm with alcohol, injected the medicine, discarded the moistened cotton swab, and dropped the syringe, needle still attached, into a basin filled with disinfectant. At the same time, working on the same patient, I injected the antigen into the buttock, discarded the cotton swab, and put the syringe with attached needle into a different basin filled with disinfectant. Once everyone in the front row had received their two injections, they moved back, and the row of patients standing in back moved up. The patients who had been injected pulled up their pants, rolled down their sleeves, and walked out.

During the hours when patients suffering from the dread disease were seen, no other patients were scheduled to be at the office. The doctor wanted to maintain the separation. It was understood that the patients, though they knew about each other, would not want outsiders to know their malady. For our own protection, the doctor emphasized again and again the danger of the used needles and of an accidental needle prick.

Not all the patients infected with syphilis were poor. There were four or five patients, mostly women, who avoided contact with the group by making appointments directly with the doctor. We were not supposed to know who they were, or why they came to see the doctor. Clad in opulent furs, they drove up in their automobiles. Affecting a haughty look, they rushed through the waiting room, the scent of exquisite perfume trailing in their wake. The office had no records that could identify them or their malady, but both Hedwig and I knew why they were there since we always prepared the correct dosage of Salvarsan in advance and subsequently sterilized the used instruments.

Every other week, Dr. Kostka attended a clinic at the infirmary of the Russian prisoner-of-war compound. "We are surrounded by camps on all sides," Hedwig told me. "In the beginning there was only Auschwitz. That's where they put all the Jews. Did you know that?"

"No," I answered.

"Yes, they did. People saw them. Early in the morning, they marched them out to work, you know with those armbands. But now they have Poles and Russians to do the hard labor. We are not supposed to talk about that, not even to know about it. Today, anyone who is smart pretends to be deaf and dumb. When you came to work here, the doctor said I should not talk about it with you. Still, sooner or later, you will have to know."

"Know what?"

"That's what I mean. How can you work here and not know?"

"I don't understand."

"Well, aside from Auschwitz, which is about fifteen kilometers south of Myslowitz, there are a number of other camps in this area. Several of them are almost within walking distance. Also, there are prisoner-of-war camps. There is a combined British-American compound, but they have their own medical officers. The doctor goes there to consult. There is the Russian compound. Then there is a small French unit, and most of the French prisoners of war have been here for quite a while. Their medic is allowed to leave the French compound, and they bring patients to our office. Jacques, their medical officer, was here yesterday. Did you see him? The one in the hunter-green uniform, wearing a black beret with a Red Cross armband on his sleeve?"

"No, I did not see him. Did he go into the doctor's office?"

"No, Jacques hardly ever goes in to see the doctor, unless he is ill himself. He brings the patients, but most of the time he brings specimens that I send away for analysis. Jacques is very capable. He has some medical training."

"Did you say this doctor sees patients at the infirmary of the Russian compound? Are there no Russian doctors?"

"Doctors? They don't even have a single a medical orderly. They have nothing, not even boots on their feet. Don't ever speak to the doctor when he gets back from the Russian compound. He hates going there, and he says it's disgusting. The compound is overcrowded, and every day new prisoners are added. They are full of lice and boils and diseases that can't be controlled. The doctor is unable to obtain the drugs and vaccines we keep requesting. I am really sticking my neck out telling you all this. Yesterday he had a telephone call informing him of a raging epidemic. The prisoners are dying like flies."

"What kind of epidemic?"

"I don't know, but some of the guards have shown symptoms, and they were taken to the hospital. Now they want to know how this happened."

I did accompany the doctor to the British-American compound, and I saw a row of barracks nearby. The few patients who were waiting in the infirmary were dressed in neat khaki uniforms, and they appeared to be well nourished. I subsequently learned that they received a steady supply of Red Cross packages addressed to individual prisoners of war in that compound.


The Russian prisoner-of-war compound I saw only once. It happened on a Friday. The doctor returned from a house call. There were no patients in the waiting room, and the door to the doctor's office was open. He walked up to the locked cabinet and opened it to remove some articles. He was in a hurry, he told me, because he and his wife had a social engagement that evening. In late morning a shipment of drugs had arrived, and he said he would deliver them before going to dinner. Suddenly, his face red, he shouted, "Hedwig? Where is Hedwig?"

"She said she felt ill and needed to lie down," I answered. "She said she was going home."

"Ill, hmmm."

The doctor went into his apartment, and I proceeded with my office work. I heard the doorbell ring, someone was admitted, and there were sounds of agitated voices. Dr. Kostka rushed into the consultation room, opened drawers and closets, gathered instruments, and proceeded to throw everything into his bag. "Get your coat and come along," he ordered.

When I got to the car, I saw Frau Kostka sitting in the driver's seat. The doctor slumped into the passenger seat, and I sat in the back. Frau Kostka raced through the town and subsequently through some unfamiliar roads. We stopped in front of a row house and were met by a weeping woman. In back of her another woman was weeping and wringing her hands.

In the apartment, lying on a bed, apparently lifeless, was Hedwig. The doctor listened to her heart, shook his head in dismay, and thumped her chest several times. Then he straightened up and shouted for a clean pail filled with warm water and for a large basin. He forced Hedwig's mouth open and inserted a long, thin rubber hose. I held the other end of a seemingly endless hose, as high as my arm could reach. Frau Kostka filled a calibrated pitcher with water, then inserted a funnel into my end of the hose. "Now," the doctor signaled. While Frau Kostka emptied pitcher after pitcher into the funnel I held high over Hedwig's head, the doctor, his shirtsleeves rolled up, kept pumping Hedwig's stomach.

The doctor worked hard. He was perspiring and breathing laboriously. After several minutes, Hedwig started to gag and pull at the hose. "Oh no, you don't," he shouted. He was angry, and he commanded his wife to keep pouring the water. He kept count on the amount of liquid used, and when he was satisfied, he pulled out the hose. Hedwig threw up a gray liquid, which flooded the bed and the floor. When the doctor was sure that all the fluid had come out, he forced Hedwig to remain on her feet, even though all she wanted to do was to slump back onto her wet bed. Her face was green. She looked exhausted. Throwing a shawl over her shoulders, the doctor compelled her to walk around the small room, while I packed up the instruments we had used. By then I knew that Hedwig had taken an overdose of barbiturates. She had taken the drug from the doctor's locked cabinet. Hedwig's mother crossed herself and went down on her knees. The doctor must have walked Hedwig for more than twenty minutes, most of the time dragging her along. He was very angry, and he rebuked her for her conduct.

"So you were going to embarrass me," he told Hedwig. "Since I refused to be involved in an abortion, you decided to implicate me by committing suicide with drugs stolen from my office. And at a time when there is trouble coming at me from all sides. That is your gratitude for all I have done for you?"

He pushed Hedwig onto a chair and told her mother that Hedwig must sit, that she may not lie down. He asked the mother to prepare a cup of tea.

As we were leaving, Hedwig's father, carrying a metal lunch pail, appeared in the doorway. He did not greet us. He looked very tired, beyond caring.

"There is something I must drop off at the Russian camp," the doctor said. "I should have been there hours ago. I won't be long, and both of you are to remain in the car. The less you see the better off you will be."

We were traveling between rows of tall, barbed-wire fences. Sentries were standing on platforms of guard towers. The towers were lit, and machine-gun barrels were clearly visible. Huge dogs, leashed to chains and straining against them, were barking furiously. Though the doctor's car was well known, he was stopped several times. Each time he produced a pass. On my left was a huge open shed. There was some sort of roof, but no walls, and within was a mass of tightly packed people swaying against each other. They were the Russian prisoners of war—feet bound in rags, remnants of uniforms on skeletal frames, white naked flesh clearly visible. They were lurching in wet mud. A gangrenous stench invaded the car through the closed windows. I felt my stomach heave. I took deep breaths. I did not want to vomit in the car. Frau Kostka, her eyes tightly shut, held a handkerchief over her nose and mouth. Within seconds we had passed the shed, and the doctor stopped the car in front of a small building. He was gone for no more than ten minutes. To me it seemed like hours. Though the open shed was no longer within range of my vision, the image of the swaying mass of prisoners stripped of their humanity was engraved on my mind. While driving us back into town, Dr. Kostka never said one word. He stopped the car near the entrance to the tenement house in which I lived. Frau Kostka said, "See you in the morning."

I felt grateful to be alive. I was continually aware of the limitless power of Hitler's army of henchmen. Murderers, spies, and informers were the fuel that kept the Nazi machine running, and they were all around us. I prayed that I might be able to remain in my hideout until the end of the war. I affirmed my resolve to carefully assess my options whenever I needed to act or to speak. Spontaneity was my enemy: I had to guard against it.

Frau Kostka's mother lived in Katowitz, and the women visited each other at least once a week. Whenever Frau Ilse came to visit, she brought cooked delicacies for her daughter. When Frau Kostka visited Katowitz, she combined her social visit with business errands for the office. She purchased items we were unable to obtain in Myslowitz, and she delivered the specimens we could not process in the office to the central laboratory in Katowitz.

My salary covered most of our needs. After working for three weeks in the doctor's office, I was able to send a fifty-mark bill to Brigitte Schultz in Essen. I thanked her, and I wrote that her kindness had helped us reach our destination. I did not post our address, and I mailed the letter from Katowitz, when I was asked to deliver material to the laboratory. From a phone booth there, I called Frau Mandola. I asked her if she had news from her niece and if there was a letter for us from Jadwiga Dembicka. There were none, but Frau Mandola asked me to give her our address, and she promised that immediately upon receipt of a letter for us, she would mail it to Myslowitz. She asked me to please not call again.

Why had Mother not written? Where was she? Why was she unable to get a message to us? Was she alive? Or had she been discovered? Was she able to use the cyanide capsule? During the day, I kept these thoughts away. But at night, they were steady visitors. The new nightmares were even grimmer than the old ones. In my dreams I saw the swaying mass of creatures, no longer human, that I had glimpsed in the Russian prisoner-of-war camp. Among the swaying creatures were the recognizable faces of my aunts and uncles, of Eva and Dollek, and, after my telephone call to Frau Mandola, even of Mother.

Unless one of my nightmares woke up Stefan, I tried hard to keep my dark thoughts to myself. When I came home at night, I would talk about what had happened in the office. My days were never dull.

Stefan, whose photography work consisted of retouching glass-plate negatives, was unhappy in his job. He worked in a dark room in front of an easel, his head beneath a black felt cloth. With a variety of special pencils and blades, he erased lines and blemishes from the illuminated plate negatives and refined facial contours. He told me that photography in Warsaw had been much more advanced.

"The emphasis was on appropriate lighting at the time the portrait was taken," he said. "You study the face, and you position the lights for each sitting. In the Pawelek Studio, lights are stationary. Reflectors are turned on for each sitting, for illumination only. Then, by means of retouching, images are produced from which all marks of individuality have been erased."

Considering our precarious situation I would have thought that Stefan would be delighted with even a tedious job. It provided him with work papers and allowed him to work outside a labor camp. Still, I understood that we viewed our predicament on the basis of our different experiences and encounters. To avoid the snares and ploys designed to entrap me, I had acquired a kind of survival dexterity. Stefan had not been called on to develop such skills. I listened to him grumbling, and occasionally I reminded him that though the room he worked in was dark, it was also heated. Fortunately for Stefan, there were high stacks of plates that needed to be processed. The subjects of the portraits were mostly young soldiers, who either had departed, or were about to depart, for the front. Their families were eager to have the photographs.

Occasionally Stefan mentioned a young coworker by the name of Alice. On the first day of his employment, she had volunteered to be his interpreter. Whenever no one was within earshot, she would either make provocative statements or ask dangerous questions. She told Stefan to be careful because Herr Pawelek only pretended not to speak or understand Polish. She said that contrary to news reports, the German army was retreating on the eastern front. She assumed that Stefan had been an active participant in the Warsaw uprising, and she told him it was an achievement to be proud of. She said that the Communists were the only friends that Poles could rely on. I was deathly afraid that in the isolation of the darkened room, Stefan might succumb to Alice's invitation to confidentiality. I begged Stefan not to trust her, or her protestations of Polish patriotism. An inadvertent slip might topple the shaky structure of our existence.

When I met Alice, I realized that my suspicions were correct. She was in her late twenties, of dark complexion and sturdy build. I was struck by the apparent discord in her features. While her jaw was square and strong, her eyes, beneath heavy eyelids, were sly and evasive. She was knowledgeable and intelligent, yet she talked too much and too fast, and she ended most of her assertions with an inflection that invited comment. The chance meeting took place late on a Saturday afternoon as we were leaving the grocery store. We were carrying our allotment of cabbage and potatoes when Alice walked into the store. We stopped to exchange a greeting, and Alice, planting her legs firmly near the door, would not move. My eyes pleaded for Stefan to disengage. He had just managed to say that we must go home, when Alice said, "I can smell it, and it's going to get worse."

"Smell what?" Stefan asked.

"You can always smell it, and on clear evenings, you can see the black smoke coming from over there."

Alice pointed in a southerly direction, and I knew immediately what she meant. I was bathed in sweat. Until the encounter with Alice, references to the proximity of Auschwitz had been vague. Whole trainloads of prisoners of war from the Warsaw uprising had supposedly arrived in Auschwitz. The Poles, even those wanting to be designated as prisoners of war subject to Geneva Convention rules, were put to work. On several occasions I had heard the doctor say that everyone must work. It was the German modus operandi, and it was strictly enforced. Frequently there were veiled references to smoke. What was it that was always burning? The black smoke and that smell Alice had referred to?

It was a cold December, and diseases proliferated. Hedwig had returned to work. She had gotten her period, and all was well again. The doctor, disregarding his office hours, saw as many patients as time would allow, and when he had to leave the office, Hedwig and I did whatever we could to help the sick patients.

Jacques brought back the sterile glass cylinders the doctor had requested, containing stool specimens Jacques had gathered from patients in the French compound. The test tubes were sealed, and it was my job to register and label them before dispatching them to the Public Health Laboratory for analysis. The doctor advised me to wear gloves whenever I touched the tubes and to wash my hands thoroughly with disinfectant before returning to more routine office tasks. I tried to be meticulous. Whenever Jacques wanted to put the vials into my hand, I pointed to the test-tube rack and told him to insert them into the slots.

Jacques knew that we had come from Warsaw. Once, when we were alone, he said, "You don't have a chance, none of us do. They want to destroy us, all of us. Then the only people left will be them. Compared to the Russian compound, we have done rather well. Now, once again they cut our food ration, and by the time it's over, all of us will have died, either of hunger or disease."

It was the week before Christmas, but the Christmas spirit was nonexistent. There was no Christmas tree in the Kostka household, and I heard that though previously plans had been made to spend Christmas day with Frau Kostka's mother in Katowitz, these plans had now been cancelled. Frau Kostka was due to deliver the baby in February. She still had two months to go, but she was having a difficult time. It seemed to me that rather than walk, she dragged her heavy body from one room to the next. Dr. Kostka, whose complexion compared to the rest of us was always ruddy, had been diagnosed with high blood pressure. Frau Kostka, a nurse, had suspected it for a while, but the doctor having been declared fit for military service had assumed that he was in fact medically fit.

One morning when I came to work, the doctor told me that I should keep my coat on because he needed to send me to Katowitz. He gave me a package to deliver to the laboratory and money for both train and trolley fare. He said to go in and see his wife. Frau Kostka gave me a string bag containing a large parcel wrapped in brown paper and tied with cord. "I wrote my mother's name and address on the parcel," she said. "I just called her, and she is expecting you. She said that if you get there by one o'clock, she would give you a sandwich and a cup of coffee."

I lifted the bag. It was heavy, perhaps weighing more than ten pounds. I smiled as if to say that the weight was of no consequence. I carefully wrote out where I should go after leaving the terminal and the number of the streetcar to get to Frau Ilse's apartment. There were also some cosmetic items Frau Kostka wanted me to purchase in Katowitz because she was unable to obtain them in Myslowitz.

After delivering the specimens to the laboratory, I noticed a telephone booth in the lobby. I had to call the Mandola number, even though I had been told not to call. I needed to know that my mother was alive. I pretended that the main reason for the telephone call was our desire to obtain news from Janka, her niece and our friend. There was none. Then I asked if mail had arrived for us from Pani Dembicka. Frau Mandola said that no mail had arrived and reiterated that she would immediately forward mail addressed to us. She had no intention to hold on longer than necessary to anything written in Polish, she said. Couldn't I see what was going on all around us? I promised that I would not call again.

At twelve-twenty I took a bus that would take me to a stop where I could board a streetcar. Holding on to the strap I looked down and into the eyes of a girl sitting between two men clad in civilian clothes. All around me were passengers wearing the red Nazi armband on their sleeves and party insignia on their lapels. I tried hard not to look at the girl, yet I could feel her eyes unobtrusively but continuously seeking mine. Was it a warning? I shifted the package so that Frau Ilse's name and address were clearly visible. It would justify my presence on the bus. I breathed a sigh of relief when the bus reached my stop. I did not think I was being followed, but I felt certain that the girl had recognized me. I had no recollection of ever having seen her before.

Frau Ilse was glad to see me and happy to receive the package. It contained food. She told me that she had prepared a jar of cooked red cabbage for her daughter. She wanted me to tell her how her daughter was feeling and if she looked well.

"My poor girl," she said. "They cut down her milk allotment. What will happen to her when the doctor leaves? As if all that mobilization into the Volkssturm could turn the tide. I told them that this was no time to be pregnant, but they would not listen to me. They really believed that the doctor would be exempt from the military. I remember the last war. When things turned bad, all exemptions were not worth the paper they were written on."

I nodded but did not say a word. That was dangerous talk. Almost daily, I heard about people who were arrested because someone had accused them of remarking about the imminent collapse of the Third Reich.

"It's going to be the Bolsheviks," Frau Ilse stated firmly. "And we know what we can expect from them. It's folly to think that it will be the British and the Americans. They'll never get here in time. I told my daughter she should move in with me the day the doctor leaves, but she is determined to remain with Marta in Myslowitz."

I could hardly wait to get home and tell Stefan everything Frau Ilse had said. When I arrived at the Katowitz train terminal, I realized that I had arrived too early for my train. I did not want to be seen loitering in the terminal for twenty minutes. Just as I had done in Poland, I walked out of the station and out in the street. I endeavored to give the appearance of someone walking purposefully, engaged in an errand.

When I boarded the train for Myslowitz, I looked for a compartment that was relatively empty. I slid open the door and nodded to a middle-aged woman and to a soldier with a swollen face and a thick head bandage. Just as the train was about to move, I heard commands being shouted and the echoes of nail-studded boots. I heard compartment doors being slid open and shut. The door to our compartment slid open and the conductor stuck his face in. He motioned to the woman and me to move to the other side, next to the soldier. Into the compartment marched two Gestapo agents in leather coats with Nazi armbands. Between them was a male prisoner, his hands cuffed. The man was well dressed. He could not have been more than thirty years old. He was tall and handsome looking. The man sat across from me, and I did not dare look in his direction.

My neighbor stared at the three men. I buried my head in the periodical I had brought along from the doctor's office, and I prayed to God not to forsake me. The two Gestapo agents talked to each other over the bent head of the prisoner. Suddenly, one of them shouted, "What are you gaping at? Have you never seen a Jew? Out, out—you too."

The last two words were addressed to me. Within seconds I was standing, the handle of the string bag in my hand. "What are you carrying?" the Gestapo agent pointed to the bag. "Red cabbage," I stammered.

"Out," he screamed. As we were leaving the compartment, he motioned to the soldier, who also had gotten up to leave, that he was to remain. The woman and I walked down the train corridor. We looked into a few compartments, and when we could not find one that had two vacant seats, she indicated that we should remain standing at a window. The woman was visibly shaken. Tears were running down her cheeks. She dried her eyes and adjusted her hat. She asked me if I had heard how she had been screamed at. She wanted to know how far I was traveling. Myslowitz, I said.

"They are taking the poor sinner to Auschwitz," the woman confided. "I work in Katowitz, at the main post office. It never fails. Whenever I go home for a visit, there are always prisoners on the train being taken to Auschwitz. Most of the time it's Jews. I don't know where they find them. It's not that I would walk into their compartment. But I was there first, and anytime they want, they can just march in and throw you out."

"Yes, yes," I commiserated.

"They can do whatever they want. I have been stopped so many times. Each time they demand that I show them my documents. My identification card says that my work is indispensable and that it contributes to the war effort. Where do you work?"

"In a doctor's office. I am a medical assistant."

"That's good. I am glad there are some doctors left to care for the people at home. My doctor was drafted a year ago, and all his patients were assigned to a health station."

I delivered the red cabbage and the items I had purchased, and Frau Kostka asked me if all had gone well. She said I looked quite pale and recommended that I get a good night's sleep. My stomach was hurting, and all I wanted was to get my head onto a pillow. That night my stomach pain was so excruciating that poor Stefan woke up Frau Ptak and asked for her help. Together they warmed pot lids, and Stefan put them on my stomach. After several hours, the spasms eased. It felt as if my intestines had coiled into a knot, which the application of heat slowly unwound.

After Christmas when I returned to the office, I saw that the sign advising patients of the doctor's office hours had been removed. In its place was a notice informing patients that as of January 10, the doctor's office would be permanently closed. We did see patients during the Christmas week, but since their records were being transferred either to Dr. Bernard, the other physician in Myslowitz, or to the public health station, we tried to discourage patients from seeing Dr. Kostka. He said that he himself was not feeling well and that his "heart was no longer in it." Hedwig and I were kept busy packing drugs and instruments into padded cartons. We stacked the doctor's books and tied them up with strings.

In the Kostka apartment, a different type of packing was taking place. Frau Kostka and Marta, sometimes I also was called in to help, wrapped stemware and china in newspaper and packed them into cartons. Several cartons were filled with their two sets of silver service and silver serving utensils. In the late afternoon, Dr. Kostka filled the trunk of his car with the closed boxes, and accompanied by his wife, they departed for some destination. When the doctor returned, the trunk was empty. Each trip lasted about two and a half hours,

Dr. Bernard contacted Hedwig, and he asked her to work for him.

Dr. Kostka told me that he had made the arrangements, but that Dr. Bernard had not been courageous enough to hire me. "You can't blame him," Dr. Kostka said. "The noose is tightening, also tightening around his neck." The doctor told me that I still would be needed to tidy things up after he left. He said that I was a good worker, even though I was a Pole, and that his wife would continue to try and find work for me.

"So near the end, we don't want you to be put into one of those camps. Not you or your husband. And Krystyna, my wife will need all the help she can get. While you are working for us, you will be paid. There is much correspondence that needs to be expedited. My wife says she can't handle it. It would be good for her to be kept occupied, but I think you better take care of it."

## JANUARY 1945 ⚔ MYSLOWITZ, FORMERLY POLAND, NOW ANNEXED TO THE THIRD REICH

Frau Ilse came from Katowitz and attempted to comfort her distraught daughter. Frau Kostka felt that the doctor was not trying hard enough to get an additional deferment. She wanted him to be nearby at the time of delivery. How could they expect him to do front-line service with his type of medical record? she asked her mother. Frau Ilse repeated what she had said to me—that the Volkssturm could not possibly succeed when military power was failing. There was a feeling of despair in the Kostka household. Frau Kostka hardly ate, yet she was putting on weight. Tears ran incessantly from her eyes, and the doctor was concerned about a premature birth. Jacques delivered a new batch of stool specimens. This time he did confer with the doctor: There was an outbreak of typhus in the French compound.

When I came to work at eight o'clock the next morning, Marta met me at the door. She told me that the doctor, dressed in uniform, had left the previous evening. When I asked if he had to travel far, she said that all they knew was that he had gone by train. Frau Kostka was in bed and did not want to see anyone. I kept myself busy typing and filing, and I knew that within a short time, I would run out of work.

Stefan and I were sure that the end was imminent. No one told us. We had no access to a radio. Signs of an impending calamity were all around us—

the grim look on people's faces as they rushed about. The stores were empty; grocery shelves bare. People did not stop to exchange a greeting. Too many residents were carrying wrapped parcels, but they were not walking to the post office. Stefan told me that the studio was busier than ever. Sixteen-year-old boys were being inducted into the Volkssturm. Dressed in uniform, the young boys and their families were eager to have their pictures taken. Stefan said it is a sure sign of defeat when children are forced to fight a man's war.

I saw Frau Kostka only once. I was standing at the stove, sterilizing instruments, when she walked into the kitchen. I had not been feeling well. My stomach was aching as if swollen inside. Frau Kostka barely looked at me and ordered that I go home immediately and go to bed.

"Do you really not know that you have a fever?" she asked. After I came home, Stefan went to see Frau Kostka and came back later with a thermometer and medicine, which she advised I take. Stefan said that this time Marta did not have to interpret for him; Frau Kostka understood and spoke Polish like a native.

At about that time, a small parcel, addressed to us, was delivered to our address. It came from Katowitz, sent to us by Frau Mandola. The original package addressed to Frau Mandola had been dispatched from a post office in Schönbrun, Austria. Only the name of the sender, Jadwiga Dembicka, was listed; there was no address.

Stefan was jubilant. "They are from your mother. She's alive! That's what you wanted to know," he kept repeating over and over again. The package contained a pair of brown felt house slippers. A short note was attached to one slipper. It read, "It's such a cold winter. I have a premonition that these warm slippers will come in handy."

Stefan helped me sit up, and he put the slippers on my feet. I was too weak to stand and too weak to rejoice at the yearned-for good news. My fever was very high. Dr. Bernard was inundated with patients and was no longer making house calls. Stefan went to Frau Kostka and begged her to intercede for us. She succeeded; Dr. Bernard did come. I have only a vague recollection of him at my bedside, bending over me. Then I lost consciousness. Later I learned Dr. Bernard had said, "There is nothing I can do at this hour of the evening. It does not look good, but if your wife makes it through the night, you can call my office in the morning, and I will try and send an ambulance."

As a result of Frau Kostka's intervention, the ambulance arrived in late afternoon of the following day. I was delirious, and Stefan was not allowed to accompany me in the ambulance. The nurse who came with the ambulance told Stefan that they were taking me to a hospital in Katowitz, and she gave him the number of the streetcar he needed to take to reach it.

I think of those days when I lost consciousness as a time of stupor and delirium. I have distinct memories of moments of consciousness. I was in a white room, in a white bed, and I was aware of another occupied white bed in the room. There was a barred window in the room, and once while trying to focus on the barred window, I saw Stefan looking at me from the other side of the window. I heard thunder, or maybe artillery fire. Large bugs were crawling over my sheets. Then I slipped once again into a stupor.

# CHAPTER 14

# Liberation

One morning when I awoke, I realized I was alive and the fever was gone. I felt very weak, but when I touched my forehead, it felt cool. I saw that I was in a small ward with four beds. The other three beds were empty and stripped of linens. Huge lice, perhaps a quarter inch in size, were crawling over my white gown and my bedclothes. I reached for my hair. It was gone. In its place, I could feel a half-inch growth of stubbly hair. I attempted to call out, but I could not raise my voice above a whisper. When I tried to raise my head from the pillow, it fell back. I must have dozed off because when I opened my eyes again, I saw a cleaning woman, holding a mop and bending over a pail.

She was old, dressed in black, peasant fashion, with a black kerchief tied beneath her chin. When I spoke to her in Polish, she shook her head, but when I asked in Polish, "Do you speak Polish?" she nodded. I pointed at the lice crawling all over me, and she said, "Typhus." Body lice transmit typhus; I realized I must have gotten infected at the doctor's office.

The woman reached for her pail, ready to move on. I stopped her and asked if she could bring me a glass of water. She shrugged her shoulders, but remained standing.

"Where am I?" I asked. The woman spoke a dialect I could hardly make out, but I understood that I was in an isolation ward in a hospital in Katowitz. She made the sign of the cross and kept repeating, "The Germans are on the run, the Russians are chasing them. God be praised." It took me a while before I fully grasped the enormity of what she was saying. I fell into a restful sleep. When I woke up, I was fully aware that the world had changed. My enemy had been defeated, and I was safe.

A nurse, a Catholic nun, walked into the room. Speaking Polish, the nun said, "May you be with God." Dressed in a voluminous black habit and hood, she moved efficiently about me, as if no earth-shaking event had just taken place. She took my temperature and checked my pulse. "We must get you cleaned up before the doctor walks in," she said.

"Is it true that the Germans have left?" I asked.

"Yes," she said, and added. "You are in the typhus ward. They took their own, and they left you behind. Do you know when you were admitted?"

I told Sister that I did not know; I had been unconscious when I was brought to the hospital. Apparently, she knew this, but that was all that was known about me. There was no record of my admission. She told me that during the previous day and through part of the night, German army authorities had evacuated the hospital. They had taken with them all German patients, the German medical personnel, and the nursing staff. The only patients who remained in the hospital were a small group of foreign workers. In the early morning hours, she said, the Russian army had taken command of the hospital. When the Russian doctor asked to see the medical charts of the remaining patients, it was learned that the Germans had taken all medical records with them when they fled.

Sister told me that since I was admitted to the typhus ward, I would be subject to a specified quarantine period before I could be released. She thought that I should consider this an advantage, because I was in very weakened condition. While in the hospital, I would be kept warm, and I would be fed. When Sister gave me the longed-for water, I could barely muster the energy to keep the straw in my mouth. A short while later, she came back with a cup of barley gruel. When I hesitated, she said, "You must eat this if you want to live. You do want to live?"

Indeed, I thought, Sister had no idea how much I wanted to live. While I ate, tears ran down my cheeks and onto my gown and the sheet. There were torrents of tears, and I could not stop them. I was alive. Despite meticulous enforcement of an unswerving Nazi decree that every single Jew be hunted, found, and destroyed, I had prevailed.

Shortly after eating the warm gruel, I was lifted off the bed and onto a gurney. I was sponge bathed, and the stubble of hair on my head was washed and rinsed with kerosene. I looked down at my naked body and noted that my breasts had disappeared. My arms and legs were spindly thin. Sister was kind but curt. She could not discuss my illness, she said, because the Germans had taken all the records.

Everything, even the mattress, was removed from my bed. The bed frame as well as the floor were washed with kerosene, then washed a second time with disinfectant. I learned that wounded Russian soldiers had been brought to the hospital and that various precautions were being taken to protect them from bacterial infections. Sister informed me that the physician in charge was aware of my presence. Since the progress of my disease could not be charted, the doctor had ordered that for the time being I remain in the isolation ward.

"For how long?" I asked.

"I cannot say. It is not up to me." Sister responded.

"Will I be allowed to see the doctor?"

"Yes, he said he would look in, perhaps this evening."

"Could I see a mirror?"

"For that you will have to wait until you leave the ward. It's better that way. You are Polish, yes? Where did you come from?"

"I am from Warsaw."

"Oh, so it's from Warsaw. You have been through much suffering, my child. What an ordeal! Dropping bombs on helpless people. For two months, yes?"

"Yes, it was a difficult time," I agreed.

I asked Sister if it would be possible to communicate with my husband, and I told her that he lived in Myslowice. Myslowice was the original Polish name of the town, now restored.

"That will not be possible, not right now," she advised. "All means of transportation have been severed. The Germans ripped up the tracks, and they cut telephone cables before they left. I understand much damage has been done. We must be patient," she concluded.

A Russian doctor accompanied by a Polish assistant came to see me. He was my first contact with the Russian people. The khaki color of his uniform was similar to that of the Polish army. The Russian doctor wore a loose-fitting tunic, gathered at the waist with a broad leather belt. There were ruby red patches on his epaulettes, and a number of medals were pinned to his chest. He was of sturdy build, and of olive complexion. His face was wrinkled. Between his eyes and his mouth were deep lines that gave the face a square appearance. When I saw his eyes, I knew that I was safe. His eyes were human.

"We found a laboratory record that confirmed your illness," he said. "You were brought in with typhus." Addressing me in Russian, the doctor had clearly enunciated each word, and I understood what he said even before his assistant had translated.

"Doctor," I ventured. "I am so very grateful that the Russian army prevailed. I would like to express my deeply felt gratitude for my liberation."

"So. I am glad you know. A lot of Russian blood was spilled."

"I am very sorry about that."

"Are you native to this area?"

"No. I am from Warsaw. We were put on cattle cars and forcibly evacuated."

"I know," the doctor snapped.

I must have said something wrong, because suddenly I felt dismissed. The doctor and his assistant were walking toward the door. "Doctor, when will I be able to leave the hospital?" I called after him, adding, "My husband lives nearby, and I have not heard from him. I am alone. My family has been scattered, perhaps murdered by the Nazis. I must look for them, and I would like to leave the hospital."

"We still need to take some tests. There has to be a period of quarantine, at least for another ten days." The assistant translated but also augmented what the doctor had said. "Don't be too anxious to leave," he cautioned. "While you are here, you will be fed. The Nazis did not leave even a morsel of food behind, and you can't expect the Russian army to take up the slack when they have yet to win the war. In your present condition, you would not last long on the outside."

"Would you have a Polish newspaper, or a book I could read?"

"I'll ask around. Those Nazi killers, they left us a starving population, and they took all the coal. We are just about managing to heat the hospital. You understand?"

"Yes, I do, and I appreciate what you said. I will do my best to recover while in the hospital. I feel quite weak. Perhaps I would get stronger if I could get up and walk around."

"Yes, you could try and walk a little. Perhaps tomorrow with Sister. I must go now."

"I have no clothes."

"I can't help you. Ask Sister, she might be able to come up with something."

Through the barred window of my room I looked out onto a courtyard. There was much snow, and at night, when the wind howled, icy gusts invaded the room. Though Sister had been able to supply me with an additional blanket, it was thin, and at night, I could only keep warm when I drew the blankets over my head and used my breath to heat the shallow tent. Throughout the day the ward was heated. Using the two blankets, I carefully walked around the room. Sister brought the New Testament for me to read.

One morning, while reading in bed, I felt someone looking at me. It was Stefan. He smiled at me through the barred window. I climbed out of bed, wrapped myself in the blanket, and walked over to the window. I was barefoot. Stefan lifted his arm and unwrapped something. He showed me the slippers my mother had sent. We tried to communicate with our eyes and hand motions. We could not hear each other, and I was so eager to convey that I was happy to be alive. I wanted to tell Stefan that during this last stretch of my clandestine journey, I could not have survived without him. I wanted to express my gratitude. Stefan's message was that I should eat, that I should be patient, and that he would come again. After he left, Sister brought in the slippers, my pajamas, and a sweater.

The next time I saw Stefan, he walked in with my winter coat over his arm and a bag containing my clothes. In his hand he held a dismissal voucher issued by the Soviet Army Hospital Administration.

Rail communication had not yet been restored, and we would have to walk several kilometers to a streetcar stop. "For the time being," he told me, "transportation to and from Myslowice begins and ends at that distant point." He was not sure that I could muster the strength to walk that far, but I assured him that I could. Although we walked very slowly, we had to stop every few minutes so that I could gather my strength. Whenever I stopped to rest, I rejoiced at the overwhelming reality of being free. I was able to breathe in the brisk air without being afraid.

It was a dreary day. There were dark clouds on the horizon and an occasional shower of snowflakes that melted on contact. I felt quite weak and thought that were Stefan to remove his arm, I would topple over. Yet all along, I was smiling within at the realization that I had survived. Whenever I saw a Russian soldier, and there were many, I experienced an emotional surge of gratitude. I wanted to run over and hug and kiss him. I told Stefan about the deep gratitude I felt and how much I wanted to express it.

"You'll get your chance," was his rejoinder. "There are many of them, and they are all around us. They will be with us for a while, so you don't have to hurry."

I scrutinized every Russian soldier I saw. Some were on foot, but most of them were in the open trucks that passed us traveling in either direction. The streets were teeming with civilians, and the trucks were moving slowly. Some of the soldiers waved to us. I noted with pleasure that almost always when I smiled, the smile was returned. There were a considerable number of female Russian soldiers. Occasionally I saw soldiers in Polish military uniform. I wanted to speak to them to find out where they had come from, but Stefan did not want to stop. We had walked for approximately two hours, and he wanted to reach the streetcar stop before dusk.

From a distance I could tell that we had reached our destination. We joined the throng of people who were lined up waiting to board the expected streetcars. Several Russian soldiers, arms resting on handheld automatic weapons, were examining bundles and checking documents. They were looking for Nazi deserters hiding among the civilian population. It was all very confusing. Several weeks ago, the only language being spoken was German, now the languages I heard were either Polish or Russian. Stefan pointed to a Polish soldier who stood in line ahead of us.

"Look at all those medals," he said. "They depict his valor while a soldier in General Berling's First Polish Army. I can't help wondering if the Berling Brigade was part of the Soviet army that was stationed across the Vistula while Polish people were dying by the thousands. They were so close they could watch us through their binoculars."

"I don't want to think about that now," I responded. "I am so grateful that they are here. For us the war is over. Not for them. They are still fighting. They have to go on fighting until the Nazis are defeated. Defeated forever."

Frau Ptak, now Pani Ptak, was happy to see me. She was excited and wanted to talk to us right away and began babbling incoherently. We told her to wait until morning.

The next morning, feeling more rested, I motioned that she sit down and slowly and clearly tell me what was on her mind. She asked us, both Stefan and me, to intercede on her behalf with both the Russian authorities and the delegation of Polish personnel that had taken charge of the town administration. She told me that she was of Polish origin and had always been a proud Pole. She had concocted a German ethnic link to retain her small apartment and continue to receive her widow's pension.

"I took you in," she said. "No one wanted Polish people in their apartment, but I took you in. I always treated you well, and I even shared my food with you. Now they are going to chase me out, and where am I going to go? I want to die here, in my own bed."

"Who is trying to chase you out?" I asked.

"All my neighbors are packing up. It's because they said that they don't want the Volksdeutsch people to remain here. Since they have pledged their loyalty to the Third Reich, they should continue to be loyal. They are advised to pack up and go to the German Reich. I don't want to go to the Reich. I want to remain in my apartment."

The old lady was in an agitated state, but after some patient prodding, I learned that no one had threatened Pani Ptak with eviction from her apartment, but that indeed there was a general panic afoot. When the Nazis invaded Poland, they had immediately annexed several border territories, and Myslowice was part of the annexed territory. Poles were forcibly evacuated into occupied Poland from all the annexed territories. The so-called ethnic German, the Volksdeutsch, moved into the houses and apartments vacated by the fleeing Poles. It was anticipated that the Poles who had been forced to flee would now want to return to their prewar homes and resume their prewar lives. Since Pani Ptak had occupied her two-room apartment before the war, and I was certain that no one would be able to accuse her of having taken part in atrocities committed by the Nazis, her existence would not be threatened. I tried to reassure her, and I said we would take up her cause should the necessity arise. Though we did manage to calm the distraught lady, she kept repeating that she felt threatened.

I had an overpowering desire to go to Auschwitz. I felt that I could walk the fifteen kilometers. Stefan told me that it was not fifteen kilometers, but rather more than twenty. He said that the only way to get there was on a Russian truck, and they were not about to take civilian passengers. The Russian army traveling on trucks and other motorized vehicles was traveling west. The movement of masses of Russian soldiers heading in a westerly direction seemed incessant.

I wanted Stefan to tell me about the liberation of Myslowice by the Russian armed forces. His experience was similar to mine. One evening, perhaps the twenty-sixth of January, he was not certain of the date, there was intermittent artillery fire, and he stayed in the apartment. The artillery exchange accelerated during the day and continued into the night, and in the morning, the Germans were gone and the Russian army was in charge of the town.

"When were you able to leave the apartment?" I wanted to know. "Were you afraid?" How did you manage to communicate, since you do not speak Russian?"

"I only approached the Polish soldiers," Stefan explained. "They told me I would have to wait before embarking on a journey to Katowice. I said that you were in the hospital and that I needed to go and take you home. You know Krysia, I came once, immediately before the liberation. I stood at the window and looked into your room. You were unconscious when the ambulance picked you up to take you to Katowice, and when I came to see you on the following day, you were still unconscious. I was very concerned."

I told Stefan that I remembered seeing him looking at me through the barred window. I reported the Russian doctor's reaction when I had mentioned that I was from Warsaw. I felt immediately that I had struck a discordant note. Stefan confirmed my perception. He had spoken to a number of Polish soldiers who were part of General Berling's brigade, the Polish battalion fighting alongside the Russian army, and he learned that mentioning Warsaw produced an adverse reaction.

"Of course, I am grateful," Stefan said. "They did liberate us. Neither the British nor the American army came to our rescue. It was the Russian army that chased the Germans from our land. Still, with regard to Warsaw, there is this festering wound. The Nazis killed our people and destroyed our city, the capital of Poland, while the Russians sat on the other side of the river, watching. Now they say they could not cross because they were waiting for supplies and additional manpower. The fact is that they refused to come to our rescue because the Polish underground had made its initial arrangements with the Polish government-in-exile in London. Was that a good enough reason? Are we supposed to forget all that?"

There was a vast difference between our respective experiences during the Nazi occupation of Poland. Aside from acquaintances who had been in the Polish army at the time of the invasion and who, it was assumed, had made their way to England, Stefan did not personally know anyone who had disappeared never to be seen again. I was grateful that for me the Russian army had come in time. There were other Jews who had been evading the ever-tightening noose of the Nazi killers. Did the Russian army arrive in time for them too? Did they arrive in time to rescue some of my relatives who had ostensibly been transported to work camps? Had Eva succeeded in staying alive? Was my mother alive? These were the questions that haunted me.

I had experienced the spiritual grandeur of the Warsaw uprising and the horror of its defeat, but I did not feel Stefan's anger. I did not share his distrust of the Russians. He now had met a number of Polish soldiers who had been taken into captivity after the defeat of the Warsaw uprising and who had subsequently been liberated by the invading Russian army. Some of them had joined their Polish comrades in the Berling Brigade to help defeat the Nazis. They had suffered mightily in Nazi forced labor camps, but they were alive.

The Russian command post in Myslowice was housed in the town's municipal building. It was called Komendatura, and the Russian officer in charge was called the commandant. Dressed in all the warm clothes I owned, I finally managed to take a short walk. There was a long line of people near the door to the Komendatura. Stefan explained that they were waiting for validation of their documents. They wanted to establish that their avowed allegiance to the German people had been a ruse to help them live through the Nazi occupation.

"That is not a task the Russians can deal with," Stefan said. "Too few of them know our language." Stefan told me that as soon as the Russians took over, the Volksdeutsch disappeared. Now everyone is Polish. Yet, they are the same people who have been here all along. Those who had means of transportation, or had appropriate connections within Germany, have left. Stefan thought that many of the ethnic Germans who had departed preferred to be under the jurisdiction of the British and American armies that were rapidly advancing from the west.

"How about Frau Kostka, Marta, and Hedwig?" I asked.

"Frau Kostka and Marta are gone. I don't know about Hedwig," Stefan said. "But do you remember Alice from the studio?"

"I do indeed. What about her?"

"Oh, she is fine, very well indeed. She now has a job in the municipal office, something to do with security. Funny, she is in fact a Communist. I did not believe her, and you suspected her of being an agent provocateur for the Nazis. She was walking with a young man when we met, and she introduced us. The young man asked me if the Kostkas were Nazis."

"What did you answer?"

"I told him the truth. I said that we never had an indication that they were Nazis. I said you had told me the doctor treated the Poles that came to see him in the same caring manner that he treated the Germans. I told him both of us thought they were decent people."

I remained firm in my belief that Alice was not a person who could be trusted, regardless of whether she was Volksdeutsch or a Communist. Both Stefan and I felt that the inquiry was perhaps related to someone eager to occupy the Kostka apartment. They had been very kind to us, and we were determined not to help others take over their apartment.

Stefan obtained a loaf of bread from a Russian storehouse. When he showed the officer in charge my dismissal slip from the hospital, the Russian motioned for Stefan to step aside and wait. When the bread distribution ended, the Russian officer brought a cup filled with dried beans and poured them into Stefan's pocket. He put two onions in Stefan's hand. Pani Ptak helped both with the cooking and the eating of the precious food.

The reports from Auschwitz were devastating. The liberating Soviet army had found mounds of skeletons, and among them human forms that, at the moment of liberation, still showed a flickering spark of life. Outside the camp, on a road going west, Russian soldiers discovered emaciated former inmates cowering in the snow. Among them were the frozen remains of dead prisoners. They were the Jews the Nazis had been unable to kill before the crematoriums were dismantled. Without food or shoes on their feet, the Nazis had been marching them to some unknown destination. When the Russian army came close, the Nazi guards ran away. Birkenau, a nearby camp, had housed

Jewish women inmates. For several weeks before the liberation, people living near Birkenau reported that human bodies were being burned there day and night. Black smoke coming from Birkenau chimneys had enveloped all the neighboring communities.

Stefan tried to dissuade me from my desire to go there and see for myself. We spoke with soldiers who had been to both Auschwitz and Birkenau, and they agreed with Stefan that the walk was arduous and that I would not find what I was looking for. We were told there was no one left in Birkenau. The Russian army had transported some Auschwitz survivors to nearby shelters. Mounds of skeletons had been buried. We heard that in Auschwitz there still remained a number of men who had accepted whatever food and supplies the Russians could spare but who had refused to be evacuated. It was these men that I wanted to see. I wanted to ask them if anyone had come across at least one of my many relatives who had disappeared into the camps. I wanted to ask about Eva. I felt that any kind of information that I could obtain would be a starting point for my search.

Stefan tried to persuade me to wait for more favorable weather, but I disagreed. The days continued to be cold, wet, and windy, and I could delay no longer. The road leading to Auschwitz was not well traveled. Occasionally, a truck filled with Russian soldiers would pass us. When one of them stopped in response to our hand motions, we managed to convey to him where we were going. He in turn motioned that he could take us for only two kilometers, then he would have to turn off and go in a different direction. True to his word, he stopped ten minutes later and dropped us off. It would have taken us an hour to get to that point. The realization that we were not the only people on the road was very reassuring. We walked for several kilometers without seeing anyone coming toward us from the opposite direction. More and more people were walking in the same direction as we were. They must have come through side roads from other localities, because when we started, we were the only people on the road.

"Look," Stefan said, "over there." He was pointing at a truck that was parked on the side of the road. "The Russian army is driving American vehicles."

"How do you know that?" It was no different, I thought, than the other khaki army vehicles I had seen since the liberation. Stefan pointed to the tires. The marking on the tires said U.S.A.

Oh my God, I thought, the trucks came all the way from America, and that's where my father lives. For the first time since the liberation, I thought of the possibility of reuniting with my father. Throughout the years of persecution I had conjured up images of my father coming to my rescue. During periods of my greatest despair, the thought of seeing my father again gave me the courage to once more to evade my pursuers. Perhaps now I did not dare rejoice until I knew that my mother and Eva were alive. Already in the hospital, my thoughts had revolved around the means I would pursue to find them. I had not yet retrieved the tiny hidden muslin square wrapped around my father's address in New York. I had hidden my talisman behind the peeling wallpaper in our room. I determined that I would now dislodge it and commit my father's address to memory.

A group of women volunteers were in the process of organizing the procession of people who were walking toward the Auschwitz camp. They wanted to greet the former prisoners with hot coffee and bread. Stefan and I were eager to help. We were directed to gather rocks from nearby fields to build fire rings. We lit fires and piled bread onto a makeshift table obtained from the Russian commissary, a symbolic offering to the resurrected inmates.

I saw them from a distance. Old men, dressed in rags and dragging their feet, were walking toward us. They were the liberated inmates who wanted to leave the camp on foot. They had not wanted to be part of a group transport to what one of them called a holding pen. Someone said *Muselman,** the name for those skeletal survivors of the concentration camp. It was the first time that I heard the word in connection with Auschwitz survivors. I forgot that I was supposed to greet them with a mug of coffee in my hand. I ran to meet them. Stefan stayed behind. Their fragility was an overwhelming sight. In ragged striped prison pajamas, ghostly forms that once were men came lurching and shuffling down the road. Death was written on their faces and in their skeletal frames.

I went from one figure to the next. I was crying, and everything I wanted to say got stuck in my throat. There was something strange in their eyes; they

--------

* German term meaning "Muslim," widely used by concentration camp prisoners to refer to inmates who were on the verge of death from starvation, exhaustion, and despair. The origin of the term is unclear.

did not acknowledge me. Their eyes weren't vacant, but rather closed off from the present. One had the impression that these eyes had seen that which no human being is supposed to know. I kept repeating the surnames of my relatives—Weissberger, David, Rinder—but the forward lurching movement never slackened and there was an almost imperceptible negative response. I instantly realized that I must not touch, that I may not get too close. Instinctively I comprehended the brittleness of the emaciated figures I approached, and I understood that all their available energy was needed for the task of forging ahead. Helplessly I stood by and watched in wonder this response to a primal urge. The survivors were going back to where once had been a home and a family.

The volunteers who had planned and organized the greeting were totally unnerved. It was beyond anything they had been led to expect. I did not feel that the former inmates intentionally spurned the offering of hot coffee and bread, but that they acted in concert with a fundamental need to reach their goal.

Perhaps thirty or forty males had passed us, but I had not seen a single female. I walked up to a man who was holding the hand of a boy who could not have been more than eleven years old. I asked, first in Polish and then in German, Where are the women? The man shook his head but did not answer. Staggering toward us were two old men. They were leaning against each other for support. One of them was dragging a lame leg, and he looked as if he was about to fall. Stefan rushed forward and helped the man sit down on a bench we had placed alongside the road. His companion wore dark glasses, and only when I saw his groping hands did I realize that he was blind.

The arduous walk had exhausted their strength, and the two men gratefully accepted the hot coffee we offered. We learned that Andre was brought to Auschwitz from Lyon, France, and that due to an untreated eye injury, he had lost all vision in his left eye. An inflammation in the right eye obscured what little vision was still remaining. He wanted to get back to France as soon as possible to obtain appropriate medical care. His frail companion had left the camp confines against advice of the Russian physician. His name was Ole, he was from The Hague in Holland, and his almost lifeless body had been found on the road by a passing Russian patrol and taken to a makeshift camp hospital. Initially, he was told that he was suffering from a severe case of frostbite. Subsequently, when the wound in his leg continued to fester, the diagnosis was changed. Amputation of the leg below the knee had been discussed, and Ole would not hear of that.

Neither Andre nor Ole understood a word of Polish, but both of them spoke German. I asked them how they would manage to get through the war zone. The Allied forces had already liberated Holland and France, but to get there, the men would have to travel through German territory, where fierce fighting was still in progress. Andre said that they were planning to take the southern route, perhaps through Austria, to avoid German territory. Both Ole and Andre were well informed, and Stefan was eager for news from the world beyond the confines of our provincial town. There were many questions he wanted me to ask. He suggested that Andre and Ole stay overnight with us in our room in Myslowice. Awaiting them was an arduous journey. Our offer was rejected. The men did not want to delay.

The men had met in Auschwitz in 1943, and throughout the remaining months of their imprisonment, they had made great efforts to stay in touch with each other. Both men were in their middle thirties, though at first glance it had seemed to us that they were in their late sixties. We exchanged whatever information we had been able to obtain, and we agreed that it was our common understanding that all of occupied Europe had been liberated and that the German Wehrmacht was now fighting on German soil.

When I told Andre and Ole that I was Jewish, they wanted to know how I had managed to survive. I learned that Ole, a banker, was a Christian and a member of the Dutch Reform Church. He was married to a Jewish woman, and he had refused to abandon her in spite of Nazi threats to his life and liberty. Despite his vigorous attempts to keep his family together, his wife and five-year-old son were forcibly taken from him. When he attempted to find out where they had been taken, he was arrested and subsequently transported to Auschwitz.

Andre, a French engineer, was Jewish. His Christian wife had been urged to abandon her husband, and then threatened when she refused. Shortly after the German invasion of France, his wife had taken their two children and had hidden them among her relatives who lived in the Provence region. When Andre was arrested, his wife and her relatives had tried to have him released. Once transported to Auschwitz, Andre lost all contact with his family. Upon meeting, the two men had bonded in friendship, and they had agreed to look out for each other. There was, however, a difference in their common plight.

Andre would look for his wife among her Christian relatives, and he knew where to find them, whereas Ole would first need to unravel the devious routes the Nazis had taken to hide the mass murder of a people. Andre repeated in front of us the promise he had previously made to Ole. He said that he would delay his return to Lyon and would instead accompany Ole to Holland. He would not leave him until he was certain that Ole could receive the appropriate medical care.

Rail service in Myslowice had not yet been restored, but we said that we would lead the two friends to the streetcar that would take them to Katowice, where we hoped they would be able to board a train traveling west. It was an arduous walk for Ole, and we had to stop quite often for him to rest his leg. Andre told us that during the past months, the women had disappeared from Auschwitz, and that in time it was learned they had been taken to a nearby camp called Birkenau, ostensibly to work. There had been rumors, Andre said, that Birkenau was equipped with gas chambers, crematoriums, and other methods of facilitating death. He said that there I would not even find the remains of former inmates. All traces leading to identification of the prisoners had been obliterated. Nazi guards charged with that gruesome task had done a very thorough job.

"It did not take me long to become acquainted with camp metaphors, a language the Nazis devised to obscure their murderous scheme," Andre explained. "All the guards were sadists, and when during this last year, the Germans realized that they were losing the war, they were determined to kill every inmate of the camp and to obliterate all traces of their monumental crime. Every day, for months, I have lived my last day. When the Gestapo could no longer proceed with murder by asphyxiation, they organized a death march. After the Russian army liberated the camp, soldiers found Ole in a ditch next to the road. He could not walk. Probably he collapsed, and when he fell down, the Nazi guards left him in the road." Andre told us that the friends thought it a good omen that they had found each other, and that once again they would be able to help each other.

We had determined that it was important for Andre to conserve his energy. Ole walked supported by a stick on one side and by Stefan's arm on the other. I held out my arm to Andre, and I asked him to let me be his guide. The four of us stood at the streetcar stop, holding hands, clinging to each other. In so short a time, we had revealed so much of ourselves. We had told them about our unregistered marriage license, the kind priest who had agreed to help us, and the German civilians flooding back into Germany from the once-conquered territories. When we saw the approaching streetcar, we felt as if we were leaving family members, and it was hard to let go. We embraced and exchanged addresses, aware that we would not meet again.

Walking back to our room, I held tightly onto Stefan's arm. Within the last few hours, I had found and lost friends; however, I had made no progress in the search for my family. Later, when I was able to access the Auschwitz camp, the only information I obtained was that transports of Jews from the Krosno and Bochnia ghettos had not arrived in Auschwitz. I did, however, learn that both within the occupied Polish territory as well as the part of Poland that had been annexed to the Third Reich, a network of camps had been constructed for the sole purpose of annihilating the Jewish people.

Since leaving Warsaw, aside from Andre, I had not met another Jewish person. Still, I reasoned, I was alive. There was the Jewish prisoner on the train in Katowice who must have been in hiding,. Why couldn't Eva still be alive? Of the many relatives who had embraced us when we arrived in Poland and whom I had come to love, there must be some who had managed to outwit the murderers. In my mind, I prepared my travel itinerary for when public transportation going east would be restored. In February 1945, travel restrictions did not permit civilian passengers to board a train. The Russian army had requisitioned all trains for the transport of soldiers and military supplies.


MARCH 1945 ≈ MYSLOWICE, LIBERATED POLAND

Getting food occupied all our waking hours. There was none. The Germans had taken nearly all the food with them when they fled. Storage depots were empty, as were the shops. Still, if someone possessed an item of value, perhaps linens or kitchen utensils, it could be bartered for food. But we had next to nothing to barter. Stefan bartered his fountain pen for bread, and a female Russian soldier gave me some soup when I offered her the set of combs I used to pin up my hair. Our only other resource was the Russian military, but their supplies were meager.

On a Thursday afternoon, as we climbed the stairs to Pani Ptak's apartment, we were met on the landing by our incoherent landlady. The woman was hysterical, shouting and cursing both in German and in Polish, and not until we calmed her down did we learn what had happened. "They took everything, everything," she sobbed, "and from your room too. I told them that you were Poles from Warsaw, but they just laughed. They would not listen to me. They walked in and took whatever they wanted, and then they left."

"Who took everything?" Stefan asked.

"They did."

*They* did not refer to a roaming band of thieves, we learned, but to the Russian soldiers, our liberators. Our room was stripped bare of all our meager possessions. Our few pieces of clothing, my underwear, the only other pair of stockings I owned, Stefan's galoshes, and the blanket we had borrowed from Frau Kostka. Everything was gone. I was beside myself with anger, and I determined to retrieve our belongings. Hatless, my coat over my shoulders, I ran down the stairs. Stefan tried to stop me, but I would not listen. I headed straight for the Komendatura, the Russian authority in charge of maintaining order. I rushed past the guard at the door and into a long corridor.

An officer rose from behind a desk. "What is it you want?" he asked. He was holding a pencil in his right hand. In an awkward combination of Polish and the little Russian I had acquired, I stated my grievance. "While I was absent," I stammered, "Russian soldiers forced their way into my room and stole all my belongings. I am Jewish. I have been persecuted and robbed by the Nazis for the past eight years. They took everything from me. I lost my family. And now the Russians, too?"

"Come with me," the officer said. Pointing with his pencil, he indicated that I walk ahead of him. I thought we were going to a storage room where I would find our clothes. He opened a door and motioned with the pencil. "In there," he said. I hesitated and felt a little shove from behind. As I stumbled into the dark room, I heard him say in a stern tone, "That will teach you that Russian soldiers don't steal."

The door was slammed shut, locked from the outside, and I found myself in a small windowless cell. The folly of my rash undertaking became abundantly clear, and I turned the momentary rage I had felt against the Russian soldiers on myself. I wept and berated myself. How could I permit myself to become so hysterical that I thought I could storm this bastion of martial law? Could I have succeeded had my approach been more circumspect? Hours later, when a guard opened the door, I rushed toward the exit and collided with an officer of high rank. In an instant he drew out his saber and stretched it across the open door barring my flight.

"Yes?" he asked. "And who are you running from?" He was a Russian who spoke Polish. I took a deep breath to calm my nerves and with as much composure as I could muster, I told my captor what had happened. Throughout, the guard outside stood at attention. I was pretty sure, though not certain, that I was addressing the Russian commandant of Myslowice. Structuring my sentences carefully, I suggested I had been a victim of a misunderstanding. The commandant nodded, as if to say that he understood my dilemma.

Speaking in accented Polish, he said, "I am sorry this happened to you. Our soldiers are at liberty to take from the German enemy whatever they need. Had you been there to explain, nothing belonging to you would have been taken. But now it is out of my hands. Whatever you are looking for you will not find here. Do you understand what I am saying?"

I indicated that I did. "It was just a few pieces of clothing and a blanket I had borrowed. I would like to retrieve the blanket," I explained, "because our room is very cold, but I understand."

"I am glad you do," was his response. "This is not a collection center for used clothes." The commandant sheathed his saber. There was a smile in his eyes as he turned and walked away.

When I stepped out into the dark street, I saw Stefan walking toward me. He said that he had not thought it prudent to come into the Komendatura to look for me. He told me that he had been waiting for an hour and forty minutes hoping that I would come out. He did not want to stand close to the guard, but throughout he had walked back and forth within sight of the building, watching and worrying. He had seen the officer draw the saber, and he had heard my voice.

"If you don't watch out," he reprimanded, "you will wind up in Siberia."

We had heard rumors of disappearing Germans, Volksdeutsch, and even some Poles. There were rumors of transports to Siberia, and Stefan said that the Bolsheviks were known for acting first and thinking later. I agreed that Stefan had been prudent to not come looking for me. Being male and a Pole from Warsaw was not an asset. Stefan feared the Russians much more than I did. He could not have understood that, while detained in that dark cell, I never for an instant feared for my life or my liberty.

We needed to find work. Ethnic Germans were leaving Myslowice, and those who remained, unless cleared of explicit Nazi collaboration, were not permitted to open up their shops. It was understood that almost all stores, and apartments, presently occupied by ethnic Germans, had belonged to Polish residents who had been forced to flee the annexed territory. Now, once again, the apartments, stores, and workshops were available to displaced Poles. When Stefan learned that Herr Pawelek would not be permitted to reopen the Cherny photography studio, Stefan applied to the district office in Katowice for a permit to open the store.

We both had agreed that we did not want to remain in that part of Poland any longer than was necessary. Stefan wanted to get back to Warsaw, and I needed to be in a metropolitan city where, in time, an American embassy or consulate would once again be established. In the meantime, we reasoned Stefan could take portraits of Russian and Polish soldiers and barter the photographs for groceries. We would remain in our room in the Ptak apartment. We had no money to pay the rent, and since the arrival of the Russian troops, Pani Ptak had not asked for payment. Whenever we were able to obtain food items, we shared them with our landlady. Moreover, she was certain that having legitimate Poles in her home would be an asset in case someone accused her of a misdeed during the four-year tenure of the Germans.

Our need to work was urgent, and Stefan attempted several times to inquire regarding the state of his application. Something was amiss. Herr Pawelek's application to open the studio had been denied. The store remained closed, but our permit had not been granted. Nothing seemed to be wrong with Stefan's application, and yet it was not being processed. Subsequently, and in a roundabout way, Stefan learned that a member of the Cherny or Pawelek family would shortly be arriving from Poland.

After receiving this information, which had not been easy to obtain, Stefan withdrew his application. During the several weeks of his employment in the Cherny studio, Herr Pawelek had shown himself to be a decent person, and Stefan had no intention of getting involved in a family feud. However, this time, before making an application for a permit to open up an abandoned photography studio in another town, Stefan wanted to be certain that the previous owner really had fled to Germany and the studio was in fact abandoned. He found a vacant photography studio in the town of Swietochlowice. Though the town was nearby, one needed to take two streetcars to get there. It was a time of great upheaval, and transportation was difficult. Streetcars often broke down and were taken out of circulation. It would not be possible to conduct a business in Swietochlowice and keep our room in Pani Ptak's apartment.

Time was of the essence, and we tried hard to move matters along. We found a vacated apartment in Swietochlowice within walking distance of the abandoned photography studio. We returned home from the district office in Katowice, pleased with our recent accomplishments. We had successfully managed to register for temporary occupation of both the shop and the apartment.

Awaiting us in our room was an official summons to appear at the UB, short for Urzad Bezpieczenstwa, or Polish security office.

"Who delivered this letter?" Stefan asked Pani Ptak.

"A civilian," she responded. "He wore breeches, boots, and a coat." The expression on her face was grave. She walked up close to Stefan's face, reached up, took his head into her hands, and whispered, "Just like the Gestapo."

"Nonsense," Stefan snapped. "You know you should not say that."

I did not feel well. In spite of my attempt to calm myself down, my stomach was reacting. There was a sharp pain below my chest and a gnawing pain in my intestines. I knew it well. It was an involuntary physical reaction to my dread of authority. I walked up to the bed; I wanted to lie down.

"Don't," Stefan urged. "Let's go. Let's get it over with. There is nothing they can do to us. We are not involved in the black market, and we can't be accused of having made derogatory remarks about the Red Army. Besides," he added, "the UB is part of the Polish government, and I will deal with them."

The UB was housed in the center of town, under the same roof as the office of the NKVD, the Soviet Secret Security Service. It was late afternoon and the summons requested that we be at the office at two o'clock that afternoon. Though I kept telling myself that it had to be a minor matter, since plans for our immediate future had been approved, I was unable to shake off my reflex reaction of anxiety. One did not want to get near either the offices of the UB or the NKVD.

Everyone knew the address of the UB, because at all times one or two soldiers guarded the entrance to the building. During the day, one could observe important-looking Russian and Polish officers entering and exiting the secret service headquarters. A Polish guard looked at us, took our summons, called for a Russian soldier, handed him the summons, and told us to follow the soldier up the stairway. We entered an office, and the guard handed the summons to the officer seated at a desk. He read the summons and pointed to the bench at the far side of the room. We sat down. What were we doing in a Polish secret security office that was administered by the Russians? The response to all our questions was *nyet.* Russians used this word often in their dealings with the indigenous population of the Polish territory they presently occupied. The word stood for no, I don't know, I don't understand, or I can't help you.

We had arrived before five o'clock in the afternoon. It was seven o'clock in the evening before we were standing in front of a middle-aged, stern-looking man—the Russian officer in charge. His tunic was covered with medals, and his multiple chins were puffed up with self-importance. Standing next to him was a soldier in a Polish army uniform. He was bilingual, and he initiated the questioning by asking why we had not appeared at the designated hour. Stefan explained that we had not been at home when the summons was delivered. Stefan told him where we had been and asked why we had been directed to appear. The answer was that Stefan was not there to ask questions but to answer them. We were asked for our respective names, my maiden name, the date of our marriage, our address before our arrival in Myslowice, the date of our evacuation from Warsaw, and the destination of the transport that took us out of Warsaw. Since the questions were precise, and since we were not given an opportunity to explain, I decided not to reveal my true identity. The question put to us was, "Why were you permitted to leave the camp in Spellen on a work-release pass?"

Stefan answered that the Allied armies were bombing the area, and it was assumed that invasion from the west was imminent. Ostensibly, on his own, the commander of the camp panicked and issued a number of work-release passes, Stefan explained. How many? he was asked. Stefan did not know the answer, but he said that immediately before leaving Camp Spellen we had learned that the camp commandant was ordered to stop issuing the work-release passes. The final question, if we still had the work-release pass in our possession, Stefan answered in the affirmative. We were ordered to leave the inner office and wait outside.

We were stunned, feeling outraged and intimidated at the same time. What were the charges against us? Who had accused us? Why were we not permitted to leave? When we had to use the toilet, a guard accompanied each of us, while another guard remained seated behind the desk. "Could it be,"

Stefan whispered, " that they found out that during the Polish insurrection I worked as a photojournalist attached to the A.K.?"

I did not think so, but neither of us could come up with a reason for what we perceived to be extremely hostile treatment. Stefan asked if I realized that no one aside from deaf and timid Pani Ptak knew of us or cared about us. I could not think of anyone who might help us. Finding my mother and Eva, seeing my father again, all my hopes and desires appeared to be once again out of reach. We had not eaten since the morning. I was in pain and felt utterly exhausted.

A short, balding man wearing thick eyeglasses walked into the room. He conversed in Russian with the guard behind the desk, and both of them laughed. By that time a different soldier was on desk duty. The bald man pointed at us, and I gathered that he was asking about us. I observed that the man was fluent in Polish and in Russian. I had the feeling that he might be Jewish, and I asked if I could speak to him for a moment. "Yes," he said, and walked toward me. I stood up, and it all came gushing out of me.

"I don't know if we are under arrest," I said. "When we returned to our room this afternoon, we found a summons waiting for us, requesting us to come to this office. We have been here for hours, waiting, and we have been forbidden to leave. We have not been told what we are accused of." I took a deep breath "I am Jewish," I revealed. "I have been persecuted by the Nazis for more than eight years. I don't know what happened to my family. I can't bear to once again live in fear." Tears were running down my face, and I was unable to halt the flow.

"What is your name and where are you from?" the man asked.

"The name I assumed was Krystyna Zolkos until I married." I pointed at Stefan who was standing next to me. "My mother and I were hiding in Warsaw, and after the defeat of the Polish insurrection, when the Germans recaptured Warsaw, we married, and now my name is Krystyna Broda. But my real name is Bertel Weissberger."

"You aren't from Warsaw?" he asked. "Where are you from?"

"I was born in Germany."

"When did you come to Poland?"

"The end of October 1938. I was forcibly transported to Poland."

"Yes, and where did you live in Poland?"

"In several places, with various relatives, but for a length of time in

Chorzow, in Krakow, and until the ghetto was liquidated, I lived in Krosno," I explained.

"In Krosno? I know Krosno. Did you have relatives there? What was their name?"

"My aunt lived in Krosno. She was my mother's younger sister. The name was Vogelhut. My aunt, my uncle, and their son were murdered by the Nazis."

"Did you know someone by the name of Freund?" he asked.

"Yes. They had a leather business. They owned a store on the main street near the town square. We used to go there in the early years and buy leather soles for our shoes. In 1941, the Freund family was forbidden to engage in trade."

"They are my cousins. Do you know what happened to them?"

"I don't know. During the first week in September of 1942 the Krosno ghetto was liquidated, and all the Jews were taken away. My sister was taken—"

The man I was speaking to held up his hand. He was upset. "I was fortunate," he told me. "They did not catch me. I met up with partisans in the forest, and we fought the Germans as best we could, until we connected with the Red Army. We have liberated all of Poland, and I have not been able to find a single member of my family. My name is Gelfand."

"Please, Pan Gelfand, tell us why they are holding us. What have we done?"

"Now calm down," he said soothingly. "I'll see what I can do. How about your husband? Was he a member of an anti-Communist organization?"

"No, of course not. It is because of him that I was able to survive the last horrifying year. He hoped that by marrying me he would save my life."

"Sit down," Pan Gelfand said. "I'll see what this is about."

Fifteen minutes later Pan Gelfand came out from the inner office. He was smiling. In his hand were our identity cards and the work-release document.

"Here are your documents," he said. "Go home and get some sleep. You won't be called again."

"Could you please tell us what we were accused of?" I pressed. "This was a frightful experience. It can happen again. If we have enemies, we would like to know who they are. We were fortunate in meeting you. I don't know what would have happened to us had you not walked in."

"I am glad I did. There are always enemies," he said, addressing me. "You know that better than most. But you won't be bothered again, believe me. It had something to do with your wanting to reopen a business—people will do anything."

"Yes, we encountered problems here in Myslowice, but as soon as we learned that a relative of the former owner was planning to take over the business, we withdrew our application and made an application for a photography studio in Swietochlowice."

"I wish you luck. There won't be any problems. It will be all right."

"Would it be possible to reach you were we to run into other difficulties?"

"No, no, I am sorry. I am attached to the Polish general staff, and I have nothing to do with the local provisional administration. I will be leaving in the morning."

Stefan and Pan Gelfand shook hands, and he walked us to the door. Once again I thanked him for intervening on our behalf. Holding on to my hand, his eyes beneath the thick lenses focusing on me, Pan Gelfand said, "Be careful. Take nothing for granted. The Nazis have not disappeared. They have moved underground, and they will continue to burrow from within. This whole territory is full of former Nazis who in an instant have shed their German skin and who are now swearing that all along they have been loyal Poles. They will get what they deserve once the Nazi murderers are wiped out. We all must unite to accomplish that goal. We must rid the Polish nation of the evil that has infiltrated our land. It's only a matter of weeks."

By the time we got back to our room, it was past ten o'clock in the evening. I was glad that Pani Ptak was asleep because I did not want to answer her questions. I felt drained of all my strength, and I fell asleep even before I had fully undressed. Several hours later, Stefan shook me awake. "What is the matter?" he asked. "Are you in pain? You were moaning, whimpering, calling for someone. I had to wake you."

I sat up. I was drenched in perspiration. I knew that I had been running, faster and faster, and that my pursuer was catching up to me. This time it happened in Krakow, on Ulica Karmelicka. A woman from Krosno had recognized me, and immediately there was the Gestapo. I had no idea why I had been there, and I was sure that my pursuer caught my arm, when in fact it was Stefan's hand on my arm, trying to wake me from my torment. Stefan wanted to help me, and he once again suggested that I stop thinking about the past. He urged that I must make a determined effort to distance myself from my self-destructive thoughts. I said that I would try, knowing full well that I neither would, nor could, detach myself from the recent past. I had no power to affect my subconscious turmoil, and once again I wondered whether Stefan would leave me.

On the following morning, when we looked through the documents that had been taken from us by the NKVD officer and then returned to us by Pan Gelfand, we noted, attached to our respective identity cards were small pieces of paper. Typed in Polish, they each read: "This identity card has been examined, and the identity of the holder has been verified by Urzad Bezpieczenstwa." There was a date, the official seal, and a signature. The slips of paper were only two inches wide by three inches long, but I felt they would be of great help in our upcoming journey. I no longer wanted to delay my trip to Krosno. That was where I wanted to begin the search for my sister and my mother. If my mother had survived, where would she start to look for me? Krosno was the logical place, I reasoned. Stefan thought it was too dangerous an undertaking. Passenger transportation had not yet been restored, and our Russian liberators urged that people remain in place and not take up space in freight trains.

In addition, Stefan feared to be designated a malingerer. Russian patrols were in the process of looking for needed laborers, and they did not look kindly on unemployed Poles who tried to avoid recruitment into the needed labor force. I argued that the clearance of our documents would pave our way. Stefan disagreed. The verification of our identity did not absolve us from our duty to perform useful work, he explained. I suggested that Stefan open the photography studio in Swietochlowice, while I proceeded with my quest to find family members. I reasoned that since concentration camp survivors who appeared to be just barely alive were embarking on train journeys in an attempt to find family members, I could do the same. Several cases of freed inmates afflicted by lapses of memory had been reported, and I had visions of Eva coming out of such a state of amnesia and not being able to find me.

"When would you leave?" Stefan asked.

"Today or tomorrow—as soon as possible."

"That soon," Stefan countered. "How can we? I want to go with you. We made an application to open the shop. It has been processed. If we are not here to claim it, it will fall in someone else's hands. Let us postpone for one more week, and I will come with you."

CHAPTER 15

# Swietochlowice: The Search for Loved Ones Begins

In the latter part of March 1945, we left Myslowice. We said good-bye to Pani Ptak and wished her well. Her incessant, mostly indecipherable flow of words had been a strain on my nervous system, and I was looking forward to a place of my own.

With our nearly empty suitcases, we moved into our assigned two-room apartment located in a modest working-class neighborhood in Swietochlowice. Though buildings appeared to be occupied, we encountered few people. It was obvious to us that the former occupants of our apartment had left in a hurry. There were no kitchen utensils or clothing in the apartment, but in a space sectioned off from the living room, we found a woman's bicycle. In their eagerness to get away, the former owners had left this coveted means of transportation behind. What a delightful surprise. I checked the wheels and the gears; all the moving parts were in working condition. I could now indulge in a newfound mobility.

There was a bed and a wardrobe in the bedroom and a small table and two chairs in the kitchen. The living room, however, was bare. It was clear to both of us that we would not get more furniture. We would leave that part

A photo I sent to my father. Swietochlowice, Poland, spring 1945.

of Poland as soon as possible, and we felt fortunate to have this temporary shelter.

We concentrated our energy on earning enough money to support ourselves. While we were scrubbing and arranging the photography studio, a number of former employees walked into the shop. They told us that the previous owner had been a woman. They had helped her pack, and she had fled as soon as she heard the Russian army was about to take charge of the annexed territory. Our visitors thought that I was the photographer, and they immediately addressed me as Pani Szefowa—Mrs. Proprietor.

When I told them Stefan was the expert and I was his assistant, they petitioned him for employment. Four former employees came in to see us. Three were female. All four were eager to assure us that neither they, nor their parents, had been Nazis; they had only pretended to be German to survive the stressful occupation. I could easily understand the need for exceptional survival strategies, and I determined not to make precipitous judgments. I took down their names and addresses. Stefan told them that we would open the studio within the next ten days, as soon as he could obtain needed equipment.

A young girl, Halina, remained behind after the other three left. She told us that some of the photography equipment had been dismantled and stored in the cellar. Halina led us downstairs. Stored away in boxes, we found a large supply of plates, photographic paper, a dismantled enlarger with an adequate lens, additional reflectors, a light meter, a filter, and even a timer. After Halina left, Stefan said that he had everything he would need to operate the studio. We agreed that we would employ Halina immediately upon opening the studio. We noted that though all the former employees had helped with the packing, only Halina came forward to lead us to the hidden equipment.

APRIL 1945 ⤝ SWIETOCHLOWICE, LIBERATED POLAND

In early April, at five o'clock in the morning, we left our apartment in Swietochlowice, each of us carrying a cloth-wrapped bundle. One bundle contained food, the other a change of underwear. We boarded a streetcar and made our way to the freight yard in Katowice. From a distance we saw many people huddled together on a narrow strip of land. As we got closer, we realized that there were hundreds of prospective passengers waiting to board passing freight trains. I learned that many of the people had been in the same spot for several days, and most of them were prepared to jump aboard any slow-moving train.

No one knew when trains were arriving or where they were headed. A long freight train passed at a rapid speed. "Bound for Russia," was the whispered comment I heard all around me. How did they know? I soon learned that freight trains bound for the Russia moved on a special wider set of rails. Russian railroad tracks were several inches wider than the tracks used all over the European continent. We were told that empty freight cars by the hundreds were arriving from Russia at frequent intervals. These closed freight cars along with flat cars loaded with coal, iron, and steel then traveled back east to Russia on those same special rails. Late in the evening, a seemingly never-ending freight train was once again traveling east, on the wider rails. Under cover of darkness, I could hear the angry voices of the people nearby. Statements such as "By the time they leave Poland, everything of value will be gone" and "They are stripping us clean" or even "Did they come to liberate us or to rob us?" were clearly audible. I did not share these sentiments. I remembered well the loaded freight cars traveling from Russia through Poland to Germany after the June 1941 German attack on the Soviet Union. I was astonished that there was so much angry resentment directed at the liberators, who, only weeks earlier, had been welcomed with rejoicing and affection.

It was past midnight when a train with several empty freight cars was passing slow enough for some to climb aboard. The crowd surged forward, propelling me toward a boxcar opening. Someone shoved me forward. I scrambled to get a foothold on an iron bar; hands reached out to pull me in. I straightened up and saw Stefan swinging a leg onto the boxcar floor. The train continued to move slowly, leaving behind the Katowice freight yard with its teeming mass of people. Even though hundreds of travelers had clambered onto the moving train, the multitude of refugees still waiting for passage had in no way diminished.

Throughout the night, despite the bone-chilling wind blowing in from the outside, the door of the freight car remained partially open. We were crowded against unwashed bodies, and foul-smelling breath enveloped me. We gathered that most of our fellow passengers, Polish workers who had either been enticed or compelled to work in the Third Reich, were returning to their homes. Most had probably been on the road for several weeks.

Toward morning when the train slowed down to a crawl, a number of men climbed up onto the roof of the freight car. The sky had cleared, and the bright dawn augured a sunny day. Stefan, watching the men climb up, determined they must know what they were doing. We decided to follow them. Anything was better than being hemmed in on all sides, within the dark cavity of the foul-smelling freight car. When I had climbed halfway up the iron ladder, I saw that the roof sloped. A center beam, perhaps eight inches wide ran the length of the car, but on either side of the beam, the roof slanted. Stefan was behind me, and in back of him, people were waiting to climb up, yet I was unable to set foot onto the slanted roof. As soon as I took a step, my foot started to slide downward. Sitting on the narrow beam in the center of the roof were men of all ages, perhaps sixteen of them, and several women. They were swaying their bodies in tandem with the rhythmic chugging of the locomotive. Some were laughing at my unsuccessful attempt to set foot on the roof. A young peasant broke into a grin, got off his haunches, and inched toward me along the narrow beam.

Reaching for my hand, he said, "Don't look down, look ahead and grab my hand." Once seated on the beam with my legs hanging down the slant, I experienced a momentary surge of joy. Stefan, moving in a crouch, sat down next to me. It had been a scary undertaking, and I had no idea how we would get back into the freight car, but Stefan and I held onto each other and basked in the warm sun and the atmosphere of goodwill. Stefan said that though he had felt my decision to embark on this trip had been reckless, he had to admit he did not regret his decision to accompany me. I did experience moments of fear when all of us had to duck down, and always at the last moment, when traveling through an underpass. But it was a totally different kind of fear than I had experienced during the past three years, when a law decreed that I was not allowed to live.

We transferred several times to different freight trains, sitting either inside a car or on its roof, and twice traveled in the wrong direction. After spending part of a night in an abandoned barn, we finally arrived in Krosno, five days after boarding the first freight car on the outskirts of Katowice. Throughout our several days of hardship, never for a moment did I feel threatened. Could the people surrounding me—some who offered to share their meager supply of food with us, men and women who sang with heartrending emotional odes to the Polish mountainmen—be kin to the Polish collaborators who had aided the Nazis in the bloody task of rounding up Jews? True, I did not tell anyone that I was Jewish, but I had never revealed my secret while hiding in Warsaw. Yet, in Warsaw, I was hunted continuously, and often by Poles. Now, I was freely speaking and answering questions, and so far no one had challenged my strangely accented Polish.

When we arrived in Krosno I was overcome by emotion, and I had to remind myself of the purpose that had brought us there. We were walking toward the market square where the liquidation of the ghetto had taken place when I saw a familiar face. I recognized the young man as an intimate of Eva's friend, Edek Gonet. I approached him and asked, "Are you Pan Janocha? My name is Bertel Weissberger, Eva's sister."

"Yes, I am. You look different. I would not have recognized you," he said. "I knew Eva."

"Edek promised he would help Eva hide should an Aktion be put in effect. But he did not help. You knew about the plans."

"How could he help her? His parents did not want him to be involved. There were threats of severe punishment. It was not our fault."

"I am not accusing anyone. I just want to find out if you—or Edek or someone—know what happened to Eva."

"There were rumors. It was a long time ago," he said reluctantly.

"What rumors? Please tell me whatever you know," I pleaded.

"It was after the liquidation of the ghetto," the young man said. "There were no more Jews. They said that all the Jews had been transported to work camps."

"Yes?" I looked into the young man's face, my eyes searching.

"They had lists with all the names. Some of the Jews were missing. All over town they had posters addressed to Krosno residents. There were warnings and death threats directed at anyone who was hiding an escaped Jew."

"I know."

"Now, Bertel, I only heard this. I did not see it with my own eyes. Apparently, Eva was caught on the street without an armband, attempting to hide her identity. There were others."

"How many? Were Salek Weinfeld and Pan Hausner with her?"

"You seem to know," Edek Janocha countered, "so why are you asking?"

"That's all I know. What happened to them? Was there shooting?" I urged.

"There were rumors that Jews caught after the ghetto was liquidated were shot on sight. Most of the shooting took place on the outskirts of town, though there were one or two killings right here in Krosno. I heard that Eva and other Jews were put on a truck, but also that there was shooting. Perhaps someone made a run for it."

"What kind of a truck?"

"I never saw it. I heard it was a small, covered truck with a steel roof that opened from the back."

"Where did they take the Jews that were put into the van?"

"How should I know that? I had no dealings with the Nazi scum. The Jews were part of the town. They had friends here. You know, more than a thousand Jews lived here at the time of the invasion, and all of them disappeared without a trace. There were attempts to find them, but no one succeeded."

I knew that I had detained the young man long enough, but still I could not let go. Stefan was standing next to me. He had not said a word. "Did any of the former Jewish residents return?" I asked. "Am I the only one?"

"No, one of the Stiefel sisters returned. Someone had helped her hide. She stayed several days, and then she left. Luzer Ellowicz is here. I think he is the only one. They say he married his family's housekeeper, and she hid him in the family barn."

While walking through the familiar streets on the way to the Ellowicz villa, I told Stefan about the Ellowicz family. I had been to their home when I visited my relatives during the summer of 1939, immediately before the invasion. I did not remember the mother, and I knew that she had subsequently died, but Pan Ellowicz the father, his son Luzer, and his daughter, I remembered well. They had been good friends of Aunt Regina and Uncle Jacub, and after we arrived in Krosno, they also became my mother's friends. They had owned a large bottling plant, but during the early war years, they operated a small carbonated beverage bottling plant in the backyard of their villa. In the early years of the occupation, Mother, Eva, and I used to visit their garden and sip sodas. The major part of the villa had been assigned to German civilians involved in engineering work. As long as the German civilians did not complain, the Ellowicz family was allowed to remain in their part of the house. The housekeeper made sure that the Germans billeted to the villa were comfortable. But once the ghetto was established, everything changed.

When Luzer Ellowicz opened the door and saw me, our eyes locked and we fell into each other's arms. There we stood, on the threshold, speechless. At that instant I understood how important it was to return to Krosno. I wanted to know. I needed to see, to touch people who had a common memory of the events. Instinctively, I knew that I could not return to what once had been my charmed refuge. In Krosno, for a brief while, I had had a carefree childhood and had rejoiced in being young. And in Krosno, within a twenty-four-hour period, I became an adult and subsequently an outcast, a prey to be hunted. Could it be that of all those many people—the families who had embraced me and lovingly tolerated my broken Polish, the friends with whom I had shared my dreams and fears and the breath-stopping anxiety of the final months—no one would return?

Zosia, previously the housekeeper and now Luzer's wife, was initially somewhat hostile, but as soon as I mentioned that we would leave on the following morning, she managed to say some words of welcome. Once again, part of the Ellowicz house was occupied, this time by the liberating Soviet army. The Soviet army personnel billeted to the Ellowicz villa made no attempts to prepare for an extended stay. The Russian officers, unlike the well-supplied former German occupiers, did not have access to an organized food supply. The Polish food stocks had been pillaged by the German occupation forces. The barns were stripped of grain. Sporadically, the Russian guests would bring provisions into the house, and when they did, they brought enough food for Zosia, and Luzer.

There was little that our hosts could offer us. All rooms were occupied by army personnel, with the exception of the bedroom occupied by the couple. Luzer said that he would share with us whatever he had. He was so happy to see me. He felt isolated in his small town in the foothills of the Carpathian Mountains, and he wanted to know what was happening in the world beyond. Again and again we returned to the topic of our common dilemma. What had been done with the Jews that were transported out of the Krosno ghetto? My brain refused to accept that they were all dead, as Luzer suggested.

"You tell me, then, what you think happened," he said. "I have been sitting here for four months, waiting, searching, trying to find out in which direction the convoy of trucks went. The Russians have liberated and opened up a number of camps. Polish workers are returning to their homes. They are reporting that they had been treated like slaves. The Germans worked them to the limits of their strength, they said, but they have come home. So tell me, where are our people?"

"I understand one of the Stiefel sisters has come back. Was it Hella or Sala?"

"It was Hella. She survived as I did. Someone helped her hide. Yes, she was here. I saw her. She came to Krosno hoping to find her sister, her brother, her parents—it was a large family."

"I was on my own with my mother. No one helped us hide," I said. Luzer shrugged and looked at Stefan.

"No," I said and smiled. "Stefan did not hide me. We met in Warsaw where I was living under my assumed identity, and I did not tell him until the end of September 1944, when the Polish insurrection failed. Then we married, and being married to a Christian Pole gave me a legitimacy that helped me through the last months until the liberation."

Luzer wanted to know how I had managed to survive, but there was not enough time for that. He asked about my mother, and I told him what I knew. I had not heard from her since I left the Spellen camp. However, I knew that she had arrived in Austria because I had received the house slippers. I told Luzer that I felt I would find my mother, and that if I kept searching, I would find a trace that would lead me to Eva.

Luzer put his arm around my shoulder and said, "Not your Eva. You have not heard what I have been trying to tell you. It's true we do not know where they have been taken, but you know, as well as I do, that there were killing camps. Not on German soil, but here in Poland. This is where the slaughter took place. They killed, they burned, and they gassed our people. There are rumors that in Russia they threw the Jews alive into a ravine and shot them from above."

Luzer told me that since the liberation he had made attempts to find out where the Jews from Krosno had been taken. He was searching for his sister. Russian officers of high rank had made inquiries on his behalf. Apparently, no one had an inkling of where the Jews from the Krosno ghetto had gone. In addition, Jews from neighboring towns and villages had been brought to the Krosno ghetto. How could so many people, perhaps more than two thousand, have disappeared without leaving a trace? That was the question Luzer and I asked each other. There must have been a region, or a camp, where they were taken. Or was there? Jewish survivors from Auschwitz had arrived in Krakow. Even if it was only a minuscule number who had survived; still, there were some. The former inmates reported the heinous crimes, and the various methods by which the killing was executed. However, there was no evidence that the large transport of Jews from Krosno ever reached Auschwitz.

That night we slept in our clothes, all four of us, on the large bed in the spacious bedroom that had belonged to Luzer's parents. The two men stretched out next to each other in the center of the bed. At each end slept their respective spouses. There was no room to move or turn, but the mattress was luxurious, the cover warm, and the mountain air coming through the wide-open window refreshing. Both Stefan and I slept well. In the morning, while Zosia went to the kitchen to cook some cereal for our breakfast, Luzer and I managed to be alone for a short period. We had said so much to each other, and so much more remained to be said. Taking my hand, Luzer said, "You and I—we are the bare tree trunks left standing in a devastated forest. They cut off all our branches and left us naked."

I briefly told Luzer about the escape from Krosno, hidden under the tarpaulin of one of Ritter's trucks, and about the patrolling Gestapo units hunting for fleeing Jews. I told him about our mutual friends who made it possible for me to stay alive. I spoke about Mennek Moszkowitz and his offer of a hiding place, his parting gift to us. I spoke about the harrowing week in the attic. I told him about Pan Majerowicz and how he had helped us and about the crucial moments when he came to our rescue at our time of despair. He helped us whenever he could. I mentioned the other Jews from Krosno who were hiding in Warsaw and whom he had helped. I told Luzer how his life ended. Both Pan Majerowicz and his daughter Ewa were killed in front of the house in which they lived, their bodies left in a ditch.

"He was a good friend, a truly noble man," I said. "I will never forget him."

"Do you think he was one of them, you know, a righteous man*?"

"We won't ever know," I responded. "All I know is that he performed many good deeds during the short span of his life."

I had dreamed of finding at least one member of the Springer family, perhaps my beloved friend Genia. The Springer family had been part of the privileged group of about twenty Jews who had been granted permission to continue working at the Krosno military airport. It was the Springer family who, at their peril, had helped us flee Krosno. That last hour before our departure, alone in the attic, Genia and I had huddled together, starring death in the face and vowing to defy it. Our common anguish—the words we said and those unsaid—were fixed in my being. Did Genia survive? Had she found someone to help her survive?

Luzer told me that, according to Poles who were working at the airport at that time, the privileged group of twenty were taken from the airport to some unknown destination. Among the twenty were the four remaining members of the Springer family.

"It was not a privileged group," Luzer said. "That's what they wanted them to believe. What it amounted to was a few additional weeks of life."

I could not bring myself to speak about my aunt Regina and Dollek, but Luzer kept insisting. He knew what had happened to my uncle Jacub. The whole Jewish community knew about the tragedy of Uncle Jacub's murder that occurred at the time of the invasion and about Aunt Regina's nervous breakdown and subsequent recovery. When I told Luzer about her fate, he wept.

"She was a spirited woman," he said. "She had such buoyancy. That was

---

*According to Jewish legend, the fate of the human race rests with thirty-six just men. These just or righteous men, who are born into each generation, are unaware of their station. Tradition has it that God will not abandon humanity as long as one just man remains in the world.

before the war. She was a good swimmer, an urbane woman, always eager to embrace life. Why would one of her Polish neighbors go out of their way to denounce her to the Gestapo? To the Germans, she was just another Polish mother living quietly in a small town."

Before Stefan and I left, we talked about our respective plans for the future. I said that I would keep searching for members of my family and that as soon as communication with America was restored, I would begin the search for my father. I gave Luzer the address of the photo studio, and I said that it was our plan to move back to Warsaw. I would forward our new address once we got there. We agreed that we would keep in touch.

Luzer said that for the time being he would remain in Krosno. He would wait and hope that his sister, or perhaps some other member of his family or his community, would return. He did not believe that this would happen; still, just in case, he wanted to be there to welcome them.

"You said for the time being." I asked. "You are in your home. You were born here, this is your house, and you have friends here. The Russians will leave."

"That's true," Luzer responded. "It is my house, and yes, I do have friends within the Christian community, but I no longer have a home. Early on, shortly after the invasion and occupation by the Nazis, long before there was an idea of a ghetto, or the liquidation of the ghetto, my family decided that there would be no future for us in Poland."

"What brought this on?" I asked. "When I visited here in the summer of 1939, you were happy, a young man about town. You loved being with your Christian friends, and I remember your father wanted you to date a Jewish girl and marry."

"Everything changed after the invasion. When the Agricultural Business Syndicate submitted a list of all the Jewish businesses in town, anticipating the German request for one, our family began to see the light. No, there is no future for me in this country. Of course, I had Polish friends—decent guys. There are good people everywhere. You remember the two German engineers who lived here with us?"

"Yes, I do."

"They were fine human beings. They tried to help us whenever they could, and yet they were the invaders, the enemy. But our neighbors, who were supposed to be our friends, supplied that list to the enemy." Luzer shook his head. "How can one live with that? In time, I plan to sell whatever I can and settle in Palestine. In that hot climate, they will surely welcome a carbonated drink–bottling plant. I will transfer my skill to another continent, to a place where I can live and work among Jews."

We thanked Zosia for her hospitality and proceeded toward the opposite end of the town and up the hill to the Villa Dunikowski. The housekeeper and I greeted each other affectionately. She told me that old Pani Dunikowska had died and that her son's fiancée, who had lived with them throughout the war, was living in the villa but had left early in the morning for her job in the post office. I thanked her for all her help during the last difficult year in Krosno, for their kindness when even just being kind to Jews was dangerous, and for keeping and then forwarding our winter coats to Warsaw.

"Please don't even mention it," was her response. "We were powerless. They ran over us and turned the world upside down. The punishment for what they did must come from God."

The housekeeper asked about my mother. About Eva she knew as much as I did. I asked her for a small shovel. "I don't know if you remember," I said, "but before we left, we dug a hole in your cellar and buried some of our papers and letters in the hole."

"Yes, I remember. We never went near it, and as far as I know no one else did. Would you want me to come with you?"

"No, thank you. I think I would like to be alone."

We had marked the spot, and I remembered it. I pushed aside some of the coal, and after breaking through the crust of the dirt floor, I extracted letters we had buried two and a half years ago. I held in my hand letters from my father. Separate letters, written to each of us, private letters. I just glanced over them. The letters to Eva and me told tales of America, the longed-for Arcadia we had not been able to reach. In each letter, Father wrote about our upcoming reunion and of the places he would take us to in the magical city of New York. Each letter ended with an exhortation to muster our courage and retain hope. In the letters to my mother, there were signs of despair, however, and a premonition of bad things to come. There was a bundle of letters sent to me by my friend Zack Schäfer—the first mailed from Hindenburg, then from Berlin, and finally from Trieste, shortly before he boarded the ship for Palestine. And there were our three Jewish identity cards, issued by the German occupation authority.

Our next stop was Bochnia. We spent the night waiting for and then riding in a freight car. We arrived in Bochnia early in the morning on the following day. Stefan, who had said very little during our time in Krosno, told me that he was exhausted. When I asked him why, he said that my emotionality was exhausting. I was not the Krysia he had come to know and love. He said he was surprised I had energy left to tackle a visit to Bochnia. I understood immediately what he was telling me. The self-control that had been my armor and had helped keep me alive was no longer necessary. At that moment in Bochnia I hardly knew which was my real self, but I understood that it was a matter I would need in time to resolve.

Once in Bochnia, we proceeded immediately to Ulica Floris, the street where my grandparents had lived. Strangers were living in their cozy little house near the Babica stream. Throughout my childhood, Eva and I spent part of our summer vacation at that little house. A horse-drawn carriage transported us from the railroad station to their house. I used to love the clip-clop of the horses' hoofs on the cobblestone street. When we arrived, my grandparents would be waiting on their front stoop. There were hugs and kisses and joyous laughter.

Stefan and I stood on the cobblestone street looking at the small house. In 1939, several of my father's brothers, who had taken us into their homes in Krakow, and their children and grandchildren fled from Krakow to Bochnia with the hope that they would have a better chance of staying alive in a small town. I wanted to share my memories of that time when twelve members of my family huddled together in the rooms below. Those were the days when there still was hope that France and England, Poland's allies, might come to our rescue—a miracle that did not happen.

I described for Stefan an incident that both Eva and I recalled years after it took place and which somehow had remained vividly in my mind. At the time of the blitzkrieg, in the early days of September 1939, Mother, Eva, and I had arrived at my grandparents' home just a day or two before the invasion. Mother's younger brother, my uncle Willek, had taken a troop train from Katowice to join up with his regiment in preparation for defending Poland. He had sent his young, attractive wife Frydia and their four-year-old son Josef to his parents in Bochnia for safekeeping. When Uncle Willek, who was six feet tall, slim, and always elegantly attired, had married self-centered Frydia, the family was surprised. They wondered how such a smart young man could not have see what he was getting into. The family said that her Grecian beauty was better suited for a sculpture than for a wife. She had raven-black hair and an olive complexion, and she spent a large part of the money Willek earned on her clothes and in beauty parlors.

On several occasions, Eva and I had visited the young couple in Katowice, and we had noted that, though always glad to see us, Frydia would invariably sit on the sofa, adjusting her hair and admiring her hands and well-manicured nails. She would say, "Willusiu, could you prepare tea for your family?" or " Willusiu, would you feed Josef?" At that time, Josef was two years old and the exact image of his mother. In the train, on our way back to Hindenburg, Eva and I would mimic Frydia and say, "Willusiu, would you . . ." Mother would reprimand us, but that mimicked remark had originated with our parents.

Immediately in advance of the German troops' arrival, the town of Bochnia had endured a twenty-four-hour bomb attack. The seven of us huddled together in my grandmother's room. The only available bomb shelter was the lower levels of the local salt mine. However, electric power had been cut, making the mine lift inoperable, and my grandmother, debilitated by Parkinson's disease, would not have been able to navigate the many stairs leading down into the salt mine. It was decided that, come what may, we would stay together in my grandmother's inside room, with a small window that looked out onto a narrow courtyard passage. The sound of bombs detonating nearby, of dishes falling to the floor, and of sirens and screams and the tremor of the floor beneath our feet were frightening.

What helped us keep our equilibrium was Frydia. Each time she heard the boom of a falling bomb, she would grab Josef and crawl under the table. Eva and I would look at each other and suppress a giggle at that ludicrous sight. Did this educated woman really think that, were a bomb to hit the house, she and her son would survive under the table?

By telling this anecdote to Stefan and adding a note of levity, I wanted to bring these family members back to life. We had heard that in autumn 1942 the Bochnia ghetto had been liquidated; its inhabitants transported to an unknown destination. I could not comprehend that word *unknown*. Poland was not an uncharted ocean.

An old woman passed by, turned around, and walked toward us.

"Are you looking for someone?" she asked.

"Yes, the people who lived here, the David family," I responded.

"The tailor. I remember him. They are not here. They, and all the others."

"Where are they?"

"They are gone. The Nazis forced them out of their houses, and for a while they had them gathered together in a ghetto. Then they were gone. All of them."

"What happened to them?" I asked. "There must have been many Jews."

"They were gone. Overnight, in one day, they were gone, all of them."

"Did any of the Jews who lived here return once the Germans were driven out?"

"Only the hairdresser. He is the only one as far as I know."

"Where can I find him?" I asked the woman.

"He lives in the same house he always lived in, behind the shop. He is quite ill, they say. He can't stand up, so he can't work."

"Is his name Gutfreund?" I asked.

"Yes, that's it. That's his name. Who are you?" she asked.

"The David family who lived in this house, the tailor. They were my grandparents."

I wished the woman the customary God's blessing, and I thanked her for stopping and giving me the information.

I remembered the hairdresser because he was my uncle Zygmunt's brother-in-law, and also because I had heard my mother say that during the occupation he had been a member of the Bochnia Judenrat—the German-appointed Jewish council. He was good at his trade, and whenever we visited Uncle Zygmunt and his family in their summer residence in Bochnia, Mother made appointments with Pan Gutfreund for the three of us.

When I knocked at his door and tried to explain who I was, he shook his head and said, "I don't remember." He pointed to his head and muttered, "It's all mixed up in there." Had I not been told where I could find him, I would never have recognized him. He had not been a handsome man. His head was too large for his body and his neck too short. Still, he had always been well groomed, and his dark wavy hair had been a testament to his talent. All that remained of that hair was a gray stubble. Moreover, one side of his face did not match the other, perhaps the side effect of a stroke. After much prodding, he acknowledged that he knew all of them. My mother's family, who had always lived in Bochnia, and the members of my father's family, who had fled the Krakow ghetto and had come to Bochnia. All have disappeared, he said. He was staying in Bochnia, he told me. He was waiting for his wife and children, for his brother and sister and their families. He hoped someone would come.

Next I needed to travel to Krakow, and my reluctant husband accompanied me. He found it difficult to understand that I was still unwilling to accept what to him had been made abundantly clear. He thought my belief that because I had survived someone from the more than hundred members of my extended family must have survived was untenable. I disagreed. That one person, I reasoned, once I found him or her, would be able to tell us what had happened to everyone and where it had taken place. There had to be graves or bodies to bury.

In contrast to Krosno and Bochnia where, except for an occasional motorized Russian vehicle, streets had been empty and sidewalks deserted, Krakow bustled with activity. Russian and Polish officers were strolling, often with good-looking women on their arms, along the gracious tree-lined avenue that encircled the center of the city. Soldiers of both armies, though not together, walked in groups, crowding the narrow sidewalks. It seemed to me that every other civilian was busy trading something for something else. The ultimate purpose was to possess an item that the peasants coming into Krakow would be willing to exchange for produce.

I was told that a Jewish agency had opened an office near Stradom. Unable to find the exact location, I approached several people who either shrugged or pointed me in the wrong direction. The implication was that either they did not know, or that it was of no interest to them. When I saw a group of people gathered in front of an old building, my eye caught some Hebrew lettering. I could not make out what it said, but I reached for Stefan's arm and headed for the entrance. It was indeed the office of the Jewish agency. Stefan waited outside, while I stood in line for my turn to speak to a gray-haired, bespectacled lady. She was seated on a kitchen chair in front of a rickety table strewn with papers. On the walls were lists of names with addresses. My stomach turned convulsively as I conjured up images of prospective reunions. While listening to the questions the man ahead of me was asking, I endeavored to organize my thoughts.

It was the first time after the liquidation of the Krosno ghetto that I had freely and openly entered an office run by Jews for the purpose of helping other Jews. The woman spoke Polish and Yiddish fluently, but she was also able to communicate in Russian and in German. "I am trying to find my sister and my mother," I said, "also, my grandfather, my uncles, aunts, and cousins. Perhaps close friends that are very dear to me. I know the ghettos they were taken from and the approximate date the Aktion was put in effect. Can you help me?"

"That is what we are here for," the woman answered. "Did you look through the lists posted on the walls?"

"No, not yet, but I would like to give you some names, at least those of my mother and sister. Perhaps you could help find a trace that would lead me to them?" I pleaded.

"We do not have the means to find anyone," the lady answered. "Perhaps in time we will. For now, all we are able to do is list your name and address. You write down the names of the relatives you are looking for. Before you do that, you should go over the names that are posted on the sheets. You might find the name of someone you know and that would be a start."

The names were not posted in alphabetical order, and I called Stefan in to help. I gave him three names: Weissberger, David, and Rinder. We were not successful. No one with a familiar name was listed at the office of the Krakow Jewish Agency. With mounting apprehension, I read the many different names of concentration camps I had never heard of before. Was it possible that the German army, while fighting a war on two fronts, had managed to set up throughout Poland such a large network of concentration camps for the sole purpose of murdering Jews? I told the woman I was grateful she was there. I left my address, and I said that shortly we would move to a different location and I would return and list my new address with her office.

"That won't be necessary," she said. "You can write to me at this office, and we will make sure that your new address is posted."

The woman wrote an address and a number on a piece of paper, rubber-stamped it, and handed me the paper; my confirmation that my name was listed.

Almost as soon as we opened the studio, we were swamped with visitors. It seemed as if the Russian soldiers had been waiting for us to open the door.

Stefan had selected a number of portraits and fitted them into available frames for display in the showcase. He restored the large box camera he had found in the cellar. He mounted a Leica, the camera he knew he could always rely on, on a tripod. The lights and reflectors were placed in advantageous positions, and all that remained was to send a customer into the back room of the studio. What we had not anticipated was the language barrier, as well as the culture barrier. My Russian vocabulary was limited, and the soldiers I tried to communicate with did not understand Polish. My attempts at sign language with eight or ten people simultaneously were futile. Occasionally, soldiers or officers with some knowledge of Polish would come in and help. I learned that the Russian soldiers who walked into the studio wanted to buy things, anything, but we had nothing to sell. They pointed at the portraits on display, frames, the ashtrays on the counter, even the extension cord that ran along the wall. After several soldiers had pointed to the Leica, and even to Stefan's wristwatch, to convey that they wanted to buy them, Stefan removed the precious camera from the tripod and put his wristwatch into his pocket.

When in time I managed to communicate that we wished to put their likeness on a postcard, a photograph they would be able to send home, they shook their heads. Often a shy smile accompanied the negative response. We later learned that for them sitting for a portrait was a serious matter one had to prepare for and not a decision made on impulse.

The Russian soldiers had currency they wanted to exchange for something of greater value. They were in transit, and they had no way of knowing where they would be on the following day. In mid-April 1945, the soldiers who walked into the studio were being gathered for a final offensive against the German enemy. Some had come from thousands of miles away. They had traveled across Asia, as well as half the European continent, and they were eager to defeat the cruel enemy in his homeland.

Though we did not have many customers, the town of Swietochlowice was crowded with Russian soldiers and officers, both male and female. They slept in barracks on the outskirts of town, and throughout the day their presence in the streets was ubiquitous. Nothing about them was reminiscent of the German soldiers who had previously occupied Poland. The soldiers I saw were either part of the infantry or the armored divisions, but the uniform did not differ. They were not arrogant, and they did not strut. There may have been small patrolling details of military police keeping an eye on the soldiers, but they were not visible. There were no units marching in a fear-inspiring lockstep.

Only a small number of officers wore high boots that reached the knee. For the most part, the soldiers were shod in work boots made of coarse leather that barely reached the calf. The khaki-brown uniform of the Soviet army resembled that of the Polish soldiers, except for their overcoats. Though some wore greatcoats, most of the overcoats were made of a quilted material, rather than of wool. The head covering varied. They wore both folded and visor hats and a variety of fur hats. Most often these fur hats were made of pelts from black or gray karakul lambs. The style in which they were fashioned reflected the region of the soldier's origin.

Often their homes were far away, not part of Europe, and they were surprised when one was unable to comprehend the many varied nationalities that comprised the Soviet Union. The Kirghiz had aquiline features and long, narrow, slanted eyes. They were tall, rather slim, and self-contained. The Cossack soldiers were more extroverted. They wore bandoliers of cartridges crossed over their chests. They were a noisy, jolly lot we wanted to keep at a distance. The nationality that seemed most strange to us were the Mongols. Of the Asiatic peoples we encountered, they appeared the most primitive. They must have been recruited from remote villages. They were enraptured with the concept of time. They wore several wristwatches on their arms, and. some even had alarm clocks hanging from ropes around their necks. In their eyes, round and shiny like black marbles, I saw the strange and wild look of a cornered animal. They appeared to be displaced, both within their army and within a country so far removed from their own.

The single unifying element, regardless of the region the soldiers came from, was the mark of hardship they had endured. It was etched into the premature aging lines in their faces. Their endurance had been pushed to the limit. Always there was an unspoken sorrow reflected in their eyes.

The enlisted men greeted a passing officer by casually lifting their right hand to their caps. There was no fraternization between the liberators and the indigenous population. The soldiers walked in groups, hardly ever alone. Groups of men and women soldiers walked together; infrequently I saw a male and female soldier couple. The couples I encountered did not hold hands; they were subdued, with little flirtatious interaction.

We eventually coaxed the soldiers into sitting for portraits. For them, it was a private undertaking to be shared with a friend or two, but hidden from strangers. In the early days of our business, when we spent most of our time encouraging the prospective customer to sit down, we managed to generate just enough business to stave off hunger. In return for the photo postcards we printed, we asked for food. The soldiers were as generous as possible. As wider areas of the former Third Reich were conquered by the Russian troops, more food storage depots were liberated. The provisions that became available were distributed among the Russian soldiers. Sometimes the soldiers brought flour, at other times beans or sugar. On one occasion three soldiers paid their bills with a piece of meat. It was wrapped in cloth and newspaper, fresh blood seeping through both. Though we were always hungry, we did not even want to look at the meat. We gave the meat to Halina and asked her to share it with our other two employees. We had no money to pay our employees; they did not really want money, anyway, but preferred to share the food that came our way.

Stefan quickly adapted to a new modus operandi. In Warsaw, in his makeshift studio, he had been quite successful in executing portraits with his Leica. For some sittings he would have preferred to use his Rolleiflex, but the latter was still buried in our cellar in Warsaw. He felt comfortable using the Leica.

To Stefan, lines and wrinkles gave the face character. But to our Russian customers, the opposite was desirable. We came to understand that the portraits they wished to send back to Russia should depict them as their family remembered them: young, trim, the weariness in their faces erased. The only way to accomplish that goal was for Stefan to use the ancient box camera with its glass plates. With skillful placing of lights, Stefan was able to enhance the positive aspects of a face and diminish those that were negative. After the photograph was printed came the slow and boring task of retouching—erasing lines and wrinkles.

When Stefan needed to experiment to find a better angle for the lighting, he used me as a model. The last photograph I had sent to my father was taken in the early months of 1941. I was looking forward to sending him a recent photo. What would he see?

Experimenting with the old camera.

MAY 1945 ⟿ SWIETOCHLOWICE, LIBERATED POLAND

After Germany's unconditional surrender on May 7, 1945, our business started to flourish. Soviet military personnel, garrisoned on the outskirts of Swietochlowice, spent several weeks in the barracks before being transported back to Russia. The soldiers were jubilant and eager to celebrate. They loved sitting for portraits now and viewed their likeness with unrestrained joy. Though we gave them several prints, always postcard size because it was the only paper size we had, they always came back for more. With them came their friends, and together they admired each other's likeness, laughing and joking, while crowding our studio. The sight of the usually stern and composed faces dissolving in laughter, sometimes to the point of tears, was a sight to behold. They arrived alone, or together with a friend, at times with a larger number of comrades than the camera lens could encompass. Some of them became our friends and would often walk in just to say hello, or because there were not many places where they could walk in and feel welcome. Having finally mastered the Polish language, I soon learned to communicate in Russian. The insurmountable problem I faced was the Russian alphabet. We were so busy, working late into the night, there was not enough time left to master the Cyrillic letters.

The soldiers were advised not to circulate their Russian rubles but instead to spend zlotys, a temporary Polish currency that no one seemed to want. Barter was the desired means of trade, preferred by all parties. When we had enough food for our employees, and ourselves, we managed by means of barter to obtain needed photography supplies and equipment.

Female soldiers were our most enthusiastic customers, and I enjoyed our mutual attempts at communication. Often the women would appear in pairs. Only days after Germany's surrender, two female soldiers walked in and made an appointment. When they appeared at the arranged time, they had several cloth bundles hanging from their arms. One contained a small sack of flour meant for us. "*Da?*" one soldier asked and pointed at me—yes? "*Da,*" I agreed. She pointed to her companion and put up four fingers. I assumed it meant that each one wanted two portraits. I nodded and ushered them into the back room. When they saw Stefan, they giggled and shook their heads. They steered me toward the mirror in a corner of the room. There they untied their bundles. One contained a comb, a hairbrush, and various cosmetics. From the other they extracted a red dress made of a silky fabric, a brassiere, white cotton stockings, and a pair of high-heeled black shoes.

The soldiers wanted to sit for one portrait in uniform and for the other in the red dress. It was a complicated procedure, and Stefan had to leave several times while they changed their clothes. As I helped each soldier into the dress that was a bit too tight, we smiled at each other. When they once again donned their black woolen stockings and linen shirts stretched tight across their ample breasts, the women laughed mischievously. They left with sparkles in their eyes. I felt quite good about the adventure, but Stefan was less than satisfied.

"Did you see that dress?" he asked me. "It was too tight for their figures, and the makeup was so artificial. Much too much rouge, and they don't know how to apply powder. The blond one has beautiful hair, but her hair was greasy.

If only I had been able to communicate with them. No matter what I do to the negative plate, these portraits will not help promote our business."

But Stefan was wrong. The two young soldiers were delighted with the photos, especially the ones with the red dress. Though I could not understand some of the exclamations they uttered while admiring themselves, their artless joy was contagious. The red dress was especially delightful to them because female soldiers had to wear the same tunics as their male counterparts, with no allowances made for the different shape of the female body.

Once at dusk, we opened up the door to the street and heard in the distance choral singing, coming from the barracks. Stefan and I decided to walk to the barracks. A curfew was in force only for Volksdeutsch residents; still, it was prudent to proceed slowly. As we got closer, it seemed to us that the whole Soviet army was singing in unison. The sound of hundreds of harmonizing voices was awe-inspiring. Thereafter, whenever we heard the singing, and if it was possible, we locked the studio and walked toward the barracks. We were not the only ones.

Although I could not understand the words, I was deeply moved by the Slavic melodies pregnant with yearning for home. At times the singing was so powerful I could not move. The sounds enveloped the countryside like an avalanche. As the unified voices reached a crescendo, all sound stopped for seconds, as if suspended in the singers' throats, only to explode and come crashing down on the listener with the power of a waterfall. All the songs ended abruptly. There was no descending from the higher to the lower register; the song ended as if in midflight, leaving the motionless listener waiting for the finale.

There were several occasions when Stefan and I walked close enough to the barracks to see the soldiers dancing around a bonfire. Though the dancing appeared to be spontaneous, one could see that the soldiers positioned themselves according to a pattern. There were usually three concentric circles around the fire. The dancers made up the first circle. In the second one were soldiers who clapped out the rhythm, while the chorus occupied the outer perimeter. Individual dancers would move up close to the fire and perform acrobatic leaps and jumps that defied imagination. The more daring the steps and the higher the leaps, the louder the accompanying clapping, while the singing stopped. The vocalists held their breaths until the dancers' feet once again touched the ground. These musical gatherings were so powerful and enthralling that momentarily we were severed from our shattered world.

One day a group of three officers came to pose for a photograph. One of them wore a canvas tunic with the high Russian collar and crossed over his chest were bandoliers. He was of medium height, but his erect posture made him appear taller. His skin was leathery, and a bushy mustache almost covered his lips. On his head he sported a dashing karakul hat. He told us he was a Cossack and that his home was in the Ural Mountains. He understood Polish, and he made an effort to speak Russian slowly so that I could understand him.

Two days after the three officers had picked up their photographs, the Cossack returned to our studio. He came alone, he told us, because he wanted to know more about us, especially because Stefan had mentioned that we were from Warsaw. He appeared to be well informed, and he told us that he had been with the advance troops of the Soviet army on the second day of August 1944—the day of the Warsaw uprising. He did not know why orders were issued to the Soviet troops not to cross the Vistula River. We were eager to hear more about it, but we were not about to trust this officer with our views. Criticism of Soviet policies, especially the sensitive subject of the Russian forces standing by for two long months, while the Polish insurgents were engaged in combat and the city of Warsaw was bombed, was strictly forbidden.

The man reached for his wallet and took out a photograph of a handsome woman. She had dark expressive eyes and an abundance of hair gathered at the nape of the neck.

"This is my wife," he said. "She died six years ago, and all my life I have loved her."

"Do you have children?" I asked.

He took out another photograph depicting three young children. "It was taken years ago," he explained, "but I wanted a photo of the three of them together. My boy," he pointed to the young male child, "died in the battle for Stalingrad. My daughter," he pointed to one of the girls, "is an officer in the Soviet army, and my youngest works in Dnepropetrovsk. She is a transportation engineer."

The Russian asked about our respective families. Stefan told him about his widowed mother, and that he was an only child. The man said he knew about the Warsaw uprising, but he wanted to know more about the Jewish revolt in the Warsaw ghetto in April 1943. When I told the Russian that I was Jewish, he told us that his wife had been Jewish and that though their children were raised to believe in God and in the commandments, they had been raised without religious affiliation. "We thought it was better for them," he said, "but sometimes I wonder."

"Is there anti-Semitism in Russia?" I asked.

"Not now," he answered. "Now, with so many thousands of Jews fighting and dying for the Motherland, you are not even allowed to say the word *Hebrew* in a derogatory tone. Ever since the revolution, the Russian people have been urged to abandon their religious affiliations. The mood of the Russian government fluctuates between aggressive measures and exhortations. During the past years, the Russian people have suffered much, almost beyond human endurance. So now they have loosened the proscription against religious practice."

"Does that also apply to Jewish Russians?"

"Yes, it should," was his reply. "But it is always more difficult for Jews. My wife's family had suffered under the Czar, and then again during the Stalin regime. Stalin's first wife was Jewish."

"Really, I did not know that," Stefan said. "Did she die?"

"No one really knows, but she has been out of favor for quite a while."

I thought about asking Stefan to invite our new friend to have tea with us in our apartment, but there was not enough time. The Russian told us that he had to get back to his barracks and pack. His regiment was withdrawing and moving east, moving closer to home. He told us that he and his two comrades belonged to the same armored division. They drove tanks. They had become friends, and ever since they met, they had tried to look out for one another. Now they were about to part, and the photographs Stefan had taken would be a memento of their friendship.

When he was about to leave, he put his arms around me and hugged me to his chest. "I hope you find both your mother and your sister," he said, "and that together you will go to America." Then he kissed Stefan on both cheeks and rushed out the door. I thought I saw tears in his eyes. I did not know his name, and he never asked to know our surname. For me, it had been an emotional encounter, and I noticed that Stefan, who shied away from emotional encounters, was also moved by this momentary bonding.

The Russian military was moving out, and both of us were impatient to see them leave. Stefan wanted to go to Warsaw and see for himself the extent of the destruction the city had suffered. We were told that regardless of money, or items of barter, there was absolutely no place where one could rest one's head for a night. Polish authorities let it be known that returning to Warsaw, even if only to come and look, was counterproductive while rubble was being cleared from the streets. The government was attempting to restore at least some basic means of transportation. We also heard that large sectors of the city were still not accessible to pedestrians. Stefan felt that regardless of prevailing conditions, we would attempt to enter the city. I wondered if it was prudent to leave for Warsaw while Russian soldiers, on their way home, were temporarily housed in neighboring barracks. Traveling to Warsaw and finding accommodation there would be expensive, and since taking photographs of Russian soldiers was our only means of support, I questioned whether it was wise to give up the opportunity to earn additional money.

I decided to once again travel to Katowice, this time alone, in an attempt to contact the Mandola family. We had been at their door in the early days of April, but no one appeared to be at home. Mother had sent the slippers to their address, and that address was our only point of contact. I felt certain that if Mother were alive, she would try to find me by means of the Mandola address.

I rang the doorbell of the apartment. I tapped the door gently, and then more firmly, and I slipped a note under the door. There was no response. A man with rolled-up shirtsleeves came puffing up the stairs. He appeared to be angry. "You come here in the early morning hours," he said, "making a lot of noise and disturbing the residents. What is it you want?"

"I am sorry," I answered. "I have been trying to reach the Mandola family. This is where they used to live. Could you tell me if they have moved away? Perhaps they have left a forwarding address? It is important that I find them."

"You are speaking to the wrong person," the man snarled. "When I moved into this house, they were already gone, and good riddance, I say. They knew that they were through. Their picnic had lasted for five years. What makes me wonder is why you would be so anxious to find these Nazi lovers."

"I know they were Volksdeutsch," I attempted to explain. "They could also have been Nazi lovers; I don't know about that. A young woman my husband and I met in camp gave us this address. She was related to Pani Mandola. I am trying to find that young woman."

"Hmmm, next thing you know, every Volksdeutsch will have a Polish patriot coming forth as his protector. I can't help you, but my advice to you is don't go chasing after Nazi lovers."

Stefan had surmised that the Mandola family had left Poland with the retreating German army. He had told me the arduous trip to Katowice would be futile. Still, I needed to explore all possible connections to my mother. It was eleven o'clock in the morning, and though I had left home very early, I did not feel that I was ready to return to Swietochlowice. Compared to the latter, Katowice was a cosmopolitan city, and the Mandola residence was not far from the center of town. When I was a child my family and I had come for visits to Katowice, and I was surprised at how much I remembered. When I had traveled to the city on behalf of Dr. Kostka, I had felt the treacherous atmosphere of the town and had never strayed far from the prescribed route to and from the railroad terminal. Now I was free to roam the city.

I remembered the location of the Katowice post office, and though I knew that communication with America had not yet started, I hoped that I could find out when it would become possible to send a telegram. The answer I got was that I could send a telegram, but that it would not be received because the necessary cables had not yet been restored. I was advised to try again four weeks hence. As I was leaving the post office, a couple holding hands crossed my path. The young woman's face was turned toward her companion, but the profile was unmistakable. I ran after them and reached for the woman's hand. "Ruth?" I asked. "Ruth Wischnitzer?"

"My God, it's Bertel!" she exclaimed. "How did you recognize me? Had you not stopped me, I would not have recognized you. You look so different, Bertel. Your hair was never that blond." Ruth turned to her companion. "Heinz," she said, "this is Bertel, a friend from Hindenburg. When I last saw her, toward the end of 1938, she was only a little girl."

I could not say the same about Ruth. Since she was my senior by perhaps five years, my image of her had always been of a grownup, a handsome young woman who never lacked boyfriends. She was as tall as I remembered her, but she had never been so skinny. Her hair, once an abundance of silky, cascading waves, was sparse and lusterless. Her large dark eyes, high cheek-bones, and generous mouth were the features I remembered. Standing in the street, holding each other's hand, we finally asked the crucial questions.

"Are you all alone?" Ruth wanted to know.

"I am married. My husband is in Swietochlowice. He is a Christian. We got married in Warsaw in October 1944. There is no one else."

"Eva?"

"They got her. I don't know what they did to her. I can't find a trace."

"Your mother?"

"I don't know. I keep searching. I have listed their names in Krakow, also the names of my closest relatives. I have posted my address. I keep wondering why no one is looking for me. Could they have murdered all of them? I think about that, and I am scared. And you?"

"You know about my father," Ruth answered. I remembered that in 1938 he had been arrested in his shoe store in Hindenburg and taken to a concentration camp. "My mother," Ruth continued, "she too was killed; I know that now. I came here in the hope of finding my brother. Günter was taken to a concentration camp, and also my cousin Friedel Teich—you remember her? I don't know which concentration camp—there were so many. Bertel, you remember that my family owns real estate in Katowice, the corner building? I thought Günter and Friedel might come here, because we have this property."

Günter had been a student at the Hindenburg gymnasium. He had been my senior by three years, and though I could easily visualize him, I did not think that he would recognize me. He had been at an age when young boys seek friendships with girls older than themselves.

"Did you survive in a concentration camp?" I asked Ruth.

"No, not quite a concentration camp," she answered. "I was sent to a slave labor section. I was among a small group of Jewish women who were sent to work in a textile mill in Grünberg in the province of Silesia. We were the lucky ones. A few of us survived. The rest died, mainly from starvation. There was this supervisor, a German. Imagine! He kept insisting that he could not release us unless he had skilled people to replace us. The Gestapo kept pressing him to return us to the concentration camp. It was a standing order. The supervisor kept postponing the date, week by week, saying all along that he was trying to find replacements. The Russian army saved us. When they entered, five of us were still alive. I was one of the lucky five."

"Did the other workers know?" I asked.

"Of course. We had to wear the yellow star at all times, and there was no food for us. At dawn, we trudged to the mill and started work on an empty stomach. The other factory workers were forbidden to communicate with us; they were not even allowed to look at us. This last winter I felt so weak I barely managed to stand up. Some women in our group just fell to the floor and died of starvation. Everyone knew that we were slowly dying. One morning, a German woman passed in back of me and touched my elbow. I looked up and on a ledge, immediately above the machine at which I worked, there was a tin cup filled with soup. Thereafter, several times a week, on that ledge, there was the same cup filled with soup, and sometimes there was even a small piece of bread. That's how the last five of us survived. Throughout these several months, there was never a word of acknowledgment on our part. We knew that it was the women's attempt to keep us alive. It was best not to know who these good Samaritans were because many of the workers were mean-spirited. Yes, there was a helping hand for me. Heinz was not that fortunate," Ruth concluded.

I looked at the tall skinny man at Ruth's side. His hair was gray and his shoulders stooped, but he was not much older than Ruth. His face was wrinkled, and there were unhealthy-looking blotches on his cheeks and chin. Ruth told me that Heinz had been quite ill when they met. He along with others had been taken on the death march, but when the Russian army closed in, the Nazi torturers left them on the road, hoping they would freeze to death, and ran away. Ruth found Heinz in a makeshift hospital for men when she went there searching for Günter. They decided to stay together. Ruth had been eager to go to Hindenburg, but Heinz was too weak to make the journey. The week before, they had finally managed to reach Hindenburg. There was no one there.

"Can you believe that?" Ruth asked me. "There were over a thousand Jewish families in our community. Some managed to flee, we know that. Your father got out, and the friends who went to Palestine. Also the children who were lucky enough to get on the list for the Kindertransport—but all the others. What happened to them? Where are they? We decided to first search for members of my family, and then go to Austria to search for Heinz's family."

"Are you going to Vienna?" I asked.

"Yes, that's where Heinz is from."

"Where are you staying? When will you be leaving?" I asked.

"We are staying in my father's building. Our family always had an apartment there, but it is occupied. The superintendent knows me, and he found a place for us in the building. We are leaving today. There is supposed to be an evening train bound for Moravska Ostrava. From there we'll find some means of transportation to Vienna. Bertel, what's the matter? You are crying. You have said nothing about yourself, and how you have managed to stay alive."

"God has sent you," I whispered. "He helped me by bringing this meeting about."

"I don't know what you are talking about," Ruth said. "Are you trying to say that after all that has happened to us, you still believe that God is guiding us?"

"Ruth," I said, attempting to explain, "five months ago I received a parcel from my mother. It contained house slippers, and they were my size. There was no note, and there was no address. But I know my mother's handwriting, and the package was mailed from Austria. Ruth, I beg you, please try to search for my mother when you get to Austria."

"You don't have to beg me," Ruth replied. "Do you have an address, a name, or the name of the camp she was in?"

"No, I don't. All I know is my mother was alive last December. Her handwriting was on the package, and the package was mailed from Schönbrun. I don't know what happened to Mother after that. We keep hearing rumors of people wandering about who can't be identified. They don't know who they are. They are thought to be Jews. I heard that Jewish survivors who have gone insane have been sighted, and that they refuse to go to hospitals. They can't be listed or reunited with their families because no one knows who they are. Do you also have such dark thoughts?" I asked Ruth.

"Don't do that to yourself," Ruth admonished. "Thoughts like these are very destructive. I have seen people like that in the hospital where I found Heinz. It's terrible. To think they were once, normal like you and me."

"I also saw some of them," I told Ruth. "On the road, they were walking out of Auschwitz. It was an awesome sight. They looked so strange, so not of this world. Will you promise me to look for my mother? Will you try?"

"Don't be silly. Of course I will do whatever can be done. That I promise you."

I took out a photograph that Stefan had recently taken of me. On the back I wrote: "For my mother. I pray that Ruth Wischnitzer will find you." I added the name and the address of the photo studio in Swietochlowice. Ruth looked at the photograph and read the words I had written. We hugged each other and wept. I watched them walk away, and I realized I wanted to go with them.

There was a continuous struggle to acquire photographic equipment, and Stefan had found a source in Katowice that so far had supplied us with the required chemicals and the postcard-size paper we needed. In late May, while Stefan was away, a young Russian soldier walked into the studio. He told me that he wanted a photograph of himself. He wanted it wallet size, so he could always have it on his person. Only one? I asked. He nodded; that was what

I gave this photo to Ruth Wischnitzer. She was to search for my mother in Austria, and deliver the photo to her. Swietochlovitz, Poland, early spring 1945.

he wanted. It seemed to me that the young fellow could not have been more than seventeen years old. He was nice looking and well groomed.

"Don't you want to send a photo to your family or perhaps to a girl-friend?"

The young soldier shook his head. "There is no one," he said. "The Soviet people are my family, and that is the family I have pledged to defend and to protect. All I wanted to do was to kill Nazis, free the world of the Nazi murderers, and I never even fired a single shot. I did have a mission, and I was willing to die for my country. Now they are sending me back, and they never gave me a chance to avenge my family."

"There must have been much sorrow in your life," I said. "You are so young."

"No, no, not young. I just turned eighteen. I don't think I was ever young. All I remember of my youth is the murderous assault of the retreating Nazi horde as it stormed through my village. When the German army first came through my village in the Ukraine, in 1941, in June, they gave us food, and they wanted us to like them. But once they were beaten, they turned into bloody killers. When we learned that they were approaching, my mother and all the other mothers sent the children to hide in the forest. Some of the men also went to hide. My father was crippled and could not go anywhere, and my mother stayed with him. When we were certain that the Germans had left, we came out of the woods. All we saw was smoke. Our house was burned to the ground, so was the barn, and all the other dwellings in the village. When we got closer, we saw all around us, hanging from trees, the villagers who had remained behind. They were old men and some women. And hanging from a tree were the bodies of my mother and my father."

The young man carefully extracted a photograph that was wrapped in a piece of cloth. There were seven bodies hanging from trees. He pointed at two of them and said, "My parents." Then he identified each of the other five people by name. It was a gruesome sight. When I told Stefan about the encounter, Stefan said that though the young man does not realize it yet, he was fortunate that the war was over. He had been much too eager to sacrifice his young life.

Swietochlowice without the colorful presence of the Russian soldiers was a drab and dreary town. Between the Volksdeutsch residents and the homeless Poles who had been urged to occupy the vacant apartments left behind by the fleeing Germans, there was mutual dislike and distrust. Ever since the defeat of the German army, there had been a continuous departure of the Volksdeutsch residents. Although the new Polish government did not urge anyone to leave, neither did they encourage the former Volksdeutsch residents to remain. There was a perception that former Polish citizens who had pledged allegiance to the Third Reich had thereby forfeited their right to protection from the new Polish government.

Even though Ruth Wischnitzer had said that she had not been able to find a single member of the former Hindenburg Jewish community, I needed to go and see for myself. I also wanted to look at our apartment and at my father's store. The war in Europe had ended. Though rail transportation, or even street-cars, had not yet been fully restored, I decided I could get to Hindenburg on my newly acquired bicycle. I had wanted to go to Hindenburg even before the German surrender, but Stefan thought it was too dangerous. Toward the end of the war, German deserters roamed the countryside. They were con-sidered to be dangerous. There had also been incidents of Russian soldiers rap-ing German females. We eventually learned that there had been a period of lawlessness when the Russians invaded Germany, but that Russian military police had restored order within twenty-four hours. Besides, during the past months I had met many Russian soldiers and officers, and I did not see them as a source of harm.

My first attempt to visit Hindenburg was a disaster. I had been told the distance from Swietochlowice to Hindenburg was about thirty kilometers. It took me five hours of hard pedaling to reach Hindenburg. Several times, trucks filled with Russian soldiers slowed down, and the drivers asked me if I wanted a ride, suggesting I could put my bicycle on the truck. When I declined, they would laugh, wave, and accelerate away. When I finally arrived in Hindenburg, I felt exhausted. Wheeling my bicycle, I walked along the empty streets. It appeared that Hindenburg had suffered little damage during the war. I could see no place to park my bicycle since I did not have a lock. I felt uncomfort-able being alone on the road and riding home in the dark. I realized that I had to turn around immediately and head back. In a way I felt good about my modest success, and I told Stefan that it had been a reconnaissance trip.

I had wanted to see if I could get there. I said that next time I would take public transportation.

Several days after my reconnoitering adventure, I took a streetcar to Chorzow, walked to a distant streetcar stop on the outskirts of town, and from there I managed to find bus transportation that connected with a streetcar bound for Hindenburg. It took four hours, and I arrived at my destination at about eleven o'clock in the morning. First I walked to our store; it was closed. The entrance door, as well as the two display windows, were locked and barred. I tried to look through the metal grate, but I could not see much. Diagonally across the street was the apartment house where we had lived: Kronprinzenstrasse, Nr. 266. The windows were open, and I recognized the sheer material of our curtains. I gathered my courage, crossed the street, and walked up the two flights of stairs.

I rang the doorbell. There was no answer. I heard voices within, and I made a quick resolve not to cry. As I lifted my hand to ring the bell again, the door opened with a jerk, and a tall Russian officer stood in front of me. From the bars on his epaulets, I deduced he was a captain. He must have just put on his tunic because it was unbuttoned.

"Yes, yes," he said in Russian. "What is it you want?"

Not having prepared for that eventuality, I was momentarily speechless. I looked into the captain's eyes, and I caught an expression of bemused impatience. I knew he would not slam the door shut while I was standing there.

"Captain, sir," I said in the best Russian I could muster, "this is my apartment."

"You said—what?" he asked. He turned and spoke to someone inside the apartment. Within seconds two more officers came out of the kitchen at the end of the corridor.

"Can you believe this?" the captain asked the two men. "This German girl comes here to tell us that we are occupying her apartment."

"No, Captain, sir," I replied. "I am a Jewish girl, and I was forcibly taken from this apartment by German police and the Gestapo. Neither I, nor a member of my family, was allowed to return. We were not permitted to take anything, not even a suitcase."

"And when was that?" the captain asked.

"In October 1938."

"In October 1938? This is May 1945."

I did not move. The captain stepped back, and for several minutes the officers exchanged words I could not understand. Perhaps, I thought, they will ask me to walk in and look around. That was all I had really hoped to achieve. I was still standing outside the apartment doorway. The captain turned back to me.

"This apartment was empty when we took possession," he said. "You must address your grievance to the German people who robbed you, not to us. I am sorry, but I don't quite see how I can help you."

The officer's tone had softened. I thought perhaps now, if I were to ask, he would let me look around, but I disregarded my impulse. I nodded and turned to go back downstairs. I looked back briefly, my glance locking for an instant with three sets of eyes fastened on me. Then I heard the familiar click of our door as the lock snapped into place.

Feeling unnerved, emotionally off balance, I stopped at the first floor landing. Why had I come? What could I have carried back with me? At that moment, there was not one golden memory associated with our apartment that I could recollect. The image my mind conjured up was of my mother, her composure shattered, sobbing inconsolably in her bedroom, while I, hovering on the other side of the door, stared into a dark future. Perhaps all I had wanted to accomplish was to view one more time the only home I had ever had.

Along Kronprinzenstrasse, the main thoroughfare that stretched almost from one end of town to the other, the apartment houses appeared to be well maintained. There was greenery and even flowers in window boxes and balconies. The stores located at street level were closed and barred. The Kochman Ecke, a complex of buildings owned and operated for several generations by the Kochman family, appeared to be unchanged. In his letters, Zack had informed me that all members of the Kochman family had left Germany after the Kristallnacht pogrom. The family had used their considerable wealth to settle in Palestine.

Peter-Paul Platz, the modern business square diagonally across the street from the Kochman Ecke, appeared ghostly in its dearth of activity. The imposing fish store, Nordsee, that had occupied one of the corners was empty. Throughout the store, walls and counters had been tiled with gleaming, white squares. Everything in the store was white except for the insides of the vast fish tanks. In the fish tanks, the tile had been sea green, a clever attempt to simulate the ocean. Now, the white tile looked gray; the tanks were chipped and dirty.

Pedestrians were conspicuously absent. The empty streets were confounding. I passed the familiar buildings, and as I looked up at the windows of the apartments where so many of my Jewish friends and neighbors had resided, I saw that they were occupied. People looked down at me from behind sheer curtains. It was noontime, and there was only an occasional passerby, though the curfew maintained by the Russian authority did not commence until evening.

I walked past the Admiralspalast Hotel, where only months earlier I had spent a sleepless night listening for dreaded footsteps in the hallway. Taking the underpass that ran parallel to the Redenhutte, the large steel mill that had provided employment for several hundred people, I was struck by the stillness engulfing the huge mill complex. In my memory, this stretch of town had resounded with an unceasing clangor. The clicking sound of the blast furnace was audible throughout the night. During the day at designated times, we heard the piercing sound of a siren, signaling the end of one work shift and the beginning of another. At night, one would see the reflection of red-hot coal from an open hearth kept in continuous operation, while the tall brick chimneys belched dark smoke into the sky. I wondered about the mill workers. I remembered some of their faces. I wondered if many of these workers had profited from Hitler's plunder. With all industry at a standstill, there must have been many thousands of unemployed workers in the area.

When I turned right at the Haendler Mühle, the flour-mill complex once owned by the Haendler family, members of the Hindenburg Jewish community, the mill also appeared deserted. The miller in charge, Herr Zimmerman, was a big and jovial man, and his wife was petite and rather timid. Their daughter Lotte, Eva's friend, was an adored only child, and she had the run of the mill. Lotte had many Jewish friends, whom the Zimmerman family graciously invited into their home. Their one-family brick house was located on the mill premises. For several years, perhaps from 1934 to 1936, our parents had urged Eva not to leave me behind when she left to meet with her friends. While Eva would have preferred to socialize without me, she would not disobey Mother's directive. For me these tagalong adventures to Haendler Mühle were happy times. With Eva and her friends, both Christian and Jewish teenagers, I played hide and seek in warehouses containing huge white flour sacks filled with grain.

Jostling each other, giggling all the time, we climbed up ladders leading to chutes from which we could slide right into a warehouse. In midafternoon we would gather at the Zimmerman house, where Lotte's mother served hot chocolate, often with whipped cream. But in 1936, Eva's association with Lotte and her other Christian friends was peremptorily terminated.

Immediately adjacent to the flour mill was the synagogue garden. Recessed, shaded by tall trees, and encircled by a fence, the children engaged in play could only be seen during the winter months when the trees were bare. In the sanctuary of the synagogue garden, we played soccer and volleyball, while little children from the Jewish kindergarten, supervised by Fräulein Preiss, played in the nearby sandbox. The synagogue, a beautiful red-brick baroque structure with twin domes and stained glass windows, was gone. In its place was an empty expanse of grass. Zack had written that during Kristallnacht the synagogue had been burned, but somehow I had not thought that it had burned to the ground without leaving a trace. The adjacent Jewish Community Building was still there. It was occupied, and I was sure that I was being watched. I was standing within the synagogue complex, and I imagined that the barely visible observer might have an idea why I was there and what I was seeking.

In the years before my expulsion from Germany, the Jewish community and its board of directors had made additional rooms available for the gathering of its young people within that community building The building became our favored meeting place, a temporary refuge from the heckling and derision spurred by the Nazis' mounting hostile propaganda. I walked around the complex for quite a while, but the only living creature I encountered was a large gray cat.

Rather than retrace my steps, I decided to walk through the tunnel, the alternate route back to the center of town. Before I left, I wanted to catch a glimpse of yet another residential part of town that was bound up with my memories. Advancing toward me was a tall, slender woman. Holding each of her hands were two little girls. Holding on to the hand of one of the girls was a boy, perhaps a year or two older than the girls. I made room on the sidewalk to let them pass. The woman hesitated; our eyes met. She let go of her children's hands, and we were in each other arms. It was Fräulein Hedel. While the three children stared and tugged at their mother's coat, we kissed, wept, and embraced each other. Hedel was visibly moved and very happy at seeing me alive, and she said so over and over again. There was no question in my mind that her joy was genuine.

Smiling through her tears, Hedel turned to her children and said, "This is Bertel." To my utter amazement, the children, seven-year-old Norbert and Gerda and Inge, about five and four years old, knew who I was. Hedel wanted to know about my mother and about Eva. I could not explain, not out in the street and not in front of her children. Besides, at that moment I was not even sure that I wanted to share my overwhelming sorrow with this once loyal family friend.

Hedel's relationship with our family was complex and deep. At one time she had been Eva's and my nanny. After we started school, she remained a cherished friend, someone my parents could count on when help was needed. With Fräulein Hedel, Eva and I would attend musical and theatrical events presented by touring companies. Most memorable were the adventurous summer vacations. Sometimes my mother would take Hedel and us to a mountain resort with a nearby lake or swimming pool and then leave us with Hedel. At other times we went alone with Hedel, and during the vacation, Mother would come and visit for a few days. Hedel was, to the full extent of the phrase, *in loco parentis*. She made all the decisions about where we went and how much money we spent. Though perhaps twelve years my mother's junior, the two women were good friends.

For many years we looked forward to celebrating Christmas day at Frau Moik's house, Hedel's mother. Under the beautifully decorated tree were presents for Eva and for me. Hedel's two married sisters, Mariechen and Mielchen, arrived with daughters close to us in age. All of us feasted on splendid food, and there was always an abundance of gingerbread in various shapes and other treats. My favorite was Mohnkuchen—poppyseed cake. Hedel, in turn, participated in our respective birthday parties and attended our piano recitals. In her gentle tone of voice, she instructed us about proper decorum and good behavior. She celebrated our Jewish holidays with us, was familiar with Jewish customs, and knew our Hebrew songs. When I participated in school performances and my mother was too distracted to fashion or obtain the appropriate costume for me, Hedel would jump into the breach. In the nick of time, she would create a costume that was both appropriate and outstanding.

The Nürnberg decrees obviated decisions on either Hedel's part or my parent's. For Hedel and our other Christian friends, who were suddenly designated "Aryans" by the National Socialists, visits to our house became impossible. At about that time, Hedel married a man who was a women's hairstylist. Subsequent meetings between us were now confined to random street encounters.

Here we were, seven years later, meeting once again in the street, our affection for each other undiminished. Yet, each of us knew that nothing would ever be as it had been, as it should have been. The world had been upended. The crimes committed against the Jewish people were too horrific to put into words. They were hovering between us, an insurmountable barrier. Hedel wanted me to come home with her. I explained that I could not stay away without notifying Stefan, and telephone communication had not yet been restored.

Hedel told me that her husband had been transported to Russia, and according to information she had been able to obtain, he had been put to work on some Russian project. Tears brimming from her eyes, she recounted how they had been duped by the invading Soviet army. Due to a health problem, her husband had been exempted from military service in the German Wehrmacht, and he had spent the war years working at his trade. Toward the latter months of 1944, all exemptions from the military were rescinded. Together with other disabled men, he was drafted into the Volkssturm, or home guard. When the Soviet army invaded, the Russian military police immediately ordered all male residents to report to the market square, ostensibly to be registered. Members of the National Socialist Party, the Russian commandant of Hindenburg advised, would be held accountable for their actions during the past years. There was an inference that the men whose "hands were clean" need not fear. They would be set to work to rebuild the damaged infrastructure of Hindenburg and its environs.

Hedel's husband, with Hedel's acquiescence, decided to report of his own free will, rather than go into hiding. Since that day, Hedel had not seen him . Apparently, the Soviet authority had decided that the restoration of the Soviet Union infrastructure should precede that of the conquered territory. Hedel obtained information that her husband had been transported to Russia, but by the time we met, she had already received notification that her husband would be able to return home in the not-too-distant future. I said that the war was over and she should not despair; what was most important was that her husband was alive and would shortly be reunited with his family. Our respective realities did not coincide. Each time Hedel referred to the treachery of the invading Soviet army, I had to call upon my self-restraint. She wanted me to understand that she and some members of her family, though not all, had also been victims of a war they did not want and of a regime they apparently had not embraced.

I told Hedel that I viewed the Soviet army as my liberators. I said that during the last few months, the relentless advance of the Russian troops had bolstered my waning courage and provided me with the strength to evade the ever-tightening noose of the Nazis.

Hedel nodded her head. She put her arm around me and said, "I will never really know what you endured. I think it is beyond human comprehension. Perhaps you will tell me? We keep hearing about terrible events that have taken place. We did not know, who knows maybe we did not really want to know. I feel that the very fact that you are standing here is a miracle. They must have pursued you; I know that much. Yes, Bertel, I understand that you were haunted and hunted, and I am so happy that they did not get you. The Jews were powerless. The evil pack of Nazis took your home, and there was no place to hide. We, however, did have an alternative. When the Russians invaded, we could have resisted. The Russians did not come to our homes to pick up our men, though they did threaten that they would. We were not smart enough to make the right decision to hide our men until things calm down. The wily Russians duped us."

I knew that Hedel did not understand. How could she know what it meant to be haunted and hunted? They were descriptive words for something she had heard, perhaps read. I had not mentioned Eva, and I sensed that perhaps she did not really want to know the gruesome truth. I wanted to get back to Stefan. I was not yet ready to sympathize with the victimization of German nationals who had been duped by Hitler, their elected leader, many years before the Russians even dreamed of invading Germany.

"You should know Bertel," Hedel continued, "all the men who did not report on that day are still sitting in their homes, enjoying their home comforts. Their wives are working for the Russians, bringing home needed food items. And you know what? There are many Nazis among them, and even some who did bad things. And we who thought we had nothing to fear, who never even belonged to the party, we have to pay the price."

It was getting late. We embraced amid tears and declarations of affection. We made a date for the following Sunday. I was to come with Stefan to Hedel's apartment. We agreed that we must see each other one more time before my departure for Warsaw. I promised that perhaps on Sunday I would tell her about Eva and my mother.

On Sunday, Stefan and I arrived at Hedel's apartment at the agreed-upon time. I wanted Stefan to meet Hedel. I wanted him to hear from someone other than me about my childhood in Hindenburg. I wanted him to have some discourse with a decent German person. He would not believe that they even existed. When I tried to explain that though there were many fine and decent Poles, too many of them had been willing to ally themselves with the Nazis and aid them in my capture, Stefan dismissed my argument. He thought Polish collaborators were an anomaly, members of an underclass beyond redemption. I, of course, knew otherwise. I knew that inherent Polish anti-Semitism had impelled many Poles to aid the Nazis in their war against the Jews.

At the neat and comfortably furnished apartment, aside from Hedel and her three children, were her sister Mariechen and her sister's husband Walter von Kolontai. I knew them well, and we embraced and kissed. They were very happy to see me. We talked about their family and about my family, but all conversation was confined to the past, our common experiences in the years before the German people empowered Hitler to become their leader. Hedel brought out photographs of my family, many with her, some just of my family. As the photos passed from one hand to the other, the children identified members of my family, including visiting relatives, even my grandmother on my mother's side. The three children, together with Hedel, sang for me in Hebrew the Hanukkah song my parents, Eva, and I had sung throughout the eight days of Hanukkah, each night lighting an additional candle. For me, the visit was full of pathos, memories of a vanished past. The fact that Hedel's German children knew a Hebrew song that was no longer part of my life was indeed amazing. Throughout the years of Hitler's tyranny, Hedel had apparently treasured her friendship with my family. Keeping in her possession the many photos of us was in itself an act of defiance.

It was a strained afternoon. Hedel and her family did not know Polish, and Stefan had never learned to speak a single German word. Yet, they did want to know about each other and how the war had affected the other. I translated as they spoke. For Stefan, the war had meant occupation of his country by an enemy, having to forego the profession he had trained for, and, most of all, the constant effort to evade the enemy by projecting himself as an insignificant person not worthy of notice.

What I knew about Hedel's family was what I had heard my parents say about them. Walter von Kolontai was not inducted into the German Wehrmacht because he had a lame leg. I thought it was an injury sustained in World War I, but of the latter I was not certain. He had always used a cane to support his lame leg. My father had mentioned that he had been a socialist. His wife, Frau Mariechen, had for a number of years assisted Fräulein Simenauer in administering an afterschool arts and crafts program, sponsored by the Jewish community and housed in the Jewish Community Building. I had no knowledge of Walter's activities during the war years. My father had spoken of him as a decent person, and I wanted to believe that he could not have been more than mildly tainted by the Nazi poison.

When I translated what Stefan was saying, I edited the pejoratives Stefan used whenever he spoke of the Boche. I also deleted the von Kolontai references to their own victimization by the Nazis. It showed a lack of sensitivity, especially after Stefan recounted the Nazi destruction of a large part of Warsaw. We had barely finished drinking our tea, when Stefan signaled he was ready to leave. Hedel told me, privately, that perhaps inviting Stefan to her home had not been such a good idea. When we were about to leave, she asked me to come for a moment to her bedroom.

From a drawer, she withdrew a cloth-wrapped bundle and proceeded to untie several knots. Within the bundle were a number of gold ladies' watches. Hedel said that it was not right that I should be without a watch on my wrist, while she had so many. She extracted a handsome gold watch with a black grosgrain ribbon and fastened it around my wrist. I was dumbstruck. She retied the bundle and tried to usher me out of the room. I said that I could not allow her to give me such an expensive gift.

"You know my sister Mielchen," said Hedel. "She wanted me to have them, to use them as I saw fit, and now I want you to have one of them, in memory of our meeting."

"Where is Mielchen now?" I asked.

"The Hoffman family left Hindenburg several months ago. They did not want to be here when the Russian army invaded. Her husband has relatives in Bavaria, so that is where they went."

Holding on to my arm, Hedel admired the look of her fine present. I understood that upon leaving, Mielchen, whose husband had owned a jewelry store, wished to make sure that her sister would have something to fall back on during the hard times ahead. When I remonstrated and said that the watch Hedel gave me could be traded for food for her family, Hedel turned a deaf ear to all my arguments. When I said that I wished I had something I could leave with her, she put a finger to my lips. We embraced and kissed. Both of us were emotionally overwhelmed. Before leaving the room, Hedel pulled my sleeve over the watch, hiding it and thereby keeping her gift secret. I promised Hedel that once settled in our next temporary home, I would write and forward my address. When we parted, there was an understanding that our paths would not cross again. Hedel's wish for me was a speedy reunion with my father in America.

I wanted to tell Stefan about the watch, but his lack of understanding about Hedel's relationship with my family prevented me from doing so. That night I could not fall asleep. For two days, the thought of the hidden watch was always on my mind, and I did not feel good about it. During our last visit to Katowice, while Stefan delivered photographs he had taken of a visiting Polish theater group that was performing at the Katowice State Theater, I spent the time looking at the display windows of newly established enterprises. In one of the windows, a woman sat in front of a knitting machine, fashioning children's garments. Hanging from wooden pegs were articles of children's clothing, among them leggings in various sizes. All articles were made from reprocessed wool. I knew what I wanted to do. Estimating the sizes of Hedel's three children, I purchased three pairs of navy leggings.

I told Stefan that I would once more return to Hindenburg to see Hedel and that I wanted to do it by myself. I showed him the leggings I had purchased for the children. Then I showed Stefan the watch. He was stunned. "Why did she do it?" he asked, and then came the inevitable question, "Why did you accept it? They so obviously are struggling to make ends meet, and for them there are rough times ahead, especially until the husband comes home. I can't understand why your friend would want to give you such a precious gift."

I did understand Hedel's generous gesture, but how could I explain to Stefan that love was the underlying motive? He agreed that it was right that I should return the watch. When I said I was going back to return the watch and that I had purchased the woolen leggings because I had noticed the children's darned cotton stockings, he shrugged his shoulders. He could understand, he said, that the watch should be returned; however, he could not understand why I would take money from our meager savings to buy such an expensive gift.

Carrying the parcel with the three pairs of navy woolen leggings, I once again made my way to Hedel's apartment. My visit came as a surprise. I saw that Hedel had been crying. When I asked her what had happened, she answered that the future looked so bleak, she often found it difficult to dispel her dark thoughts. Then she smiled and said had she known I was coming, she would have kept all dark thoughts at bay.

I gave Hedel the package. She opened it and happily spread the three pairs of leggings next to each other. "How did you know that this is what the children needed most?" she asked. "I knit, but it's impossible to obtain wool."

I asked Hedel if she had encountered problems with the newly established Polish municipalities. Was there anything I could do? Did she need me to intercede on her behalf? Hedel told me that there had been no attempts to persecute her, but she knew of many residents who had not fared that well. In any case, Hedel informed me, she had no plans to remain in an area the Allied governments had deeded to Poland. "I will remain here until my husband returns, then together we will leave and head west to the part of Germany that is now under the jurisdiction of America and England. Eventually, they will leave, everyone knows that, and we want to live in Germany."

I only stayed for a short while, and Hedel walked down with me to the lower landing where I had left my locked-up bicycle. We embraced and I slipped the gold watch into Hedel's hand. "I will never forget that you wanted me to have it," I said. "But the thought that I would have it on my wrist, while you may need it to buy food or medicine would be an unsustainable burden."

"Bertel, it was my present to you. I wanted to say something I could not put into words."

"I understand," I responded. "We are trying to say to each other what is important to both of us. We both won't forget."

Stefan was busy making inquiries regarding our trip to Warsaw. With great effort he secured access to a highly placed Polish government official in Katowice. The officer advised him that to enter the Polish capital would be against explicit orders issued by the Polish government. He would be stopped and interrogated by both the Polish and the Russian authorities. Access to Warsaw was temporarily off limits. Work crews with scarce resources were still in the process of dislodging bombs and mines and clearing debris. When Stefan said he wanted to return to the Warsaw area and did not want to stay in Katowice, they suggested he should move to the Baltic coast instead, which had once again become part of Poland.

The Baltic Sea connected to the Atlantic Ocean. Moving there, I reasoned, would bring me closer to America. The very thought of getting closer to my goal was invigorating. I did not really want to return to Warsaw. Stefan suggested that we settle in the resort town of Sopot, located midway between the seaport cities of Gdynia and Gdansk. In 1939, immediately after the invasion, Gdynia, Poland's only seaport, and the area surrounding it had been annexed to the Third Reich. The indigenous Polish residents were expelled, and German nationals as well as ethnic Germans had moved in to replace them. Gdansk, the historic medieval Hansa State of Danzig with its ancient walls and churches, I remembered well from my geography lessons. While a student, Stefan had vacationed on the Baltic Sea coast, and my parents had talked about the happy days they had spent on a steamship cruising on the North Sea. I had never seen an ocean.

It was Stefan's thought that the photo studio in Swietochlowice should continue to carry his name but that the running of the studio would be left to our employees. Elizabeth and Alice would be in charge of taking and processing the photographs, and Halina would manage the financial end of the enterprise. From the money the women earned, they would pay their salaries and the minimal rent charge—a sort of monthly tax that had to be delivered to the municipal office. It was important to me that the business continue in its location. Our present address was listed with the Jewish agencies in Krakow and Katowice. I had left my address with my contacts in Krosno and Bochnia, and I had given it to Ruth Wischnitzer when she promised to search for my mother in Austria. In addition, there were a number of letters to my father in various post offices, awaiting the resumption of overseas mail. I had put our Swietochiowice address on all envelopes and into telegrams dispatched to my father in New York.

In the midst of all this activity, I became ill. My stomach and intestines were racked with painful spasms. I lost my appetite and vomited whatever morsel of food I ate and ran a low-grade temperature. The physician we saw in Katowice suggested that an aggravated state of anxiety had affected my digestive system. He urged that I avoid stressful situations. The thought of being the only survivor of my family was sapping my strength.

I wondered if the three women left to run our affairs would be attentive to my needs. Stefan's repeated assurance that we had made sufficiently careful arrangements relieved my anxiety somewhat. He said he understood well what I was afraid of but that keeping our address in Swietochlowice would maintain all lines of communication. He pointed out that Halina was a loyal employee, as were the other two women. They had nothing to gain by withholding our mail or other information meant for us. Should someone come looking for me or for him, Stefan said, the women would direct the person to our new location. Stefan reasoned that an additional incentive for our employees' loyalty would be the larger salaries they would take home. Since we would no longer withdraw any payment for ourselves, all money earned would remain with our employees. Stefan was preparing to leave enough supplies for six months; after that time, he would return to Swietochlowice to evaluate the situation.

"All you have to do," Stefan urged, "is to concentrate on getting well. In your present condition we can't undertake what is bound to be an arduous journey. Have you changed your mind? Do you want to wait for a member of your family to contact you here? I thought we had agreed moving to the Baltic coast would bring us closer to our primary goal—to be in a position to leave Poland."

About this time, my tormenting nightmares started occurring more frequently. I woke in the middle of the night drenched in perspiration, after having once again narrowly escaped my pursuers. Once awake, the awareness that

I was safe returned. However, there were other agonizing thoughts: Had I done enough to find Mother and Eva? Was Eva roaming the countryside looking for us, perhaps bereft of reason? The fact that my many letters to Father remained unanswered added to my feeling of apprehension. Could he have died? Perhaps having learned of the mass killings he had concluded that all of us were dead and had decided to start a new family. There were days when I felt great—when I gloried in the salubrious spring weather and in my being alive to enjoy it. On those days I succeeded in banishing the anguish of the past years. It was the nights I could not control. When Stefan awoke, well rested, I made believe that I, too, had slept well.

CHAPTER 16

# On the Way to America

JUNE 1945 ✍ SOPOT, COMMUNIST POLAND

Toward the end of June, we left for the Baltic coast. We only took our clothes when we left the Swietochlowice apartment. Everything else, including the bicycle we had found there, remained behind. We had decided to continue renting the apartment for an additional three months. Though the war on the European continent had ended five weeks before, we were constantly made aware that we were living in uncertain times. Rules kept changing; laws, once put in effect, were suddenly substituted with new laws. A Communist Polish government was ostensibly in control of Poland, but the Russian military, though less conspicuous than immediately after liberation, was all around us. There was a perception that the Soviet Union and Stalin, their evil dictator, were making major decisions affecting Poland, rather than the newly constituted provisional Polish government.

Compared to the trip to Krosno, when we had been lucky to find a space to squat in the freight car, the rail accommodation to the Baltic coast was luxurious. We were able to secure seats next to each other in a passenger compartment, and there was a bathroom at the end of our railway car. Stefan was pensive, concerned about the logistics of our immediate future. There were new rules with regard to trade. All private enterprise was now subject to governmental scrutiny and permits. However, everyone had to be usefully employed, and preferably placed by governmental departments in accordance with governmental need. Still, Stefan was determined to circumvent these directives and to evade employment that would subject him to surveillance by agents of the Polish Communist government. He would not reveal that he was a licensed engineer, and since throughout the war he had managed to improve his photographic skills, he was determined to continue in this craft. The money we had earned during the past few months, both zlotys and rubles, he had managed to exchange for photographic equipment. I shared Stefan's concerns, but I felt confident that he would be nimble enough to successfully deal with the new Polish bureaucracy. This time it was my optimism that buoyed Stefan's waning courage.

The trip was uneventful until we were about eighty kilometers south of Bydgoszcz. It was half past ten in the evening when the train came to a sudden stop in the middle of a forest. Passengers seated near the window reported that soldiers were entering the train. Shortly thereafter, two Russian officers and several officers clad in Polish military uniforms entered our compartment. The Russian officers positioned themselves in the door while the Polish officers demanded that all passengers produce identification. Stefan was asked why we were traveling to the Baltic coast.

"My wife and I plan to settle in Sopot," Stefan replied.

"Your reason," the officer wanted to know.

"We were forced out of Warsaw in October 1944. Our home was destroyed, and we have been advised that we would be permitted to resettle in the liberated Baltic region."

"Doing what?"

"I will be working for the municipality in the communication department."

The officer returned our documents and moved to the passenger seated on my left.

Stefan's last statement was a total fabrication, though the idea had occurred as a passing thought when he contemplated ways to retain his independence. He had mentioned to me that if he could connect with the local newspaper covering news events as the paper's roving photographer, it would solve the problem of being "usefully employed," while allowing him to operate a photography studio.

The exchange between a woman sitting across from me and the examining officer went less smooth. "Don't you know your own name?" the officer shouted. "What! Are you telling me that you have misplaced your identity document?" The woman's male companion, speaking in a low voice, offered an explanation. There was a short exchange, and the woman produced the requested document. The officer apologized for losing his temper, and the patrolling group left the compartment.

In Bydgoszcz we had to transfer to another train, and we decided to spend the interval in the terminal. The woman whom the officer had so harshly addressed was seated on a bench. She looked ill, and her companion was trying to make her more comfortable.

"Is there something I could do to help?" I asked. "Perhaps I could get a glass of water?"

"It's all right now," the man responded. "My wife has a weak heart, and she got very upset. She is feeling better now. Still, if you would stay with her for a minute, I'll go and get something to drink."

After the man returned, we learned that the couple, a physician and his wife, were also traveling to Sopot. They told us that for the last stretch of the journey, from Gdynia to Sopot, we would have to take a bus. We had several pieces of luggage, and Stefan asked if there was much of a distance between the train terminal and the bus depot.

"There is a shortcut if you exit through the west gate," the man said. "Try to remain near us. Once we get to Gdynia, we will show you the way."

"That would be great," Stefan responded. "We feel fortunate that we met you."

By the time we boarded the train for Gdynia, the four of us felt at ease and chatted animatedly about the advantages of living in a resort town.

Pani Fala was a tall and handsome blond woman. Both her dress and her coat were made of a fine fabric and apparently custom-made. By contrast, my clothes looked dowdy, but she did not seem to notice it. She said she hoped that once settled in Sopot, we would see each other. Dr. Fala, a physician who had received his medical degree in 1937, had been licensed to practice medicine in Bydgoszcz. Before the war, he had been a cavalry officer in the Polish army. He was now attached to a military reserve unit. He advised Stefan that, immediately upon arrival, he should register with the Sopot municipal housing bureau to obtain an apartment. Apparently, residential permits to live in the town of Sopot were issued, or denied, in accordance with some discretionary policy. The German residents who had flocked to the resort town, when the area was annexed to the Third Reich, were now in the process of returning to their prewar homes in Germany, Dr. Fala said.

I asked Pani Fala what she had said that had made the officer angry, but before she could answer, the doctor said, "He asked for her name. Isn't that so, Franciszka?" Reaching for his wife's hand, he added, "Yes, at that moment my wife did not know her name, or rather at that moment, my wife did not know which name would be the appropriate one, and she hesitated. When the officer raised his voice, my wife panicked and could not find the document to substantiate the name she had given."

"Martin is right," the woman said. "For a moment my mind just stopped functioning. I was terrified because of a previous encounter we had experienced on this very train, also at night and in the middle of a forest."

Pani Fala told us that several weeks before, on a journey to Sopot, a roaming band of Polish nationalists, who proclaimed themselves to be true Polish patriots but who were, in fact, hoodlums, had stormed the train looking for Communists and Jews. Stefan said that he had read in the newspaper about roving bands of Poles who, under the guise of being part of a liberation movement, maintained themselves by robbing farmers of their livestock and produce. "I have not heard that they were also attacking trains looking for Jews and Communists. This is ridiculous," Stefan declared.

"I don't think *ridiculous* is the right word," the doctor objected. "It is well known that they have forcibly removed people from trains, dragged them into the forest, and killed them. The government is trying to hunt them down, to catch them," the doctor continued, "but so far they have not yet succeeded. I should think that this is quite an embarrassing failure for the combined effort of the Polish and Russian police forces."

Could the woman be Jewish? I wondered. In my mind, I reviewed everything Pani Fala had said. The indication that she possessed dual identity documents could suggest that. At that moment, in the train, I made the decision to not reveal my secret. I had been contemplating doing just that. I had thought that if I reclaimed my true identity, I could return to a legitimate and less stressful existence. The war was over, and Poland once again was empowered to fashion its own destiny. The realization that I was free to live as a Pole, but not as a Jew, came as a shock. I felt devastated. There were still Polish nationalists hunting and killing Jews. Apparently, the end of the war did not necessarily mean that for me the war had ended. In my eagerness for normalcy, I had wanted to believe that the terrible destruction the German nation had inflicted on Poland had also destroyed old prejudices. During our busy sojourn in Swietochlowice, we had not heard of these postwar atrocities. I was eager to be alone with Stefan. What would he now say about the Polish nationalists who, in his view, were the true honorable Polish patriots, compared to the Poles who had aligned themselves with the Polish Communist government?

## JULY 1945 ⤳ COMMUNIST POLAND

I had read many descriptions of the ocean. I had seen a number of pictures of both calm and turbulent seas, and I was aware of the wondrous predictability of the rising and falling of the tides. However, I was not prepared for actually seeing and experiencing such vast elemental power. The Baltic Sea appeared boundless and endless. A steel pier about twelve feet wide extended out for half a mile. Along the shore on both sides of the pier, stretching as far as the eye could see, was fine ivory-colored sand, glistening in the sunshine. Moving inland right up to the white stucco hotels were undulating dunes covered with sea grass.

I delighted in exploring the shore during that first leisurely afternoon by the sea. I decided to walk down the pier. I was about midway down, when a gust of wind coming from the sea whipped open my raincoat and almost toppled me to the deck. I didn't know that often with the onset of dusk, the weather could change dramatically. Storms could erupt suddenly and cause severe temperature fluctuations. The sea, which only one hour before had been dark green, turned gray. The sand had a yellow cast. The force of crashing waves shook the iron scaffolding I was standing on. I held tight to the railing as the pier swayed. Some rain fell. Just a minor storm, I was later told. On the following morning the sun shone on a blue ocean.

Each morning the sea was an exciting sight to behold, and I rejoiced in the privilege of viewing such splendor. These moments of euphoria were short. Immediately after feeling joy, I was assailed by sorrow. Wasn't there one member of my family—an aunt, uncle, or cousin—who could share my delight in being alive? Haunting thoughts about my sister cut short my moments of elation. Would Eva never again know what it meant to be young? What it felt to breathe the bracing sea air? Would she never know what it meant to be loved by a man? Was I being selfish to rejoice in being alive while ever more death camps where Jews had been slaughtered like cattle came to light? Stefan read the devastating reports, and he was stunned by the enormity of the atrocities. However, he repeatedly warned that if I continue to dwell on my sorrow, I would succeed where the Nazis had failed. He said that if I were to get sick and die, not a single member of my family would remain to tell about it.

From the Sopot housing bureau, we received two addresses of ethnic German residents who were in the process of packing and returning to Germany. We would have to share the apartment with the present occupants for several weeks until they left.

Dr. Helmut Wieland, an ophthalmologist, and his wife lived at the first address we visited. Frau Wieland said they would feel fortunate if we decided to move in with them. So far the Wieland couple had rejected three Polish applicants who had wanted to share their home. She explained that, due to the housing shortage, they had been asked to share their large apartment with a homeless Polish family, but they much preferred us. Both she and the doctor were in their late sixties and did not want young children underfoot. Dr. Wieland, she explained, kept office hours in their apartment, and members of the Russian and Polish military had come to see him with their eye ailments. In spite of that, she grumbled, he was advised that they would have to share their seven-room apartment.

Stefan and I decided to move in with the Wielands. The fact that I spoke German and Frau Wieland was able to tell me what I may or may not use facilitated the arrangement. The Wielands, educated and well informed, expressed horror at the German destruction of Warsaw, which had rendered us homeless. The housing bureau had informed us that Dr. Wieland's Nazi affiliation had been designated as "peripheral." The term was vague, but there was no question that the Wieland couple had benefited from Germany's conquests. Elegant thick Persian carpets covered the parquet floors, and Frau Wieland's silk French wardrobe was clearly fashioned by a couturier. Expensive paintings hung on the walls. The couple exuded an air of privilege.

There was quite a difference between the German residents we saw in Sopot and the natives of Polish Silesia, among whom we had lived before our arrival at the Baltic coast. From what I had been able to observe, the lifestyle of the miners and steel workers, except for minor conveniences, had not been greatly enriched by the Nazi plunder. In Sopot, the benefits of the riches plundered throughout the war from the various conquered countries were clearly visible among the Germans.

The only evidence of the collapse of one side and the takeover by the other was the burnt-out skeletal structure of what had been the luxurious Palace Hotel, which had housed the Sopot gambling casino. The new Polish residents and government officials declared with certainty that fleeing Germans had started the fire that had demolished the gambling casino. However, the German residents, including the Wielands who had lived in the town throughout the changeover, insisted with equal certainty, albeit in whispers, that it was the Russians who had torched the building before the Polish army entered the territory. Rumor had it that the Soviet army did not consult the provisional Polish government about it, because they feared resistance. The unilateral action was an expression of Soviet distrust of the Poles penchant for "capitalist decadence."

Frau Wieland never expressed surprise at my facility with the German language, and I, of course, did not think that an explanation was in order. I tried to avoid contact with Herr Wieland. When he addressed me—and it was always me, because Stefan could not understand German—he had a patronizing manner that made me feel uncomfortable. I knew some German physicians cultivated this affectation, but I found it annoying. Since both the Wielands and we used the same bathroom, it was difficult to avoid each other. One morning, in the long corridor that connected the various rooms, Herr Wieland stopped me and said, "My wife tells me you speak German like a native. Neither of us speaks your language. At our age it is difficult to twist one's tongue, ha! So for us having you as tenants is a decided advantage." I did not respond. Herr Wieland sounded jolly when he said this, but I had the distinct feeling that his joviality was a mask. I could easily detect the hard steel beneath his watery gray eyes.

The arrangement had not been a matter of choice for them; it was an assignment by governmental decree, and in their view we were the best of the lot. Between us we had agreed that the two rooms we would occupy would not be turned into a studio, but that the doctor's large office and the adjacent waiting room would be the ideal location for the studio, once the Wielands had moved out.

Stefan did not succeed in getting work with the local newspaper. However, an introduction by an acquaintance from Warsaw to an official at the local branch of the Ministry of Communication and Culture placed him in an even better position than he had dared hope for: He would be available to the department to take photographs in accordance with their requirements. He would not be employed, and he would not receive a salary. Instead, after each assignment he would present a bill. After receiving official press passes from the government's public relations department for each of us, Stefan registered his name with the various hotels. They promised to notify him regarding visits of important guests, and he in turn would supply the hotels, free of charge, with photographs of events that featured their guest. It was common knowledge that the term *culture* was a euphemism for propaganda, and none of the newspapers or publications would accept material from a reporter lacking the appropriate governmental clearance.

After searching several days for a photography studio, Stefan and I settled on a two- room unit previously occupied by a tailor. The rooms were on the first floor above an empty and ownerless camera and photographic equipment store on Ulica Rokossovsky. The street, a broad boulevard, was the main thoroughfare that led directly down to the sea. Stefan entered a limited partnership with Pan Zaczek, a Pole from Warsaw, who occupied the apartment adjoining the studio. Pan Zaczek, a bachelor, suffered from a hip injury and found it difficult to get around. He agreed to run the studio, make appointments, and help with advertising, thus freeing Stefan for several hours a day to pursue his avocation—that of a freelance photographer. Though I continued living under my assumed identity, Stefan wanted the studio to carry my real name. We registered the business under the name "Atelier Betty," and a sign with that name was prominently displayed in the window, clearly visible from the street.

I was capable of handling assignments whenever Stefan was otherwise engaged. I also could fill in at the studio and take photographs. At all times, we were on the lookout for newsworthy events and important people we felt should be photographed. Aside from Russian war heroes, such as General Konstantin Rokossovsky who had defeated the German army in Russia and General Georgi Zhukov who had commanded the Soviet armies when they reached the outskirts of Berlin, not too many Soviet functionaries visited

Sopot. We decided to concentrate on vacationing Polish dignitaries and local officials who wanted to enhance their image.

Toward evening, we rushed to the tiny darkroom, temporarily housed in the bathroom adjacent to the studio, and placed the exposed film into the developing tanks. We hung the film from clothespins and sped up the drying process with the aid of a fan. From contact prints, we selected interesting and complimentary photographs for enlargement. Not having been trained, I lacked the skills to make enlargements. Stefan would spend hours attempting to achieve the desired result. His artistry helped build up our portrait business, subsequently our major means of support. Acquaintances from Warsaw who learned of our Sopot studio traveled from Gdansk and other cities to sit for a portrait. We were saving money for the upcoming trip to Warsaw. Stefan wanted to locate his mother and I needed to visit the recently established American consulate.

Between attempts at making our living quarters more comfortable and earning enough money to support ourselves, we led a busy life. Toward the end of July, I received notice from the Sopot post office that a letter was waiting for me. It was mailed from New York and had taken almost two months to reach me. It came from my father. My joy was boundless, but it took me a while to read the letter through my tear-filled eyes. My father was in New York, and he was waiting for us—for the three of us. He was also waiting for my next letter, he wrote. He asked that I write about Mother and Eva. He couldn't understand why I had not written about Mother and Eva. Did I know where they were? Had I lost contact with them?

## AUGUST 1945 ⤶ SOPOT, COMMUNIST POLAND

My first food package from America awaited me at the post office. It was sent in my father's name, but it came from the United Nations Relief and Rehabilitation Administration (UNRRA), an agency that distributed food and clothing to the liberated countries living under American and English jurisdiction. I had read in the Polish newspaper that this fact had caused quite a bit of consternation because the UNRRA was distributing food and clothing to the Germans who had been the aggressors and not to the Polish people who had been the victims.

From the parcel I extracted a can of coffee, shortening, corned beef, powdered eggs, and powdered milk. When Stefan came home he found me sitting at the table in front of the canned goods. I was crying. I was indescribably happy, yet I could only express my emotions with tears. The following week another package arrived also from America and mailed by the UNRRA. Several days later came another letter from my father. It was seven and a half years since I had seen him last, and four years since all contact with America had ceased. For me, it had been an interminable time span. Just seeing his handwriting was overwhelming. My father wrote that he had sent many letters since he had first heard from me. Apparently, the initial news that I was alive had come via telegram. Again, he wrote that he could not understand why I had not written about Eva and Mother. He asked that I not delay. He concluded that he was attempting not to dwell on dark thoughts and that he was anxiously awaiting my reply. I kept rereading the letter. Was there something else—an implied reproach? I had not yet answered my father's first letter. My father wrote that he had contacted the U.S. State Department in Washington, and he was informed that an American consulate was about to open in Warsaw. The letter was written in German, and I translated it word for word so that Stefan could understand the portent of my father's questions.

"They are questions," Stefan assured me, "nothing else. He is very worried; that is obvious. You must sit down and write under what circumstances you were separated from your sister, and subsequently from your mother. I also think that the time has come to tell him about us." My father had also expressed surprise at my name, and he had asked me to explain.

It was a very difficult letter for me to write. My father had asked about Aunt Regina and Dollek, with whom we were living when America declared war on Germany. We had written to him about the murder of Uncle Jacub, Aunt Regina's husband. He did not ask about him, but he wanted to know about his four brothers and three sisters and their families, and of course about my mother's brothers and their families.

We received clearance to take photographs of the Stutthof concentration camp. The camp was located in an agricultural area south of Gdansk, within an hour's ride from Sopot. Until our arrival in Sopot, we had never heard about this concentration camp. Yet in the Baltic region, the camp was well known as a destination for Jews from Germany and later Jews from the Baltic countries and the Ukraine. Toward the latter years of the war, undesirable Poles, as well as Germans with "racially impure" antecedents, had also been transported to that remote camp.

At the camp, we were directed to a large iron gate. A uniformed Polish soldier stopped us at the entrance. Even after we showed him our press passes and the official permit, he appeared reluctant to let us go through the gate. "There is nothing here to see," he kept repeating. "You are wasting your time, and you could have saved yourself the bus ride."

"Well, we are here," Stefan said calmly. "We were assigned a task, and we intend to execute it."

"There is no one inside to take you around. I was informed that the camp was closed to visitors. I am here to see that these instructions are obeyed. Someday this will be a memorial."

"A memorial?" Stefan asked. "Anyway, you are wasting our time. We are here on a special mission, and I do not intend to stand around and argue with you."

The guard opened a side door, and we entered a large courtyard. Straight ahead, stretching perhaps for a quarter of a mile, were rows of wooden barracks. On the right side of the courtyard, a one-story red-brick building was conspicuous for its well-cared-for appearance. A little old man carrying a spade was walking toward us. He was puffing on a pipe that hung from a corner of his mouth.

"Be with God," he greeted us.

"And you with God," Stefan responded. "We have come from Sopot to take photographs of the camp."

"Ah, city people. For myself, I prefer the country, less trouble. You have come too late. They took everything out. They don't want any more visitors."

"Have you been here long?" Stefan wanted to know.

"No, not long, but long enough to know what has gone on here. They were cleaning up, and they needed someone to take care of the shrubs and the trees. But a man gets lonely without someone to talk to. Each day at the gate there is another guard, and they don't talk to me."

"Well, thank you very much," Stefan said. "We came to take some photographs, and we better get on with it."

The man nodded his head. There was a strange expression on his face as he pointed to a small square structure.

Stefan pushed open a heavy metal door, and we entered onto a mud floor. There was nothing in this dark windowless shack except for two huge clay ovens, taking up half the floor space. Each oven opening measured about twenty inches square. From hinges attached to the wall on both sides hung heavy iron doors, and massive sliding iron bolts were also attached to the walls with brackets. The old man had followed us, and he had put down his spade. "This is a furnace, you know, for people," he said. "That's where they burned the corpses of the Jews. When I came to work here, in the beginning of the summer, there was a chimney, a tall chimney. One Monday when I came to work, the chimney was gone. Gone, not a trace left. Next come the ovens, and that will be the end of Stutthof. Only God will know what was done here. He saw everything."

The man shook his head and muttered about sins that can never be forgiven. Several minutes later, he crossed himself, and without saying another word, he hobbled out of the shed.

Several days later when we submitted the Stutthof photographs for publication, we were advised that at the present time they would not serve a socially useful purpose and therefore would not be published. They would be preserved in the archives for future use. Stefan was angry, and he subsequently told me that when he mentioned the matter to some of his friends, he was amazed at the level of discontent with the Polish Communist regime that was building up around us. No one seemed surprised that the photographs would not be published. Information vital to the Polish nation was being withheld; the Soviet Union was suppressing historical facts that did not coincide with its propaganda. What troubled many Poles was the secrecy surrounding the massacre of Polish army officers in the Katyn forest during the early years of the war. There was a suspicion that Poland was not free to govern itself. The frustration was compounded by the fact that criticism of the Soviet Union could have dire consequences. In Sopot, we resided on Stalin Street, and our studio was located on Rokossovsky Street. How about our own heroes? Poles were asking.

I did not care whether we resided on Stalin or on Rokossovsky Street. The Soviet army had rescued me, and my gratitude was constant. Neither did I experience the visceral resentment against the Russians felt by many Poles.

Compared to the cruel and efficient German bureaucracy, the relative disorder of the Soviet government—the uncertain regulations, the vague directives—made it possible to evade contact with governmental agencies. All I wanted was to leave Poland as soon as possible. Because no one knew that I was Jewish, I heard various anti-Semitic innuendos. They were never explicit because it was understood this was not the time for intelligent people to openly express such sentiments.

I longed for contact with Jewish people, and I often thought that perhaps there were Jews nearby, people who had come to settle in Sopot and who, like me, refrained from revealing their identity. I tried hard to suppress these feelings of loneliness. Poland was not my country, and I never wanted to return to Germany. I was eager to leave Europe—to put an end to my homeless existence and establish my true identity. However, expressing a desire to leave Poland could have dire consequences. One had to be very careful to hide such seditious thoughts. Stefan shared my desire to leave Poland. Almost daily I admonished him to refrain from showing his discontent with the prevailing conditions and stifling restrictions, thereby jeopardizing my longed-for reunion with my father.

People were, in fact, disappearing. There were rumors that some Poles who had committed the treasonous act of openly criticizing the government had been taken to Siberia. An even larger number of Poles had disappeared and headed west, preferring to live in the benevolent climate of American and English occupation of Western Europe. Many Poles chose to leave their home because they did not want to live under a Communist-ruled Polish government. Illegal departure, trying to cross a border without permission by the Polish government, could result in transportation to Siberia.

The only people I felt relatively comfortable with were Fran and Martin Fala, the couple we had met on the train. Stefan and I had kept in touch with them and saw them regularly. When I asked Dr. Fala if he would be our physician, he wanted to know if I was pregnant; he was an obstetrician. Eventually, they told us that they were Jewish, and I revealed my identity to them. They said they had speculated about me because of my strained sentence structure and had wondered if during my early childhood I had had a speech defect.

Upon the invasion of Poland in 1939, Fran and Martin had fled east toward Russia. At first they were fortunate: they were far enough east to be overtaken by the advancing Russian troops and avoided the Germans. But in June

1941, when Fran was pregnant, Germany invaded Russia. With several other Jews, they managed to find a cave in a forest, and that was where their son was born. Polish partisan units were nearby in the forest, and together with them, the Jewish refugees carried out several acts of sabotage against the German enemy. The Germans spotted the source of the attacks and combed the forest. A number of Jews who were unable to run away, such as Fran and Martin with their new baby and several people who had been injured, remained in the cave. The Germans were listening for human sounds. The Fala infant was two weeks old, and Fran and Martin could not stop him from crying. There were eleven people in the cave. Martin with his own hands, with Fran looking on, had to suffocate their infant. Fran was not able to bring another child into the world. At times, Fran told me, her pain was unendurable.

I never found out why Fran could not conceive again. She was only twenty-eight years old. There was much that we did not talk about. I did not trust them enough to tell them that my father was in America, because that could indicate I was planning to leave, and plans of that nature were strictly forbidden. I could not tell them that Stefan and I had not been legally married.

Was I married? I was petrified of becoming pregnant, and it appeared to me that, since the end of the war, Stefan had been less scrupulous in taking precautions to prevent pregnancy. Yet, when I mentioned that once in Warsaw one of our first errands should be a visit to the Church of the Holy Savior to seek out the priest who had issued the provisional marriage license, I found Stefan's response vague, perhaps evasive. When I questioned him about it— when I said I could not go to America without a proper marriage certificate that validated our union—he only said, "Let's see what the priest says, and then we will consider our options."

Our first trip to Warsaw in August 1945 was a devastating blow. We had witnessed the demolition of the neighborhood I had lived in: The Nazis had wanted us to see the flaming torches and the collapsing buildings, and we had. Stefan knew that his neighborhood had undergone the same fate, and that was the reason he had brought the many rolls of exposed film—the photographs we took during the Polish insurrection in August 1944—to my apartment building. What we did not anticipate was the total destruction of Poland's capital. Only the several neighborhoods that the Germans occupied throughout the insurrection appeared to be relatively undamaged. The territory the Soviet army had occupied, the eastern bank of the Vistula River, called Warshava-Praga, also was not damaged. The rest of Warsaw resembled the Warsaw ghetto, ruins and debris and lots of ashes.

Wherever we walked, we seemed to be surrounded by people who, like us, were in a state of shock. Warsaw's architectural achievements, accumulated over hundreds of years, had been obliterated. Everyone stopped and looked and remembered. We did not speak to each other. No one had come prepared to encounter devastation of such magnitude. Occasionally there were angry outbursts, comments such as, "We got rid of the Germans, but they made sure that we will never forget them," could be heard. But for the most part, people stayed within their own groups, their eyes searching the rubble.

Thousands of people roamed the streets, everyone looking at the ruins of their former homes and the homes of their relatives and friends. But there were no hotels or accommodations to house them. We had hoped to find a shelter where we could spend the night, but the city had not yet progressed to that stage. After searching for more than six hours, we found in the Praga sector a woman who rented lodging for a night. It was about six o'clock in the evening, and the woman said that the bed in which we could sleep was presently occupied, but it would become available to us for six hours, beginning at midnight. Since a bed was difficult to come by, we felt as if we had won the lottery. We realized that we could never accomplish all we wanted to do in one day, however, and the woman could not guarantee a bed for the following night. We did make some progress. Stefan initiated a search for his mother, who had been deported from Warsaw ahead of us. We found the house I had lived in on Ulica Marshalkowska, and after an arduous walk through debris, we unearthed the two glass jars with the film we had hidden in the cellar.

The paraffin sealer was intact, the rolls of exposed film appeared undamaged. We had never seen prints of the photographs we had taken during the last weeks of the Warsaw uprising because Stefan's studio had been bombed and totally destroyed. Being once again in possession of the film was a euphoric moment. To Stefan, the metal canisters containing the rolls of thirty-five millimeter film were our most precious possessions. He thought that in America the action photographs we had taken would find an eager purchaser.

I had wanted to search for Danka. As far as we knew, her neighborhood had not sustained damage because it had been a German stronghold. We assumed that since the residents of that sector had not taken up arms against the Germans, Danka and her family would not have been deported. Stefan said we would make an attempt to travel to Ulica Falata on our next visit. I could not call Danka because telephone communication was not yet restored.

We were in the neighborhood of the Church of the Holy Savior, and I insisted that we go there before leaving Warsaw. Inside, the church was dark and dusty, though it had sustained only minimal damage. The priest who had issued our marriage license was not there. We had approached several confessionals in the hope of finding him. A young curate saw us looking around and walked up to us.

"Can I help you?" he asked. I had the certificate with me, but I did not want to show it to the young priest.

"We are looking for Father Stanislaw," I said.

"Father Stanislaw? No one answering to that name is here in this parish. Is there anything I can help you with?"

"I don't think so. We met with Father Stanislaw after the defeat of the powstanie. He was very kind. Could you tell us where we could find him?" I asked.

"I am sorry," the young curate responded. "I would like to help you, but I don't know where he is, or if he is alive. He was quite old, wasn't he? I do remember hearing the name, but three months ago when I arrived at this parish, there was no one here by that name."

The priest wanted to know where we lived, and he asked if we wanted him to hear our confession. Stefan thanked the priest and pulled me out of the church. He reproached me for insisting on this visit. He told me that even were we to find Father Stanislaw, there would be nothing he could do for us since I was not prepared to convert to Catholicism.

"Don't you understand," he asked, "that what was possible during the war would never be acceptable to the Catholic Church in peace time? There are strict rules that have to be followed, and there is little room for accommodating situations that deviate from church canon."

## SEPTEMBER 1945, WARSAW, COMMUNIST POLAND

Toward the end of September, we once again journeyed to Warsaw. We had secured two nights lodging in a rooming house in Warsaw-Praga. In the heart of the capital there were signs of commercial activity resuming. Although the skyscraper on Napoleon Square had twice been decapitated—first during the invasion and then during the Warsaw uprising—some of the lower floors appeared to be occupied. Nearby, there were cardboard shacks covered by corrugated metal. In the vicinity of the square, there was evidence of people living underground beneath the ruins. There were other signs of civilian life resuming. People carrying bundles, cartons, and scraps of metal came into view, and then disappeared from sight. There were neither doors nor gates through which they could have gone. Dignified-looking men in dark business suits were digging in the dirt and carrying pails of water. Apparently, they also were living amid the ruins.

On the following morning, I walked to the American consulate. Its temporary quarters were housed in the Polonia Hotel on Aleje Jerozolimski, located directly across from what used to be Warsaw's main train terminal. The huge steel girders that had supported the modern terminal were bent and torn apart and suggested a gargantuan broken harp. It was almost ten o'clock in the morning when I arrived at my destination, but I had to keep walking for several minutes because my stomach was in an uproar. I could feel my heart racing, and I was drenched in perspiration. I remembered how carefully my mother had dressed for each of her many visits to the American consulate in Berlin. She had hoped that her well-groomed and elegant appearance would help open the door to the office of the godlike man who held in his hands the keys to our salvation.

My outward appearance, I knew, was far from satisfactory. Several people, both male and female, had shared the room we had slept in. Everyone had slept in his or her clothes, and the amount of water apportioned to me had barely moistened a corner of my towel.

Despite my disheveled appearance, the registration I had anticipated with such trepidation went relatively smoothly. The secretary to the American consul—and she really was his secretary and not an assistant to an assistant—told me that my name had been forwarded to the consulate, but my father's affidavit had not yet arrived. The woman gave me a form that was several pages long and asked that I answer all questions to the best of my knowledge. I registered for myself, Mother, Eva, and Stefan. I wrote that my father was an American citizen, and that an American affidavit had been filed by him on behalf of the three of us, with the American consulate in Berlin in late May 1938. I wrote that I could not give my mother's or sister's address because I had not yet found them. I handed the completed form back to the secretary.

She read my statements, and while reading, she wrote brief comments with pencil in the margin. She looked up and said, "You do understand that this is only a preliminary registration. Your mother, sister, and your husband will have to appear in person. Your husband must bring a marriage certificate."

"Yes, thank you," I said. "Is there something else I should do? Will I need documents to substantiate my identity?"

"Well, no, there should be no problem once the state department forwards your father's documents. We might need the respective birth certificates, but I assume they also are part of your father's file."

"My father took copies of our birth certificates when he left Germany. I am certain of that."

"Well, I don't think that this is anything to worry about," the secretary responded. "However, there is another matter you should be aware of."

"What is that?" I asked, my senses alert to some alarming disclosure.

"There is no hurry, but you should think about obtaining a passport. Will you be able to get a German passport? If you reside in Poland legally, you might be able to obtain a Polish passport."

While she spoke to me and answered my questions, the secretary perused the questionnaire I had filled out. She got to the last page and saw that I had written Krystyna Broda when I filled out my current address. To the specific question regarding my name in the affidavit in 1938, I had written Berta Weissberger. The woman looked up and pointed out the discrepancy. I started to explain, but she interrupted me.

"I understand," she said. "There was much confusion during the war you managed to live through. Don't worry about the name, but you will need a passport."

When I closed the door behind me, I realized that tears were running down my cheeks. When the secretary said that there was a matter I should be aware of, namely securing a passport, my mind had raced ahead and supplied images of unattainable documents and inaccessible doors. I was certain that I did not want to cross the border into Germany, and I wondered what I would have to do to legitimize my residential status.

Stefan and I had agreed to meet on Ulica Marshalkowska in front of the house in which we had lived when we were evacuated. To identify the exact location, I had to count the ruins starting from the street corner. Stefan was waiting for me, sitting on top of an overturned bathtub. His face and hands were covered with dirt, and his trousers had been ripped open at the side. He had been digging in the rubble of his former apartment building and also in the ruins of his mother's building.

"Were you able to contact your mother's friends?" I asked.

"Yes, she is fine," Stefan was happy to report. "Mother is living with friends in Poznan. They are the same friends that had come to live with us when the province of Poznan was annexed to the Third Reich. They lived with us for almost a year. I am glad Mother found a safe shelter. She will be happy there."

I told Stefan what the secretary had said and that I had registered his name at the American consulate. He did not comment when I mentioned the marriage certificate. However, when I said that both of us would need a passport, he said, "Yes, you must do it now. For you that might be a problem. I think you should file an application at the Interior Department tomorrow morning, before we leave for Sopot."

"And you," I asked, "shouldn't you apply for a passport at the same time?"

"No." Stefan's response was very definite. He was certain that by registering for a passport, he would call attention to himself and become known as someone who was preparing to leave Poland. "Besides," he said, "I once had a passport, and there must be a record of it. Yours is a different situation. You never had a Polish passport. Do you have the address of the Interior Department?"

"No, I did not ask."

"That was a mistake," Stefan said. "It's probably housed in a building in Old Town, or perhaps across the river. You will never find it. Krysia, you must register for the passport before we leave," Stefan urged. "Go back to the American consulate and ask for the address. We probably will have to stay on for another day. Traveling to Warsaw is both difficult and expensive, and we should accomplish all we need to do while we are here. I also could use the extra time. We need additional supplies for the studio, and perhaps I could locate a manufacturer of photo chemicals."

On the following morning, I retraced my steps to the American consulate. The secretary reminded me that she had said I would need the passport, but there was no hurry. She explained that though the American consulate had been able to acquire temporary housing in Warsaw, the various governmental agencies were still in the process of finding a foothold in the bombed-out city. She said matters were improving daily, but the passport office was not yet open to the public and running an office in Warsaw was a constant struggle to overcome a myriad of obstacles. Her parting words were, "Here, we all have to learn to be patient."

While moving through the rubble on Aleje Jerozolimskie, one's eyes needed to be focused on the ground to avoid tripping over debris. Occasionally I would stop, straighten up, and look around. Near the intersection of Ulica Marshalkowska, I almost walked into Maryla Majerowicz. Both of us were stunned, overjoyed, and speechless at the same time. We embraced, stepped back to look at each other, and fell into each other arms, tears flowing from our eyes. We knew each others' families and shared many sad memories. Maryla's father had helped my mother and me many times. There was the unforgettable experience in Maryla's apartment in Tarnow, when I came pleading for temporary shelter. We looked at each other, and we knew that we were both thinking about that day and would remember it for as long as we lived. Maryla still looked like a young teenager. Her long, coltlike legs gave her a tall appearance. Her straight blond hair reached down to her shoulders. But there was a grief-stricken look in the widely spaced eyes set in a high forehead.

"Maryla," I said, "I will never forget your father."

"I know," she said.

"He was there for us throughout our most difficult times, advising us, helping us, a true friend to Aunt Regina and Dollek until their last days, and a loyal friend to us until his last day. Often during the night, when I am unable to sleep," I told Maryla, "I keep thinking of the many times when we came so close to the end of the road. Whenever we managed to pull away from the abyss, there was your father, helping us to get on with our lives."

In January 1944, this remarkable man was lying dead in a ditch near his rented home in Miedzeszyn, his murdered daughter Ewa at his side, their bodies unclaimed. Neither of us mentioned that traumatic event, but we were thinking about it.

During the war while living in Warsaw I had encountered Maryla only once or twice. I knew that her little sister had been hidden in a convent, and I asked about her mother, who also had been hidden. Both of them survived. I told Maryla that I had not yet found my mother, and that I was searching for her and for Eva.

"Do you believe that Eva can be found?" Maryla asked.

"It's possible. I won't give up hope," I said. "There are Jewish people who were taken away by the Nazis and who did survive—we know that."

"Yes, but no one who was taken away from Krosno survived."

"Or Bochnia or Krakow," I added. "It's overwhelming. I went to all these towns. How is it possible that no one taken away on these transports has come back?"

"I also went to Jaslo and to Tarnow," Maryla said. "No one came back. Have you been able to establish contact with your father?"

"Yes I found him, and that is my good news. Just now, I am returning from the American consulate. I am not yet allowing myself to believe that I will be reunited with my father. It's been more than seven years. Maryla, I am so glad that we met," I said. "It is so good for me to find someone from Krosno."

"When will you be leaving for America?" Maryla asked.

"It will be a while. To assemble documents, to obtain transportation—all that takes time. But most important, I must find out what has happened to my mother and to Eva. You know, Maryla, I have not yet told my father why I am alone and that I don't know where Mother and Eva are."

"You have to do it," was Maryla's response. "Your father has to know, don't you think?"

"And you?" I asked. "What are you doing in Warsaw?"

"I am passing through. I am leaving Europe, and the only way I can do that is to try and make my way first to Germany and then to Italy."

"Italy?" I asked, but I knew already.

"I am going to Palestine. My father's brother lives there. He has been living there for many years."

"Maryla," I asked, "how do you intend to get there? There is no transportation. How will you manage to cross the Mediterranean Sea? You will need to obtain a certificate from the English government."

"I can't answer all these questions. I don't know. I'll find a boat. All I'm certain of is that is where I am headed. They have been saying to us, 'Go back to Palestine. That's where Jews belong.' Well, I am going. The Balfour Declaration in support of a Jewish homeland in Palestine is meaningless until we go there and build a country. I would rather live and work in the hot desert than here on this blood-drenched earth. I am leaving Poland, and I am determined to reach Palestine. When I get there, my uncle will help me."

Only when Maryla said that she must be on her way since she was walking and had to take advantage of the remaining daylight hours, did I snap back to the present. I looked at Maryla's shoes. Will they last? This tall slender girl—how many more miles could she walk in those shoes? Would she be strong enough to reach her goal? I kept these thoughts to myself. We embraced, we kissed, we held on to each other. Our paths were leading us in different directions. We were certain that we would never again see each other.

## SEPTEMBER 1945 ⤺ SOPOT, COMMUNIST POLAND

Upon our return from Warsaw, I spent much of my time at home preparing photographs for anticipated publication. Stefan and I hardly ever had visitors, and whenever the doorbell rang, I assumed that it was a patient coming to see the doctor. One afternoon when Frau Wieland did not respond to the persistent ringing, I went to the door. Staring at me were five skinny and poorly dressed German children. The oldest, a girl, could not have been more than twelve years old. A little boy with a runny nose, who stood close behind the girl, looked to be about four years old. The girl held open a sack and asked if I could spare some food. I said that I did not have food to spare, but that I would call Frau Wieland. As I walked back to our room, I overheard our Frau Wieland say that she was sorry, but she could not help them and that German children should not be out in the street begging for food.

Feeling distressed, I stood for an instance and listened to the clatter of the children's feet as they descended the stairs. I rushed after them and called them back. When I put half a loaf of bread, several potatoes, an onion, and two apples into the sack, their little faces lit up. The act of sharing our food with the German children dissolved some of my anger, which I sensed was becoming an obsession. In Swietochlowice, I had regularly spent several hours a week as a volunteer in an orphanage. I knew that a majority of the children were of German parentage, and on one occasion I persuaded a Russian soldier who was connected to the food supply to donate a sack of flour to the orphanage. However in Sopot, the sight of the overfed callous ex-Nazis, who kept professing humanity and "culture," fueled my suppressed anger. Their self-righteous detachment from the bloody carnage they themselves had instituted and participated in had fed a growing hostility toward all Germans.

All I had done was give some food to begging children, yet I knew that I had turned a corner. That evening when I prepared our meal, consisting of some leftover cabbage with potatoes and onions, I suddenly realized that I was humming to myself. I had not done that in years.

Two days later, on a rainy afternoon, the doorbell rang. Frau Wieland called me and said a woman at the door wanted to speak with me. It was my mother. I pulled her into our room, closed the door behind her, fell down on my knees, and wept. Mother kept stroking my hair and muttering words I could not understand. All that mattered was that she was alive. I kept touching her wet clothes. I needed to be certain that she was real.

When I finally let go of her and she sat down, I went to get my father's letters from the drawer. "Look, Mother," I said as I put them in her lap. She touched the envelopes, lifted one and then another, and put them back on her lap, unread. I watched helplessly as my mother talked to herself. Her facial expression changed several times while she swallowed, nodded her head, and moved her lips.

"Aren't you going to read them?" I asked.

Speaking slowly, choosing her words carefully, Mother said, "I am very happy for you. I sent several letters to him from Vienna. I gave one letter to an American soldier. He was from New York, and he promised me that the letter would be hand-delivered."

"But you never received a letter?"

"No, there was not enough time. I left Vienna weeks ago, shortly after Ruth Wischnitzer came to see me."

"He keeps asking about you and Eva," I said. "He is very worried. I wrote that I had not yet found you. I hope that by now one of your letters has reached Father. He loves us so much. I'll read them to you."

"Eva," Mother said. "What did you do to find Eva?"

That was all she said, but it was enough to bring back the images I had fought hard to keep out of my mind. As my eyes filled with more tears, I realized that all along, while I was weeping, Mother's eyes had remained dry.

"I just returned from Warsaw," I said with as much calm as I could muster. "I registered our names—yours and Eva's—at the American consulate. The secretary told me that since Father was an American citizen, we could emigrate to America under a preference quota and that you, the wife of an American citizen, might not need a quota at all."

"Without Eva?" Mother asked. Was that a reproach? I wondered.

"Mother," I said, "I have been trying to find her. I went to Krosno. There was no one there who could tell me what had happened to the Jews who were taken away from Krosno. They heard that killing squads took trucks filled with Jews from some of the surrounding smaller towns to big city ghettos. That was already happening while we were still in Krosno. However, the Krosno residents I spoke with seemed quite certain that Jews from Krosno were not transported to Tarnow or Krakow. I went to see Luzer Ellowicz, the only Jewish person living in Krosno, and he told me about his inquiries among his Christian friends. They said that the Krosno Jews could not have been taken to Krakow, because when the Aktion took place in Krosno, the Krakow-Plaszow ghetto had already been liquidated. They were certain that the Krosno Jews had not arrived in Tarnow. Mother, what could that mean?"

"I will not even consider leaving for America without Eva," was Mother's firm response.

Stefan came home, and he and Mother greeted each other with much warmth. Mother told him that she was very grateful for all that he had done for me. She said that she would always remember that he had stood by me and helped me to survive through the final months. My mother's voice sounded tired; she appeared to be at the end of her strength. Her clothes were wet, and I had not even brought her a glass of water. I had been too eager to tell her about Father. She was obviously not yet ready to think about leaving for America.

I prepared a modest meal, but Mother hardly ate. She said that what she needed most was to rest. She told us that she could not remember when or where she last slept. It was ten months since we had parted, and I was anxious to find out how she had managed to remain alive. I made up a bed for Stefan on the sofa in our adjoining room. Frau Wieland lent me a pillow. Throughout the night, Mother and I huddled together on our bed and, sleeping intermittently, attempted to reconstruct the conditions under which each of us had survived until the liberation.

In Austria, Mother had been part of a labor detail made up of Polish and Yugoslavian women assigned to a munitions factory. As much as she tried to adapt, she somehow was unable to convince several of her coworkers that the only difference between them was that Mother was from Warsaw, the big city, while most of her fellow workers came from the provinces and rural villages. There had been too many questions and innuendos, Mother said, and attempts to trap her. Mother managed to evade the traps. She slept, ate, and went to Mass with her fellow workers, but all along Mother knew that she was viewed with suspicion. All the women in her work detail were part of the slave labor operation that had brought workers from the occupied territories to the Third Reich.

While she was working on a machine in the factory, a metal splinter entered her elbow and lodged in the bone. Several hours later, a doctor removed some of the metal fragments and ordered Mother back to work. She was in pain, and subsequently the wound began to fester. Mother was certain that part of the metal splinter had remained in the elbow. She could not straighten out her left arm. The forelady of Mother's work section agreed that additional attention was necessary, and she sent Mother back to the nurse's office for the needed medical care. The Austrian nurse told Mother that she would be wise to stop complaining. Mother tried to say that the forelady had sent her, but the nurse stopped her and said, "I don't think that you should ever again return to this medical station. Do you understand?" Mother tried to remain calm. She thanked the nurse for her kindness and said that she was sure that she would be able to continue to do her work well. Despite the pain and increasing infection in her arm, Mother continued to work.

Mother was liberated in April 1945, when the Allied forces entered Austria. The Soviet army physician who examined the wound in Mother's elbow said that it was swollen and inflamed. The infection had spread throughout the arm, and there was talk of amputation. An Italian surgeon came to her rescue. He removed the rest of the splinter and administered a powerful antibiotic. He said that appropriate surgery should have been performed immediately when the accident occurred. The doctor told Mother that she would never be able to straighten out her arm.

Ruth Wischnitzer had located my mother with the help of the Jewish agency in Vienna. When Ruth came to see her, Mother had not yet recovered from the infection in her arm, and she had a fever. Apparently, hearing that I survived speeded Mother's recovery. To reach me in Swietochlowice, Mother had to cross several occupation zones in Vienna and three borders. The American, Russian, and English soldiers on patrol in Vienna were courteous and eager to help Mother reach her destination. Crossing the Hungarian border and subsequently the Czechoslovakian border was a bit more troublesome. At each border, there were always questions she needed to answer and documents they wanted her to sign. Still, they were polite, and they helped her to obtain a meal, and in Czechoslovakia they even facilitated one night's lodging.

Crossing from Czechoslovakia into Poland was a nightmare. At the Polish border near Sanok, border guards asked to see Mother's documents and then confiscated them, ostensibly to show them to a superior officer. When Mother remonstrated and said that she was Jewish and was returning to Poland to be reunited with her daughter, the Polish guard asked "Which is it then? Your documents state that you are a Roman Catholic, but you are really Jewish— either way you did not fool us." Mother was incarcerated in a windowless room where she found herself crowded in with seven other prisoners whom the Polish guards referred to as detainees. All of them were Jewish. Conditions were abysmal.

On the fourth day when a guard led the women to the outside latrine, Mother spotted a Russian officer riding a bicycle. He was moving in the direction of the Polish guardhouse. Mother tore herself away from the group and ran toward him. She told him where she had come from, where she was going, and what had happened. The Russian officer was outraged. He said that it was about what you could expect from Poles and that Poles could not be civilized. He stomped into the guardhouse and ordered the officer in charge to immediately return all the documents to their rightful owners and to allow the refugees to return to their homes in Poland. He insisted that everyone be given a pass stating that the holder had legally crossed the border. When the group of eight expressed their gratitude to the Russian officer, he said, "I am embarrassed that liberated concentration camp survivors and slave labor camp victims should have experienced such an outrage. I am glad I came along. I will lodge an official complaint against this illegal Polish border scheme. You can be sure of that."

When my poor mother finally reached Swietochlowice, the address I had given to Ruth, she learned that we had moved to Sopot. I wanted to help heal Mother's wounds, and Stefan and I agreed that together we would endeavor to make her comfortable. Perhaps the brisk sea air would lift the darkness that engulfed her.

I don't remember if my mother wished me good morning the following day, as was customary in our family. I think her first words were, "I will not leave for America without Eva." There was determination and finality in her voice, and I knew that at this time there was nothing I could say that would make her change her mind.

"I don't think Eva is alive," I ventured.

"How can you be so sure? How can you know?" Mother demanded.

"They are telling us, Mother. There were so many concentration camps. Names we never knew in places we never heard of. They have counted the bodies of over a million victims. There are witnesses who report that millions of Jews were gassed and that their remains were burned. In Auschwitz they say the cremation process was kept going throughout the day and the night. In Myslowice the smoke was visible from Auschwitz, and there was this smell that one could not talk about. Luzer Ellowicz had been hidden on a nearby farm, and he returned to Krosno immediately after the liberation. His Polish friends, those who tried to trace the initial transport of Jews from Krosno, did not think that Jews from that area had been transported to Auschwitz."

"I must go to Auschwitz," Mother responded. "I will go there and look for myself. I will find someone who will know. I will find her body. I will not leave her here and go to America. Don't cry. I will do nothing to detain you. It is right that you should want to go. You should be reunited with your father, and I will do everything I can to help speed your departure. Does Stefan want to go with you?"

"Yes, he wants to leave. He is certain that he does not want to remain in Communist Poland. Father wrote that he is preparing an additional affidavit. We have to be very careful. We keep hearing about people who were arrested because they were planning to leave the country. We have told no one about our intention to leave. We were lucky that we moved up to the coast when we did. Now the provisional Polish government wants everyone to stay where they are unless one has a valid reason for wanting to relocate. They want people to settle down in order to better control the upcoming elections."

"I am glad that you keep yourself well informed," Mother responded. "Stefan seems to think that all the prevailing problems are caused by the Communists. After my encounter at the Polish border, I don't think he is right. There is much confusion here, and the political situation is not resolved."

"I agree, Mother, but I don't want us to get caught in another upheaval. I beg you not to do something that would keep us from leaving for America, and if you remain here, you are keeping me from leaving."

"You don't have to worry about that. You must go to your father, but don't try to stop me from doing what I have to do. Now I am very tired," Mother concluded.

Late in the afternoon Mother had a coughing spell. I stroked her back while she struggled to regain her breath. I watched her left arm. There was mobility in the shoulder and the wrist, but the arm remained stiff. My once handsome Mother looked gaunt and shrunken, though she was still several inches taller than I was. Her dark eyes were sad. The fire was gone. There were lines alongside her nose, and her hair was gray and without luster. I told Mother that we had a friend who was a physician, that I could easily locate him, and that he would come immediately. Mother said she did not need a physician; all she needed was sleep. "It's almost two months since I left Vienna," Mother said, "and I have been trying to get to you ever since. I am very tired. Just let me sleep."

Several days later I accompanied Mother to the bus station in Gdynia. She was leaving to search for Eva. She had packed a small bag. I gave her several stamps, and she promised that she would write. Shortly after Mother's departure, I realized my nightmares had changed. Rather than running from my pursuers, it was Eva, or rather Eva's shadow, that was running toward me. Her arms were outstretched, and she was reaching for me. At the moment of contact, when she was about to touch me, I woke up. Waking I could still feel her eyes on me. She was not wearing her eyeglasses, and her eyes looked so sad.

Stefan needed to travel to Warsaw, and I went with him. We managed to locate the Interior Department. Stefan waited outside while I nervously entered and approached a clerk. A guard directed me to the passport office. Before I had a chance to explain why I needed a passport, the woman behind the desk handed me a questionnaire and told me to answer all questions truthfully, and then sign my name at the bottom. When I handed back the filled-in questionnaire, she barely glanced at it and said, "You were born in Germany not in Poland. You are not a Polish citizen. Why then should the Polish state issue a passport in your name?" I tried to explain that, after my father had left Germany for America, I was expelled from Germany into Poland.

The woman was antagonistic. She said Poland needed young people, and it was not the time for Jews to leave the country. When I did not respond, she said, "You filled in the questionnaire; that's the first step. I don't make the final determination. Still I don't quite see why the Polish government should issue a passport to someone who was not born in Poland and who never applied for Polish citizenship. You will be advised of the status of your passport application." I was dismissed.

Stefan had waited impatiently for me, and he was disappointed that I had accomplished so little. He was certain that the bureaucratic red tape I had run into was Communist inspired. "If they don't allow Jews to leave, especially someone whose father is in America, can you imagine what they would say to my application?"

All I could think was that always it was documents, the need for documents, the delay of documents. The various government regulations in Germany and America had prevented our departure in 1938. Once again bureaucratic obstacles threatened to prevent our reunion with my father. Only this time it was happening in Poland in 1945.

## OCTOBER 1945 ⚹ SOPOT, COMMUNIST POLAND

When Stefan once again made preparations to travel to Warsaw, I decided to go with him. In retrospect, I felt that I had permitted myself to be intimidated by a clerk in the Polish passport office and had not adequately presented my case. My reason for wanting to leave Poland was legitimate, and this time I was determined to make a stronger request.

At the passport office a secretary referred me to Pani Rudkowa, the person in charge of administrating passport requests. The heavy-set, stern-looking woman retrieved my application, read through it, sat back in her chair, and said, "Now what is it that you wish to add? We are very busy here." Keeping my language concise, I told the woman about the events that caused my father to leave Germany and about our unconventional arrival in Poland on October 28, 1938. I explained that subsequently the American consulate in Berlin had transferred our documents to the American consulate in Warsaw and that we had been led to believe our departure for America was imminent. That was the reason, I said, why I was now unable to produce a record of ever having established permanent residency in Poland. I thought I was doing well, when the woman interrupted me.

"Why do you want to leave Poland?" she asked. "This is a time for staying on, not for leaving. I can't understand why Jews want to leave Poland now, when they should be part of the Polish nation, helping to rebuild it. You speak about your murdered family. They were not tortured and gassed by the Polish government. Poles too have suffered during the Nazi occupation. You say you want to be reunited with your father, and you will be, in time. In the meanwhile, forward us the documents we have requested. Also, I think it would be wise for you to get a job, to be socially useful. There is much work here that needs to be done."

In response to the woman's accusatory tone, all I managed to say was, "I have nothing against Poland. I only want to leave because I want to be with my father." Walking to the exit, I stopped in front of a large portrait of Wladislaw Gomulka. While he was hiding out in his parents' house in Krosno, I had delivered secret messages on his behalf. At the time, my family believed that my actions had helped him escape when he was in grave danger of being discovered by the Nazis. Now Pan Gomulka was the vice premier of Poland. His office was located in a nearby government building. A note from him, I was certain, would solve my passport dilemma.

I walked past the soldier guarding the building, but that was as far as I was allowed to go. When I told the young man seated behind a desk near the entrance hall that I would like to see Pan Gomulka, he looked at me as if I had asked for the moon.

"In reference to what?"

"It is a personal matter," I said.

"There are no personal matters here. This is the vice premier's office, not his home. In order to see the vice premier," the young man said, "you would need to make your request in advance and through the political security office."

Entering the security office, or Urzad Bezpieczenstwo, was not an option. That particular branch of the Polish government was known for its harsh and secret dealings with anyone who came within its orbit. Besides, I still remembered my bruising encounter at the UB office in Myslowice.

When I hesitated to leave, the clerk asked, "How well do you know the vice premier?"

"I met the vice premier, his wife Zofia, and their son Ryszard in Krosno in his sister's house, where he was hiding from the Nazis. He will remember me, and so will his wife. I just want to see him and say hello."

"Look, young woman," the clerk said and stood up. Attached to his belt in the back was a holster with a pistol. "The vice premier spent much of his life in hiding, and he met many people along the way. Perhaps all you say is true, but what I don't believe is that you have come here only to say hello. Everyone who comes to see the vice premier wants something. The only way that you can get past me is with an appointment memo issued by the UB."

I abandoned all thoughts of using my connection with Pan Gomulka and walked out the door.

Since I was not sure when I would again return to Warsaw, I wanted to make an attempt to find Danka. I wanted her to know that on several occasions her unquestioning friendship had helped me ward off suspicion. She was the only person aside from Stefan who had never questioned my accent or the discrepancies in my manufactured background. I wanted to tell her that I was Jewish, and I hoped that once in America I might be able to help her. Stefan agreed to come along, but he urged that I not reveal my true identity. We arrived at Ulica Falata and the Mlodzianowski apartment and learned that the family had returned to the Baltic coast, where the family had resided before the war. They were living in the town of Wejherowo.

My mother returned to Sopot after an absence of several weeks. Her quest had been futile. She looked defeated, even more tired than before, and she appeared to have shrunken into herself a little bit more. She had tried to find a trace that would lead to Eva, members of her immediate family, my father's siblings, or the many nieces and nephews. She had been to Krosno and Krakow, and she had gone to Auschwitz and to Birkenau. She had made inquiries in the municipal offices in the various towns. She had also initiated a search through a central Red Cross office in Warsaw.

Once in Warsaw, she had registered her name at the American consulate. She was assured that as the wife of an American citizen a visa to enter the United States could be obtained without delay. However, a visa could only be issued to a person with a valid passport. At the Polish passport office, Mother was more successful than I had been. Apparently in my mother's case, there was hope that a Polish passport would be issued. Mother had attended the state gymnasium in Bochnia and had concluded her studies in Krakow, and she could prove it.

I no longer heard the reproachful tone in Mother's voice that implied that perhaps I had not done enough to find our loved ones. Though she did not say it, I sensed that she was gradually accepting that Eva and the others were gone. The newspapers published photographs of mountains of dead bodies. There were piles of eyeglasses and shoes. The truth could no longer be denied; still, Mother clung to a slender hope that Eva would appear.

## NOVEMBER 1945 ~ SOPOT, COMMUNIST POLAND

My request for a passport was denied. However, I was advised that the passport office would reconsider my application were I to forward proof of Polish citizenship. At about this time, my father informed us that a representative of an American Jewish Agency, the Joint Distribution Committee, had recommended that our immigration documents should be processed through the American consulate in Stockholm, Sweden. My father wrote that he was in the process of acting on that advice. He had been assured we would not encounter difficulties when we applied for a Swedish transit visa. To facilitate our entry into Sweden and our temporary residence in Stockholm, my father's bank in New York was forwarding $3,000 to the Swedish National Bank in Stockholm.

Letters from my father were arriving twice a week, and I had to restrain my mind from conjuring up images of highly emotional reunions with my father. The letters were addressed to Mother and to me, and they always contained either a personal note or warm greeting to Stefan. Invariably, however,

Father asked what we were doing to find Eva, and he suggested that if we could supply him with more specific information, he might be able to institute a search for Eva through an American agency. He asked if he should send us money. The three of us agreed that receiving money from America would be dangerous, and since we could never be sure if mail from abroad was censored, we asked my father not to refer to money and also to be circumspect when writing about the Swedish option.

Strolling along Ulica Rokossovsky, I saw a young woman on the opposite side of the street. The face looked familiar. She was tall and blond, and she walked with a self-assured gait. Suddenly I remembered. I ran across the street, walked in back of her for a bit just to be sure, then I put my arms around her from behind and said "Stefa." She turned and recognized me immediately. "Krysia," she exclaimed. "You speak!" We hugged, kissed, and giggled. We had met in Warsaw during several very brief encounters, and we rejoiced now because we had come through the inferno and we were young. We had known some of the same people, and those relationships had been crucial to our survival during the dark days of our clandestine life in Warsaw. I had seen Stefa in Professor Glowacki's apartment on Ulica Academicka, the place where Staszek had hid and where Jerzy Krawczyk, for a limited time, had also found shelter. The professor's home had been our safe place, and it was treasured accordingly.

Because of my strange diction, I was the least welcome guest in Staszek's place. He was worried that the professor might question my accent and that I would jeopardize the few Jewish people for whom the apartment provided respite. Stefa, on the other hand, had been a most welcome visitor to the professor's apartment. She was blond and blue eyed and rather self-assured within her fabricated Christian identity. Stefa looked, acted, and spoke Polish in the manner of an educated Polish girl. She was several years older than I was, and until Germany invaded Russia in June 1941, she had been able to continue her education at the Lwow gymnasium. She had concluded her studies and had received the matura diploma. She had enough money to pay for forged documents for herself and her family, which Staszek helped arrange. She had the attributes and the means that I lacked. When we met in Sopot in the autumn of 1945, I learned that she had had a connection to the Polish underground in Warsaw.

We had not been introduced to each other at the apartment, but we had later met on the street. Though I was certain that we did talk, Stefa remembered being told, probably by Staszek, to keep her distance from me and that I was a mute. She did not recall that she had ever heard me speak.

I was unable to convince her of her erroneous memory. I remembered our meeting on the street in Warsaw when Stefa said, "I know that you are Jewish." At that time I had not been certain that she was Jewish. I had responded by saying, "That is a lie, and in times like these, it is a terrible accusation one should not make lightly." When subsequently our paths crossed, we had acknowledged each other with a nod of the head and a meeting of the eyes that indicated that now both of us knew about the other, but there had been no exchange of words.

We walked into a café, and we could not stop talking. That initial meeting must have kept us away from our respective families for several hours. Stefa knew my mother and, of course, Jerzy Krawczyk and his daughter Maryla. She did not know Stefan. She had recently married Andrzej, the proprietor of a newly opened shoe store located in the same building as our studio, Atelier Betty. She was quite surprised that the studio above her husband's store was named for me. We did not know each other's real names. For her, I continued to be Krysia, as she was Stefa for me—our link to a reality we could not easily shed. Neither Stefa's husband nor Stefan could ever understand the daily pitfalls and snares Stefa and Mother and I had been subjected to while hiding out in Warsaw. It had been Stefa, I now learned, who had interceded on our behalf through her connection to the Polish underground to funnel one hundred zlotys to us when we were on the verge of starvation.

Thereafter, Stefa and I got together whenever and wherever we could. She had met Stefan, and I had met Andrzej, but we were most happy when we could be alone. Our respective spouses resented our intimacy, as well as our whispering and giggling. Stefa knew that my father was living in America and that my mother and I would someday leave for the United States. She did not know that we had already initiated arrangements to leave Poland. Stefa and her family were remaining in Poland, and I thought that for my protection, as well as for her security, it would be better for her not to know of our "seditious" plans. I would have happily entrusted her with our secret, but not really knowing much about her husband, I was afraid. We were puzzled that Andrzej had received permission to open a shoe store. Since the Polish Communist government discouraged personal enterprise, we figured Andrzej must have a government connection that facilitated his engaging in free trade. My mother agreed that it was better if they did not know of our plans.

Through his contact in Poland's Communication Department in Sopot, Stefan learned about the imminent arrival of a ship from Hamburg, Germany. It was scheduled to arrive in Gdynia harbor, and the passengers it carried were former prisoners of war and laborers the Nazis had forcibly transported to German farms and factories. There also were Poles who had been cajoled into going to Germany through the "Travel with us to Germany" program, a German effort to recruit Polish labor for German farms. Initially, the passengers were brought home by the Polish ship SS *Batory*, and subsequently by English and American ships. We were to refer to the ships as "repatriation ships." Throughout the winter, these ships carrying returning Poles arrived at the Gdynia harbor.

We were allowed to board the ships and take photographs. Since we did not know the journalists who were interviewing the returning Poles, Stefan

Leaving ship after photo assignment to record the return of Polish workers coming home from forced labor in Germany. (From left, Polish officer from London, English captain of ship, Betty, Franciszek, officer in Polish-Communist army.) Gdynia Harbor, winter 1945–1946.

assumed that they had been sent from Warsaw. We decided to be careful and not engage in extended conversations and only snap photos of people who appeared to be happy returning to their homeland. Most of them looked apprehensive. They had been taken from their homes during the Nazi occupation of Poland, poorly housed and fed, and in many instances subjected to inferior working conditions. Now they were returning home to a Poland that was different from the one they had known before the war. They did not know what to expect from the Polish Communist government. That uncertainty was reflected in their faces as well as their voices. In addition, the weather had turned cold, and the people arriving were not adequately clothed. By contrast, the crews aboard the ships looked well dressed and appeared to be in excellent physical condition. All the ships' crews spoke English.

## JANUARY/FEBRUARY 1946 ⤷ SOPOT, COMMUNIST POLAND

During the early months of 1946, aside from meeting the Polish ship SS *Batory*, we were at the Gdynia harbor a number of times to greet other arriving ships. The disembarkation process was lengthy, and at times we waited until all the passengers had disembarked before returning to Sopot. Each ship was filled with hundreds of returning Poles. It was astonishing to see how many Poles had worked in Germany. Since I had studied English when I was a child in Germany, I sometimes managed to engage in conversation with the captain or with members of the crew. One of the captains was an American, but I was afraid to tell him that my father also was an American and that I was planning to leave for the United States. It was said that whenever a ship arrived, secret police were among the official reception delegation, but no one knew who they were. Each of the ships was accompanied by a Polish officer from the Polish government-in-exile based in England, wearing the British army uniform, and by a Polish information officer from Poland's current army, wearing the Polish army uniform.

During our third assignment, while standing on the pier shooting pictures of passengers descending the gangplank, we lingered longer than usual. When most of the passengers had disembarked, Stefan saw his friend Bogdan walking down the gangplank. He was wearing a black beret and the greatcoat of the British winter uniform, with a Red Cross armband on his sleeve. Not only had Bogdan been Stefan's friend, the two men had also been colleagues at work. Both of them were engineers and had been employed by the Warsaw municipality. Since September 1939, and throughout the war, Bogdan, an officer in the Polish army, had been an inmate of a prisoner-of-war camp in Germany. He regained his freedom during the early incursion into Germany by the Allied armed forces. Bogdan had immediately joined up with General Wladislaw Anders's regiment based in England, and he had fought with a Polish battalion at Monte Cassino, Italy.

Bogdan had taken a short leave from his regiment to visit his family in Poland, and he was to return on the next ship going back to Hamburg. He came to see us at our apartment before boarding ship for his return passage. He told us that he had wanted to see for himself how life in Poland was shaping up under a Communist-dominated government. He was disappointed and said that for the foreseeable future he preferred to remain in England. "Everything here is determined by the party," Bogdan said, "and everyone is afraid of everyone else. I thought that I might come back, but even my mother said I was better off living in England."

Stefan asked Bogdan if he would be able to get a job in his profession in England, once he crossed over into civilian life. About that Bogdan was less certain. Before leaving, Bogdan wanted us to meet his friend Lieutenant Franciszek, the Polish information officer we had met on the ship. The lieutenant had brought something from overseas for his girlfriend, but had not yet been able to find her. Bogdan said that the lieutenant, though ostensibly a Communist, was really a good man, a patriotic Pole. He did not trust politicians, Bogdan told us, and he appeared to be a resourceful middle-aged man who was looking out for his own interests. He was able to obtain goods in the black market, the one business that was flourishing in Poland, as well as throughout Europe. Lieutenant Franciszek came to our apartment, and we agreed to keep the present for his missing fiancée until his return from abroad.

Since the food items my father sent from America were assembled by the aid organization, we could not ask for specific items. To my mother's eyes I looked pale and skinny, and she determined that what I really needed was vitamins. The American and English soldiers she had met in Vienna had given her several bottles of vitamins, but at the Polish border, the guards had taken them away. Mother decided to barter some of the canned meats we had received from overseas for vitamins. Barter in the black market was strictly forbidden. Daily, we heard and read in the local newspaper about people engaging in black-market trade who had been apprehended, fined, and sometimes even incarcerated. But it was very difficult to dissuade my mother from pursuing a goal she was determined to achieve. In return for the canned meat that contained too much fat and was difficult for me to digest, Mother brought back onions, potatoes, cabbage, and even butter.

At the darkest moments of my life, I clung to my belief that a higher power was watching over me. Whenever I once again managed to evade my pursuers, I attributed it to guidance from above. The forces bent on my destruction were merely men, and I gained comfort through my connection with a higher power. Mother, unlike me, did not feel the need to put her innermost thoughts into words, but I understood that when they took Eva away, they also took away her faith. I was eager to help my mother to regain the faith I had and find respite from her disconsolate state, but I did not succeed.

At age nineteen I knew that it was wiser to keep my faith to myself. Stefan, though born and raised a Catholic, was a nonbeliever. Like my mother, he was perfectly willing to indulge what he saw as my penchant toward the supernatural. But at times I felt lonely in my comforted state.

Lately this loneliness was compounded, because my enthusiasm for a reunion with my father apparently struck the wrong chord with Mother. She was clearly conflicted about joining her husband in America. At times she talked to me about the coming reunion and wondered aloud how they would greet each other. Would my father be able to comprehend the enormity of the killing machine that had decimated the Jewish people of Europe and all members of our family? Would they find a common language? Would they be able to bridge the eight years of separation?

Then, a short while after our discussion, Mother would peremptorily announce that she would not leave for America, though she would quickly add that she would do everything in her power to expedite my reunion with my father. "As for me," she would state firmly, "how can I cross the ocean and leave Eva behind?"

When I attempted to remonstrate, Mother would raise her hand to stop me. "It's not that I don't want to leave. Of course, I will join your father in America," she would say, "but not just yet. What if Eva has been suffering from amnesia? Imagine how helpless she must be. She may not even know her name. Who would nurse her back to health and bring her to America if I leave?"

"Mother, you know that this is a dream. There was a time when I, too, believed that Eva could be suffering from amnesia," I would say.

"Perhaps it is a dream," Mother would agree, "but if I cannot find Eva alive, then I must find her remains and bury them. There has to be a grave, something to come back to."

Frequently, Mother would say, "You cannot understand what it means for a mother to be alive and not know where her child is, or under what circumstances her child has died."

CHAPTER 17

# Stowaways to Sweden

S tefan was engaged in taking portrait photographs at the studio while also adhering to his commitment to record local events for the Sopot news and publicity agency. Most of the time I worked with him. Whenever we were given advance notice of another arrival of a repatriation ship from Germany, we would take the bus to Gdynia. In my mind, being close to either an English or American ship connected me to my father.

Stefan did not share my enthusiasm, nor what he called my "sentimental pining." While Mother and I tried to devise a way that would make it possible for us to leave Poland, Stefan sat by and listened. Mother asked me if I was sure Stefan really wanted to go to America. I no longer was all that sure myself. There was no question that Stefan wanted to leave Poland, but did he really want to go to America? Mother reproached me for not thinking for myself, for letting Stefan think for me, and for being too passive.

Mother was eager to get me out of Poland, and together we wrote a letter to the Polish passport office asking to have my passport application reviewed. Mother could not understand why I did not approach one of the several ship captains I had met and ask if they could help us leave Poland. She was confident that in time she would be able to obtain a Polish passport for herself, and so would Stefan. I was the one with the problem.

Getting me out of Poland became Mother's main concern. She was hardly ever at home. Through her various contacts, originating mainly from people she met during her black-market activities, she heard that several Jewish people had returned to their prewar homes in Gdansk. She wanted to speak with them, to learn where they had been and how they had managed to survive the persecution. In the bus traveling to Gdansk, she overheard that mercantile trade was in full swing in both the Gdynia and the Gdansk harbors. Ships from the Scandinavian countries were arriving frequently. They unloaded their cargo at a pier, and after loading up with Polish coal, they departed for their respective countries. Polish harbor police kept these ships under close surveillance, and even residents living nearby were forbidden to approach these small freighters.

Lieutenant Franciszek became a frequent visitor to our apartment. Mother encouraged his visits. He was about my mother's age, shrewd but hardly cultivated. He enjoyed talking with my mother—known to him as Pani Dembicka—who apparently was part of the Polish aristocracy that, in prewar Poland, he had not been able to gain access to. Franciszek always brought news from abroad that Mother was eager to hear. His fount of stories and anecdotes was inexhaustible. He told us of encounters between impoverished Polish aristocrats and members of the English landed gentry. He mentioned the difficulties the many thousands of foreigners who had fought alongside the British army were experiencing as they attempted to remain on English soil. Will they really be able to gain a foothold in that homogenous society? Franciszek wondered. Or are the Poles who prefer not to return to their own country suffering from self-delusion? We were careful not to respond to his many rhetorical questions. He often brought packages that he would deposit with us for short periods of time. Apparently, Franciszek's fiancée had married someone else, and the present he had brought for her had been channeled into the black market. He sold Mother several yards of a fine tweed cloth, and he let her have it at cost. Mother wanted to have a suit made from the cloth.

## MARCH 1946 ≈ SOPOT, COMMUNIST POLAND

Mother was preoccupied with her mission to get me safely out of Poland. In pursuit of that goal, she spent most of her days near the Gdynia harbor. She decided that there was more activity in the Gdynia harbor than in the Gdansk harbor, and therefore also less likelihood of her being spotted in the adjacent bars and cafés. Among the sailors and the ships' personnel, there were few females, but my mother found one. She was the cook on a small Swedish freighter, and Mother invited her out to one of the better restaurants in Gdynia. The cook told Mother that in the recent past Poles had illegally entered Sweden by hiding themselves in coal bins on Swedish freighters. In the early months of 1946, the governments of Poland and Sweden had agreed to stop this illegal smuggling. Polish refugees who tried to enter Sweden would be apprehended and immediately returned to Poland.

In early March, Mother returned from a trip to Gdynia with the news that within two days she would be leaving for Malmö, Sweden. At the designated day in late evening, she would clandestinely board the Swedish vessel, and the cook would meet her and show her a hiding place. Stefan and I were stunned. The three of us huddled together to review this dangerous, illegal undertaking. My mother, who had just turned forty-six, would be a stowaway on a small ship. Though frightened about the outcome, I was not all that surprised at Mother's audacious act. It had been her audacity and her determination that had helped us survive. We pointed out the severe punishment should Mother be discovered by either the captain of the boat or the Polish harbor police, who could board any vessel departing from Poland, either at the harbor or in the open sea. Mother replied, "I know all that. That is the reason why I decided to go first. Throughout the winter while pursuing one lead after another, I had only thought of Krysia. I was determined that Krysia should go first, then Stefan, and I would go last. I thought perhaps by then I would have received the promised passport."

"What made you change your mind?" Stefan asked.

"I decided that I would rather it were me who is caught, and not my daughter, don't you agree?" Mother asked Stefan. "I should be the one to ensure this is a workable means for escape. Besides, the cook made it quite clear that she does not want the two of you—not yet anyway. She keeps repeating that she has not done this before, but I don't quite believe her. I think that she has done it before in return for payment. I don't quite trust her enough to urge her to take Krysia instead of me."

That night Mother and I slept together in the bed so we could discuss her decision and make a plan. Stefan slept in the adjacent room on the sofa.

Mother would depart under her assumed identity and reclaim her true identity once in Stockholm. She counseled me to do the same. She urged me to be very careful, to trust no one. No one must know because anyone who had this information and didn't report it to the authorities would be subject to severe punishment. Repeatedly, Mother warned me about Franciszek. "He thinks that he is very clever, and he has a habit of asking sudden and quite incisive questions. Be careful. He would not take kindly to having been deceived. Just tell him that I left to look for family members and friends. You don't know where I am, perhaps in Poznan."

From the Jewish couple Mother had met in Gdansk, she had gotten the address of a Jewish family in Stockholm. Mother told me that she would only contact the family if all went well. In our letters to each other, both Father and we had devised a simple code to communicate about our planned illegal departure from Poland. From Father's letters, we inferred he had received confirmation from both the American consulate in Stockholm and from the Stockholm Bank that his affidavits for us, as well as the money he had deposited in New York, had arrived in Sweden. He assured us that all was well. Mother felt confident that, if not apprehended by Polish border police, she could successfully manage her illegal entry into Sweden. She would rely on her affidavit at the American consulate and on the money deposited in her name in the Stockholm Bank.

The cook had said that Mother could bring one small bag, which the cook herself would take aboard on the day before departure. Also at that time, the cook would pinpoint the pier and the exact location where the ship docked. Neither captain nor crew were in the habit of remaining aboard ship during the evening hours. That was when they frequented local bars or looked for female company. Mother was to arrive at that time. She would board the ship in the late evening when the sailor on watch, the cook's friend and accomplice, would get Mother quickly below deck. Mother would send word of her arrival whenever she deemed it safe for me to receive the message. If all went well—and Mother was determined that it would—the cook would contact us, and then Stefan and I would proceed along the same route to the Swedish port of Malmö.

Throughout the night, I hugged my courageous Mother and I told her that I was certain she would succeed, while images of her being caught and thrown in jail filled my mind. My mother embraced me with her eyes only.

They were flooded with her desperate love for me. I felt that love, yet she would not utter the words I was yearning to hear. On the following morning, I did not go to the studio. I wanted to be near my mother, and I helped her pack a small bag. For the cook, Mother packed a small piece of fine luggage she had obtained on the black market. Into it she put several items that I would have liked to have for myself. On top she placed the beautiful tweed cloth she had planned to make into a suit for her arrival in America. Mother returned past nine in the evening without the two pieces of luggage. She looked exhausted, and she said that she needed all the sleep she could get. She did not know when she would once again be able to stretch out on a bed.

Throughout the next day, Mother's last day in Sopot, she had little to do except repeatedly remind me of how I was to conduct myself during the weeks ahead. Stefan left for work later than usual. He and Mother embraced, and he kissed both her hands. He told Mother that she was unique; he had never known anyone like her. She told him to watch over me; she was leaving behind her most precious possession.

Late in the afternoon I accompanied Mother to Gdynia. The sky was clear, the temperature brisk. It was a perfect day for two women to take a stroll to the harbor. I had never been near the freight harbor, and Mother pointed out the various piers and warehouses. We did not go near the ship Mother would board. At dusk, we entered a restaurant. All we carried were our respective small purses. Mother hoped that the cook would come in and sit down at our table, and in time she did. Mother had cautioned me to be reserved; I was not to ask questions. The meeting was arranged so that we could see what the other looked like. The cook ate the dinner and left. It was quite dark when Mother walked me to the bus that would take me back to Sopot. She warned that, since the harbor area was under surveillance, we might be noticed or even watched. When my bus arrived, we shook hands as if we were casual friends. Mother said, "It is for you that I am leaving." These were her last words. When I boarded the bus, I looked back and into my mother's eyes. Her face did not reveal her emotions, but the sad look in her eyes conveyed to me the dramatic moment of parting.

Though Mother had cautioned me that it could take weeks, perhaps months, before the vessel on which the cook sailed would once again return to the Gdynia harbor, the days following her departure were a time of unceasing worry. Should I have let her go? Had I been selfish? Shouldn't I have gone first? Should I have dissuaded Mother from her audacious act of smuggling herself onto a foreign ship? A stowaway at my mother's age? My mind conjured up scenarios of Mother being apprehended by Polish border police. How would I know if she had been taken off the ship and arrested? She had no document with our address in Sopot. She had taken every precaution to make sure that we would not be implicated.

Ten days after Mother's departure, I received a letter from my mother. It was mailed from Gdansk with a fictitious Warsaw return address. Glorious news. My mother had resumed life under her true identity. In the privacy of our apartment, Stefan and I rejoiced. The oppressive fear that had enveloped me was gone. My mother's unmistakable handwriting was all the assurance I needed. There were only a few words. Mother wrote that she had been unable to visit us and that she was returning to Warsaw. She wrote that Pani Kucharka (Mrs. Cook) or her nephew Olaf would be stopping by in about two weeks, and she hoped we would be ready to receive her and to treat her generously.

I contacted Stefa, my only friend in Sopot, and we arranged to meet. We took a walk along the seashore, and then stopped for a cup of tea in our favorite café. My ability to disguise my true feelings apparently had deteriorated, because several times Stefa asked if all was well, if I had a problem. She said I appeared distracted. She asked about my mother, and I told her that she had left for Krakow. "Again?" Stefa asked. We loved each other, and we felt a strong bond when we talked about our lost friends. When we talked about them, we brought them back to life and reconnected with them. We laughed together because we were happy to be safe. By not telling Stefa my secret, I was betraying her trust in me and her friendship for me. Still, I remembered my mother's words: no one, she had said. To the best of my ability, I responded warmly to Stefa's charm while at the same time holding onto my secret.

I had a powerful need to see Danka once more. This wonderful young woman during the most treacherous of times had accepted my friendship spontaneously and ungrudgingly. I had learned in Warsaw that the family had moved to Wejherowo, a small agricultural town that could be reached by bus within five hours. My mother had counseled me to forget about searching for Danka. She felt that events beyond our control had brought the relationship to a natural conclusion. The Polish uprising of August 1944 had transported us into different directions. The neighborhood Danka lived in throughout the two months of the uprising had been in German hands. Our separation had been forced by circumstances beyond our control.

Even though Danka did not have an inkling of my true identity and therefore could not know how she had helped me, I still wanted her to know that her friendship had, on several occasions, been pivotal to my survival. Danka was tall, a natural blond with a slightly up-turned nose, and she fitted the Nordic ideal the Nazis admired. On several occasions, Danka had interposed herself between me and some self-appointed Polish interrogators who wanted to know where I was from and why my diction sounded odd. I needed to tell her this before I left Poland and crossed the ocean.

I wanted to remind her of a Sunday in late April during the Jewish revolt in the Warsaw ghetto. Hunting down escaped Jews was on top of the German agenda, and Polish Nazi collaborators went to great lengths to display their loyalty by accosting and arresting people they deemed suspicious-looking. It was important to make every effort to remain incognito.

On that memorable Sunday, Danka had telephoned and said that she had not seen me. I was working too hard, she said. She wanted us to meet and attend Mass together. Her boyfriend Daniel would also be at the Church of Saint Anne. He was singing in the choir, and perhaps afterwards we would be able to spend some time together with him and his friends. Her phone call inviting me out had buoyed my spirits during a particularly dark time.

As we walked from the church, we came face to face with two uniformed Polish policemen. Addressing me, one of them demanded to see my Kennkarte. Before I had managed to produce mine, Danka had whipped out her own and turning to me, she said in a resigned tone, "What a nuisance, Krysia, not only do we need to identify ourselves to the Germans, but now also to our own, and that on a Sunday after Mass."

When the policemen signaled that we could move on, Danka hooked her arm into mine and without attempting to lower her voice, she said, "What can one expect from traitors?" She had no idea that when the policemen had stopped us my heart had stopped beating and my blood flowing.

Now was the time to tell her. I wanted her to know that each time she came to pick me up after work her very presence, her loving embrace had bought me additional respite from the ever-mounting suspicion among my fellow factory workers.

Though Stefan counseled against it, he did accompany me when he saw that I would not be deterred. On a cold blustery March morning, we left for Gdynia where we boarded a bus for Wejherowo. Toward evening, we reached the Mlodzianowski apartment. Danka was delighted to see me, and she told me of her several attempts to find me. Her fiancé Daniel had been killed during the Polish uprising, and she thought I had died too. Her parents and her sister Krystyna, now married to Mjetek and the mother of an infant daughter, greeted us with reserve. Mjetek was friendly but preoccupied. He was about to leave for an officer's training program in the reconstituted Polish air force. The family of six lived in a two-bedroom apartment.

Danka appeared to be less self-assured than I remembered. She had not received the letter in which I had apprised her of our intention to visit her in Wejherowo. She seemed lost amid the bustling activity surrounding the new baby and the impending departure of her brother-in-law. We had brought along some food, and the Mlodzianowski parents agreed that we should spend the night on their living-room floor because there was no transportation available until the following morning.

Once we were seated, Pan Mlodzianowski turned to me and asked, "Krysia, have you heard from your father?"

"Yes, I did." Perceiving that more was expected, I added, "It was wonderful to know that he is well."

"So when will he be coming home?"

"That I still don't know," I responded evasively.

"They should return home. They can't serve their country by remaining abroad. The war is over. It's finished. Our fate was determined at Yalta. The government-in-exile was stripped of all power, so why remain on foreign soil?" Pan Mlodzianowski proclaimed.

I nodded agreement. My feelings of discomfort mounted when Pan Mlodzianowski asked about Captain Dembicki. "Did your aunt hear from him?" he wanted to know.

"No, not yet," I muttered. "She is very concerned."

"Pani Dembicka is a fine lady," Danka's mother said. "She treated you like a daughter."

I realized I could not dismantle my wartime identity in the somewhat suspicious and hostile atmosphere of the Mlodzianowski household. The futility of the long and arduous bus ride became evident as the evening progressed, and I knew that I would be unable to tell Danka what I had come to say.

Danka prepared to spend the night with me, and I was delighted. Just the three of us in the living room, and if we whispered, Stefan, a good sleeper, would not even know that we were talking. Once alone together, we embraced and kissed. Danka said she was so happy I had come to find her; our visit was a good omen. She wanted to talk about Daniel. She told me she had visited his parents in Warsaw-Praga and would have liked to stay with them, but her father was against it. Danka had tears in her eyes when she reached for my hand and said passionately, "I can't bear this much longer, Krysia. I must get out of here. My parents don't understand me. They are thrilled to have a grandchild, and they would like for me also to be married. Danny is dead. Who should I marry? I am so lonely. Krysia, I need your help."

I needed to be careful about making promises I could not keep, since our departure date might come about within the next several weeks, though the exact day was uncertain, Stefan had made plans to visit his mother in Poznan during the following week. He would be away for no more than three days. That would be the ideal time for Danka to come and visit me in Sopot. Danka said she wanted to live in a city and among young people. She needed a job, and she wanted to be independent, to go to work, to go dancing, to be happy. Her father insisted that she finish her gymnasium education and receive the matura diploma. Before leaving on the following morning, Danka's father granted permission for his daughter to come visit me the following Tuesday and spend one night in our home.

During our bus ride back to Sopot, Stefan was more generous than I expected. All he said was, "Do you still believe that it was necessary to make this effort? You are in no position to help Danka, and she does indeed need help." He agreed that Danka should get out of Wejherowo and back to Warsaw, where she would have a chance to connect with her friends. He said that Danka must do this herself, and that I should not interfere.

On the following Monday, Stefan left. Danka arrived on Tuesday, in the early afternoon. She looked beautiful. Because she was tall and well shaped, her simple dress and worn overcoat looked elegant. She was excited to walk among people in the cosmopolitan atmosphere of the resort town. In contrast to Wejherowo, with its boarded-up stores, in Sopot the town supervisor had given permission for several stores to open their doors to the public. All the stores were on Ulica Rokossovsky. There was much one could purchase in Sopot if one had money to spare. Everything was very expensive. The merchants were relying on visiting tourists, who as far as I could tell, were mainly officers of high rank and their wives, members of either the Polish or the Russian armed forces. Danka was happy, and it was obvious to both of us that she was receiving flattering attention. Young men looked at her and turned around to look some more. Danka loved all of it.

Danka told me that she would like to live in Sopot, and how nice it would be for both of us if we were living near each other. We were lying in bed, and I put my arm around her. "Danka," I said gently, "I have not yet told you why I was so eager to find you."

"Tomorrow," Danka said, her voice sleepy.

"I needed to find you because I wanted to tell you that shortly I shall be leaving. I did not want to leave without saying good-bye to you. I wanted to tell you that you are a wonderful person. I am grateful that fate brought us together in Warsaw and you became my friend. I was so lonely then, and your friendship was a beautiful gift."

I had not been sure that Danka was listening, but she suddenly brushed off my arm and sat up.

"What do you mean leaving?" she demanded. "When? Leaving where? Is it England? No one is leaving now for England."

"Well, not right now, but when I leave it will be for America."

"America?" Danka had raised her voice. "What do you mean for America? Your father is a Polish officer based in England. What is he doing in America? You told my father that he would soon be coming home."

"Danka, I never said that. I said that he was alive and well. He is in America now, and I desperately want to see him again. Please be happy for me, Danka," I pleaded. "I have missed him so. It's been many years since I saw him last. You have been so lucky to have your father watch over you throughout the war. You do understand, don't you?"

But Danka did not want to understand. I knew at that moment the truth would be more than Danka could bear.

Danka turned her back to me and moved to the other side of the bed.

When I said good night, she did not respond. After a little while, I could tell by her regular breathing that she was sleeping. I was unable to fall asleep. I realized, too late, that from the moment Danka saw us in the doorway of her Wejherowo apartment, she had formulated her plan: I would be her escape route from her family entanglements. She needed a way out, and now I had let her down. Leave-taking was in my view a privilege that I had been denied in the past. I had wanted to say good-bye, and all I had accomplished by seeking out Danka was to compound her unhappiness.

On the following morning, I prepared a generous breakfast, but Danka barely ate. She wanted to catch an early bus to Gdynia. She said she would spend most of the day there. When I asked her if she wanted me to come along, she responded with a curt no. I walked her down to Ulica Pomorska, the road that ran parallel to the seashore and connected the harbor cities of Gdynia and Gdansk. Danka looked out onto the Baltic Sea and said, "If I could live here, I would never want to leave." When I hugged her, she averted her face. There were tears in her eyes.

Toward the end of March, a young man rang our doorbell. He asked for me by name. He said his name was Olaf and that he was a sailor on the *Havsmas*. I asked him to come in. Speaking in halting German, he apologized for his drunken state and said he had helped my mother arrive safely in Sweden. I thanked him and asked if I could prepare a sandwich for him. He declined, but he wondered if we had some aquavit in the house. He said he was very nervous, and he needed the alcohol to calm his nerves. I translated for Stefan. We agreed that his state of inebriation was already quite advanced. I told him that we were sorry but there was no alcohol in our house. I asked about the cook, and he said that she was no longer sailing on the *Havsmas*. She was taking a short leave and would subsequently be sailing on a larger vessel. Speaking haltingly, Olaf said that he was prepared to help us leave Poland.

I asked Olaf if he had someone to help him. He said no, it was better if he did it all by himself. *Ich allein*—I alone—he repeated several times. I translated for Stefan and added that the fewer people were involved, the safer it would be for us. Stefan agreed. Still the fact that he was drunk did not inspire confidence. He told us he had wanted to come before; since the night Mother had sailed, he had been in the Gdynia harbor twice. He did not know how much longer Gdynia would continue to be his ship's destination. His ship was returning to Sweden on the following day.

"You should be ready on a day's notice," he said, "when the ship next docks at the Gdynia harbor."

"When will that be?" I asked.

"It could be two weeks, perhaps longer." He repeated that we must be ready to leave on a day's notice starting two weeks hence. Our luggage should be very light, he said, no larger than a briefcase.

Olaf was our only option and a contact I did not want to jeopardize. I felt that he was an honorable person and would not overtly betray us. However, he appeared to be a slow thinker; that and his liking for alcohol made me wonder how effective he would be. Would he be able to make adequate preparations? Mother had said that the cook was shrewd. But when I met her at the restaurant, I had not been able to get a glimpse of her eyes; she had kept them averted. By contrast, Olaf, when he was able to focus, looked straight into my face, and what I saw was confidence-inspiring. He remained with us for over two hours and ate all the hot soup I placed before him.

"I want to help you. It is very dangerous. If I get caught or if you get caught, I lose my seaman's license." Pausing a bit, Olaf continued, "I must get something for jeopardizing my job."

"Yes, of course," I assured him, nodding vigorously.

Olaf wanted us to get him a man's gold watch and a Leica camera—the German one, he stressed, not the one made in Russia. I assured him that we would obtain what he wanted. By the time he left, it was eleven o'clock in the evening, and I needed to sit down and review everything that Olaf had told us. Stefan was upset.

"Where will we get a man's gold watch?" he demanded. "And how about the Leica? That must have been your mother's idea. I can't work without my Leica. What did your mother have in mind when she told him about a Leica? She thinks I will give up my Leica, and then be totally dependent on her generosity. Not my Leica," Stefan fretted. Once he calmed down, he suggested that he would try to find one, or that perhaps Olaf could be convinced to take our Rolleiflex, a camera of equal value, though much less versatile when taking action photographs. In the end, Stefan agreed that he would make every effort to sell some of the nonessential equipment from the studio and find a Leica.

I looked over the furnishings we would leave behind. Except for our personal belongings, there was nothing in the house to which I was attached. Most of it was there when we moved in, and the next tenant would be quite welcome to the additional items we had acquired during our residency in Sopot. Into a briefcase, I could only pack a change of underwear, socks, and a minimum of toilet articles. I would have liked to pack a suitcase with several items of clothing that I had acquired and I liked a great deal and leave the suitcase with my friend Stefa, but I remembered Mother's words. Stefa and her family would be remaining in Sopot. For their own protection, Mother had warned, they must be totally unaware of our plans.

Stefan made inquiries about a Leica, but could find no one who wanted to sell one. As for finding a gold watch, in uncertain times people would sell any other item before they would relinquish something made of gold.

Help came from the least expected source. Franciszek came to visit, but this time he was not walking. He rode up to our door on a motorcycle. He was an impressive sight, wearing a uniform, boots, cap, and holster. We were indeed surprised. He said that his tour of duty was slowly coming to an end, and he expected to be discharged at the end of the year. He did not have a home, and when he came ashore, he slept in the officer's quarters of an army barrack. He wanted to store his motorcycle with us, in our apartment, until he found a place of his own. We told him that we would, of course, store his motorcycle. Franciszek proceeded to drag the bike up the one flight of stairs. He had arrived in the late afternoon, and he told us that he needed to get back, but that he would return on the following day. We invited him to dinner. He said he would bring along a bottle of good wine he had picked up in the port of Bremen.

Even before Franciszek left, I knew that the motorcycle could be the key to solving our dilemma. We agreed that Stefan should be the one to negotiate for the motorcycle. He would need to be very circumspect when he broached the subject. Together we inspected the motorcycle. It was old and dented, but the two tires, though dirty, appeared to be relatively new.

Throughout dinner the following evening, Franciszek reported on his various adventures. We listened attentively. Stefan wanted to know if it had been difficult to buy the motorcycle, and he asked if Franciszek could buy another one for us. "No problem," Franciszek informed us. "The Germans have an abundance of them, and they can't eat them. It is strictly a matter of having the merchandise that they want in exchange. Usually I can get the items they need."

Stefan asked if he would sell us his motorcycle and buy another one for himself. Franciszek agreed. He had been too impulsive, he said, and at this time he really had no use for the motorcycle. By the time we finished the bottle of wine, and while I was in and out of the kitchen, Franciszek and Stefan had agreed on a price. Franciszek was happy to receive zlotys—the Polish currency we hoped we would no longer need. Clearing the next hurdle—getting Olaf to accept a motorcycle in lieu of a camera or watch—would be my task. I kept telling myself that every young man would be happy to own a motorcycle. I nonetheless suggested that Stefan continue to look for a Leica; I had given up obtaining a gold watch on the black market.

## APRIL 1946 ⤙ SOPOT, COMMUNIST POLAND

We continued living our lives as if no momentous events were about to occur. As we did not have a telephone, Olaf had no way of contacting us ahead of time. We told Olaf that, starting fourteen days from the day of his last visit, we would be expecting him and would endeavor to be at our apartment every evening after six o'clock. Loving letters from my father were arriving at least once a week. Circumspectly, my father wrote that he was corresponding with Mother and that shortly he hoped to hear good news from her.

Stefan hired a young woman to help us run the studio. He positioned me in front of the camera and demonstrated to her the interesting results one can achieve by manipulating light and shadow to enhance the facial structure of the sitter. He told Alicja, our new and talented employee, that shortly he might be away working on an assignment. The work could keep him away from the studio for several days, perhaps even a week. We were carefully preparing to leave our apartment and the town of Sopot, while making every effort to prevent early detection of our escape. We reasoned that our precautions might give us one week before our defection would be noted.

Shortly after our German landlords had left Sopot and returned to Germany, Mother had insisted that we find a tenant to occupy the vacated rooms. She urged that we should act before the Polish Housing Authority filled the vacated space with people that might make our lives miserable. Mother's

Jewish friends in Danzig came to our aid and introduced Mother to a prospective tenant.

Pani Biernacka was a Christian lady whose Jewish husband had been forcibly taken from their home in Gdynia, where they had been hiding during the war. The Gestapo had come to the house, and Pani Biernacka was certain that a Polish collaborator had betrayed them. Aside from the Jewish couple in Danzig, Pani Biernacka had no friends, and she trusted no one. She left early in the morning for work, and we rarely saw each other. She had told us that she worked for a freight-forwarding firm. In addition to speaking Polish, her native tongue, she was fluent in French, German, and Russian.

Mother's friends had intimated that Pani Biernacka had held an important position in prewar Poland, and from her extensive elegant wardrobe, all items apparently acquired before the war, one was able to deduce that the lady had moved in the upper circles of Polish prewar society. Though we had lived in the same apartment for several weeks, conversation between us had been confined to a few friendly but reserved words of greeting. Pani Biernacka impressed me as an interesting lady I would have liked to know better, but her stern reserve, emphasized by her tall figure and erect posture, rebuffed closer association.

Almost every, week we learned of another thwarted attempt by a Polish citizen to illegally leave Poland. Prolonged incarceration and in many instances transportation to Siberia were the frightful consequences. Although I kept my days occupied, the nights were full of dark shadows. To the question what if, my mind conjured up terrifying prospects. My stomach reacted violently, and I was afraid that I would be ill when the time came to be strong and healthy. Throughout the weeks, as we waited to hear from Olaf, Stefan was pensive, even withdrawn. When I tried to discuss steps we would need to take if our plan failed or answers we needed to prepare in case we were caught and interrogated, Stefan grumbled about too many uncertainties. "Your mother should have been a tightrope walker," he said. "This is lunacy."

I wanted Stefan to express the thoughts that really troubled him, but he kept them to himself. When we left Poland, he would have to burn all his bridges, whereas I had no bridges to burn. Yet, whenever I asked if he really wanted to leave, his answer was a clear and decisive yes. Moreover, at times Stefan did say he was very grateful to my father for giving him an opportunity to build a new life in America or in Canada. When I asked why Canada,

Stefan answered that many Poles who had been part of the Polish government-in-exile had chosen to emigrate to Canada rather than remain in England.

I tried to prepare my friend Stefa without revealing our imminent departure. She knew, of course, that my father was living in New York and was making every effort to reunite the family. Together, we complained about the Polish passport office for their refusal to grant me a Polish passport. She suggested that my father invoke the help of the American embassy in Poland, and I said I would suggest it in my next letter. I could not tell Stefa that we had moved beyond legal emigration from Poland.

Stefa at all times expressed her sympathy and regret at my ruptured family life. Miraculously, but also mainly due to Stefa's connections and her careful intervention, her immediate family had remained intact. In Sopot, she lived in a two-family house with her parents and her two siblings. The family was afraid to reestablish their Jewish heritage. Polish discontent with prevailing conditions once again looked for convenient scapegoats, and anti-Semitism was on the rise. Stefa could not understand why my mother after finding me had chosen to live apart from me. I could not tell my friend that my mother was living in Stockholm, where she was preparing to receive Stefan and me, and that she was trying to expedite our immigration to America.

The winter had been quite harsh, and we rejoiced in the visible signs of

With my friend Stefa on the beach. Sopot, early spring 1946.

spring. Stefa and I resumed our invigorating walks along the seashore, and we made a date to go sunbathing in our bathing suits. Together, we spent several joyous hours on the beach, freezing in our suits and laughing and rejoicing in our premature outing. We chased each other in the sand to keep warm. We had to admit that for our next outing on the beach we would need to wait another week or two. When we parted, we hugged and kissed affectionately. Neither one of us knew that we would not meet again.

Back home I quickly took a bath. I felt chilled to the bone, and I did not want to explain our folly to Stefan. I was busy preparing dinner, when Stefan arrived. We were sitting at our kitchen table eating, when we heard the doorbell ring. It was Olaf. He was very nervous and spoke to me first in Swedish, then in German. He was sober. He said that two days hence he would be on night-watch duty, and that we should come aboard ship no later than nine that evening. Once he had spotted us, he would whistle a tune, and as soon as we boarded the ship, he would lead us down into the cabin. Olaf said that his bunkmate, a middle-aged Finn, would need to be paid, and that he wanted payment in Swedish krona. I translated for Stefan.

I told Olaf to follow me into the living room. In the corner, hidden under an old sheet, was the motorcycle. I removed the sheet, pointed at the motorcycle, and said, "This is for you." I could see by his expression that Olaf was thrilled. He never again mentioned the Leica, the gold watch, or payment for his bunkmate. He could not take his eyes off the motorcycle. I was very relieved to see Olaf so happy. I handed him the ignition key. He said that he would need to walk out with the motorcycle that night. I assured him several times that the vehicle was in working condition and that it had been sold to us by a friend who had ridden it all the way from Gdynia. Olaf asked me if I trusted him to keep his part of the bargain once he had the motorcycle in his possession. I looked into his eyes and told him we were entrusting him with our lives.

Olaf made a drawing of the location of the pier and the exact position of his ship. He wanted to see the size of the luggage we would bring aboard. When we showed him the two briefcases, he suggested we quickly pack one of them, which he would take with him now. In parting, he told us that he in turn was entrusting us with both his livelihood and his future. I promised him that if intercepted by patrolling Polish harbor police, we would not reveal either his identity or our connection to his ship. He urged us to be very careful and to make sure that we were not seen when we boarded the ship. He wanted me to swear that under no circumstances would I reveal our connection and that I would deny we had ever met.

We watched Olaf through the window as he led the vehicle down the street. We did not know where he mounted the motorcycle or if the motor started well. We spent a restless night preparing for possible mishaps and thinking up explanations we might give for why we were at the Gdynia harbor in the evening.

The morning after Olaf's visit, I entered the kitchen while Pani Biernacka was preparing her breakfast. She knew that Mother had arrived in Stockholm, and she was aware that in time we would also depart. I told her that we would be leaving the following evening. Pani Biernacka said she was glad I was giving her at least one day's notice, because to avoid possible linkage with our departure, she would not return home that evening. She would stay away from Sopot for the next several days. I asked her to open all mail addressed to us, including my father's letters, and burn anything she did not deem crucial. Our mutual friends in Danzig were corresponding with their friends in Stockholm, and in time they would forward anything that we might need. I wrote down Mother's name and address. I told Pani Biernacka that food packages from my father would soon stop arriving, but in the meantime, all parcels would become her property.

I wanted to keep some of the personal items I had so carefully accumulated, but I knew this wasn't practical. Still, I asked Pani Biernacka if she would store them for a while. I urged her to find an appropriate tenant to share the apartment. Furnishings and linens would henceforth belong to her. I tried to express my gratitude. I wanted to embrace her, to say good-bye. Pani Biernacka's habitually stern manner relented for an instant. "No," she said. "We cannot say good-bye because I'm not supposed to know you are leaving, but I will pray for a successful outcome of your undertaking." Pani Biernacka was a pious lady who attended Mass regularly. I felt comforted by that thought.

At the appointed time, we approached the *Havsmas*. We heard a male voice whistling a soft tune, and we proceeded to the gangplank. We climbed aboard and followed Olaf down a short staircase and through a narrow passageway. He opened a door to a small cabin. We stepped inside, and he closed the door behind us. We heard the key turning the lock, and then there was silence. The tiny cabin had a bunk bed and was illuminated by a small blue bulb. On the lower bunk was the briefcase Olaf had taken the evening before. We moved it and sat down close to each other on the lower bunk. We listened for sounds from above. I prayed that Polish harbor police would not board the boat. Olaf had told us that the boat would be fully loaded when we arrived and that it would sail at about midnight at high tide. We were certain we had not been followed.

We were happy to have come that far, and both of us would have liked to doze off for a bit. We fought the urge; we needed to stay alert until we were certain that we were sailing. Olaf had warned that Polish harbor police could board the ship while at dock or while still within Polish territorial waters. Together, we had prepared for that eventuality. Olaf told us that he would take steps to arrange for enough space in a coal storage bin to hide the two of us. He hoped this emergency measure would not be needed.

At about eleven o'clock, a variety of sounds signaled the resumption of activity up above. We could hear orders shouted and chains being fastened down. Our lightbulb flickered, went out, and came on again. We heard the chugging sound of a motor starting up and felt the ship rocking. We mistakenly thought the motor was causing the rocking motion, an indication that we were about to sail. Two hours later we finally realized that the boat had in fact moved out of the harbor.

We must have dozed off because we suddenly came awake when we heard a loud bang as the cabin door was slammed shut. A large middle-aged man was lurching around the cabin. He was agitated and obviously quite drunk. We sat up on the bunk. He bent down to speak and a whiff of cheap alcohol came from his mouth. The man wanted something. He held out his hand, and though I could not understand what he was saying, the angry tone of his words could not be mistaken. He spoke in a loud voice, and we had to calm him down. I told him I didn't speak Finnish or Swedish. Russian? he asked. I nodded; I asked if he spoke German. He said yes and told us he was a Finn and used to work for the Germans. The Germans pay better than the stingy

Swedes, he said, but the Germans had lost the war. I agreed with everything he said. Then he told us that he needed money.

"This is my cabin," he informed us. "Olaf got a motorcycle. What about me? What do I get? Am I not entitled to something for keeping quiet?"

When I told the Finn that we had no money and that he must speak to Olaf, he threatened us, saying he was going to tell the captain about us and the captain would throw us overboard.

I responded by saying that I did not think the captain would do that. Maybe not, he conceded, but the captain was sure to turn the ship around and deliver us to the Polish harbor authorities. He pointed a long finger at me. "You will go to prison," he said.

Finally, the man calmed down a bit and said that all he really wanted was some money. I repeated that we did not carry currency. He asked if we were Jewish. I said no. He said that was bad, because Jews always carried money. He put his boot onto the lower berth and heaved himself up onto the upper bunk. Shortly thereafter we knew by the sound of his voluminous snoring that he had fallen into a deep sleep. Stefan and I huddled together under the thin blanket and once again dozed off.

We woke up in the early morning hours when Olaf unlocked the cabin and walked in. The Finn was gone. To my great dismay, I had vomited in the night. My stomach had been heaving all along and I had managed not to vomit, but finally I had lost control. Olaf brought a pail of water, and Stefan and I cleaned up as best we could. Fortunately, at the last moment, I had reached for a small basin, and the blanket had not been soiled.

Olaf told us that he had relieved the Finn from his deck duty because everyone could see that he was drunk. "There is nothing uglier than a drunk Finn," Olaf said. He asked us if the Finn had been badgering us.

"He wants money," I said.

"He knows he will be paid," said Olaf. "He's trying to get a bit more. All the money he earns is spent on liquor."

Our sojourn on the *Havsmas* lasted for two days and three nights. The entire time I felt seasick. All I wanted to do was lie curled on the bunk until we once again set foot on land. I could not even look at the soup and bread Olaf brought us, which Stefan consumed with a hearty appetite. Olaf urged that I drink the hot black coffee he frequently brought to the cabin. He said it would soothe my stomach spasms, and he was right.

Shortly after midnight, on our third and last night aboard ship, Olaf walked into the cabin with unexpected and unsettling news. The captain had received orders not to land in Malmö, the usual destination of the ship, but instead to proceed twenty miles north, up the western coast of Sweden to the small harbor of Landskrona.

"Why is that bad news?" I asked.

"It is bad news because we are sailing into a small harbor where a stranger could easily be noticed. It's bad luck. We hardly ever land in Landskrona, and I have only a vague notion of the harbor and of the routes that lead into town. I will speak to one of my mates. Perhaps he knows more than I do. I'll be back."

I had come aboard in a suit and had taken off my skirt while curled up under the blanket. I changed into a clean blouse and clean white socks. Stefan put on a fresh shirt, and I helped with his tie because there was no mirror. I brushed and combed my hair carefully and applied a tiny bit of lipstick and powder. Stefan said that I looked very pale, and I tried to remedy it by using the lipstick on my cheeks. We thought we looked presentable. I made every effort to restore the cabin to the same disorderly state that we had encountered on our arrival.

We could hear the easing of the engine. The rocking motion was less pronounced, and we knew that we were about to land. Olaf came back into the cabin. Though I could smell alcohol on his breath, he appeared sober. "I am determined to see it through," he said, "and I will get you off the ship. The rest is up to you. Only remember your promise."

I put my hand on my heart and said, "We will not betray you."

Olaf unfolded a piece of paper and read from it. "When you walk off the gangplank, you turn right. Go to the end of the landing pier, turn right again, and at the fork in the road you turn left. Ahead of you will be the road that will lead you into town." He looked up at me. "After that you are on your own. Don't look back," he warned. "Don't ever turn around and look in the direction you came from."

"Thank you, Olaf," I said. "May God be with you. We are grateful beyond words. I am sorry that I got seasick and made such a mess."

"It does not matter," Olaf muttered.

He walked out. A few minutes later he was back. He motioned to us to follow him.

## MAY 1946 ⤶ LANDSKRONA, SWEDEN

Once again we made our way through the narrow passageway, up the stairs, and down the gangplank. The air was brisk. There was a mist, and we were grateful for the gray predawn, which provided some cover. We followed Olaf's instructions, and shortly we turned left at the fork in the road. Neither of us could see far ahead, but there was a road, and it had to be the one that Olaf told us would lead into town. We were eager to get out of the harbor. Then out of the mist, we saw two men walking in our direction. "God Morgon," one of them said. I uttered a greeting and smiled. We kept walking, trying to keep the same pace as before.

In back of us someone called. We kept walking. The two men caught up with us. Both wore civilian clothing. There were a number of questions I could not make out, but I understood when one of them said, "Harbor administration." Subsequently, there followed a barrage of questions, the content of which was not hard to guess. I shrugged my shoulders. No, we don't understand. No, we don't have documents. No, we are not from Poland. No, we did not just arrive. No, we did not come from that pier; no, not from the other pier; and no, not from any pier.

Between German and my limited English vocabulary, I was gradually able to understand the simple questions they were asking. One of them realized that I was somewhat comprehending. Danish? he asked. I shook my head no. German? I said yes.

One of the men left. The one who remained with us continued asking questions, posing his questions in German. Stefan's eyes were focused on my face. He wanted to know what was being said, but I did not dare translate into Polish for him. I responded mainly by saying *nein*. "Do you want me to believe that you swam ashore?" he asked. Nein, I answered. The tall, handsome-looking man must have been in his late thirties. He smiled, put a hand on my shoulder, and said, "You arrived today. You came either from Poland or from Denmark." I said nein, we did not arrive today, and nein, we came neither from Poland nor from Denmark.

Ahead of us a small car, driven by the other man, stopped in front of us. We were directed to sit in the back of the car and were driven to a police station. We were ushered inside and told to sit down on a bench alongside a wall. Keeping my voice down to a whisper, I recounted to Stefan everything that had been said. A uniformed man sat behind the desk. He looked at me, and I attempted to smile. I had not eaten for several days, and I did not feel very well.

I probably did not look very well either. I remember seeing the man behind the desk speaking to another uniformed policeman, and then I must have slumped onto Stefan's shoulder. I am not sure whether I fainted or dozed off, but the next thing I remember was Stefan holding a slice of orange under my nose. I sat up and very slowly ate several slices of orange. Apparently, the police officer behind the desk had gotten a brown paper bag filled with several oranges and had given it to Stefan. I had not seen or tasted an orange since 1939.

We were asked to go into an office. When we entered, we saw the two men who had stopped us in the harbor. They introduced themselves as Herr Nielsen and Herr Ferguson. Herr Nielsen told us he represented the harbor administration and would be in charge of the investigation. He held a writing pad, a fountain pen poised between his fingers. He said that there was a trade agreement between Poland and Sweden; under the agreement, Sweden was mandated to return all illegal arrivals to Poland. There were no exceptions for asylum seekers. Most important, however, were the answers that he and his assistant were waiting to hear from us. "Nein is not an answer," he said. I was about to speak. He stopped me and added, "Whatever you say has to be the truth, so please remember to speak truthfully."

I started by saying that we did not seek asylum in Sweden. I told the two men that my father was an American citizen, living in New York, that I was Jewish, that my father had left Germany in April 1938, and that my mother, my sister, and I were forcibly deported from Germany into Poland when we were just about to leave Germany and join my father in America. The two men were watching my face as I was speaking. I paused; they motioned for me to go on.

"At the end of last year," I continued, "my father transferred $3,000 to the Swedish National Bank in Stockholm on behalf of my mother, my husband, and myself."

"If that is true, then you would not have encountered problems obtaining a Swedish visa."

"Yes, I was assured that I would be granted a Swedish visa, but I was unable to obtain a Polish passport," I answered.

"Where did you apply for the passport and why were you refused?"

"I made my application at the passport office in Warsaw. My application was rejected because I was not a Polish national and because we had never established residence in Poland. We were supposed to leave for America, when Poland was invaded by Germany."

While I was attempting to give a factual account of my distant as well as my recent past, the two men exchanged words occasionally, and subsequently Herr Ferguson left the room. When he returned, he bent down to Herr Nielsen who was seated behind the desk and whispered into his ear. Herr Nielsen told me that I was recounting quite a story; however, the problem was that they could not know if I was telling the truth.

"How can we believe what you are telling us?" Herr Nielsen asked. "Especially since the major issue we are faced with is your refusal to be truthful about how you miraculously arrived in the port of Landskrona."

Herr Ferguson went to the door and ushered into the room a tall, somewhat stooped, old man. "This is Herr Diesenhaus," he said, "and he is one of the respected elders of Landskrona. We will now proceed to examine some of your allegations." He nodded to Herr Diesenhaus. I shook hands with him, and I told him my true name.

"They told me that you arrived in Sweden illegally, and that you claim to be Jewish. You have no documents to prove that you are Jewish. You have no documents that would establish your identity, and they have not yet made a decision whether to allow you to remain here while they consult with their superior officer, or whether to put you on a boat and send you back to Poland. You did come from Poland?" he asked.

"Yes," I said.

"You say that you are Jewish?"

"Yes," I said. "Are you Jewish?"

"Yes, I am Jewish," Herr Diesenhaus answered. "This is a small town. I was born here, and I have always lived in Landskrona. Everyone knows who I am, and they brought me here to speak with you. They rely on me to tell them the truth."

"Do you know what happened in Germany on October 28, 1938?" I asked him.

He thought for a while, repeated the date, and then he said, "The Aktion. On that day, they rounded up foreign-born Jews all over Germany, and they transported them to the east and kept their apartments, their money, and all their possessions."

"My mother, my sister, and I were the victims of that Aktion."

"Where are your mother and sister now?" Herr Diesenhaus asked.

"My sister was killed. We must assume that. She was caught on the street after the liquidation of the Krosno ghetto, and we have not been able to find out what happened to her."

"And your mother?"

"My mother is living in Stockholm. I have her address."

"Did you tell that to Herr Nielsen?"

"No, not yet. I was just about to tell him when they brought you into the room."

"Were you Bar Mitzvah?"

"No, of course not." I smiled and added, "In Germany, girls do not become a Bar Mitzvah."

Herr Diesenhaus looked at me and shook his head. "This is some world," he said pensively. He shook my hand and said good-bye. Then he touched my shoulder and said in parting, "Don't worry." The three men walked out. Within seconds, Herr Nielsen was back.

"So your mother lives in Stockholm? Can you give us her address?"

I had memorized my mother's address, and they wrote it down. Herr Nielsen said that they would need to verify the truth of all my allegations, but even if everything checked out, they would still not be able to release us unless we told them the truth about our illegal entry into Sweden. Then the grilling started once more.

I was very tired. They asked the same questions over and over again. I had previously admitted that we smuggled ourselves on board a ship. We had crept aboard clandestinely in the middle of the night, and we had not been intercepted. No, no one saw us, I said. It was dark, and we could not see the name of the ship.

Herr Ferguson had walked out and he came back into the room. He looked at the writing pad, and once again he asked where we had been hiding once we came aboard.

"In a coal hold that was not quite filled with coal," I answered.

"And how long did you remain there in that coal bin, not loaded to the top with coal?"

"I don't know. It seemed like a long time. We were dozing most of the time."

"In that coal bin, with your head on the coal."

"No, we tried to keep our heads on our bags."

"There had to be someone on that boat who saw you, who took pity on you. Someone who brought you something to eat."

"No, there was no one. We did not eat."

"The whole time nothing to eat. But you did have something to drink? You could not have survived without some water. Who brought you the water?"

I kept repeating that we did not eat or drink while aboard the ship and that no one had helped us come aboard. Herr Nielsen kept insisting that we could not be released unless we revealed the name of the person who had helped us hide. We had arrived at the Landskrona Police Station before seven o'clock in the morning. The questioning had gone on for several hours. With all the sincerity I could muster, I kept repeating that no one had helped us to come aboard and no one had discovered us hiding in the coal hold.

Shortly before noon I committed a grave error. Herr Nielsen, though changing the phrasing, kept repeating the same questions. He never raised his voice. One might reason, he said, that a person could survive sleeping on the floor in a coal bin. Perhaps one could reason that a person could survive for several days without consuming food. However, a person cannot survive for several days without some liquid; therefore he argued, you must have had something to drink. He repeated this argument several times, and at last I said coffee.

Immediately, I knew that I had made a mistake. Herr Nielsen continued to reason. Of course, there had to be some liquid available. Now all you need to tell us is who brought you the coffee.

Stefan was aware of my blunder. He had heard me say coffee. He said something about not allowing myself to fall asleep, but I did not need him to tell me. I realized what had happened. I felt fully alert and ready to repair the damage.

"Just coffee. You had nothing with the coffee?" Herr Nielsen asked.

"No, nothing," I answered.

"And how many times did someone bring you coffee?"

"We had coffee only once, and no one brought it to us."

"Oh, I see, you went to the ship's galley and picked it up yourself?"

"No. One time when I woke up, I noticed on a ledge something I had not seen there before. When I went to look I realized that it was a coffee mug, half filled with coffee."

"And you drank all of it. Was it hot, cold?"

"Not quite all of it. It was lukewarm."

Shortly thereafter Herr Nielsen said, "This is enough for today. You do realize that we will not be able to release you until this mystery gets cleared up."

We were asked to pick up our bags in the outer office and follow Herr Ferguson.

"Where will he take us?" I asked apprehensively.

"Don't worry," Herr Nielsen replied. "We are not sending you back to Poland." With a stern look on his face, he added, "Not yet anyway."

"Could you please notify my mother that we are here?" I pleaded.

"Yes, your mother will be notified this afternoon. We also plan to contact the American consulate in Stockholm. The bank confirmed the information you gave us. Apparently, you were truthful about everything except for the one crucial matter, but we'll come back to that."

Herr Ferguson drove us out of the town to a large compound, which we entered through a gate. All around us were one-story red-brick buildings. They appeared to be well maintained. Off to the left, I saw a grass-covered expanse and down below a stream. It was too narrow to be a river. Had there been a castle, I would have said that it was a moat. Beyond the water, I saw meadows and trees.

Herr Ferguson left us with a woman in a gray uniform, and she led us to a small, comfortably furnished room. There were two smaller doors in the room: one led to a closet and the other to a bathroom with a tub. The woman spoke German.

"This is a transit camp," she said. "The doctor will see you tomorrow. Some tests will be taken, and after that you will be able to move freely within the compound. Until your visit with the doctor, we prefer that you remain in this room. Dinner and breakfast will be brought to you, but thereafter you will come to the dining hall and eat there."

Stefan, who had no knowledge of German, was frustrated and most unhappy. He wanted me to repeat every word that had been said during the interrogation, which had lasted for more than five hours. He had a vague idea about what was being said because of the repetitive aspect of the questions. He was sympathetic about the coffee blunder. I told him how I had tried to mend my mistake. He needed my reassurance that I would be able to withstand further interrogations and negotiate our release.

It was heavenly to be able to take a bath and fall asleep stretched out between clean white sheets, my head on a soft pillow. I slept for ten hours.

In midmorning we were asked to come to the doctor's office. He was a short robust-looking man with sparse blond hair. A nurse took some blood from our arms, and she asked us for urine samples. The medical examination was thorough and very business-like. No smiles, no conversation, and with special attention given to my lungs. I breathed in and out so many times I thought my lungs would give out. Stefan received the same attention. The doctor said that we now were free to move about the compound, but shouldn't make contact with the children until we received the return of our test results.

On the following day, a beautiful spring morning, after a generous and nourishing breakfast, we were strolling back to our room. We heard children's voices in the distance, in another part of the compound, though not fenced off from the part we were assigned to. We walked toward the sounds. Then we saw the children. Roaming about in a large grassy yard, there must have been more than two hundred children. They appeared to be between the ages of eight and twelve years. All of them were neatly dressed. Walking among them were teachers, perhaps chaperones, all female and all my contemporaries. The children were chattering away at a fast pace. We could not understand what they were saying, but Stefan and I agreed that they were speaking French.

We had just returned to our room when Herr Nielsen, accompanied by Herr Ferguson, knocked on the door and entered the room. The men sat down on the two chairs in the room and asked us to sit down on our beds. They asked if we were comfortable. I said yes. The officers told us that they were happy to inform us that we were healthy. Herr Nielsen retrieved a notebook from his breast pocket and proceeded with the same questions he had asked me two days ago. I felt more confident, and I knew that this time I would not fail. I asked him if he had been able to communicate with my mother. He brushed my question aside, and said "later." He concentrated his questions on the coffee mug.

"You want us to believe that after your first or second night aboard ship, you noticed this coffee mug. Tell us about the ledge. What kind of a ledge? And please, this time tell us the truth."

"I am sorry," I answered. "I really can't recall what the ledge looked like. We were so frightened, and it was very dark. When we stood up to stretch, we saw the mug."

"Someone just left the mug there, half filled with coffee? No one came to fetch it?"

"I don't know when it was left there or if it was picked up later. We drank most of the coffee, and after that we never thought of checking if the mug was still there. Perhaps the person who left it did come back later to fetch it."

"And it was half filled when it was left there? And sailors do like their coffee, especially at night when on duty, don't they? Why would a sailor leave his mug?"

This time the interrogation lasted for about an hour. The two men rose. Herr Nielsen said that my mother would be here, at the transit camp, at two o'clock in the afternoon, and that we could speak to each other across the moat. She would be on one side of the bank, and we on the other. He described the exact spot where she would be. At that place the stream was very narrow, and we would be able to hear each other well.

"You will not try to escape?" he asked. "No, of course not," I assured him. The four of us were standing. Herr Nielsen, who was quite tall, bent down somewhat so I would clearly understand the importance of his message.

"All you have to do is give us the name of the person who helped you to stow away on the ship," he said. "We already know which ship it was. The good news we bring you is that if you give us the name of the sailor who helped you to board the ship, you can walk out of this camp today and join your mother. But if you don't, you will give us no choice but return you to Poland. We must have the name. The decision is yours."

"Herr Nielsen," I said, "you keep asking me for a name, but I do not have a name. There was no one who helped us come aboard. There was a ship at a pier. We waited until after midnight and then snuck on board the ship. We found a dark coal hold, and that is where we stayed until we disembarked. No one saw us, and no one came to our aid, and then we met you."

Stefan and I arrived at the designated area a half hour early, but my mother was already there. She was holding a handkerchief to her eyes, but I knew that her tears as well as mine were from joy. Once again we were together, and only separated by a friendly moat. We spoke Polish so that Stefan could participate in the conversation. We did not see anyone else on either side of the bank, but we were careful.

Mother told us that Herr Ferguson had contacted her and told her that the only hindrance to our release was my refusal to tell them the name of the ship and the person who had helped us to stow away on the boat. He told Mother to urge me to reveal the name of the sailor; this alone would help us to obtain a temporary residence in Sweden. I looked straight at my mother's face—it was not possible to look into her eyes at that distance—and I said, "Mother, they keep asking me for a name, but I don't have a name because no one helped us. We just took a chance, and we boarded the ship in the middle of the night."

Mother understood. She answered that in time they would understand that I couldn't possibly give them a name, since there was no one there who had helped us. The Gdynia harbor is not well lit, Mother said, and it would be difficult to read the ship's name in such darkness. Mother told us that a recently established Jewish agency to aid refugees had helped her to find a room. She was very lucky, she said, because in Stockholm there was a short supply of furnished rooms. She said she would come again unless we were released before Sunday. She wanted to know if I had the telephone number of the Jewish family in Stockholm whose name she had gotten from the friends who lived in Danzig. Yes, I said. Mother told us that the Stockholm family had been most gracious, and she had been invited to their home for Sabbath dinners since the time of her arrival. Mother also told us that she had begun to draw money from the account my father had established for us.

Though we were not free to walk out of the compound, I felt free. Between our money in the bank and my father's attempts to bring us out of Sweden as soon as possible, I felt confident that we would be permitted to join my mother. I could not believe that Sweden, a nation that had remained neutral throughout the horrendous events that had upended most of Europe, would prevent us from being reunited with my father.

After Mother left, we walked to the children's section. The children were not in the yard, but several of the teachers were strolling along the paths. We stopped a pair of them and introduced ourselves. I asked about the children.

The young women told us that these were the orphaned Jewish French children that the Nazis had taken from their parents. After rounding them up, the Nazis had shipped them to concentration camps in Germany. Shortly before Germany surrendered to the Allied forces, and at the last possible moment, Count Bernadotte, a Swedish diplomat, had negotiated for the release of the surviving children who had been kept prisoner in the camps of Ravensbruck and Bergen Belsen. With support of the Swedish government, he had brought the children to Landskrona, together with the few fortunate teachers and chaperones who had been selected to accompany the children. At the compound several French doctors and nurses also helped to care for the children. Most of them were suffering from malnutrition, and from a number of physical and psychological illnesses. The young women told us that efforts were being made to reunite the children with a relative or, for the very lucky ones, a living parent.

I told the young Jewish women, both former concentration camp inmates, that I was Jewish and had survived in Poland. One of the women was French, the other German. My knowledge of French was very limited, but Stefan who had studied French for a number of years was able to converse with them. We also spoke German, and the two women agreed that Poland was the worst place because the Nazis had decided to make Poland the killing ground for the Jews of Europe. The women said they were fully aware that, had they been shipped to Poland, they would not have survived the persecution. How had I managed to evade the ever-tightening noose of Nazi Jew hunters while pretending to be a Pole who spoke Polish with a German accent? I understood it was a rhetorical question that required no answer. We agreed to meet at about the same time on the following day, while the children were napping.

On the next day, we missed our date with the women because Herr Ferguson met us as we were walking out of the dining hall and asked us to follow him to an office. He was very polite, and he repeated that if we didn't give the name of the sailor who helped us, we would be returned to Poland. I repeated my dismay at not being able to comply with his request because I had no answer to the question. By the time Herr Ferguson departed, the children's compound was empty, both children and chaperones were gone.

On the following day, our fifth day in Landskrona, Herr Nielsen knocked at our door and walked in. Again he asked us if we were comfortable. I assured him that we were, but that we were very eager to be released. My mother was anxiously awaiting our arrival in Stockholm.

"So, you don't think that we will send you back to Poland?" he asked.

I looked at him. "That would be a very cruel act, and I do not think that you would do it."

He said that it was not a matter of how he felt, but a matter of his responsibility to uphold the Swedish law. He wanted us to tell him what kind of work we had done while we lived in Gdynia. I told him that we had never lived in Gdynia; we had resided in Sopot. I said that Stefan was a fine portrait photographer and had also been employed by a news agency as a roving reporter. He had recorded the arrival of the repatriation ships in the port of Gdynia.

"Is that when you began to check out the possibilities for escape?"

"Yes, but that was several months ago. It took a lot of courage to linger in the harbor after dark. And then we just decided to take a chance."

"Look, young woman," Herr Nielsen said. "It is time to stop all this nonsense."

He took an envelope out of his pocket and held it out toward me. "These are your railroad tickets to Stockholm. You can leave tomorrow morning. You are free. Now let us get to the truth of the matter. Will you now give us the name of the sailor who helped you come aboard?"

"Herr Nielsen," I said, "I am so happy that we are free to leave, and we are very grateful. It's eight years since I saw my father, and we want to thank you for making it possible for us to leave for America."

"Yes, yes, I understand, but you still have not answered my question."

"I wish I could, Herr Nielsen, but I can't because I do not know the answer to the question you are asking."

"All right then," Herr Nielsen said. "You arrived on the *Havsmas* shortly before we intercepted you. The boat had just landed. We made a thorough search of the ship. In one of the cabins, on the lower berth, there were traces of face powder. You never gave us the name of the sailor who helped you, so we can't really know his name, can we?"

I did not say a word. I was stunned.

"And did you really think that even for a minute we believed your tale about hiding in a coal hold?" Herr Nielsen asked. "Have you ever heard of a stowaway who hides in a coal hold and walks off looking as if she had been a passenger in a cabin? You were wearing white socks that were sparkling clean. There was not even a smudge of dirt from all that coal you were hiding in."

I still had not said a word. Herr Nielsen put the tickets into my hand, and then he gave me a gift. "You never revealed his name," he said, "so you need not worry."

"The captain?" I asked. "Does he know?"

Herr Nielsen shook his head, "No," he said. "We did not tell him, because we could not be certain, could we? Olaf's record is clean."

Tears were running down my cheeks; I could not stop them. Herr Nielsen stretched out his arm and shook hands with Stefan, and then with me. He looked at me.

"*Välkommen i Sverige,*" he said. Welcome to Sweden.

# EPILOGUE

In Stockholm we had much to learn. Aside from looking for housing, there were the challenges of adapting to a different culture and of learning a new language. I could hardly wait to be united with my father, and I was eager to once again be my authentic self. The Stockholm Jewish community facilitated our entry into a new society, and while in their offices, Mother met a Jewish family who invited us to their home.

Stefan much preferred the Krysia he had loved than the Bertel who was beginning to emerge. While in Poland, we had begun to acknowledge our increasingly divergent needs. Once in Sweden, these differences became ever more apparent in our daily life in Stockholm. We were aware that our relationship was unraveling. To Stefan's happy surprise, there was a prewar Polish society in Stockholm in addition to a small postwar Polish community, and he eagerly embraced some of his fellow countrymen, whereas my need was to once again affiliate with a Jewish community.

Stefan, a bohemian by nature, could not acquiesce to my longing for the conventional life. We parted amicably. Years later I learned from a mutual friend that Stefan had settled in Australia. In accordance with our agreement not to keep in touch, I refrained from resuming contact. I will not forget him, and I doubt that he will forget me.

Mother leaving for America, accompanied by four friends and myself, August 1946.

In late November 1946, I sailed from Göteborg on the SS *Drottningholm* bound for New York City. My parents, standing next to each other, greeted me at customs, and I ran into their warm embrace. When I first viewed the wonders of New York City, I felt I had entered paradise.

On my way to America on the SS *Drottningholm*, late November 1946.

In August 1948, while on a summer vacation in the Adirondack Mountains, I met the young American attorney Larry Lauer, and after a courtship that lasted seven months, we got married. After the fifty-four years we happily spent together, we both agree that we were indeed fortunate to have found each other. We have two sons, Allan born in 1952 and Richard born in 1956, and four grandchildren, one of whom is named for my sister Eva.

Below are the people mentioned in the book who did survive the war:

My grandfather, Leon David, managed to escape from the Bochnia ghetto not long after my grandmother, Marja David, had died. Crossing several borders, he made his way to Hungary where his wife's family helped him hide until his liberation by the Russian army. He arrived in New York in 1950, about one year after my wedding.

My childhood friend Ernst Schäfer, Zack to his friends, lives in Israel with his wife and family.

Hedel, our childhood nanny, subsequently our companion while on summer vacations and always a friend to my parents, lives in Germany amidst a loving family. She is ninety years old.

Syga Landschaft, the only member of his family to survive, lives in Natania, Israel.

Ruth Wischnitzer, who found my mother in Austria, married an Austrian and settled in Vienna. She died in her late fifties.

Staszek, our benefactor throughout those treacherous years, lived in Israel. He died in his early sixties.

Danka, the beloved friend who never knew my true identity, has eluded my search. I have not yet given up hope that I may find her.

Maryla, though always dear to me because she was Pan Majerowicz's daughter, I now look upon as my family. She is the only person alive who knew my sister during our years in Krosno. She lives in Israel with her husband, children, and grandchildren. She is a recognized sculptor.

Stefa remained in Poland until 1969. Together with her husband and two sons, she subsequently moved to Germany.

Reunited after a separation that lasted eight and a half years, my parents lived together until my father, Oskar Weissberger, died in November 1976. My father after years of worry and loneliness was seeking a regular lifestyle with a wife who would manage a smooth-running household, while my mother throughout her remaining years kept initiating searches for that elusive trace that would lead her to Eva. Ilona Weissberger died in January 1995.

In a repository of names at Yad Vashem, the Holocaust memorial in Jerusalem, Mother and I recorded ninety-six names of our immediate family members, including the name of my sister Eva, their prewar addresses, and the names of the ghettos from which they had been deported.

## ABRAM WEISSBERGER m. CHAVA ROESEN IN KRAKOW DISTRICT, THEN AUSTRIA

| Kieve W. | Leon W. | Pearl W. | Saul W. | Henny W. | Anna W. | Josef W. | Rena W. | OSKAR W. | Nettie W. |
|---|---|---|---|---|---|---|---|---|---|
| m. | m. | m. | m. | m. | m. | m. | m. | m. | m. |
| Janka | Salla | Josef | Chana | Zalman | Mosche | Hanka | Rubin | ILONA | Maniek |
| *in Krakow* | *in Krakow* | *in Vienna* | *in Mielec* | *in Krakow* | *in Krakow* | *in Krakow* | *in Boston* | *in Bochnia* | *in Bochnia* |
| Wladek 2 | Hella | *to USA* | Salek | *5 children* | *(4 children)* | Genek | Sidney 2 | | Hella |
| Lusia 1 | Lutek 2 | *in 1920* | Renia | *(4 grandch.)* | | Ellek | Esther | | Nusia |
| Romek 1 | Rutka | *(no children)* | | | | | Allan | | |
| Anja 2 | Simon | | | | | *(1 grandch.)* | | | |
| | Hanka | | | | | | | | |
| *(6 grandch.)* | *(2 grandch.)* | | | | | | | | |

## LEON DAVID m. MARIA RINDER IN KOSICE, HUNGARY THEN AUSTRIA

| Zygmunt D. | ILONA D. | Regina D. | Wilhelm D. |
|---|---|---|---|
| m. | m. | m. | m. |
| Antonia | OSKAR | JakubVogelhut | Frieda |
| *in Lomza* | *in Bochnia* | *in Bochnia* | *in Katowice* |
| Salek D. | Eva | Dollek V. | Joesph D. |
| Bronia D. | | Berta | |
| | | m. | |
| | | Larry Lauer | |
| | | *in New York* | |

Allan L. ———— Richard L.

Jake L. — Sammy L.
Eva L. — Benjamin L.

# CHRONOLOGY

## 1938

April: Oskar Weissberger leaves Hindenburg, Germany, for Amsterdam to board the SS *Statendam* to New York.

October 28: Ilona, Eva, and Bertel Weissberger expelled from Hindenburg and illegally forced over the border into Poland.

November 9: Kristallnacht (night of the broken glass).

## 1939

March 15: Germany occupies Czechoslovakia.

August 23: Soviet-German Non-Agression Pact.

September 1: German army invades Poland, beginning of World War II.

September 3: England and France declare war on Germany.

September 17: Soviet occupation of eastern Poland.

## 1941

February: Krosno, Poland. Decree that all Jews wear armbands displaying the "Judenstern" (Star of David).

June 22: Germany attacks Soviet Union (Feldzug Barbarossa).

July: Jews are forced to move into one small area—the future ghetto.

August: Ilona, Eva, and Bertel Weissberger are forced to vacate their apartment and ordered to move into the ghetto.

December 7: United States enters the war.

## 1942

January 20: Wannsee Conference: Final Solution decreed.

February–July: Jews, mostly women, brought to Krosno ghetto from other ghettos, mainly Lodz ghetto; Jews from Krosno ghetto, mainly men, disappear to unknown destinations.

September: Liquidation of Krosno ghetto; Jews transported to unknown destination.

1943

January 18: Jews in Warsaw ghetto launch uprising against Nazi deportations.

February: German Sixth Army surrenders at Stalingrad.

April 19: Revolt of Jews in Warsaw ghetto, fighting continues for weeks.

May 16: Liquidation of Warsaw ghetto.


1944

June: Soviet offensive begins.

August 1: Warsaw Polish uprising (Powstanie).

October 2: Polish Home Army (A.K.) surrenders.

October: While Warsaw residents ordered to watch, Warsaw is torched and left burning; nearly the entire noncombatant population of Warsaw is deported, mainly in freight cars, to various camps.

Mid-October: En route to Spellen an der Wesel transit camp, the freight cars transporting us passes through Essen and is caught in an Allied forces bombing of the Ruhr district.


1945

January/February: Soviet troops liberate Poland and East Germany.

# INDEX

Betty Lauer was born in Hindenburg, Germany, on March 1, 1926, the younger daughter of Oskar and Ilona Weissberger. Her father left for the United States in March 1938. On October 28, 1938, she and her mother and sister were forcibly expelled from Germany to Poland. At the onset of the Blitzkrieg invasion of Poland on September 1, 1939, Lauer was living in Krakow. She and her family subsequently moved to Krosno, where they remained until the liquidation of the ghetto. They escaped, and Lauer survived the Nazi occupation under an assumed name and falsified documents. She was liberated by the Russian Army in Katowice, Poland, in February 1945.

Lauer escaped Poland by stowing away on a Swedish ship bound for Landskrona, Sweden. From Sweden, she sailed to America, arriving in New York City in December 1946. She met her husband Lawrence Lauer, a young attorney, in 1948, and they married in 1949. Their sons, Allan and Richard, were born in 1952 and 1956. Lauer received her BA cum laude from Queens College in 1970 and her MA from the Graduate School of CUNY in 1976. She taught German in high school and German literature in college and spent most of her free time writing. Lauer is retired and lives in Vermont.